# The Public Policy Exception in the Judicial Review of International Commercial Arbitral Awards

Shu Zhang

# The Public Policy Exception in the Judicial Review of International Commercial Arbitral Awards

## Lessons from and for China

Springer

Shu Zhang
Deakin Law School
Deakin University
Geelong, VIC, Australia

ISBN 978-3-662-67678-3 ISBN 978-3-662-67679-0 (eBook)
https://doi.org/10.1007/978-3-662-67679-0



This Springer imprint is published by the registered company Springer-Verlag GmbH, DE, part of Springer Nature.
The registered company address is: Heidelberger Platz 3, 14197 Berlin, Germany

*To Emily*

# Preface

China is currently experiencing a period of rapid economic growth and has significantly improved its position in terms of world trade. In fact, China has become one of the biggest players in international trade and inbound/outbound investment. Correspondingly, there has been an increase in commercial disputes, especially in those that are foreign-related, requiring the support of a functional and supportive legal system. In other words, for the good of China's continuing economic growth, China must have a viable and advanced legal system and legal order in place.[1] Yet China's legal system has been the subject of some criticism from international observers.[2] In an effort to improve its performance, China has introduced new domestic laws; improved the performance of its administrative departments and court systems; and increased its involvement in worldwide developments of international law, including law regulating international commercial arbitration.[3]

It is particularly notable that one major development in China's legal reform efforts is the advancement of China's arbitration law system in order to facilitate

---

[1] Kun Fan, *Arbitration in China: A Legal and Cultural Analysis* (Hart, 2013) 4.

[2] See for example, generally in Pitman B Potter, *The Chinese Legal System: Globalisation and Local Legal Culture* (Routledge, 2001).

[3] For example, the enactment of China's Arbitration Law, the enactment and amendments of China's Civil Procedure Law, and more generally, the ongoing reforms in China's judicial system. See for example,《中华人民共和国仲裁法》[Arbitration Law of the People's Republic of China](People's Republic of China) National People's Congress Standing Committee, Order No. 31, 31 August 1994;《中华人民共和国民事诉讼法》[The Civil Procedure Law of the People's Republic of China] (People's Republic of China) National People's Congress, Order No. 44, 9 April 1991 (Recently amended by National People's Congress Standing Committee, Order 106, 24 December 2021); The reforms in the court system, for example, see 中华人民共和国国务院新闻办公室 [The State Council Information Office of the People's Republic of China],《中国的司法改革》白皮书 [White Paper on China's Judicial Reforms] October 2012. Also, China's participation in international trade and law-making process. See for example, China's entering to WTO: Protocol on the Accession of the People's Republic of China, WT/L/432, 23 November 2001, and its participation in UNCITRAL as a member: see http://www.uncitral.org/uncitral/en/about/origin.html. See more detailed discussion in Chap. 3, Sect. 3.1.

international trade between the Chinese and foreigners.[4] It is widely accepted that international commercial arbitration is the preferred method of dispute resolution over litigation particularly in the context of international trade.[5] Arbitration is a private method of resolving disputes on the basis of party autonomy.[6] Allowing parties to choose arbitration means that they may play a more proactive role in how the dispute is decided, e.g. by selecting the decision-maker, the forum, and the applicable law, and further, by avoiding an unfamiliar or unfriendly national legal environment or unexpected results.[7] All these benefits are assured by the *New York Convention* (the '*NYC*' hereafter),[8] which has been adopted by China and most of the nations of the world,[9] as it promotes the enforceability of any international commercial arbitral award.

China's progress in advancing its arbitration law and practice has attracted international attention and recognition from both practitioners and scholars.[10] Despite this progress, there remain some doubts and concerns that raise questions about China's performance and its support of the arbitration system. These concerns include doubts about the lack of a consistent interpretation of the abstract concept of the legislation and the lack of transparency in the implementation of the legislation; criticisms with respect to the lack of qualified legal professionals to produce quality legal services; and an alleged adherence to local protectionism by the judiciary, which is subject to China's unique constitutional system.[11] These concerns reflect the difference between China's performance and international practice and also the difference between the

---

[4] Dejun Cheng, Michael J. Moser and Shengchang Wang, *International Arbitration in the People's Republic of China: Commentary, Cases and Materials* (Butterworths Asia, 1995).

[5] Julian D. M. Lew, Loukas A. Mistelis and Stefan Michael Kröll, 'Arbitration as a Dispute Settlement Mechanism' in *Comparative International Commercial Arbitration* (Kluwer Law International, 2003) 1, [1–19]–[1–30]; Gary B. Born, *International Commercial Arbitration* (Kluwer Law International, 2nd ed, 2014) 62.

[6] The author is of the opinion that arbitration is a dispute resolution scheme that operates under the supervision of national legal system while its fundamental nature of party autonomy shall be respected. It is notable that the understandings of the position of arbitration in a particular national legal system vary in different jurisdictions. For further discussion of this issue, though not the main purpose of this book, see.

[7] Born, above n 5, 62.

[8] *The Convention on the Recognition and Enforcement of Foreign Arbitral Awards* opened for signature on 6 July 1958, 330 UNTS 38 (entered into force 7 June 1959)art V(2)(b); Albert Jan van den Berg, *The New York Convention of 1958: Towards a Uniform Judicial Interpretation* (Kluwer Law International, 1981).

[9] 《最高人民法院关于执行我国加入的<承认及执行外国仲裁裁决公约>的通知》 [Notice of the Supreme People's Court in regard of the Implementation of the 'Convention on the Recognition and Enforcement of Foreign Arbitral Award'] Supreme People's Court, 10 April 1987.

[10] Cheng, Moser and Wang, above n 4; Jinzhou Tao, *Arbitration Law and Practice in China* (Kluwer International, 2012) 4–5.

[11] Brenda Horrigan, Felix Hess and Siew Lin Mok, 'Chapter 5: Arbitration in China: Recent Developments' in Michael J. Moser (ed.), *Business Disputes in China* (Juris, 2009) 52; Clarisse von Wunschheim, *Enforcement of Commercial Arbitral Awards in China : Business Laws of China* (West, 2011) 23.

arbitration world's understanding of China's performance and their expectation of it.

The author suggests that an understanding of how China's courts has applied the public policy exception[12] in the judicial review of arbitral awards best illustrates the concerns and questions that have been raised. The public policy exception, which is later defined in this book, is a ground upon which the court can annul an arbitral award or reject its enforcement in the context of both national arbitration legislation and international conventions governing practice in relation to arbitration law.[13] Public policy is an abstract concept that requires careful interpretation and application. It aims to protect national interests and its interpretation is dependent on the political, economic, cultural and legal traditions of a state. However, the lack of sufficient legislative guidance and the quality deficiencies of China's judiciary may result in their failure to consistently apply this ground and adopt doubtful practices that favour local protectionism, causing unexpected results for parties. In an international context of pro-enforcement of arbitral awards, the practice of interpretation and application of public policy reflects not only how China reaches a balance between international standards and local needs, but also how China's legal system makes its own contributions to world consensus on the application of public policy to international arbitration law.

Based on these understandings, this book endeavours to answer a key question:

> Can China's legal system better accommodate an application of the public policy exception that is more reflective of international standards?

In order to answer this question, this book examines and analyses how the public policy exception is applied in China's judicial review process of arbitral awards. It further compares the alleged Chinese approach to the application of the public policy exception to that of international judicial practice. This book evaluates the performance of the Chinese legal system on this issue and proposes the adoption of a more developed approach that aligns with that which is used internationally.

This book asserts that, though a pro-enforcement attitude has been formally accepted by Chinese legal practitioners, the Chinese legal system and its judiciary are yet to adopt a detailed and consistent approach to defining, interpreting and applying public policy in reviewing arbitral awards. This book asserts that such an approach would be based on a developed understanding and application of the public

---

[12] For the definition of 'public policy', including the discussion of different attributes of the 'ground of public policy', the 'public policy defence' and the 'public policy exception', see Chap. 1, Sect. 2.2. Generally, it is named as an 'exception' to the general attitude which seeks to facilitate the recognition and enforcement of international commercial arbitral awards.

[13] The *NYC*, Art V(2)(b); and also in national laws, for example, the Model Law on International Commercial Arbitration of the United Nations Commission on International Trade Law, UN GAOR, 40th sess, Supp No. 17, UN Doc A/40/17, annex I (21 June 1985); passed by the GA Res 40/72, UN GAOR, 40th sess, 112th plenmtg, Agenda Item 135, UN Doc A/RES/40/72 (11 December 1985); amended by GA Res A/RES/61/33, UN GAOR, 61th sess, 64th plenmtg, Agenda Item 77, UN Doc A/RES/61/33 (4 Dec 2006) (*the UNCITRAL Model Law on ICA* hereafter) art 34(2)(b) and art 36(1)(b).

policy exception by China's judiciary as well by the Chinese arbitration practitioners, resulting in substantial improvements of China's arbitration environment.[14]

This book is comprised of three parts, including nine chapters and a conclusion.

## Part I Literature Review

- Chapter 1 summarises the scope of the topic, identifies and defines the main terms and describes the methodology adopted.
- Chapter 2 introduces the function of the public policy exception in the context of international arbitration law and its developments and particularly categorises the elements of public policy.
- Chapter 3 further illustrates the developments of the public policy exception in China, on the basis of China's legislative and judicial structure and its unique political and cultural background, and acknowledges China's recent progress in developing its arbitration law and improving the related legal environment.

## Part II China's Public Policy Practice Compared to Other Jurisdictions

- Chapter 4 examines China's arbitration practice and the Chinese judiciary's performance in the application of public policy from a statistical perspective.
- Chapter 5 discusses the application of the fundamental substantive principles of law as one key element of public policy and examines whether the Chinese courts take the protection of state-owned properties and financial interests into consideration when making decisions.
- Chapter 6 analyses the application of fundamental procedural principles of law as a key element of public policy. Procedural principles discussed include the bias rule and res judicata. China's unique understanding of mediation-in-arbitration and the possible underlying public policy concerns are the subject of particular focus.
- Chapter 7 further examines the identification and application of public policy rules/*lois de police* as a key element of public policy and its reflections in China.
- Chapter 8 focuses on the interpretation and application of arbitrability rules in China and other jurisdictions and analyses the underlying public policy concerns.

---

[14] See generally the distinct aspects of China's social and cultural influences on the performance of arbitration practices in Kun Fan, *Arbitration in China: A Legal and Cultural Analysis* (Oxford University, 2013) Ch 8 and Ch 9; See also Wunschheim, above n 11.

## Part III Conclusion and Recommendations

- Chapter 9 summarises the current Chinese approach in applying public policy as discussed in Part II, compares it with international trends and further evaluates the performance of the Chinese legal system in responding to the issues raised in that Part II.
- The final chapter—the Conclusion—summarises the findings of the book, including an evaluation of the contribution and limitation of China's legal system in dealing with public policy, and makes suggestions and recommendations for the future development of China's approach in applying public policy.

Geelong, Australia Shu Zhang

# About This Book

This book systematically examines how the Chinese arbitration law system responds to the application of the public policy exception in the judicial review of arbitral awards, particularly those awards that are foreign-related and international. The discussion is based on a general understanding of the legal concept of public policy in international arbitration practice and the understanding developed in Chinese arbitration law and judicial practice. In focusing on both international developments and Chinese arbitral and judicial practice, this book provides some lessons from and for China.

Based on a review of both legislation and cases in China, in comparison with the international trends and consensuses, the author concludes that China's performance in defining and applying public policy in the judicial review of international commercial arbitral awards needs further improvement. Though the emergence and progress of international arbitration practice have encouraged China to restrict the application of the public policy exception in the judicial review of arbitral awards, a review of current judicial practice in identifying and applying public policy illustrates the limited progress made to date in defining and applying the legal concept of public policy. Some key questions have not yet been properly addressed or answered, including the international/national nature of public policy, the key elements of public policy, and the appropriate boundaries of judicial review. A lack of experience in dealing with the public policy exception has given rise to insufficient and problematic judicial analysis and decisions. Further steps are expected to be taken by the Chinese legal system in order to achieve a more comprehensive view of the public policy exception that is in line with the recent developments in the leading jurisdictions and consistent with the globalised trend of a converging understanding of public policy in international arbitration.

# Contents

# Part I
# Literature Review

# Chapter 1
# Scope, Terminology and Methodology

## 1 Defining the Topic: The Application of the Public Policy Exception in China's Judicial Review of International Commercial Arbitral Awards

As previously stated in the Introductory Chapter, this book reviews China's law and practice in applying the public policy exception in the judicial review of international commercial arbitral awards. Following the introduction of the main topic and its significance, this chapter further defines the scope of the topic, and explains the key terms used and methods of research adopted in this book. By doing this, this chapter aims to provide a series of basic understandings as the foundation of this book.

The application of the public policy exception in the judicial review of arbitral awards is a difficult issue because it is influenced by many factors. The rapid development of international commercial arbitration, driven by the growth in the global economy, has had an influence on the application of public policy in arbitration law, and the legal concept of the public policy exception has attracted much attention, such as in relation to economic globalisation.[1] It is influenced by time and the distinct culture of the State that applies public policy[2]; in addition, a friendly legal environment is required in order to facilitate the wide acceptance of arbitration and to limit the uncertain or unexpected result of dispute resolution. Public policy, therefore, should be applied narrowly and reserved for exceptional circumstances only.[3] It is

[1] On the influence of economic globalisation, see for example, Katherine Lynch, *The Forces of Economic Globalization: Challenges to the Regime of International Commercial Arbitration* (Kluwer Law International, 2003).

[2] Albert Jan van den Berg, *The New York Convention of 1958: Towards a Uniform Judicial Interpretation* (Kluwer Law International, 1981) 376.

[3] See Pierre Mayer and Audley Sheppard, 'Final Report on Public Policy as a Bar to Enforcement of International Arbitral Awards' (Paper presented at the International Law Association New Delhi Conference Committee on International Commercial Arbitration, New Delhi, 2002) (*'ILA Final Report'*) Recommendation 1(a).



S. Zhang, *The Public Policy Exception in the Judicial Review of International Commercial Arbitral Awards*, https://doi.org/10.1007/978-3-662-67679-0_1

also argued that the protection of a unique legal order in arbitration law, which is distinct from the legal order of any particular state, imposes additional requirements in the application of public policy; the so-called "arbitration legal order" emerges and may influence the formulation of an international consensus on the application of public policy.[4]

Contracting parties, arbitration professionals and national legal systems are all facing these complicated issues in practicing arbitration and in addressing the judicial review of arbitral awards, especially when doing this in a jurisdiction in which arbitration law is not fully advanced, for example, in China. Public policy concerns may either arise from China's distinct social and cultural background or from China's unique conduct of arbitration proceedings, or from China's mandatory law; yet none of these concerns are expressed as part of China's public policy in legislation or in judicial practice; nor is any clear test, standard or judicial approach for interpreting or applying public policy defined by its courts or observed by scholars.

This book aims to provide a thorough and detailed study on the problems and legal issues observed in China's judicial practice in relation to the application of the public policy exception. This book aims to identify the Chinese judiciary's approach in dealing with public policy through an analysis of case law and a consideration of commentary in academia. The book will also evaluate China's application of public policy by comparing it with the practices of other jurisdictions and ultimately propose is the adoption of a more developed judicial approach that aligns with that which is used internationally.

# 2 Terminology

## *2.1 International Commercial Arbitration*

As illustrated earlier in Sect. 1, this book focuses primarily on the application of public policy in the context of international commercial arbitration; the term "international commercial arbitration" is used according to its usual understanding in worldwide arbitration practices, as distinguished from other types of arbitration such as labour arbitration and sport arbitration, etc.

### 2.1.1 Arbitration

Arbitration is understood in this book as the common meaning attributed to it by the international arbitration community. Some general aspects of arbitration are well established. For instance, arbitration relies on the consent of all parties to submit

[4] Emmanuel Gaillard, *Legal Theory of International Arbitration* (Martinus Nijhoff Publishers, 2010) 35. See further Chap. 2. Whether such a legal order is applied in China's judicial practice is further examined in cases in Part II and conclude in Chap. 9.

the dispute for arbitration before a neutral and private party as the decision-maker, and the process of arbitration is distinct from the judicial proceedings that take place before national courts.[5] The practice of arbitration is understood as according with the definitions set out in the predominant legal documents such as the *NYC*[6] and the *UNCITRAL Model Law*.[7]

### 2.1.2 Commercial

Discussion in this research focuses on commercial arbitration practices unless it is stated otherwise. This limitation is consistent with the reservation made by the Chinese government that the *NYC* will only apply to "differences arising out of legal relationships, whether contractual or not, that are considered commercial under the national law".[8] "Commercial disputes" is further defined by the national law of each contracting party of the *NYC*[9]; and in particular, this term is defined as the economic right-and-obligation relationships that arise on the basis of contracts, torts or as provided by law in China.[10]

### 2.1.3 International

The arbitration practices discussed in this book are generally international ones, in which international legal elements are involved. There are several terms, such as "international", "foreign", "foreign-related" or "non-domestic", used in different legislative or research contexts,[11] illustrating that some foreign or international elements and interests are involved in the given arbitration or the enforcement of arbitral awards. Two approaches are used to identify whether the arbitration matter can be categorised as foreign or international: the nature of the dispute and the identity of the parties. National legislation and international agreements usually choose one

---

[5] For discussions of various definitions of arbitration, see Julian D. M. Lew, Loukas A. Mistelis and Stefan Michael Kröll, *Comparative International Commercial Arbitration* (Kluwer Law International, 2003) ch 1, [1–5]; Emmanuel Gaillard and John Savage, *Fouchard Gaillard Goldman on International Commercial Arbitration* (Kluwer Law International, 1999) [7]-[57].

[6] *The New York Convention,* art I(2).

[7] *The UNCITRAL Model Law of ICA.*

[8] *The NYC,* art I(3).

[9] Gaillard and Savage, above n.5, [58–77].

[10] 最高人民法院关于执行我国加入的《承认及执行外国仲裁裁决公约》的通知 [The Notice of Supreme People's Court on the implementation of the Convention on Recognition and Enforcement of Foreign Arbitral Award that China joined in](People's Republic of China) Supreme People's Court, 10 April 1987, art 2.

[11] For example, the *New York Convention* used "foreign" in its title and defined it in art I; it also referred to "non-domestic" awards in art I to enlarge the coverage of the convention. See van den Berg, above n 2, 12–51.

of these or apply them both in defining the nature of a case.[12] In this book, "international/foreign/foreign-related/non-domestic" arbitration or arbitral awards are given the same meaning, except when the terms "foreign-related" and "international" are defined distinctively by the Chinese law.[13]

It is notable that purely domestic arbitration practice is also referred to in our discussion for the purpose of comparison. With this in mind, it is important to be cautious in dealing with the nature of the disputes when reviewing cases and the application of the public policy discussed.

## *2.2 Public Policy*

### 2.2.1 Public Policy in the Judicial Review of Arbitral Award

Public policy is a widely accepted legal concept "which holds that no subject can lawfully do that which has a tendency to be injurious to the public, or against the public good"[14]; and in arbitration law specifically, public policy functions during the whole process of arbitration.[15] This book does not cover a wide range of possible public policy issues in arbitration law, but rather only focuses on its application in one specific situation: when courts review foreign or international arbitral awards, as illustrated in art V(2)(b) of the *NYC*.[16]

Public policy influences arbitration practice at many different stages and its application differs, depending on the decision-making body involved. Arbitration institutions or tribunals may consider public policy issues when deciding on the jurisdiction and choosing the applicable law for dispute resolution, because they have a general

[12] Martin Hunter et al., *Redfern and Hunter on International Arbitration* (Thomson Sweet & Maxwell, 4th ed, 2009)7–12; Okezie Chukwumerije, *Choice of Law in International Commercial Arbitration* (Quorum Books, 1994) 3–6.

[13] These terms are specifically defined by the Chinese legislation, as particularly provided by Chap. 3. Such a distinction is made on the basis that whether such arbitration proceeding is administrated by a Chinese arbitration institution.

[14] *Egerton v Brownlow* (1853) 4 HLC 1.

[15] For the function of public policy for arbitrators, see for example, Pierre Lalive, 'Transnational (or Truly International) Public Policy and International Arbitration' in Pieter Sanders (ed), *Comparative Arbitration Practice and Public Policy in Arbitration,*, ICCA Congress Series (Kluwer Law International, 1987) 258, 36–48.

[16] For this specific function of public policy, see *the Geneva Convention on the Execution of Foreign Awards,* opened for signature 26 September 1927, 92 LNTS 301 (entered into force 25 July 1929) (*'Geneva Convention'*) art 1(e); *the Convention on the Recognition and Enforcement of Foreign Arbitral Awards,* opened for signature opened for signature 6 July 1958, 330 UNTS 38 (entered into force 7 June 1959) art V(2)(b). In regards of the history of the public policy provisions in these international treaties, see Anton Maurer, *The Public Policy Exception under the New York Convention: History, Interpretation and Application* (Juris, 2012).

obligation to make an enforceable arbitral award that bind the parties.[17] Courts of the arbitration forum may also take into account public policy concerns when deciding on *lex fori*, an application for judicial intervention or the annulment of an arbitral award.[18] A final application of public policy is at the stage of enforcement of an arbitral award, as provided by the *NYC*. A typical example of the possible application of public policy at the arbitration stage is provided in a Bulgarian case, in which the Bulgarian arbitration court decided to suspend the application of the forum law to avoid violating the "fundamental rules of foreign public policy".[19]

Though multiple situations attract the application of public policy and different approaches and elements of public policy may be found, all public policy issues are most evident at the stage of judicial review.[20] The judicial review proceeding is the last chance for the parties to refer to public policy as a defence against the enforcement of an award on grounds that it will have a detrimental effect. Therefore, how public policy is applied at the stage of judicial review best illustrates the view of the legal institutions of a particular state. Also, there is international consensus on the interpretation and application of the public policy exception at the enforcement stage, as illustrated by the *NYC*. Based on the understanding of public policy's role in the judicial review, this research focuses predominantly on the ground of public policy applied in judicial review proceedings. However, the discussion of different concepts and aspects of public policy will inevitably influence the application of public policy at the earlier stages of arbitration proceedings, as they are connected to its later application in enforcement proceedings.

It is notable that scholars have referred to the legal concept of public policy in the judicial review of arbitral awards, as it is provided by the *NYC*, in different terms, emphasising different aspects and functions of this legal concept. For example, the term 'ground of public policy' focuses on its position as one of the grounds for the annulment or non-enforcement of arbitral awards[21]; the 'public policy exception' focuses on negating an arbitral award as an extreme exception to the trend in favour of enforcing arbitral awards.[22] The term 'public policy defence' emphasises the incentive of national courts or the parties who use that defence to avoid a possible

---

[17] Karl- Heinz Böckstiegel, 'Public Policy and Arbitrability' in Pieter Sanders (ed), *Comparative Arbitration Practice and Public Policy in Arbitration*, ICCA Congress Series (Kluwer Law International, 1987) 177, 185–186; Richard H. Kriendler, 'Approaches to the Application of Transnational Public Policy by Arbitrators' (2003) 4 *Journal of World Investment and Trade* 239, 242, 249–50.

[18] Stephen M. Schwebel and Susan G. Lahne, 'Public Policy and Arbitral Procedure' in Pieter Sanders (ed), *Comparative Arbitration Practices and Public Policy in Arbitration*, ICCA Congress Series (Kluwer Law International, 1987) 205, 207–210.

[19] Jacob Dolinger,'World Public Policy: Real International Public Policy in Conflict of Laws' (1982) 17 *Texas International Law Journal (Austin)* 167, 185.

[20] The *NYC*, art V(2)(b).

[21] See for example, van den Berg, above n 2, 359–60.

[22] For the exceptional nature, see in general Mayer and Sheppard, above n 3, Recommendation 1(a).

detrimental result once an award is enforced.[23] All these terms generally refer to the same public policy concept in arbitration law.

This book uses the terms ‘public policy exception’ when referring to the concept of public policy in the judicial review of arbitral awards. The choice of the term ‘public policy exception’ is made for the following reasons: firstly, this term is widely accepted in international literature[24]; secondly, it reminds us that such a ground is applied only in exceptional circumstances[25]; and thirdly, it can be applied by the courts on their own motion, which is distinguished from other grounds that negate an arbitral award.[26] The term ‘public policy’ has the same meaning of ‘the public policy exception’ in the context of this book unless it is stated otherwise.[27]

### 2.2.2 Public Policy and Other Grounds that Negate Arbitral Awards

The public policy exception, as one of the grounds in arbitration law for negating an arbitral award in the judicial review process, interacts with other grounds that have similar functions.[28] Most national legislation and international agreements expressly state a list of such grounds for the judicial review of arbitral awards, including the ground of due process, the limitations in the right to arbitrate within the scope of the arbitration agreement, arbitrability, compliance with agreed procedural rules, and public policy.[29]

Public policy is distinguished from these grounds but is still closely connected with them when it functions in arbitration and judicial practices; this is particularly notable insofar as the contents of other grounds overlap with public policy. A significant example is when procedural aspects of public policy may also be addressed by the requirements of due process.[30] Under the circumstances of overlapping grounds, public policy seems to be a residual ground and is ‘never argued at all but when other points fail.’[31] However, it is argued that public policy is not a residual ground and co-exists with other grounds; that the conditions for the application of each ground can be distinguished from each other; and that the parties or national courts may

[23] For example, Dirk Otto and Omaia Elwan, ‘Article V(2)’ in Herbert Kronke et al. (eds), *Recognition and Enforcement of Foreign Arbitral Awards* (Wolter Kluwer, 2010) 345, 365–68.

[24] For example, Mayer and Sheppard, above n 3, [10], [13] and [17].

[25] Ibid, Recommendation 1(a).

[26] This reason is adopted in Maurer, above n 16, 3, fn 9.

[27] For example, the discussion of the legal concept of public policy in Sects. 2.1 and 2.2 in Chap. 2 points to a broader legal concept of public policy which applies to private international law and arbitration law in general and is not specifically limited to the judicial review of arbitral awards.

[28] A typical set of defensive legal schemes is listed in the *NYC*, art V as the grounds for the non-enforcement of foreign arbitral awards.

[29] See the *NYC*, art V.

[30] The *NYC*, art V(1)(b).

[31] *Richardson v Melish* (1824) 2 Bing 228, 252.

choose the most appropriate ground in accordance with the specific circumstances of the case.[32]

The author agrees with the latter approach, which considers that public policy is not a residual ground to negate an award, but a distinct and independent ground that may apply when it is suitable, no matter if other grounds also apply. Based on this understanding, the discussion of the relation between public policy and other grounds in the judicial review of arbitral awards is provided for in later chapters (particularly Chap. 6).

## 2.3 The Definition of China and the Scope of the Chinese Legal System

This book focuses particularly on China's performance in applying the public policy exception to the judicial review of arbitral awards. As stated earlier, China's rapid economic growth, its expanding influence in the arbitration world, as well as its unique legal tradition and culture all contribute to the significance of this study.

The definition of the term 'China' needs to be further clarified due to China's political status. Generally, the terms 'China' and 'Chinese legal system' in this book, unless stated otherwise, refer to the jurisdiction of mainland China only—not the entire People's Republic of China ('PRC' hereafter)—and the legal system that operates in the territory of mainland China as provided by the Constitutional Law of the PRC.[33] The Hong Kong Special Administrative Region ('SAR' hereinafter) and Macao SAR are excluded in our discussion of mainland China's legal system and legal practices except when specifically noted, even though they are part of the People's Republic of China constitutionally, they have different legal systems that are governed by their Basic Laws, and the independence of their legislative and judicial branches of government is authorised by the National People's Congress of the PRC.[34] It is also notable that, though the Constitutional Law of the PRC declares that Taiwan is a part of the PRC's territory, the current legal system in Taiwan is separate from mainland China's legal system due to historical reasons.[35]

---

32 Van den Berg, above n 2, 376.

33 《中华人民共和国宪法》[The Constitutional Law of the People's Republic of China] (People's Republic of China) Chap. 3; detailed discussion, see further Sect. 2 in Chap. 3.

34 《中华人民共和国香港特别行政区基本法》[The Basic Law of the Hong Kong Special Administrative Region of the People's Republic of China] (People's Republic of China) National People's Congress, Order No.26, 4 April 1990, art 2; 《中华人民共和国澳门特别行政区基本法》[The Basic Law of the Macao Special Administrative Region of the People's Republic of China](People's Republic of China) National People's Congress, Order No.3, 31 March 1993, art 2.

35 《中华人民共和国宪法》[The Constitutional Law of the People's Republic of China] (People's Republic of China) Preamble; the constitutional documents applied to the Taiwan region was 《中華民國憲法》[The Constitution of the Republic of China], was enacted before the establishment of the current PRC. See 《中華民國憲法》[The Constitution of the Republic of China](Republic of China), National Constitutional Convention, 25 December 1947, recently amended by《中華民國

The combination of these four jurisdictions is usually referred to as 'the Greater China', which is a broader term than the term 'China' used in this book.[36] Four different jurisdictions exist in the 'Greater China' region, providing four different legal systems, These differences create difficult issues, particularly in the application of law and the enforcement of arbitral awards, because the relations among these divergent legal systems is not governed by international treaties such as the *NYC*. In dealing with these issues, mainland China has reached agreements with the Hong Kong SAR, Macao SAR and Taiwan, which serve as the foundation for the recognition and enforcement of arbitral awards in the Greater China region.[37]

Though Hong Kong, Macao and Taiwan are excluded from our major subject of study, they are still of particular significance in this research. These jurisdictions are closely connected to each other because of territorial proximity, the similarity in traditional culture, and significant economic ties between them. Nevertheless, their different legal systems and legal cultures result in each of them adopting its own distinctive approach to legal practices. For example, the Hong Kong SAR adopts a common law tradition inherited from the UK, while the Macao SAR adopts a civil law tradition from Portugal.[38] The interactions between China and the other Greater China jurisdictions, particularly in applying public policy, provide a significant volume of cases and analyses.[39] The analyses in these cases do not only provide a comparison between Chinese practice, as distinct from the legal practice in Greater China, and those of the other jurisdictions. It also provides a better understanding of traditional Chinese cultural and social notions because of the uniqueness of these Greater China jurisdictions.[40]

憲法增修條文》[The Additional Articles of the Constitution of the Republic of China], Legislative Yuan, 10 June 2005.

[36] See for example, Kathryn Sanger, Beatriz Segorbe and Jill Niu, 'Arbitration in Greater China: Hong Kong, Macau and Taiwan' (2007) 24(6) *Journal of International Arbitration* 651.

[37] See further discussion on the arrangements between Mainland China and Hong Kong SAR, Mainland China and Aacao SAR, as well as Mainland China and Taiwan Region, in Chap. 3.

[38] See generally, the Preambles of《中华人民共和国香港特别行政区基本法》[The Basic Law of the Hong Kong Special Administrative Region of the People's Republic of China] (People's Republic of China) National People's Congress, Order No. 26, 4 April 1990; and《中华人民共和国澳门特别行政区基本法》[The Basic Law of the Macao Special Administrative Region of the People' s Republic of China] (People's Republic of China) National People's Congress, Order No.3, 31 March 1993; See also Sanger et al., above n 36, 652–53, 658–59.

[39] For example, Weixia Gu, '15 Years of the Handover: The Rise, Discontent, and Positive Interaction of Cross-Border Arbitration in Hong Kong with Mainland China' (2014) 9(1) *University of Pennsylvania East Asia Law Review* 42; Xianchu Zhang, 'Enforcement of Arbitral Awards Between Mainland China and Hong Kong: Before and After Reunification' in Raymond Wacks (ed), *The New Legal Order in Hong Kong* (Hong Kong University Press, 1999); Chien-Huei Wu, 'Mutual Recognition of Arbitral Awards among Taiwan, China, Hong Kong and Macau: Regulatory Framework and Judicial Development' (2010) 3(1) *Contemporary Asia Arbitration Journal* 65; Fernando Dias Simões, 'Macau: A Seat for Sino-Lusophone Commercial Arbitration' (2012) 29(4) *Journal of International Arbitration* 375.

[40] Gu, above n 39; Simões, above n 39.

## 3 Methodology

Multiple research methodologies are adopted in this book. These include a textual analysis of legislative materials and cases, quantitative study, comparative study, historical research, and cultural analysis. A combination of these methodologies serve the purpose of examining and evaluating the performance of the Chinese judiciary in applying public policy, identifying the weaknesses of the Chinese approach and proposing a more developed approach.

### 3.1 *Textual Analysis*

First of all, it is worthwhile to examine, through a detailed textual analysis of China's legislation and court decisions, how the Chinese arbitration and judicial system operates. Textual analysis, as the most important method used in this book, is adopted to review both primary and secondary materials from both Chinese and international resources and analysed in both Chinese and English literature. A thorough review of these materials provides the foundation for further study on the Chinese approach to the application of the public policy exception and the possible factors influencing that application process.

### 3.2 *Empirical Study*

Another significant method adopted to review the practices of the Chinese legal system, particularly the Chinese judicial system, is empirical study, which illustrates the performance of the Chinese courts in applying public policy and uses statistics to identify the weaknesses in the Chinese approach.

Examples of adopting this research method can be found in many earlier studies, such as those of Wang Shengchang,[41] Randall Peerenboom,[42] Honglei Yang,[43] and also E'xiang Wan and Xiaohong Xia (most of which dealt with the Chinese

[41] Shengchang Wang, 'Enforcement of Foreign Arbitral Awards in the People's Republic of China' in Christopher R. Drahozal and Richard W. Naimark (eds), *Towards Science on International Arbitration: Collected Empirical Research* (Kulwer Law International, 2005) 277.

[42] Randall Peerenboom, 'Seek Truth From Facts: An Empirical Study of Enforcement of Arbitral Awards in the PRC' (2001) 49 *American Journal of Comparative Law* 249.

[43] 杨宏磊[Yang Honglei],《人民法院涉外仲裁司法审查情况的调研报告》[Investigation and Analysis Report on the Judicial Review of Foreign-Related Arbitration by the People's Courts](2009) 9 武大国际法评论 [*Wuhan University Law Review*] 308.

cases),[44] and other research in Drahozal and Mainmark's 2005 collection.[45] The author outlines the findings of these studies in Chap. 4.

The major component of the empirical study in this book focuses on a pool of 55 Chinese cases determined by the SPC, which deal with the application of the public policy exception. These cases, in which the application of public policy is considered, are collected from multiple sources, which include the official publication of the Supreme People's Court (the SPC), databases, news reports, journal articles and websites.[46] They are further divided into groups and described in accordance with the following factors: date; the outcome; and the element(s) of public policy considered by the courts. Based on these factors, a statistical study then traces the development of the courts' understanding of the public policy exception and its elements and evaluates these judicial practices over time. In addition to this pool of cases, this study also considered various Chinese cases, such as cases dealing with the application of the public policy by lower courts, cases addressing public-policy-related matters in other contexts.

This empirical study identifies the key elements of the public policy exception; it presents the frequency with which courts discuss those key elements and the potential acceptance of them. It also demonstrates the drawbacks in current Chinese practice that may require further improvements in the performance of Chinese courts.

## 3.3 Comparative Study

In conjunction with the review of the textual and statistical analysis, a comparative study is undertaken. From the perspective of the comparative study, the following questions will be posed: does China's understanding of public policy follow any dominant legal tradition, or is it distinctive from practices in other jurisdictions? How do the globalisation movements and foreign development of arbitration law influence China's judicial practice? Regarding the distinctions in China's approach in interpreting and applying public policy, how do differences in social, economic and political environments contribute to such distinctions?

A general literature review in Chap. 2 provides a foundation for this comparative review. It asserts the current international consensus in regard to the public policy exception, to which China's distinctive approach, as summarised in later chapters, is compared. In addition, in Chapters Five to Eight, an in-depth comparative study in dealing with each specific public policy element is included in order to provide

---

[44] 万鄂湘, 夏晓红[Wan E'xiang, Xia Xiaohong],《中国法院不予承认及执行某些外国仲裁裁决的原因——《纽约公约》相关案例分析》[Reason for the Refusals of the Recognition and Enforcement of Foreign Arbitral Awards in Chinese Courts: New York Convention Case Studies] (2010) 13 武大法学评论 [*Wuhan University Law Review*]1, and Xiaohong Xia, 'Implementation of the New York Convention in China' (2011) 1 *International Commercial Arbitration Brief* 20.

[45] Christopher R. Drahozal and Richard W. Naimark (eds.), *Toward a Science of International Arbitration: Collected Empirical Research*, (Kluwer Law International, 2005).

[46] A detailed discussion of the data collection in China, see Sect. 3.1 in Chap. 4.

determinative criteria for evaluating China's performance in dealing with each public policy element.

There are also other types of research methodologies adopted in this book in order to provide a comprehensive and in-depth review of the main topic. These methodologies include illustrating how the public policy exception is applied in China, evaluating its advantages and drawbacks, and explaining why the current approach is adopted. A historical study on the ongoing movements in China and in the international arena establishes how judicial attitudes in applying public policy change over time. Additionally, culture-based analysis and theoretical research explores the cultural and theoretical foundation supporting the distinctive approach adopted by China's courts in applying public policy to international commercial arbitration awards.

The methodology used in the individual chapters differs in order to reflect the particular focus taken. Part I is written descriptively, drawing on historical developments, legislative frameworks, and reports on the case-based statistical study. Parts II and III provide well-rounded legal research beyond the cases, including theoretical study, comparative study, and cultural analyses. The book attempts to combine these multiple methodologies, each of which has its unique position in this study and contributes to the final conclusion of presenting a full picture of China's approach in applying the public policy exception.

This chapter introduces the scope of the book, definition of key terms, and research methods and provides guidance on how to read the ensuing chapters. Chapters Two and Three further the review of a few key terms and fundamental issues mentioned in this chapter, which become the foundation of later analyses and discussion. Some key questions will be answered in Parts II (Chaps. 4–8) and III (Chap. 9 and the Final Chapter).

# Chapter 2
# Public Policy in International Arbitration Law

## 1 Introduction

Building on the definitions outlined in Chapter One, especially the definition of the term 'public policy' as a ground to negate arbitral awards, this chapter further introduces the general legal framework of the ground of public policy in arbitration law by reviewing the legal schemes that define public policy, particularly focusing on the role and limits of a national legal system. This chapter aims to introduce the current international consensus and predominant trends in the practice of applying public policy, to which the Chinese approach, as will be introduced in Chapters Three, is to be compared with and analysed in later chapters of this book.

The public policy exception is applied in both national and international legal practice, and its uniqueness is emphasised in international commercial arbitration. On the one hand, the application of the public policy exception helps the States, normally at the place of arbitration and where the award is enforced, to protect their own social order and interests that are covered by the public policy exception; on the other hand, the international arbitration community needs to limit the use of public policy by national courts in their judicial review of arbitral awards, in order to promote the universal acceptance of arbitration and to ensure the finality and enforceability of arbitral awards. The conflict between the national interests of states and the international aspirations of arbitration that transcends national interests is the source of ongoing tension in the application of the legal concept of public policy.

The resolution of such a conflict also requires national legal systems to balance their national interests on one hand against the needs of international commerce on the other. Under the influence of the internationalisation of arbitration practice, legislative and judicial systems in many jurisdictions have made efforts to respond to the international arbitration movements in developing legal schemes that define and apply the legal concept of public policy.

Section 2 of this chapter introduces the fundamental definition and characteristics of public policy in general and its adoption in arbitration law and explores its



S. Zhang, *The Public Policy Exception in the Judicial Review of International Commercial Arbitral Awards*, https://doi.org/10.1007/978-3-662-67679-0_2

historical development under the influence of ongoing globalisation movements in the economic and legal environments impacting on arbitration practice. Section 3 further examines the developments in defining and applying public policy at the national and international levels. Section 4 discusses the notions and distinctions between domestic and international public policies, and the emergence of a transnational, or "truly international public policy" in arbitration law. Sections 5 and 6 analyse the contents of public policy and its influence on arbitrators' decision-making.

## 2 The Developments of Public Policy in International Arbitration Law: A Historical Review

Before reviewing the history of the development of public policy in international arbitration, it is worthwhile clarifying the scope of public policy discussed in this book. Among the purely domestic public policy that applies to domestic matters, the international public policy that applies in the context of private international law, and the transnational or "truly international" public policy that goes beyond national law, the second and third categories of public policy are our major focus in the discussion of international commercial arbitration.[1]

### *2.1 The Origin and Fundamental Characteristics of Public Policy*

Public policy has long been accepted as a legal concept or principle of law. It is traditionally referred to as a principle of law "which holds that no subject can lawfully do that which has a tendency to be injurious to the public, or against the public good."[2] Public policy is considered as representing public goods or public interests, and aims to protect them from certain kinds of illegality or detrimental outcome. This is particularly germane in dealing with the application of foreign law and the enforcement of foreign judgments of awards.[3]

Public policy is well embedded as a traditional legal concept in a variety of jurisdictions. In continental law jurisdictions, the legal concept of public order first arose in Roman law in order to prohibit the derogation from public law by way of

---

[1] This categorisation is referred to by many scholars, e.g., Jacob Dolinger, 'World Public Policy: Real International Public Policy in the Conflict of Laws' (1982) 17 *Texas International Law Journal (Austin)* 167.

[2] *Egerton v Brownlow* (1853) 4 HLC 1.

[3] *Renusagar Power Co Ltd v General Electric Co,* [1987] SCR (3) 858, reported in (1995) 20 *Yearbook-Commercial Arbitration* 681, 24; *Deutsche Schachtbau-und TiefbohrgesellscaftmbH v Ras Al Khaimah National Oil Company* [1987] 2 *Lloyd's Rep* 246, 254.

contract.[4] In the fourteenth century, legal scholars such as Bartolus (1314–1357) first observed different treatments of foreign law in other jurisdictions and developed the use of public order in the context of private international law.[5] These observations and analyses were further developed by scholars such as Huber (1636–1694), Story (1802–1855), Savigny (1779–1861) and Mancini (1817–1888) in the continental law jurisdictions.[6] Savigny's idea of the limited effect of legal relations on the basis of space is considered a representation of public policy.[7] In common law countries, as argued by Nussbaum, the legal principle of public policy arose earlier than, and was independent from, its counterparts in the civil law jurisdictions[8]; it is reported that public policy was applied in contract law in the fifteenth century and in private international law in the eighteenth century in the common law traditions.[9]

Our discussion of public policy is limited to its application in the context of private international law. Public policy has many significant characteristics. First, public policy has an ambiguous and changing character. It is difficult to provide a comprehensive interpretation of public policy that includes all elements and situations in which such a conception might apply.[10] The application of public policy may be interpreted differently over time and in different legal contexts.[11] It is described as an "unruly horse" that may have unpredictable outcomes as "when you get astride, you never know where it will carry you."[12]

In addition, public policy has a strong connection with each state's particular legal traditions and culture. One presentation of this feature is in the distinction between "public policy" in common law countries and *"ordre public"* in continental

---

[4] For example, the law maxim "pactisprivatorumjuri public non derogatur" means that private contracts do not derogate from public law. See Herber Broom, *A Selection of Legal Maxims, Illustrated and Classified* (3rd ed, Maxwell, 1858) 620–21.

[5] Bartolus, *Bartolo on the Conflict of Laws* (J.A.Clarence Smith trans) (1970) 14 *The American Journal of Legal History* 157, 263, where Bartolus commented on the possible public policy and morality concerns underlying the law which may influence the extension of the effect of local law in other cities. See also Friedrich K. Juenger, *Choice of Law and Multistate Justice* (Martinus Nijhoff, 1993) 157. For an introduction of the historical development of public policy doctrine, see Dolinger, above n 1, 169–177.

[6] Xiao Yongping and HuoZhenxin, '*Ordre Public* in China's Private International Law' (2005) 54 *American Journal of Comparative Law* 653, 653–654.

[7] Friedrich Karl von Savigny, *Private International Law: A Treatise of the Conflict of Laws and the Limits of Their Operation in Respect of Time and Space* (William Guthrie trans, Nabu, 2010) [trans of: *System des HeutigenRomischenRechts* (first published 1840)].

[8] Arthur Nussbaum, 'Public Policy and the Political Crisis in the Conflict of Laws' (1940) 49(6) *The Yale Law Journal* 1027, 1029.

[9] Ibid.

[10] Julian D. M. Lew, Loukas A. Mistelis and Stefan Michael Kröll, *Comparative International Commercial Arbitration* (Kluwer Law International, 2003), ch 26, 721; *Renusagar Power* [1987] SCR, [24].

[11] John Westlake, *A Treatise on Private International Law* (Sweet & Maxwell, 7th ed, 1925) 51; Dolinger, above n 1, 169; *CBI NZ Ltd* v *Badger Chiyoda* [1989] 2 NZLR 669, 674.

[12] Richardson v. Mellish [1834] All ER 258,266, per Burrough, J.

legal jurisdictions.[13] Public policy is mainly discovered and defined through cases in the common law tradition, while *ordre public* is defined in continental codes and is more abstract in nature, and subject to further interpretation in accordance with the processes regulated by those codes.[14] The meaning of public policy is also strongly connected with distinctive social, economic or political needs in particular jurisdictions. The national particularities ascribed to public policy also contribute to the difficulties in reaching a unified definition of public policy in light of its distinctive interpretation in the interests of discrete states; for example, some public policy considerations in some Islamic jurisdictions may be distinct from other jurisdictions as they are based on *Shari'a*; under this public policy, interest of any form is strictly prohibited.[15]

Given the dependence of public policy on national definitions, it is used as an instrument by national courts to safeguard the interests of a state, especially when a foreign legal element would otherwise undermine those interests. It is recognised as a "safety valve" invoked by a state to protect its national interests.[16]

## 2.2 *Historical Developments of Arbitration and the Application of Public Policy Within that Context*

Arbitration has its roots in the medieval Law Merchant within the business community, where it developed as a private method of dispute resolution alternative to the mainstream "ultimate justice" provided by courts.[17] Because of its private nature,

[13] A discussion of the difference and connection between 'public policy' and 'ordre public', see further Sect. 5.

[14] It is concluded that the European Scholars such as Savigny, Mancini and Brocher preferred to explore the position of *ordre public* from the perspective of the type and character of the legal rules, while the scholars adopting common law traditions were inclined to discuss the situations where public policy would be applied. Harris P. Meidanis, 'Public Policy and *Ordre Public* in the Private International Law of EU: Traditional Positions and Modern Trends' (2005) 30(1) *European Law Review* 95, 99–100.

[15] K.T. Roy, 'The New York Convention and Saudi Arabia: Can a Country Use the Public Policy Defense to Refuse Enforcement of Non-Domestic Arbitral Awards?' (1994) 18(3) *Fordham International Law Journal* 920; Abdulrahman Baamir and Ilias Bantekas, 'Saudi Law as Lex Arbitri: Evaluation of Saudi Arbitration Law and Judicial Practice' (2009) 25(2) *Kluwer Law International* 239, 265; Naif Al-Shareef, *Enforcement of Foreign Arbitral Awards in Saudi Arabia: Grounds for Refusal under Article V of the New York Convention* (University of Dundee, 2000) 151.

[16] Herbert Kronke et al., *Recognition and Enforcement of Foreign Arbitral Awards* (Wolters Kluwer, 2010) 365; Juenger, above n 5, 157.

[17] Julian D. M. Lew, Loukas A. Mistelis and Stefan Michael Kröll, 'Arbitration as a Dispute Settlement Mechanism' in *Comparative International Commercial Arbitration* (Kluwer Law International, 2003) 1, [1–8], [1–9]; Jerome T. Barrett and Joseph P. Barrett, *A History of Alternative Dispute Resolution: The Story of a Political, Cultural, and Social Movement* (Jossey-Bass, 2004). A further discussion of the Law Merchant and its influence on the development of the modern practice of arbitration, see Leon Trakman, 'From the Medieval to the Twenty First Century Law Merchant', (2011)28(4) *American Business Law Journal* 775, Part I and II.

arbitration was conceived as having advantages in terms of speed, neutrality, flexibility, party participation and cost-effectiveness.[18] Several fundamental rules and principles of arbitration originated from its private nature, including the principle of party autonomy,[19] and the competence-competence rule.[20] Grounded in the freedom of the parties to exercise a choice of arbitration over the submission of a dispute to national courts, the choice of arbitration creates the possibility of parties choosing to adopt international rules to govern arbitration, as distinct from the national laws applied by national court judges.[21] These characteristics of arbitration are distinct from the national law and practice applied by national courts.[22]

As a private and alternative method of dispute resolution to national courts, arbitration is frequently challenged by national courts; and public policy is one the tools used by national courts to exclude arbitration. A strong hostile attitude to arbitration in judicial system was evident, particularly in common law jurisdictions, prior to the wide recognition of international commercial arbitration after the emergence of world trade. Frank J in *Kulukundis Shipping Co SA* v *Amtog Trading Corp*[23] reviewed the history of arbitration, and concluded that judicial hostility to enforcement of arbitration agreements existed long before the modern arbitration law was established in the 1920s; similar views are also evident in continental law jurisdictions.[24] The hostile attitude towards arbitration from national legal systems led to defensive legal responses to arbitration proceedings and arbitral awards, including the application of national public policy. For example, broad-based public policy objections were observed in the UK and US[25]; similarly, the principle of *ordre public*, together

---

[18] Lew, Mistelis and Kröll, above n.17, [1-19]-[1-30]; Gary B. Born, *International Commercial Arbitration* (Kluwer Law International, 2nd ed, 2014) 62.

[19] Ibid, 83–86. For a discussion of the principle of party autonomy, see Karl-Heinz Böckstiegel, 'The Role of Party Autonomy in International Arbitration' (1997) 52(3) *Dispute Resolution Journal* 24; Mo Zhang, 'Party Autonomy and Beyond: An International Perspective of Contractual Choice of Law' (2006) 20(2) *Emory International Law Review* 511; International Law Institute, 'Resolution on the Autonomy of the Parties in International Contracts Between Private Persons or Entities' (1992) 64 *Annuaire de l'Institut de Droit International*383.

[20] Lew, Mistelis and Kröll, above n.17, [14-13]-[14-18]; Alan Redfern et al., *Redfern and Hunter on International Arbitration* (Oxford University, 2009), 347–349.

[21] See Julian D.M. Lew, *Applicable Law in International Commercial Arbitration:A Study in Commercial Arbitration Awards* (Oceana Publications, 1978). Lew discussed the application of the non-legal system of private international law in Chap. 6, the application of non-legal standards in Chap. 8, and the application of an extra-legal standard in Chap. 6.

[22] The distinction is particular significant in the sense of arbitration procedure; and in regard to the applicable substantive law, though it is usually provided by a national legal system, the parties can still choose one that they think suits from multiple sets of applicable law that from different jurisdictions. For further discussion of the applicable law in arbitration, see Lew, above n 21.

[23] *Kulukundis Shipping Co SA* v*Amtog Trading Corp* [1942] 126 F.2d 978 (2nd Cir, 1942).

[24] Arthur Von Mehren, 'International Commercial Arbitration: The Contribution of the French Jurisprudence' (1986) 46(4) *Louisiana Law Review* 1045, 1048–1051.

[25] *Kill* v *Hollister* [1746] 95 ER 532, 532.

with other defensive schemes, served as a barrier to the enforcement of arbitration agreements in France.[26]

## 2.3 Developments of International Arbitration in Modern Times and the Calls for a New Definition of Public Policy

The hostility towards arbitration has gradually weakened over time, which is a consequence of the general acceptance of international commercial arbitration in responding to economic globalisation.[27] Along with this change in attitude have been adaptations in national arbitration systems, greater support for international arbitration, and exploration of the definition and scope of public policy in relation to arbitration generally. These developments are discussed further below.

In the modern economy, international commercial arbitration is preferred and promoted for its advantages, such as flexibility, party autonomy and cost-effectiveness.[28] These advantages are emphasised in particular when commercial transactions are of an international nature. In complicated and multi-cultural disputes, international commercial arbitration is likely to be more effective and attractive than litigation before national courts.[29] These advantages can be illustrated through typical transnational BOT (Build-Operate-Transfer) transactions, involving parties such as local government, foreign investors, contractors and project operators. Such contracts include long-term contract relationships on construction, rent, project operation, finance, ownership and even employee and environment issues. Compared to the uncertainty and cost of litigation proceedings before national courts, an arbitration agreement is preferred because it can provide forum, applicable law and arbitrators, ensure party-participation, and save costs for dispute resolution[30]; in the tradition of Law Merchant, arbitration is considered as providing a "speedy mercantile justice".[31]

Though it is argued that arbitration is generally independent from national legal systems and their national courts, the functioning of arbitration is not wholly autonomous. In particular, the effective conduct of international arbitration and the enforcement of arbitral awards is subject to the procedural requirements to the *lex fori*, to the *lex arbitri* adopted by the courting court, and to the applicable substantive law arising from the applicable choice of laws.[32] The parties and legal professionals, at least at the enforcement stage, still need to face diversified, unfamiliar and sometimes

---

[26] Mehren, above n.24, 1051.

[27] Born, above n 18, 37.

[28] Lew, Mistelis and Kröll, above n 17, [1–19]-[1–30]; Born, above n 18, 62.

[29] Lew, Mistelis and Kröll, above n 17, 5.

[30] W. Laurence Craig, 'Some Trends and Developments in the Laws and Practice of International Commercial Arbitration' (1995) 20 *Texas International Law Journal* 1, 5.

[31] Leon Trakman, "Legal Traditions' and International Commercial Arbitration' (2006) 17 *American Review of International Arbitration* 1, 6.

[32] Lew, Mistelis and Kröll, above n 17.

hostile legal environments of a particular state; thus, an increasing need is required for a deeper understanding and wider acceptance of international arbitration practice.[33]

During the twentieth century, many efforts were made to facilitate the universal acceptance of arbitration. This included standardising international arbitration practice, reducing state interventions in arbitration proceedings and awards, and promoting the recognition and enforcement of arbitral awards before national courts.[34] International consensus was represented by the enactment of the *Geneva Protocol on Arbitration Clauses in 1923*[35] and the *Geneva Convention on the Execution of Foreign Awards of 1927*.[36] They provided for the first time an enforcement mechanism for an arbitral award to be enforced internationally. After World War II, the International Chamber of Commerce (ICC) and the United Nations Economic and Social Council (ECOSOC) developed a new draft convention governing the enforcement of international arbitral awards, which later formed the *NYC*.[37] Despite slight discrepancies, the legal enforcement of arbitration awards has also been adopted in a variety of multilateral agreements regarding the recognition of judgments, arbitral awards and the choice of jurisdictions, such as in the *1968 Brussels Convention, the 1975 Panama Convention, 1979 Montevideo Convention, 1983 Riyadh Agreement, 1987 Amman Convention and the 1999 OHADA Uniform Act on Arbitration.*[38] The

[33] Katherine Lynch, *The Forces of Economic Globalization: Challenges to the Regime of International Commercial Arbitration* (Kluwer Law International, 2003) 1–2.

[34] *Ibid;* Born, above n 18, 63–70.

[35] *The Geneva Protocol on Arbitration Clauses in Commercial Matters*, signed on 24 September 1923, 27 LNTS 158 ('*Geneva Protocol*').

[36] *The Geneva Convention on the Execution of Foreign Awards*, opened for signature 26 September 1927, 92 LNTS 301 (entered into force 25 July 1929) ('*Geneva Convention*').

[37] *The Convention on the Recognition and Enforcement of Foreign Arbitral Awards*, opened for signature 6 July 1958, 330 UNTS 38 (entered into force 7 June 1959) art V(2)(b); Anton Maurer, *The Public Policy Exception under the New York Convention: History, Interpretation and Application* (Juris, 2012) Chap. 3; Albert Jan van den Berg, *The New York Convention of 1958: Towards a Uniform Judicial Interpretation* (Kluwer Law International, 1981) 1–10.

[38] Mauer, above n 37, Chap. 4. *The Convention on Jurisdiction and the Enforcement of Judgments in Civil and Commercial Matters*, signed at Brussels, 27 September 1968, (entered into force on 1 Feburary 1973) ('*the Brussels Convention*'); this convention was later amended by the *Accession Conventions*, and has been replaced by Council Regulation, *EC No. 44/2001 on Jurisdiction and the Recognition and Enforcement of Judgments in Civil and Commercial Matters* (entered into force on 1 March 2002) ('*Brussels I Regulation*'). The *Inter-American Convention on International Commercial Arbitration*, signed at Panama, January 30 1975 (entered into force on 16 June 1976) ('*the Panama Convention*'); the *Inter-American Convention on Extraterritorial Validity of Foreign Judgements and Arbitral Awards*, adopted at Montevideo, Uruguay, on 8 May 1979 (entered into force on 14 June 1980) ('the *Montevideo Convention*'); League of Arab States, *Riyadh Arab Agreement for Judicial Cooperation*, enacted on6 April 1983 (entered into force 30 October 1985) ('the *Riyadh Agreement*'); *Convention Arabe D'Amman Sur L'Arbitrage Commercial* [*the Arab Convention on Commercial Arbitration*] enacted on 14 April 1987 (entered into force on 25 June 1992) ('the Amman Convention'); *Organisation pour l'Harmonisation en Afrique du Droit des Affaires* [the Organisation for the Harmonization of Business Law in Africa]('OHADA'), *Uniform Act on Arbitration*, enacted 10 March 1999, implemented on 11 June 1999.

UNCITRAL also sought to produce a "unified legal framework for the fair and efficient settlement of disputes arising in international commercial relations" and later provided the *UNCITRAL Model Law* on this purpose.[39]

Following these international developments, national legal systems have made various attempts to regulate arbitration awards. The *NYC* now has 153 parties[40]; over 90 jurisdictions have also adopted the *UNCITRAL Model Law*, such as Australia, Canada, New Zealand, Hong Kong, Italy and Russia,[41] or modified national legislation incorporating the primary elements of the *Model Law*.[42] National legal systems still sometimes limit the scope of arbitral awards through judicial review of arbitral jurisdiction, proceedings and arbitral awards, but such limitations are ordinarily required to be used only in exceptional circumstances and subject to the exhaustive grounds listed by the *NYC*.[43] Because of the functioning of the *NYC* and other multilateral agreements, the enforceability of arbitral awards is now universally accepted in legislation at the national level.[44] China also participated in these activities. It adopted the *NYC* in 1987 and the *Washington Convention* (the *ICSID Convention*) in 1992 and modified its national arbitration system accordingly.[45]

Public policy, however, remains an obstacle in the universal acceptance of arbitration and arbitral awards. The ambiguity and changing character of public policy is reflected in the arbitration practice, and has caused great concerns across the whole

---

[39] Model Law on International Commercial Arbitration of the United Nations Commission on International Trade Law, UN GAOR, 40th sess, Supp No. 17, UN Doc A/40/17, annex I (21 June 1985); passed by the GA Res 40/72, UN GAOR, 40th sess, 112th plenmtg, Agenda Item 135, UN Doc A/RES/40/72 (11 December 1985); amended by GA Res A/RES/61/33, UN GAOR, 61th sess, 64th plenmtg, Agenda Item 77, UN Doc A/RES/61/33 (4 Dec 2006); Howard M. Holtzmann and Joseph E. Neuhaus, *A Guide to the* UNCITRAL *Model Law on International Commercial Arbitration: Legislative History and Commentary* (Kluwer Law and Taxation, 1989) 6.

[40] UNCITRAL, *Status: Convention on the Recognition and Enforcement of Foreign Arbitral Awards (New York,* 1958*)*, UNCITRAL, <http://www.uncitral.org/uncitral/en/uncitral_texts/arbitration/NYConvention_status.html>.

[41] *The International Arbitration Act 1974(*Cth) s 16(1), "Subject to this Part, the Model Law has the force of law in Australia".

[42] UNCITRAL, *Status of the UNCITRAL Model Law,* UNCITRAL, <http://www.uncitral.org/uncitral/en/uncitral_texts/arbitration/1985Model_arbitration_status.html> . China's reference to Model Law, see 赵秀文[Zhao Xiuwen],《中国仲裁法与建设社会主义和谐社会》[On the PRC Arbitration Law and Construction of Socialist Harmonious Society] (2006) 101 仲裁与法律*Arbitration and Law* 5, 6.

[43] Van den Berg, above n 37, 265; Kronke et al., above n 16, 209–10; Lew, Mistelis and Kröll, above n 17, [26–65]; *Parsons and Whittemore Overseas Co, Inc v Sociétégénérale de l'industrie du papier (RAKTA)* (1974) 508 F 2d 969 (2nd Cir, 1974).

[44] Lew, Mistelis and Kröll, above n 17, 6.

[45]《最高人民法院关于执行我国加入的 < 承认及执行外国仲裁裁决公约 > 的通知》[Notice of the Supreme People's Court in regard of the Implementation of the 'Convention on the Recognition and Enforcement of Foreign Arbitral Award' ](People's Republic of China), Supreme People's Court, 法(经)发(1987)5号[Supreme Court (Economic) Notice No.5], 10 April 1987;《对外经济贸易部关于认真做好执行 < 华盛顿公约 > 工作的通知》[Notice of the Ministry of Foreign Trade and Economic Co-operation in Regard of the Implementation of the Washington Convention] (People's Republic of China), The Ministry of Foreign Trade and Economic Co-operation, 1 August 1992. Discussion of the reforms in China's arbitration system, see further Sect. 3 in Chap. 3.

international arbitration system.[46] It is particularly concerning that national courts may use public policy self-interestedly for local and personal interests; the concerns are that if all nations use the public policy exception from a self-interested perspective, it will result in a high rate of non-enforcement of arbitral awards and undermine the ultimate aim of general acceptance of international commercial arbitration practice.[47] Based on the rapid development of international arbitration in general and these concerns in particular, it is important for the international arbitration community to urgently develop clear definitions or understandings of public policy. The following sections further discuss the development of public policy at both the international and national levels.

## 3 National and International Movements in Regulating the Application of Public Policy to Arbitration Practice

Promoting a unified and narrow approach in applying public policy is a significant step in the process of finding the balance between the protection of distinct national interests and the international needs of facilitating arbitration. While the international arbitration community endorses a friendly legal environment for the enforcement of arbitral awards, the national courts still engage in their own interpretations that promote national interests and public goods. The settlement of the conflicts between national legal systems and international arbitration depends on both the formulation of a legal consensus in the international arbitral community, and corresponding consensus in various national legal systems; the joint agreement of all stakeholders of international commercial arbitration are required to reach such a balance. Efforts have been made at both the international level and national levels to accomplish these goals, particularly regarding the application of public policy.

### *3.1 International Movements: Legislative Attempts to Restrict and Unify Public Policy*

The international legislative movement, which attempts to embody a worldwide consensus and unified practical framework, has responded to the application of public policy. It has provided some understanding through the development of a supportive

[46] Winnie (Jo-Mei) Ma, *Public Policy in the Judicial Enforcement of Arbitral Awards: Lessons for and from Australia* (Ph.D. Thesis, Bond University 2005) 23.

[47] Maurer, above n 37, 4.

legislative history and through processes by which public policy is applied in practice. The most important stages of this development are reflected in the *Geneva Convention,*[48] the *NYC*[49] and the *UNCITRAL Model Law.*[50]

The most influential legislative process in the twentieth century is the discussion and approval of the *NYC*. In drafting Article V(2)(b) of the *NYC*, opinions from states' representatives, governments, NGOs, and arbitration institutions were submitted and intensively discussed. Opinions were expressed for and against different variations of public policy as a legal concept. The debates reflected the diversified understandings of public policy in different jurisdictions and how the international agreements were reached. For example, European countries, such as Belgium and Sweden, expressed their preference to adopt a conception of "public order/*ordre public*", and that the definition only refers to "fundamental principles of law".[51] In contrast, common law jurisdictions preferred to identify public policy with general "principles of law" and that this should be limited to include the "subject matter thereof".[52] This position was strongly opposed by some stakeholders, not limited to European civil law countries.[53] A number of NGOs and professional institutions, such as the ILA, expressed the wish to restrict the application of public policy and suggested a narrow approach to it in legislation.[54]

After a number of conferences and meetings, the representatives finally reached agreement on the current Article V(2)(b), which only refers to the concept of public policy; the references to "subject matter" and "principles of law" were removed. Public policy was for the first time listed as a ground for refusing to recognise and enforce arbitral awards; it changed the status of public policy as a "precondition" to enforcement in the *Geneva Convention.*[55] It is also notable that the power to refuse recognition and enforcement of an arbitral award should be executed with discretion and not mandatorily.[56]

The consensus represented by the *NYC*, however, does not provide a detailed legal scheme for the application of public policy. The *NYC* did not provide further clarification of the term "public policy" but instead left much room for national interpretations in practice.[57] Also, the *NYC* is not self-executing, which means that

48 *Geneva Convention,* art 1(e); van den Berg, above n 37, 6–8.

49 *New York Convention,* art V(2)(b).

50 *UNCITRAL Model Law*, art 36.

51 Maurer, above n.37, 18.

52 Ibid.

53 One exception is that New Zealand, with Common Law tradition, expressed that they found the wording of "fundamental principles of law" sufficient. See Ibid.

54 Maurer, above n.37, 28–9.

55 Ibid, 13, 58.

56 This is emphasised by using "may", not "shall" in drafting Art V of the *New York Convention.* van den Berg, above n 37, 265. However, it is doubtful that the Convention intends to provide a discretionary power, or it is largely a by-product of the different translations of the Convention. Kronke et al., above n 16, 207–09.

57 Maurer, above n 37, 57.

its application relies on the implementation of its signatory states.[58] Similarly, the *UNCITRAL Model Law* is not binding unless the national legislative bodies choose to enact it in whole or in part domestically[59]; it also leaves plenty of key terms, including "public policy", unexplained, and relies on national legal systems, and their courts, to provide such explanations.

As a result of these international movements to provide uniform law of international arbitration, a fundamental set of principles and standards are widely respected and incorporated into national legal systems; the ground of public policy is a part of such uniform law. However, the task of clarifying the nature of public policy and setting out guidelines regarding its application, are far from satisfactory. The concept of public policy remains abstract and requires further interpretation. As a result, attempts to unify the application of public policy are still largely subject to national legal systems.[60]

## 3.2 National Schemes: The Tension Between Unification and Localisation

The detailed contexts of public policy still depend on the domestic legal system of each country. Its implementation is subject to the discretion of the contracting parties, national legislation, and the judicial practice of courts.[61] Given that the nature and application of public policy is reflected through the judicial review of arbitral awards, judicial practice is of particular significance in determining the parameters of public policy.

Tensions exist in the application of public policy in judicial review and it is evident that attempts to arrive at a consensus over public policy are subject to two disparate movements: unification movements across national jurisdictions, and localisation movements within domestic legal systems. The general trend towards unification is illustrated by the evolving consensus that public policy should be narrowly construed and limited to exceptional circumstances in which the most fundamental morals, values or principles are violated.[62] Selective consistency is also observed among

58 Ibid.

59 UNCITRAL describe the *Model Law* as "a suggested pattern for law-makers to consider adopting as part of their domestic legislation". UNCITRAL, <http://www.uncitral.org/uncitral/en/uncitral_texts/arbitration/1985Model_arbitration_status.html>

60 For example, as provided by Pierre Mayer and Audley Sheppard, 'Final Report on Public Policy as a Bar to Enforcement of International Arbitral Awards' (Paper presented at the International Law Association New Delhi Conference Committee on International Commercial Arbitration, New Delhi, 2002), the definition and application of public policy in reviewing arbitral awards still largely rely on the performance of national courts.

61 For example, the Italian representative and Israeli representative discussed whether the principle of *res judicata* should be included in public policy; the Italian representative was of the opinion that it would depend on the discretion of each jurisdiction. See Maurer, above n 37, Chap. 3.

62 Mayer and Sheppard, above n 60, Recommendation 1(a).

legislative rules by adopting identical terms when referring to public policy: for example, five countries referred to the conception of public policy in the *NYC* directly; nine used the term "public policy" generally; and seven used the phrase "international public policy".[63] Others defined public policy, *inter alia*, under private international law, or by referring to a few key issues such as fraud, corruption, breach of natural justice, the violation of good morals or a breach of public order.[64] Notwithstanding these slight differences, the legislation incorporating public policy defences were generally consistent.[65]

Localisation movements, on the other hand, are caused by reliance on the public policy "of that country" in the *NYC*[66]; furthermore, the abstract nature of public policy in the *NYC* requires further clarification and interpretation by each specific state, which is part of the localisation of arbitration law.[67] The practices in applying public policy vary from applying a general liberal conception of it in European civil law jurisdictions to applying a more restrictive conception of it in common law jurisdictions[68]; there are yet other jurisdictions that do not conceive of public policy explicitly or recognise its importance in the recognition and enforcement of arbitration awards.[69] Discrepancies in the application of public policy are observed across national legal systems.[70]

The localisation of the public policy exception in arbitration law is consistent with its diverse and changing character, as well as its connection with domestic interests and backgrounds.[71] National legislatures and courts interpret public policy at the request of local demands and on the basis of discrete legal, environmental, cultural and certain specific circumstances. Distinct national interests and values are emphasized by national courts in applying public policy; inconsistent practices and outcomes arise in regard to identical issues in different jurisdictions.[72] Arbitral awards granting legal interest, granting contractual interests, dealing with the concept of profit, or awards made by non-Muslim arbitrators, can be considered as a violation of public policy in some Muslim or Arabian jurisdictions because they may violate the

---

[63] James D. Fry, 'Desordre Public International under the New York Convention: Wither Truly International Public Policy' (2009) 8(1) *Chinese Journal of International Law* 81, 94–100.

[64] Ibid.

[65] Ibid, 100.

[66] *TheNYC*, art V(2)(b).

[67] A discussion of localisation of arbitration law is provided by Kun Fan, 'Transnational Standards Struggling with Local Norms: Through the Lens of Arbitration Transplantation in China' (2013) 18 *Harvard Negotiation Law Review* 175.

[68] Richard Garnett, 'The Legal Framework for International Arbitration in Australia: The Old and the New' in Luke Nottage and Richard Garnett (eds), *International Arbitration in Australia* (Federation, 2010) 38.

[69] Fry, above n 63, 94–95.

[70] Homayoon Arfazadeh, 'In the Shadow of the Unruly Horse: International Arbitration and the Public Policy Exception' (2002) 13 *American Review of International Arbitration* 43, 50.

[71] Section 2.1.

[72] Auldey Sheppard, 'Interim Report on Public Policy as a Bar to Enforcement of International Arbitral Awards' (2000) 19(3) *Arbitration International* 217, Part V.

Muslim *Shari'a*; such activities, however, these would not be considered as violations of public policy of other jurisdictions.[73] Similarly, arbitral awards rendering punitive damages were found to be a violation of public policy in some civil law jurisdictions, such as Japan, Germany, Switzerland and Sweden, but not in others, especially some common law jurisdictions such as the US and Australia in which punitive damages for violations of public policy arising out of commercial contracts are not ordinarily granted.[74]

Tensions regarding which goals, either unification or localisation, is recognised in applying public policy occur at the judicial stage and among academics. This difference of opinion was addressed as *"a tension …between: on the one hand, not wishing to lend the State's authority to enforcement of awards which contravene domestic laws and values; and, on the other hand, the desire to respect the finality of foreign awards."*[75] This is a precise description of the debate around how the legal concept of public policy should be developing.

## 3.3 Recent Discussions and Developments

On the basis of the current trend of unification on one hand and localisation on the other hand in arbitration practices, and the urgent requirement to further develop the legal concept of public policy, worldwide arbitration practitioners and researchers attempt to further clarify the meaning and function of public policy and unify its application in the judicial review of international arbitral awards.

Discussion of the public policy exception in arbitration practice and in the judicial review of arbitral awards has evolved along with the development of arbitration law and has always played a part in the worldwide communication relating to international commercial arbitration. As early as at the drafting stage of the *NYC*, the scope and expression of public policy was hotly debated by representatives from different jurisdictions, providing conflicting and overlapping views on its significance, use and effect.[76] The 1986 ICCA Congress further discussed several significant issues in relation to public policy in arbitration law, including its relationship with arbitrability, arbitral procedure, applicable law, the existence of a transnational(truly international) public policy, and its application in a variety of jurisdictions.[77]

---

[73] Al-Shareef, above n 15, 151;Jalal El-Ahdab, 'Saudi Arabia Accedes to the New York Convention' (1994) 11 *Journal of International Arbitration* 87, 91.

[74] Bundesgerichtshof [Federal Court of Justice], 4 June reported in 118 Entscheidungen des Bundesgerichtshofes in Zivilsachen [BGHZ] 312, 338; ICC Case No. 5946, reported in (1991) 16 *Yearbook-Commercial Arbitration* 97; *XL Petroleum NSW Pty Ltd* v *Caltex Oil (Aust.) Pty Ltd* (1985) 155 CLR 448; *Lamb* v*Cotogno* (1987) 74 ALR 188; *Willis* v *Shearson and American Express Inc* 569 F Supp 821(2nd Cir, 1983).

[75] Sheppard, above n 72, 218.

[76] Maurer, above n 37, Chap. 3.

[77] Pieter Sanders (ed.), *Comparative Arbitration Practices and Public Policy in Arbitration,* ICCA Congress Series (Kluwer Law International, 1987) 117–366.

More recently, from 2000 to 2002, the ILA conducted a detailed study on the scope and concepts of public policy in international arbitration. The outcome is contained in the "*Final ILA Report on Public Policy as a Bar to Enforcement of International Arbitral Awards*".[78] This report best illustrates the current international consensus in regard to the definition and application of public policy in relation to judicial reviews of international arbitral awards. The confirmed international consensus includes the key notions that public policy should be a well-rounded legal concept that includes both procedural and substantial public policies[79]; that the meaning of the term 'public policy' used in common law jurisdictions and '*ordre public*' used in continental civil law jurisdictions should be considered synonymous[80]; and the term of public policy should be narrowly construed.[81]

The next two sections further explore two major instances of consensus that are reflected in the *ILA Final report*: the international nature of public policy in dealing with international arbitration, and the key elements of public policy.

# 4 Domestic, International and Transnational/Truly International Public Policy

## *4.1 Domestic and International Public Policy in Arbitration Law*

One significant achievement towards international consensus in relation to the application of public policy is to distinguish the public policy applied in reviewing international arbitral awards, or usually referred to as "international public policy", from the public policy applied in purely domestic contexts, referred to as "domestic public policy". It is generally accepted that public policy applied in the international context should be narrower and more restricted than what is applied in a purely domestic context.[82]

The acceptance of international public policy as applied to international arbitral awards has now generally achieved worldwide consensus. In some national legislation, there is a reference to "international public policy" with respect to the judicial review, which is identified as "the French approach".[83] In domestic contexts, public policy safeguards the public interests of the nation, and presents the public power of the sovereign state; while in private international law, public policy is a tool used to

[78] Mayer and Sheppard, above n 60.

[79] Ibid60, Recommendation 1(c).

[80] Ibid, nn 7.

[81] Ibid, [10]-[16].

[82] Pieter Sanders, 'Commentary' in *60 Years of ICC Arbitration—A Look at the Future* (ICC, 1984); Kronke et al., above n 16, 366.

[83] Fry, above n 63, 87.

exclude the application of foreign law or foreign legal decisions when the national courts find there is a specific interest to be protected and will be otherwise infringed by such foreign law or foreign legal decisions.[84]

The distinction between private international law and domestic law is also confirmed in practice and academic research, which furthers the distinction between domestic public policy on one hand, and international public policy on the other. In *Zapata*, the Supreme Court of the United States held that the forum selection clause which had been freely negotiated in international trade should be respected and the applicable law in such arbitration should not be presumed as the domestic law.[85] In *Scherk,*[86] the court held that security disputes were arbitrable in international cases though similar disputes were inarbitrable in a purely domestic context[87]; in *Mitsubishi*, the American Arbitration Association's submission as *amicus curiae* status was accepted, which stated that non-arbitrability of antitrust matters should not be applied to the circumstance in this case, particularly when considering the international nature of this dispute.[88] Under a shared understanding to facilitate international arbitration practices, national courts must exercise great caution when applying public policy in cases conceived as being "international"; this attitude is also confirmed in the *ILA Final Report*, which provides: *"International and domestic public policy shall be distinguished, and in dealing with international commercial arbitration, a narrower approach of international public policy shall be applied."*[89] This consensus is consistent with the general purpose of the NYC, which promotes the general recognition and enforcement of international commercial arbitral awards.

It is notable that, though the term "international" is used, international public policy is still a legal concept of national law, as a part of the private international law of one particular state.[90] Its contents are still dependent on the state's legal environment, and its application heavily relies on the legal interpretation of national courts based on such legal environments. Public policy's nature as a legal notion at the national level is confirmed by the *NYC*'s reference to the public policy "of

---

[84] Pierre Lalive, 'Transnational (or Truly International) Public Policy and International Arbitration' in Pieter Sanders (ed), *Comparative Arbitration Practice and Public Policy in Arbitration,*, ICCA Congress Series (Kluwer Law International, 1987) 258, 259–260; *Rothenberger v. GEFA*, ATF 93 II 379, 382 (Swiss Supreme Court).

[85] *Bremen and Unterweser Reederei, GmBH v Zapata Off-Shore Co.* 407 US 1 [12], [17-22] (US Supreme Court, 1972).

[86] *Fritz Scherk v Alberto-Culver Co*417 US 506(US Supreme Court, 1974).

[87] Ibid, [11-18], [50-56].

[88] *Mitsubishi v. Soler,* 105 S. Ct. 3346 (US Supreme Court, 1985) See further discussion of *Mitsubishi* and arbitrability in Chaps. 7 and 8.

[89] Mayer and Sheppard, above n 60, Recommendation (2).

[90] J. Stewart McClendon, 'Enforcement of Foreign Arbitral Award s in the United States' (1982) 4 *Northwestern Journal of International Law and Business* 58,.67; Fry, above n 63, 85–89. Fry listed five types of public policy, namely domestic, international, transnational, regional and truly international. He also categorised that the first two are national public policies decided by national government while the latter three are supernational public policies which are sourced from non-national law. See further Sect. 4.1.

that country",[91] which arguably should be interpreted as the private international law rules (or in common law jurisdictions, the rules of conflict of laws) of that country. The potential confusion arises from the term "international"; this term incorporates the private international law governing public policy into domestic law but does not refer to the supernational character of that law.[92]

### 4.2 *Public Policy Approaches of Which State?*

Before proceeding to the sources of multinational or transnational laws and rules as public policy, it is important to draw attention to a question regarding the applicable law: if it is the international public policy to be applied, and such international public policy is defined by a state's private international law, then which state's approach of international public policy is to be applied in the context of international arbitration?

In arbitration and its consequent judicial proceedings, multiple rules from different jurisdictions may apply. For example, procedural law from different jurisdictions may be applied for different purposes at different stages of arbitration and the consequent judicial reviews. A court of the arbitration seat (supervisory court) will apply the *lex fori* for the procedural issues, including its approach of public policy, as illustrated by the *UNCITRAL Model Law,*[93] in the judicial review of an arbitral award.[94] The national courts of the enforcing state will review the arbitral award according to the law of the enforcing state, which is clearly illustrated by the *NYC*.[95] The expression of public policy "in that country" in the *NYC*, Art V(2)(b) is an indication of the enforcing state's power to apply its own public policy. A question then arises: For an enforcing court, should the public policy of the arbitration seat also be respected?

The current global legislative framework governing the judicial review of international arbitral awards does not provide a satisfactory answer. Generally, the dual control of the arbitration proceeding, which means that both the arbitration seat and the enforcing state would conduct a judicial review on the award, is an issue yet to be solved in the future.[96] Article V of the *NYC* provides discretionary powers

---

[91] The *NYC*, art V(2)(b).

[92] Lalive, above n 84, 284, citing *Courd'appel de Paris* [Paris Court of Appeal] 9 II 1966 264, 9 February 1966; Fry, above n 63, 96–99.

[93] UNCITRAL, *Explanatory Notes of the UNCITRAL Model Law*, 7(b), [46]-[48]. <http://www.uncitral.org/pdf/english/texts/arbitration/ml-arb/07-86998_Ebook.pdf>

[94] Lalive, above n 84, 278.

[95] *Above* Sect. 3.2.

[96] Albert Jan van den Berg, 'Should the Setting Aside of the Arbitral Award be Abolished?' (2014) 29(2) *ICSID Review* 263. The author concludes that the double control issue may continue and conflicted decisions may exist under the current regulatory scheme provided by the *NYC* and the national arbitration law systems, but propose that this issue might be solved in a distant future, by an ad hoc committee in charge of the annulment review, which is quite similar to the WTO dispute settlement scheme.

for the enforcing courts, and does not exclude the possibility of taking into consideration the public policy of other jurisdictions. Furthermore, Art V (1)(e) provides that annulment of the award at the arbitration seat might also bar its enforcement in other jurisdictions, and leaves the final decision to the enforcing court.[97] Thus, the enforcing court may consider whether the public policy of the arbitration seat would cause annulment, and further consider whether the outcome of an annulment, or more specifically, such public policy ground provided by the arbitration seat, would affect the enforceability of an award. This legislative scheme, in general, leaves the national courts with a huge discretion to apply public policy in judicial practices including in regard to the enforcement of arbitration awards.

Scholarly theoretical studies on this issue do not provide a clear answer. For instance, the enforcing courts' power to apply the approach adopted in its own jurisdiction in regard to the application of public policy is supported by Emmanuel Gaillard, who favours the view that only the judicial review of the enforcing state should be maintained, and that the state who is authorised to conduct a "seizure and forced sale of assets" is in a better position to apply its own public policy than a state that simply provides a venue for arbitration proceedings.[98] He further argues that the dual control by both the seat of arbitration and the enforcing state is "a step backwards" and is not consistent with the intention of *NYC*, which aims to facilitate the recognition and enforcement of arbitral awards and remove barriers among jurisdictions.[99] On the other hand, however, the possibility to take into consideration of the public policy of any other jurisdiction is not excluded even in Gaillard's argument, as he did not examine the situation where the public policy consideration in the arbitration seat favours the validity and enforceability of the awards while the enforcing state does not.

Issues regarding the choice of the applicable law also arise in arbitration practice and cause complicated results in the application of public policy. For example, it is particularly significant that the law of arbitrability in the arbitration seat may have some effect on the validity and enforceability of an award.[100] Also, parties' taking opportunities to argue relevant public policy issues before the tribunal or the supervisory court may also influence the consideration of any waiver or estoppel on later proceedings.[101] Though the public policy of the enforcing state and the public policy of the arbitration seat are distinguished, courts repeatedly find the importance of respecting the finality and enforceability of the arbitral awards outweigh other public policy considerations, and previous decisions of the tribunal or the supervisory

---

[97] *The NYC*, art V(1)(e) and V(2)(b); above n 56, citing van den Berg, above n 37, 265; Kronke et al., above n 16, 207–09.

[98] Emmanuel Gaillard, *Legal Theory of International Arbitration* (Martinus Nijhoff Publishers, 2010) 32–33.

[99] Ibid, 33.

[100] *The NYC*, art II(3).The supervisory court may either annul an award or refuse to enforce an arbitration agreement according to its own legislation of arbitrability. van den Berg, above n 37, 369; Dirk Otto and Omaia Elwan, 'Article V(2)' in Herbert Kronke et al. (eds), *Recognition and Enforcement of Foreign Arbitral Awards* (Wolter Kluwer, 2010) 345, 349. See further Chap. 8.

[101] Further discussed in Chaps. 6 and 9.

court might also be considered as strong persuasive support for the enforcement of the award.[102] The distinct cultural background of the arbitration seat may also be considered for the purpose of facilitating the international arbitration practices.[103] Yet enforcing courts may still review the public policy issue if such judicial review was not available in the supervisory court.[104] Also, if the winning party in arbitration succeeds in the supervisory court, a later refusal in the enforcing court might bar it from instigating a new arbitration in the arbitration seat.[105]

It is also necessary to explore whether public policy in any other jurisdictions should be taken into account in addition to the public policy of the supervisory and enforcing states. In some cases, the public policy of a third country may also be considered. For example, in *Regazonniv KC Sthia Ltd*,[106] the alleged violation of Indian law, being the jurisdiction of a third party, was also respected as a matter of human rights. Similar decisions can also be found in both German and Italian cases concerning the illegal export of artefacts,[107] and two "Borax cases" in Germany.[108] The reasons why the public policy of other jurisdictions are taken into consideration by national courts is also significant; as Lalive summarised, there are three conditions to establish a significant connection between the case and the public policy of a jurisdiction of a third state[109]:

> *(1) the contract has a sufficient connection with the foreign State the law of which has been violated;*
>
> *(2)* whether the *foreign law has a mandatory or imperative character and insists on being applied;*
>
> *(3)* whether *it aims to protect interests that are not purely* selfish *but appear worthy of protection from a supranational perspective.*

More recent developments in applying public policy have demonstrated that these difficulties in choosing and applying the applicable public policy have abated. The

[102] Sheppard, above n 72, Part IV.A.

[103] *Gao Haiyan v Keeneye Holdings Ltd* 1 HKLRD 627 (Court of Appeal Hong Kong); David Heller, 'The Public Policy Exception in Hong Kong: The Cultural Sliding Scale' (2013) 3 *The Arbitration Brief* 115; Friven Yeoh and Desmond Ang, 'Reflections on Gao Haiyan—Of 'Arb-med', 'Waivers', and Cultual Contextualisation of Public Policy Arguments' (2012) 29(3) *Journal of International Arbitration* 285.

[104] *Paklito Investment Ltd v Klocker East Asia Ltd* [1993] 2 HKLR 39, 48 (High Court Hong Kong); *Hebei Import and Export vPolytekEng'g Co.* [1999] 1 HKLRD 665, 688; Otto and Elwan, above n 100, 407–08. See further Chap. 6.

[105] *Shanghai City Foundation Works Corp* v *Sunlink Ltd* [2001] HCCT No. 83 of 200 (Court of First Instance Hong Kong).

[106] *Regazonni v KC Sthia Ltd* 1958 AC 301; [1957] 3 All ER 286.

[107] German Supreme Court, 22 June 1982, *Allg Ver. GH. v EK.*, reported in BGHZ 59; *Repubblica dell' Ecuador—Casa dellaculturaecuadoriana v. Danosso*, reported in *RDIPP* 18 (Tribunal of Turin, 25 March 1982).

[108] BGH, 27 XII 1960, BGHZ 34, 169; BGH, 24 V 1962 NJW 1962, 1436, 1962; cited by Lalive, above n 84, [77-82].

[109] Ibid, [86].

reason may be based on a trend of convergence of public policy among different jurisdictions, and the appreciation that such convergence among states may offset the distinctions.[110] International movements, including the worldwide adoption of identical legal rules provided by the *UNCITRAL Model Law* and comparative studies across national jurisdictions on public policy, all lead to shared understandings of an international conceptualisation of public policy, which is represented by converging legal practices, such as the adoption of a narrow and restrictive approach in applying public policy by many jurisdictions.[111]

## 4.3 Transnational Public Policy and a New Arbitral Legal Order?

Previous discussions have provided that the public policies of more than one nation may be applied in cases of international arbitration, and the public policies among different jurisdictions are converging under a global legal framework. Thus, it is difficult to conclude that the public policy now applied in practice remains purely and exclusively a legal concept of one single nation; it is rather a complicated product of national and international movements. For example, in dealing with corruption and bribery in commercial transactions, states share similar values in regards to commercial morality as part of public policy.[112] Under principles of economic and legal globalisation, the ideas and legal concepts shared by different jurisdictions are also rapidly evolving along increasingly consistent lines; a general trend of "delocalisation" of international arbitration practices is widely noticed.[113] There is a growing international consensus in regards to many aspects of arbitration practice, including a wider acceptance of the universal values and standards of public policy that supersede what some would call "selfish" national interests.[114]

Based on this understanding, some forms of public policy that operate beyond one national legal system are also recognised or argued. This type of public policy is referred to as "supernational", "transnational", "regional", or "truly international"

[110] Sheppard, above n 72, Part VIII; Lynch, above n 33, 466–470.

[111] Ibid; Maurer, above n 37, 331–332.

[112] ICC Case No. 1110, 15 January 1963; ICC Case No. 3916, 1982; Karl-Heinz Böckstiegel, 'Public Policy and Arbitrability' in Pieter Sanders (ed), *Comparative Arbitration Practice and Public Policy in Arbitration*, ICCA Congress Series (Kluwer Law International, 1987) 177, 200–202.

[113] Van den Berg, above n 37, 28–51; Born, above n 18, ch 25 and 26; Jan Paulsson, 'Arbitration Unbound: An Award Detached from the Law of its Country of Origin' (1981) 30 *International and Comparative Law Quarterly* 358; Jan Paulsson, 'Delocalization of International Commercial Arbitration: When and Why It Matters'(1983) 32 *International and Comparative Law Quarterly* 53; Jan Paulsson, 'The Extent of Independence of International Arbitration from the Law of the Situs' in Julian D. M. Lew (ed), *Contemporary Problems in International Arbitration* (Cambridge, 1986) 141.

[114] Lalive, above n 84, Part III and IV.

public policy by different authors.[115] Lalive argued that this is "the (really international) public policy of the law of the nations"[116]; Fry listed transnational public policy as non-national customs and *lex mercatoria*, regional public policy as the EU competition law, and truly international public policy as a pure international standard of public policy.[117] He further concluded that all three types of public policy are "supernational".[118] As the *ILA Interim Report* suggests, this type of public policy may represent "the general principles of morality accepted by civilised nations".[119] Hunter and Silva pointed out that such public policy is "narrower in scope, but more uniform" than international public policy.[120]

There is no doubt this 'superior' public policy may influence arbitration law and practice in some form. The Civil Section of the French Court of Cassation refers to public policy as "the reservation of such principles of universal justice" which has an "absolute international value"; The Italian Court of Cassation respects "a legal and moral minimum which is common to the feeling of several nations".[121] The Swiss Federal Tribunal referred to a "universal conception of public policy, under which an award will be incompatible with public policy if it is contrary to the fundamental moral or legal principles recognised in all civilised countries",[122] which may also be an interpretation of transnational public policy.

Theoretical studies on transnational public policy provide different elements and characteristics of this type of public policy. Lalive suggests that the "truly international purpose" underlying those foreign legal elements make them acceptable;[123] he also argues that arbitrators may apply the *lex mercatoria* to many aspects of international public policy.[124] Kreindler also explores the application of transnational public policy by arbitrators when deciding the applicable law.[125] Goldman argued for the existence of truly international public policy from the perspective of *lex mercatoria* rather than national policy considerations,[126] and emphasised the elements of the

115 Ibid; Fry, above n 63; van den Berg, above n 37, 361; Martin Hunter and Gui Conde e Silva, 'Transnational Public Policy and Its Application in Investment Arbitrations' (2003) 4 *Journal of World Investment and Trade* 367, 372.

116 Lalive, above n 84, Part III and IV.

117 Fry, above n 63, 87–89.

118 Ibid.

119 Sheppard, above n 72, 217.

120 Hunter and Silva, above n 115, 367–68.

121 Lalive, above n 84, [63-64].

122 *W* v *F and V*, Decision dated 30 Dec. 1994, reported in (1995) *ASA Bulletin* 217; Sheppard, above n 72, Part II.

123 Lalive, above n 84, [67].

124 Ibid, [104-105].

125 Richard H. Kreindler, 'Approaches to the Application of Transnational Public Policy by Arbitrators' (2003) 4 *Journal of World Investment and Trade* 239, 244.

126 Berthold Goldman, '*La lex mercatoria dans les contrats et l'arbitrage internationaux: réalité et perspectives*' (1979) *Journal du Droit International* 475; Dolinger, above n 1, 185.

customary norms of *lex mercatoria* in a truly international public policy[127]; alternatively, Buchanan, Gotanda and Voser all focused on the international order developed and shared by "civilised countries".[128] Gaillard and Savage emphasised public international law elements as considerations in determining the nature and application of public policy.[129]

From a more general perspective, Gaillard argues for the existence of an independent and international legal order, which is in relation to the so-argued truly international public policy. He summarised three representations of international arbitration from previous legal practices: (1) International arbitration relegated to a component of a single national legal order (the legal order of the arbitration forum); (2) International arbitration anchored in a plurality of national legal orders (the set of legal orders where the arbitral award is searching for enforcement); and (3) International arbitration as autonomous legal order, which is also known as "the arbitral legal order".[130] Gaillard further argues that the emergence of "arbitral legal order" best illustrates the current development and the future of international commercial arbitration, which means that the arbitration practices can go beyond the supervision of state sovereignty to some extent.[131] This approach is consistent with the arguments of a more uniformed public policy beyond the current understanding of international public policy as a part of one state's private international law.

Despite the growing transnational nature of international public policy, opinions are divided when deciding whether such transnational public policy should prevail in application. Advocates of transnational public policy insist that such public policy should be prioritised over purely national public policy considerations.[132] In practice, growing acceptance of truly international public policy on such issues as corruption and human rights is observed[133]; that approach is supported by the view that, under the *NYC*, states are free to apply a more favourable law according to the discretion granted them by that Convention.[134] Furthermore, arbitrators may also contribute to the establishment of a transnational public policy, as they may use their unique knowledge and experiences in their practices when dealing with cases from different

---

[127] Goldman, above n 126; Lalive, above n 84, [99].

[128] Nathalie Voser, 'Mandatory Rules of Law as a Limitation on the Law Applicable in International Commercial Arbitration' (1996) 7 *American Review of International Arbitration* 31; Mark A. Buchanan, 'Public Policy and International Commercial Arbitration' (1988) 26(3) *American Business Law Journal* 511, 530; John Y. Gotanda, 'Charting Developments Concerning Punitive Damages: Is the Tide Changing?' (2007) 45 *Columbia Journal of Transnational Law* 507, 512.

[129] Emmanuel Gaillard and John Savage, *Fouchard Gaillard Goldman on International Commercial Arbitration* (Kluwer Law International, 1999) 954.

[130] Gaillard, above n 98, 35.

[131] Ibid, 35–66.

[132] Arfazadeh, above n 70, 50–51; Voser, above n 128, 334; Richard A. Cole, 'The Public Policy Exception to the New York Convention on the Recognition and Enforcement of Arbitral Awards' (1986) 1 *Ohio State Journal on Dispute Resolution* 365, 373–74.

[133] Gaillard, above n 98, 131.

[134] Ibid.

jurisdictions.[135] The working knowledge of the arbitrators, which may include the understanding of public policy, subsequently influences the awards and their enforceability, which is further reflected in the state courts' judgments in dealing with public policy.[136]

On the other hand, some scholars argue that the idea of transnational public policy is of limited value, because it is applied in national courts or arbitration procedures only if it is deemed to be consistent with the national public policy.[137] Fry reported four reasons for the possible application of truly international public policy, including: the fear of the whole regime of the *NYC* unravelling; to feed the needs of globalisation; to accord a narrow interpretation of public policy; and to maintain consistency between all enforcing courts.[138] Yet none of these reasons provide a legitimate basis by which national courts are obliged to apply a truly international public policy and fully abandon the national character of public policy.[139]

An additional reason to limit the value of transnational public policy may be that the purpose of the *NYC*, in facilitating the enforcement of arbitral awards, should be interpreted literally in accordance with its original text, which is referred to as the public policy "of that country".[140] Furthermore, development of a truly international public policy also requests the cooperation of states and their courts. Moreover, the overly narrow approach of public policy, or undue stress placed on consistency without any further reasonable analysis, is not convincing in itself.[141] As argued by Fry, the pursuit of such a narrow approach should not be at the expense of the public policy interests of a national legal system.[142] And finally, there is still a lack of international consensus in arbitration and judicial practices in recognising such a

---

[135] Yves Dezalay and Bryant G. Garth, *Dealing the Virtue: International Commercial Arbitration and the Construction of A Transnational Legal Order* (University of Chicago, 1996) Ch 2; Teresa Cheng, 'Features of Arbitral Practice that Contribute to System-Building' (2012) 106 *American Society of International Law Proceedings* 292, 296.

[136] Lalive, above n 84, [39-49]; Yves Derains, 'Public Policy and the Law Applicable to the Dispute in International Arbitration' in Pieter Sanders (ed), *Comparative Arbitration Practice and Public Policy in Arbitration*, ICCA Congress Series (Kluwer Law International, 1987) 227, [14].

[137] For example, the *Eco Swiss* case indicates that EU public policy of competition law may also be public policy of its member countries. *Eco Swiss China Time Ltd v. Benetton International NV* (C-126/97) [1999] ECR I-03055, Christoph Liebscher, 'European Public Policy: A Black Box?' (2000) 17(3) *Journal of International Arbitration* 73, 78; William W Park, *Arbitration of International Business Disputes: Studies in Law and Practice* (Oxford University, 2012) 511.

[138] See Fry, above n 63, 120–133.

[139] Ibid.

[140] *The NYC,* art V(2)(b).

[141] Fry pointed out that the overly narrow approach in defining public policy was represented in cases where the judges expressly assumed no violation of public policy, or even when an assumption was made in the fear of being the first judge to define the limits of the public policy defence. See Fry, above n 63, 124, citing *Corcoran v Ardra Ins Co Ltd*, 156 AD 2d 70, 74 (NY 1st App Div, 1990); *Builders Federal (Hong Kong) Ltd* et al. *v Turner Construction* et al., 655 F Supp 1400, 1405 (SDNY 1987).

[142] See Fry, above n 63, 133.

transnational public policy in general, though consensus may be found in regards to several legal issues such as bribery and corruption.[143]

In summarising this section, the trend in recent years is that the sources of public policy in commercial arbitration law have become more complex. The idea of a "truly international" or "transnational" public policy, which presents the interests of the international arbitration community beyond the interests of certain states, has developed in arbitral practice as well as by arbitration scholars.[144] Yet the current situation is that the nature of public policy is still significantly determined by national legal systems, and its application is overwhelmingly influenced by legal practices at the level of national law. Based on these observations, it is too premature to conclude that courts are now bound by an approach of truly international public policy, but rather by an international public policy that is distinguished from and narrower than domestic public policy.

## 5 The Key Elements of Public Policy

Despite the changing character of public policy, national legal systems still attempt to identify a few key elements of public policy. The most famous expression of this was the "Parsons standard" adopted in the US, which referred to the "basic notion of morality and justice" of the enforcing state.[145] Other conceptions of public policy are found in various legislation, including conceptions of the "good morals" in Japanese law[146] and "fraud or corruption" and violation of natural justice in Australian law.[147] Arbitration scholars have highlighted a few issues relating to the idealised content of public policy. Lew has listed the elements of public policy, which include "an abhorrence of slavery, racial, religious and sexual discrimination, kidnapping, murder, piracy, terrorism".[148]

Many key elements of public policy are now shared across national jurisdictions under the influence of the converging international arbitration and judicial practices.

---

143 See Kreidler, above n 125, 249.

144 Dolinger, above n 1; Lalive, above n 84; Fry, above n 63; Gaillard, above n 98.

145 *Parsons and Whittemore*, 508 F.2d.

146 *Arbitration Law* (Japan), enacted on 25 July 2005, art 45(2)(ix).

147 *International Arbitration Act 1974* (Cth) s19 provides that:

*public policy was violated if:*

*(a) the making of the interim measure or award was induced or affected by fraud or corruption; or*

*(b) a breach of the rules of natural justice occurred in connection with the making of the interim measure or award.*

148 Lew, above n 21, 535.Lew also explained the public policy would "opposes any effort to subvert or evade the imperative laws of a sovereign State; upholds fundamental human rights and the basic standards of honesty and bona fides; and endorses certain rules and practices contained in the major and widely accepted uniform laws and international codes of practice".

Specifically, in relation to the key elements of public policy, the *ILA Final Report* suggests that public policy may include:

(i) *fundamental principles, pertaining to justice or morality, that the State wishes to protect even when it is not directly concerned;*
(ii) *rules designed to serve the essential political, social or economic interests of the State, these being known as 'lois de police' or 'public policy rules'; and*
(iii) *the duty of the State to respect its obligations towards other States or international organisations.*[149]

Recommendation 1(e) further provides the following examples: prohibition of abuse of rights (as a substantive fundamental principle), an impartial arbitral tribunal (as a procedural fundamental principle), anti-trust law issues (as a public policy rule), a United Nations resolution imposing sanctions (as an international obligation), and the prohibition of corruption (which falls into more than one category of public policy).[150]

This categorisation of public policy is a comprehensive conclusion on the key elements of public policy and covers most of the significant developments over the last few decades. Other possible elements of public policy, as specifically identified by scholars, are covered by this categorisation: the bribery or illegality issue is identified as a violation of mandatory rules[151]; fraudulent obtained award, rendering awards without sufficient reason and violation of time limits can be identified as a violation of procedural fundamental principles.[152]

Though Fry argued that the categorisation of public policy elements may be "unnecessarily formalistic",[153] it is undeniable that it is illustrative and useful. The ILA categorisation is highly appreciated and echoed in other research.[154] Based on this understanding, the ILA categorisation is adopted by the author of this book, with the author's adjustment, as the major tool to examine the relevant Chinese cases.[155]

## 6 Conclusion

This chapter outlines the fundamental understandings of the development of public policy in worldwide arbitration law and practices. In emphasising the role of national legal systems in defining public policy, this chapter serves as a way to focus on the conceptualisation of public policy.

---

[149] Ibid, Recommendation 1(d); Recommendation 2, 3 and 4; See further Chaps. 5, 6 and 7.

[150] Ibid, Recommendation 1(e).

[151] Also discussed in Chap. 7. Otto and Elwan, above n 100, 371.

[152] Ibid, 374–378.

[153] Fry, above n 63, nn 14.

[154] Arfazadeh, above n 70, 50.

[155] See further Sect. 6, and Sect. 3 in Chap. 3 and Sect. 4.3 in Chap. 4; the author added the category of arbitrability in addition to the key elements as identified by *the ILA Final Report;* see Mayer and Sheppard, above n 60.

This chapter reviews the general character of public policy, especially its ambiguous and changing character, and emphasises public policy's strong connection to national legal culture and national interests.[156] It also reviews the developments of public policy in arbitration law in light of the history of arbitration, and reports the significant shift of the national courts' attitude from hostile to supportive. It also observes that both national and international legal schemes have supervised and supported arbitration practice in various and increasingly interdependent ways.[157] International consensus has strongly influenced the movement to a unified set of rules governing the application of public policy considerations, while such unification is promoted by the adoption of that international consensus in national legal systems. Domestic courts' responses in dealing with public policy contribute to its clearer and more widely accepted status.

Distinctions between domestic, international, and transnational public policy, illustrate the diversity of national and international stakeholders in the development of a viable conception of public policy.[158] The tentative conclusion is that, the argument for a more truly international or 'transnational' public policy is stronger today than in decades past, yet it is still too early to conclude that such a transnational public policy has solidified in theory or is systematically applied in practice. National legal systems still define public policy in light of their national law; and national approaches in the application of public policy can therefore perpetuate divergence, just as it can lead to convergence in national and international arbitration practice.

Another crucial aspect of public policy is its key elements. The current international consensus is presented in the *ILA Final Report*'s categorisation, and such categorisation is adopted in this book for further discussion and analysis.[159] Based on the understanding of the *ILA Report* and the *NYC*, this book focuses on the following possible key elements of public policy:

*(1a) substantial fundamental principles of law;*

*(1b) procedural fundamental principles of law;*

*(2) mandatory national rules of public policy nature;*

*(3) international obligations; and*

*(4) arbitrability.*

In concluding on these fundamental aspects of public policy, this chapter provides several key notions in applying public policy in the international forum, to which the Chinese approach of public policy is to be compared: firstly, public policy remains a part of national law and to be applied by national courts; but under the trend of economic globalisation and unification of arbitration law, public policy is to be narrowly construed. Secondly, it is the international public policy or public policy in

156 Section 2.

157 Section 3.

158 Section 4.

159 Section 5.

private international law that is to be applied in the context of international commercial arbitration. And finally, there are some generally agreed categories of elements of public policy in international practices. These key notions, together with the bigger contexts of international commercial arbitration and the globalisation of arbitration law, are foundations of this book and will be frequently referred to in later chapters when comparing Chinese practices with the international consensus.[160]

[160] For example, the key elements of public policy are used as a fundamental tool to categorise cases in Chap. 4, Sect. 4. It is also the foundation of the discussion of each key element of public policy in Chaps. 5–8. The result of such comparison will be further concluded in Chap. 9 and the Final Chapter.

# Chapter 3
# Overview of China's Practice in Applying Public Policy in Arbitration Law

## 1 Introduction

As Chap. 2 suggests, the application of the public policy exception in the judicial review of arbitral awards is largely based on the legal practice of national legal systems. The application of public policy in arbitration law in China, therefore, is based on the operation of China's comprehensive national legal system. This chapter reviews the general and specific aspects of the Chinese legal system and provides the necessary context for detailed discussion in Part II (Chaps. 4–8) of this book through an examination of Chinese legislation and judicial schemes, and emphasises key, distinct features of the Chinese arbitration system; some of which will be referred to as possible influential factors in forming China's approach in applying public policy, as suggested in Part III (Chap. 9 and the Final Conclusion).

This chapter deals with several main aspects of China's legal system in relation to the application of public policy in the judicial review of arbitral awards. A general introduction of China's legislation and judicial system in Sect. 2 is the starting point to understanding China's arbitration system, and it also provides a historical review of developments in China's arbitration practices. Section 3 provides the necessary background information for understanding China's arbitration practices in regard to the application of public policy. A few key facts are emphasised, including the dual track developments at the early stage and recent developments in China's arbitration system.

Section 4 further addresses some distinctive features of China's arbitration system, including the complicated set of rules in Chinese arbitration law; the distinction between domestic, foreign-related and international awards in the Chinese legal system; and the schemes for the annulment and enforcement of arbitral awards. It introduces the significant problems with China's judicial review of arbitral awards, such as the quality of the judiciary and the trends of local protectionism, and outlines the solutions introduced to the judicial system, such as the establishment of the Prior Reporting System.

 
S. Zhang, *The Public Policy Exception in the Judicial Review of International Commercial Arbitral Awards*, https://doi.org/10.1007/978-3-662-67679-0_3

On the basis of the introduction of the Chinese arbitration system and the practices of Chinese courts in relation to arbitration, Sect. 5 introduces China's legislative schemes defining the public policy exception in the judicial review of arbitral awards, and the judicial schemes that control the application of public policy in particular cases.

## 2 General Review of China's Legal Environment: The Legislative and Judicial System in China

This section initially focuses on the legislative and judicial system of China in general as the starting point. It then provides a short introduction of the history and major aspects of China's current legislative and judicial system, which will provide the foundation for further discussion on arbitration law and practices in relation to the application of public policy in the context of the Chinese legal environment.

### *2.1 The Chinese Legislative System*

Though China has a long history of ancient laws, its development was interrupted by the influence of foreign legal movements in the early twentieth century. The current Chinese legal system was implemented after the establishment of the People's Republic of China ('PRC') in 1949, and was substantially rebuilt in the late 1970s due to the Cultural Revolution.[1] The Chinese legal system was largely re-organised for political purposes, and many pre-existing legal institutions were abandoned during the 1950s and 1960s.[2] The current legislative structure, including the regulation of arbitration in China, is governed by the *Constitutional Law*[3] and the *Legislation Law*.[4] The National People's Congress ('NPC') and its Standing Committee exercise legislative power in making national laws.[5] There are also administrative and

---

[1] Clarisse von Wunschheim, *Enforcement of Commercial Arbitral Awards in China: Business Laws of China* (West, 2011) 2–3; Jianfu Chen, *Chinese Law: Context and Transfrmation* (Martinus Nijhoff, 2008) 307–08.

[2] Jerome A. Cohen, 'Reforming China's Civil Procedure: Judging the Courts' 45(4) *The American Journal of Comparative Law* 793, 793–95; 苏力 [Su Li],《二十世纪中国的现代化与法治》[The Modernisation and Rule of Law in 20th Century's China] (1998) 1 法学研究 *Chinese Journal of Law* 3, 8; 何勤华 [He Qinhua],《法学观念本土化考: 从新中国立宪60余年之视角》[Study on the Localisation of the Legal Conceptions: Perspective from the 60-year history of the Establishment of Constitutions of the PRC] (2013) 25(2) 中外法学 *Peking University Law Journal* 270, 272–73.

[3]《中华人民共和国宪法》[The Constitutional Law of the People's Republic of China] (People's Republic of China).

[4]《中华人民共和国立法法》[The Law on Legislation of the People's Republic of China] (People's Republic of China) National People's Congress, Order No 31, 15 March 2000.

[5]《中华人民共和国宪法》[The Constitutional Law of the People's Republic of China] (People's Republic of China), art 58;《中华人民共和国立法法》[The Legislation Law of the People's

local regulations made by the State Council and lower governments subject to the Constitutional Law and national laws.[6]

China's current legislative system is significantly based on the legal transplantation of foreign legal systems and relies heavily on foreign legal experiences. The earliest modern legal reform in China happened in the 1900s when Chinese legislators generally abandoned traditional Chinese law and mostly followed the success of the Meiji Restoration in Japan, which was highly influenced by the German law.[7] After the establishment of the PRC, many aspects of the Chinese political and legal system were rebuilt, largely influenced by Soviet Union and East European legal traditions under the influence of Communist ideology. From these different origins, the Chinese legal system adopts the civil law tradition, which is generally consistent with the jurisdictions listed above. Such influences were represented by the earliest legislation after the Mao Era, such as the Economic Contract Law of 1981 and the Criminal Law and Criminal Procedure Law of 1979, which form the foundation of China's current legal system.[8]

More recent developments in Chinese legislation reflect China's desire to build an international market economy for trade and investment. The legislative structure of China's market and economic activities, such as corporation, security, and tax law, are therefore significantly influenced by powerful Western economies,[9] resulting in China's legislative movements, in the form of legal transplantation, strongly influenced by the legislation in both common law and civil law jurisdictions.[10] Nevertheless, the origins of Chinese legislation that regulated private relations in ancient

Republic of China] (People's Republic of China) National People's Congress, Order No 31, 15 March 2000, art 7.

6《中华人民共和国立法法》[The Legislation Law of the People's Republic of China] (People's Republic of China) National People's Congress, Order No 31, 15 March 2000, art 56–77.

7 Pittman B. Potter, *The Chinese Legal System: Globalization and Local Legal Culture* (Routledge, 2001) 4–5; K. W. Noerr,《法律移植与 1930 年前中国对德国法的接受》[Legal Transplantation and the Acceptance of German Law in China before 1930s] (李立强、李启欣 [Li Liqiang, Li Qixin] trans) (1988) 2 比较法研究 *Journal of Comparative Law* 55; Tsung-Fu Chen, 'Transplant of Civil Code in Japan, Taiwan and China: With the Focus of Legal Evolution' (2011) 6(1) *National Taiwan University Law Review* 389, 398–400.

8 Chen, above n 7, 413–414; 何勤华 [He Qinhua], above n 2, 277–79.

9 Potter, above n 7, 4–5; 沈宗灵 [Shen Zongling],《当代中国借鉴外国法律的实例 (下)》[Practical Examples the recent Chinese Legislation Learnt from Foreign Law (II)] (1997) 6(4) 中国法学 *Chinese Legal Science* 3, 3–5; 魏振瀛 [Wei Zhenying],《我国民法对外国法的借鉴》[Lessons Drawn from Foreign Law in Our Civil Law Legislation] (2009) 5 法学家 *Jurist* 20, 21.

10 江平[ Jiang Ping], 梁慧星 [Liang Huixing], 王利明 [Wang Liming],《中国民法典的立法思路和立法体例》[Legislative Way of Thinking and Model of Chinese Civil Code], in 王卫国 [Wang Weiguo] ed.,《中国民法典论坛 (2002–2005)》[Forum of Chinese Civil Code: 2002–2005] (中国政法大学出版社 [Chinese University of Political Science and Law Press], 2009), 4–5, 11–12.

Chinese private law still underpin and influence China's legal system today.[11] The result is a complicated mixture of Chinese private law.

In addition, the development of China's legislative system and legal culture are largely restrained by China's short history of modernisation.[12] Due to the long duration of wars and the absence of legal governance, the legal market in China is not fully developed; legal skills and experiences are not well nurtured; and the quality of the legal profession is still limited by its short history and the relevant restrictions of the social and political environments. Significant developments, in the sense that legal modernisation can be observed only after the late 1970s, occurred when the government started to make the law and implement the law. Since then the legal profession developed gradually over time in China.[13]

All of these characteristics of the Chinese legislative system influence the performance of legislative practice in China and the resultant Chinese legislation. These factors might have made it difficult for a foreigner to understand the mysteries of legislation and its functioning in China. While China has adopted a tradition of codification of its law,[14] when it comes to interpreting and applying the law, it is required that the courts' decisions give due consideration to the unique context of China's legal, economic and political environment,[15] i.e., giving due deference to the characteristics outlined above.

## 2.2 *The Chinese Judicial System*

The Chinese judicial system is huge in the sense of the number of judges and the general working load. The newest Supreme People's Court (SPC)'s Working Report

---

[11] 苏力 [Su Li],《法治及其本土资源》[*The Rule of Law and its Local Resources*] (中国政法大学出版社 [Chinese University of Political Science and Law Press], 2004); More discussions on the Theory of Local Resources, see e.g. 尹伊君 [Yin Yijun],《从 "礼教风俗"到 "本土资源"》[From 'Customs and Traditions' to 'Local Resources'] (1999) 3–4 比较法研究 *Journal of Comparative Law* 537; 邓正来 [Deng Zhenglai],《中国法学向何处去——对苏力 "本土资源论"的批判》[Where Will Chinese Legal Study Go? A Critique on Su Li's Theory of Local Resources] (2005) 23(3) 中国政法大学学报 *Journal of China University of Political Science and Law* 52.

[12] 刘思达 [Liu Sida],《失落的城邦: 当代中国法律职业变迁》[The Lost Polis: Transformation of the Legal Profession in Contemporary China] (北京大学出版社 [Peking University Press], 2008) 4–8. Liu summarised that the reforms in China's legal system are largely symbols of the modernisation of the Chinese economy, and its practical functions are not fully developed.

[13] A general review of China's historical developments in making the law before the 1970s, see a brief summary and discussion provided by Wu Jianfan, 'Building New China's Legal System' (1983–1984) 22 *Columbia Journal of Transnational Law* 1. The development of China's legal profession since 1970s, see generally in 刘思达 [Liu Sida], above n 12.

[14] A conclusion of the Chinese legislation system, see generally Wunschheim, above n 1; see also a general discussion of the origin of the traditions of civil law in China legal system, Lei Chen, 'The Historical Development of the Civil Law Tradition in China: a Private Law Perspective' (2010) 78 *Tijdschrift voor Rechtsgeschiedenis [The Legal History Review]* 159.

[15] For example, a discussion of the debate on the mother law of the Chinese Civil Code provided by Chen, above n 7, 418–21.

to the Chinese NPC in 2023 showed that the SPC have accepted 18,547 cases and finalised 13,785 cases in 2022, and the number of cases accepted and finalised in all lower courts was 33,704,000 and 30,810,000 respectively.[16]

The Chinese judicial system has distinctive vertical and horizontal structures: there are four vertical levels of Chinese courts, including the Supreme People's Court, 32 Higher People's Courts (HPC hereafter) at the level of the province (also the directly administered cities and autonomous regions), more than 400 Intermediary People's Courts (IPC hereafter) on the municipal level, and more than 3000 Basic People's Courts (BPC hereafter) at the level of districts and counties. There are also some specific courts such as maritime courts, military courts and railway transportation courts).[17] Cases are dealt with by the different level of courts according to the significance of the dispute.[18]

China does not adopt a clear separation of powers or "check and balance" scheme at either the horizontal level of government (between the legislative, administrative and judicial bodies) or the vertical level (between the State, provinces, cities and counties).[19] One consequence of this is that the Chinese judicial system is not fully independent: all the courts are responsible to the People's Congress,[20] as well as financially dependent on the national or provincial governments.[21] In addition, interference from the Chinese Communist Party ('CCP') in the whole judicial system is evident.[22] The Courts are also closely related to the procuratorate and the police. For

---

16 周强 [Zhou Qiang],《最高人民法院工作报告》[Working Report of the Supreme People's Court] (People's Republic of China), the First Meeting of the Fourteenth National People's Congress, 7 March 2023.

17《中华人民共和国人民法院组织法》[The People's Courts Organisation Law of the People's Republic of China] (People's Republic of China), National People's Congress, Order No. 3, 1 July 1979 (Most Recent Amendment by National People's Congress Standing Committee, 26 October 2018) arts 12–15.

18《中华人民共和国宪法》[The Constitutional Law of the People's Republic of China] (People's Republic of China), art 123–128;《中华人民共和国人民法院组织法》[The People's Courts Organisation Law of People's Republic of China] (People's Republic of China), arts 16–24;《中华人民共和国民事诉讼法》[The Civil Procedure Law of the People's Republic of China] (People's Republic of China) art 18–21.

19《中华人民共和国宪法》[The Constitutional Law of the People's Republic of China] (People's Republic of China) Preface, art 1, art 3(3).

20《中华人民共和国宪法》[The Constitutional Law of the People's Republic of China] (People's Republic of China) art 128.

21 龙宗智, 李长青 [Long Zongzhi, Li Changqing],《论司法独立与司法受制》[Discussion on the Judicial Independence and its Restraints] (1998) 12 法学 *Law Science* 34, 37–38; A Randall Peerenboom, 'Law Enforcement and the Legal Profession in China' in Jianfu Chen, Yuwen Li and Jan Michiel Otto (eds), *Implementation of Law in the People's Republic of China* (Kluwer Law International 2002); Yuwen Li, 'Court Reform in China: Problems, Progress and Prospects' in Jianfu Chen, Yuwen Li and Jan Michiel Otto (eds), *Implementation of Law in the People's Republic of China* (Kluwer Law International 2002) 58.

22 李建明 [Li Jianming],《论党领导下的司法独立》[Discussions on the Judicial Independence Under the Leadership of the China Communism Party] (2003) 2 政治与法律 *Political Science and Law 33*, 37; 贺卫方 [He Weifang],《中国的法院改革与司法独立——一个参与者的观察与反思》[The Reforms in Chinese Courts and the Judicial Independence: Observations and Reflections

example, the Constitutional Law of China requires the coordination and cooperation of the police, the procuratorates and the courts, especially in criminal cases.[23]

The structure and relationships among different levels of the People's Courts are also a reason why the Chinese courts are frequently criticised. In regards to the vertical structure of the judicial system, the general principle that applies to the appeal system in China is "two trials and the second one is final" for both criminal and civil cases, which means that the parties can only appeal once.[24] Thus, many disputes conclude at the level of IPCs or HPCs; and therefore, inconsistent outcomes, or conflicted opinions with respect to the application of law frequently occur among different courts. At the horizontal level, discrepancies in the practices of courts arise due to the many different features of local courts, including the quality of staff, the capacity to work, and the unbalanced distribution of resources among local courts. The result is the development of diversified "niches" for legal practitioners and unpredictable or inconsistent judicial results.[25]

The internal structure of the Chinese court system is also distinctive and may be considered as problematic in the eyes of outsiders. Each court is divided into Civil, Criminal and Economical Branches (in some courts, there are also Juvenile and other branches)[26]; in each branch, there are several sub-branches specialising in one or several major issues; and in each sub-branch, there are many tribunals. Large numbers of staff in each branch and sub-branch may contribute to inconsistency and uncertainty in decision-making. If cases were sent to different tribunals, they may get different opinions. An Adjudication Committee, which consists of administrative leaders of the courts, including the president, vice presidents and the chief of each branch of the court, deal with complicated or important cases and make the final rulings. This phenomenon is described as "those who hear the case do not rule, and

of a Participant] (2003) 2 浙江社会科学 *Zhejiang Social Science* 83, 85; Wunschheim, above n 1, 21–22.

[23]《中华人民共和国宪法》[The Constitutional Law of the People's Republic of China] (People's Republic of China), art 135. The use of the term 'procuratorate' is referred from the English version of the Constitutional Law, from the website of the Chinese National People's Congress; see http://www.npc.gov.cn/englishnpc/Constitution/node_2825.htm.

[24]《中华人民共和国民事诉讼法》[The Civil Procedure Law of the People's Republic of China] (People's Republic of China) National People's Congress, art 10;《中华人民共和国刑事诉讼法》[The Criminal Procedure Law of the People's Republic of China] (People's Republic of China) art 10.

[25] 孟建柱 [Meng Jianzhu],《深化司法体制改革》[Deepen the Reforms in the Judicial System], 人民日报 *People's Daily* (Beijing), 25 November 2013, stating that 'The developments in different areas of our country are not balanced, and the workloads of different courts significantly vary' (author trans). Meng was the Secretary of the Central Politics and Law Commission of China's Communist Party at that time. 中华人民共和国国务院新闻办公室 [The State Council Information Office of the People's Republic of China],《中国的司法改革》白皮书 [White Paper on China's Judicial Reforms] October 2012, stating that 'The lack of sufficient transparency in the execution of judicial power and non-regulated activities of the judiciaries still exist due to the reasons such as an unbalanced development of the economy and the society, the discrepancies of the ability of judiciaries, and the existence of the local-protectionism notions'(author trans).

[26]《中华人民共和国人民法院组织法》[The People's Courts Organisation Law of People's Republic of China] (People's Republic of China) art 27.

those who rule the case do not hear".[27] It is criticised as lacking transparency when the adjudication committee deals with an individual case; the procedure is not clear to parties and outsiders, and it does not make clear how many people are involved in the decision-making in each particular case[28]; also, the parties' right to be heard is not assured.[29]

The quality of the Chinese judiciary is also a major concern that may directly influence the performance of the judicial system. The judges are not considered as being any different from other governmental servants in terms of their recruitment.[30] Though the *Law on Judges* provides the fundamental requirements of judges, the requirements are generally low enough to include most legal professionals.[31] The quality of the Chinese judiciary is also significantly influenced by the method of recruitment: some judges are selected from lower-ranking personnel such as clerks; some are from other political or governmental institutions such as police and even the army; some are newly graduated law students; while yet others are professors, and

---

27《中华人民共和国人民法院组织法》[The People's Courts Organisation Law of People's Republic of China] (People's Republic of China) art 36.

28 顾培东 [Gu Peidong],《人民法院内部审判运行机制的构建》[The Establishment of an Internal System of the Courts for the Functioning of Judicial Power] (2011) 4 法学研究 *Chinese Journal of Law* 3, 5.

29 Su Li considered that the adjudication committee has its distinctive contribution and satisfied the social needs in China currently. See 苏力 [Su Li],《基层法院审判委员会的考察及思考》[Observations and Thoughts in regard of the Adjudication Committee in Basic Courts] (1998) 1(2) 北大法律评论 *Peking University Law Review* 320, 328–330; 苏力 [Su Li],《送法下乡：中国基层司法制度研究》[Sending Law to the Countryside: Research on China's Basic-Level Judicial System] (中国政法大学出版社 [Chinese University of Political Science and Law Press], 2000), 88–89. But other scholars argued for its negative effects including the lack of transparency and breach of the parties' rights. See 陈瑞华 [Chen Ruihua],《正义的误区——评法院审判委员会制度》[Misunderstanding of Justice: Comments on the System of the Court Adjudication Committee] (1998) 1(2) 北大法律评论 *Peking University Law Review* 381, 381–91; 贺卫方 [He Weifang], above n 22, 86; Cohen, above n 2, 798–99.

30 苏力 [Su Li], above n 29, Appendix.

31《中华人民共和国法官法》[The Law of Judges of the People's Republic of China] (People's Republic of China) National People's Congress Standing Committee, Order No 38, 28 February 1995 (Recently Amended by National People's Congress Standing Committee, Order No 53, 30 June 2001) art 9. A judicial candidate must (1) be of Chinese nationality, (2) be of the age of 23 or over, (3) be an advocate of the Chinese Constitutional Law, (4) have good characters and fine political and professional qualities; (5) be in good health, and (6) a graduate of law school or have tertiary education and equivalent knowledge of law, and at least two years experiences of legal practices. The judges in HPC and SPC must have more experience; for those who have post-graduate degrees the requirement of practical experience is lower. In addition, this provision also provides that the judiciary who does not satisfy those requirements can qualify via training following the SPC's direction; and for those areas where qualified candidates are rare, the requirement of tertiary education may be relaxed.

researchers.[32] Another factor is that, unlike the leading jurisdictions, legal education only recommenced in China since the late 1970s, after the Cultural Revolution. Many young professionals that are well-educated are still in junior or inferior positions in the court system due to their age and experience. Though the general educational background and performance of the judges have greatly improved recently, further improvement is still required.[33]

That being said, we acknowledge that the Chinese judiciary are taking measures to improve the quality and performance of judges. Important measures include, for example, the adoption of the quota system in the courts which caps the percentage of judges in all court staff, selects the most qualified judges to fit the quota, and requires judges within the quota to perform core adjudication roles[34]; the release of Guiding Cases,[35] the establishment of the mechanism for resolving differences regarding the application of laws[36] and the system for the retrieval of similar cases,[37] and the establishment of the China International Commercial Court in 2018 to deal with international commercial law disputes.[38]

In summary, China's historical developments and its unique political system have contributed to China's distinctive judicial system. Many of these issues have remained entrenched in the Chinese judicial system, even though judicial reform and other improvements have been implemented since the late 1970s. In considering the role of courts in the judicial review on arbitral awards, one must take into account the development of China's judicial system.

[32] 苏力 [Su Li], above n 29, Appendix of this book examines the issues of the judges who are transferred to the judicial system from the army and the problems new law school graduates might face as judges; Appendix further discusses the outcomes in local courts as a reflection of the quality of the judiciaries.

[33] .苏力 [Su Li], above n 29, Appendix; Wunschheim, above n 1, 11.

[34] 《中华人民共和国人民法院组织法》 [The People's Courts Organisation Law of the People's Republic of China] (People's Republic of China), art 46.

[35] 《最高人民法院印发《关于案例指导工作的规定》的通知》 [Notice of the Supreme People's Court on Issuing the Provisions on Case Guidance] Supreme People's Court, Fa Fa [2010] No. 51, 26 November 2010.

[36] 《最高人民法院印发 <关于建立法律适用分歧解决机制的实施办法> 的通知》[Notice by the Supreme People's Court of Issuing the Implementation Measures for Establishing the Mechanism for Resolving Differences in the Application of Laws], Supreme People's Court, Fa Fa [2019] No. 23, 11 October 2019, effective 28 October 2019.

[37] 《最高人民法院关于统一法律适用加强类案检索的指导意见(试行)》 [Guiding Opinions of the Supreme People's Court on Unifying the Application of Laws to Strengthen the Retrieval of Similar Cases (for Trial Implementation)], Supreme People's Court, 31 July 2020.

[38] 《最高人民法院关于设立国际商事法庭若干问题的规定》 [Provisions of the Supreme People's Court on Several Issues concerning the Establishment of International Commercial Courts] Supreme People's Court, 27 June 27, 2018, Fa Shi [2018] No. 11, effective July 1, 2018.

# 3 Historical Review of China's Arbitration Practices

In addition to the background provided in Sect. 2, this section will further illustrate the general history of China's arbitration system. Based on the enactment of major legislation on arbitration, the *Arbitration Law* ('*CAL*' hereafter),[39] the developments can be divided roughly into two stages: the era before the "Reforms and Open" policy being adopted in China in the 1980s, and the era since the Reforms.

## *3.1 Dual-Track Practices Before the Late 1980s*

China's arbitration practices started long before the establishment of a market economy in the 1980s. It was a dual-track model: the "foreign-related" arbitration commissions, the China International Economic and Trade Arbitration Commission ('CIETAC') and the China Maritime Arbitration Commission ('CMAC'), dealt with foreign-related disputes, and the "domestic" arbitration practices dealt with purely domestic disputes.[40]

The predominant arbitration commissions, CIETAC and CMAC, were originally established during the 1950s to resolve trade disputes between China and the USSR. Shortly after the establishment of the PRC government, China and the USSR built their economic relationship, which required the establishment of a mutually recognised scheme of government regulation of trade, including an appropriate arbitration body in China to facilitate economic communications between China and the USSR. Administrative orders were issued by the State Council to establish the Foreign Trade Arbitration Commission (later renamed as CIETAC) and the Maritime Arbitration Commission (later renamed as CMAC).[41] The two arbitration commissions were established "within and under the auspices" of the China Council for the Promotion

39 《中华人民共和国仲裁法》 [Arbitration Law of the People's Republic of China] (People's Republic of China).

40 Wunschheim, above n 1, 30–31.

41 《中央人民政府政务院关于在中国国际贸易促进委员会内设立对外贸易仲裁委员会的决定》 [Decision of the Administrative Council of the Central People's Government Concerning the Establishment of a Foreign Trade Arbitration Commission Within the China Council for the Promotion of International Trade] (People's Republic of China), Administrative Council of the Central People's Government, 6 May 1954; 《中华人民共和国国务院关于在中国国际贸易促进委员会内设立海事仲裁委员会的决定》 [Decision of the State Council of the People's Republic of China Concerning the Establishment of a Maritime Arbitration Commission Within the China Council for the Promotion of International Trade] (People's Republic of China), State Council of the People's Republic of China, 21 November 1958; Dejun Cheng, Michael J. Moser and Shengchang Wang, *International Arbitration in the People's Republic of China: Commentary, Cases and Materials* (Butterworths Asia, 1995) 7–9, 13–21.

of International Trade (CCIPT).[42] Although the foreign-related arbitration commissions were established to deal with foreign trade, there was no significant trading operation in the period from the 1950s to the late 1970s, and the number of cases taken by CIETAC and CMAC during that period was not substantial.[43]

The development of "domestic" arbitration commissions, on the other hand, followed a totally different path. This type of "arbitration" was promoted generally as an administration-oriented dispute resolution system, dealing with matters such as labour, consumer product quality matters, copyright disputes and urban real estate disputes.[44] The local administrative bureaus for industry and commerce had jurisdiction to hear those cases, and administered what could be described as a quasi-judicial procedure[45]; and these proceedings were carried out by officers of the relevant administrative departments.[46]

Without unified legislation governing arbitration practice in China, different types of arbitration practice were governed by different levels of legal rules, including several legislative acts, hundreds of administrative regulations and local regulations.[47] International and foreign-related arbitration practices were reflected in legislation governing international trade, such as the *Law on China-Foreign Equity Joint Ventures*[48] and bilateral agreements, such as the *US-China Trade Agreement*.[49] There were also numerous regulations governing the organisation of domestic arbitration, including the *Regulations of the PRC on the Arbitration of Disputes Involving Economic Contracts*.[50] With respect to the judicial review of arbitral awards, little

---

[42] CCIPT plays an important role in supervising China's foreign trade relations and activities. CCIPT's establishment and functions followed the Soviet All Union Chamber of Commerce as a governmental body in the beginning, but later transformed to a private organisation playing a "quasi-governmental" role in promoting foreign trade relations in China. Since 1988, CCIPT transformed to the China Chamber of International Commerce ('CCOIC'). But even today, CCOIC still gets involved in the arbitration practices of the two commissions in many aspects, including the appointment of the members of the Commissions and the members of the official Panel of the Arbitrators. *Ibid*, 13–14.

[43] Arthur J. Gemmell, *Western and Chinese Arbitration: the Arbitration Chain* (University Press of America, 2008; ibid, 155.

[44] Cheng, Moser and Wang, above n 41, 271–272. "Arbitration" is quoted because it is distinct from the ordinary meaning of arbitration in international practices; reasons are explained in later paragraphs.

[45] Ibid, 274.

[46] Ibid, 274–279, discussing the dispute resolution of the economic contract disputes; *Ibid*, 279–287, technology contract disputes, labour disputes and consumer disputes.

[47] Gemmell, above n 43, 141–142.

[48] 《中华人民共和国中外合资经营企业法》 [Law of the People's Republic of China on China-Foreign Equity Joint Ventures] (People's Republic of China) National People's Congress, Order No 7, 1 July 1979.

[49] Cheng, Moser and Wang, above n 41, 4–5, referring to *Agreement on Trade Relations Between the People's Republic of China and the United States of America,* United States-People's Republic of China, signed 7 July 1979, 1202 UNTS 179 (entered into force 1 February 1980) art VIII.

[50] 《中华人民共和国经济合同仲裁条例》 [Regulations of the PRC on the Arbitration of Disputes Involving Economic Contracts] (People's Republic of China), State Council, 22 August 1983. Other rules and regulations see Cheng, Moser and Wang, above n 41, 274.

guidance was provided by law. Only an enforcement scheme was provided; no further schemes of judicial supervision and intervention were established by legislation.[51]

## *3.2 Developments: Enactment of the Chinese Arbitration Law and the Current Chinese Arbitration System*

After the announcement of the "reform and open" policy in the late 1970s, foreign trade flourished in China, and the caseload of CIETAC and CMAC, who exclusively administered foreign-related cases in China at that time, rose significantly.[52] China's arbitration system grew in the late 1980s as evidenced by certain major changes: first, China adopted the *NYC* in 1987 and the *Washington Convention* (the *ICSID Convention*) in 1992.[53] Secondly, in 1995, the enactment of the *CAL* for the first time unified the legislation of China's arbitration practices at the national level, and led to the re-establishment of all arbitration commissions except CIETAC and CMAC. Thirdly, the *CCPL*[54] established the judicial proceedings relating to the annulment, recognition and enforcement of arbitral awards.

### 3.2.1 Advancement of Legislation and Regulation

From the perspective of developments at the national level, the *CAL* is the most important legislation introduced to govern arbitration practice. This legislation, enacted ten years after the *Model Law*, followed the *Model Law's* main principles and spirit by adopting the principle of party autonomy and the finality of arbitration. This forms the basis of China's current arbitration system.

---

[51] The annulment procedure was introduced by the *CAL* in 1994. 马占军 [Ma Zhanjun],《论我国仲裁裁决的撤销与不予执行制度的修改与完善——兼评 < 最高人民法院关于适用 '中华人民共和国仲裁法'若干问题的解释 > 的相关规定》[Discussions on the Amendments and Perfection of China's Legal Schemes on the Annulment and Non-enforcement of Arbitral Awards—and Comments on the *SPC's Interpretation on Several Problems in Regard of the Application of the Arbitration Law*] (2007) 2 法学杂志 *Law Science Magazine* 108, 110.

[52] Cheng, Moser and Wang, above n 41, 10; See further discussion in Sect. 3.2.2.

[53]《最高人民法院关于执行我国加入的 <承认及执行外国仲裁裁决公约> 的通知》[Notice of the Supreme People's Court in regard of the Implementation of the 'Convention on the Recognition and Enforcement of Foreign Arbitral Award'] (People's Republic of China), Supreme People's Court, 法(经)发 (1987) 5 号 [Supreme Court (Economic) Notice No. 5], 10 April 1987;《对外经济贸易部关于认真做好执行 <华盛顿公约> 工作的通知》[Notice of the Ministry of Foreign Trade and Economic Co-operation in Regard of the Implementation of the Washington Convention] (People's Republic of China), The Ministry of Foreign Trade and Economic Co-operation, 1 August 1992; Cheng, Moser and Wang, above n 41, 10–11.

[54]《中华人民共和国民事诉讼法》[The Civil Procedure Law of the People's Republic of China] (People's Republic of China).

Several other major legislative developments in the Chinese arbitration system should also be mentioned. In 2010, the enactment of the *Law on the Application of Law for Foreign-Related Civil Relations* ('*Law Application Law*' hereafter) confirmed the applicable law to the arbitration agreement.[55] The most recent *CCPL* amended in 2021 covers the judicial supervision schemes on arbitration, including various issues such as the preservation of evidence and properties to assist with arbitral proceedings, judicial review of arbitration agreements, and judicial review of arbitral awards.[56] It is also notable that China has entered into many international agreements with foreign countries and jurisdictions in regards to judicial assistance practices[57]; these international agreements and treaties take precedence over the domestic legislation if conflicts arise.[58] Besides, other national legislation also provides guidance in dealing with arbitration practices in China, such as the *General Principle of Civil Law* (*GPCL*)[59] and the *Contract Law*[60] (however, both were replaced by the *Chinese Civil Code*[61]).

It is particularly notable that judicial interpretations issued by the SPC also provide significant guidance.[62] Broadly speaking, replies and notices made by the SPC to

55《中华人民共和国涉外民事关系法律适用法》[Law of the People's Republic of China on the Application of Law for Foreign-Related Civil Relations] (People's Republic of China) National People's Congress Standing Committee, Order No 36, 28 October 2010, art 18.

56《中华人民共和国民事诉讼法》[The Civil Procedure Law of the People's Republic of China] (People's Republic of China) National People's Congress, arts 84, 104, 127, 244, 278–282, 290.

57 Cheng, Moser and Wang, above n 41, 10; Wunschheim, above n 1, 36.

58《中华人民共和国民事诉讼法》[The Civil Procedure Law of the People's Republic of China] (People's Republic of China) National People's Congress, art 267.

59《中华人民共和国民法通则》[General Principle of Civil Law of the People's Republic of China] (People's Republic of China) National People's Congress, Order No 37, 12 April 1986.

60《中华人民共和国合同法》[Contract Law of the People's Republic of China] (People's Republic of China) National People's Congress, Order No 15, 15 March 1999.

61《中华人民共和国民法典》[Civil Code of the People's Republic of China] (People's Republic of China) National People's Congress, Order No. 45, 1 Jan 2021.

62 The SPC is authorised by the National People's Congress to make judicial interpretations guiding the application of law in judicial practices; their judicial interpretations are considered to have legal effects. The can also publish guiding cases.《中华人民共和国人民法院组织法》[The People's Courts Organisation Law of People's Republic of China] (People's Republic of China) art 18;《中华人民共和国各级人民代表大会常务委员会监督法》[Law of the People's Republic of China on the Supervision of All Levels of People's Congress Standing Committee] (People's Republic of China) National People's Congress Standing Committee, Order No 10, 27 August 2006, art 31;《全国人大常委会关于进一步加强法律解释工作的决议》[Statement on the National People's Congress Standing Committee in regard of Further Enhancing the Practice of the Interpretation of Law] (People's Republic of China), National People's Congress Standing Committee, 10 June 1981, art 2. See also《最高人民法院关于司法解释工作的若干规定》[Several Regulations Issued by the Supreme People' Court in regard of the Practices of Judicial Interpretation] (People's Republic of China), Supreme People's Court, 法发 [1997] 第 15 号 [SPC Notice No 15], 23 June 1997, particularly art 4;《最高人民法院关于司法解释工作的规定》[Regulations Issued by the Supreme People's Court in regard of the Practices of Judicial Interpretation] (People's Republic of China), Supreme People's Court, 法发 [2007] 第 12 号 [SPC Notice No 12], 23 March 2007. Generally speaking, the Judicial Interpretations issued by the SPC can be applied as a legal resource in all later cases. They also make Official Replies to cases reported to the SPC for guidance; these replies

the lower courts that apply to all cases were also highly respected and followed.[63] According to the *People's Courts Organisation Law*, the SPC can issue interpretations of the application of law,[64] and these judicial interpretations are legally binding.[65] Among them are some most important judicial interpretations in relation to arbitration practice:

- *SPC's Interpretation on Several Issues in regard of the Application of the CAL* (the *'2006 Interpretation'* hereafter)[66];
- *SPC's Notice on Several Issues in regard of the Implementation of the CAL* (the *'1999 Interpretation'* hereafter)[67];
- *SPC's Regulation on the Reports and Approvals in the Judicial Review of Arbitration-related Cases* (the *'2017 Regulations on Approvals*' hereafter)[68];
- *SPC's Regulation on Several Matters in the Judicial Review of Arbitration-related Cases* (the *'2017 Regulations on Arbitration Judicial Review*' hereafter)[69];

---

are not judicial interpretations, they normally only have effects on the particular reported case. But the SPC sometimes publishes important replies as guidance for lower courts in dealing with similar issues. For example, in dealing with foreign-related commercial and maritime law issues, the SPC published their replies regularly in the series of《涉外商事海事审判指导》[Guide on Foreign-Related Commercial and Maritime Trial] (人民法院出版社 [People's Court Press]); see further Sect. 3 in Chap. 4, as the most of the cases collected for our empirical study are from these replies.

63 These notices and replies are also forms of judicial interpretations.《最高人民法院关于司法解释工作的若干规定》[Several Regulations Issued by the Supreme People' Court in regard of the Practices of Judicial Interpretation] (People's Republic of China), Supreme People's Court, 法发 [1997] 第 15 号 [SPC Notice No 15], 23 June 1997, art 9.

64《中华人民共和国人民法院组织法》[The People's Courts Organisation Law of People's Republic of China] (People's Republic of China) art 18.

65《最高人民法院关于司法解释工作的规定》[Supreme People's Court's Rules on the Issue of Judicial Interpretation] (People's Republic of China), Supreme People's Court, Fa Fa [2007] No 19, 23 March 2007.

66 最高人民法院关于适用〈中华人民共和国仲裁法〉若干问题的解释》 [Supreme People's Court's Interpretation on Several Issues in regard of the Application of the China Arbitration Law] (People's Republic of China), Supreme People's Court, Fa Shi [2006] No 7, 26 December 2005.

67《《最高人民法院关于实施 <中华人民共和国仲裁法> 几个问题的通知》 [the Supreme People's Court's Notice Concerning Several Issues in the Implementation of the China Arbitration Law] (People's Republic of China) the Supreme People's Court, 法发 [1997] 第 4 号 [SPC Notice No 4], 26 March 1997.

68《最高人民法院关于仲裁司法审查案件报核问题的有关规定》 [Supreme People's Court's Regelation on the Reports and Approvals in the Judicial Review of Arbitration-related Cases] (People's Republic of China) the Supreme People's Court, 法释 [2017] 21 号 [SPC Interpretation No. 21], 4 December 2017, modified by《最高人民法院关于修改〈最高人民法院关于仲裁司法审查案件报核问题的有关规定〉的决定》[Supreme People's Court's Decision to Modify the Supreme People's Court's Regelation on the Reports and Approvals in the Judicial Review of Arbitration-related Cases] (People's Republic of China) the Supreme People's Court, 法释 [2021] 21 号 [SPC Interpretation No. 21], 15 November 2021.

69《最高人民法院关于审理仲裁司法审查若干问题的规定》[Supreme People's Court's Regulation on Several Matters in the Judicial Review of Arbitration-related Cases] (People's Republic of China) the Supreme People's Court, 法释 [2017] 22 号 [SPC Interpretation No. 22], 4 December 2017.

– *SPC's Opinion on the Judicial Services Supporting the Development of the Chinese (Shanghai) Free Trade Trial Zone Lingang New District* (the '*2019 FTZ Opinion*' hereafter).[70]

These interpretations and replies issued by the SPC covered significant and controversial issues in China's arbitration practices, such as whether there should be an appeal procedure for the annulment of an award,[71] and the relationship between validity of arbitral agreement and the enforcement of awards.[72] The arrangements in respect of the recognition of arbitral awards between mainland China and the Hong Kong SAR,[73] and mainland China and the Macao SAR,[74] as well as the judicial assistance regarding arbitration related issues,[75] were also regulated in the form of judicial interpretations.

The author notes that the systematic reform of the *CAL* has been proposed, signalled by the release of the Drafted New Chinese Arbitration Law (*New CAL Draft*) in 2021.[76] Many of the features of Chinese arbitration and the judicial review

70《最高人民法院关于人民法院为中国 (上海) 自由贸易试验区临港新片区建设提供司法服务和保障的意见》[The Supreme People's Court's Opinion on the Judicial Services Supporting the Development of the Chinese (Shanghai) Free Trade Trial Zone Lingang New District] (People's Republic of China) the Supreme People's Court, 法发 [2019] 31号 [SPC Notice No. 31], 13 December 2019.

71《最高人民法院关于当事人对驳回其申请撤销仲裁裁决的裁定不服而申请再审, 人民法院不予受理问题的批复》[Reply by the Supreme People's Court in regard of the Application for Retrial of the Cases in which an Arbitral Award was Annulled and Such Application was Not Accepted by the People's Court] (People's Republic of China), Supreme People's Court, 法释 [2004] 第 9 号 [Judicial Interpretation No 9], 29 July 2004.

72《最高人民法院关于仲裁协议无效是否可以裁定不予执行的处理意见》[Opinions of the Supreme People's Court in regard of whether the Enforcement of an Arbitral Award should be Refused on the Basis of an Invalid Arbitration Agreement] (People's Republic of China), Supreme People's Court, [1999] 执监字第 174-1 号 [Enforcement Supervision No 174-1], 20 June 2002.

73《最高人民法院关于内地与香港特别行政区相互执行仲裁裁决的安排》[Supreme People's Court's Arrangements of the Supreme People's Court on the Mutual Enforcement of Arbitral Awards between the Mainland and the Hong Kong Special Administrative Region] (People's Republic of China), Supreme People's Court, 法释 [2000] 第三号 [Judicial Interpretation No 3], 18 June 1999.

74《最高人民法院关于内地与澳门特别行政区相互认可和执行仲裁裁决的安排》[Arrangement between the Mainland and the Macao SAR on Reciprocal Recognition and Enforcement of Arbitration Awards] (People's Republic of China) Supreme People's Court, 法释 [2007] 第 17号 [Judicial Interpretation No 17], 17 September 2007.

75《最高人民法院关于内地与香港特别行政区法院就仲裁程序相互协助保全的安排》[The Supreme People's Court's Arrangement Concerning Mutual Assistance in Court-ordered Interim Measures in Aid of Arbitral Proceedings by the Courts of the Mainland and of the Hong Kong Special Administrative Region] (People's Republic of China) Supreme People's Court, 法释 [2019] 第 14 号 [Judicial Interpretation No 14], 26 September 2019;《最高人民法院关于内地与澳门特别行政区就仲裁程序相互协助保全的安排》[The Supreme People's Court's Arrangement Concerning Mutual Assistance in Court-ordered Interim Measures in Aid of Arbitral Proceedings by the Courts of the Mainland and of the Macau Special Administrative Region] (People's Republic of China) Supreme People's Court, 法释 [2022] 第7号 [Judicial Interpretation No 7], 15 Feb 2022.

76《<中华人民共和国仲裁法 (修订)> 征求意见稿》[Draft of the Modified Arbitration Law of the People's Republic of China] (People's Republic of China), Ministry of Justice, 30 July 2021, available at: http://www.moj.gov.cn/pub/sfbgw/zlk/202107/t20210730_432958.html.

of arbitration related issues, as detailed below, might be subject to significant changes should the new law come into effect in the future.

### 3.2.2 The Transition of the Arbitration Commissions

All of China's arbitration institutions except CIETAC and CMAC were transformed and re-established under the main principles of the *CAL* after its enactment. The *CAL* regulates the establishment of arbitration commissions, their qualification, registration, selection of staff and social status. In accordance with the *CAL* requirements, the new arbitration commissions were first established in a few cities, and then in almost all cities in China, and such "re-establishment" movements were carried out with close cooperation between the local (usually the municipal level) governments and the relevant branch governing commerce and legal affairs.[77] However, in 1995 those arbitration commissions were still only authorised to hear purely domestic disputes.

It was not until the issuance of the *1996 Notice* that all the arbitration commissions, including CIETAC, CMAC and all newly established domestic arbitrations, were allowed to accept both domestic and foreign-related disputes.[78] This regulation eliminated the distinction between "foreign-related arbitration commission" and "domestic arbitration commission", though these words remain in the *CAL*.

However, CIETAC and CMAC retain some distinctive features as compared to the newly established arbitration commissions. For instance, CIETAC and CMAC are still under the supervision of CCIPT, which keeps them relatively independent from any local and domestic interests as compared with the commissions that are closely connected to municipal governmental bodies.[79] The newly established commissions, on the other hand, have some advantages because of their location, relationships with local governments and local market, and their internal structure.[80] Based on

---

77《国务院办公厅关于印发<新组建仲裁机构方案> <仲裁委员会登记暂行办法> <仲裁委员会仲裁收费办法> 的通知》[Notice of the General Office of State Council in regard of the Issuance of 'Plan of the Newly Established Arbitration Institutions', 'Interim Plan for the Registration of the Arbitration Commissions' and 'Regulations of the Charging Measures of the Arbitration Commissions'] (People's Republic of China), State Council, 国办发 [1995] 44 号 [General Office of State Council Notice No 44], 28 July 1995.

78《国务院办公厅关于贯彻实施 <中华人民共和国仲裁法> 需要明确的几个问题的通知》[Notice on Clarifying A Few Problems in the Enactment of the Arbitration Act of PRC by the General Office of the State Council] (People's Republic of China), State Council, 国办发 [1996] 22 号 [General Office of State Council Notice No 22], 8 June 1996, art 3.

79 Wunschheim, above n 1, 39. It may not be appropriate to say that these arbitration commissions at the municipal level are actually governed by municipal governments, especially those who claim independence from the government bodies, but there are still some connections between these arbitration commissions and their local government; see art 10 of the *CAL*, which provides that the arbitration commissions shall be established by the relevant governmental department and the Chamber of Commerce of the municipal government where the arbitration commission is located; it shall also be registered at the Department of Justice at the provincial level with its approval.

80 陈福勇[Chen Fuyong],《未竟的转型: 中国仲裁机构现状与发展趋势实证研究》[Unfinished Transformation: An Empirical Study of the Current Status and Future Trends of China's Arbitration

such advantages, some leading arbitration commissions, such as Beijing Arbitration Commission (BAC hereafter) developed rapidly with increasing caseloads and well-established reputation. This was not the case for all local arbitration commissions; some commissions were limited by the relatively underdeveloped local economy and stronger dependence on administrative power.[81] In the recent years, Chinese arbitration commissions developed rapidly and became more influential in the global arbitration market than ever. For example, CIETAC is among the top 5 preferred arbitration institutions in the Queen Mary International Arbitration Survey 2021. To extend its influence, CIETAC opened its Arbitration Centres in Hong Kong, North America (based in Vancouver), and Europe (based in Vienna), and allowed parties to choose places other than cities in Mainland China as the place of arbitration.[82]

### 3.2.3 Development of the Judicial Review Schemes on Arbitration

The *CAL* and *CCPL* standardised the judicial practices on arbitration law issues, which is to adhere to the principle of finality of arbitration, and states that the court will intervene in situations when: (1) deciding the validity of an arbitration agreement; (2) granting interim measures for properties or evidence in arbitration proceedings; and (3) providing the proceedings of judicial review of arbitral awards, including both annulment proceedings and enforcement proceedings. It is argued that China's judicial system provides a "minimal judicial intervention" scheme, as it will not intervene for any reason beyond those situations listed.[83] However, there is also criticism that some important schemes, such as the judicial assistance to the issuance of anti-suit injunctions or interim measures, and evidence procedures, are not yet available or fully regulated in China at the legislative level.[84]

---

Institutions] (法律出版社[Law Press], 2010). In this book Chen reviewed the unbalanced developments of different arbitration commissions in China; 袁发强 [Yuan Faqiang],《中国商事*仲裁机构*现状与发展趋势研究》[Research on the present of China's Commercial Arbitration Institutions and Their Development Trends in the Future] (复旦大学出版社 [Fudan University Press], 2011) 12–13.

[81] The top 10 arbitration commissions administered over fifty percent of China's arbitration disputes in 2006. Ibid, 12.

[82] CIETAC Arbitration Rules (2014), Chapter 6.

[83] Shengchang Wang, 'CIETAC's Perspective on Arbitration and Conciliation Concerning China' in Albert Jan van den Berg (ed), *New Horizons in International Commercial Arbitration and Beyond*, ICCA Congress Series (Kluwer Law International, 2005) vol 12, 34; See also 李虎 [Li Hu],《国际商事仲裁裁决的强制执行——特别述及仲裁裁决在中国的强制执行》[Enforcement of International Commercial Arbitration Awards: with Emphasis on Award Enforcement in the P. R. China] (法律出版社 [Law Press], 2000) 3.

[84] Weixia Gu, 'Judicial Review over Arbitration in China: Assessing the Extent of the Latest Pro-Arbitration Move by the Supreme People's Court in the People's Republic of China' (2009–2010) 27(2) *Wisconsin International Law Journal* 221, 226; Wunschheim, above n 1, 42–43. A discussion of a possible consequence of lacking these judicial interventions in supporting arbitration proceedings, see further Chap. 6, particularly a discussion of the lack of necessary guidance and standard to decide the violation of public policy in disqualification of arbitrators and taking evidences.

The *CAL* and *CCPL*, with the assistance of the SPC's judicial interpretation of arbitration law issues, added a few significant features to the process of judicial review of arbitral awards. Judicial review of all arbitral awards will not go to the BPCs but will only be dealt with by IPCs.[85] This requirement prevents the involvement of enormous BPCs, which are at the lowest end of China's judicial system. In doing so, this requirement aims to reduce the inconsistency in the judicial review and enhance the quality of the judicial decision. Parties should go to the specific court(s) based on the key features of the arbitration-related disputes.[86] The court's decision resulted from a judicial review of arbitral awards cannot be appealed, which also aims to respect the finality of arbitration.[87]

### 3.2.4 The Prior Reporting System

Before 1995 the mysterious practice and unpredictable outcomes in China's judicial practices of enforcing arbitral awards caused foreign legal practitioners to think that the enforcement of arbitral awards in China lacked natural justice and were made on the basis of local protectionism.[88] In response to those criticisms, the Chinese judicial system has made an effort to improve its performance by providing a high

---

85 The IPC's authority to hold enforcement proceedings of foreign-related awards and international awards was provided by the Prior Reporting System, and then confirmed in *CCPL*; its authority to deal with the enforcement of domestic awards was further provided by the 2006 judicial interpretation of the SPC, which is considered one of the major contributions of that interpretation. 《中华人民共和国仲裁法》[Arbitration Law of the People's Republic of China] (People's Republic of China) art 58; 《中华人民共和国民事诉讼法》[The Civil Procedure Law of the People's Republic of China] (People's Republic of China) art 281, art 290; 《最高人民法院关于适用〈中华人民共和国仲裁法〉若干问题的解释》[Supreme People's Court's Interpretation on Several Issues in regard of the Application of the China Arbitration Law] (People's Republic of China), Supreme People's Court, 法释 [2006] 第7号 [Judicial Interpretation No 7], 26 December 2005, art 29; 陆效龙, 吴兆祥[Lu Xiaolong, Wu Zhaoxiang], 《<关于适用仲裁法若干问题的解释> 的理解与适用》[Understanding and Applying 'Interpretation on Several Issues in regard of the Application of the China Arbitration Law'] (2006) 10人民司法 *People's Judicature* 28, 28–32.

86 《最高人民法院关于审理仲裁司法审查若干问题的规定》[Supreme People's Court's Regulation on Several Several Matters in the Judicial Review of Arbitration-related Cases] (People's Republic of China) the Supreme People's Court, 法释 [2017] 22 号 [SPC Interpretation No. 22], 4 December 2017, arts 2–4.

87 According to *CCPL*, the decision on an arbitral award is a "ruling", not a "judgment" under Chinese law; only three types of rulings can be appealed: (1) Rejection of a lawsuit; (2) Objection to the jurisdiction of a court; (3) Rejection of a complaint. Setting aside or not enforcing an arbitral award is not included. 《中华人民共和国民事诉讼法》[The Civil Procedure Law of the People's Republic of China] (People's Republic of China) art 157. This point is further confirmed in 《最高人民法院关于审理仲裁司法审查若干问题的规定》[Supreme People's Court's Regulation on Several Matters in the Judicial Review of Arbitration-related Cases] (People's Republic of China) the Supreme People's Court, 法释 [2017] 22 号 [SPC Interpretation No. 22], 4 December 2017, art 20.

88 Jinzhou Tao, *Arbitration Law and Practice in China* (Kluwer International, 2012) 202; Cheng, Moser and Wang, above n 41, 131. For a more detailed discussion of local protectionism and the *Dongfeng Case*, see Chap. 5.

enforcement rate of arbitral awards, showing a pro-enforcement attitude towards arbitration.[89] The most important improvement by SPC was the establishment of the Prior Reporting System ('预先报告制度) in 1995 for international arbitral awards and in 1998 for foreign-related arbitral awards.[90] This mechanism requires that, if an IPC was contemplating annulling or refusing the enforcement of an award, then that court must report the case to the HPC in the same jurisdiction for review; and if it too agrees with the IPC, then the matter must be reported to the SPC. Only when the SPC confirms the proposed decision to annul an award or to refuse the enforcement of an award, can the decision to annul or refuse the enforcement of an award be made.[91]

The operation of the Prior Reporting System is meaningful. Through this system the SPC exclusively enjoys the final say to any case negating a foreign-related or foreign arbitral award. This ensures consistency in the arbitration practice and limits, if not totally eliminates, the impact of local protectionism.[92] In addition, the determination and reasoning provided by the higher courts, especially the SPC, generated from the report and approval process might provide guidance to lower courts in dealing with similar matters.

The Prior Reporting System is not a system of appeal, but rather an internal-management mechanism adopted by the Chinese judicial system[93]; thus, the lack of transparency or clear time limit seems understandable. However, contrary to Tao's earlier comments that the Prior Reporting System was only a temporary measure and might be removed when the law improves,[94] the Prior Reporting System was seen as a huge success in China, and therefore was further confirmed and extended to domestic awards in 2017.[95] For the judicial review of arbitral awards without foreign

[89] See further Sect. 2 in Chap. 4.

[90] "Prior Reporting System" is a literal translation of the system, as it is widely used in the literature. See for example, Tao, above n 88, 202–205. Similar term such as "pre-reporting scheme" is also used for the same meaning. See for example, Michael J. Moser (ed), *Dispute Resolution in China* (Juris, 2012) 78. It is notable, however, that the essence of this mechanism is for the lower court to not merely "report", but to seek for approval, when making a decision to negate an arbitration agreement, set aside an award or deny the enforcement of an award.

[91]《最高人民法院关于人民法院处理与涉外仲裁及外国仲裁事项有关问题的通知》[Notice of the Supreme People's Court on Several Issues regarding the Handling by the People's Courts of Certain Issues Pertaining to Foreign-Related Arbitration and Foreign Arbitration; issued by the Supreme People's Court on and effective from 28 Aug. 1995 (Notice on Prior Reporting System 1995);《最高人民法院关于人民法院撤销涉外仲裁裁决有关事项的通知》Notice of the Supreme People's Court on Relevant Issues Relating to the Cancellation by the People's Court of Foreign-Related Arbitration Awards; issued by the Supreme People's Court on, and effective from 23 Apr. 1998 (Notice on Prior Reporting System 1998).

[92] Tao, above n 88, 203–05.

[93] Ibid, 205.

[94] Ibid.

[95]《最高人民法院关于仲裁司法审查案件报核问题的有关规定》 [Supreme People's Court's Regelation on the Reports and Approvals in the Judicial Review of Arbitration-related Cases] (People's Republic of China) the Supreme People's Court, 法释 [2017] 21 号 [SPC Interpretation No. 21], 4 December 2017, modified by《最高人民法院关于修改〈最高人民法院关于仲裁司法审查案件报核问题的有关规定〉的决定》[Supreme People's Court's Decision to Modify the Supreme People's Court's Regelation on the Reports and Approvals in the Judicial Review of

elements, any decision negating the award (setting aside or non-enforcement) should also be reported by the IPCs to the HPCs for approval; and if the negation was based on social public interests, it should be further reported to the SPC for approval.[96] This extension is meaningful in the context of this book, because it indicates the trend towards further unification of the interpretation and application of public policy in the judicial review of arbitral awards in China. It is yet to be determined, however, whether the public policy test in foreign-related/foreign cases and the test in domestic cases would be similar or comparable.

## 4 Distinct Aspects of the Current Arbitration System in China

This section focuses on some distinct aspects of China's arbitration system, which may influence our further discussion of the public policy exception in China's arbitration law. Section 4.1 reviews the law; Sect. 4.2 emphasises the different concepts of domestic, foreign-related and international arbitration under Chinese law; Sect. 4.3 examines the different judicial review mechanisms applying to different types of awards. Section 4.4 further explains the different schemes of annulment and enforcement proceedings. Finally, Sect. 4.5 examines the distinct features of the Chinese arbitration commissions and arbitrators and their possible influence on arbitration practices.

### *4.1 A Complicated Set of Rules Governing Arbitration Practice*

Multiple statutes and rules apply when making decisions about arbitration matters in China. They contain rules and regulations made by different authorities and based on different historical backgrounds.

China's arbitration legislation is considered to be a combination of both the distinctive aspects of Chinese characteristics and the predominant principles and values

---

Arbitration-related Cases] (People's Republic of China) the Supreme People's Court, 法释 [2021] 21 号 [SPC Interpretation No. 21], 15 November 2021, art 2.

96 《最高人民法院关于仲裁司法审查案件报核问题的有关规定》 [Supreme People's Court's Regelation on the Reports and Approvals in the Judicial Review of Arbitration-related Cases] (People's Republic of China) the Supreme People's Court, 法释 [2017] 21 号 [SPC Interpretation No. 21], 4 December 2017, modified by《最高人民法院关于修改〈最高人民法院关于仲裁司法审查案件报核问题的有关规定〉的决定》[Supreme People's Court's Decision to Modify the Supreme People's Court's Regelation on the Reports and Approvals in the Judicial Review of Arbitration-related Cases] (People's Republic of China) the Supreme People's Court, 法释 [2021] 21 号 [SPC Interpretation No. 21], 15 November 2021, art 3.

underpinning international arbitration movements.[97] The *CAL* has been strongly influenced by common practice governing international commercial arbitration, for example, those outlined by the *UNCITRAL Model Law*; it also adheres to the principles of party autonomy and the independence of arbitration.[98] Yet China's arbitration legislation is quite different from the *Model Law* in many aspects. For example, the *Model Law* allows ad hoc arbitration but the Chinese legislation does not[99]; the tribunal's right to decide its competence is fundamental in the *Model Law,* but this is limited in China.[100] Furthermore, some rules in the *CAL* have been developed in the distinct context of China's society[101]; for example, China's arbitration law has its distinctive arrangements of mediation during arbitration.[102] China's arbitration law is thus described as a "legal omelette", in which "ingredients from both Chinese and non-Chinese sources (have been) blended together to create an edible product" for all participants of arbitration in China.[103] It is overwhelmingly crucial for both practitioners and scholars to understand the origin and root of the rules of China's arbitration legislation, and identify their possible influences on how such rules are interpreted and applied.

Alongside domestic laws such as the *CAL* and *CCPL*, sit international conventions such as the *NYC*, and the SPC's judicial interpretations.[104] Given that these rules are made by different authorities and in different historical and legal contexts, it is probably inevitable that a number of out-of-date and even contradictory rules co-exist.[105]

## *4.2 Types of Arbitration and Awards*

Another significant distinction between China's arbitration law and general practice in international commercial arbitration is the categorisation of arbitration and arbitral

[97] Gemmell, above n 43, 150.

[98] Tao, above n 88, 4–8.

[99] Tietie Zhang, 'Enforceability of Ad Hoc Arbitration Agreements in China: China's Incomplete Ad Hoc Arbitration System' (2013) 46 *Cornell International Law Journal* 361.

[100] Tao, above n 88, 95–96, [244].

[101] The distinctive aspects of Chinese society include the notion of harmony, the comparison of " 礼 (Li)" (the courtesy) and "法 (Fa)" (the Law), the distinctive role of leaders in families, villages and guilds in dispute resolution, and the distinct definition of mediation and arbitration in China's society. See Kun Fan, 'Transnational Standards Struggling with Local Norms: Through the Lens of Arbitration Transplantation in China' (2013) 18 *Harvard Negotiation Law Review* 175, 193–205; Weigong Xu, 'Definition of Arbitration in China' (2011) 30 *Journal of Law and Commerce* 107, 108–110.

[102] Wang, above n 83.

[103] Gemmell, above n 43, 150–151.

[104] *Above* Sect. 3.2.

[105] One example of the out-of-date rule is the term "foreign-related arbitration commissions" as discussed in *above* Sect. 3.2.

**Table 1** Types of arbitral awards in China

| | Domestic | Foreign-related | Foreign |
|---|---|---|---|
| Parties | Chinese | Chinese/foreign | Chinese/Foreign |
| Nature of dispute | Domestic | Foreign elements included | Foreign |
| Place of arbitration | China | China | Foreign jurisdictions |
| Arbitration administers | Chinese institutions | Chinese institutions | Foreign institutions/ad hoc |
| Judicial supervisions over the procedure | Chinese courts | Chinese courts | Foreign courts |
| Legal basis of supervision procedure | Art. 58 *CAL* | Art. 70 *CAL*<br>Art.281 *CCPL* | Arbitration law of the place of arbitration |
| Legal basis of enforcement (in China) | Art.63 *CAL*<br>Art. 244 *CCPL* | Art. 71 *CAL*<br>Art. 281 *CCPL* | Art 290 *CCPL*<br>International conventions, mutual agreements… |

awards. There are three different types of arbitration as classified in China: domestic, foreign-related, and foreign arbitrations. Each of these categories is treated differently in terms of procedure and attracts different judicial review schemes, as detailed in Table 1.

Two observations can be made from the above categorisation. First, all arbitration proceedings in China are institutional and must be administered by one of the arbitration commissions established in accordance with the *CAL*.[106] Thus, when an award was made in China, it must be either domestic or a foreign-related one, resulting from a proceeding administered by Chinese institutions. This means that the legal mechanism established by the *CAL* excludes ad hoc arbitration and arbitration hearings administered by foreign arbitration institutions within China.[107]

The restrictions on ad hoc arbitration and the operation of foreign arbitration institutions were once strictly adhered to, as evidenced by many cases and judicial opinions. For example, the Fourth Branch of the SPC (specialising in international commercial and maritime disputes) published a Q&A on Practical Issues in the Adjudication of Foreign-related Commercial and Maritime Cases in 2008, which stated that an arbitration agreement selecting ad hoc arbitration in China should be

[106] 《中华人民共和国仲裁法》 [Arbitration Law of the People's Republic of China] (People's Republic of China) arts 16 and 18.

[107] Jingzhou Tao and Clarisse von Wunschheim, 'Arts. 16 and 18 of the PRC Arbitration Law: The Great Wall of China for Foreign Arbitration Institutions' (2007) 23(2) *Arbitration International* 309; Tietie Zhang, above n 99.

held invalid.[108] In Cases such as *Castel*[109] arbitration agreements selecting ad hoc arbitration and not indicating the place of arbitration were determined invalid.

However, in practice both restrictions were then loosened. As early as 2014, the SPC, in its reply to a local court, confirmed the validity of an arbitration agreement choosing ICC arbitration in Shanghai.[110] Further, to assist the development of Free Trade Zones, ad hoc arbitration and the operation of foreign arbitral institutions were both welcomed in the Free Trade Zone.[111] Several ad hoc arbitration rules were published to assist in its development and its connection with institutional support, such as the Hengqin Free Trade Zone Ad-hoc Arbitration Rules published by the Zhuhai Arbitration Commission,[112] or the China Maritime Law Association Ad Hoc Arbitration Rules.[113] It was also reported by a CMAC staff member that CMAC had acted as the appointing authority in an ad hoc arbitration seated in Mainland China.[114] In 2020, an arbitration administrated by the ICC in Guangzhou was held as a foreign-related arbitration in China, and its award should be enforced under the Chinese Civil Procedure Law[115]; an arbitration agreement selecting Singapore International Arbitration Centre to administrate its case in Shanghai was also upheld.[116]

---

108 The Fourth Branch of the SPC,《涉外商事海事审判实务问题解答》[Q&A on Practical Issues in the Adjudication of Foreign-related Commercial and Maritime Cases] (2008), art 88.

109 Guanyu Shenqingren Castel Electronics Pty. Ltd. Shenqing Chengren He Zhixing Waiguo Zhongcai Caijue Yi An De Qingshi (关于申请人 Castel Electronics Pty Ltd. 申请承认和执行外国仲裁裁决一案的请示) [Concerning Petitioner Castel Electronics Pty Ltd. Request for Instructions on the Application for Recognition and Enforcement of Foreign Arbitral Awards], 2013 Min Si Ta Zi No. 46 (Sup. People's Ct. July 10, 2013).

110《最高人民法院关于申请人安徽省龙利得包装印刷有限公司与被申请人 BP Agnati S.R.L 申请确认仲裁协议效力案的请示的复函》[Reply of the Supreme People's Court Concerning the Application to Confirm the Validity of the Arbitration Agreement between Applicant, Anhui Longlide Packing and Printing Co Ltd and Respondent, BP Agnati S.R.L] Supreme People's Court, [2013]民四他字第 13号 [Fourth Civil Branch No. 13], 25 March 2013; see also《最高人民法院关于宁波市北仑利成润滑油有限公司与法莫万驰公司买卖合同纠纷一案仲裁条款效力问题的批复》[Reply of the Supreme People's Court Concerning the Validity of the Arbitration Agreement in the Contractual Dispute between Ningbo Beilun Licheng Lubricant Oil Co and Formal Venture Corp] Supreme People's Court, [2013] 民四他字第 74 号 [Fourth Civil Branch No. 74], 5 December 2013.

111《最高人民法院关于为自由贸易试验区建设提供司法保障的意见》 [Supreme People's Court's Opinion on the Judicial Services Promoting and Supporting the Development of the Free Trade Trial Zone], Fa Fa [2016] No. 34, 30 December 2016, arts 8–9; Shanghai Municipal Justice Bureau, 'The Rules of Regulating the Branches of Foreign Arbitration Institutions Established in China (Shanghai) Free Trade Zone Lingang New District', 21 October 2019.

112《横琴自由贸易试验区临时仲裁规则》[Hengqin Free Trade Zone Ad-hoc Arbitration Rules], effective April 2017.

113《中国海商法协会临时仲裁规则》[China Maritime Law Association Ad Hoc Arbitration Rules], effective 18 March 2022.

114 https://m.yicai.com/video/101604606.html.

115 *Brentwood Industries, Inc., v. Guangdong Fa'anlong Machinery Complete Set Equipment Engineering Co Ltd.*, Enforcement of ICC Case No.18929/CYK, Guangzhou IPC, (2015) Hui Zhong Fa Min Si Chu Zi No. 62, 6 Aug 2020.

116 *BNA v. BNB*, Shanghai 1st IPC, (2020) Hu 01 Min Te No.83, 29 June 2020.

Both changes were further confirmed by the *New CAL Draft*, which expressly covered the operation of foreign arbitration institution under the supervision of the Ministry of Justice,[117] and allows the operation of ad hoc arbitral tribunals in foreign-related cases.[118] It is expected that the judicial review mechanism on arbitral awards will also apply to awards from ad hoc arbitrations and arbitrations administrated by foreign institutions under the *New CAL Draft*.

Secondly, the distinction between foreign-related and domestic arbitration, and awards generated from them, are made on the basis of the existence of any "foreign-related" element. The test was originally established by the SPC in the 1988 Opinions on Several Issues concerning the Implementation of the *GPCL*,[119] which defined a foreign-related dispute as a case where:

(1) *any or all of the parties has foreign nationality, no nationality, or is a foreign legal person;*
(2) *the subject in dispute is located in a foreign jurisdiction; or*
(3) *the legal fact creating, changing or extinguishing the rights and obligations takes place in a foreign jurisdiction.*

In the SPC's 2012 Judicial Interpretation Concerning the Application of the Chinese Choice of Law for Foreign-Related Civil Relationships (I),[120] the SPC further extended this test to where "any or all of the parties has its habitual residence in a foreign jurisdiction."

Compared with this definition, the concept of "international" stated in the *Model Law* of 2006 is much more flexible, allowing the consideration of facts such as the places of business, place of arbitration, place of the performance of substantial parts of the obligations, place most closely connected to the subject matter, and parties' intention to its international nature.[121]

In China's judicial practice, the application of foreign-related elements is subject to the discretion of the adjudicators; thus, inconsistent outcomes might occur, leaving

---

117 《<中华人民共和国仲裁法 (修订)> 征求意见稿》[Draft of the Modified Arbitration Law of the People's Republic of China] (People's Republic of China, art 12.

118 *Ibid*, art 91.

119 《最高人民法院关于贯彻执行 < 中华人民共和国民法通则 > 若干问题的意见 (试行)》[Opinions of the Supreme People's Court in regard of the Implementation of the 'General Rules of the Civil Law of the People's Republic of China' (the Trial Version)] (People's Republic of China), Supreme People's Court, Fa (Ban) Fa [1988] No. 6, 2 April 1988, art 178;《最高人民法院关于适用 <中华人民共和国民事诉讼法 > 若干问题的意见》[Opinions of the Supreme People's Court in regard of Several Issues on the Application of the Civil Procedure Law of the People's Republic of China] Supreme People's Court, Fa Fa [1992] No 22, 14 July 1992, art 304; Wunschheim, above n 1, 43–44.

120 《最高人民法院关于适用《中华人民共和国涉外民事关系法律适用法》若干问题的解释(一)》[Interpretations of the Supreme People's Court on Several Issues Concerning the Application of the Law of the People's Republic of China on Choice of Law for Foreign-Related Civil Relationships (I)] Supreme People's Court, Fa (Shi) [2012] No. 24, 28 December 28 2012, effective 7 January 2013.

121 *UNCITRAL Model Law*, Art 1(3).

a greater extent of uncertainty to parties, even in the most recent cases. In *Chaolaixinsheng*,[122] the Chaolaixinsheng Company is fully owned by a Korean investor, however, the court denied its foreign elements. Whereas, in *Landmark*, the court considered that the parties were incorporated in the Shanghai Free Trade Zone and were closely connected to foreign investors, and confirmed its foreign-related nature.[123] In *Audonline*, the foreign-related nature was again denied even though part of the performance of the contract was located in Hong Kong.[124] The existence of foreign elements also determines whether the parties can choose to arbitrate outside China Mainland; if there is no 'foreign-related' element, the Chinese courts' attitude is that the dispute should only be adjudicated in China, so the arbitration agreement or awards should not be enforced, as further illustrated in *Chaolaixinsheng* and *Audonline*.[125]

## *4.3 Application of Different Mechanisms to the Awards*

On the basis of the above categorisation, different judicial review schemes apply, as indicated in Table 1. For domestic arbitral awards, the judicial review scheme is based on Articles 58 and 63 of the *CAL* and Article 244 of the *CCPL*. For foreign-related arbitral awards the situation becomes more complicated. The judicial review for the purpose of recognition and enforcement of foreign-related awards is listed in Article 281 of the *CCPL*; Articles 70 and 71 of the *CAL* provides that the mechanism in art 281 of the CCPL also applies for the annulment of foreign-related arbitral awards.

For arbitral awards made outside the territory of mainland China, which is categorised as foreign, no unified judicial review scheme is provided by the national legislation. The *CCPL* refers to any applicable international conventions, multilateral agreements and the principle of reciprocity. Among the international conventions and agreements, the most important one is the *NYC*. It is also notable that the Chinese government has made the reciprocity and commercial reservations in

[122]《最高人民法院关于北京朝来新生体育休闲有限公司申请承认大韩商事仲裁院作出的第12113-0011号、第12112-0012号仲裁裁决案件请示的复函》[Reply of the SPC Concerning the Enforcement of KCAB Awards 12113-0011, 12112-0012 Requested by Beijing Chaolaixinsheng Sports and Leisure Co Ltd], Supreme People's Court, [2013]民四他字第64号 [Fourth Civil Branch No. 64], 18 December 2013.

[123]《西门子国际贸易 (上海) 有限公司与上海黄金置地有限公司申请承认和执行外国仲裁裁决案》[Siemens International Trade (Shanghai) Ltd Co. v. Shanghai Golden Landmark Co Ltd.—Case of the Application for the Recognition and Enforcement of Foreign Arbitral Awards], 上海市第一中级人民法院 [Shanghai 1st IPC, People's Republic of China], (2013) 沪一中民认 (外仲) 字第2号 [Recognition of Foreign Arbitral Awards No. 2], 27 Nov 2015.

[124]《爱耳时代医疗科技 (北京) 股份有限公司与领先仿生医疗器械 (上海) 有限公司合同纠纷案》[Audonline Medical Technology (Beijing) Co. v Advanced Bionics Medical Instruments (Shanghai) Co. Ltd.—Case Concerning Contractual Disputes], 上海市高级人民法院 [Shanghai HPC, People's Republic of China], (2018) 沪民申921号 [Retrial No. 921], 26 June 2018.

[125] See further Sect. 3.3 in Chap. 8.

accordance with Article I(3) of the *NYC*.[126] Another important legal framework governing the recognition and enforcement of foreign arbitral awards is the enforcement network among Greater China.[127] Based on mutual consents, China provided detailed arrangements on the recognition and enforcement of arbitral awards with the Hong Kong and Macao SARs.[128] The scheme for the recognition and enforcement activities between mainland China and Taiwan is provided by the SPC in its *Regulations on the Recognition and Enforcement of Arbitral Awards made in Taiwan ('SPC's Taiwan Regulation')*.[129] The mechanisms are summarised in Table 2.

A comparison of these mechanisms provides that the grounds to negate an arbitral award are set out differently depending on the type of the arbitral awards. The judicial review process for domestic awards and foreign-related awards is conceived as a "dual-track" system, as the judicial review scheme for foreign-related awards is generally distinct from the scheme for domestic awards, with the former being a review of procedural issues, while the latter, to some extent, allows a review of the merits.[130]

The dual-track judicial review scheme that distinguishes domestic awards and foreign-related awards has attracted the attention of both scholars and practitioners. Some have insisted that the distinction between domestic and foreign-related awards has been made on the basis of China's historical development and distinct legal environment.[131] Wang Shengming stated two main reasons that such a distinction was insisted: First, the system of credibility of individuals in China is not fully developed and cases of forgery or fraud in arbitration practices are not uncommon, and thus needs judicial supervision; secondly, the arbitration system in China, and particularly, the quality of the arbitrators, are not yet fully developed, particularly in the less developed geographic areas of China.[132] Similar statements regarding this

---

126 《最高人民法院关于执行我国加入的<承认及执行外国仲裁裁决公约>的通知》[Notice of the Supreme People's Court in regard of the Implementation of the 'Convention on the Recognition and Enforcement of Foreign Arbitral Award'] (People's Republic of China), Supreme People's Court, 法(经)发(1987)5号 [Supreme Court (Economic) Notice No. 5], 10 April 1987.

127 See Chap. 1.

128 《最高人民法院关于内地与香港特别行政区相互执行仲裁裁决的安排》 [Arrangement of the Supreme People's Court Concerning Mutual Enforcement of Arbitral Awards between the Mainland and Hong Kong Special Administrative Region] Supreme People's Court, 法释 [2000] 第3号[Judicial Interpretation No 3], 18 June 1999;《关于内地与澳门特别行政区相互认可和执行仲裁裁决的安排》[Arrangement Concerning Mutual Recognition and Enforcement of Arbitral Awards Between the Special Administrative Region of Macao and the Mainland] Supreme People's Court, 法释 [2007] 第17号 [Judicial Interpretation No 17], 30 October 2007.

129 《最高人民法院关于认可和执行台湾地区仲裁裁决的规定》[Regulations on the Recognition and Enforcement of Arbitral Awards Made in Taiwan by the Supreme People's Court] Supreme People's Court, 法释[2015]14号 [Judicial Interpretation No. 14], 2 June 2015.

130 Section 4.4.

131 肖永平 [Xiao Yongping],《也谈我国法院对仲裁的监督范围》[Comments on the Scope of Judicial Supervision of Arbitration by Chinese Courts] (1998) 87(1) 法学评论 *Law Review* 42, 49.

132 王胜明 [Wang Shengming],《在第六届中国仲裁论坛上的讲话》[Presentation at the 6th China Arbitration Forum] October 31 2012, Beijing. Mr. Wang Shengming is the Vice Chairman of the Legal Affairs Committee of the National People's Congress.

**Table 2** Comparison of judicial review schemes of different arbitral awards provided by legislation[133]

| Type of award | Annulment | Enforcement |
|---|---|---|
| Domestic | Art.58 *CAL*<br>(1) *There is no arbitration agreement between the parties;*<br>(2) *The matters of the award are beyond the scope of the arbitration agreement or not arbitrable by the arbitration commission;*<br>(3) *The composition of the arbitration tribunal or the arbitration procedure is not in conformity with the rules of arbitration;*<br>(4) *The evidence on which the award is based is falsified;*<br>(5) *The other party has concealed evidence which is sufficient to affect the impartiality of the award; and*<br>(6) *The arbitrator(s) has (have) demanded or accepted bribes, committed graft or perverted the law in making the arbitral award...*<br>*In addition, the people's court shall also annul the arbitral award if finding it violates the social public interest* | Art.244 *CCPL*<br>(1) *There is no arbitration agreement between the parties;*<br>(2) *The matters of the award are beyond the scope of the arbitration agreement or not arbitrable by the arbitration commission;*<br>(3) *The composition of the arbitration tribunal or the arbitration procedure is not in conformity with the rules of arbitration;*<br>(4) *The evidence on which the award is based is falsified;*<br>(5) *The other party has concealed evidence which is sufficient to affect the impartiality of the award; and*<br>(6) *The arbitrator(s) has (have) demanded or accepted bribes, committed graft or perverted the law in making the arbitral award...*<br>*In addition, the people's court shall also annul the arbitral award if finding it violates the social public interest* |
| Foreign-related | Art.70 *CAL*, refer to Art.281(1)*CCPL*<br>(1) *The parties have not had an arbitration clause in the contract or have not subsequently reached a written arbitration agreement;*<br>(2) *The party against whom the application for enforcement is made was not given notice for the appointment of an arbitrator or for the inception of the arbitration proceedings, or was unable to present his case due to causes of which he is not responsible;*<br>(3) *The composition of the arbitration tribunal or the procedure of arbitration was not in conformity with the rules of arbitration;*<br>(4) *The matters dealt with by the award fall outside the scope of the arbitration agreement or are not arbitrable by the arbitration commissions* | Art.281 *CCPL*, and Art.71 *CAL* refer to Art.281(1)*CCPL*<br>(1) *The parties have not had an arbitration clause in the contract or have not subsequently reached a written arbitration agreement;*<br>(2) *The party against whom the application for enforcement was made was not given notice for the appointment of an arbitrator or for the inception of the arbitration proceedings, or was unable to present his case due to causes of which he is not responsible;*<br>(3) *The composition of the arbitration tribunal or the procedure of arbitration was not in conformity with the rules of arbitration;*<br>(4) *The matters dealt with by the award fall outside the scope of the arbitration agreement or not arbitrable by the arbitration commissions*<br>Art.281(2)*CCPL* added<br>*And additionally, if the people's court determines that the enforcement of the award goes against the social public interest of the country, it shall refuse the enforcement of such arbitral award* |

(continued)

133 Translations of the Chinese legislation are adopted from the China Law Information Website, available at: <http://www.chinalawinfo.com/>.

**Table 2** (continued)

| Type of award | Annulment | Enforcement |
|---|---|---|
| Foreign | Not applicable | Art 290, *CCPL*<br>*NYC*, art V<br>*SPC's Hong Kong Arrangements*, art 7<br>*SPC's Macao Arrangements*, art 7<br>*SPC's Taiwan Regulation, art 14* |

distinction can be found in other publications regarding whether judicial review on the substance of cases should be conducted.[134] Yet there are also arguments that both domestic awards and foreign-related and international awards should be reviewed under a unified scheme; for example, the recent 2012 Amendment of *CCPL* illustrates the SPC's attempt to limit the merit review of domestic awards, which is considered as the first step towards a unified scheme of judicial review.[135] Regrettably, the dual track scheme remains till the completion of this book.

The judicial review of foreign-related awards and foreign awards, on the other hand, are identical. The grounds for judicial review of foreign-related awards follow the "no-merit review" approach adopted in the *NYC* and the *UNCITRAL Model Law* and general resemble the international instruments. This approach is also followed in the *Hong Kong Arrangements, Macao Arrangements* and *the Taiwan Regulation.*[136] The Prior Reporting System applies to both foreign-related awards and foreign awards since 1990s. It further contributes to a unified judicial review scheme and enhances the consistency of the judicial review practices.[137] For the purpose of this book, we will primarily focus on cases in these two categories, as well as the judicial review mechanisms apply to them; domestic cases will only be discussed with specific caution in limited situations.

---

134 宋连斌 [Song Lianbin] (ed),《仲裁法》[Arbitration Law] (Wuhan University Press, 2010) 242; 叶丹 [Ye Dan],《从现代司法理念角度探讨司法力渗透仲裁的合理度——以我国法院对涉外仲裁裁决的司法审查制度为现实载体》[Discussing Reasonable Involvement of Judicial Power in Arbitration from the Perspective of Modern Notions of Judiciality: Start from the Judicial Review System of the Foreign-Related Arbitral Awards in Our Courts], in 韩健 [Han Jian] (ed),《涉外仲裁司法审查》[Judicial Review of Foreign Arbitration] (Law Press, 2006)98, 106–108.

135 王亚新,陈福勇 [Wang Yaxin, Chen Fuyong]《<民事诉讼法>修改与不予执行仲裁裁决——以北京仲裁委员会为对象的实证分析》[Amendment of China's Civil Procedural Law and Non-Enforcement of Arbitral Awards: An Empirical Study on the Beijing Arbitration Commission] (2012) 5 法学杂志 *Law Science Magazine* 111–112; 宋连斌 [Song Lianbin],《司法与仲裁关系的重构: "民诉法"有关仲裁新规定之解析》[Re-establishment of the Relationship between the Judicial System and Arbitration: Analysis of the New Provisions of the Civil Procedural Law Concerning Arbitration] (2013) 33 仲裁研究*Arbitration Study* 7, 9–10. Song pointed out that the amendment unified the rules in *CCPL* and *CCA* regarding both the annulment and enforcement of the judicial review of domestic awards, but did not achieve the aim to unify the judicial review scheme over both domestic and foreign-related awards.

136 See Sect. 4.4.

137 See Sect. 3.2.

## 4.4 The Judicial Review Schemes of Annulment and the Enforcement of Arbitral Awards

The Chinese arbitration system provides two types of judicial review of arbitral awards: annulment proceedings and enforcement proceedings. Only awards made within China's geographic scope are subject to annulment proceedings in China. For domestic arbitration, annulment proceedings are regulated by Articles 58 to 61 of the *CAL*. The grounds for judicial review are listed in Article 58, and also confirmed in Article 244 of the *CCPL*. Article 70 of the *CAL* provides the annulment proceeding of foreign-related awards and refers to Article 281(1) of the *CCPL* for the same groups of grounds, which was originally enacted to govern the enforcement review.

There are different enforcement proceedings for different types of awards. Enforcement of domestic awards is regulated by Articles 62 to 64 of the *CAL*, referring to the grounds for non-enforcement for domestic awards in Article 244 of the *CCPL*, which duplicates Article 58 of the *CAL*.[138] Article 71 and 72 of the *CAL* provide enforcement proceedings for foreign-related awards, which also refers to the grounds of non-enforcement of foreign-related awards in Article 281 of the *CCPL*. The legal authority to recognise and enforce any international arbitral awards includes "international conventions or agreements in which China is a contracting party", or the enforcement may be conducted based on the principle of reciprocity.[139] The applicable rules and grounds of judicial review, thus, will be dependent on the applicable international convention or agreement in each particular case.

The co-existence of both annulment and enforcement proceedings is consistent with the practice adopted by the *UNCITRAL Model Law*,[140] yet it is a relatively new scheme in China.[141] Parties may then bring an action of annulment of an award, and when such action fails, bring an action of non-enforcement of the award on similar grounds; it was questioned whether an abuse of litigation procedures may exist under this scheme, and may negate the finality and efficiency of arbitration.[142] Also, local protectionism and inconsistency among different courts also establish

[138] In the old provision before the 2012 amendment, exceptions (4) and (5) of the judicial review scheme were that "the main evidence to ascertain the facts is not sufficient" and "the application of law is erroneous"; the 2012 amendment provided two new exceptions, "the evidence on which the award is based is falsified" and "the other party has concealed evidence which is sufficient to affect the impartiality of the award", and deleted the old exceptions (4) and (5).

[139] Before the enactment of the *CCPL*, only the enforcement proceedings were practiced in China; the co-existence was provided by the *CCPL* for the first time in 1991 and has continued since then. 《中华人民共和国民事诉讼法》[The Civil Procedure Law of the People's Republic of China] (People's Republic of China) art 290.

[140] UNCITRAL Model Law, arts 34 and 36.

[141]《中华人民共和国仲裁法》[Arbitration Law of the People's Republic of China] (People's Republic of China) arts 58 and 61.

[142] 王亚新,陈福勇 [Wang Yaxin, Chen Fuyong], above n 135, 111–112; 宋连斌 [Song Lianbin], above n 135, 9–10.

why parties choose, improperly, to use two actions in dealing with the same case.[143] In order to fix this problem, the SPC provided that the same challenge rejected in an annulment proceeding should not be considered again in the subsequent enforcement proceeding.[144] Some scholars have argued that annulment and enforcement proceedings should be merged into one proceeding in order to reduce repetition and the waste of expenses and judicial resources.[145] The calls were echoed in the *New CAL Draft*, which provides no enforcement review for awards made in China except on the ground of public policy.[146] This approach, if adopted in the future, is totally different from the approach adopted by the *Model Law*. The practical impact of this approach, therefore, remains to be seen.

## 4.5 Other Concerns of Chinese Courts and Judicial Review Practices

There are quite a number of further concerns that relate to China's judicial review scheme on arbitral awards. Many of these problems arise as a result of the distinct features of the Chinese judicial system, as indicated in Sect. 2.2. The features discussed below may influence the judicial review of arbitral awards and the application of public policy.

### 4.5.1 Amount and Quality of Chinese Judiciaries

The huge amount of IPCs[147] and problems with the quality of the judiciary may all contribute to inconsistent practices in different Chinese courts. The number of judges employed in the legal system is significant, and there are issues with respect to their qualifications and recruitment.[148] Under the particular circumstances of judicial review of arbitral awards, the establishment of the Prior Reporting System aims to

---

143 黄文艺 [Huang Wenyi], 《新《民事诉讼法》对不予执行仲裁裁决事由修改的理解与适用》 [Understanding and Applying the Recent Amendments of the Civil Procedure Law in Regard of the Grounds of Non-Enforcement of Arbitral Awards] (2012) 81 北京仲裁 *Beijing Arbitration* 106, 110–111. The author is a judge of the Enforcement Branch at the SPC.

144 Article 26 of the *2006 Judicial Interpretation.*

145 宋连斌 [Song Lianbin], above n 135, 10; 葛行军 [Ge Xingjun], 《关于仲裁裁决在执行中存在的有关问题——最高人民法院执行办主任葛行军在 "2003年仲裁员实务研讨会"上的发言》[Relevant Issues in the Enforcement of Arbitral Awards: Speech of Ge Xingjun, the Chief of the Enforcement Branch of the Supreme People's Court, at the Symposium of Practices of Arbitrators 2003] (2003) 89 仲裁与法律 *Arbitration and Law* 18, 20.

146 《 < 中华人民共和国仲裁法 (修订) > 征求意见稿》 [Draft of the Modified Arbitration Law of the People's Republic of China] (People's Republic of China), art 82.

147 Reference is only made to the IPCs because they have the jurisdiction to hold the annulment and enforcement proceedings for foreign-related or international awards. See above Sect. 3.2.

148 See Sect. 2.2.

deal with some of these problems and enhance the consistency of judicial practices across courts at different levels and among different regions of China[149]; but even under the Prior Reporting System the lower courts (normally the IPCs) still have the final say in confirming the validity of or the enforcement of an award, as only a ruling that the enforcement of an award should be rejected must be reported to higher courts; thus, their inconsistent judicial practices with respect to confirming the validity of an award or deciding to enforce an award will potentially continue.

### 4.5.2 Enforcement Difficulties

Other concerns generally relate to the efficiency of enforcement practice by Chinese courts, including delays, inactivity, local protectionism, governmental intervention,[150] all of which are concluded as a problem of "difficult enforcement".[151] Enforcement of judgments and awards is considered the weakest part of China's court system as the enforcement branch in the Chinese courts usually has inexperienced judges, insufficient funding and the working processes are usually considered to be inefficient.[152] The difficulties in enforcement procedures have been articulated as court's lacking enough incentive or sufficient funding to enforce judgments and awards, or that they are dealing with adversarial /hostile parties or even with political interference from local governments.[153] Also, the losing party may transfer properties or declare insolvency in order to prevent such judgments or awards from being enforced.[154] In *Revpower,* the governing court, Shanghai Second IPC, did not make any decision on the enforcement of the SCC arbitral award upon the request of the foreign party, but simply refused to hear the case for a period of two years.[155]

---

[149] See Sect. 3.2.4.

[150] Brenda Horrigan, Felix Hess and Siew Lin Mok, 'Chapter 5: Arbitration in China: Recent Developments' in Michael J. Moser (ed.), *Business Disputes in China* (Juris, 2009) 52.

[151] Wunschheim, above n 1, 23.

[152] William Heye, 'Forum Selection for International Dispute Resolution in China—Chinese Courts vs CIETAC' (2003–2004) 27 *Hasting International and Comparative Law Review* 535, 537; Daniel Clark, 'Power and Politics in the Chinese Court System' (1996) 10(1) *Columbia Journal of Asian Law* 1, 56.

[153] Jianfu Chen, 'Mission Impossible: Judicial Efforts to Enforce Civil Judgments and Rulings in China' in Jianfu Chen, Yuwen Li and Jan Michiel Otto (eds), *Implementation of Law in the People's Republic of China* (Kluwer Law International, 2002) 88–91.

[154] Wunschhem, above n 1, 23.

[155] *Revpower Ltd. v Shanghai Far East Aviation Technology Import–Export Company* (unreported). Xianchu Zhang, 'Enforcement of Arbitral Awards Between Mainland China and Hong Kong: Before and After Reunification' in Raymond Wacks (ed), *The New Legal Order in Hong Kong* (Hong Kong University Press, 1999) 195; Tao, above n 88, 227–229.

### 4.5.3 Implementation of the Prior Reporting System

The implementation of the Prior Reporting System may also be a reflection of inconsistent and discretionary practices in China's judicial system, reflecting the urgent need for the creation of a unified regulatory scheme of judicial review of arbitral awards. As reported, the Prior Reporting System itself is not strictly followed in practice. In quite a few cases, lower courts have rendered decisions directly to the parties, even though the Prior Reporting System required them to report the cases to higher courts for approval.[156] The SPC criticised these kinds of practices in meetings and emphasised the importance of the Prior Reporting System, but it did not remedy this implementation problem.[157]

It is also notable that the *CCPL*'s trial supervision proceeding, which is the ultimate remedy for all litigation proceedings, may also affect the judicial review of arbitral awards and limit the finality of the Prior Reporting System. This proceeding allows the president of each court to review the decision of its own courts, or higher courts to review decisions of lower courts, or the SPC to review decisions of all other courts, on its own motion, when an "definite error" is found.[158] The parties may apply for such proceedings,[159] and the relevant procuratorate may also lodge a protest to the court in order to trigger those proceedings, particularly when the situation listed in Article 207 occurs.[160] It is uncertain whether this proceeding is also applicable to judicial decisions with respect to arbitral awards. Thus, it is doubtful whether the pro-enforcement bias, as provided by the Prior Reporting System, can be implemented if

[156] 《关于上诉人利比里亚·利比里亚力量船务公司与被上诉人中国·重庆新涪食品有限公司海上货物运输合同纠纷管辖权异议一案的请示的复函》[Reply of the SPC in regard of the Jurisdictional Challenge of the Dispute of a Shipping Contract between the Appellant, (Liberia) Liberia Power Shipping Co and Appellate, (China) Chongqing Xinfu Food Co Ltd] the Supreme People's Court, [2006] 民四他字第26号[Fourth Civil Branch No 26], 21 December 2006;《最高人民法院关于原告中国·北京埃力生进出口有限公司诉被告日本·太阳航行贸易有限公司、新加坡·松加船务有限公司海上运输合同管辖权异议上诉一案的请示的复函》 [Reply of the Supreme People's Court in regard of the Jurisdictional Challenge of the Dispute of a Shipping Contract between the Plaintiff, (China) Beijing Ailisheng Import & Export Co Ltd, and Defendants, (Japan) Solar Shipping and Trading S.A. and (Singapore) Songa Shipping Pte Ltd] Supreme People's Court, [2007] 民四他字第14号[Fourth Civil Branch No 14], 29 September 2007;《最高人民法院关于上诉人武钢集团国际经济贸易总公司与被上诉人福州天恒船务有限公司、被上诉人财富国际船务有限公司海上货物运输合同纠纷管辖权异议一案的请示的复函》[Reply of the Supreme People's Court in regard of the Jurisdictional Challenge of the Dispute on a Shipping Contract between the Appellant, Wugang International Economic and Trading Co and Appellate, Fuzhou Tianheng Shipping Co Ltd and Fortune International Shipping Ltd] Supreme People's Court, [2009]民四他字第 36 号[Fourth Civil Branch No 36], 4 November 2009.

[157] 刘贵祥 [Liu Guixiang],《在全国海事审判工作会议上的总结讲话》[Concluding Speech at the National Maritime Judicial Practices Working Meeting] (2012) 25 涉外商事海事审判指导 *Guidance on Judicial Practices in dealing with Foreign-Related Commercial and Maritime Issues* 16, Part III(1). The Speaker is the Chief of the Fourth Branch of the SPC.

[158] The *CCPL*, art 205.

[159] The *CCPL*, art 206.

[160] The *CCPL*, art 207.

courts attempt to overturn a trial court's decision to enforce an award in supervising the trial proceedings.

It is notable that Chinese courts have noticed these problems and have attempted to improve their performance in many ways. For example, the SPC has made progress in enhancing its capability in dealing with foreign-related arbitration law. Its Fourth Civil Branch specialises in handling foreign-related commercial and maritime cases, including the judicial review of foreign-related and international arbitral awards. The obvious benefit of this capability within the SPC is that the cases are always dealt with by the same group of highly specialised and experienced judges. On the basis of cumulative cases and experience, the judges in the Fourth Civil Branch of the SPC have become experts in the judicial review of arbitral awards and established their reputation in dealing with international commercial arbitration law issues at both practical and theoretical levels.[161]

Empirical study also supports an optimistic conclusion in evaluating China's improvements towards arbitration law and practices. For example, both Wang's and Peerenboom's empirical studies demonstrate an increasingly favourable attitude to foreign-related and foreign awards, and the results do not show any evidence of local protectionism.[162] According to Wang, 37 of 164 CIETAC awards were rejected before 1996, and 3 of 14 foreign awards were rejected before August 1997. In 2019, the SPC reported that in 33 cases of enforcing foreign awards, only 1 was refused enforcement; it also confirmed to set aside 114 out of 201 awards reported via the Prior Reporting System (57%).[163] Regarding the comparison between foreign-related and foreign awards, Peerenboom found a "slightly higher" rate of enforcement of foreign awards (52%) than CIETAC awards (47%)[164] and concluded that local protectionism was not a "statistically significant factor" in his analysis. Nevertheless, Peerenboom pointed out that local protectionism may function differently at the recovery stage and influences the effectiveness of ultimate outcomes.[165]

---

[161] For example, the Fourth Civil Branch of the SPC is in charge of the publication of the series 《涉外商事海事审判指导》[Guide on Foreign-Related Commercial and Maritime Trial], which includes both theoretical and practical materials in relation to international commercial arbitration in China.

[162] Shengchang Wang, 'Enforcement of Foreign Arbitral Awards in the People's Republic of China' in Christopher R. Drahozal and Richard W. Naimark (eds), *Towards a Science of International Arbitration: Collected Empirical Research* (Kluwer Law International, 2005) 277, 283; Randall Peerenboom, 'Seek Truth From Facts: An Empirical Study of Enforcement of Arbitral Awards in the PRC' (2001) 49 *American Journal of Comparative Law*249, 257. Further discussion of the enforcement rate in these two empirical studies, see further Chap. 4.

[163] The Supreme People's Court,《最高人民法院中国仲裁司法审查年度报告 (2019年度)》[The Supreme People's Court's 2019 Annual Report on the Judicial Review on Abitration-related Matters in China], available at: https://www.court.gov.cn/zixun-xiangqing-281031.html.

[164] Peerenboom, above n 162, 257.

[165] Ibid, 260–264.

## 4.6 The Role of Arbitration Commissions and Arbitrators

Besides arbitration legislation and the relevant judicial system, the arbitration commissions and arbitrators are also significant players in China's arbitration practice. Due to their distinctive features under Chinese law and in arbitration practice, their positions and roles are examined below.

### 4.6.1 Arbitration Commissions

The Chinese arbitration commissions are designed as an important part of China's arbitration system, with many distinctive aspects in implementing arbitration legislation. The number of arbitration commissions in China is huge[166]; they enjoy a dominant role in Chinese arbitration practice, as it is relatively uncertain whether ad hoc arbitration or arbitration administrated by a foreign arbitration institution is allowed under the *CAL*.[167]

One major feature of Chinese arbitration practice is that arbitration commissions have significant power in nominating the arbitrators. In many arbitration rules, for example, the *CIETAC Rules (2015)*, the arbitration commissions have enormous power in appointing arbitrators.[168] Unlike the practices of most leading jurisdictions, appointments are usually made by commission insiders rather than independent outsiders or specialists.[169] Parties are not allowed access to such internal appointing procedures used by commission insiders. Some arbitration commissions are even inclined to appoint their own employees as arbitrators.[170] In addition, because of the absence of any supervisory procedure to review the decision of nomination,[171] Chinese arbitration is frequently criticised for the restrictions placed on gaining access to neutral and qualified arbitrators and the lack of fairness and transparency in decision-making procedures.[172]

---

166 According to 袁诗鸣 [Yuan Shiming], the Deputy Chief of the Legal Coordination Branch of the Legislative Affairs Office, State Council, there were 225 arbitration commissions at the end of 2013 in China.《专家建议出台全国统一的仲裁员行为规范》[Experts Suggest the Establishment of a Unified Ethical Code for Arbitrators], 法制网 *Legal Daily*, 9 June 2014, <http://www.legaldaily.com.cn/executive/content/2014-06/09/content_5581640.htm?node=32120>

167 See above Sect. 4.3 and particularly above n 110, where the possibility for foreign arbitration institutions administrating an arbitration proceeding in China is discussed.

168 See for example, the CIETAC Arbitration Rules 2015, arts 26–30.

169 Graeme Johnston, 'Bridging the Gap Between Western and Chinese Arbitration Systems—A Practical Introduction for Businesses' (2007) 24(6) *Journal of International Arbitration* 565, 568–69.

170 Ibid, 570.

171 Ibid.

172 Ibid; Jerome Cohen, 'International Commercial Arbitration in China: Some Thoughts from Experience' Address at the International Economic Law and China in Its Economic Transition Joint Conference (Nov 4 and 5, 2004). Before the amendment of the Arbitration Rules of CIETAC 2005, for CIETAC arbitrations, arbitrators have to be chosen from the list provided by the commission.

Another special arrangement in China's arbitration law is that arbitration commissions, not the tribunals themselves, determine the arbitral jurisdiction in specific cases.[173] This is distinct from the generally accepted principle of competence/competence,[174] although in practice it has shown that the tribunal's opinion on jurisdiction will sometimes be respected by the commissions, especially the opinions of leading arbitration commissions.[175]

The commissions, as well as the secretariats appointed by the arbitration commissions to administer arbitration disputes, are authorised to have discretionary powers in managing arbitration procedures, communicating with the parties, and are sometimes involved in decision-making and drafting awards. In many commissions it is normal that the secretariats—instead of the tribunal—draft the main body of the award following standard techniques adopted by the commission.[176] Some scholars even observe that a commission may force the tribunal to adopt an opinion or otherwise the arbitral award will not receive the seal of approval from the commission, or would not become effective.[177] An arbitration commission and its staff may also be involved in the mediation processes during arbitration.[178] Some Chinese practitioners and scholars defend the involvement of arbitration commissions in arbitration proceedings as a "quality-control" measure in dealing with arbitrators from diversified backgrounds.[179] The commissions also admit that they are now gradually retreating from those active roles and encouraging arbitration tribunals to be more active.[180]

All of these aspects mentioned above indicate that the Chinese arbitration commissions have an active and strong role to play in regulating arbitration practice, either

---

Even the amendments removed such requirements, the nomination only occasionally involved outsiders and arbitrators from a foreign jurisdiction, and an arbitrator from a third county would "not be advertised or encouraged" according to Cohen's observation.

173 《中华人民共和国仲裁法》 [Arbitration Law of the People's Republic of China] (People's Republic of China) art 20.

174 UNCITRAL Model Law, art 16.

175 Fan Kun has mentioned the reality on how the jurisdiction decision is made within China's arbitration commissions: "Before an arbitral tribunal is constituted, CIETAC issues a preliminary ruling on jurisdiction based on a *prima facie* assessment (as is the practice of the ICC Court, for example). If, after the arbitral tribunal has been constituted, an objection is made against its jurisdiction, the arbitral tribunal will generally express its view on the jurisdictional objection to CIETAC, which will usually respect that view. If the arbitral tribunal and the arbitration institution have conflicting views on the jurisdictional objection, then the arbitrator may have no choice but to resign from hearing the case." in Fan Kun, 'Arbitration in China, Practices, Legal Obstacles and Reforms' (2008)19(2) *ICC International Court of Arbitration Bulletin* 25, 28. This information was collected "during a research trip to China (Hong Kong, Beijing, Wuhan), undertaken by the author with Professor Gabrielle Kaufmann-Kohler in March and April 2007.

176 陈福勇 [Chen Fuyong], above n 80, 324; 袁发强 [Yuan Faqiang] above n 80, 119–143.

177 Jerome Cohen, above n 172.

178 Xi'an Arbitration Commission Rules (2008) art 37, 41; *Gao Haiyan v Keeneye Holdings Ltd* [2012] 1 HKLRD 627 (CA).

179 陈福勇 [Chen Fuyong], above n 80, 324.

180 Lijun Cao, 'A Fair Forum' (2005) 168(6) *Far Eastern Economic Review* 4.

as formally permitted by the legislation and commission rules, or through informal development based on arbitration practice not expressly excluded by law.

One of the reasons why the arbitration commissions enjoy such a distinct position under China's arbitration system is that, the establishment of these commissions was not based on businessmen's requests but was a product of governmental decision-making. Their powerful role is further promoted by their monopolistic position in the Chinese arbitration market in the last few decades. For one thing, it is uncertain whether foreign arbitration institutions would be able to render awards in China, and whether such awards could be enforced.[181] For another, disputes without any foreign-related element must be arbitrated inside China.[182] Without much competition, the Chinese arbitration commissions' strong position and their working-pattern is further emphasised.

The quasi-administrative character of these Chinese arbitration commissions is one of the major concerns with respect to their relationships with the judicial system and governmental bodies. As mentioned earlier, CIETAC and CMAC were established under the supervision and direction of the central government, while all the others were established at the municipal level. Also, the nature of arbitration commissions is not clearly defined.[183] The *CAL* only stated that the arbitration commissions are not governmental bodies but did not provide any further clarification in regards to their nature and functioning.[184] Furthermore, the members and working staff of the commissions still have close relationships with governmental bodies. The members holding leading positions on commissions are appointed by the government, and it is even common that such appointees come from or still work within governmental bodies.[185] In some commissions, staff members are still selected from and managed as governmental servants.[186] Most Chinese arbitration commissions are not self-financed and have to contribute all their income to public finance, while receiving government budgets.[187] As a result, it is undeniable that arbitration commissions in many aspects are supervised, influenced by, and economically dependent upon, governmental bodies in China.

---

[181] Moser, above 90, 3; for recent developments, see Sect. 3.2 and particularly, above n 110.

[182] See further discussion of the exclusive jurisdiction of the Chinese courts and arbitration institutions in dealing with purely domestic disputes in Sect. 3.3 in Chap. 8.

[183] 陈福勇 [Chen Fuyong], above n 80, 29–51; 袁发强 [Yuan Faqiang], above n 80, 21–26.

[184] 《中华人民共和国仲裁法》 [Arbitration Law of the People's Republic of China] (People's Republic of China), art 14, which clarifies that arbitration commissions are independent from administrative governmental bodies.

[185] 袁发强 [Yuan Faqiang], above n 80, 18. According to Yuan, in 136 arbitration commissions whose members were in their first term after the re-establishment under the *CAL*, 83.1% of the Chairmen of those commissions were "pure" governmental officers.

[186] For example, all the arbitration commissions in Shandong province are in the government servant system.《山东省参照<中华人民共和国公务员法>管理的单位审批办法》[Regulation of the Shandong Province in regard of the Approval of the Bodies that Managed in Accordance with the Public Servants Law of the People's Republic of China] Shandong Province Human Resources Bureau, 鲁发 [2006] 第19号 [Notice of Shandong Province No 19].

[187] 陈福勇 [Chen Fuyong], above n 80, 47–50.

Besides the lack of impartiality, the legal skills and effectiveness in processing arbitration are also concerns. Yet Fu states that it is not fair to make negative comments about the lack of experience and qualifications of officials within China's legal system because of China's short history in legal education and training; otherwise, an evaluation of the performance of the Chinese legal system should be made only on the basis of their practice.[188]

The relationship between arbitration commissions and the courts is also worth exploring. In China, courts and arbitration commissions are expected to cooperate rather than compete. In Chen's study of ten significant arbitration commissions, many of them were reported as having a close relationship with the courts.[189] Yuan also reported that an "interest connection" existed among courts and arbitration institutions.[190]

The *New CAL Draft* provides more detailed guidance on the internal structure and management of the arbitration commissions as non-profit institutions with checks-and-balances,[191] and proposed limiting the roles of arbitration commissions from many aspects. For example, the power to determine the jurisdiction of the tribunals was given back to the tribunal,[192] which is consistent with international practice of the competence-competence principle. It is expected that many of the drawbacks mentioned above will be gradually cured along with the reforms proposed by the *New CAL Draft.*

### 4.6.2 Arbitrators

The development of professional arbitrators is closely connected to the development of arbitration commissions. Before the 1980s, when arbitration practice was not based on a market economy and the legal profession was not well developed, arbitrators who worked for local Chinese arbitration commissions were full-time employees of the commissions and had the same status as other governmental servants; no particular expertise was required to serve on those commissions. The number of such full-time employed arbitrators was large and most of them lacked legal expertise.[193] In CIETAC and CMAC, which were originally designed to deal with foreign-related arbitrations,

---

[188] Hualing Fu, 'Putting China's Judiciary into Perspective: Is It Independent, Competent, and Fair' in Erik Jensen and Thomas Heller (eds), *Beyond Common Knowledge: Empirical Approaches to the Rule of Law* (Stanford University Press, 2003) 193.

[189] 陈福勇 [Chen Fuyong], above n 80, 219, 322, 351.

[190] 袁发强 [Yuan Faqiang], above n 80, 31.

[191] 《<中华人民共和国仲裁法 (修订)> 征求意见稿》 [Draft of the Modified Arbitration Law of the People's Republic of China] (People's Republic of China, art 16.

[192] Ibid, art 28.

[193] 王胜明,徐秀春 [Wang Shengming, Xu Xiuchun], 《关于仲裁法的若干问题》[Several Issues in Regards to the Arbitration Law], in the Research Branch of the Legislative Bureau of the State Council, 《重新组建仲裁机构手册》 [*Handbook of the Re-Establishment of the Arbitration Institutions*] (中国法制出版社 [China Legal Publishing], 1995). According to the report of Wang and Xu, there were more than 10,000 full-time employed arbitrators before the enactment of *CAL* 1995.

the parties' right to choose arbitrators was allowed but subject to strict restrictions. In particular, the parties could only choose from a restricted list of arbitrators, in which foreign arbitrators were quite limited.[194]

The enactment of the *CAL* inspired the improvement of arbitrators' independent status. It also enhanced the quality of arbitrators in general by requiring certain qualifications and specialised knowledge, and encouraged experienced professionals, including arbitration practitioners, lawyers, former judges and legal researchers to be arbitrators.[195] After the enactment of the *CAL*, CIETAC and CMAC reformed their Arbitration Rules to increase their arbitrator lists; later in 2005, they further allowed the parties to choose arbitrators who were not on the lists.[196] Other arbitration rules, such as the Rules for Shanghai Free Trade Zone by the Shanghai International Arbitration Centre (SHIAC, also the Shanghai International Economic and Trade Arbitration Commission), as well as the Shenzhen International Arbitration Court's Arbitration rules, also allows the selection of arbitrators beyond their list in the context of foreign-related arbitration.[197] The prohibition on foreign arbitrators conducting arbitrations was also gradually removed.[198] The *New CAL Draft* formally confirmed that the list of arbitrators is no longer mandatory or a close list, and that foreign arbitrators can be appointed in foreign-related arbitration proceedings.[199]

The role of arbitrators in China's arbitration procedure is relatively limited. Many procedural powers of arbitration tribunals in other jurisdictions, for example, the power to decide the jurisdiction or nominate the presiding arbitrators, are allocated to arbitration commissions by law.[200] This allocation of power is partly due to the short history of the modern legal system and limited arbitration experience in China, and the fact that the first generation of arbitrators were not experienced specialists

---

[194] For example, the CIETAC Arbitration Rules 1988, art 14–21.

[195] 《中华人民共和国仲裁法》 [Arbitration Law of the People's Republic of China] (People's Republic of China) art 13, which states that arbitrators must fulfil one of the following conditions: (1) They have been engaged in arbitration work for at least eight years; (2) They have worked as a lawyer for at least eight years; (3) They have been a judge for at least eight years; (4) They are engaged in legal research or legal teaching and in senior positions; or (5) They have legal knowledge and are engaged in professional work relating to economics and trade, and in senior positions or of the equivalent professional level.

[196] CIETAC Arbitration Rules 2005, art 21; CIETAC Arbitration Rules 2015, art 26.

[197] The SHIAC Shanghai Free Trade Zone Arbitration Rules (2014), art 27; Shenzhen International Arbitration Court's Arbitration Rules (2022), art 28(2); Beijing Arbitration Commission Commercial Arbitration Rules (2022), art 19.

[198] 《司法部关于威海仲裁委员会是否可以聘任外籍人士担任仲裁员的批复》 [Reply of the Ministry of Justice in regard of whether Weihai Arbitration Commission can employ foreign arbitrators] Ministry of Justice, 20 Aug 1996. This reply denied the newly established arbitration commissions' access to foreign arbitrators. This restriction is now removed; see for example, the Arbitrators Panel List of BAC, <http://www.bjac.org.cn/arbiter/index.asp>; the Arbitrators Panel List of Xiamen Arbitration Commission, at <http://www.xmac.org.cn>.

[199] 《<中华人民共和国仲裁法 (修订)> 征求意见稿》 [Draft of the Modified Arbitration Law of the People's Republic of China] (People's Republic of China, arts 50, 89.

[200] Manjiao Chi, 'Are We "Paper Tigers"? The Limited Procedural Power of Arbitrators Under Chinese Law' (2011) 2011(2) *Journal of Dispute Resolution* 259, 261–65.

in arbitration practice or in commercial transactions. In particular, the powers of arbitrators were limited by the design of the arbitration scheme in China and by the supervision exerted over arbitrators by arbitration commissions.[201] Though the development of China's arbitration system promoted improvements in the quality of arbitrators, the working process within those arbitration commissions continued and consequently limited the significance of the role of arbitrators. Intervention by arbitration commissions in tribunal decisions relating to jurisdiction and arbitral awards was also tolerated for many additional reasons, including worries about the quality of arbitrators, as well as to maintain formal control over the rendering of arbitration awards.[202]

The quality of arbitrators remains a major concern, especially for foreign parties participating in arbitration in China. The heavy workload in arbitration cases[203] requires a lot of arbitrators, even though it is acknowledged that the short history of China's legal and arbitration practices means that arbitrators who are well qualified are rare. This is particularly common in regional areas where there are less developed arbitration commissions.[204] There are allegations that arbitrators may lack impartiality and view their role as an opportunity to generate their own individual wealth through bribes or transferring interests.[205]

An additional concern is the lack of sufficient judicial supervision in the regulation of arbitrators. In practice, supervision is conducted by arbitration commissions as the *CAL* does not provide any legal scheme restricting this practice; there is also no unified self-regulating association for arbitrators in China. In order to ensure the performance of arbitrators, arbitration commissions can: impose requirements and restrictions when employing arbitrators; provide guidance and regulations to control the behaviour of arbitrators; track and control any potentially harmful activities of arbitrators during the arbitration procedure; and collect feedback from the parties involved and evaluate the performance of the arbitrators.[206] The Code of Conduct of Arbitrators of BAC is a leading example of the regulatory schemes that are imposed on arbitrators[207]; but in most arbitration commissions, the supervisory scheme for arbitrators is not advanced.

---

201 Ibid, 270–77.

202 陈福勇 [Chen Fuyong], above n 80, 324.

203 See further Sect. 2 in Chap. 4.

204 陈福勇 [Chen Fuyong], above n 80, 204.

205 Ibid, 278–79; in some less advanced areas, connected lawyers may be nominated as arbitrators in each other's cases and transfer interests between them.

206 Ibid, 126–27.

207《北京仲裁委员会仲裁员守则》[Beijing Arbitration Commission Code of Conducts of Arbitrators 2006], Beijing Arbitration Commission, 14 August 2006.

### 4.6.3 Other Participants in Arbitration

Other participants influencing the development of public policy in arbitration law may include the lawyers, parties and other participants of the arbitration process. The development of arbitration practice in China is significant at both the judicial and arbitration levels, but these practices are still relatively new; and they fall short of the establishment of a pattern of arbitration practice in the rapidly developing Chinese economy and legal system. Lawyers, parties and other participants in arbitration and subsequent judicial proceedings are not familiar with the public policy exception or its significance in other jurisdictions, in which the theoretical knowledge and practical experience of arbitration is more developed and consistently applied.

## 5 The Public Policy Exception in China's Arbitration Law

Based on the general understanding of China's legal system, arbitration law, and those who are involved in the arbitration process and the judicial review of arbitral awards, this section will now summarise how the public policy exception is reflected in China's arbitration law.

Public policy (or *ordre public*) is a legal concept widely accepted in China's current legal system and arbitration law in particular. The terms used in China's legislation referring to public policy in arbitration law is "social public interest",[208] which is distinct from the terms "*ordre public*" or "public policy" used in the general literature on arbitration outside of China. The term "social public interest" is not limited to private international law in China, but widely adopted in legislation regulating both governmental activities and private relationships and activities.[209] For example, in administrative regulations, social public interests are considered in evaluating government activities such as export and import control, procurement and commodity inspection.[210] *The General Principles of Civil Law* ('*GPCL*') provides,

208《中华人民共和国仲裁法》[Arbitration Law of the People's Republic of China] (People's Republic of China) art 58.

209 For this book, the term "private international law", known in the common law countries as "conflict of law" rules, is a set of rules that deals with the applicable law of legal matters that involves foreign elements. Particularly, these rules of private international law will apply in the enforcement of foreign judgments and court orders, in the judicial review of arbitration agreements and arbitral awards, in serving files of foreign parties, and other matters of international judicial assistance. The use of this term is consistent with the discussion as provided by Judge Xiaoli Gao from the SPC. See 高晓力 [Gao Xiaoli],《国际私法上公共政策的运用》[*The Functioning of Public Policy in Private International Law*] (中国民主法制出版社 [China Democracy and Rule of Law Press], 2008) 11–14.The rules of private international law in China are consist of both general rules in the *Law Application Law (2010)* and the specific rules, that govern some particular issue, for example, arbitration, in the *CCPL, CAL* and judicial interpretations.

210《中华人民共和国进出口商品检验法》[the Law of People's Republic of China on Import and Export Commodity Inspection] (People's Republic of China) National People's Congress Standing Committee, Order No 14, 21 February 1989 (amended in 2002), art 1;《中华人民共和国政府采购

as one of its fundamental principles, that all activities in private law shall "not harm the public interest"[211]; this principle is also adopted in almost all legislation governing commercial activities, such as corporation law, securities law and bankruptcy law.

The use of the term "social public interest" in private international law, however, should be clearly distinguished from its general function in other areas of law.[212] It is also generally agreed that it should be more narrowly conceived in the context of private international law than in purely domestic law.[213] According to the *GPCL* and the *Law of the Application of Law*, foreign law can only be applied in a foreign-related case, as long as it is not against the "social public interest" of China.[214] The *CCPL* further requires the "social public interest" should be considered in legal practice such as the service of legal documents, investigations, collection of evidence, and the enforcement of foreign judgments and arbitral awards.[215] *The Maritime Law* and the *Civil Aviation Law* also contain similar provisions.[216] Scholars also recognise that the distinction between the Chinese term "social public interest" and the universally accepted notion of public policy in international legal and arbitration practice may give rise to possible confusion over its meaning and application in relation to Chinese practice.[217]

There are plenty of rules referring to the legal concept of public policy in China's arbitration law. The rules are different, depending on the nature of the arbitral awards and the different ways in which they are applied in judicial proceedings. Different wording is used in dealing with different types of awards. It is particularly notable that the wording of the rules in discrete regions of Greater China differ; e.g., the *Hong*

---

法》[Law of People's Republic of China in regard of Government Procurement] (People's Republic of China) National People's Congress Standing Committee, Order No 69, 29 June 2002, art 1.

211 《中华人民共和国民法通则》[General Principle of Civil Law of the People's Republic of China] (People's Republic of China) National People's Congress, Order No 37, 12 April 1986, art 7.

212 肖永平 [Xiao Yongping], 《肖永平论冲突法》[*Xiao Yongping on Conflict of Law*], (武汉大学出版社 [Wuhan University], 2002) 100; Yongping Xiao and Zhengxin Huo, 'Ordre Public in China's Private International Law' (2005) 53 *American Journal of Comparative Law* 654, 656; 高晓力 [Gao Xiaoli], above n 209, 324.

213 . Xiao and Huo, above n 212, 656.

214 《中华人民共和国民法通则》[General Principle of Civil Law of the People's Republic of China] (People's Republic of China) National People's Congress, Order No 37, 12 April 1986, art 150; 《中华人民共和国涉外民事关系法律适用法》[Law of the People's Republic of China on the Application of Law for Foreign-Related Civil Relations] (People's Republic of China) National People's Congress Standing Committee, Order No 36, 28 October 2010, art 5.

215 《中华人民共和国民事诉讼法》[The Civil Procedure Law of the People's Republic of China] (People's Republic of China), e.g., arts 215, 244, 281, 283, 289.

216 《中华人民共和国海商法》[The Maritime Law of the People's Republic of China] (People's Republic of China) National People's Congress Standing Committee, Order No 64, 7 November 1992, art 276; 《中华人民共和国民用航空法》[The Civil Aviation Law of the People's Republic of China] (People's Republic of China) National People's Congress Standing Committee, Order No 56, 30 October 1995, art 190.

217 肖永平 [Xiao Yongping] above n 212, 655–660.

**Table 3** Public policy clauses in dealing with different types of awards in China

| | Annulment | Enforcement |
|---|---|---|
| Purely domestic | Art. 58 *CAL*<br>In addition, the people's court shall also annul the arbitral award if finding it violates the social public interest | Art.244 *CCPL*<br>In addition, the people's court shall also annul the arbitral award if finding it violates the social public interest |
| Foreign-related | Art. 70 *CAL* refer to Art. 281(1) *CCPL*<br>Did not refer to "social public interest" provision | Art.281(2) CCPL<br>Additionally, if the people's court determines that the enforcement of the award goes against the social public interest of the country, it shall refuse to enforce such an arbitral award |
| International | Not applicable | Art. V(2)(b) of the *NYC*: *"public policy of that country"*[218]<br>Art.7(5) of the *Hong Kong Arrangements: "social public interests"* in mainland China, and *"public policy"* in the Hong Kong SAR[219]<br>Art. 7(5) of the *Macao Arrangements*: *"social public interests"* in Mainland China, and *"fundamental legal principles and public order"* in the Macao SAR[220]<br>Art.14 of the SPC's Taiwan Regulation provides *"against One China policy or social public interest"*, but Art.10 of the *Taiwan Agreement* provides *"the ordre public or good morals"*[221] |

*Kong SAR Arrangements* refer to "public policy", and the *Macao SAR Arrangements* refer to "fundamental legal principles and public orders". Differences in the construction of these provisions are included in Table 3.

Articles 70 and 71 of the *CAL* only refer to grounds which can be referred to by the parties, while the "social public interest" test is a ground that can be applied

[218] *The Convention on the Recognition and Enforcement of Foreign Arbitral Awards,* opened for signature 6 July 1958, 330 UNTS 38 (entered into force 7 June 1959)art V(2)(b).

[219]《最高人民法院关于内地与香港特别行政区相互执行仲裁裁决的安排》[Arrangement of the Supreme People's Court Concerning Mutual Enforcement of Arbitral Awards between the Mainland and Hong Kong Special Administrative Region] Supreme People's Court, 法释 [2000] 第3号 [Judicial Interpretation No 3], 18 June 1999, art 7(5).

[220]《关于内地与澳门特别行政区相互认可和执行仲裁裁决的安排》[Arrangement Concerning Mutual Recognition and Enforcement of Arbitral Awards between the Special Administrative Region of Macao and the Mainland] Supreme People's Court, 法释 [2007] 第17号 [Judicial Interpretation No 17], 30 October 2007, art 7(5).

[221]《最高人民法院关于认可和执行台湾地区仲裁裁决的决定》[Regulation on the Recognition and Enforcement of Arbitral Awards Made in Taiwan by the SPC] Supreme People's Court, 法释 [2015] 14号 [Judicial Interpretation No.14], 2 June 2015, Art 14;《海峡两岸共同打击犯罪及司法互助协议》[Cross-Strait Joint Fight against Crime and Mutual Legal Assistance Agreement] Cross-Strait Relation Association and Cross-Strait Communication Foundation, 26 April 2009, art 10.

on the motion of the court. Some scholars and even practitioners initially thought it meant that the "social public interest" clause was not applicable.[222] Nevertheless, most scholars and practitioners have agreed that the whole scheme provided by Article 281 of the *CCPL*, including the social public interest provision, should apply to foreign-related arbitral awards for both annulment and enforcement review.[223] This understanding is also evident in judicial practice, as the ground of social public interest has frequently been discussed in foreign-related arbitration cases.[224]

The term "social public interest" lacks definition and guidance in regard to its application. It is an abstract and ambiguous phrase; there is no explanation given regarding the differences between "social public interest" in arbitration law and in other laws. This ambiguity is understandable for two main reasons: the ambiguity in the legal definition of "public policy" is evident in worldwide legal practice in general[225]; it is also evident in China's civil law tradition and in the limited developments in law-making in general and in legislation governing arbitration law specifically.[226] Yet such ambiguity leads to inconsistencies in the interpretation and application of the concept of public policy in judicial practice.[227]

In conclusion, the Chinese legislation governing "public policy" in arbitration law is not a single legal rule or principle, but a set of rules. It consists of a combination of international legislation and national laws, including a mixture of old and new rules, and a complicated legal framework involving different situations, types of arbitral

---

[222] See Shanghai First IPC's opinion in *Zhejiang Tianhe*, in which they denied the "social public interests" as a way of setting aside a judicial review over foreign-related arbitral awards.《最高人民法院关于浙江省天河房地产联合发展公司申请撤销中国经济贸易仲裁委员会上海分会仲裁裁决案的复函》[Reply of the Supreme People's Court in regard of the Annulment of an Award of CIETAC Shanghai Applied by Zhejiang Tianhe Real Estate Development Co Ltd] Supreme People's Court, [2003] 民四他字第 19 号 [Fourth Civil Branch No 19], 10 November 2003; 高菲 [Gao Fei],《中国海事仲裁的理论与实践》[*Theory and Practices of Maritime Arbitration in China*] (人民大学出版社[Renmin University Press],1998) 433–438.

[223] 于喜富[Yu Xifu], 《国际商事仲裁的司法监督与协助——兼论中国的立法与司法实践》[*Judicial Supervision and Assistance of International Commercial Arbitration: Comments on China's Legislative and Judicial Practices*] (知识产权出版社 [Intellectual Property Rights Press], 2006) 406–407; 刘想树 [Liu Xiangshu],《中国涉外仲裁制度与学理研究》[*Theoretical Study on China's Foreign-Related Arbitration System*] (法律出版社 [Law Press], 2001) 194–195; 赵健 [Zhao Jian],《国际商事仲裁的司法监督》[*Judicial Supervision of International Commercial Arbitration*] (法律出版社 [Law Press], 2000) 219; 郑远民等[ Zheng Yuanmin et al.],《国际司法——国际民事诉讼与国际商事仲裁》[*International Adjudication: International Civil Litigation and International Commercial Arbitration*] (中信出版社 [CITIC Publishing], 2000) 348.

[224] In *Zhejiang Tianhe*, the Shanghai First IPC's attitude was not accepted by the SPC. The SPC held that the argument for the application of social public interests was not accepted because it had no factor and legal basis.《最高人民法院关于浙江省天河房地产联合发展公司申请撤销中国经济贸易仲裁委员会上海分会仲裁裁决案的复函》[Reply of the Supreme People's Court in regard of the Annulment of an Award of CIETAC Shanghai Applied by Zhejiang Tianhe Real Estate Development Co Ltd] Supreme People's Court, [2003]民四他字第19号 [Fourth Civil Branch No 19], 10 November 2003.

[225] See Chap. 2.

[226] See above Sects. 3 and 4.

[227] Qisheng He, 'Public Policy in Enforcement of Foreign Arbitral Awards in the Supreme People's Court of China' (2013) 43 *Hong Kong Law Journal* 1037, Part IV.

awards, and legislative purposes. A clearer understanding of the rules governing the application of the public policy exception is required, but this may only be achieved through the efforts of China's law makers and courts when dealing with issues raised by practitioners in individual cases, or through the inclusion of definitions in Chinese legislation.

The most significant step towards the viable interpretation of "social public interest/public policy" in private international law area is in the recent *Judicial Interpretation on the Law Application Law*: Article 10 provides that some legislation may govern social public interest and cannot be excluded by the parties' consent or the application of conflict-of-law rules, including rules governing "(1) The protection of labour rights; (2) Food and public health; (3) Environmental safety; (4) Foreign currency control and financial safety; (5) Antitrust and antidumping; and (6)Other mandatory rules".[228] Yet it is not clear whether this clarification can be adopted when applying public policy in the judicial review of arbitral awards.[229] Judge Gao, in her analysis of this judicial interpretation, stated that the mandatory rules satisfying the listed categories above may have the same effect as the public policy reservation, which may provide useful guidance.[230]

Scholars, judges and legal practitioners have also provided various opinions in relation to the key elements of public policy, but there is little consensus. Judge Gao provides a general categorisation of China's public policy in private international law, which includes:

(a) *The fundamental spirit of China's Constitutional Law;*
(b) *China's sovereignty and national safety;*
(c) *China's international obligations under international treaties, including all multilateral and bilateral treaties that were concluded or participated in by China;*
(d) *the principles of fairness and justice recognised in international law;*
(e) *legal rules that constitute fundamental principles in China, such as the principle of good faith and honesty in contract law, the anti-terrorism law, the law against heresy, trafficking in persons, money-laundering and gambling;*
(f) *the basic morality requirement of China to protect decency; and*

---

228《最高人民法院关于适用涉外民事关系法律适用法若干问题的解释 (一)》 [The Judicial Interpretation of the Supreme People's Court in regard of Several Issues in the Application of the Law of Application of Law in Foreign-related Civil Relationship No 1] (Supreme People's Court), 法释 [2012] 第 24 号 [Judicial Interpretation No 24], 28 December 2012. For analysis of this provision in defining public policy rules, see Chap. 7.

229 He, above n 227, 1045.

230 高晓力 [Gao Xiaoli],《最高人民法院关于适用涉外民事关系法律适用法若干问题的解释 (一) 解读》 [Analysis of the Judicial Interpretation in regard of Several Issues in the Application of the Law of Application of Law in Foreign-related Civil Relationship No 1] (2013) 3 法律适用 *Journal of Law Application* 38, 42–43.

(g) *the fundamental and overall interests of China.*[231]

Judge Cui confirms the applicability of this categorisation and added the concepts of "the Four Fundamental Principles" and "national unity and the solidarity among ethnical groups".[232] A similar categorisation referred to by Tao and Wunschheim[233] considered that the arbitral award may violate public policy if it:

(a) *is in violation of the basic principles reflected and regulated in the Constitution or the Four Fundamental Principles of China;*
(b) *will damage the sovereignty or State security of China;*
(c) *is in violation of the fundamental rules of Chinese law; or*
(d) *is against the obligations that China undertook in the international treaties that China concluded or were against the public[ly]-recognised principle of fairness or justice in international law.*

Judge Huang Wenyi provides that the application of "social public interest" should be limited to issues such as land expropriation[234]; Judge Liu Guixiang also indicates several significant areas of law which may represent the national public interest, including public health, financial and economic safety, and national security.[235] Generally, these various statements are not accepted uniformly and therefore do not provide sufficient consensus regarding the key elements of public policy.

## 6 Conclusion

This chapter extends the analysis in Chaps. 1 and 2 and provides background on public policy from a Chinese perspective, which will be developed further in subsequent chapters of this book. It has also evaluated the varied approaches adopted by Chinese courts and has compared them with international conceptions of public policy, as was identified in Chap. 2.

---

231 高晓力 [Gao Xiaoli], above n 209, 131.

232 利夫糖果(上海)有限公司申请承认和执行新加坡国际仲裁中心仲裁裁决案 [Case Concerning the Application of Leaf Candy (Shanghai) Co Ltd for Recognition and Enforcement of an Arbitral Award of SIAC] Shanghai Second IPC, (2008) 沪二中民五(商)初字第 19 号 [Fifth Civil Branch (Commercial) Case of the First Instance No 19], available at <http://www.shezfy.com/view.html?id=11429>, per Judge Cui Xuejie. The Four Fundamental Principles of China are: (i) to adhere to the socialist road, (ii) to adhere to the people's democratic dictatorship, (iii) to adhere to the leadership of the Communist Party, and (iv) to adhere to Marxism-Leninism and Mao's thought. See Jingzhou Tao, 'Enforcement of SCC Arbitration Awards in China' in *Between East and West: Essays in Honour of Ulf Franke* (2010).

233 *Ibid*, 12; Wunschheim, above n 1, 283.

234 黄文艺 [Huang Wenyi], above n 143, 113.

235 刘贵祥 [Liu Guixiang], above n 157.

The chapter identifies a few key issues that may influence the establishment of a distinctive Chinese approach to applying public policy, including the limited legislative techniques that are currently used to do so, and the lack of sufficiently qualified arbitration professionals within the legal system. The chapter has also noted that the complicated definitions of "domestic, foreign-related and international" arbitration and their awards may cause difficulties in the application of public policy in the judicial review of arbitration awards. The chapter has also noted the function of the Prior Reporting System and the SPC's dominant role in making judicial decisions, which may also affect the application of public policy.

Section 5 concludes that there is no accepted definition and key elements of public policy nor a consistent approach in its application in China, and that it may prove more fruitful to undertake an analysis of the judicial decisions on the enforcement of arbitral awards. This may provide stronger evidence of China's own distinctive approach on this issue. For one thing, decisions reached by the Chinese courts, especially by the SPC, are legally significant and in turn provide guidance to arbitration practitioners and Chinese judges. Furthermore, the stability of the Prior Reporting System and the working process underlying the judicial review may provide some consistency by establishing a coherent concept of public policy in Chinese arbitration law.

Based on this chapter, Part II of this book (Chaps. 4–8) will focus on judicial practices with a view to identifying the different methods they employ in addressing public policy, and endeavour to identify as what they believe are key elements of public policy. A number of these issues arise in this chapter will be further considered in case studies in Part II (Chaps. 4–8), and their influence will be revisited in Part III (Chap. 9 and the Final Chapter).

# Part II
# China's Public Policy Practice Compared to Other Jurisdictions

# Chapter 4
# Application of Public Policy in China

## 1 Introduction

Based on the fundamental understandings of the application of public policy, as provided by Part I of this book, this Part (Chaps. 4–8) further examines in detail the performance of the Chinese courts. It reports on a statistical analysis of the Chinese judicial system's performance in relation to the application of the public policy exception in the judicial review of arbitral awards. While some primary observations are made with respect to the statistical study, this topic will be further analysed in Chaps. 5–8.

This chapter firstly reviews the arbitration practice and the judicial review of arbitral awards in Sect. 2. This general description corresponds to the discussion included in Cha. 3, which describes the development of China's arbitration and judicial practices and the general enforcement rate of arbitral awards.

It then provides a detailed statistical study on the application of the public policy exception in the judicial review of arbitral awards in Sects. 3, 4 and 5. The answers to the following questions are examined through statistical research and discussions based on a quantitative study of the following factors:

- types of cases in which public policy arguments are invoked;
- how likely these arguments are to be accepted by courts;
- what possible key elements of public policy are identified in those cases, and how frequently these key elements are discussed.

In Sect. 3, the author explains the methodology adopted in this statistical study on cases. Section 4 provides a thorough study of the 55 SPC cases in which foreign-related and international awards are reviewed and considers the developments over time; the function of the Chinese courts, especially the SPC; and examines the application of different elements of public policy. Section 5 concludes the chapter and provides the basis on which further analysis is undertaken and reported in Chaps. 5–8.



S. Zhang, *The Public Policy Exception in the Judicial Review of International Commercial Arbitral Awards*, https://doi.org/10.1007/978-3-662-67679-0_4

## 2 A General Statistical Description of China's Arbitration Practices and the Judicial Review of Arbitral Awards

### 2.1 China's Arbitration Practice

China's involvement in commercial arbitration has experienced rapid growth in recent years. A few recent statistics reports show that there has been a significant increase in the numbers of arbitration commissions and their caseloads. At the end of 2021 there were more than 270 arbitration commissions and 415,889 arbitration cases heard in China.[1] CIETAC also reported a caseload of 642 foreign-related cases in 2022.[2]

The leading arbitration commissions play a significant role in dealing with both domestic and foreign-related arbitration cases. CIETAC's general caseload increased and its amount of foreign-related cases remained stable in the last decade.[3] Similarly, BAC's case load illustrates its rapid development.[4] The development of CIETAC's and BAC's caseloads is illustrated as in Figs. 1 and 2.

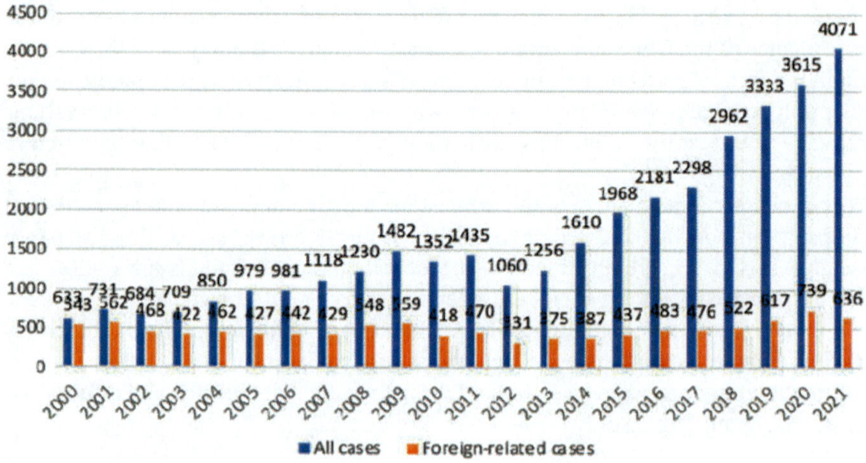


**Fig. 1** Cases accepted by CIETAC (2000–2021)[5]

[1] Legal Daily,《去年全国仲裁机构受案41.5万余件》[China's Arbitration Institutions dealt with more than 415,000 cases in 2021], at: <http://www.moj.gov.cn/pub/sfbgw/fzgz/fzgzggflfwx/fzgzggflfw/202203/t20220323_451264.html>.

[2] CIETAC's 2022 Working Report, at: <http://www.cietac.org/index.php?m=Article&a=show&id=18839>.

[3] CIETAC's Statistic Report, at <http://cn.cietac.org/AboutUs/AboutUS4Read.asp>.

[4] BAC's Annual Working Report, at https://www.bjac.org.cn/page/gybh/introduce_report.html.

[5] In this Figure and the next one, data in blue represents the overall caseload and the data in red represents the caseload of foreign-related cases.

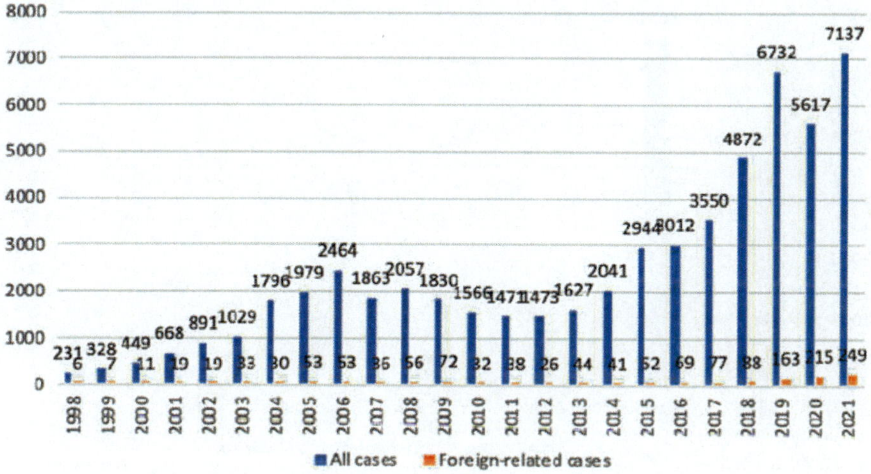


**Fig. 2** BAC caseload (1998–2021)

The caseloads of leading Chinese arbitration institutions, represented by CIETAC and BAC, are significant. The numbers are comparable to the caseloads of leading arbitration commissions such as the ICC, SIAC, HKIAC, LCIA, and SCC, which are among the five most-favoured institutions by parties in the Queen Mary 2021 Survey (excluding CIETAC and ICSID).[6] CIETAC was also ranked number five among the most favoured arbitration institutions.[7] This high caseload can probably be explained by the fact that there has been an increase in emerging trade and investment activities throughout China due to its recent economic growth; and that Chinese arbitration commissions are geographically situated to administer these cases,[8] and also favoured by the huge amount of Chinese parties involved in those trade and investment activities.

The data provided in Fig. 3 demonstrates a general description of China's position in the current world arbitration market, which serves as the background of this research.

---

[6] Queen Mary University of London School of International Arbitration, 2021 International Arbitration Survey: Adapting arbitration to a changing world, https://arbitration.qmul.ac.uk/media/arbitration/docs/LON0320037-QMUL-International-Arbitration-Survey-2021_19_WEB.pdf, at 10.

[7] Ibid.

[8] Michael Moser and Jianlong Yu, 'CIETAC and its Work - An Interview with Vice Chairman Yu Jianlong' (2007) 24(6) *Journal of International Arbitration* 555, 558–559.

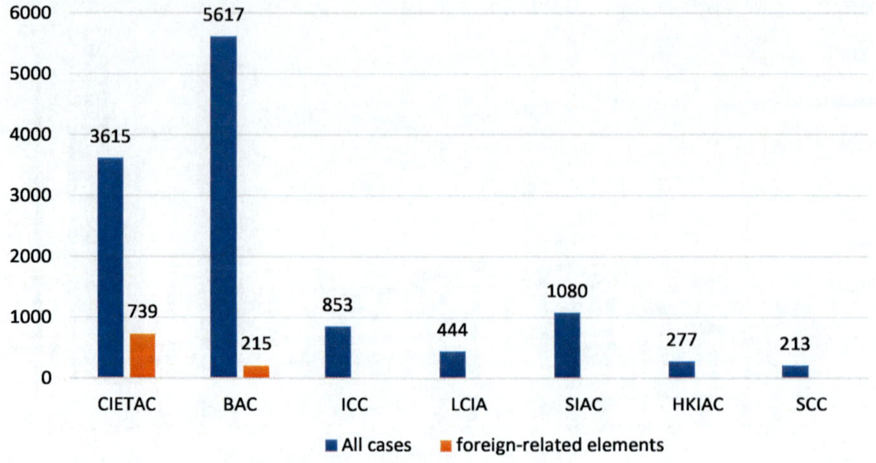


**Fig. 3** The reported caseload in 2020[9]

## 2.2 *The Annulment/Non-enforcement Rate Study*

A number of statistical reports and studies have focused on the annulment and non-enforcement rates of arbitral awards in China's judicial practice, which to some extent indicate the acceptance of international commercial arbitration in China. Before going to the most recent data, there were several important surveys in the early years, which are worth mentioning.

The SPC's 2007 report studied the annulment and enforcement rate in cases from 2002 to 2006, as illustrated in Table 1.[10] Only 4.75% of the claims of annulment were sustained; out of the cases of enforcing foreign-related awards, only 3.85% were refused, and in cases of enforcing international awards, 6.76% were refused.[11]

With respect to the judicial review of foreign-related and international commercial arbitral awards in particular, there were also two surveys conducted by CIETAC's research branch, the Chinese Arbitration Research Institute ('ARI'). In the first investigation, between 1990 and 1994 there were six reported non-enforcement cases

[9] For the number of ICC cases, For the number of the London Court of International Arbitration ('LCIA'), see <http://www.lcia.org/LCIA/reports.aspx>. For the number of SCC (Stockholm Chamber of Commerce) cases, see <http://www.sccinstitute.com/statistics/ >; For the number of Singapore International Arbitration Centre (SIAC), see SIAC 2020 Annual Report, at https://www.siac.org.sg/images/stories/articles/annual_report/SIAC_Annual_Report_2020.pdf. For the number of Hong Kong International Arbitration Centre (HKIAC), see 'Statistics', at <http://www.hkiac.org/en/hkiac/statistics>. It is notable that some of the numbers are reported without the distinction of domestic and foreign/international cases.

[10] 杨宏磊 [Yang Honglei], 《人民法院涉外仲裁司法审查情况的调研报告》[Investigation and Analysis Report on the Judicial Review of Foreign-Related Arbitration by the People's Courts] (2009) 9 武大国际法评论 *Wuhan University Law Review* 308.

[11] Ibid, 311–14.

**Table 1** Enforcement Rate in 2007 Survey of the SPC

| Type of judicial review | Annulment of awards | Enforcement of foreign-related awards | Enforcement of foreign awards |
|---|---|---|---|
| Cases annulled or not enforced | 4.75% | 3.85% | 6.76% |
| Claims of annulment or non-enforcement rejected | 85.16% | 96.15% | 78.38% |
| Case withdrawal/settled | 8.01% | Not reported | 8.1% |
| Re-arbitration | 2.08% | Not reported | Not reported |
| Others/pending | Not reported | Not reported | 6.76% |

of CIETAC arbitral awards in Chinese courts out of 30 applications. The second investigation conducted by the ARI, which covers cases before 1997, found that the enforcement rate of CIETAC cases was 77% (127 out of 164), and the rate of foreign awards was 71% (10/14).[12] The overall enforcement rate was 77% (137/178) at the end of 1997.[13]

Another important survey was conducted by Randall Peerenboom, focusing on the enforcement of both CIETAC and international awards in China between 1991 and 1999. In this report, the combined enforcement rate of both CIETAC and international awards before Chinese courts was 49%; the enforcement rate of international awards in China was 52%; and the enforcement rate of CIETAC awards was 47%.[14] None of these numbers are conclusive due to the lack of a single authoritative method of collecting data.[15]

Finally, in the report provide by the SPC in 2019,[16] there were 11,029 cases of annulment, in which 637 were annulled; in all cases reported via the Prior Reporting System for annulment or non-enforcement, only 57% were supported by the SPC; and in all 32 cases for the enforcement of foreign awards, all were enforced, except one partially enforced on the ground of *ultra vires*.[17] In a more recent review of the 2021 cases released by the JudgmentOnline and Lexis, 71 requests for annulment were upheld among 2903 cases (2.45%); and only 52 foreign-related arbitral awards

[12] Shengchang Wang, 'Enforcement of Foreign Arbitral Awards in the People's Republic of China' in Christopher R. Drahozal and Richard W. Naimark (eds), *Towards Science on International Arbitration: Collected Empirical Research* (Kulwer Law International, 2005) 277.

[13] Ibid.

[14] Randall Peerenboom, 'Seek Truth From Facts: l An Empirical Study of Enforcement of Arbitral Awards in the PRC' (2001) 49 *American Journal of Comparative Law* 249, Tables 1, 2 and 3.

[15] Ibid, 260–64.

[16] The Supreme People's Court, 《最高人民法院中国仲裁司法审查年度报告 (2019年度)》 [The Supreme People's Court's 2019 Annual Report on the Judicial Review on Arbitration-related Matters in China], available at: <https://www.court.gov.cn/zixun-xiangqing-281031.html>.

[17] Ibid.

were refused enforcement among all 464 cases (11.21%); all 9 foreign awards that sought enforcement were enforced.[18]

Besides the annulment/non-enforcement rate reported in the previous figure, which compares the case of annulment/non-enforcement to all applications of annulment and enforcement of arbitral awards, in some other surveys, the reported enforcement rates compared the number of non-enforced Chinese awards with the cases administered by the Chinese arbitration commissions. According to the SPC's 2019 report, the total number of annulled cases (637) were only 0.1% of all arbitration cases administrated by Chinese arbitration institutions in the same year (480,000).[19]

To summarise, the reported rate of awards being negated in China has varied depending on the time of research and the different reporters and is especially dependent on the method of data collection adopted. Though some disparity was found to exist between the different reports and surveys, the general and consistent trend was confirmed, i.e., the number of annulled or non-enforced cases remains small, especially in recent years. It reflects that China's practice of judicial review of arbitral awards is subject to rapid development since the adoption of the *NYC* and the *CAL*, and that the pro-enforcement trend, as promoted by the international arbitration community, is likely to be replicated in China.

## 2.3 *The Application of Different Grounds for the Annulment or Non-enforcement of Arbitral Awards*

The following grounds for annulment or non-enforcement of awards in China's practices is identified in legislation such as the *CAL, CCPL,* the *NYC* and other international and regional agreements, including the situation where the arbitral awards[20]: (a) lack a valid arbitration agreement; (b) breach the principle of due process; (c) deal with issues not covered by the arbitration agreement; (d) do not complying with the procedure requirements; (e) proceedings are invalid under the law of the seat of arbitration; (f) deal with issues not being arbitrated under the law of the seat of arbitration; and (g) violate the public policy of the country of the court.[21] In addition, an award may not be enforced because of (h) non-conformity of the enforcement procedure, particularly the time limit for enforcement. We acknowledge that there

---

[18] The numbers excluded P2P lending cases. See 朱华芳等 [Zhu Huafang et al.],《2021年度中国仲裁司法审查实践观察报告——大数据分析》[2021 Report on the Judicial Review Practice of Arbitration-related Cases: Analysis of Big Data], available at: <http://www.tiantonglaw.com/Content/2022/09-17/2316274305.html>.

[19] The Supreme People's Court,《最高人民法院中国仲裁司法审查年度报告 (2019年度)》[The Supreme People's Court's 2019 Annual Report on the Judicial Review on Arbitration-related Matters in China], available at: <https://www.court.gov.cn/zixun-xiangqing-281031.html>.

[20] See a comparison of these grounds in Sect. 4 in Chap. 3.

[21] *The Convention on the Recognition and Enforcement of Foreign Arbitral Awards,* opened for signature 6 July 1958, 330 UNTS 38 (entered into force 7 June 1959) art III.

**Table 2** Wan & Xia (2011): application of the grounds[23]

| Ground | Applied in cases | Percentage (%) |
|---|---|---|
| (a) Lack of a valid arbitration agreement | 6 | 30 |
| (b) Breach of due process | 3 | 15 |
| (c) Issues not covered by the arbitration agreement | 2 | 10 |
| (d) Non-compliance with the procedural requirements | 7 | 35 |
| (e) Not effective under the law | 0 | 0 |
| (f) Lack of arbitrability | 1 | 5 |
| (g) Contrary to public policy | 1 | 5 |
| (h) Enforcement procedure requirements | 3 | 15 |

might be other practical reasons, such as the non-existence of the enforceable property, or the lack of adequate identification of the parties, however these are not the legal grounds we intended to discuss in the context of this research.

Many researchers have commented on the non-enforcement of arbitral awards according to the grounds applied or discussed by the courts. A study conducted by Wan and Xia categorised 20 cases where the SPC applies the *NYC* to refuse the enforcement of arbitral awards during 2000 to 2010.[22] The frequencies of the application for non-enforcement on each ground are listed in Table 2.

In a more recent research by Du,[24] an examination of 194 cases of enforcement of foreign awards in China provided for 38 cases of non-enforcement. The frequency of the application of each ground is reflected in Table 3.

While acknowledging the limitation and inconsistencies in these results due to the different methods and criteria used by the authors in collecting cases, we can still summarise that the application of the public policy exception in China's judicial review of arbitral awards is quite rare in comparison with other grounds, such as validity of the arbitration agreement, as well as the procedural issues. The frequency of the application of the public policy exception is relatively low.

These findings may show the cautious attitude of the Chinese courts towards the application of public policy. The fact that public policy may only be applied when other grounds are insufficient may also contribute to its low application rate. Yet an alternative interpretation may be that Chinese courts lack the necessary understanding and experience to apply the public policy exception, and favours those grounds which are easier to understand, to explain and to apply, such as the conformity of procedural

22 万鄂湘, 夏晓红[Wan E'xiang and Xia Xiaohong],《中国法院不予承认及执行某些外国仲裁裁决的原因——《纽约公约》相关案例分析》[Reason for the Refusals of the Recognition and Enforcement of Foreign Arbitral Awards in Chinese Courts: New York Convention Case Studies] (2010) 13 武大法学评论 *Wuhan University Law Review* 1, and Xiaohong Xia, 'Implementation of the New York Convention in China' (2011) 1 *International Commercial Arbitration Brief* 20.

23 This table records all information from the original copy of Wan and Xia's case analysis table. 万鄂湘, 夏晓红 [Wan E'xiang and Xia Xiaohong], above n 22, 8.

24 杜越 [Du Yue], 大数据分析我国法院对外国仲裁裁决的承认和执行情况 [Big Data Analysis on the Recognition and Enforcement of Foreign Awards in Chinese Courts], 2020, available at: https://www.lawyers.org.cn/info/279ee53cd996446c86f5b76417a93891.

**Table 3** Du (2020): application of the grounds[25]

| Ground | Applied in cases | Percentage (%) |
|---|---|---|
| (a) Lack of a valid arbitration agreement | 12 | 32 |
| (b) Breach of due process | 7 | 18 |
| (c) Issues not covered by the arbitration agreement | 10 | 26 |
| (d) Non-compliance with the procedural requirements | 10 | 26 |
| (e) Not effective under the law | 0 | 0 |
| (f) Lack of arbitrability | 1 | 3 |
| (g) Contrary to public policy | 3 | 8 |

rules and the validity of arbitration agreement. These possible explanations are further examined in the next few sections and chapters.

# 3 Statistical Research on the Application of the Public Policy Exception: Fundamental Aspects

Based on the general understanding of China's arbitration practice, the judicial review practice of arbitral awards and the application of different grounds in the annulment/non-enforcement of arbitral awards, as provided in Chapter Three and the previous section, this section analyses the cases involving the application of the public policy exception.

## *3.1 Methodology*

This section aims to deal with all cases where there has been a judicial review of arbitral awards and where the public policy exception could potentially apply. It contains a comprehensive review of complex groups of cases and covers both reasons for and against the application of the public policy exception in judicial review.

Before describing the methodology adopted in collecting and analysing the cases, it is worthwhile to emphasise again why the research on cases is the major focus in this chapter and forms the basis of discussion in the following chapters. As suggested earlier in Chapter Three, legislation and scholars' comments provide little guidance in the application of the public policy exception before Chinese courts.[26] Thus, the

[25] This table records all information from the original copy of Wan and Xia's case analysis table. 万鄂湘, 夏晓红 [Wan E'xiang and Xia Xiaohong], above n 22, 8. Note that the percentages were calculated comparing with the case number, however multiple grounds were applied in some cases, so the adding up exceeds 100%. This also applies to the Du's analysis below.

[26] Section 5 in Chap. 3.

judiciary is the primary authority with respect to the application of public policy. Furthermore, the stability of the Chinese judicial system and the establishment of the Prior Reporting System support the idea that the judiciary is well placed to draw on a consistent pattern of judicial practices to make reliable decisions in the application of public policy.[27] Based on these reasons, the following research focuses on the cases discussing public policy issues in relation to Chinese arbitration and the judicial review of arbitral awards in China.

Cases involving the discussion of public policy can be divided into two main groups: Chinese judicial decisions on arbitral awards and international/foreign judicial decisions on arbitral awards. This book concentrates only on Chinese judicial decisions on arbitral awards. In addition, it focuses mainly on cases dealing with the judicial review of foreign-related and international awards.[28]

The book further divides the cases into two categories: the first category covers cases determined by the SPC in accordance with the Prior Reporting System.[29] Due to the uniqueness of the Prior Reporting System, the SPC have the final say in many cases. These cases are generally reported by the SPC's publication, 'China Trial Guide: Guide on Foreign-related Commercial and Maritime Trial', which publishes the SPC's replies to lower courts regularly.[30] In addition to this publication, certain secondary materials including newspaper articles, journal articles and comments from judges have been consulted, which provide additional details of these cases. They are the primary focus of the quantitative and qualitative studies as they usually cover opinions from three levels of courts and the opinion of the SPC—the highest court in the Chinese judicial system.

Apart from the SPC cases, the second category of cases is decided by lower courts. These cases were determined before the establishment of the Prior Reporting System, where the Prior Reporting system has authorised the lower courts, such as the IPC or HPC, to order the annulment, or enforceability of the arbitral award without further approval of the SPC.[31] They are collected from different sources, primarily from 'China Judgment Online'.[32] This official database of Chinese judgments has been operating since 2013 in accordance with the SPC's call for the publication of

[27] Sections 3 and 4 in Chap. 3.

[28] For a discussion of the different types of awards under judicial review in China, see Sect. 4 in Chap. 3.

[29] Sections 3.2.4 and 4.4.3 in Chap. 3.

[30] For examples of the SPC's published replies, see 最高人民法院民四庭 [the SPC Fourth Civil Branch],《涉外商事海事审判指导》[Guide on Foreign-Related Commercial and Maritime Trial] (人民法院出版社 People's Court Publishing); For databases such as the China Law Info, visit <http://www.chinalawinfo.com/>. For the difficulties of data collection, see Peerenboom, above n 14, 250–52; Clarisse von Wunschheim, *Enforcement of Commercial Arbitral Awards in China: Business Laws of China* (West, 2011) 302–304. See also Sect. 4.6 in Chap. 3.

[31] Sections 3.2.4 and 4.4.3 in Chap. 3.

[32] Wenshu.court.gov.cn. This is the official website publishing all judgments made by Chinese courts. The collection, however, is incomplete.

judgments online.[33] It is understandable, however, that the author is unable to address all cases merely mentioning public policy due to the significant volume of cases in this category. Thus, we only list cases in which public policy is substantially addressed in the judgments in Appendix, as a useful supplementary resource of public policy in Chinese practice. The non-exhaustive collection of the lower courts' decisions may undervalue the significance of this part of study from a statistical perspective, which is why the quantitative study did not cover this part of cases.

The difficulties in collecting cases and finding the necessary details in each case are always a problem in a case study. This is particularly so in the case of China, and in our study of the judicial review of arbitral awards. Most of the cases, even those that were published by the SPC, may not necessarily contain all the facts and arguments that represent the full picture of the case. The reasons for this situation may include variations in the drafting and legal skills of the judges and the informal nature of the Prior Reporting System.[34] The author acknowledges the incompleteness of the collection of cases and its impact on the quantitative study in this chapter.

In addition to the major focus being placed on Chinese decisions on international and foreign-related awards, the author also examine some Chinese judicial decisions dealing with domestic awards, although they are not a major focus of this book. There are significant differences between China's judicial review scheme on foreign-related and international awards on the one hand, and judicial review of domestic awards on the other hand. Different judicial proceedings are adopted, and different grounds to negate the awards apply.[35] Based on these differences, an analysis on these domestic awards will not contribute significantly to the understanding of the Chinese judiciary's approach in dealing with foreign-related and international awards. The applicable public policy exception in domestic arbitral awards is listed for the purpose of comparison in this chapter.[36]

Foreign judicial decisions on arbitral awards are referred to in this book primarily for comparative purposes. Some decisions targeted are those in which China's arbitral awards were sought to be enforced in foreign jurisdictions. They are targeted for the purpose of evaluating the performance of the Chinese arbitration commissions and the Chinese tribunal.[37] Other foreign judicial decisions mentioned in this research are illustrations of key points, or the typical approach adopted by foreign courts and introduced for comparative study purposes. They will not be subject to the statistical study.

---

[33] 最高人民法院关于人民法院在互联网公布裁判文书的规定》 [Provisions of the Supreme People's Court on the Issuance of Judgments on the Internet by the People's Courts], 21 November 2013, Judicial Interpretation No. 26 [2013]; updated 10 January 2016.

[34] Section 4 in Chap. 3.

[35] The different judicial review schemes applicable to domestic awards and to foreign-related and international awards, see Sect. 5 in Chap. 5.

[36] Section 5.

[37] See Chap. 6, particularly the discussion on several cases where CIETAC awards were sought enforcement in Hong Kong.

The collected Chinese cases are then grouped and analysed based on different criteria, including time, outcomes, and different elements of public policy.[38]

## 3.2 The Pool of Cases: Foreign-Related and International Awards Reviewed in China

The author examined all collected cases involving the application of the public policy exception in the judicial review of foreign-related and international awards by Chinese courts.

Table 4 presents all cases determined by the SPC, the majority of which being the cases reported via the Prior Reporting System. These cases are the main focus of this study. They provide not only the foundation for the statistical study in later parts of this chapter but also the more detailed analysis of each key element of public policy in later chapters. For the purpose of consistency, we also listed the short name of each case below, and these cases will be referred to by using the short names in this book.

In addition to the cases reported by the SPC, there are a significant volume of cases reported by the lower courts or via other means. It covers various categories of cases, such as cases determined by the lower courts when the Prior Reporting System was not yet established; cases determined by the lower courts in which the Prior Reporting System was not triggered, or the SPC's replies via the Prior Reporting System were not released; or cases that were not publicly reported by the SPC but discussed by scholars and practitioners in other contexts. These cases are listed in Appendix. Due to the limitation of the reporting methods regarding these cases, cases collected in this list are not exhaustive, and the details of these cases are sometimes incomplete. While we still extract some features and data from these cases, we must admit that the accuracy and value of the quantitative study of these cases have their own limits. Some of them, however, include substantive discussions of the concept of public policy in the Chinese context, and therefore would be used for qualitative study in the subsequent chapters.

Among the cases listed in Appendix, we note two cases in particular, the *Dongfeng case*[39] and the *Gate case*.[40] *Dongfeng* predated the commencement of the Prior

---

[38] The categorisation and definition of these different elements of public policy was introduced earlier in Sect. 5 in Chap. 2.

[39] *Dongfeng Garments Factory of Kaifeng City and Taichu International Trade (HK) Company Ltd v Henan Garment Import and Export Company.* Reported in Yongping Xiao and Zhengxin Huo, '*Ordre Public* in China's Private International Law' (2005) 53 *American Journal of Comparative Law* 654, 660.

[40] *Automotive Gate FZCO et al v Hebei Zhongxing Automotive Manufacture Co Ltd*《申请人盖特汽车自由贸易区公司、埃及盖特汽车制造公司等与被申请人河北中兴汽车制造有限公司申请认可和执行香港特别行政区仲裁裁决民事裁定书》[Civil Decision on the Application for the Recognition of a Hong Kong SAR Arbitral Award among Automotive Gate FZCO et al. and Hebei Zhongxing Automotive Manufacture Co Ltd], Yichang IPC, (2015)鄂宜昌中民认字第00003号之一 [Civil Recognition No. 00003-A], 15 August 2019.

**Table 4** Table of cases: foreign-related and international awards in China discussing public policy, reported by the SPC

| Case number | Decided year | Name | Short title |
|---|---|---|---|
| 1 | 1997 | *USA Production, Tom Hulett and Associates v Chinese Women Travel Agency*[41] | *Heavy Metal* |
| 2 | 2000 | *Misuer v Shenzhen Guangxia Cultural and Industrial Co et al.*[42] | *Guangxia* |
| 3 | 2001 | *Glencore UK v Chongqing Mechanical Machinery Import & Export Co*[43] | *Glencore* |
| 4 | 2003 | *Macau Daming Group Co v Guangzhou Dongjian Industrial Co*[44] | *Daming* |
| 5 | 2003 | *Zhejiang Tianhe Real Estate Corp v Asian Lake Ltd (Hong Kong)*[45] | *Zhejiang Tianhe* |
| 6 | 2003 | *ED & F Mans (HK) v China Sugar & Wine Co (Group)*[46] | *ED & F Mans* |

(continued)

[41]《最高人民法院关于北京市第一中级人民法院不予执行美国制作公司和汤姆·胡莱特公司诉中国妇女旅行社演出合同纠纷仲裁裁决请示的批复》[Reply of the SPC to the Request of the Beijing First Intermediate People's Court in regard of the Non-Enforcement of the Arbitral Award regarding the Dispute between USA Production Co, Tom Hulett & Associates and Chinese Women Travel Agency] Supreme People's Court, 他[1997]第35号 [Other Cases No. 35], 26 December 1997.

[42]《最高人民法院关于深圳市广夏文化实业总公司、宁夏伊斯兰国际信托投资公司、深圳兴庆电子公司与密苏尔有限公司仲裁裁决不予执行案的复函》[Reply of the SPC on the Non-enforcement of an Arbitral Award concerning Shenzhen Guangxia Culture Industry Company, Ningxia Islamic International Trust and Investment Company, Shenzhen Xingqing Electronics Company and Misuer Co Ltd] Supreme People's Court, [2000]执监字第96-2号 [Enforcement Supervision No. 96-2], 20 April 2002.

[43]《最高人民法院关于英国嘉能可有限公司申请承认和执行英国伦敦金属交易所仲裁裁决一案请示的复函》[Reply of the SPC on the Recognition and Enforcement of an Arbitral Award Made by the UK London Metal Exchange Applied by Glencore UK] Supreme People's Court, [2001] 民四他字第2号 [Fourth Civil Branch No. 2, 19 April 2001.

[44]《最高人民法院执行工作办公室关于澳门大明集团有限公司与广州市东建实业总公司合作开发房地产纠纷仲裁裁决执行案的复函》[Reply of the SPC Enforcement Branch Concerning Macau Daming Group Co. Ltd v Guangzhou Dongjian Real Estate Co Disputes on Developments of Real Estate] Supreme People's Court, [2003] 执他字第9号 [Other Enforcement Case No. 9], 5 August 2003.

[45]《最高人民法院关于浙江省天河房地产联合发展公司申请撤销中国经济贸易仲裁委员会上海分会仲裁裁决案的复函》[Reply of the SPC Concerning the Application of Zhejiang Tianhe Real Estate Developments Co for Annulment of the CIETAC Shanghai Award] Supreme People's Court, [2003] 民四他字第19号 [Fourth Civil Branch No. 19], 10 November 2003.

[46]《最高人民法院关于ED&F曼氏(香港)有限公司申请承认和执行伦敦糖业协会仲裁裁决案的复函》[Reply of the SPC Concerning the Application of ED & F Mans (Hong Kong) for Recognition and Enforcement of an Arbitral Award of the London Sugar Association] Supreme People's Court, [2003] 民四他字第3号 [Fourth Civil Branch No. 3], 1 July 2003.

**Table 4** (continued)

| Case number | Decided year | Name | Short title |
|---|---|---|---|
| 7 | 2003 | *Hong Kong Xiangjin Cereal, Oil and Foodstuffs Co., Ltd. v Anhui Cereal, Oil and Foodstuffs Import and Export Corporation*[47] | *Xiangjin* |
| 8 | 2004 | *Weimao International (Hong Kong) Co Ltd v Shanxi Tianli Industrial Co Ltd*[48] | *Weimao* |
| 9 | 2005 | *Tianjin Xianda Hotel v (Korean Company)*[49] | *Tianjin Xianda* |
| 10 | 2005 | *Mitsui Co. (Japan) v Hainan Textile Industry General Co*[50] | *Mitsui* |
| 11 | 2006 | *Shenzhen Baosheng Jinggao Environment Protection Co et. al. v Wildcat Mfg Co Inc (US)*[51] | *Wildcat* |
| 12 | 2006 | *Luoding Energy Supply Bureau v Finenco China Investment Corp*[52] | *Finenco* |

(continued)

47《最高人民法院关于香港享进粮油食品有限公司申请执行香港国际仲裁中心仲裁裁决案的复函》[Reply of the SPC Concerning the Application of Hong Kong Xiangjin Food & Oil Co Ltd for Enforcement of an Arbitral Award of HKIAC] Supreme People's Court, [2003] 民四他字第9号[Fourth Civil Branch No. 9], 4 November 2003.

48《最高人民法院关于不予执行国际商会仲裁院10334/AMW/BWD/TE最终裁决一案的请示的复函》[Reply of the SPC Concerning the Non-Enforcement of ICC Final Award No. 10334/AMW/BWD/TE] Supreme People's Court, [2004] 民四他字第6号 [Fourth Civil Branch No.6], 5 July 2004.

49《最高人民法院关于天津先达大酒店申请撤销 [2003] 津仲裁字第364号仲裁裁决一案的请示的复函》[Reply of the SPC to the Request Concerning the Application of Tianjin Xianda Hotel for Annulment of [2003] Jin Zhong Cai Award No 364], Supreme People's Court, [2005] 民四他字第26号[Fourth Civil Branch No. 26], 11 August 2005.

50《最高人民法院关于对海口中院不予承认和执行瑞典斯德哥尔摩商会仲裁院仲裁裁决请示的复函》[Reply of the SPC to the Haikou Intermediate People's Court's Request Concerning the Non-Enforcement of SCC's Arbitral Award], Supreme People's Court, [2001] 民四他字第12号 [Fourth Civil Branch No. 12], 13 July 2005.

51《最高人民法院关于是否裁定不予执行中国国际经济贸易仲裁委员会仲裁裁决的复函》[Reply of the SPC Concerning Non-Enforcement of CIETAC's Award], Supreme People's Court, [2005] 民四他字第45号 [Fourth Civil Branch No. 45], 23 January 2006.

52《最高人民法院关于是否裁定撤销中国国际经济贸易仲裁委员会华南分会仲裁裁决的请示的复函》[Reply of the SPC Concerning the Annulment of CIETAC South Branch's Arbitral Awards], Supreme People's Court, [2005] 民四他字第47号 [Fourth Civil Branch No. 47], 1 March 2006.

**Table 4** (continued)

| Case number | Decided year | Name | Short title |
|---|---|---|---|
| 13 | 2006 | *Expert Assets et al v Jiangsu Huayuan Medical Co*[53] | *Huayuan* |
| 14 | 2007 | *Bunge Agribusiness Singapore Pte Ltd v Guangdong Fengyuan Oil and Grains Co Ltd*[54] | *Bunge* |
| 15 | 2008 | *FIC v Mawei Shipbuilding*[55] | *Mawei* |
| 16 | 2008 | *Shin-Etsu Chemical v Jiangsu Zhongtian Technologies Co Ltd*[56] | *Shin-Etsu v Zhongtian (No. 1)* |
| 17 | 2008 | *Hemofarm et al. v Shandong Yongning Corp*[57] | *Yongning* |
| 18 | 2008 | *Shin-Etsu Chemical v Tianjin Xinmao Co Ltd*[58] | *Shin-Etsu v Xinmao* |

(continued)

53《最高人民法院关于是否裁定撤销中国国际经济贸易仲裁委员会[2004]中国贸仲京裁字第0222号仲裁裁决请示的复函》[Reply of the SPC Concerning the Annulment of CIETAC Award [2004] Zhong Guo Mao Zhong Jing Cai Zi No 222], Supreme People's Court, [2006] 民四他字第2号 [Fourth Civil Branch No. 2], 7 March 2006.

54《最高人民法院关于邦基农贸新加坡私人有限公司申请承认和执行英国仲裁裁决一案的请示和复函》[Reply of the SPC Concerning the Application of Bunge Agribusiness Pte Ltd (Singapore) for Recognition and Enforcement of a British Arbitral Award], Supreme People's Court, [2006] 民四他字第41号 [Fourth Civil Branch No. 41], 25 June 2006.

55《最高人民法院关于马绍尔群岛第一投资公司申请承认和执行英国伦敦临时仲裁庭仲裁裁决案的复函》[Reply of the SPC Concerning First Investment Co of Marshall Islands' Application for Recognition and Enforcement of an Ad-hoc Arbitral Award of London, UK], Supreme People's Court, [2007] 民四他字第35号[Fourth Civil Branch No. 35], 27 February 2008.

56《最高人民法院关于不予承认日本商事仲裁协会东京04-05号仲裁裁决的报告的复函》[Reply of the SPC to the Request Concerning the Non-Recognition of JACC's Tokyo Award No. 04-05], Supreme People's Court, [2007] 民四他字第26号 [Fourth Civil Branch No.26], 3 March 2008.

57《最高人民法院关于不予承认和执行国际商会仲裁院仲裁裁决的请示的复函》 [Reply of the SPC Concerning Non-Enforcement of an ICC Arbitral Award], Supreme People's Court, [2008] 民四他字第11号 [Fourth Civil Branch No. 11], 2 June 2008.

58《最高人民法院关于裁定不予承认和执行社团法人日本商事仲裁协会东京05-03号仲裁裁决的报告的答复》[Reply of the SPC to the Order to Refuse the Recognition and Enforcement of JACC Tokyo Award No. 05–03], Supreme People's Court, [2008]民四他字第18号 [Fourth Civil Branch No. 18], 10 September 2008.

**Table 4** (continued)

| Case number | Decided year | Name | Short title |
|---|---|---|---|
| 19 | 2009 | *China Medical and BioSicence Ltd (Hong Kong) v Shantou Xinyuan Trade Ltd et al*[59] | *China Medical* |
| 20 | 2009 | *Noble Group Ltd (Singapore) v Zhoushan Zhonghai Grain and Oil Industrial Co Ltd*[60] | *Noble* |
| 21 | 2009 | *Shanghai Feilun Industrial Co Ltd v GRD Minproc Ltd (Australia)*[61] | *GRD Minproc* |
| 22 | 2009 | *Wu Chunying v Zhang Guiwen*[62] | *Mongolia* |
| 23 | 2009 | *Ningbo Yongxin Motor Component Products Co v Korea Central et al*[63] | *Yongxin* |
| 24 | 2009 | *Leroy Merlin France, etc v Tianjin Home World Group Co Ltd, et al*[64] | *Leroy* |

(continued)

59《最高人民法院关于撤销中国国际经济贸易仲裁委员会[2008]中国贸仲京裁字第0044号裁决的请示的复函》[Letter of Reply of the Supreme People's Court on Request for Instructions Regarding Revocation of Award No. 0044 [2008] of China International Economic & Trade Arbitration Commission], Supreme People's Court, [2009] 民四他字第1号 [Fourth Civil Branch No. 1], 18 March 2009.

60《最高人民法院关于舟山中海粮油工业有限公司申请不予执行香港国际仲裁中心仲裁裁决一案的请示报告的复函》[Reply of the SPC to the Request Concerning the Application of Zhoushan Zhonghai Food & Oil Industrial Co Ltd for Non-Enforcement of a HKIAC's Arbitral Award], Supreme People's Court, [2009] 民四他字第2号 [Fourth Civil Branch No. 2], 18 March 2009.

61《最高人民法院关于GRD Minproc 有限公司申请承认并执行瑞典斯德哥尔摩商会仲裁院仲裁裁决一案的请示的复函》[Reply of the SPC Concerning the Application of GRD Minproc Co Ltd for Recognition and Enforcement of SCC's Arbitral Award], Supreme People's Court, [2008] 民四他字第48号[Fourth Civil Branch No. 48], 13 March 2009.

62《最高人民法院关于不予承认及执行蒙古国家仲裁庭仲裁裁决的请示的复函》 [Reply of the SPC Concerning Non-Enforcement of Mongolian National Arbitration Court's Arbitral Award], Supreme People's Court, [2009] 民四他字第33号 [Fourth Civil Branch No.33], 2 September 2009.

63《最高人民法院关于宁波永信汽车部件制造有限公司申请撤销宁波仲裁委员会甬仲裁字[2007]第44号裁决一案的请示报告的复函》[Reply of the SPC Concerning the Application of Ningbo Yongxin Motor Components Production Co for Annulment of Ningbo Arbitration Commission's Award Yong Zhong Cai Zi [2007] No 44], Supreme People's Court, [2009] 民四他字第45号 [Fourth Civil Branch No. 45], 29 October 2009.

64《最高人民法院关于是否不予承认和执行国际商会洛桑12330/TE/MW/AVH仲裁裁决的请示的复函》[Reply of the SPC to the Request Concerning Non-Recognition and Non-Enforcement of ICC Award No. 12330/TE/MW/AVH (Lousanne)], Supreme People's Court, [2009] 民四他字第38号 [Fourth Civil Branch No.38], 5 November 2009.

**Table 4** (continued)

| Case number | Decided year | Name | Short title |
|---|---|---|---|
| 25 | 2010 | *Louis Dreyfus Commodities Asia Pte Ltd (Singapore) v Guangdong Fuhong Oil Products Ltd*[65] | *Louis Dreyfus* |
| 26 | 2010 | *Tianrui Hotel Management (Samoa) v Hangzhou Yiju Hotel Management*[66] | *Tianrui* |
| 27 | 2010 | *Shin-Etsu Chemical Co Ltd v Jiangsu Zhongtian Technologies Co Ltd*[67] | *Shin-Etsu v Zhongtian (No. 2)* |
| 28 | 2011 | *Qingdao Jiacheng Construction Co. v VEM S.P.A & SIMEST S.P.A*[68] | *Jiacheng* |
| 29 | 2011 | *Debao (Fareast) v Hubei Yingtai Economic Developments*[69] | *Debao* |
| 30 | 2012 | *Western Bulk Pte Ltd v Beijing Sinosteel Tiantie Iron & Steel Trade Co Ltd*[70] | *Western Bulk* |

(continued)

65《最高人民法院关于路易达孚商品亚洲有限公司申请承认和执行国际油、种子和脂肪协会作出的第3980号仲裁裁决请示一案的复函》[Reply of the SPC Concerning the Application of Louis Dreyfus Commodity Asia Co Ltd for Recognition and Enforcement of International Federation of Oils, Seeds & Fats Association's Arbitral Award No 3980], Supreme People's Court, [2010] 民四他字第48号 [Fourth Civil Branch No. 48], 10 October 2010.

66《最高人民法院关于申请人天瑞酒店投资有限公司与被申请人杭州易居酒店管理有限公司申请承认仲裁裁决一案的请示报告的复函》[Reply of the SPC to Request Concerning Application of Tianrui Hotel Investment Co Ltd for Enforcement of Arbitral Award against Hangzhou Yiju Hotel Management Co Ltd], Supreme People's Court, [2010] 民四他字第18号 [Fourth Civil Branch No. 18], 18 May 2010.

67《最高人民法院关于不予承认日本商事仲裁协会东京07-11号仲裁裁决一案的请示的复函》[Reply of the SPC to the Request Concerning the Non-Recognition of JACC's Tokyo No 07-11 Arbitral Award], Supreme People's Court, [2010] 民四他字第32号 [Fourth Civil Branch No. 32], 29 June 2010.

68《最高人民法院关于撤销中国国际经济贸易仲裁委员会 (2009) CIETACBJ 裁决 (0355) 号裁决案的请示的复函》[Reply of the SPC to the Request Concerning the Annulment of CIETAC's (2009) CIETACBJ Award No (2009) 0355], Supreme People's Court, [2011] 民四他字第13号 [Fourth Civil Branch No. 13], 22 April 2011.

69《最高人民法院关于德宝 (远东) 有限公司申请执行湖北省鹰台经济发展公司合作合同纠纷一案中不予执行涉外仲裁裁决的请示的复函》[Reply of the SPC to the Request Concerning the Non-Enforcement of a Foreign-Related Arbitral Award in the Disputes Regarding Hubei Yingtai Economic Development Co's Contract of Coordination], Supreme People' Court, [2011] 民四他字第62号[Fourth Civil Branch No. 62], 14 December 2011.

70《最高人民法院关于韦斯顿瓦克公司申请承认与执行英国仲裁裁决案的请示的复函》[Reply of the SPC to the Request Concerning the Application of Western Bulk Co Ltd for Recognition and Enforcement of a British Arbitral Award], Supreme People's Court, [2012] 民四他字第12号[Fourth Civil Branch No.12], 21 May 2012.

**Table 4** (continued)

| Case number | Decided year | Name | Short title |
|---|---|---|---|
| 31 | 2012 | *Xu Jianwen v Zhongwei Urban and Rural Construction & Development Co Ltd*[71] | *Zhongwei* |
| 32 | 2012 | *Singapore Zhongtian Investment (Group) Co v Huludao Harbour Logistics Co Ltd*[72] | *Huludao Harbour* |
| 33 | 2012 | *Beijing Kangwei Medical Consulting v Asian Medical Resources Developments (Group) Co Ltd*[73] | *Kangwei* |
| 34 | 2013 | *Beifang Wanbang Logistics v JMT Mining SPRL Ltd et al*[74] | *Wanbang* |
| 35 | 2013 | *Sri Trang International Pte Ltd v Triangle Tyre Co., Ltd*[75] | *Triangle* |
| 36 | 2013 | *Xiamen Hulishan Fortress Management Bureau v Yi Zhao Precious Stones (Singapore)Pte Ltd*[76] | *Hulishan* |

(continued)

[71]《最高人民法院关于宁夏高院请示不予执行(2011)中国贸仲深裁字第36号仲裁裁决的复函》[Reply of the SPC to Ningxia HPC Concerning the Non-enforcement of CIETAC Shen Cai Award No (2011) 36], Supreme People's Court, [2012]民四他字第27号 [Fourth Civil Branch No. 27], 30 July 2012.

[72]《最高人民法院关于新加坡中天投资 (集团) 有限公司申请撤销中国国际经济贸易仲裁委员会仲裁裁决一案的复函》[Reply of the SPC to the Request Concerning the Application of Singapore Zhongtian Investment (Group) Co Ltd for Annulment of CIETAC's Awards], Supreme People's Court, [2012] 民四他字第47号[Fourth Civil Branch No. 47], 25 October 2012.

[73]《最高人民法院关于北京康卫医药咨询服务中心有限公司申请撤销中国国际经济贸易仲裁委员会仲裁裁决案件的请示的复函》[Reply of the SPC to the Request Concerning the Application of Beijing Kangwei Medical Consulting Service Centre Co Ltd for the Annulment of CIETAC's Arbitral Award], Supreme People's Court, [2012] 民四他字第57号 [Fourth Civil Branch No. 57], 19 December 2012.

[74]《最高人民法院关于申请人北方万邦物流有限公司申请撤销(2012)海仲京裁字第001号仲裁裁决一案的请示的复函》[The Reply of the SPC Concerning the Request to Set Aside CMAC Jing Cai Award No.(2012)001 submitted by Beifang Wanbang Logistics Co Ltd], Supreme People's Court, [2013] 民四他字第5号 [Fourth Civil Branch No. 5], 22 January 2013.

[75]《最高人民法院关于对诗董橡胶股份有限公司与三角轮胎股份有限公司涉外仲裁一案不予执行的请示的复函》[Reply of the Supreme People's Court to the Request for Instructions on Non-Enforcement of the Foreign-Related Arbitral Award between Sri Trang Agro-Industry Plc. and Triangle Tyre Co., Ltd], Supreme People's Court, [2013] 民四他字第12号 [Fourth Civil Branch No. 12] 22 March 2013.

[76]《申请人厦门湖里山炮台管理处申请撤销(2011)中国贸仲京裁字第343号仲裁裁决案》[Case Concerning the Application for the Annulment of (2011) CIETAC Beijing Arbitration Award No.343 by Xiamen Hulishan Fortress Management Bureau], Supreme People's Court, [2013] 民四他字第27号, date not reported. The SPC's reply was not published. The case was reported in 李娜[Li Na], 仲裁司法审查实践中的"公共政策"研究 [Research on the Public Policy in the Judicial Review of Arbitration Matters], (2022) 119 北京仲裁 [Arbitration in Beijing] 50, 65. The author is a clerk of the Fourth Civil Branch of the SPC.

**Table 4** (continued)

| Case number | Decided year | Name | Short title |
|---|---|---|---|
| 37 | 2013 | *Castel Electronics Pty Ltd v TCL Air Conditioning (Zhongshan) Co Ltd*[77] | *Castel* |
| 38 | 2013 | *Beijing Chaolaixinsheng Sport and Leisure Co Ltd v Suowangzhixin Co Ltd*[78] | *Chaolaixinsheng* |
| 39 | 2015 | *Siemens International Trade (Shanghai) Ltd v Shanghai Golden Landmark Co Ltd*[79] | *Siemens* |
| 40 | 2015 | *Luntai County Lvyuan Agriculture and Forestry Development Co Ltd v Productos Agrovin Sociedad Anonima*[80] | *Luntai* |
| 41 | 2015 | *FSG Automotive Holding AG v Wuhan Fanzhou Mechanic Manufacturing Co Ltd*[81] | *FSG Automotive* |
| 42 | 2015 | *Spliethoff's Bevrachtingskantoor B.V. v China National Electronic Import & Export (Shandong) Co Ltd et al*[82] | *Spliethoff* |

(continued)

[77] 《最高人民法院关于申请人Castel Electronics Pty Ltd申请承认和执行外国仲裁裁决一案请示的复函》[Reply of the Supreme People's Court Concerning the Applicant, Castel Electronics Pty Ltd's Application to Recognise and Enforce a Foreign Arbitral Award] Supreme People's Court, [2013] 民四他字第46号[Fourth Civil Branch No.46], 10 October 2013.

[78] 《最高人民法院关于北京朝来新生体育休闲有限公司申请承认大韩商事仲裁院作出的第12113-0011号、第12112-0012号仲裁裁决案件请示的复函》[Reply of the SPC Concerning the Enforcement of KCAB Awards 12113-0011, 12112-0012 Requested by Beijing Chaolaixinsheng Sports and Leisure Co Ltd], Supreme People's Court, [2013] 民四他字第64号 [Fourth Civil Branch No. 64], 18 December 2013.

[79] 《最高人民法院关于西门子国际贸易(上海)有限公司申请承认与执行外国仲裁裁决一案的请示的复函》[Reply of the SPC Concerning the Recognition and Enforcement of a Foreign Award Requested by Siemens International Trade (Shanghai) Co Ltd], Supreme People's Court, [2015] 民四他字第5号 [Fourth Civil Branch No. 5], 10 October 2015.

[80] 《最高人民法院关于对北京市高级人民法院就轮台县绿源农林开发有限责任公司申请撤销中国国际经济贸易仲裁委员会[2014]中国贸仲京裁字第0526号仲裁裁决案件的请示的复函》[Reply of the SPC Concerning the Report from the Beijing HPC Regarding the Request to Set Aside CIETAC Jing Cai Award No. [2014] 0526 by Luntai County Lvyuan Agriculture and Forestry Development Co Ltd], Supreme People's Court, [2015] 民四他字第40号 [Fourth Civil Branch No. 40], 28 Oct 2015.

[81] 《最高人民法院关于湖北省高级人民法院就申请人FSG汽车工业控股公司与被申请人武汉泛洲机械制造有限公司申请承认和执行奥地利联邦经济会仲裁中心SCH-5239号仲裁裁决一案请示的答复》[Reply of the SPC Concerning the Report from Hubei HPC Regarding the Request to Recognition and Enforcement of International Arbitral Centre of the Austrian Federal Economic Chamber Vienna Award No. SCH-5239 between FSG Automotive Holding AG and Wuhan Fanzhou Mechanic Manufacturing Co Ltd], Supreme People's Court, [2015] 民四他字第46号 [Fourth Civil Branch No. 46], 24 December 2015.

[82] 《最高人民法院关于西特福船运公司申请承认英国伦敦仲裁庭作出的 "HULL XXK06-039"号仲裁裁决案件请示的复函》[Reply of the SPC Concerning the Report Regarding the Recognition of an Award made in London UK No. HULL XXK06-039 Requested by Spliethoff's Bevrachtingskantoor B.V.], Supreme People's Court, [2015] 民四他字第48号 [Fourth Civil Branch No.48], 25 December 2015.

**Table 4** (continued)

| Case number | Decided year | Name | Short title |
|---|---|---|---|
| 43 | 2015 | *Dongcheng International Trade Ltd v Tianjin Tarrif-free Zone Tiangong International Trade Co Ltd*[83] | *Dongcheng* |
| 44 | 2016 | *Wicor Hold-ing AG v Taizhou Haopu Investment Co Ltd*[84] | *Wicor* |
| 45 | 2016 | *J&D IB Ltd v Tian et al*[85] | *J&D IB* |
| 46 | 2016 | *Chenco Chemical Engineering and Consulting GmbH v Duofuduo Chenical Engineering Co*[86] | *Chenco* |
| 47 | 2017 | *Bright Morning Limited and Respondent Yixing Leqi Textile Group Co Ltd*[87] | *Bright* |

(continued)

83《最高人民法院关于东成国际贸易有限公司申请执行涉外仲裁裁决一案的请示的答复》[Reply of the SPC to the Report Concerning the Enforcement of A Foreign-related Arbitral Award Requested by Dongcheng International Trade Co Ltd], Supreme People's Court, [2015]民四他字第53号[Fourth Civil Branch No. 53], 9 December 2015.

84《最高人民法院关于不予执行国际商会仲裁院第18295/CYK号仲裁裁决一案请示的复函》[Reply of the SPC to the Report Concerning the Non-enforcement of the ICC Award No.18295/CYK], Supreme People's Court, [2016] 最高法民他字第8号 [SPC Civil Other Cases No. 8], 22 March 2016.

85《最高人民法院关于株式会社 J&D IB 申请承认国外仲裁裁决一案请示的答复》[Reply of the SPC to the Report Concerning the Recognition and Enforcement of a Foreign Award Requested by J&D IB Ltd], Supreme People's Court, [2016] 最高法民他38号 [SPC Civil Branch Other Cases, No. 38], 17 May 2016.

86《最高人民法院关于对河南省高级人民法院就申请人成可化学工程和咨询公司与被申请人多氟多化工股份有限公司申请承认和执行外国仲裁裁决纠纷一案请示的复函》[The Reply of the SPC to the Report from Henan HPC Concerning the Recognition and Enforcement of a Foreign Award Regarding the Dispute between the Applicant Chenco Chemical Engineering and Consulting GmbH and Respondent Duofuduo Chenical Engineering Co], the Supreme People's Court, [2016] 最高法民他66号 [SPC Civil Branch Other Cases No. 66], 20 December 2016.

87《最高人民法院关于江苏省高级人民法院就申请人 Bright Morning Limited与被申请人宜兴乐祺纺织集团有限公司申请承认和执行新加坡国际仲裁中心2011年第130号(ARB130/11/MJL)仲裁裁决一案请示的复函》[The Reply of the SPC to the Report from Jiangsu HPC Concerning the Recognition and Enforcement of SIAC 2011 Award No. ARB130/11/MJL Regarding the Dispute between the Applicant Bright Morning Limited and Respondent Yixing Leqi Textile Group Co Ltd], Supreme People's Court, [2017] 最高法民他44号 [SPC Civil Branch Other Cases No. 44], 23 June 2017.

**Table 4** (continued)

| Case number | Decided year | Name | Short title |
|---|---|---|---|
| 48 | 2017 | *Guangdong Sanmao Railway Industrial Development Co Ltd v Respondents Zhuhai Special Economic Zone Ciangzhou Jindu Real Estate Development Co Ltd and Best Fair Asia Limited*[88] | *Sanmao* |
| 49 | 2017 | *IP Cathay II, L. P., Cayman Island v Zhou et al*[89] | *IP Cathay* |
| 50 | 2018 | *Palmer Maritime Inc v Zhongmu Industrial Co*[90] | *Palmer* |
| 51 | 2018 | *Pixelplus Co. Ltd v Shenzhen JSL Technology Co Ltd*[91] | *Pixelplus* |

(continued)

88《最高人民法院关于广东省高级人民法院就广东三茂铁路实业发展有限公司与珠海经济特区香洲金都房产开发有限公司、佳建亚洲有限公司申请不予执行仲裁裁决一案请示的复函》[Reply of the SPC to the Report from Guangdong HPC Concerning the Non-enforcement of an Arbitral Award Regarding the Disputes between the Applicant Guangdong Sanmao Railway Industrial Development Co Ltd and Respondents Zhuhai Special Economic Zone Ciangzhou Jindu Real Estate Development Co Ltd and Best Fair Asia Limited], Supreme People's Court, [2017] 最高法民他115号 [SPC Civil Branch Other Cases No. 115], 26 December 2017.

89《最高人民法院关于北京市高级人民法院就英属盖曼群岛商智龙二基金公司申请认可和执行香港特别行政区仲裁裁决一案请示的复函》[Reply of the SPC to the Report from Beijing HPC Concerning the Recognition and Enforcement of a Hong Kong Arbitral Award Requested by IP Cathay II, L. P., Cayman Island], Supreme People's Court, [2017] 最高法民他131号 [SPC Civil Branch Other Cases No. 131], 25 December 2017.

90《最高人民法院关于天津市高级人民法院就申请人帕尔默海运公司与被申请人中牧实业股份有限公司申请承认和执行外国仲裁裁决一案请示的复函》[Reply of the SPC to the Report from Tianjin HPC Concerning the Recognition and Enforcement of a Foreign Arbitral Award Regarding the Dispute between the Applicant Palmer Maritime Inc and the Respondent Zhongmu Industrial Co] Supreme People's Court, [2017]最高法民他140号 [SPC Civil Branch Other Cases No. 140], 9 March 2018.

91《最高人民法院关于广东省高级人民法院就派视尔有限责任公司申请承认和执行韩国商事仲裁院仲裁裁决一案的请示的复函》[Reply of the SPC to the Report from Guangdong HPC Concerning the Recognition and Enforcement of an KCAB Award Requested by Pixelplus Co. Ltd], Supreme People's Court, [2018] 最高法民他15号 [SPC Civil Branch Other Cases No. 15], 29 March 2018.

**Table 4** (continued)

| Case number | Decided year | Name | Short title |
|---|---|---|---|
| 52 | 2018 | *Triton Container International Ltd v Yangpu Economic Development Zone Construction and Investment Co Ltd*[92] | *Triton* |
| 53 | 2020 | *Zhang Lan et al v La Dolce Vita Fine Dining Group Holdings Limited*[93] | *Zhang Lan* |

Reporting System; the IPC held that the public policy ground should apply and the arbitral award should be refused, however, it was later reported that the outcome was overturned by the SPC. In the *Gate case*, ruled in 2019, the IPC applied the public policy ground to refuse the recognition and enforcement of the award. It was presumed that such ruling, as well as the reasoning, was confirmed by the SPC as an outcome of the operation of the Prior Reporting System. Thus, we include these two cases in the statistical analysis of the SPC's approach below, despite the absence of the SPC rulings. We did not include the *Pepsi case*; *Pepsi* may have been another example which confirmed the SPC's preferences, in which case the SPC ruled in favour of non-enforcement on the basis that the arbitration was initiated before the expiration of a "period of negotiation" in the original agreement, however the SPC considered this as being a procedural irregularity.[94]

This pool of cases might not be complete, however it is more comprehensive than the pool of cases in all other existing literature, for example, He's study in 2014

[92]《最高人民法院关于海南省高级人民法院就承认与执行美国国际争议解决中心50-125-T-00029-13号仲裁裁决一案再次请示的复函》[Reply of the SPC Concerning the Second Report from Hainan HPC regarding the Recognition and Enforcement of ICDR Award No. 50-125-T-00029-13], Supreme People's Court, (2018) 最高法民他108号 [SPC Civil Branch Other Cases No. 108], 21 December 2018.

[93]《张兰、盛兰控股集团(BVI)有限公司 [Grand Lan Holdings Group] 申请撤销仲裁裁决特别程序民事裁定书》[Civil Order of Special Procedure on the Setting Aside of An Arbitral Award Requested by Zhang Lan and Grand Lan Holdings Group], Supreme People's Court, [2019] 最高法民特4号, 5号 [SPC Civil Special Procedure No. 4, 5], 29 December 2020.

[94] *Pepsi* is included in Appendix rather than in the statistical analysis. It was reported by some scholars that the public policy argument was once raised but turned down during the reporting process (See 邓莉莉,《解析: 百事仲裁案》[Analysis: Pepsi Arbitration] (2006)12 大经贸 *Foreign Trade and Economy*), however none of the replies or the rulings, or quotes of such rulings relating to the public policy, were made public. Thus, it is hard to precisely describe the attitude of the parties and courts, especially the SPC, in this case.

(covering 19 cases),[95] Guo's study in 2016 (covering 20 cases)[96] and Li's study in 2022.[97]

## 4 Statistical Study: Public Policy in Chinese Courts' Judicial Review of Foreign-Related and International Awards

The application of the public policy exception in the judicial review of foreign-related and international arbitral awards by the SPC is summarised in Table 5. The arguments of the parties and opinions of different levels of courts are included according to the published materials.

An overall conclusion that can be drawn from this table is that the public policy exception was ultimately applied in 10 cases (including four on arbitrability) in China's judicial review of foreign and foreign-related arbitral awards, a relatively small number compared with the total volume of cases of judicial review of arbitral awards. This is consistent with the low application rate of public policy as observed by other scholars.[98] 10 out of the 55 cases is still quite significant, because the SPC would only intervene in the significant and difficult cases reported by the lower courts, in which the public policy is more likely to be applied. Taking into account the cases reported by lower courts in Appendix, in which the application of the public policy was simply turned down, the rate of the application of public policy is much lower. In all cases listed in Appendix except *Dongfeng* (predating the Prior Reporting System and intervened by the SPC), *Xinwei* (predating the Prior Reporting System) and *Gate* (presumably confirmed by the SPC), the public policy argument raised by the parties were rejected, or in rare cases, omitted, by the IPCs or the Maritime courts.

---

[95] 何其生[He Qisheng],《国际商事仲裁司法审查中的公共政策》[Public Policy in the Judicial Review of International Commercial Arbitration Matters], (2014) 7 中国社会科学 *Social Science in China*.

[96] 郭浩 [Guo Hao],《我国国际商事仲裁裁决的司法审查中公共政策运用的实证研究》[An Empirical Study of the Application of Public Policy in the Judicial Review of the International Commercial Arbitral Awards in China] (2016) 95 北京仲裁 *Arbitration in Beijing* 77, 79–82.

[97] 李娜 [Li Na],《仲裁司法审查实践中的 "公共政策"研究》[Study of the Public Policy in the Practice of the Judicial Review on Arbitration Matters], (2022) 119 北京仲裁 *Arbitration in Beijing* 50. This article covers domestic, foreign-related and foreign arbitral awards, while the author of this book only compares the latter two.

[98] See Sect. 2.3. Please note that arbitrability cases were not included in some of the other reports. Also, the author did not cover those cases where the public policy exception is not referred to.

**Table 5** Application of public policy in the SPC cases

| No | Year | Short title | Place of arbitration | Parties argued | IPC/ MC | HPC | SPC | Validity confirmed / enforced |
|---|---|---|---|---|---|---|---|---|
| 1 | 1992 | *Dongfeng* | Hong Kong | / | A | | NA | C |
| 2 | 1997 | *Heavy Metal* | China | / | / | / | A | NC |
| 3 | 2000 | *Guangxia* | China | / | / | / | A | NC |
| 4 | 2001 | *Glencore* | UK | / | A | A | / | NC on other grounds |
| 5 | 2003 | *Daming* | China | A | / | / | NA | C |
| 6 | 2003 | *Zhejiang Tianhe* | China | A | NA | / | NA | C |
| 7 | 2003 | *ED & F Mans* | UK | A | / | A | NA | C |
| 8 | 2003 | *Xiangjin* | Hong Kong | / | A | A | NA | C |
| 9 | 2004 | *Weimao* | Hong Kong[99] | A | / | NA | / | C |
| 10 | 2005 | *Tianjin Xianda* | China | A | A | NA | NA | C |
| 11 | 2005 | *Mitsui* | Sweden | / | / | A | NA | C |
| 12 | 2006 | *Wildcat* | China | / | A | A | NA | C |
| 13 | 2006 | *Finenco* | China | A | / | / | NA | C (partially annulled on other grounds) |
| 14 | 2006 | *Huayuan* | China | A | NA | A | A | NC |
| 15 | 2007 | *Bunge* | UK | A | / | NA | / | NC on other grounds |
| 16 | 2008 | *Mawei* | UK | A | / | / | / | NC on other grounds |
| 17 | 2008 | *Shin-Etsu v Zhongtian (No. 1)* | Japan | A | A | A | / | NC on other grounds |
| 18 | 2008 | *Yongning* | France | A | A | A | A | NC |
| 19 | 2008 | *Shin-Etsu v Xinmao* | Japan | A | | A | / | NC on other grounds[100] |
| 20 | 2009 | *China Medical* | China | A | / | / | / | C |
| 21 | 2009 | *Noble* | Hong Kong | A | A | A | NA | C |
| 22 | 2009 | *GRD Minproc* | Sweden | A | A | A | NA | C |
| 23 | 2009 | *Mongolia* | Mongolia | / | / | A | A | NC |

(continued)

[99] In this case, the arbitration was administrated by ICC and award was made in Hong Kong. The SPC, however, considered the award as a French award rather than a Hong Kong award. See the *Weicao Case*.

[100] The case was initially handled by the Tianjin HPC, not an IPC.

**Table 5** (continued)

| No | Year | Short title | Place of arbitration | Parties argued | IPC/ MC | HPC | SPC | Validity confirmed / enforced |
|---|---|---|---|---|---|---|---|---|
| 24 | 2009 | *Yongxin* | China | A | A | A | NA | C |
| 25 | 2009 | *Leroy* | Switzerland | A | / | / | / | NC on other grounds |
| 26 | 2010 | *Louis Dreyfus* | UK | A | A | A | NA | C |
| 27 | 2010 | *Tianrui* | UK | A | A | A | NA | C |
| 28 | 2010 | *Shin-Etsu v Zhongtian (No. 2)* | Japan | A | A | A | NA | NC on other grounds[101] |
| 29 | 2011 | *Jiacheng* | China | A | A | A | A | NC |
| 30 | 2011 | *Debao* | China | / | / | A | NA | C |
| 31 | 2012 | *Western Bulk* | UK | / | / | A | NA | NC on other grounds |
| 32 | 2012 | *Zhongwei* | China | A | A | NA | / | C |
| 33 | 2012 | *Huludao Harbour* | China | A | NA | / | / | C |
| 34 | 2012 | *Kangwei* | China | A | NA | / | / | C[102] |
| 35 | 2013 | *Wanbang* | China | A | / | / | / | NC on other grounds |
| 36 | 2013 | *Triangle* | China | / | A | / | / | NC on other grounds |
| 37 | 2013 | *Hulishan* | China | / | / | / | A | NC |
| 38 | 2013 | *Castel* | Australia | A | NA | A | NA | NC on other grounds |
| 39 | 2013 | *Chaolaixinsheng* | Korea | A | A | A | NA | NC on other grounds |
| 40 | 2015 | *Siemens* | Singapore | A | / | A | NA | C |
| 41 | 2015 | *Luntai* | China | A | / | / | / | NC on other grounds |
| 42 | 2015 | *FSG Automotive* | Austria | A | NA | / | / | C (partially refused on other grounds) |
| 43 | 2015 | *Spliethoff* | UK | A | A | NA | NA | C (partially refused on other grounds) |
| 44 | 2015 | *Dongcheng* | China | A | / | / | / | C |

(continued)

[101] In this case, the SPC confirmed the application of the principle of *res judicata* but refused to include it as a public policy exception. The analysis of the SPC's attitude is provided later in Chap. 6.

[102] In this case, the Beijing HPC and the SPC's discussion on the principle of *res judicata* were also subject to the procedure requirements, not public policy. See further Chap. 6.

**Table 5** (continued)

| No | Year | Short title | Place of arbitration | Parties argued | IPC/ MC | HPC | SPC | Validity confirmed / enforced |
|---|---|---|---|---|---|---|---|---|
| 45 | 2016 | *Wicor* | Hong Kong | A | A | / | A | NC |
| 46 | 2016 | *J&D IB* | Korea | A | A | A | NA | C |
| 47 | 2016 | *Chenco* | Switzerland | A | A | NA | / | C (partially refused on other grounds) |
| 48 | 2017 | *Bright* | Singapore | A | A | NA | / | C (partially refused on other grounds) |
| 49 | 2017 | *Sanmao* | China | A | NA | / | / | C |
| 50 | 2017 | *IP Cathay* | Hong Kong | A | NA | / | / | NC on other grounds |
| 51 | 2018 | *Palmer* | UK | / | / | / | A | NC |
| 52 | 2018 | *Pixelplus* | Korea | A | / | / | / | NC on other grounds |
| 53 | 2018 | *Triton* | US | / | A | A | NA | C (partially refused on other grounds)[103] |
| 54 | 2019 | *Gate* | Hong Kong | A | / | / | A | NC |
| 55 | 2020 | *Zhang Lan* | China | A | / | / | NA | C |

In this table, A = Argued by parties/Applied by courts; NA = Not Argued by parties/Not Applied by courts; / = Not Specified; C = the validity of the award or its enforceability was confirmed, NC = Not confirmed

Particularly, the Parties Argued column shows whether the parties raised the public policy argument. / = information not available; A = Argued; NA = Not argued

## *4.1 Change Over Time*

Figure 4 lists the number of cases covered by Table 5 in each year between 1992 and 2022.

As noted above, despite the generally low volume of cases in which the public policy ground is ultimately applied, the number of cases in which the public policy exception is discussed before Chinese courts has increased in the past two decades.

The number of cases reported till 2000 (inclusive) is not large.[104] This may partly be due to the smaller scale of economic disputes at the earlier stages of the period of

[103] In this case, the SPC's comment on public policy was actually provided in its earlier reply (2016) 最高法民他25号 [SPC Civil Branch Other Cases No. 25], which was not published. The comments, however, are adopted by Haikou Maritime Court's final ruling on this case: (2015) 琼海法他字第7号 [Other Cases No.7], 30 Dec 2019.

[104] This pro-2000 and post-2000 division is a rough division according to the decades. It is particularly notable that many changes in China's arbitration law system and China's judicial review practice in dealing with arbitration happened during 1990–2000 (including the enactment of the

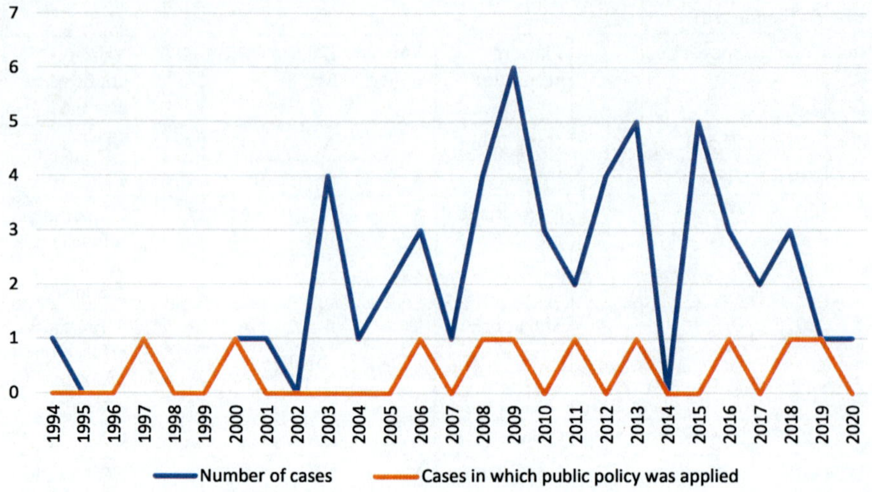


**Fig. 4** Number of cases decided by the SPC each year on public policy

study,[105] and also the lack of a sufficient method of publication of cases.[106] Only seven cases were reported during this period and two of them were refused enforcement on the ground of public policy.

After 2000, the number of cases significantly and steadily increased. Most of them were finally decided by the SPC through the Prior Reporting System. This fact, again, confirms the significance of such a system both in the judicial review practice, and also as a publishing method of these judicial decisions. The public policy exception was applied in eight cases after 2000 and there is no significant trend of an increase in its application.

## *4.2 Roles of Parties and Courts*

The roles of the parties and the different levels of courts in the application of the public policy exception are detailed in the following discussion.

---

*CCPL* in 1991, *CAL* in 1994, reforms of arbitration commissions started from 1995, the establishment of the Prior Reporting System in 1995–1998 etc., see Sect. 5 in Chap. 3), so the distinction between pro-2000 and post-2000 is significant. Though the date illustrates a sudden rise of the cases in the year 2002, this does not necessarily mean a significant change in judicial approach in applying public policy in that year, and there is no evidence or materials supporting such a change in the specific year of 2002.

[105] For the economic growth in China, see the Introductory Chapter.

[106] See above Chap. 3.

### 4.2.1 The Role of the Parties

The public policy exception is categorised as being applied by the court "on its own motion" in both Chinese legislation and the *NYC*.[107] This does not mean that public policy cannot be argued by the parties; the legislation simply provides that the court has the discretion to review the public policy issues when the parties do not raise them in argument.[108]

Of the 55 cases, public policy arguments were raised by the parties in at least 41 cases; in other cases, either the courts actively introduced the public policy issue on their own motion, or the parties' arguments were not available.[109] This indicates that, despite the fact that the legislation provides the courts with discretion in reviewing public policy issues, the parties can and do successfully make public policy arguments to draw the courts' attention to them. This may be a positive reflection of the fact that Chinese arbitration practitioners understand the importance of public policy arguments; but on the other hand, it may increase the instances of public policy arguments being raised inappropriately by the parties, though such a trend of inappropriate use of public policy arguments by parties has not yet been reported as a serious problem in China.

### 4.2.2 The Role of the SPC and Lower Courts

In the judicial review stage, three levels of the Chinese courts may potentially be involved. Among them, the role of the SPC, particularly in the functioning of the Prior Reporting System, can be confirmed by statistics. In 34 out of the 55 cases, the SPC made a ruling on the public policy arguments made by the parties or reasonings submitted by lower courts.[110] The SPC confirmed the application of the public policy ground (including arbitrability) in 10 cases and rejected it in 24 of the cases. In many cases, for example *Noble, GRD Minproc, Louis Dreyfus, Tianrui, Shin-Etsu (No 2) and Castel*, the SPC directly overturned the opinions of the IPCs and HPCs that proposed a rejection of enforcement. The SPC clearly stated the purpose of limiting the application of public policy to exceptional circumstances. This attitude represents the aim of the Prior Reporting System and is consistent with international practice.[111] In addition, it is evident from the reasoning used that the SPC has improved its use of legal techniques in recent years. In the early cases, particularly the cases before the year 2000, the SPC rarely provided substantial legal reasons in applying public policy, whereas in most recent cases, the SPC consistently attempts to provide more detailed legal reasoning.[112]

---

[107] Section 5 in Chap. 3; also the *NYC*, art V(2).

[108] Section 5 in Chap. 3.

[109] See Table 5: Application of Public Policy.

[110] See Table 5: Application of Public Policy.

[111] See Chaps. 2 and 3.

[112] For example, *the Palmer case* (2018).

The other 21 cases can be divided into two categories. The public policy arguments or reasoning was rejected by lower courts in 10 cases. In these cases, if the public policy argument or reasoning was correctly turned down by lower courts, the SPC would not further this line of argument. In cases such as *Weimao* and *Bunge*, the public policy arguments raised by the parties were clearly refused by lower courts and unlikely to be further discussed by the higher courts in subsequent proceedings. In *Zhejiang Tianhe*, the SPC rejected the public policy argument by holding that it "lacks factual and legal basis", which is consistent with the Shanghai First IPC's conclusion. Only when the public policy issue is complicated or significant enough and the lower court cannot decide on it, does the SPC decide. For example, in *Wildcat* and *Louis Dreyfus*, the lower courts were not able to form a decision because their judges had different and even contradictory opinions. The SPC responded to the contradictory opinions provided by the HPCs in these cases. Due to the lack of complete information, this observation may not represent all situations, but such a trend is consistent with the design and function of the Prior Reporting System.

In another 11 cases, the public policy arguments or reasonings were simply ignored in the SPC's reply, or the series of reports and replies after it was raised. This might show that the SPC, or the Chinese courts in general, are reluctant to comment on the public policy grounds when the arbitral award is likely to be refused enforcement on other grounds, or the public policy argument lacks substance. Examples can be found in early cases like *Glencore* (2001, enforcement refused on the basis of Art V(1)(a)) and *Dongcheng* (2015, the argument raised by the parties were never responded to by three levels of courts). *Shin-Etsu (No. 2)* expressed the view that public policy would be applicable only if no other ground is available. This point of view, however, is not consistent with the predominant view in international practice, which favours the co-existence between public policy and other grounds of non-enforcement on the basis of different conditions and standards-of-proof in the application of different grounds.[113] It also corresponds to the fact that the Prior Reporting System is not an appeal system; the SPC enjoys the ultimate determining power and discretion in the Prior Reporting System and does not need to deal with all issues raised in previous proceedings.[114]

Chinese courts play both the role of the supervisory and the enforcing court. Though these two roles are distinct from each other from a theoretical perspective, in both cases the judicial review practices are generally identical according to Chinese legislation,[115] and the role of the supervisory court in China is not significant in regard to the application of public policy in judicial practice. In the 55 cases decided by the SPC, 23 dealt with Chinese-made arbitral awards.[116] In 13 of these, the Chinese courts were the supervisory courts, and in the remaining 10 the Chinese courts were the enforcing courts. The public policy grounds were applied twice in annulling the

[113] See Chap. 2.

[114] For the Prior Reporting System, see Sect. 3.2.4 in Chap. 3; see further in Chap. 9.

[115] See Sect. 3.2 in Chap. 3.

[116] See Table 2.

awards and three times in the context of enforcement,[117] showing that the SPC deals with these cases in a similar manner.

There are some exceptional cases that did not follow the Prior Reporting System. In *Huayuan*, the Beijing 2nd IPC held that the arbitral award was not annulled, but later this decision was overturned by the Beijing HPC and the SPC; according to the Prior Reporting System, however, the decision not to annul an award made by the Beijing 2nd IPC need not be submitted to the higher courts for further confirmation.[118] Also, in *Guangxia*, both Shenzhen IPC and Beijing 2nd IPC confirmed the validity and enforceability of the involving award, but the losing parties complained to the SPC through various avenues and the SPC eventually took this case and denied such enforcement.[119] Seven years after the SPC's decision, Shenzhen IPC re-started the enforcement proceeding, and the decision to enforce such an award was also sustained by the Guangdong HPC, against the SPC's previous decision.[120] These two cases reflect that the higher courts might follow some alternative proceedings other than the Prior Reporting System, for example, the retrial system in *CCPL*[121]; also, the SPC's reply may not guarantee the outcome of cases. The uncertainty shown in this procedure provides additional unpredictability in the application of public policy.

The performance of the SPC in establishing a consistent approach of applying the public policy exception, even in its most recent cases, is far from satisfactory. In quite a few cases, the SPC merely avoided addressing the issue or was reluctant to discuss the possibility of the application of public policy by finding it "inappropriate" without further explanations.[122] Furthermore, in many cases, the SPC attempted to apply other grounds while avoiding the discussion of public policy. One typical preference of the SPC is to address any detailed procedural flaw as a "procedural irregularity" for non-enforcement, rather than trying to deal with the public policy issue, despite it being raised by the parties or the lower courts. For example, in *Shin-Etsu (No. 2)*, the SPC clarified the principle of *res judicata* as a requirement of "fundamental procedural principles" that it applied as part of procedural rules

[117] It is particularly notable that in *Guangxia*, the award is eventually enforced despite the SPC held not to enforce it on the basis of Element (4); thus, it is not certain whether the SPC's holding in this case is binding. See the next paragraph. For the complicated procedural history of the *Guangxia* Case, see further Sect. 3.2.1 in Chap. 8.

[118] For an example of the final decision supporting the validity and enforcement of an award by the IPC, see the Ningbo IPC's decision in *Duferco S.A v Ningbo Art Crafts Import & Export Co.* (2008), reported in 赵秀文 [Zhao Xiuwen],《从宁波工艺品公司案看我国法院对涉外仲裁协议的监督》[The Supervision of Our Courts on Foreign-Related Arbitration Agreement: Insights from the Ningbo Arts & Crafts Co Case] (2010) 5 时代法学 *Present-day Law Science* 3.

[119] As reported by the website of WunschARB, "it seems that during the 9th CPC National Congress in 2000, NPC delegates from Ningxia, and during the 2001 session of the National People's Congress and the Chinese People's Political Consultative Conference, an NPC member from Guangdong, protested against the handling of the case and forwarded relevant materials to the SPC."

[120]《广东省高级人民法院执行裁定书》[Enforcement Order of the Guangdong High People's Court] (2013) 粤高法执复字第43号 [Enforcement Reconsideration No 43].

[121]《中华人民共和国民事诉讼法》[The Civil Procedure Law of the People's Republic of China] (People's Republic of China) ch 16, the Trial Supervision Procedure.

[122] This expression is repeatedly used in cases such as *Wildcat* and *Debao*.

governing the arbitration, rather than as a possible element of public policy.[123] In *FSG Automobile*, the SPC dealt with the matter of whether the tribunal's ruling on liquidation-related matters was enforceable in the context of *ultra vires* rather than arbitrability or public policy. In *Castel,* the SPC denied the application of public policy and referred to "invalid arbitration agreement" under art V(1)(a) of the *NYC*, despite a possible misunderstanding of the applicable law to decide the invalidity of such arbitration agreement.[124]

These observations may serve as reasons why the SPC has failed to achieve a more precise and consistent approach in identifying and applying public policy. Even though the SPC is generally recognised as sitting in the predominant position in the legal system, a clearer legal position established by legislation and formally designed proceedings in the judicial review of arbitral awards may help the SPC to improve its performance by providing a more consistent and thorough legal reasoning to explain how it determines whether the public policy exception applies in cases it examines.

## 4.3 *Different Elements of Public Policy*

Further analysis relates to the frequency with which each element of public policy is discussed in dealing with foreign-related and international awards. According to a thorough review of all cases, they can be categorised as outlined in Table 6. The categorisation of the key elements of public policy, as introduced in Chapter Two, includes: (1) the Fundamental Principles of law, including (1a) the substantive fundamental principles of law and (1b) the procedural fundamental principles of law; (2) the Public policy rule, also known as *lois de police*; (3) International Obligations, and (4) arbitrability. Detailed elements mentioned by parties and the courts of each level can be found in Table 6.

It is noteworthy that the information in the table is not complete because of the difficulties in collecting materials.[125] Thus, discussion of the following aspects, particularly dealing with the numbers reflected in the previous table, may not be accurate; yet it still presents a general trend in China's judicial practice.

### 4.3.1 The Application Frequency

The frequencies with which each element of public policy is referred to are included in Table 7.

According to this result, the frequency of (1b) procedural principles and (2) *lois de police* and (1a) substantive principles being cited were quite similar, on 24, 21

[123] For the analysis of the element of *res judicata* and *Shin-Etsu (No 2)*, see Sect. 4.2 in Chap. 6.

[124] See further discussion in Sect. 4.2 in Chap. 6.

[125] See Sect. 3.1, in which the limitation of China's case reporting system and its possible influence on this book is discussed.

**Table 6** Elements of public policy mentioned by parties or considered by the courts[126]

| Short title | Year | Parties | IPC | HPC | SPC | Conclusion | Outcome |
|---|---|---|---|---|---|---|---|
| *Dongfeng* | 1992 | / | (1a) | / | (1a) | (1a) | Not applied |
| *Heavy Metal*[127] | 1997 | / | / | / | (1a)(2) | (1a)(2) | Applied |
| *Guangxia* | 2000 | / | / | / | (4) | (4) | Applied |
| *Glencore* | 2001 | / | (1a) | (1a) | / | / | Not Applied |
| *Daming* | 2003 | (1a)(1b) | (1b) | (1b) | (1b) | (1a)(1b) | Not applied |
| *Zhejiang Tianhe* | 2003 | Not specified | / | / | Not specified | Not specified | Not applied |
| *ED& F Man* | 2003 | (2) | / | (2) | (2) | (2) | Not applied |
| *Xiangjin* | 2003 | / | (1a) | (1a) | (1a) | (1a) | Not applied |
| *Weimao* | 2004 | (1a) | / | (1a) | / | (1a) | Not applied |
| *Tianjin Xianda* | 2005 | (1a) | / | / | / | (1a) | Not applied |
| *Mitsui* | 2005 | / | (2) | (1b)(2) | (2) | (1b)(2) | Not applied |
| *Wildcat* | 2006 | / | / | (1a) | (1a) | (1a) | Not applied |
| *Finenco* | 2006 | (1a) | / | / | (1a) | (1a) | Not applied |
| *Huayuan* | 2006 | (4) | (4) | (4) | (4) | (4) | Applied |
| *Bunge* | 2007 | (2) | / | (2) | (2) | (2) | Not applied |
| *Mawei* | 2008 | (1b) | / | / | / | (1b) | Not applied |
| *Shin-Etsu v Zhongtian (No.1)* | 2008 | (2) | (2) | (2) | (2) | (2) | Not applied |
| *Yongning* | 2008 | (1b) | (1b) | (1b) | (1b) | (1b) | Applied |
| *Shin-Etsu v Xinmao* | 2008 | (1a)(2) | / | (1a)(1b)(2) | / | (1a)(1b)(2) | Not applied |
| *China Medical* | 2009 | (2) | / | / | / | (2) | Not applied |
| *Noble* | 2009 | (2) | (2) | (2) | (2) | (2) | Not applied |

(continued)

[126] The result "/" represents that the discussion of public policy elements was not available. This may be for several reasons: it may be the absence of relevant material, or such information is not provided by any reported material, or omitted by the judges, or refused to be discussed by the judges; or otherwise, the discussions regarding public policy are too general to identify any elements from it.

[127] It is arguable that the *Heavy Metal* case can be counted for (1a) or (2), or both of them, as the language used in the original decision is not clear enough to provide an answer; therefore, in this paper, this case is counted twice for both grounds.

**Table 6** (continued)

| Short title | Year | Parties | IPC | HPC | SPC | Conclusion | Outcome |
|---|---|---|---|---|---|---|---|
| *GRD Minproc* | 2009 | (1b)(2) | (1a)(2) | (1a) | (1a) | (1a)(1b)(2) | Not applied |
| *Mongolia* | 2009 | / | / | / | (4) | (4) | Applied |
| *Yongxin* | 2009 | (4) | (4) | (4) | (4) | (4) | Not applied |
| *Leroy* | 2009 | (1a) | / | / | / | (1a) | Not applied |
| *Louis Dreyfus* | 2010 | (1b)(2) | (2) | (2) | (2) | (1b)(2) | Not applied |
| *Tianrui* | 2010 | (1a)(1b)(2) | (1b)(2) | (1a)(2) | (1b)(2) | (1a)(1b)(2) | Not applied |
| *Shin-Etsu v Zhongtian (No.2)* | 2010 | (1b)(2) | (1b)(2) | (1b) | / | (1b)(2) | Not applied |
| *Jiacheng* | 2011 | (1b)(4) | (1b)(4) | (4) | (4) | (1b)(4) | Applied |
| *Debao* | 2011 | / | / | (1a) | (1a) | (1a) | Not applied |
| *Western Bulk* | 2012 | / | / | (1a) | (1a) | (1a) | Not applied |
| *Zhongwei* | 2012 | (1b) | (4) | (1a) | / | (1a)(1b)(4) | Not applied |
| *Huludao Harbour* | 2012 | (1b)(2) | (1b)(2) | (1b) | (1b) | (1b)(2) | Not applied |
| *Kangwei* | 2012 | (1b) | (1b) | (1b) | (1b) | (1b) | Not applied |
| *Wanbang* | 2013 | Not specified | / | / | / | Not specified | Not applied |
| *Triangle* | 2013 | / | (1a) | / | / | (1a) | Not applied |
| *Hulishan* | 2013 | / | / | / | (2) | (2) | Applied |
| *Castel* | 2013 | (1b) | (1b) | (1b) | (1b) | (1b) | Not applied |
| *Chaolaixinsheng* | 2013 | (1b) | (1b) | (1b) | (1b) | (1b) | Not applied |
| *Siemens* | 2015 | (1b) | / | (1b) | (1b) | (1b) | Not applied |
| *Luntai* | 2015 | (2) | / | / | / | (2) | Not applied |
| *FSG Automotive* | 2015 | (2) | (2) | / | / | (2) | Not applied |
| *Spliethoff* | 2015 | (1b) | (1b) | (1b) | (1b) | (1b) | Not applied |
| *Dongcheng* | 2015 | (1b) | / | / | / | (1b) | Not applied |

(continued)

**Table 6** (continued)

| Short title | Year | Parties | IPC | HPC | SPC | Conclusion | Outcome |
|---|---|---|---|---|---|---|---|
| *Wicor* | 2016 | (1b) | (1b) | / | (1b) | (1b) | Applied |
| *J&D IB* | 2016 | (2) | (2) | (2) | (2) | (2) | Not applied |
| *Chenco* | 2016 | (1a) | (1a) | (1a) | / | (1a) | Not applied |
| *Bright* | 2017 | (1b)(2) | (1a)(2) | (2) | / | (1a)(1b)(2) | Not applied |
| *Sanmao* | 2017 | (2) | / | / | / | (2) | Not applied |
| *IP Cathay* | 2017 | (1a)(2) | / | / | / | (1a)(2) | Not applied |
| *Palmer* | 2018 | / | / | / | (1b) | (1b) | Applied |
| *Pixelplus* | 2018 | (1b) | / | / | / | (1b) | Not applied |
| *Triton* | 2018 | / | (2) | (1a)(2) | / | (1a)(2) | Not applied |
| *Gate* | 2019 | (1b) | / | / | (1b) | (1b) | Applied |
| *Zhang Lan* | 2020 | (1b) | / | / | (1b) | (1b) | Not applied |

**Table 7** The frequency and proportion of each element of public policy[128]

| Element | Frequency | % out of 55 cases |
|---|---|---|
| (1a) Substantive principles | 21 | 38.2 |
| (1b) Procedural principles | 24 | 43.6 |
| (2) *lois de police* | 21 | 38.2 |
| (3) International Obligations | 0 | 0 |
| (4) Arbitrability | 6 | 10.9 |

and 21 occasions respectively. These arguments may be favoured by the parties and courts because they are easily based upon the mandatory law and the broad coverage of abstract conceptions of fundamental substantive and procedural principles. The less frequently mentioned element is (4) arbitrability, on five occasions, and (3) international obligations was never used. The frequency of the discussion on arbitrability is lower and may be limited by the codified rules regulating arbitrability. It is particularly notable that in 14 out of 55 cases, more than one element of public policy is discussed; and in 2 cases, the detailed reasoning relating to public policy was not specified.

[128] As it is not uncommon for more than one element to be discussed in a case, the total of the rate of frequency is more than 100%.

**Table 8** Frequencies of reference to different elements of public policy

| Element | Frequency | Success | Percentage (%) |
|---|---|---|---|
| (1a) Substantial principles | 21 | 1 | 4.8 |
| (1b) Procedural principles | 24 | 4 | 16.7[129] |
| (2) *lois de police* | 21 | 2 | 9.5 |
| (3) International obligations | 0 | 0 | / |
| (4) Arbitrability | 6 | 4 | 66.7 |
| Not specified | 4 | 0 | 0 |

### 4.3.2 The Possibility of Success

The possibility of success in applying each public policy element is illustrated as in Table 8.

According to this result, the conclusion is that all of the elements of public policy are indicated by international consensus, except (3) international obligations, are discussed and applied.[130] The overall rate of application of each public policy element is generally low except for (4) arbitrability, which enjoys a high rate of application. With 4 cases, the application of (1b) procedural principles of law is also high, 3 of which are in the last decade (2016, 2018 and 2019). The arguments based on (1a) and (2), though favoured by parties and lower courts, are rarely confirmed by the SPC. However, this conclusion may not be a comprehensive description of China's current attitude towards public policy due to the limitations of the research methodology, as discussed in Sect. 3.1.

### 4.3.3 Developments in the Judicial Analysis of Each Element Over Time

In order to describe more precisely the development of each element in China's practice, the book further reviewed the changes in judicial attitudes towards public policy over time. According to records, the reference to the different elements of public policy and its successful application by Chinese courts are shown in Figs. 5, 6, 7 and 8.

[129] This result does not contain *Shin-Etsu (No. 2)* as it expressly excluded the application of public policy despite its application of *res judicata.* For further discussion of the principle of *res judicata,* see Chap. 6.

[130] For the elements of public policy, see Sects. 5 and 6 in Chap. 2.

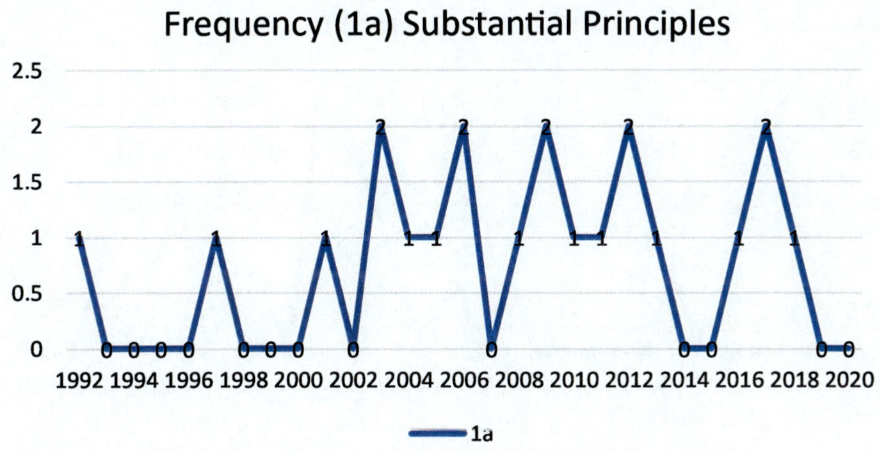


**Fig. 5** Frequency of discussions of (1a) substantial principles (1992–2020)

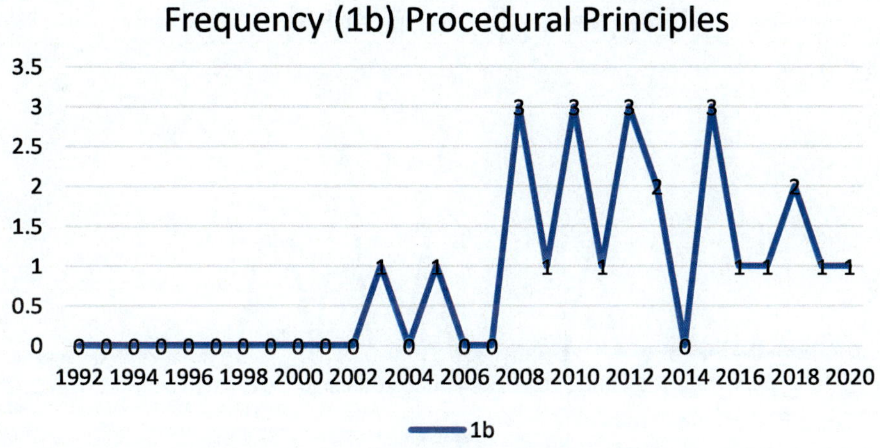


**Fig. 6** Frequency of discussions of (1b) procedural principles (1992–2020)

It is noted that the discussions of all elements are more frequent after 2000. While the discussion of (1a) has a minor increase from pre-2000 to post-2000, such increase for the discussions of (1b) and (2) is more significant, and the trend of increases for both is also observed during 2005–2010. The discussions of (4) appeared around 2000 and peaked between 2005 and 2015 but have ceased to occur in recent years.

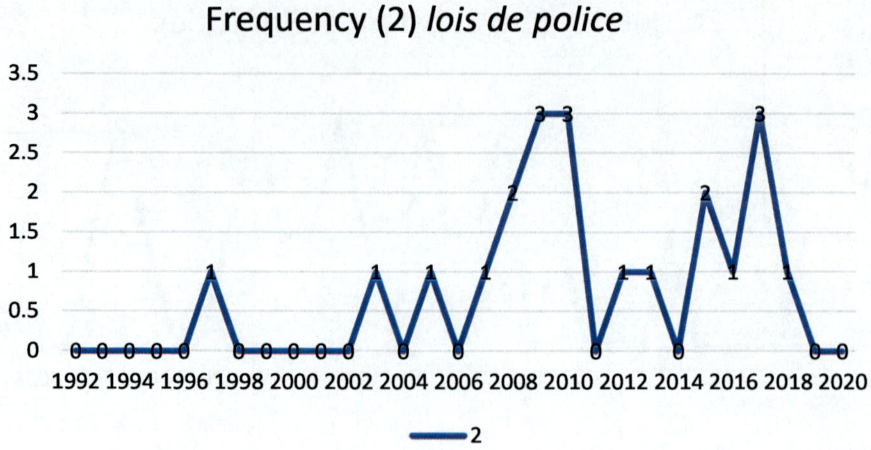


**Fig. 7** Frequency of discussions of (2) *lois de police* (1992–2020)

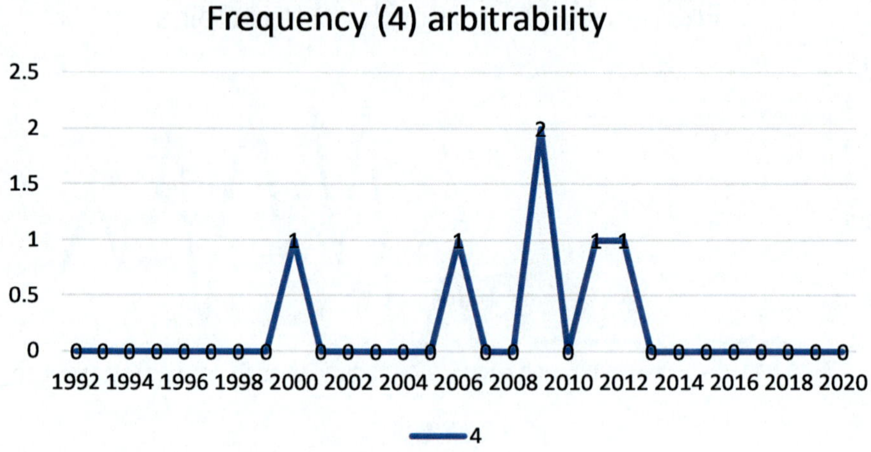


**Fig. 8** Frequency of discussions of (4) arbitrability (1992–2020)

### 4.3.4 Frequencies of the Discussion of the Different Elements, and *the Interaction Between Parties and Different Levels of Courts*

Table 9 presents the frequency with which public policy elements are raised by the parties and are discussed by the different levels of courts.

A primary observation is that most of the public policy elements are more frequently raised by the parties than by the courts. The parties initiated a large amount

**Table 9** Reported frequencies of public policy elements argued by parties and raised in each level of courts

| Element | Parties | IPC | HPC | SPC | Application |
|---|---|---|---|---|---|
| (1a) Substantive | 9 | 7 | 12 | 8 | 1 |
| (1b) Procedural | 21 | 11 | 11 | 13 | 4 |
| (2) *lois de police* | 16 | 12 | 11 | 10 | 2 |
| (3) International obligations | 0 | 0 | 0 | 0 | 0 |
| (4) Arbitrability | 3 | 4 | 3 | 5 | 4 |

of the public policy arguments and many of those arguments are included in subsequent analysis before the court. It is notable, however, that some of the public policy arguments raised by the parties are not responded to.

In addition, it is noteworthy that Element (2) *lois de police* is most frequently discussed by the parties, while all levels of Chinese courts discuss (2) *lois de police* and (1b) procedural principles in a similar frequency. The discussion of (1a) substantive principles is also significant. The least mentioned element was (4) arbitrability.

It is also interesting to trace how public policy elements were argued and responded to through the Prior Reporting System. It is significant that the HPC and SPC are reluctant to respond to the discussion of public policy elements, even when the parties have so argued and the lower courts have so reported, particularly in the discussion of (1b) procedural principles and (2) *lois de police.* There may be various reasons for the different rates of response. On the one hand, arguments of (1a) substantive principles, (1b) procedural principles and (2) *lois de police* may be deficient and clearly refused by the lower courts, and needed no further response from the higher courts; also, the SPC may specify the possible issues under (1b) procedural principles under other grounds, for example, under the procedural irregularity.[131]

Sometimes, however, the court would raise discussions of a different element of public policy despite the element not being mentioned by the parties or lower courts, as reflected in the discussion of (1a) substantive principles. As previously discussed, public policy is a ground which the court can apply "on its own motion". *GRD Minproc* clearly illustrates this phenomenon. While the parties argued for a breach of the principle of procedural fairness and impartiality in the evidence proceedings, and the violation of China's environment law, which fall in the scope of (1b) procedural principles and (2) *lois de police*, the opinions of the courts clearly go beyond these arguments. The Shanghai First IPC considered the violation of principle of substantial fairness (as part of (1a) substantive fundamental principles), and a breach of labour protection law (as part of (2) *lois de police*); the Shanghai HPC and the SPC discussed the principle of substantial fairness (1a) only.

[131] For example, in *Huludao Harbour* and *Beijing Kangwei.* See further discussions in Sect. 4 in Chap 6.

Similarly, in *Tianrui,* the Respondent argued the violation of China's mandatory law regulating a franchising business (under (2) *lois de police*), and that the arrangement of such an agreement breached the principle of good faith (1a); and also a violation of the jurisdiction of courts and the principle of *res judicata* (1b). These issues were not fully responded to by the courts. The Hangzhou IPC confirmed a breach of the regulation of franchising businesses that infringed upon China's fundamental economic interests, and violated the principle of *res judicata,* may give rise to the application of (1b) and (2). The Zhejiang HPC rejected the arguments of (2) but suggested the application of (1a) by finding Tianrui's breach of the principle of good faith. The SPC, instead, rejected the argument of (2) and (1b). None of the courts fully responded to the arguments raised by the parties, but rather developed their own reasoning. The courts' use of the discretion to not respond to discussions of one particular public policy element and initiate discussion of a new element also indicates that the mechanism of the Prior Reporting System is not an appeal.

The discussions of (4) arbitrability, on the other hand, is generally consistent. This may be based on the fact that the law governing arbitrability is reasonably clear in the context of the *CAL,* so the argument would be persuasive enough to gain the SPC's attention, or the SPC may be more confident to comment on the arbitrability issue. Alternatively, it may be argued that (4) arbitrability was not considered as a public policy element in China, and thus the public policy concerns underlying arbitrability were not fully recognised.[132]

## 4.4 Primary Observations Arising from the Cases

After a comprehensive review of the cases dealing with foreign-related and international arbitral awards, the following material conclusions are made.

First, the general trend to limit the application of public policy is adopted in the practices of Chinese courts, and particularly, in the functioning of the Prior Reporting System. This is evidenced by a relatively low rate of application of the public policy exception in general, at each level of courts, throughout the process of litigation, and in particular, a low rate of application of almost all major elements of public policy except arbitrability.

Second, Chinese courts have made progress in advancing their understanding of the public policy elements. This is represented by an increase in the judicial reference to almost every public policy element over the last three decades. This trend is also consistent with the Chinese courts' attempts to improve the quality of legal reasoning over the last few decades.[133] A general increase in the number of cases may also have contributed to the increase and may constitute one reason for the evolving judicial analysis of public policy.

---

132 See also, e.g., the *Mitsui case*. See further Chap. 8.

133 See above Chap. 3.

Third and more specifically, the frequencies of reference to different public policy elements vary, indicating an unbalanced trend in its development. Elements of public policy such as (1b) fundamental procedural principles and (2) *lois de police* are favoured both by the parties and the courts. The ways courts have scrutinised and applied these elements is explained through cases.[134] Arbitrability is also confirmed in some cases, yet the frequency of the discussion and application of this element is generally limited due to the restrictive approach adopted by the legislation that defines arbitrability.[135]

International obligations, another widely respected public policy element, is neither discussed nor applied in China's judicial practice. This may stem from a lack of sufficient opportunity or readiness among Chinese legal practitioners to argue this issue, and because of its sensitivity in the Chinese legal environment, or for both reasons. It is notable that the international relation and international obligation issues were rarely discussed in China, especially within the legal context. For example, the Chinese government avoided responding to the *South China Sea Arbitration* brought by Philippines.[136] Yet it is also observed that in the area of international commercial and investment law, the awareness of international obligations and super-national dispute resolution schemes is emerging in China. The Chinese government actively participated in several ICISD arbitration cases.[137] It is expected that in the near future the public policy element of international obligations can draw the attention of the Chinese legal practitioners as well as the Chinese judiciary.

The statistics confirm that the Prior Reporting System is not arranged as a system of appeal, making the Prior Reporting System is a double-edged sword. On one hand, the higher courts in the Chinese judicial system need not necessarily reply to every public policy concern raised by the lower courts; on the other hand, they may consider the public policy exception, or some specific elements of public policy which have not been raised by the parties or by lower courts. Thus, higher courts are not obliged to respond to public policy arguments; and may either avoid further argument on the subject or actively encourage it. In reality, however, ignorance of public policy analysis before Chinese courts is more frequently observed in cases than courts engaging in public policy analysis of their own volition.[138] This may indicate that Chinese courts, even higher courts, attempt to avoid analysis of public policy and do not feel confident in engaging in legal reasoning related to the application of public policy.

---

[134] See further Chaps. 5, 6 and 7.

[135] See further discussion in Chap. 8.

[136] See Stefan Talmon, Bing Bing Jia, *The South China Sea Arbitration: A Chinese Perspective* (Hart Publishing, 2014).

[137] See for example, *Ansung Housing Co., Ltd. v. People's Republic of China* (ICSID Case No. ARB/14/25); *AsiaPhos Limited and Norwest Chemicals Pte Ltd v People's Republic of China* (ICSID Case No. ADM/21/1).

[138] See discussions in Sect. 4.3.

Based on these primary observations, the author emphasises two factors that will be further discussed and analysed in subsequent chapters: first, the unbalanced development of public policy elements and second, a general reluctance among courts to initiate or engage in public policy analysis. The remainder of Part II will explore the reasons of these facts further. Part III will present proposals for developing such public policy analysis, including suggesting some solutions.

## 5 Conclusion

This chapter provides a comprehensive statistical description of Chinese arbitration practices and the judicial review of arbitral awards in general and illustrates the distinct features of the application of public policy in China's judicial review of foreign-related and international arbitral awards.

The general statistical description provides an overall picture of the emergence of the Chinese arbitration practice and the large number of cases on the judicial review of arbitral awards that has evolved in response to China's increasingly important position in the worldwide arbitration market.[139] A short summary of the empirical studies on the enforcement rate of arbitral awards further indicates the success of the Chinese judiciary in supporting China's possible approach towards public policy in relation to arbitral awards.[140] Based on these indications as the background of this research, the main body of this chapter has examined several aspects of public policy in the judicial review of foreign-related and international awards. These include: its developments over time, the development of different public policy elements, and the role of the parties and different levels of courts in providing arguments and analyses of public policy.

Some generally positive observations can be drawn from this statistical study. First, the legal concept of public policy has gradually gained the attention of legal practitioners and the Chinese judiciary; the frequency of public policy discussion in Chinese cases has increased significantly after the year 2000, and the legal reasoning in later cases is provided for in significant detail. The development of each public policy element is also consistent with general trends in the development of public policy in China's practice. Secondly, Chinese courts, especially the SPC, have adopted a narrow approach to public policy and limited the application of this legal concept. The number of cases in which public policy is applied is small, and particularly so in comparison with the number of cases in which other grounds for annulment or non-enforcement are applied.

Yet it must be admitted that the Chinese judiciary's achievements in developing the legal concept of public policy is far from satisfactory. Given the low number of cases in which public policy is discussed, guidance provided by and to practitioners and the Chinese judiciary arising from these cases is far from sufficient. The notion

139 Section 2.

140 Section 3.

of considering public policy as a residual ground and the enormous discretion of the courts under the Prior Reporting System have all contributed to the insufficient public policy discussion and the limited development of public policy before Chinese courts.

The chapter has observed that the different elements of public policy have developed unevenly. While cases discussing the fundamental principles (especially the procedural ones) and *lois de police* are substantial, no cases have referred to international obligations. Also, it is notable that arbitrability is frequently applied. The following chapters in Part II (Chapters Five to Eight), will engage in a further review of the development of each key element of public policy and will include a detailed analysis of the Chinese courts' performance in dealing with these public policy elements.

# Chapter 5
# Substantive Notions, Public Morals and Fundamental Principles Under Public Policy

## 1 Introduction

As introduced in earlier chapters, one of the key elements of public policy in the judicial review of arbitral awards is the element of fundamental principles of law (Element (1)).[1] This element can be further divided into (1a), substantive fundamental principles, and (1b) procedural fundamental principles.[2] The substantive fundamental principles are dealt with in this chapter, while the procedural issues will be discussed in Chap. 6.

Before analysing the relevant law and cases relating to substantive fundamental principles, this chapter will initially distinguish between Element (1a), substantive principles of law, and Element (2), *lois de police*, the latter of which are to be further discussed in Chap. 7. There is consensus in the international community that both the notion of justice and/or morality and public policy rules are major elements of public policy; and they are distinct from each other.[3] The substantive fundamental principles refer to the basic morality and principles of substantive fairness and justice, which is abstract and sometimes implied, while the public policy rules focus on the interests of a nation represented by its law in the form of legislation and regulations.[4]

---

[1] Section 5 in Chap. 2.

[2] Section 5 in Chap. 2; for the division of substantive and procedural aspects of public policy, see also Report of the United Nations Commission on International Trade Law on the Work of Its Eighteenth Session, UN GAOR, 40th sess., UN Doc A/40/17, (21 June 1985) [297], [303].

[3] Pierre Mayer and Audley Sheppard, 'Final Report on Public Policy as a Bar to Enforcement of International Arbitral Awards' (2003) 19 *Arbitration International* 249 ('The ILA Report' hereafter), Recommendation 1(d).

[4] See further Sect. 2 in Chap. 7. Also, a possible consequence of such distinction is that court may apply different standards to decide whether they would re-open the discussion of the underlying disputes or accept new facts and evidence in dealing with a violation of (substantive) fundamental principles of law on the one hand, and in dealing with a breach of public policy rules on the other hand.



S. Zhang, *The Public Policy Exception in the Judicial Review of International Commercial Arbitral Awards*, https://doi.org/10.1007/978-3-662-67679-0_5

An example of the former is the principle of good moral, which is quite abstract, while an example of the latter, for instance, a mandatory law protecting market competition, is straightforward and governed directly by legislation. Yet both of these two elements guard the State's substantive interests and some scrutiny is required to identify whether the interests protected by either the principles or the rules of national law are considered to be fundamental and essential enough for the principles of public policy to apply. Some of such scrutinies may arise in applying to both substantive (1a) fundamental principles and (2) *lois de police*. Based on this understanding, the establishment of such scrutiny is to be discussed in this chapter, and then developed further in Chap. 7.

This chapter reviews the application of substantive fundamental principles and national interests in the judicial review of arbitral awards. This chapter is organised as follows: Sect. 2 outlines the general developments relating to the application of the substantive fundamental principles of law. Sections 3, 4 and 5 deal with the possible concepts of substantive fundamental principles of law, including the notions of fairness and justice, good morals and public order, and fundamental national interests. A review of the cases reveals a distinctive Chinese approach to these concepts, as concluded in Section 6.

## 2 Overview of the Developments of Substantive Fundamental Principles

### *2.1 International Developments in Defining the Substantive Notions and Principles of Public Policy*

It has long been recognised that the application of the public policy exception in international arbitration includes substantive public policy, such as the substantive fundamental principles of law, notions of public morality, and national interest. However, the terms used to describe these substantive elements may vary in different contexts of arbitration and judicial practice. One example is the often cited quotation from *Parsons & Whittemore*,[5] which states that the public policy exception that serves to deny the enforcement of a foreign arbitral award can be applied "only where enforcement would violate the forum state's most basic notions of morality and justice".[6] Also, as we observe from the drafting history of the *NYC*, "fundamental principles of law" come within the definition of public policy.[7] Nevertheless, even long after the

[5] *Parsons & Whittemore Overseas Co Inc. v. Société Générale de l'Industrie du papier* (*RAKTA*), 508 F.2d 969 (2d Cir. 1974).

[6] Ibid.

[7] Anton G. Maurer, *The Public Policy Exception under the New York Convention* (Juris, 2012) 37–46. For example, Mr. Coloma-Silva (Ecuador) stated that, the reference to "incompatibility with public policy" is sufficient without further mentioning the fundamental principles of law. See Summary Record of the Second Meeting, U.N.Doc.E/CONF.26/SR.2, at 10; In the final discussion

enactment of *NYC*, the possible scope of the substantive fundamental principles of law has not been clearly defined. Thus, before a thorough discussion is undertaken, the author will initially review a few limitations affecting the development of this element of public policy.

First, the pro-enforcement trend in regard to the enforcement of arbitral awards, which is widely accepted in international practice,[8] limits the discussion and application of public policy, especially when dealing with issues relating to the substance of the arbitral award. The international consensus is that the national court would generally respect the finality of the arbitral award,[9] and courts are generally cautious when applying public policy, and especially when deciding whether they should examine the subject matter or substance of the arbitral award.[10]

Secondly, it is a major question for the courts as to whether a notion or principle is "fundamental" enough to be considered as public policy of a state before finding any breach of such principle. The national law or courts must first identify the particular types or categories of substantive fundamental principles and such a decision is made within the context of a particular legal system. For example, the *Swiss Private International Law Act (1987)* requires the identification of particular fundamental principles being violated when setting aside an arbitral award.[11] These include such principles as *pacta sunt servanda* (the sanctity of promises), the prohibition of the misuse of the law, the principle of good faith, the prohibition of uncompensated expropriation, the prohibition of discrimination and the protection of those incapable to act.

Because the task of identification and definition of the substantive fundamental principles is fulfilled by national courts based on each distinct judicial environment, the outcomes may vary from one jurisdiction to another. For example, understandings regarding the term "fundamental principles of law" are clearly divided between the common law and civil law jurisdictions.[12] As observed by Sheppard, the use of

---

of the public policy clause, the suggestions to add "fundamental principles of the law (*ordre public*)" by Brazil and agreed to by some other delegates, was finally rejected by vote at the 1958 Conference (the 17th Meeting, June 3 and 4). See UNDocE/CONF.26/SR.17, 15.

[8] For example, see Albert Jan van den Berg, *The New York Convention of 1958: Towards a Uniform Judicial Interpretation* (Kluwer Law International, 1981) 265; Fora review of the "pro-enforcement bias" adopted by the US courts, see Joseph T. McLaughlin and Laurie Genevro, 'Enforcement of Arbitral Awards under the New York Convention—Practice in U.S. Courts' (1986) 3 *International Tax and Business Law* 249; See also Sect. 3.1 in Chap. 2.

[9] Audley Sheppard, 'Interim Report on Public Policy as a Bar to Enforcement of International Arbitral Awards' (2000) 19(3) *Arbitration International* 217, 232–35.

[10] *Parsons & Whittemore*, 508 F 2d. Discussion of the extent of judicial review, see Sect. 4 in Chap. 9.

[11] Robert Briner, 'Switzerland' in Jan Paulsson (ed), *International Handbook on Commercial Arbitration* (Kluwer International, 1992) 13.

[12] Maurer, above n 7, 24–49. In the drafting history of *the New York Convention*, the term "fundamental principles of law" is frequently debated. While the representatives from civil law jurisdictions such as Sweden recognised the meaning and favoured the inclusion of this term, the common law jurisdictions, such as England, were against the term, as the "fundamental" principles were not meaningful and were difficult to distinguish from other rules of law in the English jurisdiction.

good faith as an element of "fundamental principles of law" in some jurisdictions is significant; while in others, the reference to the principles of good faith is unusual.[13] Another example relates to the award of punitive damages: while courts in Switzerland consider awarding punitive damages to be against public policy, some US courts do not take that approach.[14]

Yet the *ILA Interim Report* demonstrates some degree of consensus and lists several categories of substantive public policy, including the substantive fundamental principles of law; good morals/public order; and possibly, national interests/foreign relations.[15] The *ILA Final Report* also recognises that one major category of public policy is: "*fundamental principles, pertaining to justice or morality, that the State wishes to protect even when it is not directly concerned*", and includes both substantive and procedural ones.[16] It refers to several examples of substantive fundamental principles, including: protection of good faith and prohibition of abuse of rights; *pacta sunt servanda*; prohibition against uncompensated expropriation; prohibition against discrimination, and the prohibition of activities that are *contra bonos mores*, including "the proscription against piracy, terrorism, genocide, slavery, smuggling, drug trafficking, and paedophilia",[17] and bribery and corruption.[18]

The *ILA Final Report* also notes that it is the national standard of the particular enforcing state regarding the fundamental principles that is to be considered in the application[19]; but the court may also take into consideration of the international consensus in order to find a sufficiently fundamental principle. In other words, the court might possibly consider international or even "transnational" public policy rather than the purely domestic public policy standard in seeking to determine the fundamentality of these principles, which might be evidenced by international conventions or agreements.[20] Examples are listed by the *ILA Report* to establish the standard of fundamentality, including: "fundamental rules of natural law; principles of universal justice; *jus cogens* in public international law; general

[13] Sheppard, above n 9, 234, citing *Republique de Cote d'Ivoire v Norbert Beyrard* (1993) Rev Arb 685, 12 Jan 1993.

[14] Sheppard, above n 9, 238–42, provides a comparison between *ICC Case No. 5946*, where an award with punitive damages was held against Swiss public policy, and *Willis v Sherson and American Express Inc* 569 F Supp 821 (DCNC, 1983), where the arbitrability of punitive damages was confirmed in the United States. Furthermore, the award with punitive damages was found also enforceable under US law. See also Sheppard, above n 9, n 102.

[15] Sheppard, above n 9, IV.B. Regarding the national interests in the context of international relations, they may also be covered by the element of international obligations. See Sect. 5 in Chap. 2.

[16] Mayer and Sheppard, above n 3, Recommendation 1(d).

[17] Mayer and Sheppard, above n 3, [28].

[18] Mayer and Sheppard, above n 3, [32]; bribery and corruption are considered not only covered by the *contra bonos mores*, but may also be covered under national laws and international agreements, so may fall into more than one category. In this book, the author discusses this issue only under this category as the issue of corruption is not particularly raised in either the public policy rule case or the international obligation cases in China.

[19] Mayer and Sheppard, above n 3, Recommendation 2(a).

[20] Mayer and Sheppard, above n 3, Recommendation 2(b) and [40–43]. For the discussion of transnational public policy, also see Sect. 4 in Chap. 2.

principles of morality accepted by what are referred to as "civilised nations".[21] Cases supporting the admission of alleged transnational public policy in recognising substantial fundamental principles, however, are rare.

## 2.2 *The Overview of China's Approach in Defining Substantive Fundamental Principles*

The particular focus in this chapter is to review China's practice regarding the substantive principles of public policy, including the fundamental principles of law, the notion of justice, and public morality. Many Chinese scholars refer to the public policy exception by listing its substantive elements. Judge Gao's categorisation includes:

> (a) The fundamental spirit of China's Constitutional Law; (b) China's sovereignty and national safety; ...(d) the principle of fairness and justice that is recognised in international law; (e) legal rules that constitute fundamental principles in China, such as the principle of good faith and honesty in contract law, the anti-terrorism law, the law against cults, traffic in persons, money-laundering and gambling; (f) the basic morality requirement of China to protect decency; and (g) the fundamental and overall interest of China.[22]

Judge Cui adds the concepts of "the Four Fundamental Principles" and "national unity and the solidarity among different ethnic groups".[23] Tao and Wunschheim also refer to public policy as:

> (a) the basic principles reflected in the Constitution or the Four Fundamental Principles of China; (b) the sovereignty or State security of China; (c) the fundamental rules of Chinese law; and (d) the obligations that China undertook in the international treaties that China concluded or against the publicly recognised principle of fairness or justice in international law.[24]

These categorisations exhibit a strong preference for respecting China's political values, system and notions. The fundamental aspects of China's state sovereignty, such as the principles in the Constitution, national unity and national safety, the political system and notions such as the Four Fundamental Principles, are all considered to attract the application of public policy. However, these elements focus on political

---

[21] Mayer and Sheppard, above n 3, [43].

[22] 高晓力 [Gao Xiaoli],《国际私法上公共政策的运用》[The Functioning of Public Policy in Private International Law] (中国民主法制出版社 [China Democracy and Rule of Law Press], 2008) 131, translated by the author. The clause (c) is omitted because it is irrelevant to the substantive fundamental principles of law.

[23] The Four Fundamental Principles of China are: (i) to adhere to the Socialist road, (ii) to adhere to the people's democratic dictatorship, (iii) to adhere to the leadership of the Communist Party, and (iv) to adhere to Marxism-Leninism and Mao's thought. See Jingzhou Tao, 'Enforcement of SCC Arbitration Awards in China', in Kaj Hobér, Annette Magnusson and Marie Öhrström (eds), *Between East and West: Essays in Honour of Ulf Franke* (2010), nn 25.

[24] Clarisse von Wunschheim, *Enforcement of Commercial Arbitral Awards in China: Business Laws of China* (West, 2011) 283; Tao, Above n 23, 12.

interests rather than private law and are not closely related to arbitration practice. It is understandable that a State's political system, notions and values are crucial and will generally be protected. However, their practical significance in the particular context of international commercial arbitration should not be over-estimated, as they are rarely dealt with in contractual or commercial disputes that are arbitrated; alternatively, even if such political elements are involved, as shown in *Parsons*,[25] such political elements should be carefully dealt with and should generally be distinguished from the underlying disputes.[26]

Furthermore, these lists and categories do not provide sufficient guidance to arbitration practitioners and the judiciary. The terms referred to by these categories, for example, "the fundamental rules of Chinese law", or the reference to the principles of fairness and justice, are broad and ambiguous; they are not defined in legislation or through any judicial interpretation. The international consensus, which provides detailed categories of substantive fundamental principles of law, is not well represented in the categories listed above.

A general review of scholars' opinions shows a lack of sufficient interpretation and depth of understanding of the substantive fundamental principles of law in China, particularly those principles that would be applicable to commercial disputes. Yet the categories suggested by the scholars at least identified a few key principles, including the State's sovereignty and political interests, the notion of fairness and justice, public morality, and the overall interests of the State. Based on this understanding, the next sections of this chapter will examine some of these elements as they are discussed by the Chinese judiciary.

## 3 Substantive Fairness and Justice

The principle of fairness and justice has long been accepted as part of public policy. However, applying the principle of substantive fairness and justice in the judicial review of arbitral awards may result in a substantive review of the merits of the dispute which is questionable under the pro-enforcement purpose of the *NYC*.[27] Thus, the courts, when making their decisions, often need to balance the finality of the award on the one hand, and their appreciation of the value of substantive fairness and justice on the other.

---

[25] 508 F.2d 969 (2d Cir. 1974).

[26] See further discussions of the details of the Parsons Case in Sect. 5.1.

[27] Maurer, above n 7, 37, 46. Also, a discussion of the possible judicial review of the merits or substance of a case, see Sect. 4 in Chap. 9.

### 3.1 International Practices and Controversies

In limited situations, the principle of substantive fairness and justice has been dealt with by some national courts in the judicial review of arbitral awards; but the issues are still quite controversial.

One example previously mentioned regarding the substantive fairness and justice of the award, is whether punitive damages can be ordered in relation to an arbitral award. In an early case, a Swiss court found that punitive damages, which were not for the purpose of compensation, were actually a punishment against one party, and therefore against Swiss law and public policy.[28] A similar ruling occurred in an early case in the United States.[29]

Nevertheless, claims of punitive damages have been upheld in other jurisdictions, particularly in common law jurisdictions[30] and might be acceptable in arbitration practice.[31] Even in the US, a later case provided that the enforceability of an international or foreign arbitral award rendering punitive damages should be distinguished from purely domestic awards and may be upheld.[32] This attitude indicates that the US courts sometimes prioritise the finality of arbitration practice over their tendency to discourage punitive damages generally.[33] This point of view is also promoted by many scholars.[34] It is also notable that these discussions largely focus on whether

---

[28] *Seller v Buyer*, Final Award, ICC Case No. 5946, 1990, reported in (1991) 16 *Yearbook—Commercial Arbitration* 97, 118.

[29] *Larminoirs-Trefilieries-Cableries de Lens, S.A. v Southwire Co.*, 484 F Sup 1063, 1069 (US District Court for the Northern District of Georgia, 1980).

[30] The significant example is the US law; also accepted in Australia for particular types of cases, eg. fraud (*XL Petroleum NSW Pty Ltd v Caltex Oil (Aust) Pty Ltd* (1985) 155 CLR 448) and deliberate misstatement in a policy of insurance (*Lamb v Cotogno* (1987) 74 ALR 188). Also see Markus Petsche, 'Punitive Damages in International Commercial Arbitration: Much Ado about Nothing?' (2013) 29(1) *Arbitration International* 89, 93, n 27, citing John Y. Gotanda, 'Punitive Damages: A Comparative Analysis' (2003) 42 *Columbia Journal of Transnational Law* 391.

[31] *Willis* 569 F Supp (DCNC 1983); this case confirmed the arbitrability of claims of punitive damages under the federal law of the United States. However, case law under the *New York Convention* or *UNCITRAL Model Law* remains rare. Petsche, above n 30, 99–100.

[32] Ward, 'In the Matter of an Arbitration between Marco Barbier and Shearon Lehman Hutton Inc' (1991) 6 *Mealey's International Arbitration Reports* 14, B1. The author is a judge in the District Court of the Southern District of New York. He distinguished the enforceability of a foreign award rendering punitive damages from *Garrity v Lyly Stuart Inc* 40 NY 2d 354 (1976), in which the enforcement of a domestic award with punitive damages was refused. See also Sheppard, above n 9, 245–248.

[33] See Sheppard, above n 9, 245–248.

[34] Van den Berg, above n 8, 360; Allan Farnsworth, 'Punitive Damages in Arbitration' (1990–1991) 20 *Stetson Law Review* 395, 407; the author stated that the punitive damages would not violate the "international" public policy, even in countries where such a remedy is not available in domestic law. Yet there are other scholars who consider that the enforceability of an award of punitive damages would be problematic in civil law countries, or even in England, where punitive damages are not generally accepted in domestic law, or not available for contractual disputes. See also Niccolo Pietro Castagno, 'International Commercial Arbitration and Punitive Damages' (2011) 4 *Revista*

such an award itself constitutes a violation of public policy, rather than whether there is a violation of public policy in relation to the merits of a case.

Despite the possible inconsistent practices in different jurisdictions with respect to ordering punitive damages, the general trend across jurisdictions is that the judicial review rarely deals with the issues of substantive fairness and justice arising in the cases. National courts generally respect the finality of the arbitral award and are reluctant to go beyond the award, and as such the judicial review process leaves little space for a thorough evaluation of the substantive fairness or justice of the matter.[35] Consistent with this trend, an argument based on the fraud underlying a contract or transaction, is itself not considered a violation of public policy. Distinguished from a fraudulent arbitration,[36] fraud in an underlying contract relating to the merits of the case should be reviewed by the tribunal; courts, on the other hand, should resist the urge to review the merits if such a claim has already been dealt with by the tribunal.[37]

### *3.2 Reflections on China*

There are some cases in which the Chinese courts dealt with substantive fairness and justice issues raised by the parties. The following cases illustrate the approach taken by the Chinese courts.

- *Glencore*

The IPC reviewing this case opined that Glencore unjustly benefited from the arbitral award by taking advantage of the contract and its arbitration clause, which had not actually been formed, and which was also against the public policy. The majority opinion in the HPC agreed to this ruling, while the minority view was that the substance of the award should not be reviewed at the enforcement stage. The SPC refused the enforcement of the award on the basis of no valid arbitration agreement and avoided any further comments on the public policy matter. It is possible that the SPC considered it was not necessary to apply public policy in this case, given the

---

*de Arbitraje Comercial y de Inversiones* 729, 747; Alan Redfern et al., *Redfern and Hunter on International Arbitration* (Oxford University, 2009) 530–531.

[35] One example is that the English court limits the re-opening of the facts of the dispute; see *Westacre Investments Inc v Jugoimport SDPR Holding Co Ltd* [1999] 2 Lloyd's Rep 65. For the discussion regarding the extent of the judicial review, see further Sect. 4.3 in Chap. 9.

[36] See further the discussion of fraudulently obtained contracts in Chap. 6 and Sect. 4.3 in Chap. 9.

[37] Dirk Otto and Omaia Elwan, 'Article V(2)' in Herbert Kronke et al. (eds), *Recognition and Enforcement of Foreign Arbitral Awards* (Wolter Kluwer, 2010) 345, 375, citing *KarahaBodas Co. LLC v Perusahaan Pertambangan Minyak Dan Gas Bumi Negara* [2007] HKCA 429 (Court of Appeal, Hong Kong), also reported in (2008) 33 *Yearbook—Commercial Arbitration* 574); *Europcar Italia S.p.A. v Maiellano Tours Inc.*, (1998) 156 F 3d 310, 315(US Court of Appeals for the 2nd Circuit, US) also reported in (1999) 29(a) *Yearbook—Commercial Arbitration* 860, 865.

enforcement of this award could be refused on the grounds of an invalid arbitration agreement.

- *Xiangjin*

The contract between Xiangjin and Anhui Oil was signed by Zhang Genjie, who stole the documents from Anhui Oil, forged the seals, and represented himself as an agent of Anhui Oil. A dispute arose in relation to the performance of this contract, and HKIAC rendered its award in favour of Xiangjin, who consequently sought enforcement. Both the Hefei IPC and the Anhui HPC preferred to reject such enforcement based on a violation of public policy. They were of the opinion that, given that the consent of Anhui Oil to the contract was forged, such a contract should not be binding on Anhui Oil; thus, to hold Anhui Oil responsible "would be against the aims and purpose of the civil laws in China, would violate the fundamental principles of voluntariness, fairness, equality and honesty in civil and commercial activities, and would disturb the economic order and infringe the public interest".[38]

Similar to *Glencore*, the SPC opined to refuse enforcement of such an award but was reluctant to apply the public policy exception and based its decision on the invalidity of the arbitration agreement instead.[39] The SPC further stated that it was inappropriate to apply the ground of public policy but did not provide any reason for this statement.

- *Weimao*

The ICC award favoured the Hong Kong party regarding a contractual dispute in this case. The Chinese party at the enforcement stage argued that the enforcement would let the Hong Kong party take possession of USD 410,000 worth of goods and also entitle them to damages of up to USD 330,000, which would be a result significantly contrary to the notion of fairness and justice "as a fundamental value of the law and the society".[40] The Shanxi HPC and the SPC did not accept this argument, finding that the claim was unfounded.[41]

- *Shin-Etsu v Xinmao*

The party resisting the enforcement of the award argued that the enforcement of the award would be assisting the anti-dumping activities of the Japanese party and against the decision of the Chinese Ministry of Commerce (MOFCOM). It further argued that such outcome would be against the fundamental principles in civil law such as fairness, equality and mutual benefit, good faith, and prohibition of the abuse of rights. The argument relating to substantive fairness was also picked up by Tianjin

---

38 Citing the opinion of Hefei IPC.

39 The *Hong Kong Arrangements*, art 7 (1).

40 林一飞 [Lin Yifei],《公共政策作为抗辩仲裁裁决的一项理由》[Public Policy as a Defense Against an Arbitral Award], at <http://www.cnarb.com/Article/swzn/200807/4492.html>, 15 July 2008.

41 Ibid.

HPC. This argument, however, was not commented by the SPC, which refused the enforcement on the ground of the breach of natural justice.

- *Western Bulk*

In this case, the Tianjin HPC, in its report to the SPC, highlighted its public policy concerns, stating that the tribunal's decision requiring the Chinese party to pay for damages that did not exist and were not covered by the contracts was an obvious violation of fairness, and was detrimental to the interests of the Chinese party and China's social public interest. The SPC found that this opinion was "inappropriate" as it evaluated the substantive outcome of the discussion. The SPC further emphasised that the public policy exception should only apply in circumstances where there was a violation of fundamental legal principles, a violation of the State's sovereignty, damaging the State's and the social public safety, or a violation of good morals.

- *Chenco*

In this case, the parties argued that the damages awarded by the tribunal were much too high and therefore punitive in nature. Such argument was supported by the IPC which stated that the punitive damages would be against the fundamental principles in the Chinese law of remedies. Such reasoning, however, was rejected by the Henan HPC by referring to the tribunal's power to determine the amount of damages and the parties' obligation to respect such determination when they choose to arbitrate. The court also stated that the amount of damages awarded should not be referred to in assessing whether China's public policy was violated. It is notable that this reasoning was repeatedly used by lower courts in cases handed down in the past decade when dealing with punitive damages, like in *Ecom No.* 1 (2016)[42] and *GS Global* (2017).[43]

- *Triton*

Both the Haikou Maritime Court and the Hainan HPC were of the opinion that the arbitral award was inconsistent with the rules in the Chinese bankruptcy law and therefore would infringe the interests of other debtors and breach the principle of substantive fairness. Such submissions, however, was rejected by the SPC.[44]

In addition to the cases mentioned above, similar rulings were also found in cases determined by lower courts. For example, arguments based on excessive or

---

[42]《EcoM Agro-industrial 申请承认和执行外国仲裁裁决民事裁定书》[Decision on the Application for the Recognition and Enforcement of A Foreign Arbitral Awards by Ecom Agro-industrial Corp Ltd Switzerland], Shenzhen IPC, (2014) 深中法涉外初字第60号 [Foreign-related First Instance No. 60], 25 May 2016.

[43] GS Global Corporation (佳施国际株式会社)诉上海市振戎石油有限公司申请承认和执行外国仲裁裁决一案民事裁定书》[Civil Ruling on the Application for the Recognition and Enforcement of a Foreign Arbitral Award between GS Global Corporation and Shanghai Zhenrong Oil Corp], Shanghai 1st IPC, (2016) 沪01协外认12号 [Judicial Assistance Foreign Recognition No. 12], 22 February 2017.

[44] The SPC referred to an earlier reply which they did not publish on the public policy matters ([2016] 最高法民他5号). In the final ruling, the Haikou Maritime Court simply stated that the award was not against China's public policy. Thus, we are unable to extract more detailed analysis provided by the SPC when rejecting this argument.

punitive damages were consistently rejected by courts in cases like *GS Global*[45] and *Henghao.*[46]

### 3.3 Analysis

The discussion in Chinese judicial practice, as provided by the cases discussed above, is not in line with international practice. Generally, in international practice, the application of substantive fairness and justice is quite limited and very controversial in the judicial review of international commercial arbitral awards. While in Chinese practice, discussions of substantive fairness and justice from the original disputes are frequently made, either by the parties, or by the lower court on its own motion. In *Weimao, Shin-Estu v Xinmao* and *Western Bulk*, the arguments were based on the evaluation of the fairness and justice of the substantive outcome of the award. In *Glencore and Xiangjin*, the arguments were based on flawed or fraudulent underlying transactions.

None of these arguments established in China's lower courts have been confirmed by the SPC. This may indicate that a "no merit review" attitude is adopted, and the substantive fairness is never applied as an element of public policy. However, the approach adopted by Chinese courts fails to distinguish between the substantive aspects of the underlying disputes on one hand and the fairness of the awards on the other.[47]

## 4 Good Morals/Public Order

### 4.1 International Practice in Defining Good Morals and Public Order

The *ILA Interim Report* reports several examples of *contra bonos mores*, including piracy, terrorism, genocide, slavery, smuggling, drug trafficking and paedophilia. This category of substantive public policy is further confirmed in the *ILA Final*

---

[45]《GS Global Corporation (佳施国际株式会社)诉上海市振戎石油有限公司申请承认和执行外国仲裁裁决一案民事裁定书》[Civil Ruling on the Application for the Recognition and Enforcement of a Foreign Arbitral Award between GS Global Corporation and Shanghai Zhenrong Oil Corp], Shanghai 1st IPC, (2016) 沪01协外认12号 [Judicial Assistance Foreign Recognition No. 12], 22 February 2017.

[46] 执行申请人奥卓布克有限公司与被申请人红河恒昊矿业股份有限公司执行异议执行裁定书》[Ruling on Enforcement Dispute between the Applicant Ultrabulk A/S and the Respondent Honghe Henghao Mining Co], Kunming IPC, (2017) 云01执异54号 [Enforcement Dispute No. 54], 18 September 2017.

[47] See further Sect. 4 in Chap. 9.

*Report*.[48] In this book, they are summarised as good morals and public order. One illustration of the concerns regarding good morals and public order is the famous case of *Soleimany*,[49] where the arbitral award dealt with a contract between father and son regarding smuggling carpets out of Iran in breach of Iranian law. The arbitrator applied Jewish law and confirmed the proceeds of such dealing, but the UK court later refused to recognise the award on the ground of a violation of UK's public policy. Other illustrations of public order or good morals include the bribery and corruption of public officials.[50]

The developments of different categories of good morals vary. The most significant and universally accepted notion of good morals is the prevention of corruption and bribery, and it is even arguable that there is an international public policy against corruption and bribery in commercial dealings.[51] Thus, in many cases, an award dealing with such a matter is held as not enforceable because of the violation of public policy.[52] Good morals, such as the anti-terrorism policy, are also universally accepted in most countries; while other categories of good morals may not be universally accepted, and may be dealt with differently in different jurisdictions based on the distinctive considerations or on the particular legal environment in that jurisdiction. For example, gambling is respected as a legal contract in some jurisdictions, but in others, gambling is considered as a serious breach of the State's public morality or social order.[53] Some other notions and rules of morality are limited to particular jurisdictions, for example, the Muslim *Shari'a* in Muslim society; an arbitral award against the Muslim *Shari'a* may not be enforced in Muslim jurisdictions such as Kuwait or Saudi Arabia.[54]

The application of good morals or public order is also limited by the extent of the judicial review. In *Westacre Investments Inc v Jugoimport-SPDR Holding Co Ltd*,[55] the losing party claimed the contract was obtained through bribes in Kuwait

---

48 Sheppard, above n 9, 249–51; Mayer and Sheppard, above n 3, [28].

49 *Soleimany v Soleimany*, [1998] 3 WLR 811, [1999] QB 785 (CA).

50 For example, see *Westacre Investments Inc v Jugoimport-SPDR Holdings Co Ltd and Others* [1999] 2 Lloyd's Rep 65; [2000] QB 288 (CA); *European Gas Turbines SA v Westman International Ltd*, Rev Arb 359 (1994), also reported in (1995) 20 *Yearbook—Commercial Arbitration* 198; Julian D. M. Lew, Loukas A. Mistelis and Stefan Michael Kröll, *Comparative International Commercial Arbitration* (Kluwer Law International, 2003) 423, n 47.

51 For example, see *The Convention on Combating the Bribery of Foreign Officials in International Transactions*, OECD, signed 17 December 1997, 31 ILM 1 (entered into force 15 February 1999).

52 Sheppard, above n 9, 240–245.

53 Ibid.

54 For example, the cases granting legal interests under Egyptian or Syrian law, contractual interests under Libyan law, or profits, or rendered by non-Muslim arbitrators, or dealing with aleatory contracts, may be considered at least partially against the Muslim Shari'a and may be denied enforcement in Kuwait or Saudi Arabia. See Jalal El-Ahdab, 'General Introduction on Arbitration in Arab Countries', in (1998) 27 *International Handbook on Commercial Arbitration*, Annex 1, 23; Jalal El-Ahdab, 'Saudi Arabia Accedes to the New York Convention' (1994) 11 *Journal of International Arbitration* 87; Jalal El-Ahdab, 'Arbitration in Saudi Arabia under the New Arbitration Act 1983' (1986) 3 *Journal of International Arbitration* 23.

55 [1998] 4 All ER 570, [1999] QB 740, [1998] 3 WLR 770.

and an award upholding such contract would breach the fundamental principle of law. A UK court recognised the public policy against international corruption but refused to re-open the facts of a case based on the notion that the value of finality of international arbitral awards should outweigh the concerns about corruption and bribery under the particular circumstances of that case.[56]

## 4.2 *Practice in China*

Very few Chinese cases deal with the issue of good morals or public order.

- *Heavy Metal*

In this case, the US party employed actors and singers to perform in China based on a Contract of Performance with the Chinese party, which provided that the actors should obey the relevant rules and regulations in China, and that the Chinese authorities were entitled to review and approve the details of the performance before it took place. An American band did not follow the performance details that were previously approved by the Ministry of Culture and performed heavy metal music. The Ministry considered the music was "not appropriate" in accordance with the social environment of China and against China's social public interests and consequently cancelled the remainder of the band's performances. The band could therefore not perform in accordance with the contract and did not get payment from the Chinese party. The US party brought arbitration before CIETAC and won.

At the enforcement stage, however, the SPC found that the loss suffered by the US party was caused by their own breach of the contract and non-compliance with the prior approval of the Ministry of Culture. The SPC decided that the arbitral award was "wrongful" because it ignored these facts, and held that "the social and public interest of our country would be harmed if the award was enforced", because the US party's performance was beyond the scope of the Ministry's approval and was not appropriate under China's social environment.[57]

The significance of this case is that the ground of social public interest in the *CCPL* was applied by the SPC for the first time. It is accepted that this decision was made on the basis of protecting public morality and decency as an element of the social public interest/public policy,[58] particularly in dealing with arbitral awards involving foreign elements.[59]

---

[56] See Colman J, [1998] WLR 770. Further analysis, see Sect. 4 in Chap. 9.

[57] Ibid.

[58] The use of term "social public interest" in Chinese legislation when referring to public policy, see Sect. 5 in Chap. 3.

[59] See for example, 赵秀文 [Zhao Xiuwen],《国际商事仲裁法》[International Commercial Arbitration Law], (人民大学出版社 [Renmin University Press], 2nd Edition, 2008) 464; 葛行军 [Ge Xingjun],《关于仲裁裁决在执行中存在的有关问题—最高人民法院执行办主任葛行军在2003年仲裁员实务研讨会上的发言》[Relevant Issues in the Enforcement of Arbitral Awards: Speech by Ge Xingjun, the Chief of the Enforcement Office in the SPC, at the Symposium

However, the author is of the opinion that this case failed to make any significant progress in recognising China's good morals or public order because of its poor legal reasoning and its conservative and out-of-date view on China's standard of good moral. First of all, in this case the SPC referred to two different possible rationales: that there was a breach of public morality or decency due to the performance being considered "inappropriate" as it created a negative influence on society; and a breach of contract and administrative order, as the SPC emphasised that the reason the contract could not be performed was based on an administrative decision to cancel such performance, and pointed out the wrongfulness of CIETAC's ignorance of such administrative regulatory actions.[60] It is therefore difficult to identify which reason was relied upon by the SPC in refusing enforcement.

Furthermore, no explanation was provided as to why the heavy metal music was detrimental and what category of interests or good moral, if there is any, was infringed by the heavy metal music. Also, this case is of limited significance because the judgment was made in 1997, and therefore could be argued to be out of date. Similar legal decisions were not made during the following two decades, and it is likely that China no longer considers heavy metal to be "inappropriate", and therefore if a similar argument is made, it is very unlikely to succeed.[61]

## 4.3 Analysis

Compared with the international consensus regarding good morals and public order, which generally deals with activities contrary to the public good, the practice of identifying public order or good morals in China is neither consistent nor significant. Most of the generally recognised good morals and public order in international practice are not discussed in China's current arbitration and judicial practice.

It is arguable that the only case that deals with morality or public order is *Heavy Metal*,[62] where the negative influence on Chinese society is considered relevant. However, the legal reasoning of this case is neither coherent nor clear in identifying any element of public order or good morals in China, and the timing and social background of this case also discredits its significance.[63]

of Practices of Arbitrators 2003] (2003) 89 仲裁与法律 *Arbitration and Law* 20, 24–25; 赵秀文 [Zhao Xiuwen],《从永宁公司案看公共政策作为我国法院拒绝执行外国仲裁裁决的理由》[Public Policy as a Ground Adopted by our Courts for Refusal of Foreign Arbitral Awards: Review from the Perspective of the *Yongning* Case] (2009) 4 法学家 *Jurist* 98, 103–04.

[60] It is arguable that such a ruling is made on the basis of public policy rules/*lois de police* as further discussed in Chap. 7.

[61] Wunschheim, above n 25, Appendix D, Case No. 7. The background of China's arbitration law developments, see Sects. 3.1 and 3.2.2 in Chap. 3.

[62] See Sect. 2.

[63] See further Sect. 4 in Chap. 9.

## 5 National Interests as Elements of Public Policy

### 5.1 International Developments

It is both arguable and controversial whether the general interests of a particular state should be considered in relation to public policy. This issue is of particular significance in the context of international relations, and the attitudes of national courts in different jurisdictions vary.

The US courts seem to take a more liberal approach in treating foreign-relation issues in the enforcement of arbitral awards under the *NYC*. In *Parsons,*[64] a dispute arose between an American party and an Egyptian party. When the relationship between the Egyptian and American parties became conflictual, the American party stopped performance of a construction project in Egypt, and later was held liable by the arbitration tribunal. When the Egyptian party sought enforcement of the award in the US, the US court held that the tensions between the two countries and the national policy in foreign relations should not be treated as equal to public policy, and could not bar the enforcement of the arbitral award. It was further confirmed in *National Oil Corp. v Libyan Sun Oil Corp*[65] that the arbitral award favouring a Libyan party would not be refused enforcement merely because of the United States' "national political interests".[66] As the judgment stated, it is not the aim of the *NYC* to "enshrine the vagaries of international politics under the rubric of 'public policy'."[67]

An English court adopted a different approach by distinguishing the relationship between England and an enemy alien from the relationship between two other countries at war. This approach justified enforcing the arbitral award between India and Pakistan, which were at war at the time, but both maintained a friendly relationship with England.[68] However, regarding a contract with an enemy alien or a contract causing injury to a friendly government, the English court would possibly have made a negative response.[69]

### 5.2 Chinese Practice: Overview

It remains a problem to decide whether the State's substantive interest would be considered as an element of public policy in China. A traditional description of the function of the public policy exception is that it would be a "safety valve" guarding

[64] 508 F.2d 969 (2d Cir. 1974).

[65] 733 F Supp 800 (Del 1990).

[66] Ibid, 819–820.

[67] Ibid.

[68] *Dalmia Bairy Industries Ltd v National Bank of Pakistan* [1978] 2 Lloyd's Rep 223.

[69] Ibid.

national interests in a general sense.[70] The term "social public interest" used in Chinese legislation also reflects the respect of the interests of the State to some extent.[71] The reference to general national interests is also evidenced by the categorisation provided by Gao, which respects "*(g) the fundamental and overall interest of China*" as an element of China's public policy.[72]

In the last few decades, the instances where the term "fundamental and overall interests" is defined are rare, and it is questionable whether there have been any instances at all in China's arbitration and judicial practice. The following subsections further examine cases in which different categories of interests in relation to the State are discussed by Chinese courts.

## *5.3 The Economic Interests of the State*

According to a series of cases discussed below, the protection of economic and financial interests of a particular entity, without any further reference to a State's overall interests, would not be accepted as public policy in the judicial practices of Chinese courts.

### 5.3.1 Dongfeng

This point of view was first expressed in the SPC's reply to *Dongfeng*.[73] The dispute arose between the parties based on a cooperation agreement of exporting products. The winning Hong Kong company sought enforcement of a CIETAC arbitral award in Kaifeng IPC, but this was refused because the court found that "according to current State policies and regulations, enforcement ... would seriously harm the economic influence of the State and public interest of the society, and adversely affect the foreign trade order of this State."[74] No further analysis of what kind of state and public interests would be infringed was provided. It is believed that this decision aims to protect domestic interests, because the domestic enterprise held a

---

[70] Herbert Kronke et al., *Recognition and Enforcement of Foreign Arbitral Awards* (Wolters Kluwer, 2010) 365; Friedrich K. Juenger, *Choice of Law and Multistate Justice* (Martinus Nijhoff 1993) 157.

[71] Yongping Xiao and Zhengxin Huo, 'Ordre Public in China's Private International Law' (2005) 53 *American Journal of Comparative Law* 654, 655. Also, general discussion of this term, see Sect. 5 in Chap. 3.

[72] 高晓力 [Gao Xiaoli], above n 23, 131.

[73] Xiao and Huo, above n 71, 660; also reported at <http://www.wunscharb.com/court-decisions/dongfeng-garments-case-1992>.

[74] Anne-Marie Loong, 'Steps toward an International Arbitration Culture? A Dissenting View from the People's Republic of China' (2007) 1(5) *World Arbitration and Mediation Review* 665, 675, citing Michael Moser, 'China and the Enforcement of Arbitral Awards' (1995) 61(1) *ARB* 132, 134.

significant role in the economy of the municipality, and the awarded damages would detrimentally affect the local economy.[75]

The decision of Kaifeng IPC was later overturned by the SPC, which held that Kaifeng IPC erred in rejecting the enforcement.[76] The SPC did not provide any further explanation of its opinion in *Dongfeng*. Scholars generally conclude that this case illustrates that mere interests of an enterprise or a local area cannot amount to the 'social public interest', or public policy, of the State.[77] As indicated below, in a subsequent series of cases, the SPC confirmed its attitude in *Dongfeng* under different situations where the interests of a State enterprise, a local area or State-invested project were involved.

### 5.3.2 The State's Investment and State-Owned Enterprise

- *Tianjin Xianda*

In this case, a dispute arose between a Chinese party, a state-owned enterprise, and a Japanese company regarding a contract of cooperation. Tianjin Arbitration Commission's award held the contract invalid and the Chinese party liable to compensate the Japanese company. The Chinese party then sued for annulment of the arbitral award, arguing that there were errors made in relation to both procedural and substantive issues, and that the award infringed the interests of the State-owned enterprise and therefore violated the "social public interest" of China. This argument was rejected by both the Tianjin HPC and the SPC. Both courts commented on the procedural issues only. The SPC found that there was no ground that could support the annulment of the arbitral award, which may imply that the interest of State-owned enterprises cannot be held as a "social public interest" or public policy.

- *Wildcat*

In this case, Wildcat, a US company, obtained a favourable CIETAC award in a contractual dispute regarding the manufacture of waste disposal equipment, and sought enforcement of the award before the Hefei IPC. Both the Hefei IPC and the Anhui HPC refused the enforcement of the award on the ground of public policy. The majority of the Anhui HPC's judicial committee, in particular, opined that the enforcement of such an award would diminish the value of the State's substantial investment in a waste disposal factory, and therefore violate the social public interest in China.

The SPC denied that such a circumstance would violate the social public interest or create a situation that could "not be tolerated by China's legal order" and thus effect the enforcement of an award. It further clarified that the aim of public policy/ social public interest is to "maintain the fundamental legal order" of the jurisdiction.

---

[75] Ibid; See also Xiao and Huo, above n 71, 660.

[76] Ibid.

[77] Ibid.

It may be implied from this case that the State's investments would not amount to public policy and consequently justify the refusal of the enforcement of an award.

### 5.3.3 The Financial Interests of State Governmental Authorities

The interests of governmental bodies in arbitration are also alleged to be relevant to the application of public policy in some cases. Nevertheless, all these allegations have been rejected by the Chinese courts.

- *Finenco*

The two parties were in the process of establishing a joint venture and then a dispute arose because of the failure of the proposed joint venture. CIETAC rendered an award favouring Finenco. Luoding Bureau of Electric Power Supply later sued for annulment of this award. One of its arguments was that the award infringed the interests of the bureau, which was an administrative body that represented the State. The SPC in its reply to Guangdong HPC denied this argument by clarifying that the governmental bodies in civil and commercial activities were merely civil entities that have the same individual responsibilities as other entities. Thus, the public policy argument for protection of the interests of any governmental body in civil and commercial transactions was not accepted.

## *5.4 Other Discussion on China's National Interests*

Other discussions provided by cases reported by the SPC regarding China's fundamental state interests within the scope of public policy are rare and insignificant. In *Debao,* the lower courts were of the opinion that the properties subject to enforcement were owned by the State and unable to be transferred, and therefore constituted a situation where the public policy exception might apply. The SPC held that the fact that the properties were State-owned was not a sufficient reason for the application of the public policy exception. It also suggested that the transfer of State-owned properties might be dealt with under Article 204 of the then effective *CCPL,*[78] according to which the administrative body governing the State-owned properties might bring an objection and have the enforcement procedure suspended. In *IP Cathay*, the party put forward an argument that the public interest would be infringed because the Valuation Adjustment Mechanism (VAM) in the contract was against the public nature of the entity, and the enforcement of the award would interfere in the operation of the party (which is a university and public in nature). However, such an argument is quite weak and was rejected by the IPC. No further comments were provided on this argument by the HPC and SPC, which chose to refuse the enforcement on the ground of *ultra vires.*

[78] Now art. 263 of the *CCPL.*

In addition to the cases reported above, there are also cases determined by the lower courts discussing the element of national interest. The occasions in which the national interest were discussed include the interests of state-owned entities or shares in the *David Dein Case*[79]; the health and safety of the general public in a case dealing with the public health industry, as shown in the *Ciming Case*[80]; and in two cases of *Rich* and *Sean*, against the State's political position with Korea during the THAAD deployment controversy.[81] None of these arguments were supported by courts. The court in many of these cases adopted a similar line of reasoning which emphasises that the awards only dealt with the commercial interests of two specific parties and did not involve the broader interests of the general public or the State.[82]

## 6 Conclusion

After reviewing how Chinese courts have applied substantive fundamental principles in the judicial review of arbitral awards, the following preliminary observations are made.

Generally, only limited substantive fundamental principles of law are recognised as international public policy in the judicial review of arbitral awards. The *ILA Final Report* represents some international consensus, but also warns that its application should be limited and applied with great caution.[83] As a result, only those substantive principles that are universally recognised by worldwide jurisdictions should be

79 《大卫戴恩咨询有限公司、布拉姆利有限公司申请执行香港仲裁裁决案》[Case of Application for the Recognition and Enforcement of a Hong Kong arbitral award by David Dein Consultancy Ltd and Bramley Corp Ltd], Beijing 4th IPC, 2020) 京04认港5号 [Recognition Hong Kong No. 5], date not reported, reported in the SPC, 《内地与香港特别行政区发布相互执行仲裁裁决的典型案例》[Typical Cases of the Enforcement of Arbitral Awards between China Mainland and the Hong Kong SAR], 27 November 2020.

80 《慈铭博鳌国际医院有限公司与海南亨延顿医院管理咨询有限公司等申请撤销仲裁裁决民事裁定书》[Civil Decision on the Application for the Annulment of An Arbitral Award between Ciming Bo'ao International Hospital Co Ltd and HRC-Hainan Holding Company LLC et al.], Beijing 4th IPC, (2021) 京04民特26号 [Civil Special No. 26], 5 March 2021.

81 《利奇食品株式会社、元春秋申请承认与执行法院判决、仲裁裁决案件裁定书》[Decision on the Application for the Recognition and Enforcement of Judgments or Arbitral Awards between Rich Food Co Ltd and Chunqiu Yuan], Tianjin 1st IPC, (2018) 津01协外认1号 [Judicial Assistance Foreign Recognition No. 1], 4 March 2019 (the *Rich Food Case*); 《世安株式会社、天津市天锻压力机有限公司申请承认与执行法院判决、仲裁裁决案件裁定书》[Decision on the Application for the Recognition and Enforcement of A Foreign Award between Sean Inc and Tianjin Tianduan Press Machine Co Ltd], Tianjin 1st IPC, (2018) 津01协外认13号 [Judicial Assistance Foreign Recognition No. 13], 27 March 2019. The THAAD controversy, see for example, Ethan Meick and Nargiza Salidjanova, 'China's Response to U.S.—South Korean Missile Defense System Deployment and its Implications', US.—China Economic and Security Review Commission Staff Research Report, 26 July 2017, at: <https://www.uscc.gov/sites/default/files/Research/Report_China%27s%20Response%20to%20THAAD%20Deployment%20and%20its%20Implications.pdf>.

82 For example, the *Rich Food Case*.

83 Section 2.

considered as public policy in the judicial review of international awards, particularly if public policy is to be construed consistently and coherently across jurisdictions.[84] More specifically, national courts should recognise limitations regarding the extent of judicial review of arbitration awards.[85]

The progress towards formalising a consistent approach in applying substantive fundamental principles ascribed to public policy is not quite significant in China. Given that developments in clarifying this approach at the legislative level are absent, and the categories listed by the scholars is generally abstract, limited guidance is provided for the judiciary.[86] The finding of any particular set of fundamental principles as part of China's public policy is rare in China's judicial practice. Only in *Heavy Metal*,[87] was public order or good morals considered, yet this case is of limited value. The principles of substantive fairness and/or justice, or the overall interest of the State, were not applied at all.[88] Notably, the SPC has made a concerted effort to distinguish between the interests of one party from the overall interests of the State in a series of cases.[89]

Also, it is generally clarified that the Chinese judiciary will not review the substance of the original dispute and open up a discussion of the facts. In cases like *Western Bulk*, the Chinese courts expressed the view that they would not evaluate the substantive outcome of the cases.[90] Such attitude is also observed in some cases determined by the lower courts such as *GS Global*.[91] It is yet to be determined whether this attitude is clearly and consistently applied in all cases. This problem is also reflected in judicial attitudes in dealing with public policy rules, as will be noted in Chap. 7 and summarised in Chap. 9.

It is interesting to note that the observations made in relation to the analysis of the cases discussed in this chapter, which deals with the other elements of public policy, are echoed in other chapters. For example, the issue of fraudulent contractual issues (distinguished from fraudulently obtained awards) are further referred to in Chap. 6, while the standard of evaluation of a state's comprehensive and overall interests is discussed in Chaps. 7 and 8. All these observations contribute to the final analysis and conclusion reached in Chap. 9 and serve as the basis for the recommendations made in the Final Chapter.

---

[84] Section 5.1.

[85] Section 3.1 and further Sect. 4 in Chap. 9.

[86] Section 2.2.

[87] Sections 4.2 and 4.3.

[88] Sections 3 and 5.

[89] Section 5.3.

[90] Sections 3.2 and 3.3.

[91] 《GS Global Corporation (佳施国际株式会社)诉上海市振戎石油有限公司申请承认和执行外国仲裁裁决一案民事裁定书》.[Civil Ruling on the Application for the Recognition and Enforcement of a Foreign Arbitral Award between GS Global Corporation and Shanghai Zhenrong Oil Corp], Shanghai 1st IPC, (2016) 沪01协外认12号 [Judicial Assistance Foreign Recognition No. 12], 22 February 2017.

# Chapter 6
# Procedural Fundamental Principles in Public Policy

## 1 Introduction

As Chap. 5 discussed the substantive fundamental principles, this chapter deals with the procedural fundamental principles, the combination of which constitutes the fundamental principles of law as element (1) of public policy.[1]

A broad notion of public policy includes all procedural issues. From this point of view, other grounds in the judicial review scheme under the *NYC*, such as "lacking due process" in Article V(1)(b), and the "irregularity of the composition of arbitral tribunal or arbitration proceedings" in Article V(1)(d) may also be closely connected with and restricted by the procedural public policy.[2] Some scholars argue that the grounds of public policy provided by Article V(2)(b), when dealing with the procedural issues of arbitration, may function as a corrective and residual ground of Articles V(1)(b) and V(1)(d), and only apply when the other arguments fail.[3] Yet van den Berg points out that these three different procedural grounds are independent from each other, and the ground of public policy is not residual.[4] Based on this understanding, parties and courts may choose the applicable grounds that suit their arguments, in accordance with the particular circumstances of a specific case.

---

[1] Pierre Mayer and Audley Sheppard, 'Final Report on Public Policy as a Bar to Enforcement of International Arbitral Awards' (Paper presented at the International Law Association New Delhi Conference Committee on International Commercial Arbitration, New Delhi, 2002), Recommendation 1(b); Section 5 of Ch 2.

[2] For a discussion of the relationship of different grounds of refusal of arbitral awards, see Chap. 2. See also Stephen M. Schwebel and Susan G. Lahne, 'Public Policy and Arbitral Procedure' in Pieter Sanders (ed), *Comparative Arbitration Practices and Public Policy in Arbitration*, ICCA Congress Series (Kluwer Law International, 1987) 207–208.

[3] Ibid, n 7; Albert Jan van den Berg, *The New York Convention of 1958: Towards a Uniform Judicial Interpretation* (Kluwer Law International, 1981) 299–301.

[4] Ibid.



S. Zhang, *The Public Policy Exception in the Judicial Review of International Commercial Arbitral Awards*, https://doi.org/10.1007/978-3-662-67679-0_6

In practice, quite a few fundamental principles of procedural law may be covered by the public policy exception. As Goldman summarises, the procedural rules protect the parties on at least two distinct grounds: first, they ensure the parties have the opportunity to fully develop their claims; and secondly, they also ensure that issues be decided only when each party is afforded the opportunity to discuss the position of the other party.[5] The principle of natural justice requires the parties to exercise their rights to a fair hearing (*audi alteram partem*) and that a decision is not biased in favour of one particular party (*nemo judex in sua causa*).[6] Other procedural issues also include important procedural principles, for example, the principle of *res judicata*. The *ILA Report* summarised the procedural fundamental principles as:

> The requirement that tribunals be impartial; other examples of breaches …the making of the award was induced or affected by fraud or corruption; breach of the rules of natural justice; and the parties were on an unequal footing in the appointment of tribunal;…to enforce an award that is inconsistent with a court decision or arbitral award that has res judicata effect in the enforcement forum.[7]

Though procedural public policy is considered fundamental and critical in arbitration and in the judicial review of arbitral awards, few arbitral awards are refused because of the violation of procedural public policy.[8] In China, the application of procedural public policy is also rare. Yet quite a few issues arise in practice and cover many aspects of the arbitration processes in China.

This chapter reviews issues that may constitute a violation of procedural public policy in the following aspects: Sect. 2 reviews the issues relevant to the impartiality of the tribunal and the parties' right to be equally treated in an arbitration proceeding, including equal treatment at the stage of the nomination of arbitrators, the hearings, and decision-making. The particular issue of the institutional impartiality is also discussed. Sect. 3 examines the protection of the parties' procedural rights in order to ensure a fair hearing. Sect. 4 reviews a series of cases dealing with the principle of *res judicata* and the position of this principle in China. Sect. 5 further discusses the relationship between public policy and other grounds that may be applied in dealing with procedural errors in arbitral proceedings. Finally, Sect. 6 discusses the distinct positions and roles of the Chinese arbitration commissions, their staff, and the arbitrators, as well as their involvement in the procedural issues.

---

[5] Berthold Goldman, 'The Complementary Roles of Judges and Arbitrators in Ensuring that International Commercial Arbitration is Effective' in *60 Years of ICC Arbitration: A Look at the Future* (ICC Publishing, 1984) 257, 267.

[6] David Phillip Jones and Anne S. de Villars, 'Natural Justice and the Duty to be Fair' in *Principles of Administrative Law* (Carswell, 5th ed, 2009) 208, 209.

[7] Mayer and Sheppard, above n 1, [31].

[8] As concluded by Schwebel and Lahne, the cases dealing with procedural public policy are rare because it is rarely disputed under the judicial review. See also Michael John Mustill, 'Transnational Arbitration and English Law' (1984) 37(1) *Current Legal Problems* 133, 134, which states that English judiciaries were reluctant to review arbitration proceedings under procedural public policy.

## 2 Impartiality and the Equal Treatment of Parties

### *2.1 Impartiality of Arbitrators in the Composition of the Tribunal*

The major aspect of impartiality is to select neutral arbitrators at the very beginning of the arbitration procedure. The essential requirement of impartiality, therefore, must be adopted in the rules and regulations dealing with the composition of an arbitration tribunal. Impartiality demands that there should not be any possibility for a conflict of interest to exist with the arbitrators. Any possible conflicts must be properly disclosed by potential arbitrators, and they should be subject to challenge with respect to possible bias prior to the composition of the tribunal.[9] The *UNCITRAL Model Law* and *UNCITRAL Arbitration Rules* both confirm that a challenge on the basis of bias may result in the non-enforcement of an arbitral award.[10] A few issues in relation to impartiality then arise in the following aspects during the composition of arbitration tribunals.

#### 2.1.1 Impartiality in the Nomination of Arbitrators

From an international perspective, most arbitration legislation and arbitration rules, as well as arbitration agreements, recognise the parties' rights to select their own arbitrators. It is quite unlikely that such rights would be infringed in arbitration practice, as long as the arbitration agreement and the selected arbitration rules are generally followed. Where a perception of bias is observed in the composition of arbitrators, for example, all arbitrators are from one country in the situation of an international dispute, it may not be held as a violation of public policy if the parties voluntarily agree to accept such an arrangement.[11] A similar case further illustrated that the mere fact that one party played a predominant role in the composition of the arbitration tribunal would not amount to a violation of public policy.[12] The courts generally prefer to focus on the actual bias that occurs in the performance of the tribunal, rather than the possibility of bias that may be caused by the composition of the tribunal.[13] One exception to the general respect of the parties' autonomy in

[9] Schwebel and Lahne, above n 2, 209.

[10] *UNCITRAL* Arbitration Rules, art 6(4), art 9 and art 10(1).

[11] *Czechoslovak Firm C. (claim assigned to a German Company) v. German* (*F.R.*), Oberlandesgericht Hamburg; Bundesgerichtshof [Supreme Court], 14 October 1964; 6 March 1969, reported in (1977) 2 *Yearbook-Commercial Arbitration* 235 (FR Germany No.5); *Not indicated v. Not indicated*, Oberste Gerichtshof, 3, 11 June 1969, reported in (1977) 2 *Yearbook-Commercial Arbitration* 232 (Austria No. 3).

[12] *German Charterer v. Romanian Shipowner*, *Bundesgerichtshof* [Supreme Court], 15 May 1986, reported in (1987) 12 *Yearbook-Commercial Arbitration* 489 (Germany No. 30).

[13] See eg., Sam Luttrell, *Bias Challenges in International Arbitration: The Need for a 'Real Danger' Test*, (Kluwer Law, 2009).

nominating arbitrators, however, is that, in a case where the parties were denied the possibility to know the identity of the arbitrators (although the rule of the institution they had chosen is not breached by not providing the arbitrators' identity to the parties). The refusal of the enforcement of the award was ordered on the basis that the practice fundamentally infringed German and international public policy.[14]

In China, however, the situation is somewhat distinct because the parties' agreement in relation to the composition of an arbitration tribunal is restricted by the current legal scheme under the *CAL* and the arbitration rules of the Chinese arbitration commissions. Quite a few restrictions in these rules are still followed in China's arbitration practice in relation to the composition of arbitration tribunals. Based on these facts, it is doubtful that the impartiality of arbitration tribunals can generally be assumed as it is understood in international practice. The *CAL* requires that the arbitration commissions must introduce arbitrators from people who have the characteristics of fairness and good morals,[15] and lists a few circumstances when the arbitrators are obliged to withdraw from the tribunal either by their own motion or at the request of the parties, including the situation that the nominated arbitrator:

(1) is a close relative of the parties or the attorneys;
(2) has a conflict of interest with the dispute;
(3) is connected with the parties or the attorneys in any other form that may influence the fair decision-making of the dispute; or
(4) meets the parties or the attorneys in private, or accept gifts and services from them.[16]

A general requirement of independence and impartiality is also adopted by many arbitration commissions.[17] Some arbitration rules also provide a set of factors for a chairman to consider in appointing arbitrators.[18] Yet it is very difficult to observe whether procedural fairness is achieved during this process, due to a lack of written regulation on how the nomination criteria should be applied in China's arbitration commissions' internal management procedures.

One distinct requirement, especially adhered to in 1990s and early 2000s, is that only arbitrators whose names are on a list provided by the Chinese arbitration commissions should be selected; parties were not allowed to choose arbitrators

[14] *Danish Buyer v German (F.R.) Seller*, Oberlandesgericht Köln [Higher Regional Court of Koeln], 10 June 1976, reported in (1979) 4 *Yearbook-Commercial Arbitration* 258 (Case Germany No. 14).

[15] 《中华人民共和国仲裁法》 [Arbitration Law of the People's Republic of China] (People's Republic of China) National People's Congress Standing Committee, Order No 31, 31 August 1994, art 13.

[16] Ibid, art 34.

[17] For example, *CIETAC Arbitration Rules* (2015), art 24; it states that the arbitrators shall be independent from any party and treat them equally.

[18] CIETAC Arbitration Rules (2012), art 28; it provides that the relevant considerations would include "*the law as it applies to the dispute, the place of arbitration, the language of arbitration, the nationalities of the parties, and any other factor(s) the Chairman considers relevant*."

whose names were not listed.[19] This requirement is stipulated by the *CAL* and old versions of many arbitration rules.[20] This requirement, however, is inconsistent with the worldwide common practice that the institutions' list is provided for guidance only,[21] and is not to be considered as imposing limits on a party's autonomy,[22] as well as their access to foreign arbitrators and having sufficient information about the potential arbitrators.[23] Also, arbitrators chosen from the list may be more closely connected with the commission, and have stronger motives to build their relationship with the arbitration commission and its employees; some of them are even employed by the commission directly.[24] Jerome Cohen reports that the nomination of self-employed arbitrators usually happened in nominating the sole arbitrator or presiding arbitrators, and emphasises that the nomination of its own staff as arbitrators is "one of CIETAC's biggest defects".[25] Though the leading arbitration commissions, such as CIETAC and BAC, have modified their arbitration rules and provided the parties with the opportunity to choose any potential arbitrators without the restriction of the panel list,[26] the old-fashioned practice remains in other arbitration commissions in

---

19《中华人民共和国仲裁法》[Arbitration Law of the People's Republic of China] (People's Republic of China) art 25(1), art 38.

20 宋连斌 [Song Lianbin],《仲裁法》[Arbitration Law] (Wuhan University Press, 2010) 144; CIETAC Arbitration Rules (2005), art 20(1).

21 For example, American Arbitration Association (AAA) provides a reference list of arbitrators from a National Roster of Arbitrators established and maintained by AAA only when no appointment or appointment methods have been provided; parties are free to nominate anyone who follows the R-17 requirement of impartiality and independence unless otherwise agreed to by the parties, and can seek assistance from AAA by referring to a list from the National Roster as well. See AAA Arbitration Rules, R-11, R-12 and R-17; See also HKIAC Administered Arbitration Rules, Rule 8–11.

22 宋连斌 [Song Lianbin],《中国仲裁员制度改革初探》[A Preliminary Exploration of Reforms of China's Arbitrator System] (2001) 4 中国国际私法和比较法年刊 *Yearbook of Chinese International Private Law and Comparative Law* 575.

23 袁发强 [Yuan Faqiang],《中国商事仲裁机构现状与发展趋势研究》[Research on China's Present Commercial Arbitration Institutions and Their Development Trends in the Future] (Fudan University, 2011) 98.

24 Michael J. Moser, 'CIETAC Arbitration: A Success Story?' (1998) 15(1) *Journal of International Arbitration* 27, 30; Russell Thirgood, 'Critique of Foreign Arbitration in China' (2000) 17(3) *Journal of International Arbitration* 89, 97–98. Particularly, arbitrators that employed by the arbitration commissions and work on a full-time basis like government servants are of significant scale in most of Chinese arbitration commissions, which are frequently criticised.

25 Jerome A. Cohen, 'Time to Fix China's Arbitration' (2005) 168(2) *Far East Economic Review* 31, 33–35.

26 *CIETAC Arbitration Rules 2015*, art 26 provides that parties can nominate arbitrators from the panel list as prepared by CIETAC, or, when the arbitrator is nominated (by the parties) or appointed (as *CAL* allowed, by the chairman of arbitration commission) from people not listed, such a nomination or appointment shall be confirmed by the Chairman of CIETAC. BAC does not allow the selection (either nominated by parties or appointed by the chairman) of arbitrators outside the panel list for domestic arbitration, but allows the nomination of people not on the list in foreign-related arbitrations as long as such nomination is confirmed by the Commission. See BAC Arbitration Rules (2022), art 19, art 64.

China, and consequently influences the behaviour of experienced arbitrators, lawyers and arbitration commission employees.

Another problem with the panel list is the inability of the parties to choose foreign nationals as arbitrators in Chinese arbitration practice. Article 67 of the *CAL,* when it was originally legislated, only allowed CIETAC and CMAC to appoint arbitrators from foreign nationals. Further, in 1996, the Ministry of Justice expressly denied the possibility of other arbitration commissions introducing arbitrators of foreign nationalities.[27] However, this restriction has now been abandoned in practice, as the panel lists of most arbitration commissions now include foreign arbitrators.[28]

Furthermore, the predominant decision-making power of the chairman of the arbitration commission is evident in the composition procedure of the arbitration tribunal in both domestic and foreign-related arbitrations in China. According to the *CAL*, the chairman of the commission enjoys extensive powers that include appointing arbitrators.[29] In many circumstances, the commission functions as the decision-maker in determining the composition of the tribunal, rather than the parties.[30]

Although it is generally not an issue that one party or both parties are reluctant to participate in the nomination of arbitrators, or there is an imbalance of bargaining power at this stage,[31] it is not so if some fundamental right of the parties is violated in relation to choosing the arbitrators and getting access to sufficient information about them.[32] When combining these issues, it is difficult to conclude that an assumption of impartiality can be assured under the current legislative scheme in China. Despite the progress made in relation to relaxing the restrictions, e.g., the rigid requirements of selecting arbitrators solely from a panel list; limited access to foreign arbitrators; and the extensive involvement of the arbitration commissions, to ensure party autonomy, these restrictions continue to influence the current arbitration practices in China.

[27] 《司法部关于威海仲裁委员会是否可以聘任外籍人士担任仲裁员的批复》 [Reply of the Ministry of Justice Concerning Whether Weihai Arbitration Commission Can Employ Foreign Arbitrators] (People's Republic of China) Ministry of Justice, 20 August 1996. The Ministry of Justice is the government body governing the establishment and operation of all arbitration commissions in China.

[28] See for example, the Panel List of BAC, at <http://www.bjac.org.cn/arbitrator/list>.

[29] The chief arbitrator or sole arbitrator can be appointed by the chairman of the arbitration commission who is "jointly entrusted by the two parties", should the parties fail to jointly nominate one. The chairman of the arbitration commission can also nominate arbitrators if the parties fail to do so within the time limit prescribed by the applicable arbitration rules. Given that the parties involved in dispute have tight time constraints, it is highly likely that the arbitrators, especially the presiding or sole arbitrator, would be nominated by the chairman, rather than selected by the parties. If a conflict of interest emerges, a party may request for the withdrawal of arbitrators and the decision is made by the chairman of the arbitration commission. Only when the chairman of an arbitration commission acts as an arbitrator in the presenting cases, is the decision to be made collectively by the arbitration commission. See 《中华人民共和国仲裁法》 [Arbitration Law of the People's Republic of China] (People's Republic of China) art 31, art 32.

[30] Cohen, above n 25, 33.

[31] Bundesgerichtshof [Supreme Court], 15 May 1986 (Germany No 30).

[32] *Danish Buyer v. German (F.R.) Seller,* Oberlandesgericht Köln [Higher Regional Court of Koeln], 10 June 1976, (Case Germany No 14).

They also reduce the opportunities for parties to be able to identify prejudices on the part of arbitrators.

While some of these issues may increase the possibility of arbitral prejudice, they may not necessarily be considered prejudicial in all cases. Even in international arbitration practice, claims are rarely brought merely on the basis of the composition of the tribunal, and even if a claim is made, they are not likely to be supported by the courts.[33] Courts generally prefer to focus on the particular acts of the tribunal in identifying bias.[34] Yet the criticisms currently levelled by practitioners and scholars suggest that further reform is needed in order to reduce the risk of bias in nominating the arbitrators to ensure party autonomy.

### 2.1.2 Disclosure of Conflicts of Interest and Challenges to Arbitrators

International practice generally provides a very narrow construction of bias and prefers to deny the enforceability of arbitral awards only under extreme circumstances, particularly in dealing with international arbitral awards.[35] Yet the approach adopted by courts has differed in discrete jurisdictions and in various cases.

There are plenty of standards adopted or suggested for judicial review by Chinese courts in relation to the impartiality of arbitrators. Generally, it is considered that "actual bias", which is construed on the basis of a close and direct relationship, must be shown to justify the refusal of enforcement of arbitral awards.[36] Minor prior relationships between one party and the nominated arbitrator are not sufficient to negate the award.[37] This is so even if such a relationship is not particularly disclosed.[38] However, in some other cases, "apparent bias" is also considered as a ground for refusal to enforce an award.[39] It may also be considered as lack of impartiality if the parties are denied their right to challenge and remove arbitrators. For example, in a case where a lawyer acted for both of the parties, nominated himself as the sole

---

[33] An example can be found in early practices that a claim of lack of independence merely based on the limitation imposed by a list of available arbitrators was denied. *Billerbeck Cie v Bergaban-Handel GmbhH, Berlin-East*, Tribunal Fédéral (Bundesgericht), 3 May 1967, reported in (1976) 1 *Yearbook-Commercial Arbitration* 199, 199.

[34] Ibid.

[35] See for example, Schwebel and Lahbe, above n 2, 208.

[36] See *Fertilizer Corp of India v IDI Management Inc*, 517 F Supp 948 (1981), 530 F Supp 542, reported in (1983) 3 *Yearbook-Commercial Arbitration* 419; *Transmaine Seaways Corp v Marc Rich & Co AG*, 480 F Supp 352 (SDNY 1979).

[37] *Fertilizwer Corp of India*, reported in (1983) 3 *Yearbook-Commercial Arbtiration* 419.

[38] *Andros Compania Maritime SA v Marc Rich &Co AG*, 579 F 2d 691 (2nd Cir, 1978). In this case, the court held that the failure to disclose a "close personal and professional relationship" with one party's broker and agent was not sufficient to be a ground to vacate the award because the relationship was common knowledge and could not demonstrate a close business relationship to justify "bias".

[39] *Commonwealth Coating Corp v Continental Casualty Co*, 393 US 145, 89 S Ct 337 (1986). In this case, the award was vacated on the basis that one arbitrator was engaged with and paid by one party as its consultant prior to the arbitration proceedings, and such a fact was not disclosed.

arbitrator of all disputes between the parties and granted himself the power not to be removed under any circumstances; such a situation is considered as a violation of impartiality.[40] Some scholars have also suggested a "real danger" test, which indicates a real danger of bias is to be adopted in evaluating the impartiality of arbitrators.[41]

The Chinese law and arbitration rules require the disclosure of conflict-of-interest issues and impose requirements that arbitrators must withdraw upon challenge when certain issues exist. The *CAL* provides four circumstances when arbitrators must withdraw and the parties are entitled to challenge those arbitrators;[42] *CIETAC Arbitration Rules* also provide that the arbitrators shall disclose "any facts or circumstances likely to give rise to justifiable doubts as to his/her impartiality or independence."[43] The parties may challenge the arbitrator based on the disclosure of any evidence that gives rise to a reasonable doubt about the impartiality or independence of the arbitrators. When both parties agree to challenge an arbitrator, the arbitrator voluntarily withdraws, or such a challenge is affirmed by the chairman of the arbitration commission, the arbitrator will be removed from the tribunal.[44]

Because detailed disclosure and withdrawal requirements are provided by the *CAL* and Chinese arbitration rules, Chinese courts prefer to require strict compliance with these procedural requirements in dealing with impartiality issues. However, the requirement of strict compliance with procedural rules falls outside the public policy framework. For example, in *Huludao Harbour*, the SPC evaluated the possible conflict-of-interest issue as claimed by the party, but only discussed this issue under the ground of procedural irregularity. Similarly, in *DMT S.A. v Chaozhou Huaye Packing Materials* et al., the discussion of the arbitrators' competence and impartiality was also dealt with under the ground of violation of arbitration rules.[45]

An extreme example is *Louis Dreyfus*, in which the SPC totally denied a review to the issue of impartiality. In this case, the Chinese party claimed that the sole arbitrator failed to disclose his previous working experience as an attorney in the law firm representing the foreign party. Both the Guangdong HPC and the SPC were of the opinion that the impartiality of arbitrators did not fall within the scope of

---

[40] Bezirksgericht [Court of First Instance], Affoltern am Albis, 26 May 1994, affirmed by the Court of Appeal in Zurich on 26 July 1995, reported in (1998) 23 *Yearbook—Commercial Arbitration* 754 (Switzerland No 30).

[41] Luttrell, above n 13.

[42]《中华人民共和国仲裁法》[Arbitration Law of the People's Republic of China] (People's Republic of China) National People's Congress Standing Committee, Order No 31, 31 August 1994, art 34.

[43] CIETAC Arbitration Rules (2015), art 31.

[44] CIETAC Arbitration Rules (2015), art 32.

[45]《最高人民法院关于申请人DMT有限公司 (法国) 与被申请人潮州市华业包装材料有限公司、被申请人潮安县华业包装材料有限公司申请承认和执行外国仲裁裁决一案请示的复函》[Reply of the Supreme People's Court to the Request Concerning the Application of a Foreign Arbitral Award between the Applicant, DMT S.A. (France) and the Respondents, Huaye Packing Materials Company of Chaozhou City and Huaye Packing Materials Company of Chaoan County] Supreme People's Court, [2010] Min Si Ta Zi No 51, 12 October 2010.

the judicial review for the purpose of recognition and enforcement of the award. A total denial of judicial review of impartiality significantly excludes any possibility of developing a standard in evaluating impartiality at the stage of the composition of the tribunal and including such evaluation as a procedural public policy consideration.

## 2.2 *Impartiality of Arbitrators in Trial Proceedings*

The international practice of defining impartiality generally focuses on how the arbitrators behave during arbitration proceedings. Many cases in international practice have illustrated the general concern that arbitrators should not prejudice any party during the arbitration proceedings. For example, an arbitrator acting in parallel proceedings was held to be biased in the decision-making of one proceeding, not merely because of his involvement in dual proceedings, but because he was wrongfully influenced by erroneous information conveyed during the other proceeding.[46] Also, the failure of arbitrators to forward the evidence of one party to another party,[47] or relying on *ex parte* evidence,[48] may be considered a breach of public policy. However, procedural errors that did not prejudice any party would not necessarily amount to a violation of public policy as a ground to overrule arbitral awards.[49]

Chinese law and arbitration rules, however, make no real effort to regulate the impartiality of arbitrators during arbitration proceedings. Little guidance is provided by the *CAL* or the arbitration rules as to how the procedure would be structured, and plenty of discretion is provided to the tribunals. Furthermore, little supervision of the behaviour of arbitrators is provided in the current Chinese arbitration system. It is best illustrated by the *Gao Haiyan et al. v Keeneye Holdings Limited* ('*Keeneye*'),[50] in which the arbitral award, made by Xi'an Arbitration Commission ('XAAC' hereafter) from Mainland China, was challenged before the Hong Kong Court.[51] In this case, the

---

46 *Excelsior Film TV, srl v. UGC-PH*, Cour de Cassation [Supreme Court], 24 March 1998, reported in (1999) 24a *Yearbook-Commercial Arbitration* 643–44 (France No 30).

47 *Firm P v. Firm F*, Oberlandesgericht Hamburg [Higher Regional Court of Hamburg], 3 April 1975, reported in (1977) 2*Yearbook-Commercial Arbitration* 241 (Germany No 11).

48 *Totem Marine Tug & Barge v North American Touring* 607 F 2d 649 (5th Cir 1979).

49 *Parsons & Whittemore Overseas Co Inc. v. Société Générale de l'Industrie du papier (RAKTA)*, 508 F.2d 969 (2d Cir. 1974).

50 HCCT No. 41/2010; CACV No. 79/2011.

51 Gao Haiyan and Keeneye, parties of a share sale agreement, disputed on the issue of whether the agreement was void on the ground of duress and misrepresentation, and submitted it to XAAC as agreed. At the end of the first hearing, the tribunal obtained the parties' mutual consent to mediate. The tribunal then appointed the Secretary General of the XAAC, Pan Junxing, and one of the arbitrators, Zhou Jian, to mediate. Pan and Zhou then met a third party, Zeng Wei, who was regarded as "friendly with the Respondent" or described as "a person related to" the Respondent, at the Xi'an Shangri La Hotel, and asked him to persuade the Respondent to accept a settlement plan, which confirmed the validity of the share transfer and held the Respondent to pay RMB 250 million to Applicants. Neither Gao nor Keeneye accepted this settlement plan and the arbitration proceedings continued. In the final award, however, the share transfer agreement was revoked and

impartiality issue arose during the arbitration proceedings that commenced in China, in which the arbitrators' behaviour was argued to be either apparently or substantively biased. Though the challenge was eventually denied by the Hong Kong court in the appeals proceeding, the case reminds Chinese practitioners of the risk of partiality in commencing arbitration proceedings in China. A detailed discussion of this case helps us understand this risk.

The most controversial part of the arbitration proceeding in *Keeneye* is the mediation proceedings provided during the arbitration process, also known as "mediation-in-arbitration" in modern arbitration practice.[52] In the mediation there was an informal, *ex parte* communication between Pan (the Secretary General of XAAC), Zhou (an arbitrator) and Zeng (a related party of the Respondent, Keeneye); during this communication, Pan and Zhou promoted a settlement plan, which was considered as strongly favouring Gao.[53] Particularly, this settlement plan was significantly different from the later award. These activities were held by the trial judge as showing apparent bias.[54]

The combination of mediation (or conciliation)[55] and arbitration itself is a controversial practice; it is criticised that arbitrators "wearing double hats" would lose their impartiality and infringe the fundamental neutrality of the arbitration process.[56] This double-hats problem is particularly significant in the Chinese style of mediation-in-arbitration, which allows extensive involvement of mediator-arbitrators and is

---

the tribunal only "recommended" the Respondent to pay RMB 50 million "based on fairness and reasonable arbitration principles" and "not binding and not included in the arbitral matters." Based on the magnificent difference between the suggested settlement plan and the ultimate outcome, the Respondent alleged that Pan manipulated the outcome, and the tribunal showed "favouritism and malpractice" at the supervisory court in Xi'an. Nevertheless, its submission to Xi'an Court was dismissed as it held it was not sufficient to prove Pan had manipulated the case. They subsequently objected on the same basis in the Hong Kong court where enforcement of the award was sought. The trial judge denied enforcement on the basis of "apparent bias", but the decision was later reversed by the Court of Appeal.

[52] The character of mediation-in-arbitration is also noticed by the trial judge. See HCCT41/2010, [19]. The cited facts below are all selected from the "minimalist version" as illustrated by the trial judge in para 22, as it is agreed by both parties.

[53] Ibid, [5].

[54] The trial judge found no basis for actual bias but had an apprehension of "a real risk of bias" (see Ibid, [52, 53]), and such bias was not waived by the Respondent's subsequent participation in arbitration proceedings (EEE para 81–91), or limited by Xi'an Court's decision; see Ibid, [92]–[96]. Enforcing such an award, therefore, is "an affront to this Court's sense of justice" and was refused on the grounds of Hong Kong's public policy. This judgment was later overturned by the judge of the Court of Appeal.

[55] In this book "conciliation" and "mediation" are generally used interchangeably unless noted otherwise.

[56] Michael Schneider, 'Combining Arbitration with Conciliation' in Albert van den Berg (ed), *International Dispute Resolution: Towards an International Arbitration Culture*, ICCA Congress Series (1998) 57, 77.

different from a mere combination of two separate procedures.[57] Limited party autonomy to obtain procedural fairness is provided under the Chinese style of mediation-in-arbitration, and the tribunal enjoys enormous discretionary power to participate actively in managing a dispute.[58]

This research does not aim to challenge the adoption of mediation-in-arbitration in China and the role of the tribunal at the mediation stage. The concern of this research is the risk of a breach of impartiality. On the one hand, the flexible arbitration proceedings and the involvement of mediation-in-arbitration practice have increased the efficiency of dispute resolution; as indicated by Tang, it assists the communication of parties and increases the settlement rates in arbitration.[59] But on the other hand, the risk of a breach of impartiality also increases because of the double-hat problem. With respect to the advantage of mediation-in-arbitration practice, the officers of CIETAC frequently promote their working experiences in mediation-in-arbitration as a useful tool to facilitate dispute resolution.[60] Similar trends can also be found in other civil law countries, especially Japan and Germany.[61] However, the greatest concern of practitioners about this particular type of practice is whether impartiality and independence of the tribunal can be ensured when the discretionary powers of the tribunal in organising arbitration procedures are provided without sufficient guidance. Furthermore, the Chinese courts (as courts of the arbitration seat) prefer rigid compliance of the arbitration rules rather than evaluating whether impartiality was

---

[57] Ibid, 60–72. Schneider divided mediation-in-arbitration into two categories, one "Conciliation followed by Arbitration" and another "Conciliation during arbitration". Both categories are generally understood as a combination of two separate procedures, not as what was discussed above, where there is only one procedure of arbitration and a mediation component then emerges during it and is conducted by the same people. He also notes in this situation where arbitrators as mediators is a distinct problem from the two categories in his paper.

[58] Regarding the initiation of mediation during the arbitration process, it is a universal principle that mediation must only be conducted upon the consent of the parties, and both the CIETAC and BAC rules generally respect this principle. However, art 51 of *CAL* states, "The arbitration tribunal may mediate a case before rendering the award. Whereas the parties voluntarily require mediation, the arbitration tribunal shall mediate". Such a provision suggests a positive move of the tribunal to initiate the mediation; although the right to accept or reject mediation is still in the hands of the parties, it is very difficult to distinguish whether the arbitrators can impose any further influence on the parties when initiating mediation, which may amount to the determinative factors of the parties' decision.

[59] Houzhi Tang, 'Is There an Expanding Culture that Favors Combining Arbitration with Conciliation or Other ADR Procedures?' in Albert Jan van den Berg (ed), *International Dispute Resolution: Towards an International Arbitration Culture*, ICCA Congress Series (Kluwer Law International, 1998) vol 8, 101; Houzhi Tang, 'Combination of Arbitration with Conciliation—Arb-Med' in Albert Jan van den Berg (ed), *New Horizons in International Commercial Arbitration and Beyond, 2004 Beijing*, ICCA Congress Series (Kluwer Law International, 2005) vol 12, 547.

[60] Shengchang Wang, 'CIETAC's Perspective on Arbitration and Conciliation Concerning China' in Albert Jan van den Berg (ed), *New Horizon in International Commercial Arbitration and Beyond* (2005) vol 12, 27.

[61] Schneider, above n 56, 70–74; See also Tatsuya Nakamura, 'Brief Empirical Study on Arb-Med in the JCAA Arbitration' (2009) 22 *JCAA Newsletter* 10, 12.

achieved and pay little attention to evaluating the tribunal's behaviour in executing its discretionary powers.[62]

More importantly, the understanding of impartiality differs from one national jurisdiction to another due to the distinct legal environments and legal cultures of each country. As a result, it is important that there is sufficient legal guidance and judicial supervision of mediation-in-arbitration. Quite a few key issues were disputed in *Keeneye*, including the use of mediation-in-arbitration itself, the active involvement of arbitrators, the *ex parte* meetings, and the settlement plan positively proposed by the mediator.[63] These issues are understood differently by arbitration practitioners with different backgrounds, because the recognition of mediation-in-arbitration is significantly differentiated between Western and Eastern jurisdictions.[64] German practitioners suggest that an arbitration tribunal should play an active role in initiating mediation, while the US and other European Civil Law jurisdictions do not so provide.[65] *Ex parte* meetings are common in China's mediation-arbitration practice,[66] but this type of practice is opposed by 66 percent of practitioners in a global survey.[67] Differentiated positions can also be found in relation to whether the arbitrator, who also played a role as a mediator, can actively pursue a settlement plan,[68] provide opinions and evaluate cases.[69] Due to various differences in understanding,

[62] See discussion in Sect. 2.1; also, Clarisse von Wunschheim, *Enforcement of Commercial Arbitral Awards in China: Business Laws of China* (West, 2011), 267–68.

[63] For the disputed facts of *Keeneye*, see above n 51.

[64] Shahla F. Ali, 'The Morality of Conciliation: An Empirical Examination of Arbitrator "Role Moralities" in East Asia and the West' (2011) 16(1) *Harvard Negotiation Law Review* 1, 3–10.

[65] Christian Bühring-Uhle, Lars Kirchhoff and Matthias Scherer, 'Two Surveys on Arbitration and Settlement' in Christian Bühring-Uhle, et al. (ed), *Arbitration and Mediation in International Business* (Kluwer Law International, 2006) 105. The authors opined that the arbitrator's role to make an independent and neutral decision is distinct from the mediator's role to facilitate the settlement. The distinctions between the different roles of arbitrators and mediators subsequently causes the different requirement of qualifications, or possibly the inappropriate disclosure of information in the mediation-in-arbitration practice. See also 韩健 [Han Jian],《现代国际商事仲裁法的理论与实践》[The Theory and Practice of Modern International Commercial Arbitration], (China Law Press, 2000) 191; 乔欣 [Qiao Xin],《仲裁权论》[The Research on Arbitration Power], (China Law Press, 2000) 27.

[66] Ibid, 27–28.

[67] Bühring-Uhle, Kirchhoff and Scherer, above n 65, 110–116.

[68] Ibid; The positive expectation regarding the tribunal's suggestion of settlement formula is 51% in Eastern countries and 58% in Western countries. The actual frequency is 40% and 16% respectively.

[69] The overall attitudes towards this practice is not positive, although a clear difference is made between those disclosing with the consent of the parties (known as "case evaluation"), and those disclosing without the consent of the parties (known as "hint at the possible outcome"). The acceptance of the former is higher (62%) than the latter (about 25%). The influence of different legal cultures is also significant, as the German participants reflect a higher recognition in both practices while others do not. See also Shahla F. Ali, 'Barricades and Checkered Flags: An Empirical Examination of the Perceptions of Roadblocks and Facilitators of Settlement Among Arbitration Practitioners in East Asia and the West' (2010) 19 *Pacific Rim Law and Policy Journal* 243, 248–53; Ali, above n 64, 15–20. According to Shahla Ali, the acceptance is 35% in East Asia and 24% in the West; the actual frequency in practices is 4% in East Asia and 8% in the West.

the *CEDR Reports* strongly recommend that mediation-in-arbitration practice, particularly active movements proposed by arbitrators, should be carried out with great caution and on the basis of the mutual consent of the parties.

The mediation-in-arbitration practice in China poses a real risk of violating impartiality in many ways, due to the lack of sufficient guidance and supervision from both the arbitration commissions and through judicial review. As illustrated by *Keeneye*, the active role in proposing a settlement plan of the arbitrators/mediators would cause some defects in mediation-in-arbitration.[70]

Significant procedural issues were identified by Chinese practitioners, especially after *Keeneye*. Some leading Chinese arbitration rules now regulate the inappropriate disclosure and use of information obtained during mediation by providing that such information obtained during mediation shall not be used in later arbitration proceedings.[71] However, this is not a perfect solution to the information asymmetry between the parties, as the arbitrators may also get *ex parte* information or form their own impressions during mediation, which may consequently cause distrust of the arbitrators and prevent the parties from being proactive in mediation. An alternative solution provided by the *Hong Kong Arbitration Ordinance* is that the arbitrators shall disclose all private information they obtain during mediation as long as it is "material" in relation to the case.[72] *CEDR Reports* reviewed both solutions and concluded that neither can fully resolve the problem of using private information, but suggested that a more flexible structure of the tribunal may provide cost-efficient yet impartial mediation-in-arbitration procedures.[73]

An overall conclusion of the mediation-in-arbitration procedures in Chinese arbitration practices, such as represented by *Keeneye*, is that plenty of procedural steps are taken under the discretionary powers of the tribunal, and it is difficult to conclude that impartiality is achieved during the process. The discretionary power of the tribunal in mediation-in-arbitration is only one example of the procedural issues in China's arbitration practices with respect to impartiality. Similar procedural issues are also reflected in other cases such as *Polytek*.[74] In that case, the arbitrators failed to give

---

70 Although, practically, experienced arbitrators in China would like to limit the use of settlement proposals to only when the facts and positions of the parties are clear, and try not to impress upon the parties that a refusal of the plan would cause an unfavoured award. See Tang Houzhi, above n 59, 554, which provides the mediation techniques of CIETAC arbitrators, including: firstly, in CIETAC practice, the arbitrator-turned-conciliator never makes a concrete settlement proposal before the facts of the case become ninety percent clear and the parties know where they are; and secondly, a concrete settlement proposal is made at the late stage of conciliation when the gap (difference) between the parties has been narrowed to the minimum extent.

71 *CIETAC Arbitration Rules* (2015), art 47(9); *BAC Arbitration Rules* (2022), art. 43(5).

72 S33(4), Cap 609 *Arbitration Ordinance (Hong Kong)*, 1 June 2011. Similar provisions can also be found in the *Commercial Arbitration Act 2010* (NSW) s 27D(7), although applied only in domestic arbitration in NSW.

73 Kun Fan, 'The Risks of Apparent Bias when an Arbitrator Acts as a Mediator: Remarks on Hong Kong Court's Decision in *Keeneye*' (2011) 13 *Yearbook of Private International Law* 93, 102–105.

74 *Polytek Engineering Company Ltd v Hebei Import & Export Corp.*, High Court of the Hong Kong Special Administrative Region. Court of Appeal, 16 January 1998, Civil Appeal No 116 of 1997, reported in (1998) 23 *Yearbook—Commercial Arbitration* 666–84 (Hong Kong No. 12); Albert

notice to one party when inspecting the other party's factory during the arbitration procedure. The Hong Kong court held that such behaviour breached the principle of impartiality and denied enforcement of the CIETAC award on the ground of public policy.[75]

A further issue is whether the Chinese courts have provided sufficient supervision on impartially issues that arise in arbitration proceedings. It is likely that the judicial supervision provided by the Chinese courts, such as provided by the Xi'an Court in *Keeneye*, which merely focused on the compliance of the XAAC's rules, was not satisfactory. Although the Hong Kong Court of Appeal later held that it is more appropriate for the domestic courts of the seat of arbitration to review these activities, as they may have a better understanding of the distinct legal culture and practical customs,[76] it is doubtful that the Chinese courts really fulfilled their role in providing supervision on the issue of breach of impartiality in the *Keeneye* Case.[77] Similarly, in *Polytek,* it is arguable that the supervisory courts in China also failed to address it in accordance with an evaluation of impartiality.

Generally, the impartiality issue during arbitration proceedings is rarely exposed in Chinese courts' review of foreign cases and foreign-related cases. This does not prove that impartiality is largely assured, but that it is largely ignored by the whole arbitration system in China. As stated in *Louis Dreyfus*, the SPC not only denied the review of impartiality during the composition of the tribunal, but also stated that the behaviour of arbitrators would not be covered by its judicial review.[78] Without sufficient respect for party autonomy, regulation and guidance on the behaviour of the arbitrators, and an evaluation of impartiality in the judicial review stage, it is difficult to conclude that a standard of impartiality—exclusion of real bias or apparent bias—is achieved and adopted under the Chinese arbitration system. Cases such as *Polytek* and *Keeneye* clearly remind Chinese practitioners that much needs to be done in ensuring the impartiality of China's arbitration practices, and for the Chinese judiciary to understand impartiality within the scope of procedural public policy to the same level as their international counterparts.

---

Jan van den Berg, 'New York Convention of 1958: Refusals of Enforcement' (2007)18(2) *ICC International Court of Arbtiration Bulletin* 1, 20–21; Weixia Gu, '15 Years of the Handover: The Rise, Discontent, and Positive Interaction of Cross-border Arbitration in Hong Kong with Mainland China' (2013) 9 *East Asia Law Review* 42, 63–67.

[75] Ibid.

[76] [2011] CACV No. 79; Weixia Gu, above n 74, 55–60; Kun Fan, 'Transnational Standards Struggling with Local Norms: Through the Lens of Arbitration Transplantation in China' (2013) 18 *Harvard Negotiation Law Review* 175, 188.

[77] The roles of the supervisory and enforcing courts will be discussed in Sect. 6.2 in Chap. 9.

[78] See discussion in Sect. 2.1.2.

### 2.3 Impartiality in Decision-Making

In international practice, the impartiality issue may also be considered when evaluating the decision-making of arbitrators. Sometimes, impartiality may be challenged on the basis that the arbitrators' decision-making was influenced by their personal knowledge and understanding of a particular issue. For example, in *Sidarma Societa Italiana di Armamento v Holt Marine Indus Inc*,[79] a challenge was brought on the basis of the dissenting arbitrator's opinion that the other two arbitrators failed to "pierce the corporate veil" due to their own personal business considerations. This claim was supported by the district court by referring to the "evident partiality" standard, but the court was reluctant to vacate the award when considering the international nature of the disputes and possible consequences for the entire industry.[80]

This issue is not addressed in Chinese arbitration practice. It is consistent with judicial practice in China that the courts focus on compliance with arbitration rules and are reluctant to go deeper in reviewing the behaviour of arbitrators not expressly regulated by arbitration rules. Though impartiality issues at the decision-making stage are not specifically dealt with in Chinese legislation, the arbitration commissions may provide guidance for dealing with these issues. For example, BAC's internal regulation provides a time limit for decision-making to prevent any delay that may benefit any party.[81]

### 2.4 Institutional Impartiality

It is also an issue when the impartiality of the arbitration institution is challenged. Chinese arbitration commissions may face a particular type of claim that argues that there is institutional partiality given their distinct position and role under Chinese arbitration law.[82] Such claims were observed in earlier cases. In *Tianjin Stationary & Sporting Goods Import and Export Corporation (PR China) v Verisport BV* (*Netherlands*), a Dutch party alleged that CIETAC lacked impartiality because "Tianjin Corporation is a State enterprise and CIETAC is a State arbitral institution" and "it comes as no surprise that an award was rendered which saves Tianjin's face".[83]

---

[79] 515 F Supp 1302 (SDNY 1981).

[80] Schebwel and Lahne, above n 2, 211–212.

[81] 陈福勇 [Chen Fuyong],《未竟的转型: 中国仲裁机构现状与发展趋势实证研究》[Unfinished Transformation: An Empirical Study of the Current Status and Future Trends of China's Arbitration Institutions] (Law Press China, 2010) 130;《北京仲裁委员会关于提高仲裁效率的若干规定》[Several Regulations of the BAC for the Enhancement of Arbitration Efficiency] (2003), art 9.

[82] For the significant position and role of the Chinese arbitration commissions, see Sect. 4 in Chap. 3. G.1.

[83] Arrondissements rechtbank [Court of First Instance], Zutphen, 3 September 1996, reported in (1997) 22 *Yearbook-Commercial Arbitration* 766–767 (Netherlands No 23).

Similarly, in another case in which a CIETAC arbitral award sought enforcement in Japan, the defendant argued that CIETAC lacked impartiality because both CIETAC and the Chinese party were subject to the supervision of the Ministry of Commerce (formerly the Ministry of Foreign Trade and Economic Co-operation, 'MOFCOM') in China.[84] Nevertheless, both arguments challenging the impartiality of CIETAC were rejected. The courts found no factual basis for the challenge to the impartiality of CIETAC and stated that the connection between CIETAC, a State-established arbitration commission and the State-owned enterprises, was not a sufficient ground for such a challenge.[85]

It is doubtful whether any claim of "institutional partiality" can be accepted by the court. Professor Huang concludes that the claim of bias against the arbitration commissions in China does not exist because it is neither expressly provided for by national law and the *NYC*; nor is it consistent with the general principle that a judicial review of the enforceability of an arbitration award cannot be conducted on the merits of the case.[86] The author, however, questions this opinion. Even though the challenges in the previous cases failed, it was because the challenges were based on the relationship between CIETAC and the Chinese government. Yet it is undeniable that impartiality concerns may occur as a result of the behaviour of the arbitration institution and its staff's activities, as shown in *Keeneye,* which shall be covered later when discussing the bias rule in arbitration law.[87]

In other jurisdictions, arbitration institutions are generally exempted from liability unless their activities are held to be dishonest or fraudulent.[88] Besides dishonest and fraudulent behaviour, an arbitration institution's impartiality is rarely discussed by the court. For example, in *Gong Benhai v HKIAC*, the issue of the impartiality of an arbitration institution was raised by a Chinese party before a Hong Kong court and the argument was rejected.[89] The core issue was whether the arbitration institution could be sued on the basis of their decision in dealing with the challenge of impartiality of the arbitrators. The court held that the HKIAC was not the right defendant; that

---

[84] *Buyer v Seller*, High Court of Tokyo, 27 January 1994, reported in (1995) 20 *Yearbook-Commercial Arbitration* 742 (Japan No 5).

[85] See also Chap. 5, Sect. 5.3.

[86] 黄亚英, 李薇薇 [Huang Yaying, Li Weiwei],《中国仲裁裁决在外国的承认和执行》[Enforcement of the Chinese Arbitral Awards in Foreign Jurisdictions] (2002) 6 中国对外贸易 *China's Foreign Trade* 17, 18–19.

[87] See Sect. 2.2.

[88] For example, such immunity is provided by legislation in Hong Kong; Section 105, Cap 609 Arbitration Ordinance (Hong Kong), 1 June 2011.

[89] 宮本海對香港國際仲裁中心 [Gong Benhai v Hong Kong International Arbitration Centre], High Court of Hong Kong Special Administrative Region, Court of the First Instance, HCMP 325/2014, 28 April 2014. The case summary can also be found at: <http://www.hkiac.org/sc/news/457>. In this case, Mr. Gong, and Dandong Tyre Factory submitted their dispute to the HKIAC. During the arbitration proceeding, Gong challenged independence and impartiality of two arbitrators after the tribunal refused to order the disclosure of some evidence as requested by Gong; the challenge was later rejected by the HKIAC in accordance with HKIAC's Challenge Rule 2008. Gong then challenged such a rejection before the Hong Kong Court of First Instance and the HKIAC was listed as the only defendant.

the application for court intervention of an arbitration proceeding was not within the time limit; and the HKIAC had not shown any dishonesty and was therefore not liable for exercising its function.[90] This case illustrates that the issue of impartiality of the tribunal is unlikely to extend to an arbitration institution when the latter exercises its functions appropriately. It is also a lesson for Chinese practitioners in understanding the position and status of the Chinese arbitration commissions and their impartiality, as the current legislation and arbitration rules are silent on this issue.

## 3 Protection of the Parties' Rights: The Hearing Rule

### *3.1 Introduction: The Hearing Rule*

Principles of procedural law generally require the parties to be heard fairly. Such principles include the protection of the parties' rights to be represented, to know the claims and evidence against them, and to defend their position. In European countries, these rights are protected under Article 6 of the *European Convention on Human Rights*.[91] The *UNCITRAL Model Law* and the national arbitration laws also provide parties' rights to fair notice and fair opportunity to present their own arguments.[92]

The requirement of a fair trial is covered by the ground of due process in Article V(1)(b) of the *NYC* and the ground of public policy in Article V(2)(b).[93] It is notable, however, that these grounds may apply only when the arbitration proceeding was an "egregious departure from the due process of law"[94]; in many cases, procedural errors that did not egregiously depart from due process or the principle providing for a fair trial are found not to be a ground for non-enforcement of an arbitral award. For example, in a series of cases, it was the actual reception of the notice, rather than the fulfilment of the law of service of documents that was emphasised; as long as the party received sufficient notice, no matter whether the format of service was satisfied, it was generally considered not to be a reason to negate the award.[95] Also, if

---

[90] Ibid; *UNCITRAL Model Law,* art 13(3); Section 105, Cap 609 Arbitration Ordinance (Hong Kong), 1 June 2011.

[91] This provision applies to both criminal and civil cases. In particular, it provides the person under criminal cases minimum rights such as adequate time and facilities to prepare their defence, access to legal representation, the right to examine witnesses against them or have them examined, and the right to the free assistance of an interpreter.

[92] *UNCITRAL Model Law*, art 18, art 23(3), and art 24(2).

[93] For the relationship between the ground of due process (Art V(1)(b)) and public policy (Art V(2)(b)), see Sect. 2.2.2 in Chap. 1; see further discussion in Sect. 6.

[94] Schwebel & Lahne, above n 2, 217.

[95] *English Company X v. Spanish Company Y*, Tribunal Supremo [Supreme Court], 10 February 1984, reported in (1985) 10 *Yearbook-Commercial Arbitration* 493 (Spain No 5); *X (Finnish shipowner) v. Y (Spanish charterer)*, Tribunal Supremo [Supreme Court], 11 February 1981, reported in (1982) 7 *Yearbook-Commercial Arbitration* 356 (Spain No1); *Intercommerce, Sofia v.*

a party voluntarily and intentionally defaulted in attending the arbitration proceeding and abandoned their right to present evidence, it then could not claim that the other party failed to present any evidence that would favour the defaulting party, and such failure constituted a fraud that would cause a refusal of enforcement.[96]

## 3.2 *Practice in China*

Both legislation and arbitration rules provide detailed guidance to tribunals in China in regulating arbitration proceedings and to courts in supervising such proceedings. Chapter 4 of the *CAL* provides the general requirement of oral hearings, the confidentiality of hearings, procedures on notifying the parties of the hearing, and provisions for the withdrawal of claims and award by default.[97] The *CAL* also provides guidance regarding the onus of proof and evidence. The parties' right to present their case and participate in the hearing is further provided and ensured in Articles 47, 48 and 69.[98]

Beside the legislative requirements, the Chinese arbitration commissions also provide detailed rules in regulating arbitration proceedings in order to ensure the fulfilment of the rights of the parties. The *CIETAC Rules* expressly provide that the tribunal shall "*afford a reasonable opportunity to all parties to make submissions and arguments*".[99] The *BAC Rules* also require the arbitral tribunal to treat the parties "fairly and impartially" and to "give each party a reasonable opportunity to present and argue its case".[100] Both rules deal with the procedural issues in details and mainly focus on the organisation and process of oral hearings. The parties' procedural rights, such as to get timely notice, to present their case, and to have the arbitration proceedings properly organised and arranged, are covered by the applicable arbitration law

---

*Menaguale Eugenio*, Corte D'Appello Di Roma, 24 September 1973, reported in (1976) 1 *Yearbook-Commercial Arbitration* 192 (Italy No9); *European Grain & Shipping Ltd. v. Seth Oil Mills Ltd.*, High Court of Bombay, 29 January 1983, reported in (1984) 9 *Yearbook-Commercial Arbitration* 411 (India No 9).

[96] *Biotronik Mess-und Therapiegeraete GmbH v Medford Medical Instrument*, 415 F Supp 133 (CDNJ 1976), reported in (1977) 2 *Yearbook-Commercial Arbitration* 250. (USA No. 8).

[97] *CAL*, art 39–42.

[98] The right to debate during the hearing is ensured in *CAL*, art 47. A final statement of each party shall be requested by the chief or sole arbitrator at the end of such debate. A written record of the hearing shall be made for all cases, and anyone involved in the hearing enjoys the right to correct their own statements in such written record. Arbitrators, record-makers and all parties involved in the hearing shall sign or seal the record; See CAL, art. 48. Art. 69 echoes the wordings in art.48, but uses "may" (可以) instead of "shall" (应当).

[99] *CIETAC Arbitration Rules* (2015), art 35(1).

[100] *BAC Arbitration Rules* (2022), art 25(5).

and chosen arbitration rules. As a result, most of the procedural errors may not necessarily be reviewed with the referrence to the principle of due process or the notion of fairness or natural justice.[101]

In relation to other issues not covered by the parties' right to be given proper notice and to make submissions and arguments, insufficient guidance is provided. Claims of infringed procedural rights are rarely made in China's arbitration practice and in subsequent judicial reviews. But there are still some reported instances of allegedly infringed procedural rights, as illustrated below. In *Mitsui*, the Chinese party argued that procedural fairness was breached for the following reasons: First, the tribunal proposed to introduce a neutral Chinese law expert to explain the disputed legal issues and later failed to do so; second, the tribunal did not exclude the foreign party's attorney from acting as its expert of Chinese law. However, the SPC did not respond to either of these claims.

Similarly, in *Shin-Etsu*, a series of claims in relation to the procedural errors were made, including the claim that there were inconsistent approaches adopted by the tribunal in accepting evidence and applying the law, the claim of accepting forged evidence, and the claim of depriving the Chinese party's right to fully represent their case. Neither of these claims was answered by the SPC, which refused enforcement purely on the basis of a failure to comply during the arbitration period regulated by the *JCAA Arbitration Rules*.

It is also not clear whether the evidence rule applied in arbitration procedures should be interpreted as strictly as that which is applied in civil litigation, and whether evidence not questioned and challenged by the other party can be accepted. The SPC did not respond to any of these issues in considering claims in relation to a violation of procedural public policy. For example, in *Zhejiang Tianhe*, the Chinese party argued that some evidence and materials were not sent to it and not questioned during the hearings, and they lost the opportunity to fully respond to such evidence due to the tribunal's behaviour. This claim was confirmed by the Shanghai HPC, but denied by the SPC, which did not comment on the acceptance of some particular evidence. Instead the SPC held that the tribunal generally "complied with the fundamental requirements of the arbitration rules" in organising the trial and hearings and decided that "the parties shall not claim to annul the award on the ground of whether and to what extent evidences are questioned and accepted". Again, the SPC adhered to the strict compliance of the arbitration rules only and did not go further to evaluate whether the parties' right to be given proper notice was actually satisfied.

In comparison, in quite a few cases the enforcement of CIETAC's awards was sought before Hong Kong courts, where procedural errors were held to be a violation of due process and public policy. In *Paklito v Klockner*[102] it was claimed that the CIETAC tribunal made their award on the basis of an opinion by an expert appointed by the tribunal, and that the parties were not accorded a sufficient opportunity to

[101] Therefore, the Chinese courts rarely apply the due process or public policy exception when the procedural errors fall in non-compliance with the arbitration rule or law. The relation of compliance of arbitration rules or law, and the due process and public policy exceptions.

[102] *Paklito Investment Ltd. v. Klockner East Asia* [1993] 2 HKLR 39.

challenge the opinion. In *China Nanhai Oil Corp Shenzhen Branch v Gee Tai Holdings Co Ltd*,[103] the CIETAC tribunal conducted an investigation on their own motion without notifying the parties about the investigation or the results and provided no opportunity for the parties to challenge them. Even though this conduct was permitted by the CIETAC rules at that time, it was held by the Hong Kong court to be a violation of due process. In *Polytek*, the failure to notify the defendants requiring their presence at an inspection of the factory conducted by the tribunal-appointed experts was considered to be a violation of Hong Kong's public policy.[104] These cases remind the arbitration practitioners in China to be vigilant in protecting the parties' right during the arbitration proceedings. In responding to these cases, CIETAC later modified its arbitration rules and improved its guidance for arbitrators. Similar modifications are also observed in other leading arbitration commissions in China.[105] However, little progress has been observed in Chinese courts when dealing with similar issues.

## 4 The Principle of Res Judicata and China's Judicial Sovereignty

### 4.1 International Developments and Discussions

Arbitral awards may also be challenged when dealing with issues that have already been determined; a common situation of a determined matter is a previous arbitral award or judgment. In almost all jurisdictions, such an issue is covered by the principle of *res judicata*, which means that: "*an earlier and final adjudication by a court or arbitration tribunal is conclusive in subsequent proceedings involving the same subject matter or relief, the same legal grounds and the same parties...*"[106] As a widely accepted principle in procedural law, *res judicata* is respected under common law as a rule of evidence, codified in civil procedural laws in many continental law jurisdictions, and also acknowledged in international law.[107] Furthermore, in many

---

[103] *China Nanhai Oil Joint Service Corp. Shenzhen Branch v. Gee Tai Holdings Co Ltd.* [1995] 2 HKLR 215.

[104] *Polytek Engineering Company Ltdv Hebei Import &Export Corp*, High Court of the Hong Kong Special Administrative Region, Court of Appeal, 16 January 1998, Civil Appeal No. 116/1997, reported in (1998) 23 *Yearbook-Commercial Arbitration* 666 (Hong Kong No. 12); van den Berg, above n 74, 20–21. Although the court was of the opinion that it would be a violation of public policy, it opined that the right to claim so was waived by the party as it kept silent during the entire arbitration process and only brought it out in the enforcement stage.

[105] *CIETAC Arbitration Rules* (*2012*) art 41 provides that the outcome of the investigation by the tribunal's own motion should be handed to the parties, and the parties should also be provided sufficient opportunity to challenge such an outcome. See also BAC Arbitration Rules (2008) art 31.

[106] Filip de Ly and Audley Sheppard, 'ILA Interim Report on Res Judicata and Arbitration' (2009) 25(1) *Arbitration International* 35, 36.

[107] Ibid, 41–49 (common law jurisdictions); 49–54 (European Civil Law jurisdictions); 55–60 (international law).

jurisdictions, it is considered a public policy issue, and the failure to respect such a principle would cause a judicial decision or award to be annulled or its enforcement refused.[108] It is notable that some scholars distinguish a negative effect of *res judicata* from its positive effect. The positive effect means the final and binding effect of the judgment or award, while the negative effect prevents the same issue from being re-litigated; such a negative effect, however, is highly controversial, as discussed below.[109]

In the context of international arbitration, the situation is more complicated because of the difference between arbitration proceedings and court proceedings. There are four situations in which *res judicata* may be applied in arbitration: (1) a partial award and a final award; (2) two arbitral tribunals; (3) a state court and an arbitral tribunal, and (4) a super-national court or tribunal and an arbitral tribunal.[110] The current legal theory and practices does not provide a complete answer to all these scenarios. Also, the issue of *res judicata* is not regulated at the stage of arbitration proceedings, as no arbitration rules have yet provided any guidance on it.[111]

The opinions of scholars are also divided. Some argue that the arbitration tribunal shall not be bound by any prior judicial decisions in the arbitration seat, because in modern arbitration practice, the connection between the arbitration seat and the substance of the dispute is weak.[112] It is also argued that the arbitral tribunal would be competent and independent to hear a dispute according to a valid arbitration agreement even if a court in another jurisdiction has made a decision on this issue, if the judicial decision breaches the arbitration agreement.[113] It is notable that the force of *res judicata* on domestic judgments should be distinguished in national and transnational forums; in *Lucchetti v Peru*, ICSID's Annulment Committee held that, in the arbitration of an ICSID dispute (which is of a supernational or transnational nature), a domestic judgment did not have the force of *res judicata*.[114] Scholars also suggest a number of courses of action and theories to solve this issue. Schlosser is of the opinion that a prior foreign judgment does not enjoy the fully force of *res judicata* at all times upon subsequent arbitration tribunals. In comparing the application of the principle of international comity,[115] he prefers to establish the theory on the basis

---

[108] Ibid, 66. Yet in some other countries, such as France, Netherlands and Belgium, this issue must be brought forward by the parties, as it is not a public policy consideration which can be reviewed by the courts on their own motion.

[109] Ibid, 36.

[110] Ibid, 37.

[111] Peter R. Barnett, *Res Judicata, Estoppel and Foreign Judgments: The Preclusive Effects of Foreign Judgments in Private International Law* (Oxford University Press, 2001) 23.

[112] Christer Söderlund, 'Lis Pendens, Res Judicata and the Issue of Parallel Judicial Proceedings' (2005) 22 *Journal of International Arbitration* 301, 310.

[113] Bernardo M. Cremades and Ignacio Madalena, 'Parallel Proceedings in International Arbitration' (2008) 24 *Arbitration International* 507, 509.

[114] *Industria Nacional de Alimentos, S.A. and Indalsa Perú, S.A. v The Republic of Peru*, ICSID Case No ARB/03/4—Annulment Proceeding, dated 5 September 2007, [87].

[115] Peter Schlosser, 'Arbitral Tribunal or State Court: Who Must Defer to Whom?' in (2001) *ASA Special SeriesNo.15: Arbitral Tribunal or State Court, Who must defer to whom?* 32, 32–34. As

of a "vested right" as identified by Dicey, which means that the winning party of the prior litigation is entitled to claim a vested right under such judgment in any other foreign jurisdiction (including arbitration tribunals). Thus, unless the prior litigation manifestly disregarded the arbitration award, its judgment would be respected by the arbitration tribunal.[116] Poudret points out that the arbitration tribunal should review the foreign judgment following the national law of the arbitration seat to recognise and enforce the foreign judgment, and such a decision is only subject to the judicial review of a court of the arbitration seat.[117]

Other scholars and practitioners suggest that it is the tribunal's discretion to decide on the *res judicata* of a prior foreign judgment if the parties have reached any agreement otherwise.[118] Some have also argued that the *res judicata* problem is in fact an issue of jurisdiction. It largely depends on whether the arbitral tribunal can successfully establish its jurisdiction to govern the case by distinguishing the prior judgment.[119] Gao Wei also suggests that the situation can be further divided into three categories: the arbitral award is contradictory to the judicial decision of (1) the arbitration seat; (2) the enforcing state, and (3) any other state, and the approach in judicial review shall be adjusted in accordance with each category.[120]

Another significant issue is the scope and effect of *res judicata*. Courts in different countries diverge in deciding whether issues beyond *dispositif* (rulings on the subject matter) enjoy a *res judicata* effect. Generally, in common law countries (including the UK and the US), not only do rulings on subject matter of a dispute have a *res judicata* effect, but so do the essential elements of the legal reasoning because of the application of issue estoppel.[121] In civil law jurisdictions, Germany, Sweden and Switzerland insist on a strict approach and opine that only *dispositif* has a *res judicata* effect, while jurisdictions such as France, Netherlands and Belgium provide that key reasoning may also have a binding effect, with certain conditions and limitations.[122]

---

reported by the author, such a principle is applied in US courts in recognising and enforcing foreign judgments.

[116] Ibid.

[117] Jean-Francois Poudret, 'Concluding Remarks on the Relationship Between State Courts and Arbitral Tribunals?' in (2001) *ASA Special Series No. 15: Arbitral Tribunal or State Court: Who must defer to whom?* 163.

[118] *HRH Constr.Corp.v.Bethlehem Steel Corp.*, 384 N.E.2d 1289 (NY 1978), where the court is of the opinion that even a general provision in agreements recognising the binding effect of a prior foreign judgment does not preclude the tribunal's contradictory decision. Randy D. Gordon, 'Only One Kick at the Cat: A Contextual Rubric for Evaluating Res Judicata and Collateral Estoppel in International Commercial Arbitration' (2008) 18 *Florida Journal of International Law* 549, where the author is of the opinion that the binding effect of a prior foreign judgment shall be provided in arbitration agreements if the parties intend to enjoy such effect.

[119] 高薇[Gao Wei],《论诉讼与仲裁关系中的既判力问题》[Comment on the Issue of Res Judicata in the Relationship between Arbitration and Litigation], (2010) 6 法学家 *The Jurist* 153.

[120] Ibid, 127–29.

[121] De Ly and Sheppard, above n 106, 42, 47.

[122] Ibid, 51–52; see particularly Swiss Federal Supreme Court, 3 April 2002, ATF 128 III 191; *Eco Swiss v. Benetton*, Hoge Raad, 20 January 1984, NJ 1987, 295; and Hoge Raad, 21 March 1997, NJ 1998, 207.

The latter approach is also favoured in international practice and by many scholars.[123] As Professor Lasok stated,

> *the 'extent of the effect of res judicata is defined by reference to the operative part of the judgment and to the reasoning in the judgment which supports it. The effect covers only those questions of fact and law actually or necessarily decided in the judgment'.*[124]

The *ILA Final Report* attempts to summarise the international consensus and provide guidance in regard to the preclusive effect of arbitral awards against any further arbitration proceedings.[125] It suggests that the arbitral award has a conclusive and preclusive effect if:

> 3.1 it has become final and binding in the country of origin and there is no impediment to recognition in the country of the place of the subsequent arbitration;
>
> 3.2 it has decided on or disposed of a claim for relief which is sought or is being reargued in the further arbitration proceedings;
>
> 3.3 it is based upon a cause of action which is invoked in the further arbitration proceedings or which forms the basis for the subsequent arbitral proceedings; and
>
> 3.4 it has been rendered between the same parties,

And such conclusive and preclusive effects as to

> 4.1 determinations and relief contained in its dispositive part as well as in all reasoning necessary thereto;
>
> 4.2 issues of fact or law which have actually been arbitrated and determined by it, provided any such determination was essential or fundamental to the dispositive part of the arbitral award.[126]

On the basis of the complicated practice in different jurisdictions and disparate discussions, it is not easy to predict the possible outcome of the application of the *res judicata* principle even with the guidance of the *ILA Reports* and *Recommendations.* Further developments may be observed on a case-by-case basis. The following sections discuss some of these issues in China's practice by reference to decided cases, though no clear approach of the Chinese courts is identified. We also noticed that the Chinese courts frequently refer to "judicial sovereignty" in a similar context and include these cases in our discussion, as detailed below.

## 4.2 *Cases in China's Arbitration Practice*

- *Shin-Etsu (No. 2)* and *Daming*

---

[123] De Ly and Sheppard, above n 106, 59–60.

[124] Paul Lasok, *The European Court of Justice: Practice and Procedure* (Butterworths, 1994) 120.

[125] Filip De Ly and Audley Sheppard, 'Final Report on Res Judicata and Arbitration' (2009) 25(1) *Arbitration International* 67.

[126] Filip de Ly and Audley Sheppard, 'ILA Recommendations on Lis Pendens and Res Judicata and Arbitration' (2009) 25(1) *Arbitration International* 83, Recommendation 3 and 4.

In *Shin-Etsu (No. 2)* and *Daming*, the involved arbitral award deals with the same issue which have been decided in a previous award and therefore arguably breached the *res judicata* principle.

Shin-Etsu brought arbitration claims against Zhongtian before the Japan Commercial Arbitration Association ('JCAA' hereafter) because of a contractual dispute. The tribunal rendered an award favouring Shin-Etsu, and awarded them damages calculated based on the period of January 2004 to July 2005 on the basis of breach of the disputed contract. This award was later refused enforcement in China (*Shin-Etsu (No. 1)*).[127] Shin-Etsu again brought a claim for damages for breach of contract, or the price of the goods, from August 2005 to July 2007 (later amended to March 2008) on the basis of the same arbitration agreement.

The JCAA tribunal of *Shin-Etsu (No. 2)* supported the claim of Shin-Etsu. In respect to the *res judicata* issue involved in this case, it stated that it would "strictly and cautiously" decide on the issue, and particularly, from a perspective of equity, considering that the previous award was refused enforcement in China. It further decided that the foundation of its decision in the second arbitration was the Japanese civil law, which was distinguished from the first award which was based on the agreement between the parties; thus, such a decision was made on the basis of different legal reasoning and therefore was not influenced by the *res judicata* effect of the first award.

At the enforcement stage, the Nantong IPC found several grounds for refusing to enforce this second award, including the public policy exception, on the basis that it was against the Chinese government's antitrust policy and disregarded the decision of the Chinese courts. The Jiangsu HPC also confirmed the application of the public policy exception, as the award disregarded the binding decision of the Chinese courts. It is notable, however, that both courts referred to the principle of finality of the arbitral award as a procedural conformity issue, rather than a public policy one. In a more recent case, *SIPC v UNI-TOP*, the SPC considered two conflicting CIETAC awards as a violation of Art 9 of the *CAL* (finality of the arbitral award) Art 274(4) of the *CCPL* (*ultra vires*) and did not consider it within the scope of public policy.[128]

The SPC held that this award violated the principle of *res judicata* by dealing with the damages between 2005 and 2008, which was already denied by the tribunal in the first arbitration. It also opined that the breach of *res judicata* was a procedural irregularity under Article V(1)(d) of the *NYC* rather than a violation of public policy.

---

[127] The dispute arose when the Chinese party, Zhongtian, signed a purchase agreement with the Japanese party, Shin-Etsu, purchasing fibre-optical products. Shortly after that agreement was signed, the Chinese government decided to impose anti-dumping duties against imported fibre-optical products, which seriously influenced the execution of the original agreement between the two parties. Since the Japanese party refused to re-negotiate the price, the parties were in dispute and the agreement was not fully performed.

[128] 中国石化集团国际石油勘探开发有限公司与UNI-TOP Asia Investment Limited申请撤销仲裁裁决案裁定书[Decision on the Application for the Annulment of the Arbitral Award between SINOPEC Group International Petroleum Exploration and Production Corp. and UNI-TOP Asia Investment Limited], Beijing 4th IPC, (2017)京04民特39号[Civil Special Procedure No.39], 27 April 2020.

It denied the application of the ground of public policy, on the basis that other grounds had already established the refusal of enforcement and therefore there was no need to apply such a residual ground.

A similar issue rose in *Daming*, in which two arbitral awards between the same disputed parties were rendered.[129] The first award was made by CIETAC's Southern Branch (Shenzhen) and the later award was rendered by CIETAC Beijing Headquarters. Both arbitration proceedings were based on the same arbitration agreement, which only referred to "CIETAC" and did not identify the particular branch. The SPC held that both arbitration proceedings were legally enforceable as the parties did not challenge the jurisdiction during the proceedings; and that the two proceedings were brought by different parties, who made claims based on different factual grounds and different causes of action; and found that the award made by CIETAC Beijing was lawful and not covered by the *res judicata* effect of the Shenzhen award.

- *Yongning* and *Mitsui*

*Yongning* and *Mitsui* illustrate another scenario where the issue of *res judicata* arises: a previous judicial decision and a later arbitration award.

In *Mitsui*, a dispute arose between Hainan Textile and Mitsui in relation to the payment of a debt. The Arbitration Institute of the Stockholm Chamber of Commerce ('SCC' hereafter) rendered an award in favour of Mitsui. At the enforcement stage, Hainan HPC provided that the award was contradictory to an earlier judgment of the Hainan HPC, which held that the provisions in the contract governing the debt did not have legal effect, and that the tribunal's decision, in ignoring the previous judgment, was a breach of *res judicata*, and China's public policy. Nevertheless, the SPC never responded to that opinion and enforced the award.

In *Yongning*, the foreign parties and the Chinese party established a joint venture, Jinan Hemofarm, and an ICC arbitration clause was included in the joint venture contract. Later, the Chinese party sued the joint venture on the basis of property disputes, and the foreign parties brought jurisdictional objections based on the arbitration clause to Jinan IPC, and then appealed to the Shandong HPC. Such objections were repeatedly rejected as the courts found the joint venture was not a party of the arbitration clause. The Jinan IPC then granted a property reservation measure towards the joint venture, and later rendered its judgments favouring the Chinese party, and such judgments were confirmed by the Shandong HPC in appeal.

At the same time, the foreign party started an ICC arbitration based on the joint venture agreement for the same property dispute. The ICC tribunal rendered an award holding that the application of the property reservation before the Chinese court breached the arbitration agreement, and the decision to grant such a property reservation could not be justified in both a legal and commercial sense; the failure of the joint venture was a direct consequence of this grant and the foreign parties were entitled to damages.

---

[129] Wunschheim, above n 62, App.D.16-17; also <http://www.wunscharb.com/court-decisions/daming-case-2003>.

In deciding whether to enforce the ICC award, the Jinan IPC opined that the ICC award ignored the judgments of the Chinese courts, infringed the judicial power of China, and violated China's public policy. The Shandong HPC also held that China's public policy was violated as the ICC award infringed both the jurisdiction of the Chinese courts and the *res judicata* of their judgment and was detrimental to China's judicial system. The SPC confirmed these opinions and concluded that both the jurisdiction and the "judicial sovereignty" of China would be infringed if such an award was enforced. This is the first case in which the SPC referred to the concept of "judicial sovereignty".

- *Kangwei*

Kangwei illustrates a more complicated scenario regarding the application of *res judicata.* In this case, disputes arose between Kangwei and Asian Medical with respect to the supplementary agreement of a joint venture contract. In 2003, Asian sued Kangwei for the joint venture's license and seal. Beijing 1st IPC ruled in favour of Asian, confirming the validity of the supplementary agreement and supporting Asian's rights to the licence and seal; the judgment was further confirmed on appeal by Beijing HPC. In 2005, Kangwei brought arbitration proceedings for unpaid interest and sought to rescind the supplementary agreement. A CIETAC tribunal supported the claim for unpaid interest but rejected the application to rescind the agreement. After that award was rendered, Kangwei brought a second arbitration claiming subsequent interest under the supplementary agreement. In this proceeding, Asian argued that the supplementary agreement contained provisions violating the mandatory law of China and should be *void ab initio.* The tribunal accepted this argument and made further decisions on the basis of the invalidity of this supplementary agreement.

In dealing with Kangwei's application to annul the second CIETAC award, both the Beijing 1st IPC and Beijing HPC opined that the second CIETAC award breached the principle of *res judicata.* Particularly, the Beijing 1st IPC referred to the SPC's decision in *Shin-Etsu (No. 2)* in supporting its opinion. Their opinions, however, were rejected by the SPC, who distinguished the second CIETAC award from the previous judgment and first CIETAC award on the basis of different claims sought in these cases. The SPC further held that the validity of the supplementary agreement was determined on the merits in this case which the lower courts should not review. This holding did not respond to whether the matter of the validity of the supplementary agreement in this case, which is a matter beyond *dispositif*, would have the *res judicata* effect.

- *Castel*, *Wicor*, *Palmer,* and *Gate*

This group of cases deal with one scenario, in which the Chinese party challenges the validity of the arbitration agreement before a Chinese court, pending the parallel arbitration proceeding.

*Castel* confirmed that a later court decision to negate the validity of the arbitration agreement will not affect the enforceability of a previous arbitral award made on the basis of that arbitration agreement in China; the principle of *res judicata* or *lis pendens* will not apply in this situation. In this case, a Chinese court had made an order negating the validity of the arbitration agreement in the disputed contract between Castel and the Chinese party, while a foreign arbitral award was made in accordance with this arbitration agreement. The Guangdong HPC preferred not to enforce the award on the basis of a violation of public policy, holding that such award was in conflict with the Chinese court's decision. The SPC found that such award was made prior to the Chinese court's decision on the validity of this arbitration agreement, and the Chinese party never argued the invalidity of this arbitration agreement during the arbitration proceedings, but actively brought it as a counterclaim. Thus, the SPC held that the tribunal's jurisdiction on this case was in accordance with the arbitration rules and *lex arbitri* and the enforcement of the tribunal's award would, therefore, not infringe the "judicial sovereignty" of China and violate China's public policy.

In this way the SPC distinguished this case from *Yongning* and denied the application of the ground of public policy. It is notable that, in Castel, the timing of the arbitral award and court decisions are crucial to determine whether there is any infringement of such "judicial sovereignty".[130]

An implication arising from this case is that the "judicial sovereignty", which was referred to by the SPC in both *Yongning* and *Castel,* but not formally defined by any legislation or judicial interpretation, may have a similar effect as the principle of *res judicata* or *lis pendens.*

In *Wicor*, the arbitration agreement between the parties referred to the ICC rules without a designated place of arbitration. In July 2011, Haopu sued Wicor for breach of contract before the Taizhou IPC, and in response, Wicor filed a jurisdictional challenge based on the existence of the arbitration agreement. Meanwhile, in November 2011, Wicor brought an arbitration claim against Haopu to the ICC, and the ICC Court of Arbitration designated Hong Kong as the place of arbitration. The SPC rejected the jurisdiction challenge via the operation of the Prior Reporting System in March 2012 by applying the *CAL* in determining the validity of the arbitration agreement, which resulted in the Taizhou IPC's ruling in March 2012 confirming its own jurisdiction to hear the dispute and HPC's decision upholding this ruling in December 2012. Despite Haopu's submission to the ICC and Taizhou IPC's notice on its jurisdictional ruling soon after March 2012, the ICC tribunal proceeded with an interim award in November 2012 confirming the validity of the arbitration agreement and the final award favouring Wicor in 2014.

Wicor sought enforcement of the ICC award before the Taizhou IPC, who then reported the case to Jiangsu HPC, referring to the infringement of China's judicial sovereignty under Art V(2)(b) of the *New York Convention.* Jiangsu HPC erroneously referred to Art V(1)(a), the invalid arbitration agreement under the *lex arbitri*, in its report to the SPC. In 2016, the SPC replied to Taizhou IPC refusing the enforcement of the ICC award but correctly pointing out that the *Hong Kong Arrangement* rather than the *New York Convention* should apply, and that, because the final award in the

[130] This is not to say the "judicial sovereignty" is exactly equal to these two principles in the context of the SPC. Another reference to the term "judicial sovereignty", see the discussion of the exclusive jurisdiction of the Chinese courts or arbitration commissions in dealing with purely domestic issues, in Sect. 3.3 in Chap. 8.

ICC arbitration was made (in 2014) after the Jiangsu HPC's ruling on the arbitration agreement being in effect (in 2012), enforcing such an award would conflict with the effective court ruling and therefore violate China's social public interest, under the wording of the *Hong Kong Arrangement*.[131] This suggests that the time gap between the arbitral award and the effective Chinese judicial decision is crucial in determining whether China's judicial sovereignty has been infringed.

A breakthrough was observed in the *Palmer* case, which involved a similar scenario. In May 2016, Zhongmu sued Palmer for damages before the Guangzhou Maritime Court under a bill of lading, on the back of which there was an arbitration clause. Palmer disputed the jurisdiction of the court on the basis of the arbitration clause. Upon the SPC's reply via the Prior Reporting System,[132] in October 2017 the Guangzhou Maritime Court held that the arbitration clause could not bind the subsequent holder of the bill of lading, which was further confirmed by Guangdong HPC in January 2018. Meanwhile, Palmer brought a parallel arbitration case for the same dispute against Zhongmu in London, and the tribunal made an award favouring Palmer in September 2016.

Palmer sought the enforcement of the London award before the Tianjin Maritime Court in January 2017. The Tianjin Maritime Court reported the case to Tianjin HPC, both opining that the enforcement should be refused on the basis of the lack of a valid and binding arbitration agreement between the parties (Art V(1)(a)). The SPC avoided the argument on the basis of Art V(1)(a), as the arbitration agreement may have been seen as binding and valid under *lex arbitri* (in this case, the UK law), but instead, determined that the enforcement of the award would be refused on the ground of public policy. According to the SPC, enforcing this award would implicitly affirm the binding effect of the arbitration agreement and would be against the effective ruling made by the Guangzhou Maritime Court negating the same arbitration agreement. "The outcome, therefore, would lead to inconsistent judicial decisions and violate the uniformity and consistency of the legal values in a State, which will definitely be a part of a State's public policy no matter how narrow and restrictive such a concept should be."

It is particularly notable that in this case the final arbitral award was made well before the Chinese courts' negative ruling on the arbitration agreement. Despite that, the award was still refused. This approach seems different from, and more expansive than, the approach adopted in *Castel* and *Wicor*, which still appreciates the sequence and time gap of the rulings of the Chinese court and the arbitral award.

*Gate* was another case following this rationale. In this case, the parties agreed to arbitration in China "as per ICC" in English, while the Chinese translation stated "ICC Rules". When a dispute arose from the performance of the contract, the Chinese party sought a review of the validity of the arbitration agreement before the Shijiazhuang IPC in May 2011. In Oct 2011, the foreign parties filed arbitration to the ICC, during which the Chinese party resisted the jurisdiction and notified the ICC and later the tribunal that the had filed the case for the review of the arbitration agreement before

[131] Art 7(3) of the *Hong Kong Arrangement.*

[132] (2017) 最高法民他 83 号 [SPC Civil Other Matters No. 83].

the Chinese court. Despite the objection of the Chinese party, the ICC designated Hong Kong as the place of arbitration and constituted tribunal, which made a partial award in 2013 to proceed with the substance of the dispute and the final award favouring the foreign party in 2015.

The foreign parties sought the recognition and enforcement of the arbitral award before Yichang IPC in 2015. However, Yichang IPC decided to postpone the proceeding pending Shijiazhuang IPC's judicial review on the arbitration agreement. Only when the Shijiazhuang IPC determined the arbitration agreement invalid (presumably, following the SPC's reply via the Prior Reporting System), did Yichang IPC resume the enforcement review, and refused the recognition and enforcement of the arbitral award on the ground of public policy (presumably, also following the SPC's reply). As the SPC reply was not released, we can only presume the SPC's reasoning from the Yichang IPC's ruling, which stated, "On the condition that the People's Court has already negated the validity of the arbitration agreements between the parties, the recognition and enforcement of any arbitral award made on the basis of those arbitration agreements would be conflicted with those legally effective orders made by the People's Court and violated the social public interest of the Mainland." It was emphasised in their reasoning that the review of the arbitration agreement was filed in May 2011, earlier than the arbitration filed in October 2011, the sequence of when the cases were filed were taken into account rather than the when the determination was made, as distinguished from *Castel* and *Wicor*.

- *Spliethoff*

In *Spliethoff*, Spliethoff's Bevrachtingskantoor B.V., signed a contract with two Chinese companies regarding the building of a ship. The 2011 arbitration arose from the performance of the shipbuilding contract. A few months earlier, the Chinese shipbuilder sued Spliethoff and two other parties for torts in the sale of the engine of the same ship before the Qingdao Maritime Court, alleging that they fraudulently supplied a second-hand engine as a new engine. The dispute was then appealed to Shandong HPC, which rendered the judgment in 2014, affirming such claim.

The Chinese parties resisting the arbitral award argued that the arbitral award made in 2012, which held that Spliethoff complied with all contractual duties, conflicted with the Chinese courts' final ruling. Such view was supported by the Qingdao Maritime Court, which held that the two rulings were in conflict despite the differing causes of action, and the recognition and enforcement of the arbitral awards would deny the Chinese court's 'judicial sovereignty'. This view, however, was rejected by majority view of the Shandong HPC on the basis of the different parties involved, the different nature of the underlying legal relationships (a building contract and a sale of engine contract) and the different causes of action (contract and torts). The SPC confirmed this view, and further added that there was a time gap between two disputes, that the engine dispute arose 210 days after the expiration of the due date for the handover of the ship under the shipbuilding contract. Thus, the two rulings were not in conflict, and the judicial sovereignty was not infringed.

## 4.3 Discussion: Practice in China

As summarised by scholars, Chinese legislation and arbitration rules provide limited guidance with respect to the principle of *res judicata*. The finality of the judgment and award is defined by law without sufficient elaboration on the relevant effect of *res judicata*.[133] Previous cases in China's judicial review practice have shown various situations in which the principle of *res judicata* would apply, including various situations, yet Chinese courts do not systematically apply this principle.[134]

### 4.3.1 Res Judicata and Judicial Sovereignty

In the context of our case pool, it seems that the Chinese courts are reluctant to adopt this principle as part of China's public policy. The express mentioning of *res judicata* was rare. In *Shin-Etsu* (*No.* 2), the principle of *res judicata* was recognised as provided by the *CAL* and the relevant arbitration rules; so the violation of this principle was construed as a procedural irregularity rather than a violation of public policy. In *SIPC v UNI-TOP*, another ground, ultra vires, was referred to justify a ruling dealing with the *res judicata* effect of a prior arbitral award. Only the discussion by the Hainan HPC in *Mitsui* referred to public policy concerns in dealing with the *res judicata* issue, but these opinions were not confirmed by the SPC.

Rather, the SPC had chosen to refer to a different concept, "judicial sovereignty" which had only some of the features of *res judicata*. In a series of cases, the SPC developed this concept and actively considered it as an element of public policy. While cases such as *Yongning*, *Castel* and *Wicor* appreciated the sequence of the Chinese judicial decisions and the arbitral awards, this attitude was abandoned in *Palmer* and *Gate*, in which the Chinese court's ruling on the arbitration agreement was upheld even though it was made after the tribunal's award. While in *Gate*, the court referred to the sequence of the dates of start of the Chinese court proceeding and the date when the arbitration was filed, in *Palmer* the timeline of the arbitration was never clearly reported in the analysis and therefore did not bear any weight.

The application of public policy, in the context of arbitral awards conflicting with the Chinese court's rulings, is further confirmed by the SPC in a systematic manner. In the *2021 Minutes of the National Symposium of the Chinese Court System on the*

---

[133] For finality of judgment, see CCPL art 10; For finality of arbitral awards, see *CAL* art 9(1). 江伟, 肖建国 [Jiang Wei and Xiao Jianguo],《论既判力的客观范围》[Discussing the Objective Scope of the Res Judicata Effect], (1996) 18(5) 法学研究 *CASS Journal of Law* 37, 37–38, 48; 傅攀峰 [Fu Panfeng],《普通法系国际商事仲裁裁决既判力问题的处理经验及其启示—以 Associated Electric v European Re 为例》[Experiences of the Common Law Jurisdictions in Dealing with the Res Judicata Effect of International Commercial Arbitral Awards and Lessons From Them: Taking the Associated Electric v European Re as an Example] (2012) 30 仲裁研究 *Arbitration Study* 64, 72–74.

[134] 高薇 [Gao Wei], above n 119.

*Adjudication of Foreign-related Commercial and Maritime Law Matters*,[135] the SPC confirmed that,

> *if the Chinese court had made a ruling holding the arbitration agreement was not formed, invalid, cease to be effective, or not enforceable, and the recognition and enforcement of an arbitral award would be conflicting with the Chinese court's ruling, the enforcing court should hold that China's public policy, as so defined in Art V(2)(b) of the New York Convention, was violated.*[136]

Based on the observation above, the author suggested that the most recent development of the SPC's rationale in handling this line of cases emphasises the authoritative nature of the Chinese judgments, especially those that negatively affect tribunal's jurisdictions. Rather, the sequence of the conflicting decisions was no longer of concern, as reflected in *Palmer* and *Gate*, as well as the SPC's *2021 Minutes*. From this perspective, the Chinese court's approach clearly deviates from the principle of *res judicata*.

The influence of adopting this approach could be far-reaching. As shown in the line of cases in which the Chinese courts' decision on arbitration agreement contradicts the foreign tribunals', namely, *Castel*, *Wicor*, *Palmer* and *Gate*, and taking into account that three out of four awards in these cases were refused enforcement, the Chinese courts proactively and expansively uphold and maintain their own assessment on the effect of the arbitration agreement and the jurisdiction of an arbitral tribunal. This approach is also echoed in recent cases like *Jiachuan Mechanical* (2020), in which an award made in the UK sought enforcement. In this case, Meikesi raised the claim against the validity of the arbitration agreement before the Shanghai Maritime Court pending the arbitration proceeding. The court held that both the tribunal and the Shanghai Maritime Court favoured the validity of the arbitration agreement, so China's public policy was not violated.[137] Should there be any inconsistency between the tribunal's and the Chinese court's determination on the arbitration agreement, the answer would be different.

Taking into account the restrictive and rigid approach in determining the validity and scope of the arbitration agreement under Chinese law,[138] there is a real danger that China is utilising the public policy ground to bypass the restriction imposed by Art V(1)(a) of the *NYC*, that the law used to review the arbitration agreement should

---

135 《全国法院涉外商事海事审判工作座谈会会议纪要》[Minutes of the National Symposium of the Chinese Court System on the Adjudication of Foreign-related Commercial and Maritime Law Matters], the SPC, released 31 December 2021.

136 Ibid, art 108.

137 《上海佳船机械设备进出口有限公司、美克斯海洋工程设备股份有限公司申请承认与执行法院判决、仲裁裁决案件其他民事裁定书》[Civil Ruling on the Application for the Recognition and Enforcement of A Foreign Arbitral Award between Shanghai Jiachuan Mechanical Equipment Import and Export Co Ltd and Meikesi Maritime Engineering Facility Co], Jiaxing IPC, (2019) 浙 04 协外认 1 号, 2 号 [Judicial Assistance Foreign Recognition No.1 and No.2], 1 July 2020.

138 See above Sect. 4.2 in Chap. 3.

be the *lex arbitri*, and to apply the Chinese law to the arbitration agreement even though the arbitration took place in other jurisdictions.[139]

### 4.3.2 The Scope of the Potential Res Judicata Effect

While it has been said that the SPC does not favour the recognition of the principle of *res judicata*, it is interesting, though, to see that the SPC adopted an approach similar to *res judicata* when distinguishing two rulings governing different but related matters in determining whether China's "judicial sovereignty" was infringed. In *Daming*, the SPC emphasised the distinction between the two awards on the basis of the different parties who brought the claim, the different content and scope of the claims, and the different causes of action. A similar approach was also observed in *Spliethoff*, in which the SPC reiterated the elements mentioned above, and further examined the sequence of, and time gap between, the two disputes. These identified elements are similar to those that have international consensus and are set out in the *ILA Recommendations.*[140] Yet the limited details provided in this case did not provide sufficient information to demonstrate that the SPC actually applied all of these tests to the facts.

In another line of cases that arguably touched on the notion of *res judicata*, it is noteworthy that Chinese courts have failed to establish a clear standard in deciding whether issues beyond the *dispositif* can have the *res judicata* effect. In *Shin-Etsu (No. 2)*, the SPC held that the principle of *res judiciata* was violated because the arbitral award dealt with damages between 2005 and 2008, which were already denied by the tribunal in *Shin-Etsu (No. 1)*. This is clearly a subject matter that falls within the scope of the *dispositif*. In *Mitsui*, the Hainan HPC commented on the possible *res judicata* effect of an earlier judgment negating the legal effect of a contract provision, which was the legal foundation of the awarded interests by the tribunal. This opinion, however, was not responded to by the SPC. In *Kangwei,* the Beijing 1st IPC and the Beijing HPC discussed the *res judicata* effect of the validity of the contracts in an earlier judgment and an earlier award, which were later negated in a second arbitral award. The SPC refused to review the issue regarding the validity of the underlying contract, holding that it was a substantive issue. In fact, it would have been better if the court had based its decision to uphold the award on a strict approach of limiting the scope of the *res judicata* effect to the *dispositif*, and denying the *res judicata* effect of other legal reasoning, in this case, the validity of the contract. In *Spliethoff*, while the lower courts referred to the conflicting conclusions made by the tribunal and the Chinese courts in dealing with the same or related facts, the SPC was silent on this matter and adopted the analysis to compare the different causes of action.

---

[139] For a more detailed analysis, see Shu Zhang and Peng Guo, 'The (ab)use of the public policy ground in the New York Convention in the judicial review of foreign arbitral awards: Recent developments in China', (2021) 43 *Houston Journal of International Law* 553.

[140] De Ly and Sheppard, above n 125.

It would not be a surprise if the Chinese courts insisted on such a strict approach in limiting the *res judicata* effect to the *dispositif* as suggested by scholars. This is because China's theory of *res judicata* was adopted from civil law jurisdictions such as Germany and Japan; and in these jurisdictions, such a strict approach is adopted.[141] It is noteworthy, however, that even in civil law jurisdictions the effect of legal reasoning is not totally ignored, especially when connected with the understanding of the *dispositif*.[142] As introduced earlier, though the civil law jurisdictions are more conservative in recognising the effect of legal reasoning compared with the common law's estoppel theory, they have been showing more flexibility in doing so in recent judicial practices. Even Chinese scholars have commented that the legislation in providing the finality of judgments and arbitral awards is abstract, and leaves room for judges to explain the scope of the *res judicata* effect.[143] The SPC's refusal to review the possible *res judicata* effect of legal reasoning in this situation may thus be a failure to distinguish the judicial review of the *res judicata* issue from the judicial review of merits.[144] The Chinese courts' limited ability and incentive to provide a high-quality, logical and comprehensive legal reasoning may also contribute to the ignorance of the *res judicata* effect on legal reasoning.[145]

All of these cases reflect that the principle of *res judicata* is not fully developed in China's judicial practice, as it is not formally recognised as an element of public policy. Also, its applicability in the judicial review proceedings is doubted in inconsistent practice, and even if it is ever applied, it is not clarified whether issues beyond *dispositif* would have a *res judicata* effect. A more detailed understanding of the *res judicata* principle, including its scope, the condition of application and applicable tests, would help the Chinese courts provide a more consistent approach in dealing with similar issues in the future.

## 5 Fraud and Dishonesty in Arbitration Practices

It is also generally accepted that fraud and dishonesty in arbitration proceedings should be recognised as a violation of procedural public policy. In a Swedish case, the enforcement of an award was refused because the arbitration was conducted so that the parties could take advantage of it in a bankruptcy proceeding. The Swedish court held that an award under such fraudulent circumstances was a violation of

141 江伟, 肖建国 [Jiang Wei, Xiao Jianguo], above n 133, 43–45. See also Sect. 2 in Chap. 3 regarding China's legal transplantation of German and Japanese law.

142 Section 4.2.

143 傅攀峰 [Fu Panfeng], above n 133, 72–74.

144 According to the *ILA Interim Report*, it is generally accepted that the *res judicata* issue is a procedural law issue rather than a substantive law issue. See de Ly and Sheppard, above n 106, 66.

145 江伟, 肖建国 [Jiang Wei, Xiao Jianguo], above n 133, 43.

public policy.[146] Similarly, in *Westacre*, the English High Court also stated that an award obtained by perjured evidence might lead to the application of public policy.[147] The English court further provided the conditions upon which a court may adduce additional evidences to decide on the possible perjury or fraud.[148]

In China, two possible types of fraudulently obtained awards are considered in the *CCPL*, but only for domestic awards. Article 244 of the *CCPL* provides that a domestic arbitral award may be annulled when: "…(iv) the main evidence that supports the award is forged; and (v) the opposing party intentionally hides evidence that is significant enough to influence the making of a fair award".[149] Such grounds are not applicable to foreign-related awards and international awards. The distinction between dealing with domestic and foreign-related or international awards in judicial review proceedings is clearly confirmed by many practitioners and scholars.[150] They acknowledge that a substantive judicial review of arbitral awards is limited to domestic awards only, and a review of the forged or hidden evidence would be subject to such a substantive judicial review for domestic awards. On other words, according to this division, forged and hidden evidence should not be reviewed in dealing with foreign-related or international awards.[151]

This understanding which separates the judicial review on forged evidence from public policy and insists that such judicial review should only be limited to domestic awards, however, is somewhat problematic. First, separating these two instances of fraud from public policy may result in a questionable interpretation concluding that fraud in taking evidence is not covered by public policy; secondly, indicating that the judicial review approach for these two situations should only be limited to

---

[146] Högsta domstolen, NJA 2002, 45 (Supreme Court, Sweden), reported by Lars Heuman and Göran Millqvist, 'Swedish Supreme Court Refuses to Enforce an Arbitral Award Pursuant to the Public Policy Provision of the New York Convention' (2003) 20(5) *Journal of International Arbitration* 493, 497.

[147] *Westacre Investments Inc. v. Jugoimport-SDPR Holdings Co. Ltd.*, Beogradska Banka and others, High Court of Justice, Queen's Bench Division (Commercial Court), 19 December 1997, reported in (1998) 23 *Yearbook-Commercial Arbitration* 836 (UK No. 51), 878; Further confirmed in appeal: *Westacre Investments, Inc. v. Jugoimport*—SDPR Holding, Court of Appeal, Civil Division, 12 May 1999, [2000] 1 QB 288, also reported in (1999) 24 *Yearbook-Commercial Arbitration* 753 (UK No 54), 769.

[148] See further Chap. 9, discussing the introduction of new evidences in the judicial review.

[149] *CCPL*, art 244.

[150] See Sect. 4.3 in Chap. 3, discussions around n 108.

[151] 肖永平 [Xiao Yongping],《也谈我国法院对仲裁的监督范围》[Comments on the Scope of Judicial Supervision of Arbitration by Chinese Courts] (1998) 87(1) 法学评论 *Law Review* 42, 49;王胜明 [Wang Shengming],《在第六届中国仲裁论坛上的讲话》[Presentation at the 6th China Arbitration Forum] October 31 2012, Beijing. Mr. Wang Shengming is the Vice Chairman of the Legal Affairs Committee of the National People's Congress; 叶丹 [Ye Dan],《从现代司法理念角度探讨司法力渗透仲裁的合理度—以我国法院对涉外仲裁裁决的司法审查制度为现实载体》[Discussing Reasonable Involvement of Judicial Power in Arbitration from the Perspective of Modern Notions of Judiciality: Start from the Judicial Review System of the Foreign-Related Arbitral Awards in Our Courts], in 韩健 [Han Jian] (ed),《涉外仲裁司法审查》[Judicial Review of Foreign Arbitration] (Law Press, 2006) 98, 106–108.

domestic cases may imply that the possibility of fraud in foreign-related and international awards would not be reviewed, even taking into consideration public policy concerns.[152] Combining these two possible implications, it may be concluded that the applicability of procedural public policy may be restricted by this understanding, not only in domestic cases but in foreign-related and international cases also.

In some SPC cases, there were arguments made by the parties regarding fraud in the underlying transactions or in the evidence submitted to the tribunal, such as in *Zhongwei* and *FSG Automotive*. In the latter, the majority of the Hubei HPC, as well as the SPC, determined that the evidence admission should be within the discretion of the tribunal and not reviewable at the enforcement stage.

Before the SPC's holding in 2015 in *FSG Automotive*, we also observe some analysis from the lower courts. In *Foshan*,[153] for example, the original dispute arose between Foshan Investment and Foshan Chemical Fabrics, and the tribunal held that Chemical Fabrics should repay a debt to Investment. The award was later cnforced on the basis of settlement. Gaoxin, a third party who was also a creditor of Chemical Fabrics, applied for an annulment of the award on the basis that such arbitration was fabricated by the two parties, who were both governed by the Foshan Financial Bureau, in order to avoid any debt-repayment to other creditors. This claim was rejected on the basis that Gaoxin, as a third party, was not a qualified plaintiff for an annulment judicial review under current Chinese law.[154] The Foshan IPC did not analyse whether the award was obtained fraudulently, and refused to apply the ground of public policy, but provided its legal reasoning on a factual-based analysis that the debt between Investment and Chemical Fabrics existed first and was repaid prior to the debt between Gaoxin and Chemical Fabrics, and such repayment of debt was therefore not fraudulent.[155]

Some domestic cases also dealt with the fraud issue but provided only limited guidance to courts in reviewing foreign-related or international awards. In one case, the court held that the tribunal failed to review whether there was any violation of mandatory rules, and whether the dispute was fabricated by the parties to take advantage of a third party; and further opined that the disputed interests rendered to the winning party should be submitted to the State, and that an award rendering

---

152 See further in Chap. 9.

153 高新 (香港) 有限公司与佛山市投资咨询公司等申请撤销仲裁裁决纠纷案广东省佛山市中级人民法院民事裁定书》[Civil Order of the Guangdong Foshan Intermediate People's Court in regard of the Application of Goldensail (Hong Kong) Ltd and Foshan Investment Consulting Co for Annulment of an Arbitral Award] Foshan Intermediate People's Court, (2004) 佛中法民四初字第 133 号 [Fourth Civil Branch, Case of First Instance No. 133]. It is arguable whether this case is a domestic or foreign-related case; the original award seems a domestic one, but the annulment claim was brought by a Hong Kong party. We classified it as a foreign-related case because the Foshan IPC declared it as so and might be applied to the judicial review scheme for foreign-related cases accordingly.

154 Ibid.

155 For an analysis of such a factual-based analysis approach, see further in Sect. 4.3 in Chap. 9.

such interests infringed the State's public interests.[156] As Wang and Chen reported, in another series of cases in Beijing, two parties signed 21 contracts in relation to the sale of apartments—nine of them were disputed. The buyers eventually won the case. In the annulment proceeding, the seller (the losing party of the arbitration) argued that the contracts were signed for the purpose of illegal financing and the contracts were in fact fabricated to provide a guarantee for such financing transactions. When this argument was rejected, the seller provided additional evidence and argued that the apartments were in fact sold to and actually pre-occupied and used by other parties before signing the disputed contract in the enforcement stage. The court eventually refused to enforce these awards on the basis that the tribunal's decisions were made without the proper presentation of the main evidence, but the public policy exception, though discussed by the parties and courts, was not applied.[157]

These two domestic cases provide totally different understandings of the issue of fraud in arbitration proceedings in China's judicial practice. The first case may imply that fraud in arbitration, which is not covered by Article 244(iv) and (v) of the *CCPL*, should be covered by the ground of public policy, at least for domestic cases; conversely, the other series of cases provided that a lack of evidence, or intentionally hiding the main evidence, is covered by Article 244(iv) or (v), and therefore did not fall under the public policy exception; thus, the lack of evidence or intentionally hiding evidence may not be reviewed when dealing with foreign-related or international awards, as Article 244(iv) and (v) does not apply. Furthermore, in the latter series of cases, the seller took advantage of the judicial review by adducing evidence about its own behaviour in hiding main evidence during the arbitration proceeding. As Wang and Chen suggested, this type of litigation strategy is not covered and regulated by the current judicial review scheme.[158] Generally, these domestic cases provide limited and inconsistent responses to whether in China the principle against fraud is part of procedural public policy in dealing with foreign-related and international cases.

Finally, it is also notable that fraud in arbitration proceedings, if it is ever covered by public policy, should be distinguished from fraudulent activities in relation to the underlying contract. It is generally agreed that the latter type of fraud should be "brought before and decided by" the tribunal and should not be a reason for non-enforcement.[159]

---

156 王亚新, 陈福勇 [Wang Yaxin, Chen Fuyong] «《民事诉讼法修改与不予执行仲裁裁决—以北京仲裁委员会为对象的实证分析》» [Amendment of China's Civil Procedural Law and Non-Enforcement of Arbitral Awards: An Empirical Study on the Beijing Arbitration Commission] (2012) 5 法学杂志 *Law Science Magazine* 111, 118.

157 Ibid. 117–118.

158 Ibid. 118. Also, for the extent of judicial review in regard of taking new evidence, see further Sect. 5 in Chap. 9.

159 Dirk Otto and Omaia Elwan, 'Article V(2)' in Herbert Kronke et al. (eds), *Recognition and Enforcement of Foreign Arbitral Awards* (Wolter Kluwer, 2010) 345, 375; also see Sect. 3 in Chap. 5, discussing fraud in the substantive underlying dispute.

# 6 Approaches to Judicial Review

## *6.1 Determining Which Ground to Apply to Procedural Errors*

Procedural issues can be considered under three major grounds for the non-enforcement of arbitral awards under the *NYC* scheme: irregularity (Article V(1)(d)), lack of due process (Article V(1)(b)) and public policy (Article V(2)(b)).[160] First, those activities contrary to the agreement of parties, or the *lex arbitri*, are subject to review under Article V(1)(d) ('irregularity'). Secondly, an arbitral award is also subject to the requirement of due process under Article V(1)(b), especially regarding the protection of the parties' right to be properly notified and the right to present their case. Public policy in Article V(2)(b) may also apply to any situation that violates fundamental procedural principles. It is therefore a practical problem for the parties and the court to choose from the three grounds in their judicial review of the arbitral award.

The relationship between the three grounds is complicated, and opinions are divided among practitioners and scholars in different jurisdictions. Van den Berg suggests that the grounds of irregularity should be subject to the fundamental requirement of due process.[161] The opinion that procedural fairness and due process are covered by Article V(2)(b) is also confirmed in many cases.[162] Van den Berg provides that the public policy exception is not residual, but is a ground that co-exists with other grounds.[163] In some cases, parties even prefer to use the public policy defence rather than the due process defence when dealing with some procedural errors, because different standards of judicial review apply to these different grounds.[164]

The understanding of the elements and scope of these grounds are also influenced by national legislation and distinct approaches adopted by national courts in different jurisdictions. For example, a breach of natural justice is considered a violation of due

---

160 Section 2.

161 Albert Jan van den Berg, *The New York Arbitration Convention of 1958: Towards a Uniform Judicial Interpretation* (Kluwer Law and Taxation Publishers, 1981)324; For example, see *Danish buyer v. German (F.R.) seller*, Oberlandesgericht Köln [Higher Regional Court of Cologne] 10 June 1976, reported in (1979) 4 *Yearbook—Commercial Arbitration* 323. In this case the provisions of the agreed arbitration rules provided that the name of arbitrators were not made known to the parties; such provision was held against the fundamental requirement of due process (under art V(1)(b)), although the satisfaction of parties' agreement (under V(1)(d)) was not explicitly breached.

162 *Dutch seller v. Swiss buyer*, Obergericht of Basle, 3 June 1971, Obergericht of Basle [Appeal Court of Basel], 3 June 1971, reported in (1979) 4 *Yearbook—Commercial Arbitration* 309.

163 Van den Berg, above n 160, 376.

164 *Compagnie de Saint-Gobain-Pont* à Mousson v The Fertilizer Corp., of India Ltd, Cour d'appel of Paris (1st Chamber) 10 May 1971, reported in (1976) 1 *Yearbook—Commercial Arbitration* 184; U.S. Biotronik Mess-und Therapiegerate GmbH & Co. v Medford Medical Instrument Com, 415 F Supp 133 (D.N.J., 1976), decided by District Court of New Jersey, 12 May 1976, reported in (1977) 2 *Yearbook—Commercial Arbitration* 250.

process under Article V(1)(b) in the US[165]; but in Singapore, New Zealand and the Philippines, a breach of natural justice is considered as being covered by the public policy exception.[166] Particularly, in New Zealand, such an inclusion in public policy has been formalised in legislation.[167]

A clear trend observed in China's judicial practice is that the ground of irregularity is heavily relied upon, while the application of due process and public policy is relatively rare. According to Xia's statistical research of 17 cases in which enforcement was refused by the SPC under the *NYC* since 2000, irregularity is the most frequently applied ground for such refusal (seven times, 41.2%); while due process was only applied three times, and public policy was only applied once.[168]

We can also observe interactions between these three grounds in China's judicial practice from Xia's report. The most significant trend observed is that the application of a lack of due process was usually coupled with the application of irregularity. In Xia's report, due process was applied three times, and in these instances, while procedural irregularity was applied twice.[169]

Public policy, however, was rarely applied and never applied together with other grounds covering procedural errors; in fact, the SPC clearly stated that public policy should not be applied when other grounds are applicable, in *Shin-Etsu (No. 2)*.[170] This attitude is also observed in other cases. For example, in *Wildcat*, the defendant argued for a violation of public policy on the basis that the expert report was accepted without cross examination; the SPC held that the alleged procedural issues were not sufficiently covered by public policy, but rather covered by irregularity (*CCPL* Article 281); and such argument was eventually rejected on the basis that no procedural rule of CIETAC was found to have been violated. Similarly, in *Weimao*, the ground of public policy was considered by the Taiyuan IPC, which found that the composition of the tribunal was not in accordance with the arbitration agreement, and the defendant had not been given an opportunity to present its counterclaim.[171] However, the SPC based its decision not to enforce the award on the fact that the application for enforcement was out of time, rather than considering the argument in relation to public policy.

---

[165] *Parsons & Whittemore*, 508 F.2d.

[166] Michael Hwang and Shaun Lee, 'Survey of South East Asian Nations on the Application of the New York Convention' (2008) 25(6) *Journal of International Arbitration* 873, 880, n 34.

[167] Article 34(6)(b), which is to be read with article 34(2)(b)(ii) of the First Schedule to the *Arbitration Act 1996*. It states that:

(6) For the avoidance of doubt, and without limiting the generality of paragraph (2)(b)(ii), it is hereby declared that an award is in conflict with the public policy of New Zealand if— …

(b) A breach of natural justice occurred—

(i) During the arbitral proceedings; or

(ii) In connection with the making of the award.

[168] Xiaohong Xia, 'Implementation of the New York Convention in China' (2011) 1 *International Commercial Arbitration Brief* 20, 22.

[169] Ibid. 23.

[170] See Sect. 4.2.

[171] Wunschheim, above n 62, Case Note 40, App.D-56.

Why is the ground of irregularity preferred over the grounds of due process and public policy by the Chinese courts? A first indication may be that the detailed and rigid procedural requirements in China's arbitration law and rules provide little space for the application of other grounds. For this reason, the ground of due process can be considered as "indirectly covered" by the ground of irregularity.[172] Thus, as long as the detailed procedural guidance has been provided, the court is reluctant to consider other grounds. Also, it is much easier for the court to identify an irregularity than a violation of public policy. A breach of procedural rules, or a failure to give timely notice, is more easily identified by the courts than public policy, which can be rather obscure. In dealing with violations of procedural public policy, the courts face more difficulties justifying its legal reasoning, particularly given that little guidance is provided in China. And finally, courts that show a general reluctance to apply public policy seem in line with the global trend to narrow down the interpretation of public policy in order to facilitate the enforcement of international arbitral awards,[173] though not all the decisions to not apply public policy are well-grounded and logically reasoned.

The overwhelming dependence on the regulation of arbitration proceedings and the limited application of public policy in China's arbitration practice have largely limited the development of the understanding of public policy. On the one hand, the reliance on strict compliance with arbitration law and rules provide limited space for the courts to further address the public policy concerns. On the other hand, without sufficient understanding and experience in dealing with procedural public policy, the courts would hesitate to review the activities that are not governed by arbitration rules. Particularly, an explicit emphasis on the residual nature of the ground of public policy may devalue the distinct requirements for the application of public policy.[174] Clear criteria regarding the application of public policy considerations in dealing with procedural issues are generally required if the Chinese courts are to improve their performance.

## 6.2 *The Criteria Governing the Application of Public Policy in Dealing with Procedural Issues*

Given that the Chinese judiciary needs to further develop the criteria governing the procedural fundamental principles of law as an element of public policy, this section attempts to provide some guidance from international experiences. For example, in dealing with the bias issue, the Hong Kong court adopted the "actual or apparent

---

[172] Wunschheim, above n 62, 256–57.

[173] Illustrated in Chap. 2.

[174] See Wunschheim, above n 62, 267, 284.

bias" standard. In American cases, the standard of "evident partiality" under the *Federal Arbitration Act* was frequently used and confirmed.[175]

More comprehensive criteria are provided in regard to broader procedural principles such as "natural justice". In *Minmetals Germany GmbH v Ferco Steel Ltd*,[176] the court provided that the determination of natural justice should be evaluated from the following perspectives:

(i) the nature of the procedural injustice;
(ii) whether the enforcement has invoked the supervisory jurisdiction of the seat of arbitration;
(iii) whether a remedy was available under that jurisdiction;
(iv) whether the court of that jurisdiction has conclusively determined the complaint of the person seeking enforcement in favour of upholding the award; and
(v) if the claimant has failed to invoke that remedial jurisdiction, for what reason, and in particular whether he was acting unreasonably in failing to do so.[177]

Compared with these clearly identified criteria provided by international practice, the Chinese courts' approach is neither well-developed nor consistent, and no clear criterion is ever identified. Different procedural principles are treated differently in Chinese judicial practice. While in *Yongning*, the facts of the violation of *res judicata* were easy to identify, and the SPC confirmed that the principle of *res judicata* was part of China's procedural fundamental principle and public policy, the same principle was denied as a concept of public policy in *Shin-Etsu No.* 2; the interpretation of the concept of "judicial sovereignty" was also inconsistent in cases such as *Castel, Palmer* and *Gate*. The principle of impartiality was excluded from the scope of judicial review in *Louis Dreyfus*.[178] It is then less likely that any judicial criteria would be developed in regard to impartiality.

Another statement in relation to the possible criteria adopted by the Chinese judiciary is in *Wildcat*, where the SPC stated that public policy does not work for "merely maintaining the procedural fairness" but is also responsible for "the maintenance of the fundamental legal order of the country". The SPC held the latter standard was not reached without any further explanation to "fundamental legal order", and did not explain why "procedural fairness" would not amount to a fundamental principle and was not covered by public policy in China.

According to these observations, much needs to be done by the Chinese judiciary in applying the procedural fundamental principles and in recognising these principles as part of China's public policy. Not only the most significant procedure principles,

---

175 9 USC § 10(a)(2); *Sidarma Societa Italiana di Armamento v Holt Marine Indus Inc,* 515 F Supp 1302 (SDNY 1981). For a more recent discussion of the "evident partiality" standard, see Gary Born, 'The Different Meanings of an Arbitrator's "Evident Partiality" Under U.S. Law', blog article published in March 2013, at <http://kluwerarbitrationblog.com/blog/2013/03/20/the-different-meanings-of-an-arbitrators-evident-partiality-under-u-s-law/>.

176 [1999] 1 All ER739.

177 Ibid; See also Jean-François Poudret, Sébastien Besson and Stephen Birti, *Comparative Law of International Arbitration* (Sweet & Maxwell, 2nd ed, 2007) 867.

178 See Sect. 2.

such as the impartiality and the *res judicata,* should be respected, but the criteria in relation to their application in cases need to be further developed. For the purpose of deepening the understanding of these principles and improving the judiciary's performance in applying these principles in practice, international consensus and discussions from scholars should also be taken into consideration.

# Chapter 7
# Public Policy in the Form of Public Policy Rules

## 1 Introduction

In current arbitration practice and judicial review, the definition and application of public policy still relies largely on national law.[1] One significant question is whether a breach of national law, particularly mandatory rules in domestic law, amounts to a violation of public policy; and if so, under what circumstances will courts reach that conclusion?

International practice does not provide a clear consensus on the extent to which a breach of national law, or fundamental rules in national law, would amount to a violation of public policy leading to non-enforcement of an arbitral award. During the drafting of the *NYC*, the Indian and Israeli representatives proposed that any violation of national law would amount to a violation of public policy.[2] Alternatively, the majority of the participating parties preferred a narrow application of public policy. Though the Indian and Israeli suggestions were eventually rejected in the final draft, the *NYC*, in fact, did not exclude the possibility that a breach of the mandatory rules would constitute a violation of public policy.

Different jurisdictions attempt to provide their own solution for dealing with mandatory rules of law.[3] Although their practices vary, there is still general consensus that, at least to some extent, mandatory rules of a national law may embody public policy, even international ones, and the breach of mandatory rules of this type may become a ground to negate the enforcement of the arbitral award. As the *ILA Final Report* provided, public policy includes: "…(ii) rules designed to serve the essential

[1] See Sect. 4 in Chap. 2.

[2] The submission of the Indian Representative in Summary Record of Fifth Meeting, U.N.DOC.E/AC.42/SR.5, 7–8; the submission of the Israeli Representative, see UN.DOC.E/CONF.26/L.33/Rev.1, 7. See also Anton G. Maurer, *The Public Policy Exception under the New York Convention* (Juris, 2012) 20–21, 40–41.

[3] See further Sect. 2.



S. Zhang, *The Public Policy Exception in the Judicial Review of International Commercial Arbitral Awards*, https://doi.org/10.1007/978-3-662-67679-0_7

political, social or economic interests of the State, these being known as "*lois de police*" or "public policy rules".[4]

Such a consensus provides guidance to practitioners, but problems that arise in applying this consensus in judicial practice are not fully resolved. Though it is generally accepted that some national rules of law are of a public policy nature, it remains a difficult task for national courts to determine which detailed categories of these national rules are, and under what circumstances a breach of a national law rule may constitute a violation of public policy. Courts face further difficulties of establishing a consistent approach to support such a finding. In particular, the phrase, "essential political, social or economic interests"[5] needs further interpretation by national courts on a case-by-case basis.

This chapter explores the influence of mandatory rules on the approaches adopted by the Chinese judiciary. Section 2 distinguishes the role of mandatory rules from public policy rules/*lois de* police. It first reviews the mandatory rules that are applied in arbitration proceedings and in the judicial review of arbitral awards. It then focuses on their influence in deciding arbitrability and enforceability of arbitral awards in the arbitration and subsequent judicial review. It also clarifies that only limited mandatory rules may constitute public policy rules/*lois de police.* Section 3 explores several categories of public policy rules/*lois de police*, and also the approaches employed in Chinese legislation and by the courts to identify public policy rules/*lois de police*, particularly in relation to specific areas of law such as competition law, export/import control and foreign-investment policies. The practice of Chinese courts in dealing with public policy rules/*lois de police* is systematically examined. Section 4 focuses on the legislative purpose of mandatory rules and its possible effect in identifying public policy rules/*lois de police.*

## 2 The Development of Mandatory Rules in Arbitration Law: A General Review

### *2.1 Major Aspects of Mandatory Rules*

Before reviewing the major legal issues, the term "mandatory rules" discussed in this chapter needs to be defined. Though there is no one predominant and conclusive definition of "mandatory rules of law" in all jurisdictions, this term generally refers to the "imperative rule(s) of law that cannot be excluded by agreement of the parties"

---

[4] Pierre Mayer and Audley Sheppard, 'Final Report on Public Policy as a Bar to Enforcement of International Arbitral Awards' (2003) 19 *Arbitration International* 249, Recommendation 1(d).

[5] Ibid.

as provided by the *ILA Final Report*.[6] The term is recognised in the context of both domestic law and also private international law. For example, Switzerland's *Federal Code on Private International Law (CPIL)* recognises both public policy and the mandatory application of law as grounds which can preclude the application of foreign law.[7] For the purpose of this research, the distinction between the role of mandatory rules in the arbitration process and their role in judicial review is emphasised; the latter of which is our focus.

Mandatory rules of law have influenced the process of arbitration law in many different ways. First of all, the arbitrability of some disputes may be excluded by mandatory rules of law; mandatory rules of law may also influence the decisions of tribunals in choosing the applicable law[8]; and mandatory rules of law can also prevail over the terms of an arbitration agreement.[9] During arbitration proceedings, arbitrators may also be under specific duties to apply mandatory rules of law in order to execute their powers, or to ensure the enforceability of awards rendered.[10] Thc final and ultimate role of mandatory rules of law is as an element of the public policy exception in the judicial review of arbitral awards.

There are significant distinctions between the mandatory rules of law applied by the arbitrators and by the courts. Arbitrators consider whether a particular rule of mandatory law is applicable in a case,[11] while courts are required to evaluate whether awards conflicting with a particular set of mandatory rules of law would constitute a violation of public policy. As the narrow approach to interpret public policy is widely accepted in the judicial review of arbitral awards, it is likely that the courts' consideration of mandatory rules would be more limited and applied with greater caution. The judicial review of arbitral awards ordinarily entails a court taking a "second-look" at the award to determine whether mandatory rules were complied

---

[6] Mayer and Sheppard, above n 4, 261, nn 46, citing *UNIDROIT Principles of International Commercial Contracts (1994)* art 3.19, which provides 'The provisions of this Chapter [concerning fraud, threat and gross disparity] are mandatory, except insofar as they relate to the binding force of mere agreement, initial impossibility or mistake'.

[7] *Federal Code on Private International Law (CPIL)*(Switzerland), 18 December 1987, art 17.V, which states, "The application of provisions of foreign law shall be precluded if it would produce a result which is incompatible with Swiss public policy (*ordre public*)". Art. 18(Mandatory application of Swiss law) states," this Code does not prevent the application of those mandatory provisions of Swiss law which, by reason of their particular purpose, are applicable regardless of the law designated by this Code".

[8] Luca G. Radicati di Brozolo, 'Mandatory Rules and International Arbitration' (2012) 23(1) *American Review of International Arbitration* 49, 50–52. See further Chap. 8.

[9] Richard M. Buxbaum, 'Public Law, Ordre Public and Arbitration: A Procedural Scenario and a Suggestion' in Peter Hay et al. (eds), *Resolving International Conflicts: Liber amicorum Tibor Varady* (Centre European University Press, 2009) 83, 85–89.

[10] For example, see *UNIDROIT Principles of International Contracts* (2016) art 1.4; *Hague Principles on Choice of Law in International Commercial Contracts*, art 11.5. This instrument had been approved in 2015 and used as guidance by various arbitration institutions. See also di Brozolo, above n 8, 54.

[11] For the role of arbitrators in deciding the application of mandatory rules, see Mohammad Reza Baniassadi, 'Do Mandatory Rules of Public Law Limit Choice of Law in International Commercial Arbitration?' (1992) 10 *International Tax and Business Law* 59.

with in reaching agreement on the award.[12] Based on this understanding, this research mainly focuses on the mandatory rules of law that apply at the stage of a judicial review of arbitral awards.

## 2.2 *Mandatory Rules, Arbitrability and Public Policy*

In early legal practice, mandatory rules of law were first introduced into arbitration at the arbitrability stage. Such a function of mandatory rules of law was once fundamental in the area of arbitration.[13] The most significant representation of mandatory rules of law relates to a discussion of the non-arbitrability of security law and antitrust law claims in the US.[14]

The recent trend, however, is that courts have gradually relaxed their judicial review requirements relating to arbitrability. Many issues that were once excluded by reason of arbitrability are now held to be arbitrable. Such a significant change in the role of mandatory rules is best illustrated by US case law, such as *Scherk* and *Mitsubishi*,[15] cases in which the courts revisited the arbitrability of security law and antitrust law claims and confirmed the arbitrators' decision-making powers in relation to them. This is also observed in many other jurisdictions and in other areas of mandatory law, such as in anti-racketeering law and anti-discrimination law in the US, and in consumer protection claims in Australia.[16]

The consequence, then, is that mandatory rules of law that once barred some disputes from being arbitrated no longer function in that way. In fact, their main role is now reflected at the judicial review stage as part of the enforcing courts' public policy,[17] which is the focus of this chapter. It is also notable that, as indicated in the

---

[12] The term "second look" is from *Mitsubishi Motors Corporation v Soler Chrysler-Plymouth Inc*373 US 614 (1985), though some scholars provided the court did not take a "second look" in this case. See Phillip J McConnaughay, 'The Risks and Virtues of Lawlessness: A "Second Look" at International Commercial Arbitration' (1998–1999) 93 *Northwestern University Law Review* 453, 457; Horatia Muir Watt, Luca G. Radicati di Brozolo,'Party Autonomy and Mandatory Rules in a Global World', (2004) 6 *International Law Forum* 90, 91–92. See further Chap. 8.

[13] McConnaughay, above n 12, 475.

[14] Ibid.

[15] *Scherk v Alberto-Culver Co*, 417 US 506 (1974); *Mitsubishi*373 US.

[16] Leanne Rich, 'The Arbitrability of TPA Claims: To Stay or not to Stay?' (2010) 18 *Trade Practices Law Journal* 7, 7–9; Sam Luttrell, 'Public Policy Conflicts in the Arbitrability of the Trade Practice Act 1974 (Cth)' (2007) 4 *Macquarie Journal of Business Law* 139,147; Romauld Andrew, 'The ILL-Favour Child of Litigation: International Commercial Arbitration and the Australian Trade Practices Act 1974' (2004) 21(3) *Journal of International Arbitration* 239, 240.

[17] As Sects. 5 and 7 in Chap. 2 provided, arbitrability is also a ground for non-enforcement of arbitral awards. This section, however, only focuses on the element of public policy rules (ground (2)), not the ground of arbitrability (ground (4)), and all discussions referring to public policy are subject to this condition. In this Chapter, arbitrability and public policy (for the purposes of ground (2)) are clearly distinguished.

next section, only some of the most significant rules of mandatory rules of law are recognised in the application of public policy.[18]

## 2.3 *Mandatory Rules of Law not Equivalent to Public Policy*

Arbitration does not require the strict application of the national law of a particular jurisdiction, which is especially illustrated in the existence of amiable arbitration in which the tribunal need not adhere to the strict application of the law, but decide on the basis of the notion of fairness and justice.[19] Also, under the pro-enforcement approach in international arbitration practice, it is now generally accepted that a breach of national law does not necessarily lead courts to decline to enforce or annul arbitral awards. Yet the situation may become difficult if mandatory rules of law are involved in and become part of a court's deliberations in relation to the applicability of the public policy exception.

Quite a few mandatory rules of law are respected by judges, especially in earlier cases, the breach of which could constitute a violation of public policy under judicial review of an arbitration award. In *Laminoirs-Trefileries-Cableries de Lens, S.A. v Southwire Co.*, the US court found that the interest rate applied by the arbitral award was excessive and rejected its enforcement based on public policy grounds.[20] Similarly, in *Soleimany,* the British courts found that because the arbitral award applied Jewish law, confirming the transaction on the basis of a contract, which was *void* ab initio under the UK law, this violated the public policy of the UK and should not be enforced.[21] Both of the judgments were later criticised for imposing domestic law on international commercial activities, thus extending the scope of public policy, and consequently undermining the value of international arbitration.[22]

---

18 See further Sect. 2.3.

19 *Model Law on International Commercial Arbitration of the United Nations Commission on International Trade Law*, UN GAOR, 40th sess, Supp No. 17, UN Doc A/40/17, annex I (21 June 1985); passed by the GA Res 40/72, UN GAOR, 40th sess, 112th plenmtg, Agenda Item 135, UN Doc A/RES/40/72 (11 December 1985); amended by GA Res A/RES/61/33, UN GAOR, 61st sess, 64th plenmtg, Agenda Item 77, UN Doc A/RES/61/33 (4 Dec 2006) art 28(3). Although the Explanatory Note of the Model Law noted that amiable arbitration is not universally accepted or used in all jurisdictions, the recognition of it in UNCITRAL Model Law itself already indicates its consistency with the major aims of international arbitration practice. See also generally Leon Trakman, 'Ex Aequo et Bono: De-mystifying An Ancient Concept' (2008) 8(2) *Chicago Journal of International Law* 621, which discusses the possibility of arbitrators to decide cases on the basis of the principle of justice and fairness rather than rules of law.

20 [1980]484 F Supp 1063 (N.D. Ga).

21 *Soleimany v Soleimany* [1999]QB 785.

22 See Ramona Martinez, 'Recognition and Enforcement of International Arbitral Awards under the United Nations Convention of 1958: The Refusal Provisions;' (1990) 24(2) *The International Lawyer* 487, 495, where the author criticises *Laminoirs-Trefileries-Cableris.* As the public policy was ambiguous and subjectively construed, which is not consistent with the Purpose of the New York Convention. See also Hakeem Seriki, 'Enforcement of Foreign Arbitral Awards and Public

It is accepted that more guidance is needed in distinguishing mandatory rules of law from public policy and to identify when the breach of mandatory rules of law would also be a violation of public policy. Consistent with the promotion of worldwide economic development and co-operation, it is now widely accepted that a breach of mandatory rules of a national law is not necessarily a breach of public policy. In *Society of Lloyd's v Saunders*,[23] Lloyd's marketing activities breached securities legislation in Canada, especially the regulation governing the sufficient disclosure of information. This breach was not considered a violation of public policy by the English court, which held that contracts violating Canadian law can be enforced in England as long as English public policy is not violated. When enforcing this English judgment, the Canadian courts held that the breach of Canada's mandatory rules of law was not necessarily a violation of its public policy, and recognised that it was important to maintain a consistent approach in the international insurance market.[24] Professor Geneviève Saumier commented that the Canadian decision represented "the triumph of internationalism over parochialism."[25]

The trend to limit the scope of national mandatory rules of law in international commercial activities is also reflected in the practice of judicial review of arbitral awards. An interim statement of the committee charged with drafting the *NYC* stated that only breaches of "fundamental" principles of national law can ground claims to refuse the enforcement of international commercial arbitration awards,[26] and rejected the opposition from Australia, India and the UK. This approach clearly illustrates an intention to limit the application of public policy.[27] As the *ILA Final Report* states,

> An award's violation of a mere "mandatory rule" (i.e. a rule that is mandatory but does not form part of the State's international public policy so as to compel its application in the case under consideration) should not bar its recognition or enforcement, even when said rule forms part of the law of the forum, the law governing the contract, the law of the place of performance of the contract or the law of the seat of the arbitration.[28]

---

Policy-A Note of Caution' (2000) 9 *The Arbitration and Dispute Resolution Law Journal* 192, 194–98, which reported the criticisms to *Soleimany* as it only presents the public policy of the UK but not the public policy applicable to the international transactions. It is also arguable that in both cases, some underlying standards or scrutinies have been met in order to apply the public policy exception. Regarding *Laminoirs-Trefileries-Cableris*, it might be the abuse of rights or a breach of fairness and justice (although this attitude in the judiciary is not so likely now, see Sect. 3.1 in Chap. 5); and in *Soleimany*, an arguable point is that the smuggling transactions of carpets may violate not only the mandatory law but also good morals or *ordre public*; See Sect. 4.1 in Chap. 5.

[23] (2001) 210 PCR(4th) 519, 55 OR(3d) 688.

[24] *Sanders* (2001) 210 PCR (4th), per Feldman JA.

[25] Genevieve Saumier, 'What's in a Name—Lloyd's, International Comity and Public Policy' (2002) 37(2) *Canada Business Law Journal* 388, 418.

[26] The ad hoc Committee on the Enforcement of International Arbitral Awards (established by the United Nations Economic and Social Council). Report of the Committee on the Enforcement of International Arbitral Awards, United Nations Economic and Social Council, U.N.DOC.E/2704, 13. See also Anton Maurer, *The Public Policy Exception under the New York Convention: History, Interpretation and Application* (Juris, 2012) 25.

[27] *Ibid.*

[28] Mayer and Sheppard, above n 4, recommendation 3(a).

Such statements summarise cases in which this approach was adopted. For example, in *Inter Maritime Management SA v Russin and Vecchi*,[29] the court declared that public policy was not violated if a foreign arbitral award was rendered against mandatory rules in Swiss law.[30] Such a conclusion is further observed and confirmed by scholars.[31] Voser argues that public policy might imply a higher moral standard than mandatory rules of law, and that the latter may not necessarily express a moral standard.[32] Villiers also concludes that, the term "mandatory rules" has a broader content than the term "public policy rules/*lois de police*", and that only the latter would lead a court to refuse enforcement.[33]

Even though both practitioners and scholars have attempted to distinguish mandatory rules of law from public policy, they cannot deny that in some particular circumstances a breach of mandatory rules of law may amount to a violation of public policy. Examples are clearly provided in case law such as *Eco Swiss*,[34] and in legal instruments such as the *2009 European Community Regulation on the Law Applicable to Contractual Obligations*.[35] Similarly, if the enforcement of an award is against the US government's decision to freeze assets of particular States and their nationals, the US court would grant the enforcement order upon the approval of the Office of Foreign Assets Control.[36]

Thus, based on the conclusion that mandatory rules are not equivalent to public policy, it is then crucial for courts to identify the circumstances in which a breach of mandatory rules of law can amount to a violation of public policy, and to develop a method by which such breaches should be scrutinised through judicial review proceedings. Guidance may be gained from legislation and judicial practice, and also academic discussion. Based on these understandings, the next section discusses both international and Chinese practices in dealing with public policy rules/*lois de police* in the judicial review of arbitral awards.

---

29 Tribunal Fédéral [Supreme Court], Not Indicated, 9 January 1995, reported in (1997) 22 *Yearbook-Commercial Arbitration* 789.

30 Ibid, [23].

31 Pierre Mayer, 'Mandatory Rules of Law in International Arbitration' (1986) 2 *Arbitration International* 274, 275; Luke Villiers, 'Breaking in the 'Unruly Horse': The Status of Mandatory Rules of Law as a Public Policy Basis for the Non-Enforcement of Arbitral Awards' (2011) 18*Australian International Law Journal* 155.

32 Nathalie Voser, 'Mandatory Rules of Law as a Limitation on the Law Applicable in International Commercial Arbitration' (1996) 7 *American Review of International Arbitration* 319, 347.

33 Villiers, above n 31,165.

34 *Eco Swiss China Time Ltd. V. Benetton International* Nv(C-126/97) [1999] ECR-I 3055. See further Sect. 3.1.

35 *Regulation (EC) No 593/2008 of the European Parliament and of the Council, of 17 June 2008, on the Law Applicable to Contractual Obligations (Rome I)* [2008] OJ L 177/6, art 9.It provides the courts should have the obligation to ensure the compliance of the overriding mandatory provisions. See further Sect. 4.

36 Auldey Sheppard, 'Interim Report on Public Policy as a Bar to Enforcement of International Arbitral Awards' (2000) 19(3) *Arbitration International* 217, 237.

# 3 The Judicial Review Practice in Applying Public Policy Rules/*Lois De Police*

## *3.1 International Practice*

This section attempts to resolve the major question i.e., under what circumstances will a breach of a mandatory rule of law constitute a violation of public policy? In discussing what mandatory rules may also be held to be public policy rules, this section also recommends the approach that should be adopted by courts in applying public policy rules.

### 3.1.1 Possible Categories of Public Policy Rules

Based on these developments in judicial practice, the *ILA Final Report* has illustrated several examples of *lois de police*, including "*anti-trust law*[37]*; ... currency controls; price fixing rules; environmental protection laws; measures of embargo, blockade or boycott; tax laws; and laws to protect parties presumed to be in an inferior bargaining position (e.g., consumer protection laws).*"[38]

This conclusion reached by the *ILA Final Report* is based on a summary of international practice prior to the ILA Conference, including a series of key cases such as *Eco Swiss,* which recognises that EU Competition law is part of both the public policy of the EU and its member states. In this case, the European Court of Justice (ECJ hereafter) held "the provision of art 81 of EC may be regarded as a matter of public policy within the meaning of the *New York Convention*".[39] A similar approach was also adopted in *Gallay* and *Ingmar.*[40]

Some of these examples were confirmed in later judicial practice. For example, the public policy nature of the consumer law rules is identified in *Case C-168/05 Elisa María Mostaza Claro v Centro Móvil Milenium SL.*[41] In this case, the ECJ found that Directive 93/13, Art 3(1)(t) and 6(1), which aims to protect the consumer from unfair contractual terms, was of a public policy nature, following *Eco Swiss.*[42] The dispute arose regarding an arbitral award enforcing an arbitration agreement that was claimed to contain terms that were unfair to consumers. It was then the ECJ's task to interpret Articles 3(1) and 6(1) and to decide whether rendering an arbitral award

---

37 *Eco Swiss China* [1999] ECR-I 3055; *Gallay v Fabricated Metals INC* [2000] Rev Arb 805(French Cour de Cassation, 5 January 1999).

38 See in the *ILA Interim Report*, Sheppard, above n 36, 231; and in the *ILA Final Report*, Mayer and Sheppard, above n 4, 256.

39 *Eco Swiss China* [1999] ECR-I 3055 [39].

40 *Gallay* [2000] Rev Arb 805; *Ingmar GB Ltd v Eaton Leonard Technologies Inc,* (C-381/98) [2000] ECR I-9305.

41 *Elisa María Mostaza Claro v. Centro Móvil Milenium SL.* (C-168/05) [2006] ECR I-10421.

42 *Elisa María Mostaza Claro* [2006] ECR I-10421, [34], [35], which refers to the Benetton case in considering the significance of the consumer protection rule.

against such a rule would require the annulment of the award. The ECJ annulled the award and confirmed the nature of this public policy rule. The court found that this public policy rule was important in "raising the standard of living and the quality of life in its territory" and considered "the nature and importance of the public interest underlying the protection" in its analysis. In doing so, the court also held that Articles 3(1)(t) and 6(1) of the *Directive 93/13* constitute public policy rules of both the EU and its member states and should be taken into consideration in deciding whether an arbitral award should be annulled.

Some international consensus has been established in order to identify public policy rules/*lois de police*: the most common rules of public policy nature are in competition law and consumer law. Other examples illustrated by Otto and Elwan include bankruptcy law, exchange control restrictions, export/import restrictions and other governmental restrictions.[43] Villiers also provides that public policy rules in Australia include competition laws, currency control, environmental protection laws, embargo measures, as well as consumer law.[44] Furthermore, in forming such a general approach, the *ILA Final Report* suggested that the legislative history must be taken into consideration and international elements in case law should be approached with great caution.[45] It is also observed that the identified mandatory rules of law usually have a specific economic purpose.[46] This conclusion was confirmed by cases such as *Gallay* and *Ingmar*,[47] in which the protection of competition in EU are emphasised, illustrating that the economic purpose of these competition law rules is sufficient to "elevate the law to a fundamental legal principle" that amounts to public policy.[48]

### 3.1.2 Application of Public Policy Rules in Cases

The previous discussion lists categories of law in which mandatory rules of law would be respected as public policy rules. Further guidance is needed to aid the courts in deciding whether a breach of mandatory rules would constitute a violation of public policy. The *ILA Final Report* recommended that:

> A court should only refuse recognition or enforcement of an award giving effect to a solution prohibited by a rule of public policy forming part of its own legal system when: (i) the scope of the said rule is intended to encompass the situation under consideration; and (ii) recognition or enforcement of the award would manifestly disrupt the essential political, social or economic interests protected by the rule.[49]

---

43 See Otto and Elwan, "Art.V(2)", in Kronke et al., *Recognition and Enforcement of Foreign Arbitral Awards: A Global Commentary on the New York Convention* (Wolters Kluwer, 2010)378–386.

44 Villiers, above n 31, 158–159.

45 Mayer and Sheppard, above n 4, 261.

46 Ibid, 262.

47 Villiers, above n 31, 170, citing *Gallay*[2000] Rev Arb 805; *Ingmar* [2000] ECR I-9305..

48 See Villiers, above n 31, 170.

49 Mayer and Sheppard, above n 4, Recommendation 3(b).

According to this suggested approach, national courts should first determine whether the mandatory rule of law has sufficient connection with the particular case under judicial review; secondly, they are expected to explore the intention of the alleged "public policy rules"; to identify the meaning of "essential political, social or economic interests"; and to evaluate whether such interests are "manifestly" disrupted in the particular circumstances of each case.

In relation to the standard governing the decision whether a mandatory rule of law should be applied in a particular case, scholars' opinions vary. Some scholars have referred to common preconditions of application, and common conceptions of transnational public policy, in order to ensure consistent international practice.[50] Others have referred to a "real connection" between the law and the underlying transaction.[51] Though such guidance is provided to arbitrators in deciding the application of mandatory rules of law, they may also be useful for the courts.

More recent developments in dealing with mandatory rules of law further require that the application of public policy rules be limited in their scope of application. As *Thales* provided, public policy is applied only when the violation of mandatory rules of law is "flagrant, effective and concrete" from a summary review of an arbitral award.[52] This trend to limit the application of public policy rules is also consistent with the pro-enforcement trend of the *NYC*. Conversely, there are also opinions promoting the application of mandatory rules of law[53]; however, these cases are criticised as adopting a "one-sided approach" that only addresses the interests protected by the rules and ignores the broader interests of finality of arbitration.[54]

Based on these understandings, the following sections focus on the reflections in Chinese jurisprudence, and further explore the approaches by Chinese courts' to evaluate whether there is a violation of public policy. Most of the cases, in fact, arguably fall into the exemplary scope of the categories listed by the *ILA Report* and global practice in regard to public policy rules and are therefore significant to illustrate the recent Chinese approach.

---

[50] Yves Derains, 'Public Policy and the Law Applicable to the Dispute in International Arbitration' in Pieter Sanders (ed) *Comparative Arbitration Practice and Public Policy in Arbitration* (Kluwer Law International, 1987) 228; Emmanuel Gaillard and John Savage, *Fouchard, Gaillard, Goldman on International Commercial Arbitration* (Kluwer Law International, 1999) 996–997.

[51] Simon Greenberg, Christopher Kee and Romesh Weeramantry, *International Commercial Arbitration: an Asia–Pacific Perspective* (Cambridge University Press, 2011) 122.

[52] *Thalès* v *Ingénierie des Technologies Nouvelles* (2002–2003) 2 *Cahiers de l'arbitrage*362 (Paris, January 18, 2003).

[53] Alexis Mourre, Luca G Radicati di Brozolo, 'Towards Finality of Arbitral Awards: Two Steps Forward, One Step Back' (2006) 23(2) *Journal of International Arbitration*171, 174, citing opinions of French scholars such as Jean-Baptiste Racine, *L'arbitrage commercial international et l'ordre public* (LGDJ,1999); Christophe Seraglini, *Lois de police et justice arbitrale internationale* (Dalloz, 2001); Walid Abdelgawad, *Arbitrage et droit de la concurrence* (LGDJ, 2001); Sylvain Bollée, *Les methodes du droit international prive a l'epreuve des sentences arbitrales* (Economica, 2004).

[54] Mourre and Brozolo, 176.

## *3.2 Possible Categories of Public Policy Rules in China: The Law and Academic Discussion*

Before going through the cases, it is necessary to summarise the current law and discussion of the possible categories of public policy rules/*lois de police* in China.

China's arbitration legislation provides no guidance regarding the definition of public policy rules in the context of arbitration law. Most of the discussion of mandatory rules of law and public policy rules is provided by scholars. Gao's general categorisation of China's public policy under private international law includes "...(e) legal rules that constitute fundamental principles in China". She further provides examples such as "the principle of good faith and honesty in contract law, the anti-terrorism law, the law against cults, traffic in persons, money-laundering and gambling".[55] The categorisation provided by Tao and Wunschheim refer to the public policy rules as "fundamental rules of Chinese law".[56] Both of these categorisations refer to the fundamental rules in China's legislation, particularly the public law ones. Many scholars have also considered the *ILA Report* and refer to it as a useful reference.[57] Yet these references are still abstract, and their applicability is yet to be tested in judicial practice.

Guidance, however, may be found in the broader context of private international law in China. The most recent and significant achievements in this area may be found in the Law of the People's Republic of China on the Application of Law for Foreign-Related Civil Relations *(Law Application Law hereafter)*, and the SPC'*s Judicial Interpretation of the Law Application Law.*[58] According to Article 4 of the *Law Application Law*, mandatory rules of law shall apply in dealing with foreign-related civil relationships. The SPC's judicial interpretation includes six instances where mandatory rules of law are held to be public policy. These include:

(1) protection of the interests of labourers;
(2) safety of food and public health;
(3) environmental safety;
(4) financial safety, notably foreign exchange administration;
(5) anti-monopoly or anti-dumping; or

[55] 高晓力[Gao Xiaoli],《国际私法上公共政策的运用》[The Functioning of Public Policy in Private International Law](中国民主与法制出版社[China Democracy and Rule of Law Press], 2008) 131.

[56] See Jingzhou Tao, 'Enforcement of SCC Arbitration Awards in China' in *Between East and West: Essays in Honour of Ulf Franke* (2010) 12; Clarisse von Wunschheim, *Enforcement of Commercial Arbitral Awards in China: Business Laws of China* (West, 2011) 283.

[57] 高晓力[Gao Xiaoli], above n 55, 131.

[58]《中华人民共和国涉外民事关系法律适用法》[LAW of the People's Republic of China on the Application of Law for Foreign-Related Civil Relations](People's Republic of China) National People's Congress Standing Committee, Order No36, 28 October 2010, art 4.

(6) other situations that should be recognised as mandatory rules.[59]

These examples may provide useful guidance for the judiciary in determining the scope of public policy rules/*lois de police*; yet their effect on the judicial review of arbitral awards is still doubtful and further clarification by the SPC is required.[60] In particular, the distinction between the application of law in dealing with substantive law issues and the judicial review of arbitral awards should be respected. In addition, the courts' ability to apply the national law in the latter proceeding, even mandatory national laws, should be limited.[61]

Finally, regarding the standard of or approach to identifying a category of public policy rules/*lois de police,* there is some suggestion that the fundamentality of the protected interests and the foreign-related nature of the disputes are helpful when courts consider the application of public policy rules in the context of international arbitration law.[62] It is thus the court's task to evaluate each particular national law rule involved in the arbitral award.

## *3.3 The Economic and Financial Regulations and Approvals*

In a series of cases dealing with economic and financial regulations, the Chinese courts, especially the SPC, consistently emphasised that a breach of China's mandatory rules of law was not necessarily a violation of China's public policy.

### 3.3.1 Forbidding Future Transactions

In *ED and F Mans*, the SPC for the first time pointed out that a breach of China's mandatory rules of law and regulation was not necessarily a violation of China's public policy. In this case, the disputed offshore future transactions conducted by the China Sugar Group, a domestic enterprise, were prohibited by Chinese law at that time. The London Sugar Association rendered the award against the China Sugar Group. In enforcement proceedings, the Chinese party claimed that the contract was "valid in its formation with invalid purposes" by constituting speculative future transactions, which breached both the mandatory rules and the fundamental legal

---

59《最高人民法院关于适用(中华人民共和国涉外民事关系法律适用法)若干问题的解释 (一)》[Interpretation No.1 of the Supreme People's Court Concerning Several Issues in Applying Law of the People's Republic of China on the Application of Law for Foreign-Related Civil Relations] Supreme People's Court, [2012] Fa Shi.No24, 10 December 2014.

60 Qisheng He, 'Public Policy in Enforcement of Foreign Arbitral Awards in the Supreme People's Court of China' (2013) 43 *Hong Kong Law Journal* 1037, nn 112.

61 See above Chap. 2; for the extent of judicial review, see further Sect. 4 in Chap. 9.

62 He, above n 60, nn 113, nn122.

system and social public interest of China. *Soleimany*[63] was substantially considered by Chinese courts in deciding the application of *lois de police*.

Both the Beijing 1st IPC and the Beijing HPC opined that the breach of China's mandatory regulation on future transactions was also contrary to public policy under the *NYC*. The SPC, however, stated that the breach of mandatory rules in China was not equal to the violation of China's public policy, and that the breach of China's mandatory regulation on future transactions in this case did not constitute a violation of China's public policy. Thus, the arbitral award was held enforceable.

### 3.3.2 Currency Control

The SPC's legal reasoning in *ED & F Mans* was further confirmed in *Mitsui*. In this case, there were a few major alleged breaches of China's mandatory rules of law.[64] First, it is arguable that the guarantee provided by the local government breached China's prohibition on governmental guarantees. Second, the agreement by the parties to repay the guarantee in Japanese Yen (JPY) was reached without any foreign debt registration or the approval of the State Administration of Foreign Exchange, which breached the regulatory scheme of foreign debts at that time.

Regarding the first claim, the discussion of the courts and the final opinion of the SPC did not mention whether the disputed governmental guarantee breached the relevant Chinese law. Judge Gao later commented that it was not a breach of a mandatory rule of law, because the prohibition on governmental guarantees was only imposed by administrative notices and orders at the time of this case and only codified by law after 1995. It is then difficult to conclude that the governmental guarantee was a breach of a mandatory rule of law of a public policy nature.

The decision on the registration and approval of foreign exchange issues, however, is more controversial. Opinions were divided on this issue among practitioners and scholars before the final judgment was rendered.[65] Some pointed out that China's foreign exchange policy was flexible; the requirement of administrative approval in economic practice was common; and treating such a requirement of approval as a fundamental one would undermine the predictability of contract dealings and the economic order in general. Alternatively, others argued that China's foreign exchange policy had long been one of China's fundamental policies, and that the violation of such a policy, especially when the disputed amount was large, as was the situation in this case, would infringe the national interests and transaction order, which was an outcome to be prevented by the application of the public policy exception. Some commentators also stated that the SCC tribunal did not reasonably take into

---

[63] *Soleimany* [1999]QB 785.

[64] There are also doubts that in this case, the Hong Kong Company's activities in transferring its own foreign debt to the Chinese company was against the general rule of fairness and justice in substance. However, this was not responded to on all levels of judicial opinions, and beyond our discussion of mandatory rules and the violation of Chinese law in this chapter. 高晓力[Gao Xiaoli], above n 55, 258–259. See also Chap. 5.

[65] 高晓力[Gao Xiaoli], above n 55, 258–259.Gao is one of the SPC judges.

consideration that the award had manifestly disregarded China's foreign exchange regulations, which should have been construed as a violation of public policy.[66]

The SPC eventually held that the breach of the foreign exchange regulation in this case did not constitute a violation of China's public policy and enforced the SCC arbitral award. Similar rulings were found in later cases such as *J&D IB* (2016) and *IP Cathay* (2017) in which the SPC repeatedly rejected arguments based on violations of currency control policies.

Despite the rulings mentioned above, Judge Gao of the SPC, in her book, maintained that the foreign exchange regulation should be construed as being of a public policy nature, because the strict foreign exchange restrictions in China were universally known. Thus, the SCC's award ignored this mandatory restriction and violated China's public policy.[67] Although Gao's comment, as well as the opinions favouring the application of public policy in the SPC's international discussion, was not accepted by the SPC in this ruling, it remains a reminder for Chinese arbitration practitioners and scholars to note the importance of running a specific analysis on the particular nature and character of mandatory law and the interests protected by the law, in order to create some possibility to identify a rule of a public policy nature.

### 3.3.3 Restrictions on the Scope of Foreign-Invested Business

In *Starr Cayman*, the Fuzhou IPC upheld the enforceability of a HKIAC award, in which the losing party argued that the disputed contract breached the mandatory requirements of a foreign investment business. In this case, the parties executed a Share Purchase Agreement and an Investor Rights Agreement and then disputed the use of the investment funds. Starr brought arbitration proceedings against the Chinese party and then sought the enforcement of the HKIAC's award in China. The Chinese party argued that the disputed investment via VIE (Variable Interest Entities) was a breach of China's mandatory rules of law which required the proposed foreign investment in a telecommunications business to pass a national security review and obtain prior approval[68]; that the VAM (Valuation Adjustment Mechanism) in this

---

[66] Ibid, 258–259. These opinions were collected by Gao J during 15–16 November 2004, in a symposium organised by the Fourth Civil Branch of the SPC (which is the branch in charge of all judicial review over foreign and foreign-related arbitral awards), the Southern Branch of CIETAC and the Chinese Arbitration Academy in Shenzhen. This symposium was organised before the final decision of this case.

[67] 高晓力[Gao Xiaoli], above n 55, 258–259, 258–259.

[68] According to the following regulations, foreign investors shall not attempt to use any form of "substantial control" in domestic companies to avoid the security review on acquisitions by foreign investors: 《外商投资电信企业管理规定》[Provisions on the Administration of Telecommunications Enterprises with Foreign Investment] (People's Republic of China) State Council of the PRC, State Council Order No333, 11December 2011, recently amended by State Council Order No534, 10 September 2008, art 17; 《关于加强外商投资经营增值电信业务管理的通知》[Notice on Strengthening the Administration of Operation in Value-Added Telecommunications Service by Enterprise with Foreign Investment] (People's Republic of China) Ministry of Information Industry, Xin Bu Dian Han [2006] No342, 13 July 2006, art 1.1.These two regulations require that the foreign

transaction structure was a breach of Chinese law[69]; and that the application of US law in the arbitration proceedings, not the Chinese mandatory rules of law, was a breach of China's social public interest.[70] Nevertheless, the Fuzhou IPC referred to the SPC's ruling in *Mitsui,* and held that the HKIAC's award was not against China's social public interest, even if it was a breach of Chinese mandatory rules of law. It is not clear whether this reasoning is confirmed by higher courts or even the SPC due to the distinctive feature of the Prior Reporting System.

It is arguable that this decision may not be an outstanding example in the area of foreign-investment law. The use of VAM and VIE arrangements has long been controversial under Chinese law. For example, there were rulings by the SPC and CIETAC tribunals that rejected the validity of those arrangements.[71] We also note that there are cases in other jurisdictions confirming that the law controlling foreign investments is of a public policy nature, as it protects "the public interest, the balance of economic and financial relations with the rest of the world, by controlling the movement of capital across the border."[72]

Despite the concerns above, the SPC kept silent when it had the opportunity to clarify whether VIE and VAM arrangements would be against China's public policy in the *IP Cathay* (2017) case. In this case, the party resisting the enforcements raised

---

investor must establish a foreign-invested enterprise in China if they intend to invest in a telecommunications business in China, and obtain a license for the telecommunication business in accordance with Chinese law. Also,《国务院办公厅关于建立外国投资者并购境内企业安全审查制度的通知》[Notice of the General Office of State Council on the Establishment of the Security Review System Relating to Acquisition of Domestic Enterprises by Foreign Investors] (People's Republic of China) State Council, Guo Ban Fa [2011] No.6, 3 February 2011;《实施外国投资者并购境内企业安全审查制度的规定》[Regulations on the Implementation of the Security Review System Relating to the Acquisition of Domestic Enterprises by Foreign Investors] (People's Republic of China) Ministry of Commerce, Notice [2011] No53, 25 August 2011, art 9.

69《苏州工业园区海富投资有限公司诉甘肃世恒有色资源再利用有限公司 (以下简称甘肃世恒) 、香港迪亚有限公司、陆波公司增资纠纷案》[Haifu Investment Co., Ltd. of Suzhou Industrial Park v Gansu Shiheng Nonferrous Metals Recycling Co., Ltd., Hong Kong Diya Co., Ltd. and Lu Bo], 最高人民法院(the SPC), (2012) 民提字第11号[Civil Re-trial No11], 7 November 2011. The SPC in this case denied the validity of the VAM agreement between the PE investor and the target company, which would harm the interests of other shareholders and the third party, but confirmed the validity of the VAM agreement between the PE investor and other shareholders, as long as no other parties' interest would be harmed. See Qian Yaozhi, Xia Dongxia, Liu Xiangwen and Zhou Wei, 'The Haifu Case Review: Interpreting the Supreme People's Court's Retrial Judgment and Its Implications for PE Investors', (2012) *China Bulletin*, at http://www.kingandwood.com/Bulletin/ChinaBulletinContent.aspx?id=ebf3a7f9-a2a1-4e81-b55f-35314939e93.

70《最高人民法院关于贯彻执行<中华人民共和国民法通则>若干问题的意见 (试行》[Opinions of the Supreme People's Court on Several Issues Concerning the Implementation of the General Principles of the Civil Law of the People's Republic of China (For Trial Implementation)] (People's Republic of China) the Supreme People's Court, Fa Ban Fa [1988] No6, April 2, 1988, art 194 stated that 'Where any party has any act of evading the compulsory or prohibitive legal criterions of our country, the foreign law shall not apply.'.

71 The ChinaChem case, The Supreme People's Court, [2002]民四终字第30号, 29 Oct 2012; and the GigaMedia Case, see: https://www.mondaq.com/unitedstates/contracts-and-commercial-law/258650/china-vies-recent-developments-and-observations.

72 *Courreges Design v Andre Courreges* (1992) Rev Arb 110 (Paris Court of Appeal), 5 April 1990.

various arguments, one of which being that the VAM and VIE arrangements in dispute breached the mandatory law in China and therefore would lead to the non-enforcement of the award. This argument was not responded to by any of the courts, although the award was eventually refused enforcement on the basis of *ultra vires* (Art V(1)(c)). In 2019, the new *Foreign Investment Law of PRC* came into force, which did not expressly prohibit the use of VIE and left some room for the VIE to be utilised in practice,[73] which might signal that the use of VAM and VIE might be dealt with on a case by case basis and not subject to an overall ban based on public policy concerns in China.

### 3.3.4 Excessive and Compound Interest

While there are no SPC cases dealing with compound interest, this issue has been deal with by the Shenzhen IPC in *Itochu.*[74] Shenzhen Petrochemical argued at the enforcement stage that the calculation of compound interest by a tribunal in London was "against the social public interest or public morality" of China. The Shenzhen IPC opined that the calculation of interest only affected the debtor's interest, not the public interest in China, and therefore could not constitute a violation of public policy. Yet it should be noted that this case does not clearly decide whether compound interest is an issue of substantive fundamental principle or a mandatory rule of law. The parties argued that a calculation of compound interest would be against public morals, but in its ruling denying the application of public policy, the Shenzhen IPC referred to China's financial regulations and provided that compound interest is not prohibited in China. It seems that the Chinese court's approach is to deny a claim suggesting that compound interest is a violation of public policy by excluding it as a mandatory prohibition in China.[75]

This decision is an interesting response to the cases in other jurisdictions where compound interest is considered. Generally, compound interest is not considered a public policy issue, even though it is prohibited under the mandatory rules of law of some jurisdictions. In *Inter Maritime Management SA v Russin and Vecchi,* the calculation of compound interest was held not to be a violation of public policy.[76] In

---

[73] The foreign-invested companies are dealt with by the Foreign Investment Law in 2019. See《中华人民共和国外商投资法》[Foreign Investment Law of the People's Republic of China] (People's Republic of China) National People's Congress, Order No 26, passed on 15 March 2019, effective on 1 January 2020, art 2; this definition abandoned the test of the 'actual controller' in the proposed draft in 2015, which was once seen as a more rigid approach excluding the VIE. Similarly, in art 4, there was a negative list for foreign investments, and VIE was not in the list.

[74] 伊藤忠石油 (香港) 有限公司申请承认执行英国仲裁裁决案 [Case Concerning the Application of Itochu Petroleum (Hong Kong) Co Ltd for the Recognition and Enforcement of a UK Arbitral Award] Shenzhen Intermediate People's Court, (1999) 深中法经二初字第190号[Second Economic Branch No 190], reported in 高晓力 [Gao Xiaoli], above n 55, 259–260.

[75] This is why this case is discussed in this chapter, though the author is of the opinion that both substantive fundamental principles and public policy rules are discussed. See Sect. 3 in Chap. 4.

[76] *Inter Maritime Management SA* (1997) 22 *Yearbook- Commercial Arbitration* 789.

this case, the defendant argued that the fees and interest were excessive and against the prohibition of compound interest in Swiss law, while the Supreme Court found that such a prohibition was not mandatory, and even if it was, it would not constitute a bar to the enforcement of the arbitral award.[77] A similar conclusion was reached in other cases such as *Renusagar Power Co. Ltd v. General Electric Co.*[78]

Beside the issue of compound interest, it is notable that excessive interest, especially extremely high interest rates, is considered a violation of public policy in many jurisdictions. Egypt's Supreme Court held that an award that consisted of an interest rate beyond the maximum interest rate allowed by Egyptian law violated public policy.[79] Also, an Austrian court held that an award that involved a default interest rate of over 107% per annum violated Austria's international public policy.[80]

China People's Bank used to regulates the rate of interest for loans between private entities,[81] however the interest rate provided by the People's Bank is now replaced by the Loan Prime Rate (LPR) released by the National Interbank Funding Centre, as authorised by the People's bank. Up to this point, however, the Chinese courts have not had an opportunity to comment on whether an excessive rate of interest in an arbitral award, particularly those rates of interest that are higher than the capped rate provided by the SPC, is a violation of China's public policy.

### 3.3.5 Other Administrative Approvals

There are many other administrative regulations and rules that are considered mandatory in nature in China's economic and financial businesses. A breach of these regulations and approvals is also a commonly disputed issue in arbitration. An example is *Tianrui,* which involved a breach of a restriction of a franchise license. In this case, the licensing agreement between the parties did not get the approval of the relevant administrative body, which was a mandatory requirement by law. Ultimately, the

---

[77] Ibid, [23].

[78] *Renusagar Power Co Ltd v General Electric Co* AIR 1994 SC 860, reported in (1995) 20 *Yearbook-Commercial Arbitration* 681(India No 22).

[79] Unpublished Case No815/52 of May 21, 1990 (Supreme Court, Egypt). In a later case, an excessive rate of 5% per annum, which is allowed under Egyptian law, was enforced: Court of Cassation, decided January 22, 2008, reported in (2009) *Journal of Arab Arbitration* 174, 177; Dirk Otto and Omaia Elwan, 'Article V(2)' in Herbert Kronke et al. (eds), *Recognition and Enforcement of Foreign Arbitral Awards* (Wolter Kluwer, 2010) 345, 393.

[80] OGH SZ 2005, reported in (2005) 30 *Yearbook-Commercial Arbitration* 421(Supreme Court, Austria, decided 2005) 433.

[81]《最高人民法院关于人民法院审理借贷案件的若干意见》[Opinions of the Supreme People's Court Concerning the Judicial Review on Loan Disputes]Supreme People's Court, Fa Min Fa [1991] No21, 2 July 1991, art 6; replaced by《最高人民法院关于审理民间借贷案件适用法律若干问题的规定》[Regulation of the Supreme People's Court Concerning Several Issues Arising from the Adjudication of Loan Disputes in Civil Contexts]Supreme People's Court, Fa Shi [2020] No 6, effective 20 August 2020, art 26, modifying Fa Shi [2015] No 18, effective 1 September 2015. It provides that the highest interest rates in loan contracts between private parties shall not exceed four times the LPR provided by the Chinese banks on the same types of loan.

SPC held that such a breach was an administrative management matter, which did not impinge on the effectiveness of the agreement and held that such an award did not breach Chinese law and China's public policy.

Similar issues also arose in *Leaf Candy*[82] determined by lower courts. A dispute arose between Leaf Candy, a foreign-investment enterprise established in China, and Shanghai Lianfu, a Chinese company, in relation to an assets purchase agreement.[83] The dispute was then arbitrated before the Singapore International Arbitration Centre and an award was rendered in favour of Leaf Candy. Leaf Candy consequently sought the enforcement of the arbitral award before the Shanghai Second IPC. One issue in this case was whether the asset-transfer in the award would be a ground of non-enforcement of the award, because it was against Article 23 of the *Detailed Rules for the Implementation of the Foreign-Invested Enterprise Law*,[84] which required all asset transfers from a foreign-investment enterprise to other entities to be approved by the appropriate administrative and regulation authorities. The Shanghai Second IPC held that such a mandatory rule was not fundamental and declined to apply the public policy exception.

Also in *Huludao*, a dispute arose in relation to a contract of equity trust for shares in a foreign-investment company. One party argued that it was in fact a contract for the transfer of shares, which must be approved by the relevant authorities; thus, the award confirming the contract and ignoring the lack of sufficient approval violated the mandatory rules of Chinese law. This argument was denied by the Beijing 1st IPC, holding that the arbitral award clearly distinguished the contract of equity trust from a share transfer. Thus, the award was not held to be a breach of the mandatory rules of law. The Beijing HPC and the SPC did not comment further on this issue.

It is particularly notable that, in his comment on *Leaf Candy*, Judge Xuejie Cui provided some distinctive comments on the categorisation of mandatory rules under contract law, which may contribute to the division between mandatory rules of law and *lois de police* in practice.[85] He referred to Article 52(5) of the *Chinese Contract Law,* which provides that a contract is void if it is against mandatory rules of law or

---

[82] 利夫糖果(上海)有限公司申请承认和执行新加坡国际仲裁中心仲裁裁决案 [Case Concerning the Application of Leaf Candy (Shanghai) Co Ltd for Recognition and Enforcement of an Arbitral Award of SIAC] Shanghai Second IPC, (2008) 沪二中民五 (商) 初字19号[Fifth Civil Branch (Commercial), Case of First Instance No.19], available at <http://www.shezfy.com/view.html?id=11429> .

[83] This dispute is categorised as foreign-related and therefore its arbitration can be conducted by foreign arbitration institutions. This is because one of the contracting parties, a natural person, is of Malaysian nationality; therefore, a "foreign-related element" of the disputed contract can be successfully established and the arbitration did not violate the exclusive jurisdiction of China in dealing with pure domestic disputes. See *CCPL*, art 278; see also Sect. 4.3 in Chap. 3, discussing the definition of "foreign-related element" in China.

[84]《中华人民共和国外资企业法实施细则》[Detailed Rules for the Implementation of the Foreign-Invested Enterprise Law of the People's Republic of China]State Council, 28 October 1990, amended in 12 April 2001, 19 February 2014, art 23.

[85] See http://www.shezfy.com/view.html?id=11429. It is notable that this part of the comments is not included in the judgment, but as commentary published on the website of the court.

administrative regulations,[86] and that the distinction between "regulatory mandatory rules" and "validating mandatory rules" provided by the SPC is that the former aims to regulate the activities of the contracting parties, while the latter aims to affect the validity of the contract.[87] Only a breach of the "validating mandatory rules" can render a contract void, while a breach of "regulatory mandatory rules" would only result in possible negative effects under administrative regulations, but not necessarily influence the validity of the contract.[88] Based on these distinctions of the two categories of mandatory rules of law, Cui further opined that the requirement of administrative approval did not affect the validity of the contract because (i) the rule in Article 23 of the *Detailed Rules for the Implementation of the Foreign-Invested Enterprise Law* did not expressly provide so, and (ii) upon the violation of such a rule, the continuing recognition of the validity of the contract would not infringe upon national interest and the social public interest. This analysis, although not directly related to the application of public policy, clearly shows that the mandatory rules in China are narrowly construed. Therefore, the consequence of a breach of mandatory rules of law should not be over-estimated, not only in determining the validity of the contract, but also in the application of public policy.

## *3.4 The Competition Law Rules*

*Eco Swiss*[89] confirmed that a breach of competition law might amount to a violation of public policy in the enforcement of arbitral awards. In this case, Benetton argued for the refusal of enforcement of the award by claiming that the contract in issue breached the previous Article 85 of the *Treaty Establishing the European Community*[90] regarding competition law rules, and therefore was against public policy defined in Article 1065(1) of the *Netherlands Code of Civil Procedure*. The Court of the European Community (the EC Court) held that such a law was "essential for the accomplishment of the tasks entrusted to the Community and the functioning

86 《中华人民共和国合同法》[Contract Law of the People's Republic of China] (People's Republic of China) National People's Congress, Order No15, 15 March 1999, art 52(5).

87 《最高人民法院关于适用<中华人民共和国合同法>若干问题的解释(二)》[Interpretations of the Supreme People's Court on Several Issues in the Application of the Contract Law of the People's Republic of China (Second)] Supreme People's Court, 24 April 2009, art 14.

88 《最高人民法院关于当前形势下审理民商事合同纠纷案件若干问题的规定》[Regulations of the Supreme People's Court in Regard of the Judicial Review of Civil and Commercial Contractual Disputes under Recent Circumstances] Supreme People's Court, Fa Fa [2009] No40, art 15. It provides that the courts should hold a contract void based on a violation of validating mandatory rules; and should decide on the validity of a contract based on the specific circumstance of the case if there is only a violation of regulatory mandatory rules.

89 *Eco Swiss China* [1999] ECR-I 3055.

90 *Treaty Establishing the European Community*, opened for signature 7 February 1992, [1992] OJ C 224/6 (entered into force 1 November 1993), as amended by the *Treaty of Nice Amending the Treaty on the European Union, the Treaties Establishing the European Communities and Certain Related Acts*, opened for signature 26 February 2001, [2001] OJ C 80/1 (entered into force 1 February 2003).

of the internal market",[91] and that a national court could decline to enforce an arbitral award if that award was contrary to such a rule.[92] The EC Court also confirmed that the competition rules in Article81 of the *EC Treaty* constituted both the domestic public policy of each member country and the public policy of the EU.[93] The significance of the competition law is also confirmed in *Gallay.*[94]

In China, cases arising from the context of antidumping law are observed. For example, in *Shin-Etsu (No. 1)*, there has been arguments based on the violation of the anti-dumping policy. This case dealt with the administrative decision made by MOFCOM regarding the anti-dumping policy. Shin-Etsu and Zhongtian entered into a contract to export raw fibre-optic materials from Japan to China for five years, commencing on 1 January 2003, at a particular price. Later in 2003, MOFCOM started an anti-dumping investigation against imported fibre-optic products (the product of such raw materials in this case) from the US, Japan and Korea. MOFCOM provided its primary decision to require a deposit for such dealings in 2004, and the final decision in 2005, requiring a 46% anti-dumping tariff on all products imported from Japan. Due to this decision, the price of the fibre-optic products of Zhongtian fell dramatically. Zhongtian required Shin-Etsu to re-negotiate the price but such negotiations eventually failed; performance of the contract then failed. In the arbitration, the Japan Commercial Arbitration Association (JCAA) rendered its award in favour of Shin-Etsu.

The award was challenged by Zhongtian and thoroughly discussed before the Nantong IPC, the Jiangsu HPC and the SPC. The discussion of public policy arose regarding MOFCOM's anti-dumping decision. The Nantong IPC's opinions were divided. Some of the judges in Nantong IPC considered that the enforcement of the JCAA award would be detrimental, not only to Zhongtian, but also to all importers in a similar position to Zhongtian (given that the JCAA made similar awards in other cases with identical facts). Judges also commented that this decision would affect all fibre-optic producers in China, and eventually damage China's fibre-optic industry, a result that MOFCOM tried to avoid. Thus, China's public policy would be infringed if such an arbitral award was enforced. On the contrary, some other judges favoured a narrow interpretation of public policy and refused to apply the public policy exception based on the facts that only the interests of one particular entity, Zhongtian, was involved in this case; that the raw materials in dispute were not the final product being regulated by the anti-dumping decision; and that there was no evidence that Shin-Etsu was involved in the dumping activities regulated by MOFCOM.[95]

---

[91] *Eco Swiss China* [1999] ECR-I 3055, [36].

[92] *Ibid,* [41].

[93] Nevertheless, the EC Court also held that the application of such public policy is subject to time limits provided by domestic procedural law, and in this case the delay in bringing such a claim might result in a failure to argue the annulment of arbitral awards. Ibid, [43]-[48].

[94] *Gallay* [2000] Rev Arb 805.

[95] The opinion of the Nantong IPC.

The Jiangsu HPC accepted the argument relating to the possible effect of the price of the raw materials and products and found that the original price of the contract would cause Zhongtian's production costs to rise significantly. Thus, Shin-Etsu's activities amounted to it taking "advantage of its monopoly position" as a provider and that it sold such raw materials at a "monopoly price" to Chinese companies (not only Zhongtian but also other major fibre-optic producers). Based on these facts, the Jiangsu HPC held that this award would have the same effect as dumping the final product, infringe China's fibre-optic industry, offset the effect of MOFCOM's anti-dumping tariff, and violate China's public policy.

Neither of these opinions was responded to by the SPC, which again kept silent on the application of public policy. Rather, the SPC refused enforcement on the ground of procedural irregularity, based on the tribunal's failure to render its award within the prescribed time limit; and the ground of due process, based on the tribunal's failure to properly notify the parties of the time limit.

Similarly, in *Shin-Etsu v Xinmao*, another case arising in a similar context, the Tianjin HPC attempted to apply the public policy ground to refuse the enforcement of the arbitral award favouring the foreign party. It was considered that the Japanese party committed to dumping, and the enforcement of such award would facilitate the dumping activity and breach the Chinese law as well as the MOFCOM's tariff. Again, the SPC kept silent on this point and refused the enforcement on the ground of the breach of procedural fairness (Art V(1)(b)).

It was notable that the SPC refrained from confirming that the rules of competition law would amount to public policy rules in the context of the judicial review of arbitral awards. It is further observed, however, that the SPC expressed its view on various occasions that the arbitrability of competition law matters would be their major concern, at least in the context of domestic law.[96] It is yet to be seen whether this attitude would be extended to the context of international arbitration, and if so, how it would impact the construction of public policy in the judicial review of the arbitral awards resulting from, or relating to, a competition law dispute.

## 3.5 *The Import/Export Controls and Public Health/ Environmental Protection*

In some cases, it is also considered a violation of public policy when import and export control orders are breached. For example, Indian courts once held that the performance of a contract of coal exports violated Indian public policy because such export was against India's export restrictions and therefore illegal.[97] On the other

[96] See further Sect. 3.2.5 in Chap. 8.

[97] *COSID v Steel Authority of India*, AIR 1986 Del.8(22)(Delhi High Court, India).

hand, if the law only affects the performance, but not fully forbids such performance,[98] or if the party's failure to perform may attract the risk of governmental interference,[99] it is not likely that public policy would be violated. These results are generally consistent with the narrow construction and limited application of the public policy exception.

The following are a series of cases in which the courts discussed whether China's public policy may have been violated when the arbitral award was made arguably against the Chinese government's export/import decisions. In *Bunge* (2006), the Singapore party sought enforcement of a London FOSFA award in China. The defendant, the Chinese party, argued that the enforcement would be contrary to China's social public interest and public order because the arbitral award violated the banning notice of the General Administration of Quality Supervision, Inspection and Quarantine of the People's Republic of China (AQSIQ); when the disputed contract was subject to performance, the applicant was on a "blacklist" of exporters and was temporarily disqualified from exporting soybeans from Brazil to China by order of AQSIQ.[100] The Yangjiang IPC did not comment on this issue and neither did the SPC in its final reply, refusing to enforce the award on other grounds.[101]

The only discussion of the possible application of public policy is provided by the Guangdong HPC, which found that the AQSIQ's notice regarding the temporary disqualification of the Singapore party was not directly related to the particular products disputed in the case. Therefore, there was a lack of sufficient evidence to prove the connection between the case and the disqualification. In adopting this factual

---

[98] *Smita Conductors Ltd v Euro Alloys Ltd*, Appeal (civil) 12,930 of 1996, Supreme Court of India, reported in (2002) 27 *Yearbook-Commercial Arbitration* 482, 489–491. See also Otto and Elwan, above n 43, 386.

[99] *KarahaBodas Company LLC v Perusahaan PertambanganMinyak Dan Gas Bumi Negara,* [2004] A.J.No.1440, reported in (2005) 30 *Yearbook-Commercial Arbitration* 488, 496 (Alberta Court of Queen's Bench, Canada); For cases with similar outcomes in the US and Hong Kong courts, see *KarahaBodas Company LLC v Perusahaan PertambanganMinyak Dan Gas Bumi Negara,*364 F 3d 274, 306, reported in (2004) 29 *Yearbook-Commercial Arbitration* 1262, 1291(US Court of Appeals for the 5th Circuit); and *KarahaBodas Company LLC v Perusahaan PertambanganMinyak Dan Gas Bumi Negara,* HKCA Civil Appeal No.121/2003, reported in (2008) 33 *Yearbook-Commercial Arbitration* 574. See also Otto and Elwan, above n 43, 386–87.

[100] 《国家质量监督检验检疫总局公告》[Notice of the General Administration of Quality Supervision, Inspection and Quarantine of the People's Republic of China], the General Administration of Quality Supervision, Inspection and Quarantine, [2004] No 71, June 14, 2004. The legal foundation of this decision-making is provided by《中华人民共和国进出口商品检验法》[Law of the People's Republic of China on Import and Export Commodity Inspection] National People's Congress Standing Committee, Order No14, 21 February 1989; Modified by National People's Congress Standing Committee, Order No67, 28 April 2002, art 3; and《中华人民共和国进出口商品检验法实施条例》[Regulations for the Implementation of the Law of People's Republic of China on Import and Export Commodity Inspection] State Council, 31 August 2005, art 19.

[101] The Yangjiang IPC focused on the inappropriate notice to the defendant, which caused their failure to nominate the arbitrator and present their case before the tribunal. The SPC, instead, focused on the fact that the final arbitrator was directly appointed by the Association without notifying the defendant after the first arbitrator withdrew from the tribunal, which is inconsistent with the applicable arbitration rules.

analysis, the Guangdong HPC denied the possibility of a breach of such a rule, and avoided further discussion on whether the administrative disqualification would be a category of public policy rules/*lois de police*. It may be implied, though, that the Guangdong HPC would consider the public policy argument if a connection could be established between the dispute and the AQSIQ notice.[102]

Had the courts in this case adopted the two-step analysis,[103] first identifying the public policy rules/*lois de police* and then reviewing whether there was a breach, it is arguable that public health or environmental protection considerations underlying the AQSIQ's banning order against the Singapore party[104] might fall within the scope of public policy. In addition, the import/export control based on public health considerations might also be regulated under international agreements and treaties, such as the multilateral trade agreements and the WTO agreements, and might be recognised as key elements of public policy on the basis of the international consensus on the importance of these issues, which is provided by these multilateral agreements. These questions, however, were not answered by the SPC in this case.

Similar disputes are repeated in *Noble* and *Louis Dreyfus*. In *Noble*, the Chinese party argued that its failure to comply with the contract was caused by the AQSIQ's banning order on the foreign party, and the award against such a banning order should be refused enforcement. The SPC rejected this argument on the basis that the soybeans had already been delivered when the banning order was issued; and that later such a banning order was terminated and licences and approvals were obtained by Noble; thus, the award was not against the AQSIQ's order. In *Louis Dreyfus,* a dispute arose with respect to the AQSIQ's temporary banning order. Opinions in the Guangdong High Court were divided, with the majority preferring to refuse such enforcement on the ground of public policy based on concerns relating to the protection of food safety and the environment. The SPC again refused to apply the public policy exception, and enforced this award by holding that the disputed soybeans did not cause any damage to the public health or the environment, and that such an award was thus not a breach of the AQSIQ's order and a violation of China's public policy.[105]

In recent years, the SPC's reluctance to respond to similar arguments was also followed in the practice of lower courts. When dealing with another case involving the banned Brazilian soybeans in *Beiliang* (2018),[106] the Rizhao IPC simply held that the

---

102 This is because their clarification of the lack of that connection was directly followed by the conclusion that "the application of public policy lacks sufficient factual basis". It is arguable that the lack of connection is a factual reason that public policy could not be applied in the eyes of the Guangdong HPC.

103 See Sect. 3.1.

104 《国家质量监督检验检疫总局公告》[Notice of the General Administration of Quality Supervision, Inspection and Quarantine of the People's Republic of China], the General Administration of Quality Supervision, Inspection and Quarantine, [2004] No 71, June 14, 2004.

105 Ibid.

106 北良（香港）有限公司、日照兴裕嘉贸易有限公司申请承认与执行法院判决、仲裁裁决案件裁定书[Decision on the Application for the Recognition and Enforcement of Judgments or Arbitral Awards between Beiliang (Hong Kong) Co Ltd and Rizhao Xingyujia Trade Co Ltd], Rizhao IPC, (2016)鲁11协外认1号[Judicial Assistance Foreign Recognition No.1], 9 January 2018.

award only resulted in monetary payments between the parties and therefore did not involve public policy. In other cases, the lower courts repeatedly rejected arguments based on the violation of import and export quotas, in cases such as *Olam*,[107] *Ecom No.1* (2016),[108] or the violation of the controls of import and export of precursor chemicals in *CAO Singapore* (2017).[109]

## *3.6 Other Cases*

Many other rules are referred to as different categories of public policy rules/*lois de police* in foreign jurisdictions. The *ILA Final Report* includes issues such as embargo measures, blockades or boycotts, tax laws and consumer laws. The violation of sanctions and boycott legislation was considered to be a ground to refuse the enforcement of an arbitral award in *Harris Adacom Corp v Perkom Sdn Bhd,*[110] where the court held that an award offending a boycott against Israel's interest would be refused enforcement.[111]

These possible categories of public policy rules have not yet been raised in cases in China, but there are cases in China where other mandatory rules of law are occasionally discussed, in most of which government approvals are concerned. In two of them, the public policy ground was upheld by the SPC. In *Heavy Metal*, while the morality of the performance was concerned,[112] another major reason referred to by the SPC was that the performance was against the government's approval and therefore against the law.

The *Hulishan* case is quite similar to *Heavy Metal*. Xiamen Hulishan Fortress Management Bureau agreed with a Singaporean company for the display of certain historical relics and jewels in their exhibition. However, the items in the display were later found to be counterfeit and the extension of the exhibition was rejected

[107] 翱兰国际有限公司、淄博银花棉麻有限公司等申请承认和执行外国仲裁裁决民事裁定书 [Civil Decision on the Application for the Recognition and Enforcement of a Foreign Arbitral Award between Olam International Ltd and Zibo Yinhua Cotton and Linen Co Ltd], Zibo IPC, (2015)淄民特字第1号[Civil Special No.1], 19 January 2016.

[108] EcoM Agroindustrial 申请承认和执行外国仲裁裁决民事裁定书 [Decision on the Application for the Recognition and Enforcement of A Foreign Arbitral Awards by Ecom Agroindustrial Corp Ltd Switzerland], Shenzhen IPC, (2014) 深中法涉外初字第 60 号[Foreign-related First Instance No.60], 25 May 2016.

[109] 中国航油（新加坡）股份有限公司、成都欣华欣化工材料有限公司申请承认与执行外国仲裁裁决裁定书 [Decision on the Application for the Recognition and Enforcement of a Foreign Arbitral Award between China Aviation Oil (Singapore) Corp Ltd and Chengdu Xinhuaxin Chenical Engineering Materials Co Ltd], Chengdu IPC, (2017)川01协外认1号[Judicial Assistance Foreign Recognition No.1], 23 June 2017.

[110] [1994] 3 MLJ 504.

[111] This was accepted by both parties in this case. Nonetheless, the court did not rule on whether the boycott legislation should be a ground for refusal of enforcement but ruled on the fact that such boycott legislation was not violated in the given transaction. See ibid.

[112] See Sect. 4 in Chap. 5.

by the government. The Bureau then discontinued the display and packed the items under the supervision of Customs. The Singaporean company brought an arbitration claim before CIETAC, claiming for damages on the basis of the discontinuation of the display, which was upheld by the CIETAC tribunal. The Bureau sought an annulment of the award. The Beijing First IPC held that the award was in fact requiring the Bureau to perform the contract against the government's approval and violate the law, and therefore, was against China's public policy.

In contrast, in *Ciming*, the party resisting the award argued that the arbitral award's dealing with, and assessment of, the value of the administrative approval violated the mandatory law. The court held that the dispute only dealt with the financial interests of the parties, not the interest of the general public, and therefore was not against the public interest.[113]

It may be observed from these cases that the Chinese court's major concern in assessing the illegality is whether the awards, or the effect of the award, would lead to breaches of the Chinese law or government approval, rather than focusing on the breaches of the Chinese law that leads to the arbitration or in the existing dispute. This approach, however, is not consistent with the analysis of the fundamentality of the rules in breach, as illustrated in international practice above; nor is it consistent with the other rulings of the SPC, like the competition law cases in which the award might in effect support the dumping activities of foreign companies. As both rulings in *Heavy Metal* (1997) and *Hulishan* (2013) were at least a decade ago, it remains to be seen whether this rationale would be reflected in any rulings in the future.

# 4 Conclusion: Establishing a Consistent Approach in Dealing with Public Policy Rules

## *4.1 China's Problem: Lack of a Practical Approach*

After reviewing the cases mentioned, it can be concluded that none of the mandatory rules of law involved in these China-related arbitral awards have been recognised as categories of public policy rules/*lois de police* in China's judicial review practice. Yet one further question remains to be answered. Have the Chinese courts, in identifying any category of public policy rules and finding breaches of them, adopt a consistent approach in making their decisions?

Some progress in developing a consistent approach is evident in China's judicial practices in dealing with public policy rules. The most significant development is that Chinese courts, in general, have realised that there are differences between mandatory rules of national law on the one hand, and public policy on the other hand, particularly

[113]《慈铭博鳌国际医院有限公司与海南亨延顿医院管理咨询有限公司等申请撤销仲裁裁决民事裁定书》[Civil Decision on the Application for the Annulment of An Arbitral Award between Ciming Bo'ao International Hospital Co Ltd and HRC-Hainan Holding Company LLC et al.], Beijing 4th IPC, (2021)京04民特26号[Civil Special No.26], 5 March 2021.

when applied in the context of international commercial arbitration. This approach is clearly adopted in a series of cases such as *ED and F Mans* and *Mitsui*, and further confirmed in recent cases such as *Starr Cayman.*[114]

A fundamental problem in Chinese courts in establishing a practical approach to dealing with public policy rules is that they generally fail to follow a two-step analysis, which is generally adopted in other leading jurisdictions: to initially evaluate whether a mandatory rule of law is significant enough to become a public policy rule, and then decide whether the award breaches such a public policy rule, and if there is a breach, whether this breach is significantly detrimental to the fundamental interests protected by such a public policy rule.[115] In most Chinese cases, the discussions of public policy are not fully developed. For example, in *ED &F Mans* and *Mitsui*, the courts, especially the SPC, generally denied the public policy nature of many mandatory law rules in China without further explanation.[116] Alternatively, the courts in *Shin-Etsu (No. 1)* avoided any discussion of public policy rules and instead based their decisions on other grounds.[117] In *Bunge* and *Louis Dreyfus,* the courts skipped the analysis of whether there is a relevant public policy rule, and directly jumped to the second question, finding no breach of a mandatory rule of law or administrative decision.[118]

In regard to identifying some categories of public policy rules or establishing a consistent approach in evaluating the public policy nature of mandatory rules, no significant progress is observed. Chinese courts do not expressly confirm any public policy rules, though they have dealt with some cases in areas of law in which public policy rules are recognised in international practice e.g., anti-dumping laws, currency control, foreign-investment security review, and export/import control. There is a possible category of public policy rules discussed in *Leaf Candy,* where Judge Cui referred to Judge Gao's categorisation, but did not apply it.[119] The most significant debate in regard to the public policy nature of a rule is *Mitsui,* in which different opinions towards or against the public policy nature of the foreign currency control rule were reported by Judge Gao, though its public policy nature was eventually denied.[120] To summarise, Chinese courts only make it clear that mandatory rules of law are not necessarily public policy rules, but do not further clarify which mandatory rules of law are significant enough to become one.

In addition, there are a few problematic understandings and unresolved issues under the current approach adopted by Chinese courts. One typical misunderstanding

---

[114] Section 3.3.

[115] Section 3.1.

[116] Section 3.3.

[117] Sections 3.3 and 3.5.

[118] Section 3.5.

[119] The categorisation of Gao provided: "…*(e) the legislative rules that constitutes the fundamental legal principle of China, such as the principle of good faith and honesty, the law of anti-terrorism, the prohibition against cult, traffic in persons, money laundering, and gambling*". 高晓力[Gao Xiaoli], above n 55, 131.

[120] 高晓力[Gao Xiaoli], above n 55, 254.

made by some lawyers and possibly some judges is that the court should only focus on whether the outcome of the enforcement would influence social public interests, rather than whether the award breached a possible public policy rule.[121] This is a clear misunderstanding, because the direct outcome of the enforcement of an award in a particular case is that it will only influence the losing party, not the whole country. If we decide that no public policy is violated because only limited numbers of private parties bear the burden to pay an amount as an outcome of enforcement, the ground of public policy would become meaningless and would never be applied.

Another problem is that Chinese courts appear to lack the confidence to comment on any issue relation to the violation of public policy, except procedural errors, and particularly, they are reluctant to comment on the tribunal's failure to apply Chinese mandatory law.[122] In order to decide whether there is a manifest violation of public policy rules, however, it is necessary to discuss the non-application of a particular mandatory rule of law, as well as its possible consequences.[123] If these misunderstandings cannot be resolved, it is very unlikely that Chinese courts will make significant progress towards identifying which rules can impinge on China's public policy.

## 4.2 *Legislative Purpose as a Possible Indicator of Public Policy Rules*

Given the primary conclusion that the general progress of Chinese courts towards confirming public policy rules is disappointing to date, the author suggests that some positive indicators may be introduced into the judicial review process to help the Chinese judiciary improve its performance. It is particularly notable that both international experience and current Chinese legislative movements suggest that the identification of legislative purposes may contribute to the identification of public policy rules.

International experience provides that a legislative purpose may expressly or implicitly influence the construction of public policy rules by arbitrators, as well as the enforcement of arbitral awards; but that the legislative purpose must be clear enough to be identified.[124] As provided by the *EC Regulation on the Law Applicable to Contractual Regulations*, some legislation may be considered as "overriding

---

[121] For example, in *Shin-Etsu (No. 1)*,this opinion was taken by some judges in the IPC; also in *Starr Cayman*, this opinion was taken by the foreign party and also taken by the case comment in Eric Liu, Yaxing Zhang, Yuhao Lu and Delong Zou, 'Mainland court's standards for identifying social public interests when recognizing off-shore arbitration awards', 25 December 2014, at http://www.hankunlaw.com/downloadfile/newsAndInsights/6ac7910a05c1ec017cfde99f1de18053.pdf.

[122] See for example, *Louis Dreyfus* and *Starr Cayman*.

[123] See further discussions in Chap. 9 in regard to the approach of the judicial review in respect to the substance of the arbitral award.

[124] Villiers, above n 31, 169.

mandatory provisions", and the failure to recognise and apply such provisions might lead to the non-enforcement of awards.[125]

Further standards of judicial review might be required in order to identify the legislative purpose. For example, both the *ILA Report* and the *EC Regulation* suggest that the public policy rules or the overriding mandatory provisions should emphasise the significance of those rules in safeguarding essential political, social and economic aspects of interests and also ensure its application in all situations.[126] It may be clear if the legislation clearly expresses such a purpose; however, if the legislation is not clear, then the task of interpreting the legislation becomes complicated.

It is particularly notable that recent legislative movements in China may contribute to the identification of the public policy purpose underlying a particular mandatory rule of national law, which may qualify it to be a public policy rule/*lois de police*. As discussed in Sect. 3.2, the recent enacted *Law Application Law* and the SPC's judicial interpretation of the implementation of the *Law Application Law*[127] have identified some categories of mandatory rules of law that are considered to be significant enough to be applied, which may indicate their public policy nature. It is also notable that some other laws in China may also contribute to the identification of public policy rules. One example is the recent *Foreign Investment Law,*[128] which emphasises the compulsory application of this law in any foreign investment in China and introduced a series of compulsory schemes on foreign investment. For example, if an investment shall be subject to the national security review, such review can be done either by voluntary submission of the investor or by the governmental body on its own motion; and such review is not appealable.[129] These provisions may contribute to the identification of a public policy rule in the law of foreign-investment control when Chinese courts deal with this issue in the future.

[125] Regulation (EC) No 593/2008 of the European Parliament and of the Council, of 17 June 2008, on the Law Applicable to Contractual Obligations (Rome I) [2008] OJ L 177/6, art 9 provides:

'Overriding mandatory provisions.

1. Overriding mandatory provisions are provisions the respect for which is regarded as crucial by a country for safeguarding its public interests, such as its political, social or economic organisation, to such an extent that they are applicable to any situation falling within their scope, irrespective of the law otherwise applicable to the contract under this Regulation.

2. Nothing in this Regulation shall restrict the application of the overriding mandatory provisions of the law of the forum.

3. Effect may be given to the overriding mandatory provisions of the law of the country where the obligations arising out of the contract have to be or have been performed, in so far as those overriding mandatory provisions render the performance of the contract unlawful. In considering whether to give effect to those provisions, regard shall be had to their nature and purpose and to the consequences of their application or non-application'.

[126] Mayer and Sheppard, above n 4, Recommendation 1(d).

[127] Section 3.2.

[128] 《中华人民共和国外商投资法》[Foreign Investment Law of the People's Republic of China] (People's Republic of China) National People's Congress, Order No 26, passed on 15 March 2019, effective on 1 January 2020.

[129] Ibid, art 35.

The author also suggests that the court should identify whether the disputed issue was intended to be covered by such a clearly defined legislative purpose. As the *ILA Report* suggests, public policy should apply only when: "*(i) the scope of said rule is intended to encompass the situation under consideration…*" This is also reflected in judicial practice; for example, the Indian courts held that a rule completely forbidding the performance of a contract would be respected as a public policy rule; but a rule affecting, but not completely forbidding, such performance, would not bar enforcement.[130]

In some of the Chinese cases discussed above, Chinese courts also faced similar issues when disputed contracts and their performance were not directly covered by the mandatory law or regulations referred to but were strongly influenced by them. For example, in *Bunge*, the disputed transaction was not directly covered by the AQSIQ notice, but was influenced by it.[131] The situation in *Shin-Etsu (No 1)* was much more complicated, as the disputed contractual activities were not covered by the anti-dumping decision of MOFCOM; but it is reasonable to predict that the continuation of the disputed contract would cause detrimental results which the anti-dumping decision aimed to avoid.[132]

However Chinese courts, especially the SPC, have not focused on analysing the legislative purposes and exploring their possible scope. Their approach, in general, has been to deny any possible violation of a particular administrative order on a factual basis, as illustrated in *Bunge* and *Louis Dreyfus,*[133] without further exploring whether the involved law or regulation was violated. Without discussing and properly applying the legislative purpose, it is hard to conclude that such an approach satisfactorily addressed the real issues in deciding such cases. The author thus suggests that the Chinese courts, after finding the possible involvement of a legislative or mandatory rule in the disputed arbitral award, should decide whether the issues in dispute are covered by the purpose of such legislation. A detailed exploration of the purpose of the applicable law and regulations is required to make such a decision.

It may be that progress has been made by the Chinese courts with respect to exploring the function of the legislative purpose when reviewing arbitral awards in order to distinguishing between validating mandatory rules of law and regulatory mandatory rules. Though this distinction is provided by the SPC in terms of deciding on the validity of contract, it may also be a useful exercise in determining whether such mandatory rules of law are intended to protect the public policy of the State.[134]

---

130 *COSIDAIR* 1986 Del.8(22)(Delhi High Court, India); *Smita Conductors*in (2002) 27 *Yearbook-Commercial Arbitration* 482, 489–491.

131 Section 3.5.

132 Section 3.4. This detrimental consequence is predicable by any reasonable person with basic economic knowledge, and also adopted bythe Jiangsu HPC in this case. The author is of the opinion is that such analysis is a comprehensive and well-rounded analysis of the legislative purpose of the applied law and regulation in this case.

133 Section 3.5.

134 Cui's comment on the Shanghai IPC's decision on the *Leaf Candy Case*, available at <http://www.shezfy.com/view.html?id=11429> .

The SPC, in distinguishing these two different types of mandatory rules determines whether the contracting activities covered by the validating mandatory rules infringe upon the State's interests or social public interests, in order to d hold such a contract void when there is a violation. On the other hand, if the mandatory rule relates to the qualification to enter a particular market, or regulates the performance of such a contract rather than the validity of the contract, the courts take a cautious approach in deciding upon its validity and may request an interpretation by the legislative authority or the higher courts on the purpose of such a rule.[135] The courts also consider the characteristics of the involved rights and interests, the security of transactions, and the objects of such a regulation, in distinguishing "validating mandatory rules" from "regulatory mandatory rules".[136] This approach provides a useful guide for practitioners in recognising the effect of the legislative purpose in China's commercial practice. However, it is worthwhile to also consider whether they will be employed by the courts in identifying public policy rules in the judicial review of arbitral awards.

Finally, if the newly enacted legislation expressing such public policy effects is intended to govern pre-existing disputes, it must expressly so provide. The *ILA Report* indicates that public policy rules may not apply unless *"it is plain that the legislator intended said rule to have effect as regards awards rendered prior to its enactment",*[137] *which may also be an important reminder for legislators and legal practitioners regarding the establishment and interpretation of the legislative purposes underlying mandatory rules.*

The author suggests that the Chinese courts, as well as arbitration practitioners and even legislators, take these indicators into account when establishing the standards required identifying public policy rules. In adopting these standards, the Chinese courts may more confidently recognise the public policy nature of some mandatory rules in China, and this development may more closely align China's practices to those of the leading jurisdictions in the area of arbitration law.

---

135 《最高人民法院关于当前形势下审理民商事合同纠纷案件若干问题的规定》[Regulations of the Supreme People's Court in Regard of the Judicial Review of Civil and Commercial Contractual Disputes under Recent Circumstances] Supreme People's Court, FaFa [2009] No40, art 16.

136 Ibid; 叶阳[Ye Yang], 《效力性规定在司法实践中的辨识》[Identification of "Validating Mandatory Rules" in Judicial Practices], 人民法院报*People's Court Daily,* 23 November 2011. See also Judge Ye Yang from the SPC, who provides that: firstly, the detriment to public interests caused by a violation of validating mandatory rules is direct and realistic, not indirect and possible; secondly, the extent of such detriment should be significant, not merely remote; and finally, the court should also consider and balance the public interests on one hand, and transaction safety and reliance interests on the other hand.

137 Mayer and Sheppard, above n 4, Recommendation 3(d), and [30].

# Chapter 8
# Arbitrability and Public Policy

## 1 Introduction

This chapter deals with arbitrability as a possible element of public policy. As introduced earlier, arbitrability may also be an element of public policy, though it is separately stated in the *NYC* as a ground to refuse the enforcement of an arbitral award.[1] It is particularly notable that arbitrability is closely connected with mandatory rules of law, especially those that contain public policy considerations.[2] For these reasons, this chapter examines the possible public policy nature of arbitrability as a ground for negating arbitral awards in judicial practice.

Section 2 of this chapter deals with some significant issues of arbitrability identified in the general literature, including its definition and development, the criteria used to decide arbitrability, national and international approaches in dealing with arbitrability, and its relationship with public policy. Section 3 examines the references to arbitrability in China's legislation and in relevant judicial review of arbitral awards cases. Section 4 concludes this chapter by summarising the approach adopted by the Chinese legal system in dealing with arbitrability and evaluating the performance of Chinese courts.

---

[1] Sect. 5 in Chap. 2. Also see Pierre Mayer and Audley Sheppard, 'Final Report on Public Policy as a Bar to Enforcement of International Arbitral Awards' (2003) 19 *Arbitration International* 249, Recommendation 1(d).

[2] See Sect. 2.2 in Chap. 7



S. Zhang, *The Public Policy Exception in the Judicial Review of International Commercial Arbitral Awards*, https://doi.org/10.1007/978-3-662-67679-0_8

# 2 General Literature Review on Arbitrability

## 2.1 *Definition of Arbitrability*

Arbitrability is generally defined as the determination of whether a dispute can be referred to and resolved through the mechanism of arbitration. As the *NYC* provides, arbitrability means that disputes are "capable of settlement by arbitration".[3] Although the general concept of arbitrability is universally accepted, it is difficult to define arbitrability in a consistent manner. Quite a few different definitions are proffered by scholars, reflecting different aspects of this legal concept. Brekoulakis focuses on arbitrability as a pre-condition to the establishment of jurisdiction, and distinguishes it from a pre-condition relating to the validity of an arbitration agreement[4]; Youssef defines it as the freedom to arbitrate, and delineates its role within the parameters of the principle of party autonomy[5]; Carbonneau emphasises the categorisation between public and private justice in relation to the arbitrability issue.[6] These definitions illustrate different aspects and characteristics of arbitrability.

In addition, there are broad and narrow approaches in defining arbitrability. In some jurisdictions, such as the US, the limitations on the issues to be arbitrated are referred to as "objective arbitrability", which is *ratione materiae*; there is also a "subjective arbitrability" that is *ratione personae*, which considers whether the parties have the capability to submit a dispute to arbitration.[7] Many scholars combine the subjective and objective elements of arbitrability to propose a broad definition of arbitrability.[8] An even broader definition of arbitrability, as reported by Bermann, covers any reason that bars a dispute from being arbitrated.[9] All of these definitions

---

[3] *The NYC*, art II(1), art V(2)(a).

[4] Stavros L. Brekoulakis, 'Chapter 2—On Arbitrability: Persisting Misconceptions and New Areas of Concern ' in Loukas A. Mistelis and Stavros L. Brekoulakis (eds), *Arbitrability: International and Comparative Perspectives* (Kluwer Law International, 2009) 19, 39.

[5] Karim Youssef, 'The Death of Inarbitrability ' in Loukas A. Mistelis and Stavros L. Brekoulakis (eds), *Arbitrability: International and Comparative Perspectives* (Kluwer Law International, 2009) 47, 48–49.

[6] Thomas E. Carbonneau, 'Liberal Rules of Arbitrability and the Autonomy of Labor Arbitration in the United States' in Loukas A. Mistelis and Stavros L. Brekoulakis (eds), *Arbitrability: International and Comparative Perspectives* ( Kluwer Law International, 2009) 143, 143.

[7] For the broad definition under US law, see Loukas A. Mistelis, 'Arbitrability: International and Comparative Perspectives' in Loukas A. Mistelis and Stavros L. Brekoulakis (eds), *Arbitrability: International and Comparative Perspectives* (Kluwer Law International, 2009) 1, 5.

[8] Laurence Shore, 'The United States' Perspective on "Arbitrability"' in Loukas A. Mistelis and Stavros L. Brekoulakis (ed), *Arbitrability: International and Comparative Perspectives* (Kluwer Law International 2009) 69; Domenico di Pietro, 'General Remarks on Arbitrability Under the New York Convention' in Loukas A. Mistelis and Stavros L. Brekoulakis (ed), *Arbitrability: International and Comparative Perspectives* (Kluwer Law International, 2009) 85, 85–86.

[9] George A Bermann, 'Arbitration Fundamental: Arbitrability Trouble' (2012) 23 *American Review of International Arbitration* 367, 368. It argues for a broad definition of arbitrability that includes

focus on different aspects of arbitrability, showing different understandings of its nature and content.

A broad definition of arbitrability, however, is of little significance to this research, as the latter only focuses on arbitrability in the context of the judicial review of arbitral awards. It is notable that such a reference to arbitrability may imply that there are public policy implications,[10] especially those that take account of the state's public interests. Subjective arbitrability is more likely to serve as a private mechanism adopted by the parties to protect their own interests, and is therefore less relevant to this research.[11] Based on this understanding, this chapter adopts the narrow definition of arbitrability, excludes any reference to subjective arbitrability, and only refers to arbitrability as applied in the judicial review with possible public policy considerations.

## 2.2 Developments in Broadening the Scope of Arbitirability

Arbitrability was once narrowly construed by national courts which applied it as a means of ensuring the exclusive jurisdiction of the domestic judicial system.[12] Many national law rules were once not arbitrable, including bankruptcy law, governmental contracts, company and security law, and competition law.[13] Generally, such a rigid approach towards arbitrability was a reflection of a hostile attitude towards arbitration by national judicial systems.[14]

Nevertheless, hostility is no longer present in general arbitration law or in defining arbitrability in particular. In *Scherk* and *Mitsubishi*, the Supreme Court of the United States revisited the arbitrability of security law and antitrust issues and found them arbitrable, at least in the context of international commercial disputes.[15] These two cases illustrate that the importance of arbitrability as an independent ground of non-enforcement has gradually diminished. Some disputes, once considered to be exclusively handled by courts, are now arbitrable as long as the mandatory rules of the national law can be applied by the tribunal. Significant examples can be observed in areas of law such as administrative contracts, security law, competition law, and

---

both legal and factual reasons that bar a dispute to be resolved by the method of arbitration. For example, the issue of *res judicata* would be included by such a definition.

[10] See Sect. 2.5.

[11] Mistelis, above n 7, 5–7; Emmanuel Gaillard and John Savage (eds), *Fouchard Gaillard Goldman on International Commercial Arbitration* (Kluwer Law International, 1999) [533].

[12] Homayoon Arfazadeh, 'Arbitrability under the New York Convention: the *Lex Fori* Revisited' (2001) 17 *Arbitration International* 73, 81–82.

[13] Dirk Otto and Omaia Elwan, 'Article V(2)' in Herbert Kronke et al. (eds), *Recognition and Enforcement of Foreign Arbitral Awards* (Wolter Kluwer, 2010) 345, 349–364. See also the relationship between mandatory rules and arbitrability discussed in Chap. 7.

[14] For example, see Otto and Elwan, above n 13, 348.

[15] For the discussion of the second-look doctrine, see Chap. 7.

consumer protection law,[16] though there are variable practices in different jurisdictions.[17] As observed by many scholars, arbitrability is now rarely a controversial issue in arbitration practice in most jurisdictions.[18] In many jurisdictions, the scope of arbitrablity is clearly enlarged by both legislation and case law.[19]

International practice has also confirmed the discretionary power of states in deciding arbitrability. In the past, such power allowed national courts to limit arbitrability, but recent developments show that such attempts to impose limitations have gradually been relaxed or abandoned altogether. Article I(3) of the *NYC*, drafted in the 1950s, allows states to reserve their right to limit the application of the Convention on commercial disputes. Article V(2)(a) provides that a breach of the arbitrability criteria of the enforcing state can be a ground for non-enforcement. A similar rule is available for the supervisory courts in annulment proceedings, as indicated in the *UNCITRAL Model Law*.[20] It is however recently reported that the commerciality reservation has lost most of its significance,[21] and that the application of arbitrability as a ground for non-enforcement is rare.[22] Youssef remarks that this is a change "from restriction to expansion".[23]

Despite the expansion of the scope of arbitrability there are still some areas of law that are not considered to be arbitrable under national and international law, such as family law and criminal law issues. Although arbitrability in current arbitration practice is not as frequently contested as it was a few decades ago, such an element still exists in current legislative schemes. It remains worthwhile to further explore the understanding of arbitrability and the public policy considerations behind it.

---

[16] Loukas A. Mistelis and Stavros L. Brekoulakis (eds), *Arbitrability: International and Comparative Perspectives* (Kluwer Law International, 2009) Ch 12; Otto and Elwan, above n 13, 356–363.

[17] For example, in regardsto the competition law issues, the US and EU countries generally accept their arbitrability; the Austrian approach is that competition law issue is not arbitrable, but this would not negate the arbitration of the whole dispute; the practical solution is to let the tribunal deal with all non-competition issues and to leave only the competition law issue for the national courts. See *GmbH v. O B.V. (Netherlands), O Co Ltd (Japan) and others*, ObersterGerichtshof [Supreme Court], 4Ob80/08f, 26 August 2008, reported in (2009) 34 *Yearbook-Commercial Arbitration* 404 (Austria No.19). On the other hand, the dominant view in Australian courts is that the competition law issue is not arbitrable, though some recent cases show otherwise. See *Walter Rau Neusser Oel und Fett AG v. Cross Pacific Trading Ltd* [2005] FAC 1102 (Federal Court of Australia).See also Otto and Elwan, 356–363.

[18] For example, Youssef concluded it as "the least of a modern practitioner's problems", in Youssef, above n 5, 47.

[19] See Chap. 8, Sect.2.3.

[20] *UNCITRAL Model Law* art 34.

[21] Youssef, above n 5, 66.

[22] Julian D. M. Lew, Loukas A. Mistelis and Stefan Michael Kröll, *Comparative International Commercial Arbitration* (Kluwer Law International, 2003), 721; Otto and Elwan, above n 13, 348.

[23] Youssef, above n 5, 48.

## 2.3 The Revised Criteria for Defining Arbitrability

One significant trend that signifies the expansion of arbitrability is the revised criteria for defining arbitrability. A traditional criterion to limit arbitrability, as confirmed by the *NYC,* is the commerciality reservation. Other criteria also include the public nature of the applicable law in regulating the dispute.[24] As observed, these traditional criteria have been removed in most jurisdictions.[25] Instead, broader and more flexible criteria have been adopted in order to decide the arbitrability of certain issues and thus the scope of arbitrability has significantly expanded.[26]

The existence of economic or financial interests is a widely accepted consideration in determining arbitrability in many jurisdictions. In Switzerland, for example, all disputes that involve "financial interests" are arbitrable.[27] In adopting this approach, a matter would not necessarily be held to be inarbitrable just because some public law concerns are raised.[28] This approach to define arbitrability by the economic interests involved is also adopted in Germany, but together with another criterion in relation to the parties' right to settle a dispute. According to the *German Code of Civil Procedure*, disputes involving economic interests can be arbitrated; and disputes with no economic interests but which can be settled by the parties themselves may also be arbitrable.[29] This latter approach is known as the autonomy principle, which is also widely adopted in many jurisdictions.[30] Beside France and Italy,[31] this approach is also observed in Spain and Sweden.[32] Such an approach further expands the scope of arbitrability, as it may also include the arbitrability of non-economic disputes as long as they can be settled.[33]

---

[24] Otto and Elwan, above n 13, 349–364.

[25] For the erosion of the commerciality requirement, see above Sect. 2.2. For the erosion of the significance of public policy concerns, see further Sect. 2.5. One example may be found in the French statute, which limits the reference to public policy to "international public policy" only. Youssef, above n 5, 58–60.

[26] Gaillard and Savage, above n 11, 568.

[27] Swiss Federal Code of Private International Law 1987, art 177(1).

[28] For example, in *Fincantieri-Cantieri Navali ItalianiS.p.A. et Oto Melara S.p.A. v M. et Tribunal Arbitral,* ATF 118 II 353 (June 23, 1992), the Swiss Federal Tribunal did not consider the UN embargo on commercial activities with Iraq would make the dispute in regards to a contract for sale of military equipment to Iraq inarbitrable. See also Youssef, above n 5, 60.

[29] *Zivilprozessordnung (ZPO)* [The German Code of Civil Procedure], promulgated on 5 December 2005 *(Bundesgesetzblatt (BGBl., Federal Law Gazette)* 3202; 2006, 431; 2007, 1781), last amended by Article 1 of the Act dated 31 August 2013 (Federal Law Gazette, 3533), Sect. 1030.

[30] Youssef, above n 5, 59.

[31] Lew, Mistelis and Kröll, above n 22, 194–195; For the French approach, see also Youssef, above n 5, 58–60.

[32] Ibid; the *Spanish Arbitration Act* (Act 11/2011, of May 20, reforming Act 60/2003, of December 23) art 2(1); the *Swedish Arbitration Act* (SFS 1999:116) art 1.

[33] For example, s1030 of *the ZPO* combined the criteria of economic interests and the autonomy principle, which covers disputes of both economic and non-economic natures. Youssef, above n 5, 60–61.

Other instances that illustrate the expansion of arbitrability include the relaxed restrictions on arbitrability. For example, Arabian laws used to restrict arbitrability by limiting the state and administrative bodies' eligibility to enter into an arbitration agreement.[34] In recent years, such restrictions on eligibility have been removed. Instead, the law now tends to restrict the specific forum of such arbitration.[35] This attitude reflects the strong pro-arbitration bias driven by economic globalisation, and significantly affects the application of arbitrability in judicial practice.

Recent developments in worldwide practice indicate that arbitrability is now rarely a practical barrier to arbitration. In most countries, disputes are considered *prima facie* arbitrable. For example, legislation in the Canadian province of Quebec provides that the arbitration tribunal is the default jurisdiction for dealing with certain types of disputes.[36] At a national level, Canada's case law also favours the jurisdiction of the tribunal in dealing with copyright issues by adopting a similar approach.[37] The US also adopts a general principle that if there is any doubt with respect to interpreting arbitrability, the courts favour arbitrability.[38] Similarly, a liberal approach in defining arbitrability is also observed in France, where the development of the principle of autonomy favours the finding of arbitrability, and arbitrability has been relegated to a residual and restrictive position.[39] All this progress indicates that the recent criteria in judicial review in deciding arbitrability favour the facilitation of arbitration practice, and traditional restrictions imposed by the old criteria are no longer strictly followed.

[34] Dhisadde Chamlongrasdr, 'Tension in Domestic and International Law on Capacity to Enter into Arbitration Agreements: A Survey on Legal Restrictions' (2005) 16 *European Business Law Review* 275, 302–303; it provides that public entities have limited power in reaching arbitration agreements under Egyptian law.

[35] Ibid, 302–03; Habib Malouche, 'Recent Developments in Arbitration Law in Tunisia' (1991) 8(2) *Journal of International Arbitration* 23, 29; Tarek F. Riad, 'Arbitration and the Legal Business Environment in Egypt' (2000) 17(5) *Journal of International Arbitration* 169, 187; Youssef, above n 5, 62.

[36] *Professional Artists Act 1988*(Quebec) s 37: In the absence of an express renunciation, every dispute arising from the interpretation of the contract shall be submitted to an arbitrator at the request of one of the parties. See also Youssef, above n 5, 61.

[37] Richard Boivin and NocolaMariani, 'International Arbitration in Canada' (2003) 20(5) *Journal of International Arbitration* 507, particularly 514.*ÉditionsChouetteinc. v. Desputeaux*, 2003 SCC 17.

[38] See eg, *Apache Bohai Corp. LDC v. Texaco China BV*, 2007 WL 587,233 (5th. Cir. Feb. 27, 2007); *Brook v. Peak Intern* Ltd. 294 F 3d 668 (5th Cir. 2002); *Action Indus., Inc. v. US Fid & Guar Co.*, 358 F 3d 337 (5th Cir. 2004) 343; *Moses H. Cone Memorial Hospital v Mercury Construction Corp.* 460 US 1 (US Supreme Court, 1983) 24.

[39] Youssef, above n 5, 58, citing Jean-Baptiste Racine, *L'Arbitrage Commercial International etl'ordre Public* (LGDJ, 1999) 34; See also CA Paris (1991) *Rev Arb* 478, 29 March, 1991.

## 2.4 National or International Approaches to Arbitrability

It has been argued and accepted that arbitrability should be an issue of purely domestic law. In most jurisdictions, the issue of arbitrability is expressly regulated by national law. The trend of unification or harmonisation is "at its lowest" level, if any, in regard to arbitrability.[40] Various different approaches are found in different jurisdictions.[41]

Insisting on the domestic nature of arbitrability is evidenced by legislative and judicial practices in many jurisdictions. On the one hand, most national legislation governing arbitrability did not refer to any rules of applicable law; instead they directly provided an inclusive or exclusive list of matters that could or could not be arbitrated, and such lists were usually based on political, economic and social considerations and interests of the particular nation. On the other hand, the international legislation and agreements on arbitration respect states' discretionary power in deciding arbitrability. The *UNCITRAL Model Law* did not cover the issue of arbitrability and intended to leave it to the discretion of the national law.[42] The *NYC*, which distinguished the arbitrability issue from the applicable law issue,[43] allows the courts to decide arbitrability on the basis of its national law.[44]

The purely national character of arbitrability is criticised, particularly in the context of the development of cross-border arbitration practice, because such a character of arbitrability may result in the courts evaluating international arbitration practices based on a purely domestic standard.[45] Inconsistent national legislation with respect to arbitrability may cause an arbitral award made in one jurisdiction, where such a matter is held as arbitrable, to be refused enforcement in other jurisdictions where such a matter is held as not arbitrable.

More recently, there is a move to recognise the international nature of arbitrability, which is consistent with the general pro-arbitration bias under the *NYC*. Proponents of this approach argue that arbitrability should be broader in the international context.[46]

---

[40] Youssef, above n 5, 48.

[41] For example, the arbitrability of bribery and corruption issues is inconsistently practiced in different jurisdictions. See Mistelis, above n 7, 9–10; Lew, Mistelis and Kröll, above n 22,198–199.

[42] Model Law on International Commercial Arbitration of the United Nations Commission on International Trade Law, UN GAOR, 40th sess, Supp No. 17, UN Doc A/40/17, annex I (21 June 1985); passed by the GA Res 40/72, UN GAOR, 40th sess, 112th plenmtg, Agenda Item 135, UN Doc A/RES/40/72 (11 December 1985); amended by GA Res A/RES/61/33, UN GAOR, 61th sess, 64th plenmtg, Agenda Item 77, UN Doc A/RES/61/33 (4 Dec 2006) art 1(5).

[43] Mistelis, above n 7, 12–13; Arfazadeh, above n 12, 83; Lew, Mistelis and Kröll, above n 22, 193.

[44] The *NYC*, art V(2)(a), "the subject matter of the difference is not capable of settlement by arbitration under the law of that country".

[45] The French delegate's statement, in the UN Conference on International Arbitration, Summary Record of the Eleventh Meeting, UN DOC E/CONF.26/SR/11 (Sept.12, 1958) 7, reprinted in Giorgio Gaja (ed), *International Commercial Arbitration-New York Convention* (Oceana Publications,1978) III.C.89.

[46] Jay R Sever, 'The Relaxation of Inarbitrability and Public Policy Checks on US and Foreign Arbitration: Arbitration out of Control?' (1991) 65 *Tulane Law Review* 1667, 1673.

The US Supreme Court in *Mitsubishi,* for example, based its ruling on the international nature of the dispute and the need to broaden the scope of arbitrability in such an international context.[47]The French practice aims to limit the considerations of arbitrability to French law and international public policy.[48] The adoption of flexible and broad criteria in deciding arbitrability in most jurisdictions is also consistent with the internationalisation of arbitration.[49] According to this trend, courts rarely find a matter is notable to be arbitrated.[50] Thus, even if the arbitrability is still a national law matter, it rarely functions as a barrier to arbitration practice.

## 2.5 *Arbitrability and Public Policy*

It is also worthwhile to explore the relationship between arbitrability and public policy before further analysing the Chinese practice. Some insist that arbitrability is mainly based on public policy considerations, or that public policy is the major criterion in identifying arbitrability. Thus, the separation of Article V(2)(a), arbitrability, from the public policy ground in Article V(2)(b), is purely "superfluous",[51] and is adopted merely for the purpose of respecting the historical provisions from early international agreements such as the *Geneva Convention.*[52]

Based on this understanding, public policy in Article V(2)(b) informs the standard by which a decision on arbitrability is made according to Article V(2)(a).[53] This approach has also influenced the legislative and judicial practice of many national jurisdictions.[54]In many cases, courts have examined the public policy concerns underlying arbitrability.[55] The proposed draft of the US *Arbitration Fairness Act* (2007)

---

[47] However, the arbitrability of antitrust claims was later confirmed in domestic disputes in the US. Ludwig von Zumbusch, 'Arbitrability of Antitrust Claims under US, German and EEC Law– the "International Transaction" Criterion and Public Policy' (1997) 22 *Texas International Law Journal* 291, 304–12.

[48] Youssef, above n 5, 59, citing Arrêt Dalico, Cass, 1ere, (1994) Rev Arb 116, 20 December 1993.

[49] See above Sect. 2.3.

[50] Ibid.

[51] Pieter Sanders, 'The New York Convention' in *International Commercial Arbitration* (Martinus Nijhoff, 1960) vol II, 292, 323; Albert Jan van den Berg, *The New York Convention of 1958: Towards a Uniform Judicial Interpretation* (Kluwer Law International, 1981) 360.

[52] *The Geneva Convention on the Execution of Foreign Awards,* opened for signature 26 September 1927, 92 LNTS 301 (entered into force 25 July 1929) (*'Geneva Convention'*) art 1(b). See also Berg, above n 51, 360.

[53] Brekoulakis, above n 4,20, nn 8; Alan Redfern et al., *Redfern and Hunter on International Arbitration* (Oxford University, 2009) [3–13].

[54] Brekoulakis, above n 4,21.

[55] Ibid, nn 6, listing famous cases such as *Mitsubishi Motors Corp v. Soler Chrysler Plymouth Inc*473 U.S. 614 (1985) (United States); *Ganz v. Nationale des Chemins de FerTunisiens (SNCFT),* (1991) Rev Arb 478 (France); *Fiona Trust & Holding Corporation and Others v. Privalov and Others,* [2007] 2 Lloyd's Rep. 267 (UK); C-126/97, *Eco Swiss China Time v Benetton International,* [1999] ECR I 3055 (ECJ, 1 June 1999).

imposed restrictions on the scope of arbitrability under public policy considerations. Similarly, Article 2060–1 of the *French Civil Code* also expressly referred to public policy in defining arbitrability.[56]

One argument that supports the view that public policy considerations underlie arbitrability is that, some issues, particular those that are complex, multiparty, and relate to public law areas or affect the general public, are considered inarbitrable.[57] There are also concerns that the arbitration proceeding may not satisfy the requirement of due process, and that the arbitrators may not have sufficient ability and competence to deal with public interest issues.[58] Some of the concerns are rooted in the origin of arbitration practice as a mechanism used by commercial parties, and are based on an assumption that the arbitrators, as "commercial men", are biased towards commercial entities and against the public in general, and therefore either fail to consider public concerns or lack the capacity to deal with them properly.[59]

Alternatively, other scholars argue that arbitrability and public policy are separate and distinct from each other, particularly under the *NYC* scheme.[60] As Böckstiegel argues, the distinction is clear because arbitrability rules are always mandatory, and most of them are directly imposed by the statute, while the public policy exception requires further qualifications such as the underlying value of morality and justice and the fundamentality of these rules.[61] Born is also of the opinion that these two principles run parallel to each other, sharing exceptional characteristics, but can be distinguished in their application.[62]

In regard to recent developments and trends, scholars have observed that there has been a decline in the role of public policy in defining arbitrability. Youssef reports such a trend in the last 25 years when observing the role of public policy in both Europe and the US.[63] Brekoulak has also argued that arbitrability is restrained in today's practice by the inherent nature of arbitration as a dispute resolution mechanism based on contractual consent, rather than public policy considerations.[64] According to his analysis, the reason for referring to public policy considerations to

---

[56] French Civil Code, art 2060–1; similarly, see Singapore International Arbitration Act 1994(Chapter 143A)(Revised 2002), art 11. See also Brekoulakis, above n 4, 21.

[57] Gary B. Born, *International Commercial Arbitration* (Kluwer Law International, 2nd ed, 2014) 950.

[58] Brekoulakis, above n 4, 22–30.

[59] Youssef, above n 5, 50.

[60] Karl- Heinz Böckstiegel, 'Public Policy and Arbitrability' in Pieter Sanders (ed), *Comparative Arbitration Practice and Public Policy in Arbitration*, ICCA Congress Series (Kluwer Law International, 1987) 177.

[61] Ibid. He re-confirmed these points in his later speech, Karl-Heinz Böckstiegel, 'Public Policy as a Limit to Arbitration and its Enforcement', presented at 11th IBA International Arbitration Day and United Nations New York Convention Day, "The New York Convention: 50 Years" in New York on 1 February 2008, published (2008) *IBA Journal of Dispute Resolution Special Issue: The New York Convention—50 Years* 123.

[62] Born, above n 57, 950.

[63] Youssef, above n 5, 60.

[64] Brekoulakis, above n 4, 32–36.

support the concept of arbitrability was the assumption that the legislation protecting specific social groups cannot be applied by a particular forum which is inherently biased towards such social groups.[65] The assumption, however, is questionable, because there is no evidence to support a general conclusion that judges would apply the legislation differently from arbitrators, particularly if the legislation's purpose is clearly stated,[66] and especially since the arbitrators' ability to decide arbitrability and consider the underlying public policy concerns is generally confirmed in practice.[67]

The declining function of public policy as a concern underlying the ground of arbitrability is particularly emphasised because of the development of public policy as an independent ground to negate an arbitral award, which functions after the arbitration proceeding, or as was concluded in *Mitsubishi*, as a "second-look".[68] While arbitrators have the discretion to consider and balance all relevant factors, courts now prefer to delay their intervention until later in the process of judicial review of the arbitral awards. Thus, the role of arbitrability as a pre-condition to arbitration fades because public policy considerations can function afterwards.[69]

Despite the different opinions on the relationship between arbitrability and public policy, it is undeniable that these two principles are closely connected, or at least have been so during the historical approach to arbitration. Based on the legal regimes mentioned above and for the purpose of this research, the author includes the issue of arbitrability as one possible key element of public policy in the judicial review of arbitral awards, though the declining role of public policy considerations in dealing with arbitrability in international practice is also appreciated.

## 3 Reflections in China

### 3.1 *The Arbitrability Issues in China in General*

In China, the issue of arbitrability is generally regulated by the following legislative provisions. The *CAL* provides that the contractual and other proprietary disputes between equal identities such as citizens, legal persons and other organisations can be arbitrated; and excludes disputes relating to marriage, adoption, custody, guardianship and succession, and the administrative disputes which should be decided by administrative bodies.[70] It also excludes labour disputes and disputes of contracts

---

65 Discussion around above fn 59.

66 Detailed analysis, see *Ibid,* 27–29.

67 *Mitsubishi Motors Corp,* 473 U.S. 614.

68 Ibid; see also discussions in Chap. 7.

69 Pilar Perales Viscasillas, 'Arbitrability of (Intra-) Corporate Disputes', in Loukas A. Mistelis and Stavros L. Brekoulakis (eds), *Arbitrability: International and Comparative Perspectives* (Kluwer Law International, 2009) 273, 284. See also Chap. 7, Sect.2.

70 The *CAL,* arts 2 and 3.

undertaking agriculture projects within agricultural-collective economic organisations in China.[71] Arbitrability for certain specific types of disputes are further provided in other statutes, for example, the *Copyright Law*.[72] Furthermore, China has made the reservation under Article I(3) of the *NYC*, which limits arbitration to commercial disputes under the Convention scheme.

Thus, the arbitrability issue in China is regulated by mandatory legislation, which provides a list that covers matters that can be arbitrated (the positive list) and a list of those matters which cannot be arbitrated (the negative list). Many highly controversial types of disputes in leading jurisdictions, or at least where they were once controversial, are now accepted in China as arbitrable as confirmed by legislation, including consumer and security disputes.[73] Conversely, the arbitrability of antitrust and bankruptcy law issues seem to be excluded by legislation.[74]

One major problem in the Chinese regulation of arbitrability is that the term "other proprietary disputes" in the positive list is expressed in abstract terms without any further clarification.[75] It is not clear whether an issue not mentioned in the negative list, but which has a proprietary nature, would be covered by such an inclusive

---

71 The *CAL*, art 77.

72《中华人民共和国著作权法》[The Copyright Law of the People's Republic of China](People's Republic of China) National People's Congress Standing Committee, Order No 31, 7 September 1990, recently amended by National People's Congress Standing Committee, Order No26, 26 February 2010, art 55.

73《中华人民共和国消费者权益保护法》[The Protection of Consumer Rights Act of the People's Republic of China](People's Republic of China)National People's Congress Standing Committee, Order No18, 31 October 1993, recently amended by Order No7, 25 October 2013, art 39;《股票发行与交易管理暂行条例》[Trial Rules for Management of Share Issuance and Trade](People's Republic of China) State Council, 22 April 1993, arts 79 and 80.

74《中华人民共和国反垄断法》[Antitrust Law of People's Republic of China](People's Republic of China)National People's Congress Standing Committee, Order No68, 30 August 2007, art 53, which provides that the only remedies under the law to challenge the administrative decisions are merit review by administrative appealing bodies and administrative litigation. The arbitrability of bankruptcy law issues are also considered as excluded by the current bankruptcy law, as it does not expressly note any possibility of arbitration. It is notable, however, that the international awards dealing with bankruptcy issues may be enforced in China according to international conventions, agreements or the principle of reciprocity. See《中华人民共和国企业破产法》[The Law of People's Republic of China Concerning Bankruptcy of Enterprises](People's Republic of China) National People's Congress Standing Committee, Order No54, 27 August 2006, particularly art 5. See also 齐湘泉[Qi Xiangquan],《外国仲裁裁决承认及执行论》[Study on Recognition and Enforcement of Foreign Arbitral Awards], (Law Press, 2010) 299–300.

75 梁慧星[Liang Huixing],《民法总论》[General Issues of Civil Law], (Law Press, 1996) 88. As Professor Liang provides, there is no clear definition of "property" under current Chinese law. 陈治东[Chen Zhidong],《国际商事仲裁法》[International Commercial Arbitration Law], (Law Press, 1998) 50, which provides that the test of "proprietary disputes" lacks sufficient legislative interpretation to give its full meaning. See also 黄进, 马德才[Huang Jin, Ma Decai],《国际商事争议可仲裁范围的扩展趋势之探析——兼评我国有关规定》[Review and Analysis of the Expanding Scope of Arbitrability of International Commercial Disputes: With Comments on Relevant Rules in Chinese Law] (2007) 143 法学评论 *Law Review* 54, 58.

definition. A particular example is the controversial arbitrability of the proprietary interests in torts disputes as discussed below.[76]

Another problem may be that the scope of arbitrability lacks sufficient consistency. For example, arbitrability of similar intellectual property rights is treated differently: Copyright issues are respected as arbitrable, while patent and trademark issues are not.[77] Furthermore, it is considered that copyright, which is a type of intellectual property right, has both personal nature and proprietary nature, and it is uncertain that arbitrability as provided by the *Copyright Law* would be limited by the general rule in the *CAL,* which limits arbitrability to disputes arising from contractual and proprietary rights.[78] As reported by Huang and Ma, copyright disputes are generally arbitrated by the CIETAC and there is no reported case that such awards were not held to be enforceable because of the possible involvement of its personal nature.[79] Similar conflicts are also observed in family law disputes that contain both personal and proprietary elements.[80]

These difficulties related to interpretation and consistent application of the arbitrability rules that arise in China's practice may be caused by the short history of arbitration in China. Because China did not define arbitrability in similar terms to that of the leading jurisdictions, and most of the provisions governing arbitrability have been imported,[81] there is a lack of understanding on the part of the practitioners of the rules regulating arbitrability. Most theoretical research on arbitrability in China also focuses on developments overseas rather than focusing on the real problems experienced in China, and thus provides limited contributions to the advancement of the understanding of arbitrability in practice.[82]

---

76 See further Sect. 2.2.1.

77《中华人民共和国著作权法》[The Copyright Law of the People's Republic of China](People's Republic of China) National People's Congress Standing Committee, Order No 31, 7 September 1990, recently amended by National People's Congress Standing Committee, Order No26, 26 February 2010, art 55, which provides that copyright disputes can be mediated or arbitrated. But the dispute resolution method provided by Trademark Law and Patent Law in China only provides administrative review and litigation for dispute resolution. See《中华人民共和国商标法》[Trademark Law of the People's Republic of China](People's Republic of China)National People's Congress Standing Committee, Order No59, 23 August 1982, recently amended by the National People's Congress Standing Committee, Order No6, 30 August 2013,art 53;《中华人民共和国专利法》[Patent Law of the People's Republic of China](People's Republic of China) National People's Congress Standing Committee, Order No11, 12 March 1984, recently amended by the National People's Congress Standing Committee, Order No8, 27 December 2008, art 57.

78 齐湘泉[Qi Xiangquan], above n 74, 301–302.

79 黄进, 马德才[Huang Jin, Ma Decai], above n 75, 58.

80 钱宇宏, 马伯娟[Qian Yuhong, Ma Bojuan],《从可仲裁性的发展看司法权的让渡》[Viewing the Alienation of Judicial Power from the Development of Arbitrability] (2004) 93 仲裁与法律 *Arbitration and Law* 18, 22.

81 齐湘泉[Qi Xiangquan], above n 74, 317.

82 For example, see张超[Zhang Chao],《浅析我国对可仲裁争议事项的立法》[Primary Analysis of the Chinese Legislation of Arbitrable Issues] (2012) 323法制与经济*Rule by Law and Economics* 63, 63–64; 扈媛媛[Hu Yuanyuan],《我国争议可仲裁性标准的确立》[Establishment of the Standard of Arbitrability in China](2009) 111司法改革论评*Judicial Reform Review* 32, 43–46.

## 3.2 *Arbitrability in China's Judicial Practice*

The particular focus of this research is the role of arbitrability as a ground in the judicial review of arbitral awards. In China, Article 244 (for domestic awards) and 281 (for foreign-related awards) of the *CCPL* provides that the court shall refuse enforcement of a foreign-related arbitral award if the issue being arbitrated is not provided for in the arbitration agreement or "not authorised to be arbitrated by arbitration institutions". Similar language is also found in Article 58 of the *CAL* regarding the annulment of judicial review proceedings.[83] For the judicial review of international awards, Article V(2)(a) of the *NYC* and other corresponding provisions in international and regional agreements apply.[84]

Before a thorough study of the cases is undertaken, it is worthwhile mentioning that there is a significant difference between the approaches taken by the *CCPL* and the *NYC*. Under the *NYC*, the ground of arbitrability can be applied by the court *ex officio*. In Chinese legislation, however, the ground of inarbitrability, which is defined by law as "matters that are not authorised to be arbitrated", is an issue that the parties bear the onus of proof.[85] This section further explores arbitrability issues in the judicial review of arbitral awards in a series of Chinese cases, which are divided according to their subject matter: tort, succession, dissolution of company, and administrative approval.

### 3.2.1 Tort Law Disputes

Whether a tort law dispute is arbitrable is controversial under current Chinese law. It is clearly not covered by the negative list in Article 3 of the *CAL*, and it is arguable that a tort law dispute would be considered one of the "other proprietary disputes" in the positive list in Article 2. Judicial practice in China does not provide a consistent approach either.[86] For instance, *China National Technical Import & Export Corp. v Swiss Industrial Resources Corp* provides that a tort dispute was not arbitrable,[87] but later, in *Textile & Other Light Industries Co. Ltd. of the Commodities Group vs Topcapital Holdings Ltd. (Hong Kong) and Prince Development Ltd. (Canada)*, the SPC confirmed the arbitrability of tort disputes arising from the performance of a contract.[88] Scholars argue that the SPC's notice to announce China's participation in

[83] *CAL*, arts 58, 70 and 71; *CCPL*, arts 244 and 281.

[84] Chap. 3.

[85] *CCPL*, arts 244 and 281.

[86] 陈治东[Chen Zhidong], above n 75, 63–64.

[87]《中国技术进出口总公司诉瑞士工业资源公司侵权损害赔偿案》[China National Technical Import & Export Corp. v. Swiss Industrial Resources Corp—Case of Appeal for Damages in Tort)][1989] 1中华人民共和国最高人民法院公报[Gazette of Supreme People's Court of People's Republic of China] 26.

[88]《江苏省物资集团轻工纺织总公司诉 (香港) 裕亿集团有限公司、(加拿大) 太子发展有限公司侵权损害赔偿纠纷上诉案》[Textile & Other Light Industries Co. Ltd. of the Commodities

the *NYC* referred to both contractual and non-contractual disputes, which may cover tort disputes and other economic relationships.[89]

Yet such confirmation of the arbitrability of tort disputes is not found in the judicial review of arbitral awards in China. In *Guangxia*, the SPC ruled that the award dealt with tort disputes among the parties, and that this was not allowed by arbitration law and the *CIETAC Arbitration Rules*, which only refer to "contractual or non-contractual civil and commercial disputes". It is also interesting that the SPC considered it as a breach of arbitration rules rather than a breach of arbitrability as a ground to negate an award. It is reported, however, that the SPC's ruling was not the end of this case. In 2010, long after the reply was made, the Shenzhen IPC recommenced enforcement proceedings and, in 2011, the Guangdong HPC decided to sustain such enforcement despite the SPC's previous non-enforcement ruling.[90] It is uncertain whether the SPC's ruling on the tort law issue remained binding in this case.

### 3.2.2 Family Law Issues: Succession

In *Mongolia*, a dispute arose because Ms Wu, the legal successor of her late husband, claimed her contractual rights against the other party. The SPC found that the award made by the Mongolian National Tribunal was in fact recognition of the right of succession of Wu, rather than a resolution of proprietary disputes. Applying Article 3 of the *CAL* and Article V(2)(a) of the *NYC*, the SPC confirmed the non-arbitrability of succession disputes and refused enforcement accordingly.

Family law issues, particularly those of a personal nature, have long been held as not arbitrable. Such a position is also supported by Article 3 of the *CAL*. However, it is arguable whether the proprietary issues under family law could be arbitrated. Some scholars in China argue for their arbitrability as long as the proprietary issues are severable from personal claims.[91] Also, proprietary disputes may be considered arbitrable as long as they fall within the positive list provided by Article 2 of the *CAL*. Others argue against such a proposal because it is not practical and convenient

Group (Jiangsu Province) vs. Topcapital Holdings Ltd. (Hong Kong) and Prince Development Ltd. (Canada)—Case of Appeal for Dispute of Liabilities of Tort], [1998] 3 中华人民共和国最高人民法院公报[Gazette of Supreme People's Court of People's Republic of China] 109.

[89] 齐湘泉, [Qi Xiangquan], above n 74, 302; 黄进[Huang Jin],《国际私法与国际商事仲裁》[Private International Law and International Commercial Arbitration](Wuhan University Press, 1994) 210–211.

[90] WunschARB, *Misuer v. Guangxia Industry* et al. Guangdong HPC [2011] 粤高法执复字第43号[Guangdong HPC Enforcement Reply No43], 19 May 2011, available at: <www.kluwerarbitration.com. See also above Sect. 4.2.2 in Chap. 4.

[91] 乔欣,李莉[Qiao Xin, Li Li],《争议可仲裁性研究》[Research on the Arbitrability of Disputes](2004) 53 北京仲裁 Beijing Arbitration 35, 39.

to divide a family dispute into personal and proprietary issues and to deal with them separately in different forums.[92] No answer was provided in the legislation.

As explained by the SPC, the award dealt with "the confirmation of Wu's status as legal successor to her husband and her proprietary right under the contract". Due to the fact that only limited details of the award have been published, it is not certain whether the dispute arose with respect to the status of the successor, which may be personal, or in relation to the contractual rights of Ms Wu as her husband's successor, which may arguably be classified as proprietary. It would be arguable, then, if the dispute was about proprietary rights, it may be severable from the personal family law issue and may even be covered by the positive list provided by Article 2 of the *CAL*, and therefore be arbitrable.[93]

### 3.2.3 Dissolution of Companies

In *Jiacheng,* the SPC declared that the dissolution of a company could not be arbitrated. The dispute arose between Jiacheng, VEM and SIMEST, who intended to establish a joint venture through a series of agreements. The CIETAC tribunal rendered an award holding the agreements invalid and that the joint venture established on the basis of such agreements should be dissolved accordingly. The Beijing 1st IPC, the Beijing HPC and the SPC all opined that the dissolution of the company, as regulated by the *Company Law*, should only be dealt with by the courts, and not by arbitrators.[94] Thus, the arbitration institution's ruling was annulled according to Article 258 of the (then) *CCPL* and Article 70 of the *CAL*.

This judicial ruling is different from the SPC's earlier decision in *Ningbo Yongxin*, in which a dispute arose in relation to joint venture agreements. The Ningbo Arbitration Commission's award ruled that the joint venture established in accordance with the disputed agreements should be dissolved and the joint venture wound-up. The SPC held that the ruling regarding dissolution was merely a declaration of the consequence of the termination of the joint venture agreements, rather than a decision under the *Company Law*; thus it did not violate the arbitrability of the matter. In finding no breach of Article 258 of the then *CCPL*, the SPC upheld the validity of the award. These two cases, based on identical facts and decided by the SPC, had different outcomes. Leaving aside the possible inconsistent rulings arising from the lack of a sufficient internal control system of the SPC,[95] the contradictory results

---

92 武雁冰[Wu Yanbing],《国际商事争议之可仲裁性研究》[Research on the Arbitrability of International Commercial Disputes], (Master Degree Thesis, China University of Political Science and Law, 2011).

93 乔欣, 李莉[Qiao Xin, Li Li], above n 91, 39.

94《中华人民共和国公司法》[Company Law of the People's Republic of China](People's Republic of China) National People's Congress Standing Committee, Order No16, 29 December 1993, recently amended by the National People's Congress Standing Committee, Order No 8, 28 December 2013, art 182, art 183, art 187, art 188.

95 See Chap. 3 and further analysis in Chap. 9.

illustrate the difficulties in the judicial construction of arbitrability in relation to the dissolution of companies.

The dissolution of a company is an intra-corporate issue, and its arbitrability is controversial because it affects third parties.[96] Generally speaking, the dissolution of a company is similar to other infra-corporate issues, such as the nullity of a shareholder meeting and the nullity of a company, the arbitrability of which is controversial and little international consensus is presented.[97] This is particularly so because these issues are governed by mandatory law and might be covered by the exclusive jurisdiction of national courts. Also, these issues are considered to have public policy connotations as third party interests may be affected.[98] It is notable, however, that Chinese courts have adopted a more favourable attitude in confirming the arbitrability of these issues. Furthermore, in the case of a partnership or joint venture, which is generally established on the basis of a contract rather than the *Company Law*, the attitude favouring arbitrability is understandable. For example, the dissolution of a partnership is considered arbitrable in Singapore, which is distinguished from the dissolution of a company.[99]

In particular, regarding the arbitrability of the dissolution of a company, judicial practices vary in different jurisdictions. In recent years, leading jurisdictions, such as France, Belgium and Finland, have favoured arbitrability in relation to the dissolution of a company.[100] In Singapore, the dissolution of a company was once reported as being inarbitrable, but a more recent case may suggest otherwise.[101] Various discussions are also reported in leading jurisdictions such as the United States, Spain and Italy.[102] Generally, an attitude favouring the arbitrability of the dissolution of a company is observed in these jurisdictions, especially in recent years. Under Chinese law, however, the procedure for such dissolution or winding-up of a company can

---

[96] Viscasillas, above n 69, 287, citing Bernard Hanotiau, "*L'arbitrabilité*", in *Recueil des Cours - Collected Courses of The Hague Academy of International Law* (Martinus Nijhoff Publishers, 2003) 169; Daniel Cohen, *Arbitrage et Société* (LGDJ 1993) 141.

[97] Viscasillas, above n 69, 290–292.

[98] Ibid,285.

[99] Ibid, nn 49.

[100] Court of Cassation 30, January 1967. See also Viscassillas, above n 69, nn 47.

[101] Michael Hwang and Rajesh C Muttath, 'Arbitration in Company Matters' (2001) 5 *International Business Law Journal* 555, 562–563; Viscasillas provides that a later case may provide a possibility for the arbitrability of dissolution issues. See Viscasillas, above n 69, nn49, citing *Four Pillars Enterprises Co Ltd v. BeiersdorfAktiengesellschaft* (1999) 1 SLR 737.

[102] Note, 'Arbitration as a means of settling disputes within close corporations' (1963) 63(2) *Columbia Law Review* 267, 283–284; S.S.J.Jr, 'Mandatory Arbitration as a remedy for intra-close corporate disputes' (1970) 56 *Virginia Law Review* 271, 281–282; Viscasllas, above n 69, citing Gabriele Silingardi,*Ilcompromesso in arbitrinellesocietà di capitali* (Giuffrè, 1979) 93–95, 191–210; and Perales Viscasillas, *Arbitrabilidad y convenio arbitral: Ley 60/2003 de Arbitraje y Derecho Societario* (Thomson-Aranzadi, 2005) 186–188. All of these authors generally favour the arbitrability of dissolution issues.

only be brought to the courts,[103] which is arguably not in line with the practice in the leading jurisdictions as discussed.

Beside the arbitrability in the dissolution of a company, Chinese courts also face another general issue, in deciding whether a tribunal's decision was made on the basis of the underlying contractual relationship among the parties, or the possible effect of that dissolution. The dissolution of a company may be a natural outcome of the resolution of a dispute arising between the parties of the joint venture contract and arguably arbitrable.[104] Otherwise, if the award dealt with the detailed plan governing that dissolution, it may arguably violate current Chinese legislation in regard to the arbitrability of intra-corporate issues.

Based on this understanding, the problem underlying these two conflicting judicial decisions is to decide whether arbitration tribunals should deal with the contractual issue or with the company law issue. In *Yongxin*, the SPC properly held that the award, which mentioned the dissolution of the joint venture company, was no more than a mere declaration of the consequence of the termination of the contract, which should not constitute a breach of inarbitrability in the dissolution of the company. Based on this ruling, the disputed contractual issue was held to be arbitrable.

It is then doubtful that the whole arbitral award of *Jiacheng* followed the same logic, as its award held that two disputed contracts were void and the company registered according to one of these contracts should be dissolved; it further rendered an award that Jiacheng should bear the costs of the foreign party in negotiating these contracts, their loss of capital investment, and depreciation in the value of the machines and equipment. As argued by the foreign party, it is doubtful that the award provided a dissolution plan for the disputed joint venture, because the only ruling dealing with dissolution was a mere declaration of that dissolution arising from the voided contracts: all of the other rulings dealt with the economic liabilities of the parties in reaching and performing these agreements and are distinguishable from the issue of dissolution in corporate law, such as in winding-up procedures, debtor-creditor issues, and payments to employees.[105] In addition, the award would not impact on third party interests as long as it dealt only with the interests of the parties to the joint-venture contract. In the author's view, it is erroneous to hold that the award violated the courts' exclusive jurisdiction over the dissolution of a company.

---

103《中华人民共和国公司法》[Company Law of the People's Republic of China](People's Republic of China) National People's Congress Standing Committee, Order No16, 29 December 1993, recently amended by the National People's Congress Standing Committee, Oder No 8, 28 December 2013, art 182, art 183, art 187, art 188.

104《中华人民共和国中外合资经营企业法》[Law of the People's Republic of China on China-Foreign Equity Joint Ventures](People's Republic of China) National People's Congress, Order No7, 1 July 1979, recently amended by National People's Congress, Order No 48, 15 March 2001, art 16.

105《中华人民共和国公司法》[Company Law of the People's Republic of China](People's Republic of China) National People's Congress Standing Committee, Order No16, 29 December 1993, recently amended by the National People's Congress Standing Committee, Order No 8, 28 December 2013, art 181–191.

These two cases are a reminder to the Chinese judiciary to analyse the real issue dealt with by the tribunal and its legal effects, before deciding on the violation of arbitrability by dealing with the dissolution matters. If the arbitral award deals only with contractual issues and not with the interests of any third party or the general public, it is unlikely that the principle of arbitrability would be violated.

### 3.2.4 Administrative Approvals

Both *Jiacheng* and *Yongxin* dealt with the dissolution of a joint venture, which the courts considered inarbitrable not only because of a violation of *Company Law,* but also because of the parties' possible breach of the requirement of administrative approval for the dissolution of foreign-related joint ventures.[106] It is noteworthy that, in China's foreign investment law, many administrative approvals are required in practice. These requirements frequently arise as issues in arbitration and in subsequent judicial review.

The *Guangxia* case also dealt with the conflicted outcomes of administrative decisions and arbitral awards.[107] Beside the tort law issue discussed above,[108] the SPC also refused the enforcement of the award by holding that the arbitral award confirmed the performance of Misuer's obligation to contribute to the joint venture, which was actually a denial of the Shenzhen Industrial and Commercial Administration Bureau's decision that Misuer failed to contribute to and had breached the joint-venture contract. It was also held that such an award was in conflict with the Shenzhen Bureau's decision to cancel Misuer's qualification as a shareholder in the joint venture. The SPC further opined that the arbitration tribunal did not have the authority to rule on the validity of the administrative decisions of the Shenzhen Bureau, and this resulted in the non-enforcement of the award.[109]

The *Huayuan* case illustrated a similar situation. In that case, disputes arose among several parties of a joint venture established upon the approval of the MOFCOM, in regard to the share composition of the different parties. The CIETAC arbitral award decided on the share composition that was inconsistent with MOFCOM's previous approval. According to the *PRC Law on Chinese-Foreign Equity Joint Ventures,* any change in the shares of such joint ventures require the approval of the relevant administrative governing bodies, and the identification of any shareholder should be confirmed in conjunction with that approval.[110]

---

[106] Above 3.2.3.

[107] The outcome of this case, see above 3.2.1 and also Chap. 9.

[108] Above 3.2.1.

[109] However, the award is eventually enforced long after this decision to not enforce was made. See 3.2.1.

[110]《中华人民共和国中外合资经营企业法》[Law of the People's Republic of China on China-Foreign Equity Joint Ventures](People's Republic of China) National People's Congress, Order No7, 1 July 1979, recently amended by Order No48, March 15 2001, art 14.

Chinese courts differ in their opinions on this issue. The Beijing 2nd IPC held that the dispute was of a contractual rather than an administrative nature, and that administrative approval should only confirm the contractual relationship and should not affect the performance of an effective contract or the tribunal's finding of such performance. Thus, the Beijing 2nd IPC opined that the issue was arbitrable and not a violation of the *PRC Law on the China-Foreign Contractual Joint Ventures.*[111]

However, this opinion was rejected by both the Beijing HPC and the SPC. The Beijing HPC referred to a 2004 civil litigation case published by the SPC, which decided that any claims requesting a correction in the composition of shares and in their administrative approval should be dealt with only in administrative litigation, and the court should notify the parties to use administrative litigation if faced with such a claim in civil proceedings.[112] In applying the rules in this case, Beijing HPC held that the change in the share composition in the equity joint venture was not arbitrable and could only be decided through administrative litigation. This opinion was later confirmed by the SPC, which also found that the award not only affected third parties' interests, but also "changed the approved share composition", and thus was an issue not authorised to be arbitrated. The SPC then annulled the award.

In the author's opinion, the decisions of the Beijing HPC and SPC are problematic for several reasons. First of all, the Beijing HPC and the SPC may have erred in recognising the legal effect of the administrative approval. As the Beijing 2nd IPC pointed out, the approval is a consequent confirmation and should not affect the effectiveness and status of the underlying joint-venture contract, or the contractual relationship between the parties in performing such a contract. Parties might still have disputes regarding their share proportions within the scope of their contracts, and they are entitled to solve such contractual disputes by choosing arbitration.

Another reason supporting the SPC and the Beijing HPC's decision is that the issue of the allocation of shares is not arbitrable. In particular, the Beijing HPC referred to the procedures that a corporation should follow in requesting administrative approval in changing a share proportion, and the remedies available in administrative litigation when such a change in share proportion is erroneous.[113] Again, this reference was problematic when applied to that case, as the claim did not mention the failure to apply for administrative approval, but instead sought confirmation of the actual share proposition in performing the contract. Nothing barred the parties from further claiming a change in the proposition to the administrative bodies, through an administrative application or administrative litigation according to the outcome of a dispute resolution process.

[111] 《中华人民共和国中外合作经营企业法》 [Law of the People's Republic of China on China-Foreign Contractual Joint Ventures](People's Republic of China) National People's Congress, Order No82, 23 February 1997, Order No55, 27 August 2006, art 85–92.

[112] The Beijing HPC did not specify the name of the SPC case referred to here.

[113] Ibid.

On the basis of the previous discussion, it is likely that the Beijing 2nd IPC's opinion, rather than the HPC and SPC's opinions, is more appropriate in distinguishing between the underlying contractual dispute and the subsequent administrative approval confirming the contractual relationship. We also observed that the Prior Reporting System is not followed in this case when the Beijing HPC and the SPC overturned the Beijing 2nd IPC's opinion to enforce this award.[114]

### 3.2.5 Competition Law Matters

While there is no specific case law in the context of China's judicial review of international arbitral awards that deals with the arbitrability of competition law disputes, the Chinese courts, especially the SPC, made significant moves towards the determination of the arbitrability of competition law related disputes in the domestic context. In some cases, the Chinese courts, especially the SPC, determined that the existence of the arbitration agreement in certain contracts do not exclude the Chinese courts' jurisdiction in dealing with competition-law related cases. Yet in some other cases, the Chinese courts upheld the effect of the arbitration agreement when competition-law related issues arose.

In *Shell v Huili* (2019),[115] a high-profile case, the SPC concluded that the arbitration agreement could not exclude the Chinese court's jurisdiction to hear antitrust disputes. Huili brought the claim before the Chinese court claiming compensation for the horizontal monopoly activities committed by Shell. The SPC emphasised that the antitrust law is public in nature, and the *Chinese Antitrust Law* only allows determination on the commitment of antitrust activities and the consequences to be made via the execution of the administrative power or via civil litigation and does not expressly mention arbitration. Further, the antitrust dispute between Huili and Shell, which involved the determination on whether Shell committed horizontal monopoly, exceeded the civil, contractual, or property-related relationships between the parties, and therefore went beyond the arbitrable matters defined by Art 2 of the *CAL*. Thus, the SPC upheld the lower court's opinion that the arbitration agreement between Shell and Huili could not exclude the jurisdiction of the Chinese court to hear the dispute regarding the horizontal monopoly.

---

[114] See Chap. 3, Sect. 4; also see further discussion in Chap. 9, Section 4.2.

[115]《上诉人壳牌 (中国) 有限公司与被上诉人呼和浩特市汇力物资有限责任公司横向垄断协议纠纷民事裁定书》[Civil Ruling Concerning the Horizontal Monopoly Agreements Between Shell (China) Co and Hohhot Huili Supplies Co Ltd - Appeal], The SPC, (2019)最高法知民辖终46,47号[Intellectual Property Civil Jurisdiction Final No.46, No.47], 21 August 2019.

Similarly, in *Beijing Longsheng*[116] the SPC held that the existence of the arbitration agreement could not exclude the People's Court's jurisdiction over matters arising from antitrust agreements. The SPC stated, "the antitrust dispute arises from the formality and performance of the monopoly agreement, in which the contract is merely a vehicle or tool for the parties to commit the monopoly-related conducts, and the monopoly itself is the origin of the infringement. Further, the determination on the commitment of the monopoly, as well as the consequences, goes beyond the rights and obligations of the parties. Thus, the dispute exceeds the scope of the arbitration agreement." Taking into account the public nature of the antitrust law, the court held that the arbitration agreement in the contract could not exclude the Chinese court's jurisdiction to hear the antitrust dispute. Similar reasoning could also be found in a series of cases between 2018 and 2022.

In another series of cases, however, some courts, even the SPC, upheld the arbitrability of competition law related disputes. In *Shell v Shanxi Changlin* (2020),[117] the SPC denied Changlin's request that the Chinese court, instead of the arbitration tribunal, should hear the dispute relating to Shell's abuse of dominance. The ruling took into account that the dispute was closely related to the rights and obligations of the parties of the franchising distribution under the distribution agreement, and, therefore, could be seen as a dispute that arose from that agreement. Further, the arbitration agreement was broad enough to cover "any dispute arising from the agreement". Thus, the SPC refrained from letting the courts intervene.

The inconsistencies beteween these two lines of determinations seemed to be ended by the SPC's proposed judicial interpretation in 2022,[118] which proposed that the Chinese courts still have the jurisdiction to hear an antitrust dispute even when there had been a contractual relationship and an arbitration agreement between the disputed parties; however, if the court determined that the dispute was not in the nature of an antitrust dispute, it may decline its jurisdiction. If this provision comes into force, then a civil dispute relating to antitrust law is principally not arbitrable in China, despite a general absence of express wording in the *CAL*. The consequence of this move is far-reaching. Potentially, it would affect the judicial review of both foreign and foreign-related arbitral awards, as Art V(2)(a) of the *NYC* clearly allows

---

116《北京龙盛兴业科技发展有限公司与域适都智能装备 (天津) 有限公司、霍尼韦尔自动化控制 (中国) 有限公司纵向垄断协议纠纷案民事裁定书》 [Civil Ruling on the Dispute Concerning the Vertical Agreements among Beijing Longsheng Xingye Technical Co. Ltd, Resideo Smart Home Technology (Tianjin) Co Ltd and Honeywell Automation and Control Solutions (China) Co Ltd], The SPC, (2022) 最高法知民终1276号[Intellectual Property Civil Final No.1276], 19 August 2022.

117《山西昌林实业有限公司、壳牌 (中国) 有限公司滥用市场支配地位纠纷再审审查与审判监督民事裁定书》 [Shanxi Changlin Industrial Co. Ltd v Shell (China) Co. Ltd—Dispute Concerning Abuse of Dominance—Retrial—Civil Ruling], the SPC, (2019)最高法民申6242号[Civil Retrial No.6242], 10 June 2020.

118《最高人民法院关于审理垄断民事纠纷案件适用法律若干问题的规定 (公开征求意见稿)》[The Supreme People's Court's Rules Concerning Various Matters on the Application of Law in the Adjudication of Civil Disputes in Relation to Antitrust Law (Draft for Public Consultation)], The SPC, 18 November 2022.

a Contracting State to apply its own standard of arbitrability to awards made in other jurisdictions.

### 3.3 *The Exclusive Jurisdiction in China*

As well as the non-arbitrability issue, the exclusive jurisdiction of the Chinese forum may also be a relevant factor in deciding jurisdiction. Although it is not considered to be an arbitrability issue,[119] a determination on jurisdiction may also have the effect of negating the validity and enforceability of an arbitral award; some discussion on exclusive jurisdiction may also involve public policy considerations.

*Leaf Candy* is an example of the exclusive jurisdiction of China in relation to purely domestic issues.[120] In that case, the disputed facts focused on whether the dispute was a purely domestic matter and, if so, whether it would be a violation of the exclusive jurisdiction principle and could be refused enforcement under the *NYC*. The Shanghai 2nd IPC held that Mr. Huang, a Malaysian party, was a party to the agreement, and found it to be a foreign-related matter, even though he did not actually take any rights or obligations under such agreement. Based on this fact, the court denied the application for non-enforcement.

More direct answers to whether a purely domestic issue can be arbitrated by foreign arbitration institutions arose from a series of cases such as *Hengding Industry*[121] and *Chaolaixinsheng*. In *Hengding Industry*, the SPC ruled that an arbitration agreement relating to a purely domestic dispute heard by a foreign arbitration institution was outside what is authorised by the current law and constituted a breach of "judicial sovereignty" and the State's public policy.

In *Chaolaixinsheng*, the Beijing 2nd IPC opined that the parties were not authorised by law (*CCPL* and *CAL*) to submit a purely domestic issue to foreign arbitration institutions, and that such an arbitration agreement would be a breach of Chinese law and public policy. The SPC upheld the Beijing 2nd IPC's decision in refusing to enforce the Korean award, but did not apply the public policy exception; instead, it relied on the ground of an invalid arbitration agreement, holding that "the applicable law of the underlying contract and its arbitration clause…shall be deemed as PRC

---

[119] Youssef, above n 5, 62; Chamlongrasdr, above n 34, 302–303; Above Sect. 2.3.

[120] 利夫糖果(上海)有限公司申请承认和执行新加坡国际仲裁中心仲裁裁决案 [Case Concerning the Application of Leaf Candy (Shanghai) Co Ltd for Recognition and Enforcement of an Arbitral Award of SIAC] Shanghai Second IPC, (2008) 沪二中民五 (商) 初字19号[Fifth Civil Branch (Commercial), Case of First Instance No.19], available at <http://www.shezfy.com/view.html?id=11429> .

[121]《六盘水恒鼎实业有限公司与张洪兴采矿权转让合同争议管辖权异议案》 [Liupanshui Hengding Industry Co v Zhang Hongxing—Case of Jurisdictional Disputes Regarding a Dispute Occurred in a Transfer of a Mining Contract], reprinted in苏泽林[Su Zelin], 景汉朝[Jing Hanchao] and 最高人民法院(the Supreme People's Court) ed., 最高人民法院立案一庭、立案二庭[the First and Second Case Filing Branches of the Supreme People's Court],《立案工作指导》[Guidance on Case Filing] (2011)(1), Vol.28, 94–98. This case dealt with the jurisdictional issue only and therefore is not covered by the case pool of this book.

law", and that the PRC law did not authorise the parties to refer a purely domestic dispute to foreign arbitration.

Thus, it is notable that the violation of exclusive jurisdiction may be a ground for non-enforcement of an arbitral award in China. Yet, it is not certain whether it is an issue of arbitrability, public policy or an issue of an "invalid arbitration agreement" under Article V(1)(a) of the *NYC*, as all of these possible grounds were referred to by the courts. Practitioners have argued that the SPC's opinion erred in *Chaolaixinsheng* in referring to Article V(1)(a) of the *NYC*, because this provision only requires the validity of the arbitration agreement under *lex arbitri* in order for an arbitration award to be enforced.[122] Thus, it does not matter whether the arbitration agreement is invalid under Chinese law as long as it is valid under Korean law, the *lex arbitri* in this case.[123]

The judicial determination that the involved arbitration agreement is invalid is also problematic. The Beijing 2nd IPC's ruling states that, foreign arbitration institutions and tribunals are not authorised by the *CAL* and *CCPL* to deal with disputes that do not involve a foreign-related element; this explanation is based on Art 278 of the *CCPL*, which states that.

> 'in the case of a dispute arising from the foreign economic, trade, transport or maritime activities in China, if the parties have had an arbitration clause in the contract concerned or have subsequently reached a written arbitration agreement stipulating the submission of the dispute for arbitration to an arbitration institution in the People's Republic of China handling foreign-related cases or any other arbitration institution, they may not bring an action in a people's court.'

Similarly, Art 128 of the *Chinese Contract Law* states,

> 'The parties to a foreign-related contract may, according to the arbitration agreement, apply to a Chinese arbitration institution or any other arbitration institution for arbitration.'[124]

It is doubtful, however, that these provisions imply that the power to arbitrate is authorised by law rather than the parties' consent; and even if it does, it does not expressly exclude the arbitration of purely domestic disputes by foreign arbitration institutions or tribunals; furthermore, these provisions are considered out-dated.[125] In addition, it is doubtful whether a foreign arbitration institution would follow the

---

122 The NYC, art V(1)(a), "...under the law where the award is made". Also Born, above n 57, 492–501.

123 牟笛[Mou Di],《再议无涉外因素争议能否在外国机构仲裁》[A Re-Discussion on Whether A Purely Domestic Dispute without Any Foreign-Related Element Can Be Arbitrated By Foreign Arbitration Institutions], 7 January 2015, at <http://www.aiweibang.com/yuedu/8943990.html >. He also argues that the invalidity of this arbitration agreement is not found on the basis of the *CAL* and Chinese contract law.

124《中华人民共和国合同法》[Contract Law of the People's Republic of China] (People's Republic of China) National People's Congress, Order No 15, 15 March 1999. This rule is now removed when the Chinese Contract Law was replaced by the Chinese Civil Code in 2020.

125 In Chinese research and practice there is still a leading opinion that the power to arbitrate does not arise from the parties' consent, but from judicial authorisation, or sovereign power. See for example, 钱宇宏, 马伯娟[Qian Yuhong, Ma Bojuan], above n 80, which provides adiscussion that the power to arbitrate derivves from the transfer of the judicial power (a power comes from the

Chinese law to decide whether they are authorised to arbitrate on an issue which is categorised as "purely domestic" in China.[126] What is also doubtful is whether that issue related to arbitrability or public policy, as the SPC itself denied the application of the ground of arbitrability or public policy in *Chaolaixinsheng*.[127]

A further uncertainty in relation to this issue is that Chinese legislators and the judiciary may update the definition of foreign-related elements from time to time. The modification is reflected in the SPC's judicial interpretation on the Civil Procedure Law[128] as well as in other cases including*Siemens*,[129] the Chinese court determined that disputes involving enterprises invested in exclusively by foreign investors and incorporated in the Free Trade Zones could be seen as satisfying the definition of "foreign elements", and therefore, could be arbitrated by foreign arbitration institutions overseas; enforcement of arbitral awards resulted from such arbitration agreement should not be refused on the basis of a lack of any valid arbitration agreement. Nor did the public policy ground apply in this scenario. The extension of the foreign-related element is further confirmed by the ***SPC's Opinions on Facilitating the Development of the Free Trade Zones*** in 2016,[130] which stated that, "arbitration agreements

sovereignty) to the private parties. But even if so, there is no clear rule that in the area of arbitration, all activities not explicitly authorised by the CAL or the CCPL shall be forbidden. See牟笛[Mou Di], above n 123. Also, it is notable that this provision is out-dated now, because there is no distinction between 'foreign-related arbitration commission' and 'domestic commission' in China now, and foreign arbitrations that accepted by Chinese law are not restricted to institutional arbitration; ad hoc awards are now recognisable and enforceable in China. See Chap. 3, Sect. 4.

[126] It is, however, arguable that the foreign arbitration institution may consider the parties' capacity to reach an arbitration agreement to bring a purely domestic issue in China to a foreign arbitration institution. Given that such capacity is to be decided according to the parties nationality, which would be Chinese law in this situation, it may be held that the parties of a purely domestic dispute lack the capacity to reach an international arbitration agreement and to select a foreign arbitration institution. However, the question of whether the capacity of a party should be decided according to the law where they reside or are domiciled is still controversial in international practice, as more and more practitioners and scholars argue for a broad rule to confirm such capacity (eg., the validity principle, the non-discrimination principle, rather than rules from a particular national law). See Born, above n 57, 625–631.

[127] Lijun Cao, Leilei Lu, 'To Be or Not to Be: The Practical Implications of Choosing Foreign Arbitration for Purely Domestic Contracts', at Kluwer Arbitration Blog, 6 March 2015, at http://kluwerarbitrationblog.com/blog/2015/03/06/to-be-or-not-to-be-the-practical-implications-of-choosing-foreign-arbitration-for-purely-domestic-contracts/.

[128] A new list of foreign elements, see《最高人民法院关于适用《中华人民共和国民事诉讼法》的解释》[The SPC's Judicial Interpretation on the Application of the Civil Procedure Law of the People's Republic of China](People's Republic of China), Supreme People's Court, 法释(2015)5号[Judicial Interpretation No 2015–5], issued 30 January 2015, modified on 23 December 2020 and then 22 March 2022, effective 10 April 2022, art 520.

[129]《最高人民法院关于西门子国际贸易(上海)有限公司申请承认与执行外国仲裁裁决一案的请示的复函》[Reply of the SPC Concerning the Recognition and Enforcement of a Foreign Award Requested by Siemens International Trade (Shanghai) Co Ltd], Supreme People's Court, [2015]民四他字第5号[Fourth Civil Branch No.5], 10 October 2015.

[130]《最高人民法院关于为自由贸易试验区建设提供司法保障的意见》[The Opinions of the Supreme People's Court on Providing Judicial Safeguard to the Construction of Free Trade Zones], Supreme People's Court, 法发[2016]No.34[Law Issue No.34], 30 December 2016.

choosing arbitration overseas between enterprises solely invested by foreign investors and incorporated in the Free Trade Zones should not be held as invalid."[131]

While the approach adopted by the SPC in *Chaolaixinsheng* is problematic, it seems that the general attitude to exclude foreign arbitration institutions to hear purely domestic arbitration between Chinese parties has been adopted by the Chinese legislator. In the *New CAL Draft*,[132] it was proposed that the foreign arbitration institutions, which are authorised to operate within China, could only deal with "foreign-related" business. It remains to be seen whether the exclusive jurisdiction of Chinese arbitration commissions to hear purely domestic matters will be formally confirmed as a distinctive factor in China's public policy.

## 4 Comments and Conclusion

The legal concepts of arbitrability, mandatory rules and public policy intersect. Mandatory rules, particularly those that have public policy implications, shape the scope of arbitrability. Along with the globalisation of international arbitration, the definition of arbitrability has expanded, as is signified by such cases as *Scherk* and *Mitsubishi*. The result is that not all mandatory rules or public rules are inarbitrable. The role of arbitrability in the judicial review of arbitral awards has diminished in judicial practice in different national legal systems; courts have relaxed the criteria used to identify arbitrability; and domestic courts and arbitration tribunals increasingly take international concerns into account in limiting the scope of issues that are not arbitrable.[133] Despite these recent trends, arbitrability is still heavily influenced by public policy and, at least to some degree, public policy concerns underpin the criteria used to identify arbitrability.[134]

Though these developments are widely accepted in the international context, they are not fully accepted in China's arbitration and judicial practice. Chinese legislation provides both positive and negative lists, which are rigidly delineated compared to the more flexible definitional lists in other leading jurisdictions. Such Chinese legislation also fails to provide a sufficiently clear interpretation of the term "proprietary" in relation to disputes. Nor does it refer to any public policy concerns or to the international context.[135]Chinese courts' have adhered strictly to inclusive and exclusive lists in legislation and have applied them literally in cases such as *Mongolian*. In other cases, especially in dealing with controversial areas of law, such as tort law and

[131] Ibid, art 9.

[132]《<中华人民共和国仲裁法 (修订) >征求意见稿》[Draft of the Modified Arbitration Law of the People's Republic of China](People's Republic of China), Ministry of Justice, 30 July 2021, available at: http://www.moj.gov.cn/pub/sfbgw/zlk/202107/t20210730_432958.html, art 12.

[133] Chapter 7; Chap. 8, Sect. 2.3.

[134] Ch 8, Sect. 2.5.

[135] Ch 8, Sect.3.1.

company dissolution, Chinese courts have failed to adopt a consistent approach.[136] Generally, underlying public policy concerns are not observed in these rulings, and Chinese courts do not display sufficient experience or technical skill in distinguishing between disputed contractual and proprietary issues from the relevant administrative approvals.[137] Also, regarding the exclusive jurisdiction of the Chinese institutions in dealing with purely domestic disputes, Chinese courts also adopt a rigid approach.

The rigid approach of Chinese courts in dealing with arbitrability and their exclusive jurisdiction over disputes involving purely domestic issues may be a natural outcome of its understanding of the power to arbitrate as a consequence of a transfer of judicial power and authorisation by the State. Thus, party autonomy is not fully respected, and a flexible approach favouring the validity and enforceability of the arbitral awards, is not adopted.

The author suggests that the Chinese judiciary might like to consider adopting the recommendations of academic commentators on China's legal practice and abandon its rigid judicial approach in adopting a literal interpretation of inarbitrability without taking into consideration underlying public policy concerns. In particular, it is evident that Chinese academics appreciate the connection between arbitrability and public policy. For instance, Cao suggests that public policy concerns play a key role in the interpretation of the ambiguous definition of arbitrability in China, particularly when the legislation is not well rounded[138]; Huang also argues that the nexus between public policy and arbitrability should be respected under the *NYC* scheme when applying them in judicial review.[139] In addition, a more flexible interpretation of arbitrability would also be inconsistent with China's pro-arbitration position.

It is also suggested that the Chinese court may pay more attention to the nature of the disputed matter and to identify whether such matter is categorised as inarbitrable. In particular, it is the author's view that in cases such as *Mongolia* and *Jiacheng,* a more detailed interpretation should have been made in deciding whether the disputed matter is covered by an inarbitrability rule (succession or administrative registration of a company), or is of a proprietary nature and generally arbitrable under Chinese law. A narrowly constructed coverage of inarbitrability would help the court maintain consistent decision-making and it would also contribute to a pro-arbitration environment in China.

---

[136] Ch 8, Sects.2.1 and 2.3.

[137] Particularly in Ch 8, Sects.2.3 and 2.4.

[138] 曹志勋[Cao Zhixun],《论可仲裁性的司法审查标准——基于美国反垄断仲裁经验的考察》[Discussion on the Judicial Review Standard of Arbitrability: A Review on the Basis of US's Antitrust Law Arbitration](2012) 83 华东政法大学学报 *East China University of Political Science and Law* 56, 63–64.

[139] 黄卉[Huang Hui],《论 < 纽约公约 > 里的不可仲裁性》[Discussion on Inarbitrability in the New York Convention](2011) 知识经济 *Knowledge Economy* 41.

# Part III
# Conclusion and Recommendations

# Chapter 9
# An Evaluation of the Application of Public Policy in the Chinese Legal System

## 1 Introduction

On the basis of a detailed case study of the Chinese cases dealing with public policy in the judicial review of arbitral awards, as provided by Chaps. 4–8, this chapter summarises the author's observations and evaluations of the general performance of the Chinese legal system in defining and applying the public policy exception in the judicial review of international commercial arbitral awards.

Sections 2 and 3 focus on how the concept of the public policy exception in arbitration law is defined in China. Section 2 demonstrates that the international nature of public policy is not specifically reflected in China's legislation and judicial practice, and Sect. 3 concludes that the key elements of public policy defined in Chap. 2 have not been fully developed in China. Sections 4 and 5 further examine the approach adopted by the Chinese judiciary in practice, including their attitude towards merit review, acceptance of new facts and evidence, and the possible application of a waiver or estoppel in applying public policy.

Sections 6 and 7 further examine the performance of the Chinese courts, the Chinese arbitration commissions, arbitrators and other participants in Chinese arbitration, and the subsequent judicial review of arbitral awards. Section 6 evaluates the role and performance of the Chinese courts in applying public policy; Sect. 7 comments on the activities and possible influence of the Chinese arbitration commissions and arbitrators.

By examining these issues together, the author attempts to illustrate some distinctive characteristics of Chinese arbitration and judicial practice. Based on these understandings, Sect. 8 examines how the development of public policy in arbitration law reflects the influences of globalisation and localisation in China's legal system and legal culture, and how these influences function as a means of shaping China's arbitration law and practice. This section also identifies the international legislative and judicial practices that are most likely to influence China's practice, and suggests how



S. Zhang, *The Public Policy Exception in the Judicial Review of International Commercial Arbitral Awards*, https://doi.org/10.1007/978-3-662-67679-0_9

China should develop its approach to applying the public policy exception in the future.

## 2 Domestic, International and Transnational/Truly International Public Policy in China

In international practice, distinctions are usually drawn between domestic and international public policy. The notion of transnational public policy is also acknowledged as the basis of converging international practices in applying public policy.[1] Acceptance by the Chinese legal system of international public policy, however, is limited, and questions of acceptance are even more evident in relation to the more sophisticated notion of transnational public policy.

The distinction between domestic arbitral awards and awards with foreign elements, including foreign-related awards and international awards, are generally appreciated in China's judicial review of arbitral awards, but such a distinction is not emphasised in the application of public policy in the judicial review of arbitral awards.[2]

The author has observed that one achievement attained by the Chinese judiciary is that it has adopted a narrow approach in applying public policy when dealing with foreign-related awards and international awards. This narrow approach is confirmed in a series of cases. In *Tianjin Xianda* and *Wild Cat*, as well as on various other occasions, the SPC repeatedly stated that the facts and application of the law in deciding the substantive issues of disputes should not be reviewed because the disputes were of a foreign-related nature.[3] The non-enforcement of foreign-related and international awards is further limited by the Prior Reporting System.[4]

With respect to the application of public policy, however, the distinction between domestic and international public policy,[5] which is widely accepted in international practice, is rarely expressed in China's legislation or judicial practice. Though some Chinese courts have noted that public policy that is applied in reviewing foreign-related and international arbitral awards is based on private international law, and should be interpreted in a narrow sense,[6] no particular features of international public

---

[1] Section 4 in Chap. 2.

[2] For the different types of awards, and the schemes provided by Chinese legislation in differentiating the judicial review schemes of domestic awards and foreign-related/international awards, see Sects. 4.3, 4.4 and 4.5 in Chap. 3.

[3] Discussed in Sect. 4.3 in Chap. 5.

[4] Section 3.2.4 in Chap. 3; further confirmed by the statistical study in Chap. 4.

[5] Section 3 in Chap. 2.

[6] 高晓力 [Gao Xiaoli],《国际私法上公共政策的运用》[The Functioning of Public Policy in Private International Law] (中国民主法制出版社[China Democracy and Rule of Law Press], 2008) 11–14; Sect. 3 in Chap. 3. Such a distinction is also confirmed by Cui J's additional comments on the decision of *Leaf Candy*; see 利夫糖果(上海)有限公司申请承认和执行新加坡国际仲裁中心仲裁裁决案 [Case Concerning the Application of Leaf Candy (Shanghai) Co Ltd for Recognition

policy were identified and distinguished from domestic public policy. A narrow approach in applying public policy was insisted on because of the general nature of the dispute, rather than the recognition of it having the particular feature of international public policy.[7]

The only possible discussion of a distinction between domestic and international public policy can be seen in the different attitudes of the courts dealing with mandatory rules in the judicial review of domestic awards, and in the judicial review of foreign-related and international awards. In the domestic case of *Beijing Star Factory* a violation of mandatory rules of financial regulation was considered to be a violation of public policy[8]; while in cases such as *ED & F Mans* and *Mitsui* in which a foreign-related or international award was reviewed, the SPC repeatedly emphasised that the violation of mandatory rules was not necessarily a violation of public policy. Given the similar nature of the applicable mandatory rules regulating the financial market in *Beijing Star Factory, ED &F Mans* and *Mitstui,* such a distinction between domestic and international public policy may be implied; yet such a distinction is never expressly confirmed in judicial practice.[9] Similarly, it is unclear whether the denial of the arbitrability of competition law matters in the domestic context should be applied in an identical manner in the context of the review of a foreign-related or international award.[10]

Along with the limited recognition of international public policy, it is difficult to argue that a transnational public policy has ever been recognised or extensively adopted in China's judicial practice. The notion of transnational public policy is only expressly recognised by scholars,[11] and some of these scholars consider that it is "not practical" to expect China's judiciary to adopt a truly international public policy within the current legal environment.[12]

A tentative conclusion is that the distinction between domestic and international public policy, as well as the concept of a truly transnational public policy, is not well accepted or acknowledged in China's practice. The distinction between different types of arbitration and awards, as indicated in Chap. 3, may provide some guidance for the courts to apply public policy, but limited progress is made in relation to

---

and Enforcement of an Arbitral Award of SIAC] Shanghai Second IPC, (2008) 沪二中民五 (商) 初字19号 [Fifth Civil Branch (Commercial), Case of First Instance No. 19], available at <http://www.shezfy.com/view.html?id=11429>; See also Sect. 5 in Chap. 3.

7 See for example, *Tianjin Xianda*and *Wildcat*.

8《北京星工场音乐娱乐有限公司诉北京中鸿房地产开发有限公司申请撤销仲裁裁决案》[Beijing Star Factory Music and Entertainment Co Ltd v Beijing Zhonghong Real Estate Development Co Ltd-Case of Annulment of Arbitral Award] Beijing Second IPC, 2004, case number not available.

9 Section 3.3 in Chap. 7.

10 Section 3.2.5 in Chap. 8.

11 齐湘泉 [Qi Xiangquan],《外国仲裁裁决承认及执行论》[Study on the Recognition and Enforcement of Foreign Arbitral Awards] (法律出版社[Law Press], 2010) 319–323; Emmanuel Gaillard, translated by 黄洁[Huang Jie],《国际仲裁的法理思考和实践指导》[Legal Theory of International Arbitration], (北京大学出版社[Peking University Press], 2010), 110–117.

12 齐湘泉 [Qi Xiangquan], above n 11, 319–323.

distinguishing among the different contexts in which domestic and international public policy is applied. Transnational or truly international public policy is not generally recognised in China's arbitration practice.

## 3 The Possible Key Elements of Public Policy in China's Practice

This research reviews China's judicial practice in relation to the application of the following key elements of public policy, including (1a) substantive fundamental principles of law, (1b) procedural fundamental principles of law, (2) public policy rules, (3) international obligations, and (4) arbitrability.[13] Based on this categorisation, our review of the Chinese cases illustrates that the arbitration and judicial practices in China are yet to make substantial progress in identifying and applying any particular key element of public policy.

Such a conclusion is reached on the basis of the unsatisfactory performance of the Chinese legal system in identifying and applying the key elements of public policy, as provided by Part II of this book (Chap. 4–8). Generally, legislation provides limited guidance for the clarification of any particular element in the judicial review of arbitral awards.[14] Developments in theoretical studies with respect to the key elements of the application of public policy by the judiciary are also limited; most theoretical interpretations and discussions provided by scholars on possible elements of public policy focus generally on political notions, which are rarely involved in arbitration practice. Only limited guidance is provided in these scholarly discussions about arbitration and judicial practice.[15]

Similarly, detailed discussion in regard to the elements of public policy is generally rare in China's judicial practice. With respect to the identification of public policy elements, progress has been observed, but only in limited aspects. There are only a limited number of cases in which public policy is applied, and the public policy elements are still to be identified. Element (3), international obligations, was not mentioned at all during the last two decades.

Element (1)(a) Substantive fundamental principles of law, and (2) public policy rules, were arguably applied in *Heavy Metal,* but the SPC's legal reasoning did not

---

[13] Sections 5 and 6 in Chap. 2; also, its application is reflected in Sect. 4.3 in Chap. 4.

[14] Section 5 in Chap. 3; though a categorisation of possible public policy rules is listed in the *Law Application Law.* Its possible application in identifying public policy rules (Element(2)), see Sect. 3.2 in Chap. 7.

[15] Section 5 in Chap. 3 and Sect. 2.2 in Chap. 5, discussing the elements of public policy that identified by Gao Xiaoli, Tao, and Wunschheim; 高晓力[Gao Xiaoli], above n 6, 131; Clarisse von Wunschheim, *Enforcement of Commercial Arbitral Awards in China: Business Laws of China* (West, 2011) 2–3; Jingzhou Tao, 'Enforcement of SCC Arbitration Awards in China' in *Between East and West: Essays in Honour of Ulf Franke* (2010), fn. 25. See also Jianfu Chen, *Chinese Law: Context and Transfrmation* (Martinus Nijhoff, 2008) 283.

specify which element the decision was applied to.[16] Similarly, the reasoning in *Hulishan,* or even the decision itself, which might be arguably based on Element 1(a), was never disclosed.

Element (1)(b), procedural fundamental principle of law, was considered as applied in *Yongning*, but the SPC referred to "judicial sovereignty" as China's public policy, rather than the commonly known principle of *res judicata.*[17] In a series of cases, this element seems to be further developed to uphold the Chinese courts' determination on the jurisdictional matters of the arbitration, especially on the issue of the validity of arbitration agreements, while the approach largely ignores the sequence of the arbitration and judicial determinations, which is neither consistent nor comparable to international practice.[18] On other occasions, *res judicata* was applied as a requirement of arbitration law and rules rather than a procedural fundamental principle, or an element of public policy.[19] Similarly, the SPC excluded the impartiality of arbitrators as a possible procedural public policy in *Huludao Harbour* and *Louis Dreyfus.*[20]

Besides *Heavy Metal*, Element (2), *lois de police/* public policy rules, is also discussed in a number of cases, yet with limited experiences of successful application or clarification; Some of these decisions are controversial because they have involved mandatory rules which may have a public policy nature, including rules regulating financial markets, anti-dumping laws and public health rules.[21]

Element (4), arbitrability, was consistently and repeatedly applied in a series of cases. Yet the possible public policy concerns were not recognised in these cases, but instead these decisions were made on the basis of a rigid application of the positive and negative lists provided by mandatory legislation rather than on the basis of the analysis of any underlying public policy concern.[22]

A typical line of reasoning frequently adopted in the current practice, especially in various cases determined by the lower courts in rejecting the public policy arguments, is that the arbitral awards under judicial review only deal with the interests of particular parties and awarded monetary relief, and therefore are not reflecting the interests of the general public, and therefore, not supporting China's social public interest or public policy.[23] While this line of reasoning makes sense in some cases, like when

---

[16] Chapter 4, nn 106; Sect. 4 in Chap. 5, discussing *Heavy Metal.*

[17] See Sect. 4 in Chap. 6.

[18] See Sect. 4 in Chap. 6, discussions of cases such as *Castel, Wicor, Palmer* and *Gate.*

[19] Section 4.2 in Chap. 6, discussing *Shin-Etsu No. 2.*

[20] Section 2.3 in Chap. 6.

[21] Section 3 in Chap. 7, discussing significant cases including *ED & F Mans, Mitsui, Shin-Etsu No. 1* and *Bunge.*

[22] Section 2.2 in Chap. 8.

[23] See for example,《中国航油 (新加坡) 股份有限公司、成都欣华欣化工材料有限公司申请承认与执行外国仲裁裁决裁定书》[Decision on the Application for the Recognition and Enforcement of a Foreign Arbitral Award between China Aviation Oil (Singapore) Corp Ltd and Chengdu Xinhuaxin Chenical Engineering Materials Co Ltd], Chengdu IPC, (2017)川01协外认1号 [Judicial Assistance Foreign Recognition No. 1], 23 June 2017.

the State-owned enterprises are involved,[24] it fails to address the broader concerns underlying the distinctive public policy elements listed above, like the fundamental principles or the public policy rules.[25] This approach, therefore, denies any meaningful discussion in examining the essence of each of the public policy elements and the opportunity to further elaborate those elements in the context of Chinese law.

Though the general progress relating to the identification and application of key elements of public policy is not totally satisfactory in China's practice, the following developments have been achieved during the last few decades. First, significant exclusions were made by the Chinese courts in clarifying the scope of the key elements of public policy. For example, the Chinese courts generally have refused to apply public policy when it is argued that the underlying contract or transaction is fraudulent,[26] which is consistent with international practice.[27] It is also significant that Chinese courts have denied the interests of state government bodies, State-owned enterprises or domestic and regional interests as an element of public policy.[28] These are significant steps taken by the Chinese courts to control local protectionism in the judicial review of arbitral awards.

Progress is also observed when the SPC has attempted to establish some standards in evaluating the fundamentality of some key elements of public policy. An illustration of "fundamental legal order" is observed in cases such as *Wildcat*. Such a reference is also adopted in the evaluation of the "essential political, social or economic interests"[29] in identifying *lois de police*.[30] Particularly, the differences between validating mandatory rules and regulatory mandatory rules may be a useful reference in recognising the legislative purpose and identifying public policy rules.[31]

Based on these primary conclusions, the author suggests a comprehensive category of public policy elements, which would cover the elements provided in previous

---

[24]《来宝资源国际私人有限公司、中煤京闽（福建）工贸有限公司申请承认与执行法院判决、仲裁裁决案件民事裁定书》[Civil Decision on the Application for the Recognition and Enforcement of Judgments or Arbitral Awards between Noble Resources International Pte Ltd and China Coal Jingmin (Fujian) Industry and Trade Co Ltd], Fuzhou IPC, (2019) 闽01认港1号 [Recognition Hong Kong No. 1], 29 September 2019.

[25] See for example,《北良（香港）有限公司、日照兴裕嘉贸易有限公司申请承认与执行法院判决、仲裁裁决案件裁定书》[Decision on the Application for the Recognition and Enforcement of Judgments or Arbitral Awards between Beiliang (Hong Kong) Co Ltd and Rizhao Xingyujia Trade Co Ltd], Rizhao IPC, (2016)鲁11协外认1号 [Judicial Assistance Foreign Recognition No. 1], 9 January 2018.

[26] Section 3.2 in Chap. 5.

[27] Section 3 in Chap. 5; Dirk Otto and Omaia Elwan, 'Article V(2)' in Herbert Kronke et al. (eds), *Recognition and Enforcement of Foreign Arbitral Awards* (Wolter Kluwer, 2010) 345, 375.

[28] Section 5 in Chap. 5.

[29] Pierre Mayer and Audley Sheppard, 'Final Report on Public Policy as a Bar to Enforcement of International Arbitral Awards' (2003) 19 *Arbitration International* 249, Recommendation 3(b); discussed in Sect. 3 in Chap. 7.

[30] Section 3.2 in Chap. 7, discussing the opinions of the scholars in recognising the fundamental rules of Chinese law; also see Sect. 3.3.2 in Chap. 7, the discussion of the fundamentality of the rule of currency control in *Mistui;* 高晓力[Gao Xiaoli], above n 6, 258–259.

[31] Section 3.3 (discussing *Leaf Candy*) and 4 in Chap. 7.

discussions, including (1) substantial and procedural fundamental principles, (2) *lois de police*, (3) international obligations, and (4) arbitrability, in China's legislative and judicial practice in relation to arbitral awards. The ultimate goal of developing such public policy elements is to connect the Chinese approach in dealing with public policy with the worldwide consensus in dealing with similar issues.

It is understandable that the establishment of such a comprehensive category may be a huge and continuing task, and such goal may not be achieved for a number of years. It is possible, however, for Chinese legal scholars and practitioners to make the following significant and urgent modifications that will lead to the establishment of a basic legal framework of public policy:

First of all, a few commonly accepted elements and principles covered by public policy can be identified and recognised in China's practice. For example, the issue of impartiality and *res judicata*, which are universally regarded as procedural fundamental principles as a part of public policy, should be recognised and applied. These principles have been repeatedly construed and tested in international practice,[32] and a recognition of them would shift them from the 'negative list' to the 'positive list' of public policy elements. Errors in excluding these principles can be corrected immediately in order to avoid confusion, particularly for international practitioners.

In addition, certain criteria in distinguishing the substantive principles, or *lois de police*, which are part of public policy, from other principles and mandatory laws, which are not considered to be of a public policy nature, can be established. Evaluation of the national interests, or the protected interests expressed as part of the legislative purpose, can be taken into consideration.[33] By applying these considerations and referring to international experiences, progress may be achieved in establishing the "fundamental" standard of legal principles, laws and interests in certain areas of law, for example, the foreign-investment regulation and antitrust law.[34]

In the meantime, the Chinese court should abandon its rigid reliance on arbitration law and rules and apply public policy elements with a working knowledge of their nature and characteristics. For example, procedural public policy, such as the protection of the parties' rights in arbitration proceedings, or impartiality of arbitrators, should be ensured. Whether there is a fundamental procedural principle, and whether there is a serious breach of such principle, should be evaluated apart from compliance with arbitration rules. As illustrated by *Keeneye*, an arbitral proceeding fully complying with the provided arbitration rules may still cause concerns about a breach of impartiality.[35]

Similarly, the arbitrability of proprietary matter can be evaluated by the courts on the basis of the underlying public policy concerns even if it is not expressly declared as arbitrable, or even if it relates to other non-arbitrable matters. The court shall discern the nature of the disputes, for example, the disposition of a proprietary right from a succession case, or confirming the underlying proprietary rights

[32] Sections 2 and 4 in Chap. 6.

[33] Section 5 in Chap. 5; Sect. 4 in Chap. 7.

[34] Section 3 in Chap. 7.

[35] For example, the *Keeneye Case* as illustrated in Sect. 2.2 in Chap. 6.

of the shareholders/partners, which is arbitrable, from the prima facie issues of succession or administrative registration of a company/partnership, which is arguably non-arbitrable.[36]

By undertaking these moves, the Chinese courts may establish a primary category of public policy elements that are understandable and acceptable to international practitioners, and may become more experienced in dealing with similar cases in the future. In the meanwhile, the unique understandings of Chinese courts and practitioners about these public policy elements can be explored and interpreted based on this category; for example, an understanding of mediation-in-arbitration practice may be connected to the impartiality principle, and an understanding of the fundamental national interests may be linked to fundamental principles that are substantive in nature. The undeveloped public policy elements, such as the international obligations, may also be explored when Chinese courts have such an opportunity to deal with them.

## 4 The Extent of Judicial Review

### *4.1 International Progress*

An issue of determining the extent of judicial review is an issue which every court faces when dealing with an arbitral award. A few questions may be asked: How should the court deal with the merits of the awards? How should it deal with the underlying transactions and disputes? And how should courts accept new evidence and find new facts, if that is even allowed?

It has long been the international consensus to generally prohibit the review of the merits of arbitration awards, which aims to respect the finality of arbitration decisions.[37] However, because the judicial review of arbitral awards is distinguished from an appeal, a review of an arbitral award on the merits is generally excluded from judicial review. As a result, mistakes in fact or law made by arbitrators would not be reviewed.[38] The *NYC* and extensive international case law confirms that a merit review is not allowed, or is restricted to truly exceptional occasions in the judicial review of international arbitral awards in different circumstances.[39] It is also

[36] See Sect. 3.2 in Chap. 8.

[37] Albert Jan van den Berg, *The New York Convention of 1958: Towards a Uniform Judicial Interpretation* (Kluwer Law International, 1981) 269–273; Alexis Mourre and Luca G. Radicati di Brozolo, 'Towards Finality of Arbitral Award: Two Steps Forward and One Step Back' (2006) 23(2) *Journal of International Arbitration* 171.

[38] Van den Berg, above n 37, 269.

[39] *AB Götaverken v. General National Maritime Transport Company*, Supreme Court of Sweden, 13 August 1979, reported in (1981) 6 *Yearbook-Commercial Arbitration* 237, 239–240 (Sweden No. 1); in this case, the Swedish court clearly refused to review the merits when the party argued that two issues in the awards were contradictory.

generally accepted that judicial review should focus on the awards and avoid the evaluation of the tribunal's findings of underlying disputed facts or decisions in the application of law in relation to the merits.[40]

These general notions are also widely accepted by courts in national jurisdictions in applying public policy in the judicial review of arbitral awards, and particularly, in applying substantive principles that are fundamental (1a), public policy rules (2) and arbitrability (4).[41] For example, in dealing with issues of fraud, national courts have consistently emphasised that fraud in arbitration proceedings, as an element of public policy, should be distinguished from fraud in the underlying transactions, the latter of which would be subject to a merit review and is inappropriate under judicial review of an arbitration award.[42] As *Karaha Bodas* provided, when holding that fraud in the underlying transaction would bar the enforcement of awards, a court must not review the merits of the award, which is inappropriate.[43] Similarly, courts frequently rejected arguments such as a "manifest disregard of law" as a possible element of international public policy on the basis that such an evaluation of the tribunal's application of law would in fact be a review of the merits.[44]

National courts also do not generally review arbitral awards in a comprehensive and substantive manner—especially those of an international character—and as illustrated by *Westacre*, in which the court adopted a strict approach that it would re-open discussion of facts and evidence only in "truly exceptional circumstances".[45] In this case, the defendant sought to submit new evidence regarding claims of bribery of Kuwaiti officials before the court. English courts rejected such an application by emphasising the finality of the award and the courts' respect for the arbitration tribunal's efforts in appropriately dealing with the alleged bribery issue.[46] A similar

---

[40] Van den Berg, above n 37, 271.

[41] Procedural fundamental principles (Element (1b)) are less involved in this discussion, as the judicial review on arbitration proceedings is less likely to be a merit review.

[42] Section 3.2 in Chap. 5; Otto and Elwan, above n 27, 375.

[43] *KarahaBodas Co. LLC v Perusahaan PertambanganMinyak Dan Gas Bumi Negara* [2007] HKCA 429, Court of Appeal of Hong Kong SAR, reported in (2008) 33 *Yearbook-Commercial Arbitration* 574, 588–590 (Hong Kong No. 20).

[44] Manifest disregard of law is a ground negating the enforceability of an award in the US for domestic cases; yet it is doubtful whether it can be covered by the ground of public policy for international cases. See for example, *Parsons &Whittemore Overseas Co v SocieteGenerale de L'Industrie du Papier (RAKTA)*, 508 F.2d 969 (2d Cir. 1974) 977.

[45] *Westacre Investments Inc v Jugoimport-SDPR Holding Co Ltd* [1998] WLR 770; [1999] 2 Lloyd's Rep 65; Auldey Sheppard, 'Interim Report on Public Policy as a Bar to Enforcement of International Arbitral Awards' (2000) 19(3) *Arbitration International* 217, 244–245. See also Alexis Mourre, Luca G Radicati di Brozolo, above n 37, 172–174.

[46] *WestacreInvestments Inc* [1998] WLR 770, per Colman J. See also Jonathan Harris and Frank Meisel, 'Public Policy and the Enforcement of International Arbitration Awards: Controlling the Unruly Horse' (1998) 1 *Lloyd's Maritime and Commercial Law Quarterly* 568; Shai Wade, 'Westacre v Soleimany: What policy? Which public?' (1999) *International Arbitration* 97; Erwan Brown, 'Illegality and Public Policy: Enforcement of Arbitral Awards in England' (2000) *International Arbitration* 31.

approach was also adopted in *Sonic SACI v Novokuznetsk Aluminium Plain.*[47] Only in limited circumstances have courts conducted a more comprehensive review of awards. In an earlier case, *European Gas Turbines SA v Westman International Ltd*, the Paris Court of Appeal conducted a comprehensive judicial review which included "all legal and factual elements justifying or not the application of the international public policy rule", including the validity of the disputed contract.[48]

The arguments for or against a comprehensive judicial review of the facts and merits is controversial. In particular, to what extent and under what "exceptional" circumstances will courts go beyond the awards themselves and re-open the facts and examine evidence of the disputes? The *ILA Report* provides a response to this question, stating that the re-opening of facts is accepted under particular exceptional circumstances regarding the violation of public policy rules:

> *When the violation of a public policy rule of the forum alleged by a party cannot be established from a mere review of the award and could only become apparent upon a scrutiny of the facts of the case, the court should be allowed to undertake such reassessment of the facts.*[49]

A review of the details of arbitration proceedings may also be required in finding a violation of procedural fundamental principles of law; but in practice, the court may also take into consideration whether such claims have already been dealt with by the supervisory court.[50]

More general responses to the controversy over the judicial review of facts in relation to the merits are provided by scholars who comment on diversified practices of judges in different jurisdictions and under different circumstances, and when multiple public policy elements are involved. Two different approaches to judicial review are described as the maximalist, or maximal judicial review, which prefers a full review of the facts and law of the dispute; and a minimalist, or minimal judicial review, which consists of a limited review in respect of the arbitrators' competence and ability to decide on the relevant issues.[51] For example, in dealing with public policy rules (2), a discretionary analysis and evaluation of the particular situation of the case may be required, though the courts may not be in a better position to revisit such situations or cannot justify revisiting the facts under current enforcement schemes. Yet in order to emphasise the application of a particular public policy rule/*lois de police*, the court may prefer to delve deeper to ensure the implementation

---

[47] [1998] CLC 730; Sheppard, above n 45, 245.

[48] (1994) Rev Arb 359, 30 September 1993, reported in (1995) 20 *Yearbook-Commercial Arbitration* 198; Sheppard, above n 45, 245.

[49] Mayer and Sheppard, above n 29, Recommendation 3(c).

[50] The relationship between the supervisory and enforcing courts is discussed furher Sect. 6.

[51] Abdulhay Sayed, *Corruption in International Trade and Commercial Arbitration* (Wolters Kluwer, 2004) 391–394; Sayed provides examples of minimal judicial review in Switerland; see *Federal Code on Private International Law (CPIL)* (Switzerland), 18 December 1987, art 182 and 190(2); and the maximal judicial review in France's judicial practices, such as in *Westman International Ltd*, 30 September 1993, (1994) Rev. Arb. 359, and reported in (1995) 20 *Yearbook-Commercial Arbitration* 198. See also Luca G. Radicati di Brozolo, 'Arbitration and Competition Law: The Position of the Courts and of Arbitrators' (2011) 27(1) *Arbitration International* 1, 4–8.

of the law.[52] However, if the judicial review is too detailed, it may in fact lead to a retrial of the case, which indirectly denies the arbitrability of the case and creates an abuse of litigation procedure.[53]

Similarly, in dealing with arbitrability (4), opinions are also divided. Some argue the issue of arbitrablity should be solely decided by arbitration tribunals. Others insist that court intervention remains necessary under current legal schemes.[54] While the advocates of the "maximal judicial review" demand total control over the arbitrability issue by direct reference to arbitrability rules,[55] other scholars who propose the "minimal judicial review" suggest a limited review and, particularly when the tribunal or another court has made a decision on arbitrability, giving rise to an indirect review only.[56]

A more appropriate description of the courts' task should be to seek a balanced approach between the maximum and minimum review of the awards. By setting general rules to limit the judicial review of awards and create exceptions for a more comprehensive review beyond the award under limited circumstances, a balance may be achieved. In trying to achieve such a balanced approach, a few arbitration practitioners and scholars have attempted to identify the occasions in which such an exception to the general denial of re-opening the facts may exist. Di Brozolo pointed out a few conditions: first, where the award is poorly drafted and there is at least *prima facie* evidence that a deeper review is necessary; second, where there is a well-founded suspicion that the arbitrators made the award fraudulently which constituted a violation of the relevant mandatory rules; and third, where issues relating to the mandatory rule were not raised or pleaded in the arbitration proceedings, and there is a strong case to be made on that ground.[57] Di Brozolo also pointed out that, even a genuine review of the award may need to address necessary details in order to help assess whether the tribunal has properly dealt with the mandatory law issues.[58] The *ILA Final Report* also suggests that the reassessment of the underlying facts in

---

52 Ibid, 4–5, the author discusses the implementation of competition law in EU jurisdictions.

53 Ibid, 5–8; Luca G. Radicati di Brozolo, 'Mandatory Rules and International Arbitration' (2012) 23(1) *American Review of International Arbitration* 49, 55–58.

54 See for example, Stavros L. Brekoulakis, 'Chapter 2—On Arbitrability: Persisting Misconceptions and New Areas of Concern' in Loukas A. Mistelis and Stavros L. Brekoulakis (eds), *Arbitrability: International and Comparative Perspectives* (Kluwer Law International, 2009) 19, 46, suggesting tribunals should have an "exclusive" power in deciding arbitrability in the pre-arbitration stage. See also Laurence Shore, 'The United States' Perspective on "Arbitrability"' in Loukas A. Mistelis and Stavros L. Brekoulakis (ed), *Arbitrability: International and Comparative Perspectives* (Kluwer Law International 2009) 69, 73–74, discussing the *First Option* Case and the US approach.

55 Domenico di Pietro, General Remarks on Arbitrability Under the New York Convention' in Loukas A. Mistelis and Stavros L. Brekoulakis (eds), Arbitrability: International and Comparative Perspectives, (Kluwer Law International, 2009) 85, 97.

56 Ibid, 97–98.

57 Di Brozolo, above n 53, 55–60.

58 Ibid.

the dispute should be done only when there is a "strong *prima facie*" argument for a violation of public policy.[59]

In extreme circumstances, as previously defined, the courts are allowed to re-open the facts of the dispute in relation to the merits and review the evidence that was submitted before the tribunal. For example, in *Hilmarton v OTV*, the Geneva court overturned the tribunal's finding and decision on a violation of Algerian mandatory law, and held that there was no violation of the applicable Swiss law and Swiss public policy.[60] In other situations, not only may the original evidence be reviewed, but also new evidence allowed. The English courts require conditions to be met to introduce additional evidence when the original award was made on the basis of perjured evidence:

(i) *the evidence sought to be adduced is of sufficient cogency and weight to be likely to have materially influenced the arbitrators' conclusion had it been advanced at the hearing; and*
(ii) *the evidence was not available or reasonably obtainable either (a) at the time of the hearing of the arbitration; or (b) at such time as would have enabled the party concerned to have adduced it in the court of supervisory jurisdiction to support an application to reverse the arbitrators' award if such procedure were available.*[61]

Similar requirements have been identified by American courts in *Bonar v Dean Witter Reynolds Inc*, which also indicated the necessity of introducing new evidence in the judicial review stage and discussed the relevant circumstances.[62]

## 4.2 Chinese Practice

### 4.2.1 Lack of Guidance in Legislation

Chinese legislation does not provide any direction in regard to a discussion of the merits in the review of an arbitration award; there is also no guidance in regard to the acceptance of new facts and evidence at the judicial review stage in general, or in regard to facts related to the merits in particular in the judicial review of arbitral awards. Similarly, Chinese legislation does not provide any comment in dealing with the judicial review of the application of law by the tribunal and evidence in relation

[59] Mayer and Sheppard, above n 29, 262.

[60] [1999] 2 Lloyd's Law Rep. 222, reported in (1994)19 *Yearbook-* 214; Sheppard, above n 45, 245–246.

[61] *Westacre* [1998] WLR 770, also reported in (1998) 23 *Yearbook-Commercial Arbitration* 836, 878; confirmed in appeal, [1999] 2 Lloyd's Rep 65, reported in (1999) 24 *Yearbook-Commercial Arbitration* 753, 769.

[62] 835 F. 2d 1378 (11th Circ., 1988); Sheppard, above n 45, 247.

to the merits.[63] The only possible indication provided in Chapter 19 of the *CCPL* is that both the parties and any third party whose interests are involved in a case can bring objections during the enforcement stage, which may imply the introduction of new facts and evidence in a general sense at that stage.[64]

In regard to the merit review and the acceptance of new evidence in relation to the merits, one further possible indicator may be an emphasis on the distinction between a domestic award and a foreign-related and international award.[65] Some scholars have alleged that there are distinctions among judicial review schemes, particularly in regard to different sets of applicable grounds for negating awards that apply to domestic awards on the one hand, and foreign-related and international awards on the other.[66] The result is that no merit review should be allowed for the latter categories of awards.[67] This distinction is also reflected in some judicial practice.[68] Such a distinction, however, focuses mainly on general judicial review schemes; no particular attention is paid to the application of public policy.

Other scholars have observed that the rule of not reviewing the substance of an award may not be applied when considering the ground of public policy, because public policy is complex enough to include both substantive and procedural elements.[69] With little guidance from legislators, a more cautious attitude might be developed on a case-by-case basis in judicial practice, as is discussed in the next section.

### 4.2.2 The SPC's Approach and Possible Problems Arising from It

Regarding the application of public policy, one major achievement is that the SPC declared that the substantive outcome of cases should not be regarded as a basis for applying public policy. In *Dongfeng*, the Kaifeng HPC's opinion to refuse the enforcement of an award was made on the basis that such award might have an adverse

---

63 An early version of the *CCPL's* provision in regulating judicial review of domestic awards included the wrongful recognition of facts and erroneous application of law, as distinguished from the judicial review scheme of foreign-related awards, which may indicate that the latter would not review factual issues and application of law. This provision, however, is deleted in the 2012 *CCPL*.

64 *CCPL*, art 281.

65 Sections 4.3, 4.4 and 4.5 in Chap. 3.

66 Sections 4.4 and 4.5 in Chap. 3; particularly, the grounds to negate domestic awards, including the fraud in taking forged evidence and hiding evidence, but the grounds to negate foreign-related or international awards do not include these grounds.

67 赵秀文[Zhao Xiuwen],《民诉法关于国际仲裁规定的不足与完善》[The Drawbacks in the CCPL's Provisions Concerning International Arbitration and Their Perfection] (2013) 9 法治研究 *Research on Rule of Law* 35, 38–39. Zhao states that such an approach for domestic awards is in fact a review of the substance of the case.

68 See the next paragraph further.

69 赵秀文[Zhao Xiuwen], above n 67, 39; 于喜富[Yu Xifu],《国际商事仲裁的司法监督与协助——兼论中国的立法与司法实践》[Judicial Supervision and Assistance of International Commercial Arbitration: Comments on China's Legislative and Judicial Practices] (Intellectual Property Rights Press, 2006) 404.

influence on State property, and that opinion based on facts and the substance of the dispute was rejected by the SPC. The SPC also made similar statements in a series of cases, including *Gaoxin, Xiangjin* and *Weimao*.[70] As it stated in *Tianjin Xianda*:

> ... the People's courts do not have the sufficient power to review the nature of the legal relationship being recognised by the tribunal as well as the arbitral result in accordance with the relevant provisions regarding foreign-related arbitration in the *CCPL* and *CAL*.[71]

Similar statements were also found in *Handiboke*.[72] Judge Liu Chunmei also stated that the public policy exception should not include the five situations that invalidated the applicable contracts.[73] These statements reflect the international trend to restrict the judicial review of underlying contracts.

It is notable, however, that the SPC did not clarify whether any discussion of the substance of a case should be excluded in applying public policy. Some scholars have referred to *Tianjin Xianda,* and have argued that the SPC suggested that the judicial review should focus solely on procedural issues. It is notable, however, that the SPC only referred to the first paragraph of the *CCPL's* Article 281 when stating that only procedural issues are to be reviewed, which does not cover the public policy exception; thus, the alleged strict exclusion of any review of substantive issues in arbitral awards may not apply to public policy issues.[74] In reality, some public policy elements would undeniably be relevant to the substance of a case, including substantive fundamental principles (1a), public policy rules (2), and arbitrability (4).[75]

A problematic consequence of such an alleged exclusion in dealing with substantive aspects of the arbitral awards is that the courts in China lack sufficient guidance when actually facing substantive issues and in dealing with requests to review the substance of an award, and even in considering previous or new evidence in their judicial review. On one hand, lack of guidance may lead courts to avoid any discussions of the substantive aspects of an award. Furthermore, if the judiciary denies any possibility of reviewing the substantive aspects of an award, arbitration practitioners—both the arbitrators and counsels—would not have an incentive to bind themselves to a consideration of substantive public policy. On the other hand, though the SPC declared that the substance of cases is not to be reviewed, judicial practice shows otherwise. Discussion of the substance of an award is observed at different

---

[70] Section 3.2 in Chap. 5.

[71] See Chap. 5.

[72] See 胡建新 [Hu Jianxin],《汉迪波克公司申请承认和执行外国海事仲裁裁决案》[Handiboke Co Applying Recognition and Enforcement of a Foreign Maritime Arbitral Award] (2010) 中国水运报 China Water Transport, 16 June 2010.

[73] 刘春梅[Liu Chunmei],《申请撤销涉外及外国仲裁裁决案件司法审查中发现的具体问题》[Detailed Issues in Judicial Review of Cases Dealing with Application of Annulment and Enforcement of Foreign-Related and Foreign Arbitral Awards], in 韩健[Han Jian] (ed.),《涉外仲裁司法审查》[Judicial Review of Foreign-Related Arbitral Awards]386, 408. Liu is a judge of the Beijing Second HPC.

[74] See discussions around above n 66 and n 67.

[75] Section 2 in Chap. 5.

levels of courts. Many lower courts have discussed the substance of arbitration cases: in *Foshan*, the Foshan IPC based its ruling on its evaluation of the significance of the factual issues and held that the failure to pay the debt was not significant enough to constitute a violation of public policy. In *Wildcat*, the Anhui HPC held that the enforcement of the arbitral award would cause the abandonment of all State-invested machinery, and thus infringed the State's economic interests and was contrary to China's public policy.

Even the SPC itself, in some cases, went beyond the award and evaluated the substance of the dispute. In *Heavy Metal*, the SPC adopted a factually based analysis by holding that the breach of the contract was caused by the US party's activities and therefore that such a breach in itself (performing heavy metal music) was in violation of China's social and public order; that the CIETAC award ignored such facts including the administrative order based on those facts; and that the enforcement of the award was contrary to China's social public interests.[76] In *Bunge*, the SPC analysed the applicability of the mandatory rules or administrative order directly, such as AQSIQ's notice in the particular dispute, rather than by referring to the tribunal's relevant decision on the issue.[77]

These discussions of the facts in the underlying dispute rather than the awards may actually conflict with the alleged exclusion of any review of the substance of an award. The lack of sufficient guidance provided by legislation and judicial interpretations may be a major reason for such inconsistencies. The traditional hostility adopted by Chinese courts in dealing with the jurisdiction of arbitration may also contribute to this phenomenon, particularly given that the power of the tribunal is not fully respected in China's arbitration practice.[78] A reassessment of the court's role in judicial review would remind the Chinese judiciary to focus on the review of awards, rather than positioning themselves as the ultimate decision-maker of the dispute. In doing so, more attention may be given to distinguishing the award from the underlying transaction and to establishing the exception by which a court can examine the substance of a dispute beyond that award.

Lack of sufficient guidance in regard to the acceptance of new evidence and facts is also observed and has influenced the application of public policy specifically. One area of progress made by Chinese courts in dealing with new evidence is that they have consistently rejected claims to submit evidence that was once rejected by the tribunal. They have also clearly confirmed the tribunal's right to accept or not accept evidence. The SPC has also denied the claim that some evidence was forged which was accepted without question during arbitration proceedings in *Tianhe*; a similar ruling was made in *Tianjin Xianda*, where the SPC decided that the tribunal's refusal to review a particular piece of evidence in the execution of their powers should not be reviewed.

[76] Sections 4.2 and 4.3 in Chap. 5.

[77] See Chap. 7. As the SPC states, their decision is made based on "the facts stated in the report" of the AQSIQ notice, rather than an evaluation of the award.

[78] Section 4 in Chap. 3, discussing the limited power of the tribunals under the Chinese arbitration system.

However, the practice of Chinese courts is not clear in dealing with newly submitted evidence on other occasions, particularly when such evidence may be relevant in making to public policy arguments. In *Shin-Etsu (No. 1)*, the Nantong IPC and Jiangsu HPC relied on new evidence in dealing with forged affidavits. Also in *Foshan*, the Foshan IPC, in negating the argument that there was a possible violation of public policy, held that the existence and repayment of a debt by one party to another was an event prior to the creation of a debt to a third party (who claimed the annulment of the arbitral award), and thus was not a violation of any public policy element. It is more likely that such a conclusion was reached on the basis of new submissions than a mere confirmation of the original award, given that the third party was not involved in the arbitration proceedings and its submissions were new to the arbitration proceeding.[79]

The SPC, however, seems more cautious when dealing with new evidence; yet such an attitude is not expressly and consistently presented. In *GRD Minproc*, the Shanghai 1st IPC sought an explanation from research institutions in relation to the new evidence submitted by Feilun in order to evaluate the pollution caused by the disputed machine. The evidence given by those institutions formed the basis of the court's finding that there had been a violation of public policy. This opinion, however, was overturned by the SPC, which held that the tribunal's decision to take evidence on the merits should be generally respected. In *Louis Dreyfus*, the Zhanjiang IPC required the relevant governmental body, the AQSIQ, to interpret the meaning, scope and consequences of their administrative orders and evaluated the possible breach of public policy rules on that basis.[80] The SPC did not directly respond to this new evidence, but made its decision on the basis that the disputed soybeans, after they had been carefully treated, were not detrimental to environment and public health in China. It was not possible to determine whether such an evaluation, which was crucial to the decision, was made with respect to the original award, or whether the newly submitted AQSIQ interpretation was also taken into consideration.

It is also notable that the SPC has recognised that the application of law in arbitration proceedings is a part of fact-finding and should not be reviewed as an issue that is subject to public policy. In *Louis Dreyfus*, for example, the tribunal ruled against the application of Chinese law, declaring that it was "differently applied in practice than it looks" and should not be respected in the arbitration proceedings. The SPC did not consider this declaration as a violation of public policy, but rather as a mere declaration that did not influence the result of the ruling and enforcement of the award. Similarly, in *Handiboke*, the wrongful acknowledgement of the relevant Chinese law was considered as the fact-finding of the tribunal, and excluded from the

---

[79] See also discussion in Sect. 5.3.2 in Chap. 5.

[80] The *Louis Dreyfus Case* in Chap. 7.

scope of judicial review; thus, public policy was not considered.[81] This recognition is an important development in narrowing the scope of judicial review.

In concluding that the Chinese courts' performance in limiting its extent of judicial review and its acceptance of new facts and evidence is not satisfactory, particularly when compared with the international practices, the author suggests the following improvements ought to be considered by Chinese legislators and judicial practitioners:

- Introducing some preliminary steps e.g., by implementing the SPC's judicial interpretations;
- That courts should adopt a consistent approach;
- That this approach should be based on Chinese experience, international trends, as expressed through practice and academic study; and
- Clearly defined in the *Civil Procedure Law* outlining both general rules restricting what can be considered in judicial reviews, and exceptions relating to new facts and evidence that might apply in extreme circumstances.

It is also suggested that the *ILA Report*'s approach, as well as the English courts' discussion in *Westacre* may be considered in structuring the rules for exceptions.

## 5 Waiver and Estoppel in Applying Public Policy

An additional issue in relation to the application of public policy is whether there is any waiver or an estoppel that bars the application of public policy. An example of a waiver may be found in *Techno v IDTS*,[82] in which the US Court of Appeals for the 2nd Circuit held that IDTS had already waived its claims of fraud and bribery against the tribunal, as they did not bring forward such a claim during the arbitration proceeding after noting the facts and evidence.

The applicability of waiver or estoppel, however, is controversial, and the courts' attitude towards its application may vary, depending on the particular situation of a case and the different elements of public policy involved. For example, it is likely that a waiver or estoppel is applicable in dealing with procedural public policy elements when the parties fail to argue the relevant public policy issues before the tribunal.[83] This is probably because procedural issues not argued during the arbitration proceedings are assumed to be implicitly consented to by the parties. Also, parties are not encouraged to take a "wait and see" strategy, and benefit at a later stage from an

[81] See http://www.wunscharb.com/court-decisions/handiboke-case-2009; 胡建新 [Hu Jianxin],《汉迪波克公司申请承认和执行外国海事仲裁裁决案》[Handiboke Co Applying Recognition and Enforcement of a Foreign Maritime Arbitral Award] (2010) 中国水运报 China Water Transport, 16 June 2010.

[82] *AAOT Foreign Economic Association (VO) Technostroyexort v International Development and Trade Services Inc*,139 F 3d 980(2nd Cir, 1998).

[83] Mayer and Sheppard, above n 29, 260, Recommendation 2(c).

earlier silence.[84] A waiver may also be argued in dealing with arbitrability, particularly when the tribunal may have already dealt with the issue with the consent of the parties, despite the issue being arguably non-arbitrable in some national legal systems.[85] Generally, a tribunal would have a prior opportunity to review the issue before its arbitrability was argued later at the stage of the enforcement of the arbitral award[86]; thus, the tribunal's power to balance the relevant facts and the possible applicable law should be generally respected in dealing with arbitrability.[87] Conversely, *lois de police* may still apply, even if the parties fail to argue it at first instance. This is consistent with the commonly accepted mandatory nature of *lois de police* that cannot be waived or contractually excluded.[88]

In representing the international consensus, the *ILA Final Report* confirmed that the parties' failure to raise the argument in relation to fundamental principles before the arbitration tribunal during arbitration proceedings might constitute a waiver.[89] Such a waiver is particularly applicable to procedural public policy,[90] as noted by the report, and evidenced by the time requirement imposed to bring challenges of bias against anarbitrator.[91] But the *ILA Final Report* also noted its limitations: first, it depends on the capability of the party to note the violation of the principle and to raise it before the tribunal during arbitration proceedings, or to challenge it in court or in the arbitration forum.[92] Secondly, the waiver may only be established when the involved fundamental principle is universally accepted as international public policy. For example, the impartiality of an arbitration tribunal operates as a universal principle, while shari'a law is only recognised as a fundamental principle in Muslim jurisdictions.[93]

In China's arbitration and judicial practice, the discussion about waiver is limited to procedural issues. Most of the arbitration rules provide such a waiver. For example, the *CIETAC Rules* 2012 state that,

> *A party shall be deemed to have waived its right to object where it knows or should have known that any provision of, or requirement under, these Rules has not been complied with and yet participates in or proceeds with the arbitration proceedings without promptly and explicitly submitting its objection in writing to such non-compliance.*[94]

---

[84] For example, represented *Gao Haiyanet al v Keeneye Holdings Limited,* HCCT No. 41/2010; CACV No. 79/2011 (Hong Kong, 2011).

[85] Gary B. Born, *International Commercial Arbitration* (Kluwer Law International, 2nd ed, 2014) 3311–3312.

[86] Ibid.

[87] Brekoulakis, above n 54, 41–42.

[88] Sections 2.1 and 2.2 in Chap. 7. It is also confirmed in cases dealing with EU competition law; *Linde AG v Halyvourgiki AE,* 2010 Rev arb 124 (Paris Courd'appel, 22 October 2009).

[89] Mayer and Sheppard, above n 29, recommendation 2(c).

[90] Ibid, 260.

[91] For example, art 13(2) of the *UNCITRAL Model Law* provides that a challenge to an arbitrator on basis of bias shall be made within a specific period since the bias issues were noted by the party.

[92] Mayer and Sheppard, above n 29, 260.

[93] Ibid.

[94] *CIETAC Arbitration Rules* (2012), art 10.

In *Contestar*, the Guangzhou Maritime Court held that the Chinese party abandoned its own opportunity to claim nonconformity by not responding to the arbitration procedures and the tribunal's orders, and thus was not entitled to argue the later proceedings as procedural errors. However, this issue is considered under the ground of nonconformity with an arbitration rule rather than as a violation of public policy.[95]

Yet a waiver subject to arbitration rules cannot fully solve all the problems arising in arbitration proceedings, because there are still many procedural issues not covered by the arbitration rules; this happens particularly when proceedings are conducted within the discretion of the tribunal or under the internal case-management of an arbitration commission. Also, some discretionary powers of the tribunal, which may be permitted by arbitration rules, still constitute a breach of due process or public policy. In practice, most of the challenges in later judicial reviews arise in relation to issues that are not covered or justified by the applicable arbitration rules.

Examples can be found in a series of challenges when enforcement of CIETAC arbitral awards was sought in Hong Kong. In *Polytek*,[96] the Hong Kong Court of Final Appeal found that the losing party intentionally held the procedural issue as a "back up" during the entire arbitration proceeding and waited until after the awards—which were not beneficial to them—were made to make such a claim. It then held that this activity amounted to a situation in which the court would use its discretionary power and not apply public policy.[97] Such an approach was also adopted in *Keeneye*, where the challenge to the use of mediation practices in arbitration was also brought after the award had been rendered. Such a challenge was also rejected on the basis of a waiver.[98]

These cases remind us of the incomplete regulation scheme provided by Chinese legislation and arbitration rules to govern arbitration proceedings, which may cause the application of public policy when a procedural error occurs[99]; and the lack of guidance to apply a waiver to negate the application of public policy in the absence of rules provided by legislation and arbitration rules. The author suggests that the waiver of certain public policy arguments should be governed by a comprehensive

---

[95] 塞浦路斯康特斯达航运有限公司申请承认和执行伦敦仲裁裁决案 [Case Concerning the Application of Cyprus Contestar Shipping Co Ltd for Recognition and Enforcement of London Arbitral Award] Guangzhou Maritime Court, (1997) 广海发湛字5号[Zhanjiang Tribunal No. 5], 15 July 1998.

[96] *Polytek Engineering Company Ltd v Hebei Import &Export Corp.*, High Court of the Hong Kong Special Administrative Region, Court of Appeal, 16 January 1998, Civil Appeal No. 116 of 1997, reported in (1998) 23 *Yearbook- Commercial Arbitration* 666 (Hong Kong No. 12).

[97] Ibid; see also Weixia Gu, '15 Years of the Handover: The Rise, Discontent, and Positive Interaction of Cross-border Arbitration in Hong Kong with Mainland China' (2013) 9 *East Asia Law Review* 42, 65–66, commenting on the waiver issue.

[98] *Gao Haiyan et al. v Keeneye Holdings Limited* [2011]CACV No. 79, [2012] 1HKRD 650 (Court of Appeal).

[99] See also Chap. 6, particularly Sect. 6.1, for the discussion of the relationship between Art V(1)(d), "inconformity", and Art (2)(b), "public policy", in China's judicial practice.

set of rules provided by Chinese arbitration legislation; and that the scope of these public policy arguments should be considered in detail.

## 6 Evaluation of the Performance of the Chinese Courts

### *6.1 General Performance of the Chinese Courts in Applying Public Policy in the Judicial Review of Arbitral Awards*

The Chinese judiciary have gradually acknowledged that it is important to limit the application of public policy in the judicial review of arbitral awards and have intended to do so.[100] The current trend to limit the application of public policy, as indicated in recent cases such as *Bunge*,[101] can be clearly distinguished from the expansive approach adopted by some lower courts in earlier cases, such as *Dongfeng*. The latter may no longer be a representation of the understanding of public policy in China.[102] This progress signals the rapid development of the modern Chinese arbitration system, together with China's economic prosperity. Other developments include some theoretical studies written by judges, which further influence decision-making in judicial practice.[103]

The overall impression, however, is that the Chinese judiciary is reluctant or not confident enough to handle the issue of public policy. Judges appear to be more comfortable relying on the grounds that are easier to apply, and thus avoid the opportunity to develop several key elements of public policy. This is widely reflected in cases such as *Shin-Etsu (No. 2)*, where the SPC held that *res judicata* is a procedural rule provided by law and arbitration rules, rather than procedural public policy.[104] Also, it seems that the Chinese judiciary is not yet ready to recognise any public policy rules/ *lois de police* based on their significance, even though some of them have been recognised in other jurisdictions.[105] Furthermore, there is no clear answer as to whether the Chinese courts have developed a comprehensive approach in applying public policy, e.g., establishing rules for deal with the facts and merits of the underlying disputes and accepting new evidence, or considering whether there is a waiver if the parties have failed to argue certain public policy issues in previous proceedings.[106]

---

[100] For the detailed data and analysis of the enforcement rate, see Sects. 2 and 4 in Chap. 4.

[101] Section 3.5 in Chap. 7.

[102] Section 5 in Chap. 5; Yongping Xiao and Zhengxin Huo, 'Ordre Public in China's Private International Law' (2005) 53 *American Journal of Comparative Law* 654, 660.

[103] For example, Judge Gao's study as discussed in Sect. 5 in Chap. 3 and further in Sect. 2.2 in Chap. 7. Its influence is discussed in Sect. 3.7 in Chap. 7.

[104] Section 4 in Chap. 6.

[105] Particularly the regulation of financial markets, in Sect. 3.3 in Chap. 7; and the rules of competition law, in Sect. 3.4 in Chap. 7.

[106] See above Sects. 4 and 5.

It is also observed that many judicial decisions, particularly early ones, are abstract, which also highlights the Chinese judiciary's limited capability to deal with complicated legal reasoning in relation to public policy.[107] In recent years, however, the SPC has made progress in providing more comprehensive discussion of public policy in a series of cases. The explanation and interpretation of public policy adopted by the courts has significantly increased.[108]

An overall conclusion is that a lack of consistent and advanced discussion of public policy is observed in China's judicial practice. The reluctance of the judiciary to develop and apply public policy makes this legal concept less meaningful in the context of judicial practice.[109] Such reluctance is based on a lack of a formal and consistent scheme that covers and regulates judicial review, particularly in the following respects: the internal management of the courts, the improvement of case-management, the distinction, if any, between the court's role as a supervisory court or an enforcing court, the relationship between different levels of courts, and a consistent approach in applying public policy. The following sections further examine how the current Chinese judicial system performs in these aspects.

## 6.2 *Chinese Courts as Supervisory Courts and Enforcing Courts*

The Chinese judiciary plays a significant role as both the supervisory court of arbitral awards made in China, and as the enforcing court of both these awards made in China and awards made outside China whose enforcement is sought in China. Generally, the two roles are identical in many respects, particularly when dealing with foreign-related awards and international awards. Thus, in our discussion of the performance of courts in applying public policy in reviewing these awards, the distinction between their roles as supervisory courts or enforcing courts is not addressed.

There are also several other reasons why the distinction between the Chinese courts' role as supervisory courts and enforcing courts are not emphasised. One reason is that the *CCPL* has adopted schemes of judicial review that are identical to the *NYC* and the *UNCITRAL Model Law* for the judicial review of foreign-related awards, making it identical to the judicial review of international awards in China. This equivalence is consistent with the schemes provided in the *UNCITRAL Model Law*.[110] In addition, the Prior Reporting System applies to both foreign-related awards

[107] For example, *Dongfeng* and *Heavy Metal* in Chap. 5.

[108] For example, *Louis Dreyfus, the Tianrui,* and *Shin Etsu (No. 2).* See Sect. 3 in Chap. 7; Sect. 4 in Chap. 6.

[109] 张宪初 [Zhang Xianchu],《外国商事仲裁裁决司法审查"公共政策"理论与实践的新发展》[Recent Theoretical and Practical Developments in Applying Public Policy in the Judicial Review of Arbitral Awards in Foreign Jurisdictions], in 韩健[Han Jian] (ed),《涉外仲裁司法审查》[Judicial Review of Foreign-Related Arbitration] (法律出版社 [Law Press], 2006) 359, 394.

[110] Section 3 in Chap. 3.

and international awards and helps to maintain consistency in the practice of Chinese courts engaged in the judicial review of arbitral awards generally.[111]

Based on these identical schemes, Chinese courts generally adopt the same approach in the general practice of judicial review and in identifying and applying public policy in particular when performing as a supervisory court and an enforcing court. The rate of recognition in upholding arbitration awards is similar, and the trend to limit the application of public policy is observed in both categories of cases.[112] Chinese courts do not distinguish between the different wording in the *CAL* and the *CCPL* as "social public interest" and "public policy" in the *NYC*.[113]

### 6.2.1 Chinese Courts as Supervisory Courts

The role of Chinese courts in the annulment of foreign-related awards is not particularly emphasised in legislation. According to the *CCPL*, their power in annulment proceedings is generally identical to their power in enforcement proceedings; the public policy exception is generally recognised within this scheme of judicial review.[114]

The overall performance of the Chinese courts in supervising arbitration awards on the ground of public policy is also rarely contested. The conflict between the Chinese courts' role as supervisory courts and their role as enforcing courts is also not significant. However, the co-existence of supervisory and enforcement judicial reviews in China may produce the problem of "double-checking", meaning that an arbitral award can be reviewed twice by different courts. This problem is likely to be resolved by Article 26 of the *2006 Interpretation,*[115] at least for foreign-related cases. "Double-checking" is not a big problem in interpreting public policy, because of the function of the Prior Reporting System.[116] This is also confirmed by statistical studies.[117]

The discussion on Chinese courts as supervisory courts is more significant in the global context, and particularly in regard to the application of public policy. Foreign courts, when reviewing an arbitral award made in China, may consider the Chinese courts' decision as that of a supervisory court. Generally, the public policy argument that is not dealt with, or not supported by the courts at the place of arbitration, may not necessarily influence later judicial proceedings for the enforcement of arbitral awards

[111] Section 3 in Chap. 3.

[112] Sections 2 and 4 in Chap. 4.

[113] Section 5 in Chap. 3.

[114] Section 4 in Chap. 3.

[115] 《最高人民法院关于适用〈中华人民共和国仲裁法〉若干问题的解释》[Supreme People's Court's Interpretation on Several Issues in Regards of the Application of the China Arbitration Law] (People's Republic of China), Supreme People's Court, Fa Shi [2006] No 7, 26 December 2005, art 26. It states that if an award that was held not annulled by a supervisory court in China, if challenged on the same grounds in the enforcement stage, the challenge should be refused.

[116] Section 4 in Chap. 3.

[117] Section 4 in Chap. 4.

in other jurisdictions.[118] This is confirmed in *Polytek*, where the court clearly stated that a party need not pursue its remedy in the supervisory court before bringing its argument to the enforcing court, because public policy in the forum of the enforcing State may be different.[119] It is also confirmed by the *ILA Report* that it is not generally accepted that exhausting the remedies of the forum is a pre-condition to claiming public policy in the enforcing State.[120]

In some cases, however, the enforcing court has taken into consideration the decision of the supervisory court at the place of arbitration, in this discussion, the Chinese courts dealing with public policy issues. In *Ferco*,[121] in dealing with a "natural justice" argument raised by Ferco as a public policy defence, the English court recognised that the issue had already been dealt with by the court at the arbitration seat, and that its decision should be taken into consideration.[122] The English court found the decision of the Chinese court confirming the finality of the award as a strong policy consideration, subject only to exceptional situations involving "an obvious and serious disregard for basic principles of justice by the arbitrators or where for unjust reasons, such as corruption, they decline to do so".[123]

In this case, Ferco applied to annul the original award before the Beijing 2nd IPC, arguing that they were not given an opportunity to challenge some evidence. However, when the Beijing 2nd IPC annulled the award and ordered the matter to be arbitrated again, Ferco failed to raise the issue that they argued before the Beijing 2nd IPC and did not challenge that evidence again. Thus, the tribunal made an award on the same terms as in the original arbitration. When Ferco again sued to annul that award, the Beijing 2nd IPC rejected its argument and held it was a waiver, as it was given the opportunity in the second arbitration proceeding to present evidence on the issue, but failed to do so. The English court also considered it as a waiver by taking into consideration the decision of the Beijing 2nd IPC.[124] Similarly, in *Keeneye*, the Hong Kong court also respected the judgment of the supervisory court, the Xi'an IPC in China, when it rejected the impartiality argument of the tribunal and staff from the arbitration commission.[125] Even though the Hong Kong court's judgment was made on the basis of Hong Kong public policy, they also respected that the court at

---

[118] See the *NYC*, art V(2)(b), … "public policy of that country".

[119] Gu, above n 97, 65–66.

[120] Mayer and Sheppard, above n 29, 260.

[121] [1999] 1 All ER (Comm) 315, reported in (1999) 24 *Yearbook-Commercial Arbitration* 739 (UK No. 53).

[122] Minmetals sought enforcement of a CIETAC arbitral award in UK. Ferco argued that the evidence relied upon by the tribunal in determining the case was not shown to Ferco, and therefore natural justice was breached. However, before the enforcement proceedings, Ferco had brought forward the same argument in the Beijing Court in order to set aside the award, and the argument had been rejected. *Ferco*[1999] 1 All ER, [24]-[26].

[123] *Ibid,* [25].

[124] *Ibid,* [26].

[125] See Sect. 2 in Chap. 6.

the place of arbitration was in a better position to determine the nature of mediation activities based on the distinct legal culture of that forum.[126]

These cases show the enforcing courts' general reliance on the finality of awards and the decision of the supervisory court regarding possible procedural errors in an arbitration case. The influence of this reliance is particularly significant in the application of procedural public policy. In *Ferco*, the English court listed the following factors to decide whether a supervisory court's decision should be taken into consideration in the application of procedural fundamental principles:

(i) the nature of the procedural injustice;
(ii) whether the enforcee has invoked the supervisory jurisdiction of the seat of the arbitration;
(iii) whether a remedy was available under that jurisdiction;
(iv) whether the courts of that jurisdiction have conclusively determined the enforcee's complaint in favour of upholding the award;
(v) whether the enforcee has failed to invoke that remedial jurisdiction, for what reason and in particular whether he was acting unreasonably in failing to do so.[127]

Though the recognition of the supervisory court's decision by the enforcing court is not a universally accepted practice,[128] the supervisory court's role in the proceedings of arbitration and enforcement should not be ignored in general and in particular in the practice of applying public policy. This reminds both the Chinese courts and the Chinese arbitration system of the significance of the courts' role as the supervisory court, and their influence in applying public policy. It also reminds both courts and arbitrators of the need to recognise the possibility of an award being enforced in China and for a consistent approach to applying public policy in different local courts. They also need to recognise the possibility of the award being enforced in foreign jurisdictions and for supervisory courts to provide qualified and reliable decisions, in order to obtain the general respect of enforcing courts.

### 6.2.2 Chinese Courts as the Enforcing Courts and Public Policy

Most of the significant cases regarding the identification and application of public policy are cases in which the Chinese courts have functioned as the enforcing court of foreign-related and international awards. The overall performance of Chinese courts has been in favour of the enforcement of such awards. This conclusion is reached on the basis that there is a reasonably high enforcement rate.[129]

---

[126] Keeneye [2012] 1HKRD 650, 659; Gu, above n 97, 82.

[127] *Ferco*[1999] 1 All ER, [26].

[128] For example, the French courts' attitude is that the annulment of the award in the place of arbitration would not necessarily cause the non-enforcement of the award in other jurisdiction. Emmanuel Gaillard and John Savage (eds), *Fouchard Gaillard Goldman on International Commercial Arbitration* (Kluwer Law International, 1999) 33–34.

[129] Section 2.2 in Chap. 4.

Generally, Chinese courts adopt a very cautious attitude and are usually reluctant to comment on the application of public policy.[130] This is consistent with the facilitation of the enforcement of arbitral awards in a global context, but it may also be an illustration that the Chinese courts have not established a consistent and comprehensive understanding of public policy, nor developed a well-rounded approach in applying it.[131] It is also notable that, Chinese courts have not yet expressly emphasised China's own public policy when enforcing a foreign award, which is distinguishable from the public policy of the place of arbitration, nor appreciate the similarities between them under the converging public policy in international practice.[132]

## 6.3 The Functioning of the Prior Reporting System in Applying Public Policy

One major feature of the judicial review of arbitral awards in China is the Prior Reporting System, which requires the decision to annul or not enforce foreign-related and international arbitral awards to be reported to HPCs and the SPC.[133] It is a major scheme that covers the judicial review of arbitral awards, including the application and interpretation of public policy. As noted previously, the Prior Reporting System is not a system of appeal, but rather an internal management scheme in the court system.[134]

Many commentators have recognised the significance of the Prior Reporting System, as it limits the chance of non-enforcement of foreign-related awards and international awards. The Prior Reporting System was established as a response to the abuse of public policy as shown in *Dongfeng*, and functions well in limiting the application of the public policy exception, which is represented by the SPC's frequent rejection of lower courts' attempts to apply public policy.[135] Such a strategy was adopted by the SPC to prevent the trend of local protectionism in the application of public policy.

Yet the Prior Reporting System's contribution to the clarification of the concept of public policy, or the identification of several key elements of public policy, is limited. This is partly due to the inherent characteristics of the system as an internal-management scheme rather than a system of appeal.[136] The higher courts, particularly the SPC, are less motivated to reply to each issue and to provide detailed legal

---

[130] Section 4 in Chap. 4, particularly Sects. 4.2, 4.3 and 4.4.

[131] Sections 4 and 5.

[132] Discussions of the national nature of public policy under the NYC and the converging trend in recent practice, see Sect. 4 in Chap. 2. See also Sect. 2 for China's approach.

[133] Sections 3 and 4 in Chap. 3.

[134] Ibid.

[135] Jinzhou Tao, *Arbitration Law and Practice in China* (Kluwer International, 2012) 204–05. See also Sects. 4 in Chap. 3 and Sect. 4 in Chap. 4.

[136] Section 4 in Chap. 4.

analyses, because the reporting system is not an appeal system and does not impose on them an obligation to reply and to provide detailed legal reasoning. The lower courts also lack the motivation to perfect their statements in their reports, as it is not a formal judicial decision; all they need to do is to list all possible grounds and conflicting opinions.[137]

It is also notable that the Prior Reporting System has other practical limitations and cannot cover all aspects of arbitral awards. The Prior Reporting System is not established by legislation but by the SPC's judicial interpretation; limited by this fact, its implementation is not regulated by law, but is largely a self-regulatory aspect within the court system. It does not ensure that all cases are properly reported, which tends to undermine its effectiveness.[138] Also, it is doubtful whether the Prior Reporting System is the final procedure in the judicial review of an arbitral award because of the trial supervision proceedings in China's judicial system.[139] None of these factors assist the Prior Reporting System in fulfilling its purpose to limit the non-enforcement of awards or to establish a comprehensive and well-rounded approach in applying public policy.

To summarise, the Prior Reporting System contributes to the advancement of China's performance in the judicial review of arbitral awards in general and the application of public policy in particular.[140] Yet the functioning of the Prior Reporting System is restricted by its nature as a temporary tool of case-management, and its distinctive characteristics sometimes even bar the development of the comprehensive and consistent approach of interpreting the public policy in the judicial review of arbitral awards.[141] Even though it is undeniable that the Prior Reporting System functions as part of China's current judicial system in applying public policy, and will continue to function in this way in the near future, the judiciary and arbitration practitioners should be aware of how it functions and make best use of this scheme in developing their understanding of public policy.

## *6.4 Problems and Proposed Reforms in China's Judicial System*

This study also highlights a number of problems that may arise in China's judicial system in the judicial review of arbitral awards, as listed in Chap. 3. Some of these were reflected and discussed in the case study in Part II (Chaps. 4–8). This section focuses on some of the significant issues that may influence the interpretation and

---

[137] Ibid.

[138] Section 4 in Chap. 4, nn 123, referring to cases in which the Prior Reporting System was not followed.

[139] Ibid; this is further confirmed by *Huayuan*; see Sect. 2.2 in Chap. 8; see also *Guangxia*, as illustrated in Sect. 4 in Chap. 4.

[140] Section 4 in Chap. 4.

[141] Discussed in Chaps. 3 and 4.

application of public policy in particular and further examines the Chinese judiciary's progress towards resolving these problems.

The internal structure of the Chinese courts, which provides possibly uncertain proceedings and an unpredictable decision-making process,[142] significantly influences the application of public policy. Judicial committees have been substantially involved in some cases and have played an important role in providing opinions with respect to the application of public policy[143]; while in most of other cases, judicial committees they have not been involved. The uncertain nature of the procedures may be a significant barrier to the development of a comprehensive understanding of public policy, as it may either be discussed thoroughly or omitted from discussion, depending on the decision-maker's knowledge and understanding. In addition, different tribunals of the same court, for example, the SPC, may reach different decisions on similar issues due to the lack of an efficient internal-management system.[144]

In addition, the SPC's role in dealing with arbitral awards and applying public policy is yet to be fully respected and emphasised in judicial practice. Though the SPC generally enjoys the final say through the Prior Reporting System, the SPC's opinions in regard to arbitration is only binding in the particular case and is not generally applied as its formal judicial interpretation. Only selected cases of the SPC cases are published.[145] The lack of a systematic case-reporting system within the SPC probably accounts for the slow development of a consistent approach to public policy.

Furthermore, the large number of local courts and the quality of the judiciary in these courts has also restrained the developments of public policy. These concerns include the quality of judicial decisions, inconsistencies in judicial decisions, errors in distinguishing a review of the underlying disputes from a review of the award, and a reluctance to evaluate public policy.[146] Also, some erroneous ideas and problematic approaches to judicial review, for example, a denial of the impartiality of arbitrators as a possible element of public policy, have been reported.[147] The lack of a consistent approach in taking into account new facts and evidence may have also caused the judiciary's limited and inconsistent understanding of public policy.[148]

Based on these comments on the current performance of the Chinese courts, the author suggests that such performance need to be improved and that there needs to be ongoing reform of the Chinese judicial system to resolve the problems inherent

---

142 Section 2.2 in Chap. 3.

143 See for example, *Wildcat* and *GRD Minproc*as discussed in Chap. 5.

144 One significant example is where the SPC gave significantly different opinions with respect to the arbitrability of two cases that had substantially identical facts. See Sect. 3.2.3 in Chap. 8, discussing *Jiacheng* and *Yongxin*.

145 Section 3.2 in Chap. 3.

146 Section 4 in Chap. 3; Discussed in Chaps. 4–8, for example, the distinction between the underlying disputes and the awards in Chap. 8, as concluded in Sect. 3.

147 Section 2 in Chap. 6.

148 Section 4.

in the system, such as the quality of staff, lack of transparency and efficiency, the problem of corruption, as well as local protectionism.[149] While the introduction of specialisation has improved the performance of the Chinese judiciary, the Fourth Civil Branch of the SPC should emphasise its specialisation in dealing with foreign-related commercial and maritime disputes and continue to publish its important case decisions, guiding the practice of lower courts and legal practitioners.[150] The Chinese International Commercial Court may also play a significant role in centralising and furthering the development of a high-quality case pool in the context of the judicial review of international commercial arbitration.[151] These efforts will hopefully reduce the negative effects previously discussed.

In addition, the author also suggests that the improvement of the Chinese judiciary's performance in defining and applying public policy also depends on the clarification of the role of the courts in the judicial review of arbitral awards. The author notes that the Chinese judicial system is now promoting the establishment and advancement of a multi-perspective dispute resolution mechanism combining litigation, arbitration and mediation for international commercial disputes,[152] and consider the improvement of the performance in applying the public policy ground in the judicial review of arbitral awards a significant step towards this aim.

In this regard, it is proposed by the author that an internal control system among different levels of courts (for example, advancement of the current Prior Reporting System) be established; a clear definition of the roles of supervisory and enforcing courts be provided in legislation; and that this guidance provided by legislation be part of the reforms suggested above.

---

[149] Sections 2 and 4 in Chap. 3. See also, the Supreme People's Court, 《最高人民法院关于全面深化人民法院改革的意见》[The Opinion of the Supreme People's Court on Comprehensively Deepening the Reforms in People's Courts], Fa Fa [2015] No 3, 4 Feb 2015.

[150] For example, the series of《涉外商事海事审判指导》[Guide on Foreign-Related Commercial and Maritime Trial] (人民法院出版社 [People's Court Press]) is published by the Fourth Civil Branch of the SPC. It provides most significant judicial materials in the area of international trade, commercial law and maritime law. See Sect. 3.2 in Chap. 3. Also see the book "The Functioning of Public Policy in Private International Law" by Judge GaoXiaoli, 高晓力[Gao Xiaoli], above n 6.

[151]《最高人民法院关于设立国际商事法庭若干问题的规定》[Provisions of the Supreme People's Court on Several Issues concerning the Establishment of International Commercial Courts] (promulgated by the Sup. People's Ct., June 27, 2018, effective July 1, 2018), Fa Shi [2018] No. 11, CLI.3.316419 (Chinalawinfo);

[152] 周强 [Zhou Qiang],《最高人民法院工作报告》[Working Report of the Supreme People's Court], the First Meeting of the Fourteenth National People's Congress, 7 March 2023.

## 7 The Role and Contributions of Arbitrators and Other Participants in Arbitration

### *7.1 Arbitration Commissions*

Arbitration commissions, particularly the leading ones, play a significant role in shaping Chinese arbitration proceedings.[153] Their distinct position and power may influence the legal concept of public policy in two contradictory ways.

First, the distinctive procedural aspects of Chinese arbitration procedures and approaches to judicial review shape the particular understanding of public policy among Chinese courts and arbitrators. In many cases, Chinese courts respect the Chinese arbitration commissions' decisions, activities and arbitration rules in arbitration proceedings. Specifically, Chinese courts rely heavily on the arbitration rules provided by arbitration commissions in relation to the judicial review process, which in effect "squeezes out" the possibility of the application of procedural public policy elements.[154] This is observed in many cases where the public policy exception was discussed but ultimately the decision to refuse to enforce the award was based on a procedural non-conformity.[155]

Yet, in some cases, Chinese arbitral awards were challenged when such awards sought enforcement in foreign jurisdictions and reviewed under the concerns whether they were held not compatible with the jurisdiction's foreign public policy. In two Japanese cases, CIETAC was challenged because of its close connection with governmental bodies[156]; in *Keeneye*, the activities conducted by the commissions' Secretary General were also criticised as inappropriate.[157] Though these challenges were denied in subsequent judicial proceedings, the position, rules and activities of these Chinese arbitration commissions may still create some doubts, as they may be contrary to some universally accepted elements of procedural public policy.[158]

These challenges remind the Chinese arbitration commissions that they should respect public policy, and particularly the procedural elements in arbitration practice, in order to ensure the enforceability of arbitral awards. The connection between Chinese arbitration commissions and Chinese governmental or semi-governmental

---

153 Section 4 in Chap. 3; See also the discussion of CIETAC and BAC's Arbitration Rules regarding arbitration proceedings in Chap. 6.

154 Section 6 in Chap. 6; Wunschheim, above n 15, 256–57.

155 Ibid; also, the discussion in Sect. 4.3 in Chap. 4 and Sect. 6 in Chap. 6.

156 Section 2.4 in Chap. 6.

157 Section 2.2 in Chap. 6.

158 Section 2.2 in Chap. 6.

bodies may also raise doubts about their impartiality.[159] And, the diversified development of different arbitration commissions in China further increases the possibility that some activities of Chinese arbitration commissions, particularly those that are undeveloped, may infringe upon public policy elements and hinder the creation of a universal understanding of public policy in China.

### 7.2 Arbitrators

As noted in Chap. 3, there are concerns regarding the diversified quality of arbitrators and the lack of a sufficient supervision scheme, which would negatively affect the application of public policy.[160] Particularly, arbitrators may not consider the possible violation of public policy in a foreign jurisdiction when making their award, which may cause subsequent non-enforcement. This conclusion is accentuated by the fact that public policy issues challenged at the judicial review stage are rarely discussed by arbitrators at the arbitration stage in China.[161]

There are also concerns about the arbitrators' performance in organising arbitration proceedings and concerning international public policy during these proceedings. One significant example is the possible involvement of procedural public policy when the Chinese style of mediation is involved in arbitration proceedings and the arbitrators may take on the role as mediators.[162] The "double-hat" problem cannot easily be fixed, particularly when some Chinese arbitrators sometimes confuse the distinctive characteristics and different functions of mediation and arbitration; or act cautiously when dealing with information obtained during mediation when communicating with the parties; or positively encourage a settlement between the parties, or make *ex parte* communications and settlement proposals on their own motion.[163] All of these behaviours, although arguably tolerable in Chinese mediation, are extremely dangerous in the eyes of foreign legal practitioners, particularly those with a common law background, and may violate some elements of public policy in jurisdictions outside Mainland China.[164]

---

[159] Sections 3.2 and 4.7 in Chap. 6; For example, CIETAC has a quite close relationship with CCIPT, a semi-governmental body of the Central Government. See also 陈福勇 [Chen Fuyong],《未竟的转型: 中国仲裁机构现状与发展趋势实证研究》[Unfinished Transformation: An Empirical Study of the Current Status and Future Trends of China's Arbitration Institutions] (法律出版社 [Law Press], 2010).

[160] Section 4.7 in Chap. 3.

[161] Section 3.1 in Chap. 4.

[162] Section 2.2 in Chap. 6, discussing the *Keeneye* Case.

[163] Section 2.2 in Chap. 6; The distinctions are particularly emphasised in common law jurisdictions; Kun Fan, 'The Risks of Apparent Bias when an Arbitrator Acts as a Mediator: Remarks on Hong Kong Court's Decision in *Gao Haiyan*' (2011) 13 *Yearbook of Private International Law* 93, 102–105; Shahla F. Ali, 'The Morality of Conciliation: An Empirical Examination of Arbitrator "Role Moralities" in East Asia and the West' (2011) 16(1) *Harvard Negotiation Law Review* 1, 3–10.

[164] Section 2.2 in Chap. 6.

## 7.3 Lawyers and Other Participants

Generally, the participating parties and their counsel in China do not contribute significantly to the clarification of the meaning of public policy. In many cases the parties and their lawyers who argued for and against the public policy exception did not fully understand its meaning. As illustrated in Chap. 4, in quite a few cases, particularly the early ones, this ground was merely noted without any proper interpretation and was generally rejected by courts.[165] In other cases, parties and their counsels insisted upon some erroneous understandings of public policy, including that public policy should be used to protect the interests of State-owned properties and enterprises, or some domestic group. These allegations were obviously not consistent with the current understanding of public policy in China's judicial practice and were generally rejected.[166]

Yet the role and contribution of these arbitration participants during the last twenty years should not be undervalued. Their most important contribution is that they are more active in bringing many possible elements of public policy in the judicial review of arbitral awards. Compared with courts' cautious attitude and reluctance to deal with public policy, the parties and lawyers were generally more active and open-minded in introducing different elements of public policy into judicial proceedings. For example, the procedural elements of impartiality were brought out in cases, such as *Shin-Etsu (No. 1)* and *Louis Dreyfus*.[167] Similarly, the issue of *lois de police* was argued by the parties in cases such as *ED & F Mans* and *Noble*.[168] In *Zhang Lan*,[169] the parties even referred to the French case of *Dutco*[170] to support their public policy argument regarding the equal rights of appointing arbitrators in the context of multiparty arbitration.

The participants' efforts in raising public policy arguments are one of the reasons why Chinese courts have improved their understanding of public policy and such efforts should be appreciated. This is particularly meaningful when more legal practitioners with an international view of arbitration are involved in China's arbitration practice and subsequent judicial review of arbitral awards; the contribution of broad views from international and foreign practitioners to China's approach of applying public policy should be fully respected. However, attempts by the parties and their

165 For example, the *Shanghai Dental* Case, published in《中国涉外仲裁年刊》[*China Foreign-Related Arbitration Yearbook*]. See also Sect. 4.2.3 in Chap. 4.

166 Examples can be found in *Tianjin Xianda*, in which the parties argued for the interests of the State-owned enterprise and its employee; and *Daming*, in which the parties argued for the interests of 200 peasants. Both arguments were rejected. See Sect. 5 in Chap. 5.

167 Section 2.2 in Chap. 6.

168 Section 3.3 in Chap. 7.

169 张兰、盛兰控股集团(BVI)有限公司 [Grand Lan Holdings Group 申请撤销仲裁裁决特别程序民事裁定书》[Civil Order of Special Procedure on the Setting Aside of An Arbitral Award Requested by Zhang Lan and Grand Lan Holdings Group], Supreme People's Court, [2019]最高法民特4号, 5号[SPC Civil Special Procedure No. 4, 5], 29 December 2020.

170 *Siemens AG and BKMI Industrienlagen GmbH v Dutco Construction*, Court of Cassation, First Civil Chamber, Decision of 7 January 1992, Case No. 89-18708/89-18726.

counsel to abuse the judicial review process by raising meaningless and abstract public policy arguments must be discouraged. Both the legislators and the judiciary need to provide guidelines with these matters in mind.

## 8 China's Legal System and Legal Culture: Globalisation and Localisation of Public Policy in China?

In the previous chapters and sections details of the application of public policy in China's arbitration and judicial practice have been discussed and compared with foreign practice. In this section the whole issue is reviewed in the broader context of globalisation in the sense of economic and legal globalisation and, particularly, the worldwide development of international arbitration law.[171]

The application of public policy in arbitration practice and the judicial review of arbitral awards is a complex legal process, and in many situations more than one legal system and legal culture are involved.[172] On that basis, the author will now evaluate the performance of Chinese arbitration practitioners and the judiciary through the perspective of globalisation and localisation.

### *8.1 Internationalisation?*

Generally, we have observed that international practice has had a limited influence on the application of public policy in China, and there are significant differences between international practice in relation to public policy and China's corresponding practice. The international nature of public policy is not significantly appreciated in China.[173] Generally, the discussion of public policy in China's judicial practice rarely responds to the relevant international developments.[174] For example, the reference to "judicial sovereignty" rather than the principle of *res judicata*[175] and the exclusion of the impartiality of arbitrators as an element of public policy, indicate that Chinese legal practitioners, legislators and the judiciary are generally not familiar with international contexts and commonly accepted conceptions of public policy, asset out in the *ILA Final Report.*[176] Some elements of public policy, such as *lois de police*, are

---

[171] For a brief discussion of globalisation of international law, see Chap. 2.

[172] Sections 2 and 3 in Chap. 2.

[173] Section 2.

[174] For examples and conclusions in discussing different elements of public policy, see Sect. 6 in Chap. 5 (concluding the Chinese practices in dealing with substantive fundamental principles), Sect. 2 in Chap. 6 (discussing the rule of impartiality), Sect. 4 in Chap. 6 (discussing the *res judicata* principle) and Sect. 4.4 in Chap. 7 (discussing the competition law rules).

[175] *Yongning* discussed in Sect. 4 in Chap. 6.

[176] Section 4 in Chap. 4; Sect. 3.

recognised, but not well-developed or consistently applied before Chinese courts.[177] By evaluating the application of public policy on a case-by-case basis, it is also hard to conclude that the globalisation of arbitration law plays a significant role in China's arbitration and judicial practice.

Despite these limitations in the judicial conception of public policy before Chinese courts, this study has also noted some general, and to some extent indirect, progress in the internationalisation of China's practice in applying public policy. Lynch has provided several key indicators that exhibit the influence of economic globalisation on international commercial arbitration practice; among these are two major indicators relating to the application of public policy: the unification of arbitration law and arbitration procedures; and the establishment of a uniform scheme to enforce arbitral awards.[178] Developments in these two aspects can be seen in China's current legal system, particularly after the implementation of the *NYC*, the enactment of the *CAL*, the amendments to the *CCPL*, and reforms in China's judicial system and arbitration commissions.[179] Developments in these two aspects illustrate the internationalisation of China's arbitration system and constitute the foundation of the internationalisation of the legal concept of public policy in China.[180] Furthermore, "international public policy" may be recognised by indirect means, such as in the distinction drawn between domestic awards and foreign-related and international awards and in the narrow approach adopted in the judicial review of the latter types of awards.[181]

## *8.2 Localisation?*

The issue of localisation and de-localisation has long been a hot topic for debate in the literature on international arbitration, and focuses particularly on the validity of an award and its connection to the *lex fori* in determining the procedural requirements governing that award.[182] This book, however, does not intend to discuss this issue and uses the term "localisation" to refer to the efforts to introduce international legal schemes and adjust them to meet local needs: this "localisation" occurs in China's arbitration law system and shapes the distinctive nature of China's judicial review of international commercial arbitral awards. In the context of the judicial review of arbitral awards, the possible aspects of "localisation" of arbitration law

---

[177] Section 4 in Chap. 4; also the discussion of element (1a) in Chap. 5 and element (2) in Chap. 7.

[178] Katherine Lynch, *The Forces of Economic Globalization: Challenges to the Regime of International Commercial Arbitration* (Kluwer Law International, 2003) 22–34.

[179] For the development and current status of China's arbitration institutions, see Sects. 3 and 4 in Chap. 3.

[180] Section 4 in Chap. 3.

[181] Section 2.

[182] For example, Jan Paulsson, 'Delocalisation of International Commercial Arbitration: When and Why it Matters' (1983) 32 *International Commercial Law Quarterly* 53, 57; also Simon Greenberg, Christopher Kee and J. Romesh Weeramantry, *International Commercial Arbitration: An Asia–Pacific Perspective* (Cambridge University, 2010) 68–80.

includes: the introduction and application of international conventions such as the *NYC*; the reference to international legislation, for example, to the *UNCITRAL Model Law* and the adoption of legislation from leading jurisdictions in drafting Chinese legislation, as a reflection of the transplantation of foreign law;[183] the combination of distinctive features of Chinese arbitration with international law in the design of the recognition and enforcement of foreign-related and international arbitral awards.

From the perspective of localisation of arbitration law, there are many distinctive factors that shape Chinese-style arbitration practice and influence the application of public policy. Significant examples can be found in the establishment and functioning of the Prior Reporting System,[184] and the strict reliance on procedural rules.[185] Other distinctive aspects in China that directly or indirectly influence the application of public policy include: the distinct role and performance of the Chinese arbitration institutions and their staff,[186] the quality and resources of the judiciary,[187] enforcement difficulties and local protectionism.[188] The distinct culture and particular moral values in China may be a consideration taken by Chinese arbitrators and courts in recognising the substantive fundamental principles of law, which are possible elements of public policy.[189] The Chinese-style of mediation in arbitration and its underlying cultural value may be worthy of respect as part of China's procedural public policy.[190] China's mandatory regulation of currency exchange and export/import activities may also impliedly influence China's public policy.[191] Participants in arbitration and enforcement proceedings must also take account of these aspects in arguing for or against the application of public policy in China. It is important, too, that Chinese legislators, judges and scholars acknowledge these factors in further developing a viable legal conception of public policy in China.

It is particularly notable that some of these factors that influence the Chinese legal system are considered problematic in the eyes of foreign legal practitioners, especially common law lawyers and those who are not familiar with China's distinctive social and legal cultures.[192] This may be one of the reasons why Chinese legal practices relating to arbitration are sometimes criticised or are not trusted. It is arguable that the performance of the Chinese legal system in responding to international standards of arbitration and judicial practice is not wholly satisfactory. The author, however, is of the opinion that it may be worthwhile for these critics to become

---

[183] Section 2 in Chap. 3.

[184] Sections 3.2 and 4.6 in Chap. 3, and Sect. 4.3.

[185] Section 6 in Chap. 6 and Sect. 3.

[186] Section 4.7 in Chap. 3 and Sect. 8.

[187] Section 4.6.1 in Chap. 3 and Sect. 6.

[188] Section 4.6 in Chap. 3.

[189] Section 5 in Chap. 5.

[190] Section 2 in Chap. 6.

[191] Sections 3.2 and 3.3 in Chap. 7.

[192] See the criticism reported in Sects. 4.6 and 4.7 in Chap. 3, such as the difficult enforcement issue, the behaviour of arbitrators and judiciaries, and the controversies of mediation-arbitration discussed in Sect. 2.2 in Chap. 6.

familiar with the Chinese legal environment and the underlying legal culture to obtain a more comprehensive understanding of China's distinctive position, and to note China's recent developments in addressing these problems, before making such criticisms.

## 8.3 China's Choice and Future

In summarising this section, we observe both trends towards internationalism and the movement towards localisation in China's arbitration practice with respect to public policy. The international trend to promote transnational arbitration legal orders and unify and limit the application of public policy is generally respected; but the identification of public policy elements and the application of them in discrete cases may still depend largely on the distinct legal environment and legal culture of China. It is then a major task for Chinese legal professionals to maintain a balanced approach in further developing an understanding of the public policy exception and how it should be applied.

It is particularly noteworthy to acknowledge China's distinctive position in the world economy and how this potentially influences how China will respond to international directions in judicial practice governing arbitration. As a recently emerged developing country, it is more difficult for China than leading developed countries to formulate its own distinctive approach towards public policy while making itself more influential in contributing to international consensus on the legal conception of public policy.[193] It is not disputable that leading developed jurisdictions, in serving as legal markets for arbitration including the law governing arbitration, have significant advantages in making the rules and influencing the formulation of international consensus. Many scholars have observed that the development of international arbitration is not simply "globalised", but also "Americanised".[194] Other observers have noted that the most influential part of the worldwide arbitration market is under

[193] For example, the leading jurisdictions that have advanced legislation of arbitration law and become the major players of arbitration include: the US, the UK, France, Sweden and other leading EU countries. In Asia, Hong Kong and Singapore are also influential in arbitration practices. Lynch, above n 178, Sect. 6, particularly discussed the reforms in Asia, Arabian countries, Latin America and Africa following the leading jurisdictions and showing a trend of convergence. See also Sects. 2 and 3 in Chap. 2, discussing the international developments of arbitration law in general and public policy in particular.

[194] See generally Steven Seidenberg, 'International Arbitration Loses Its Grip: Are U.S. Lawyers to Blame?' (2010) 96 *ABA Journal* 50; For another opinion, see George M. von Merhen and Alana C. Jochum, 'Is International Arbitration Becoming too American?' (2011) 2 *Global Business Law Review* 47, which argues that the US did not overwhelmingly influence the developments of international arbitration and did not make it a fully American-style practice. See also 'New World Order? How Americanised has International Arbitration Actually Become?' (2013) 18(2) *Arbitration Newsletter*.

the control of a small class of professionals, or elites.[195] China is yet to join the leading jurisdictions that dominate international trends in regulating transnational arbitration.[196] It is also under pressure from these leading jurisdictions to follow the international consensus governing arbitration that was formed prior to the development of China's arbitration practice.[197] This distinct position may thus contribute to the confusion regarding the public policy exception in Chinese practice.

Based on its distinct position, Chinese legal practitioners face multiple tasks: first, to follow the leading trends in international practice relating to arbitration and second, to protect China's distinctive interests. In response, the Chinese legal system needs to improve its understanding of public policy in alignment with what is subscribed to internationally.[198] This includes determining the elements of public policy and how to apply them in judicial practice.[199] These developments would encourage both the internationalisation of China's arbitration law in general, and the development of China's conception of international public policy in particular.

China needs to establish its own position on the application of public policy and to make its own distinctive contribution to the international arbitration community. In so doing, it needs to further explore its own legal culture and legal traditions in order to shape its distinct approach to the application of public policy.[200] It also needs to improve Chinese judicial review schemes and judicial practice in relation to public policy; and to work towards defining public policy in legislative and arbitration practice.[201] In other words, China should adjust its local legal system, legal culture and arbitral and judicial practices in order to better connect them to international trends and understandings. It also needs to integrate international elements of public policy into its domestic legal system. In the meanwhile, it needs to protect its local culture and interests by carefully designing a dispute-resolution scheme. It also needs to make an effort to explain the distinctive features of such a scheme to foreign

---

[195] Yves Dezalay and Bryant G. Garth, *Dealing in Virtue: International Commercial Arbitration and the Construction of a Transnational Legal Order* (University of Chicago Press, 1998) 18–29.

[196] Generally in Sects. 2 and 3 in Chap. 2. An example of rule-making may be the recognition of competition law as a possible element of public policy in EU countries and the US; see Sect. 3.4 in Chap. 7.

[197] For example, China only became a contracting party of the New York Convention in 1985, which was long after the drafting this predominant Convention in the international arbitration law, which was reached in 1958. China's first arbitration law, which came into force in 1995, was also influenced by the legislation of leading jurisdiction and the UNCITRAL Model Law. See detailed discussion in Sect. 3.2 in Chap. 3.

[198] Generally in Sect. 5 in Chap. 2 and particularly in Sect. 2 in Chap. 5, Sects. 2, 3 and 4 in Chap. 6, Sect. 3 in Chap. 7 and Sect. 2 in Chap. 8, and summarised in Sect. 2.

[199] Sections 2 and 4.

[200] For example, the further clarification of the Chinese style mediation in arbitration, as discussed in Chap. 6, and the possible Chinese public policy rules in competition law and anti-dumping law as discussed in Chap. 7.

[201] For the discussion of the performance of the judicial system, see Chaps. 3, 4 and summarised in Sect. 6; for the functioning of other participants of arbitration in defining and applying public policy, See Chap. 3 and summarised in Sect. 7.

participants in order to promote the exchange of information and to arrive at a 'win–win' result in a commercial sense.[202] Only when these goals are achieved will the Chinese legal system and its arbitration practices develop, and such developments will be recognised internationally.

[202] An example of the distinct local scheme that is based on Chinese culture is the mediation in arbitration as discussed in Chap. 6, which may benefit both Chinese and foreign participants in the commercial sense. Yet the possible risk in such practice should also be noted and prevented by careful design of a dispute-resolution process and communication between participants from different legal jurisdictions. See Chap. 6.

# Conclusion: A Lesson from and for China

This research has systematically examined how the Chinese arbitration law system responds to the application of the public policy exception in the judicial review of arbitral awards, particularly those awards that are foreign-related and international in nature. The discussion is based on a general understanding of the legal concept of public policy in international arbitration practice, and the understandings developed in Chinese arbitration law and judicial practice. In focusing on both international developments and Chinese arbitral and judicial practice, this book provides some lessons from and for China.

A general conclusion is that China's performance in defining and applying public policy in the judicial review of international commercial arbitral awards is not satisfactory. This is due in part to the difficulty in defining and applying public policy in the context of international arbitration law. In particular, it is difficult to interpret such an abstract term as public policy, to go through its different possible key elements and to formalise a consistent approach to the judicial review of arbitration awards based on public policy grounds. All of these tasks involve a struggle to find a balance between two opposing aims: protecting national interests on the one hand and facilitating international commerce by not subjecting arbitral awards to domestic interests on the other. Finding such a balance is a mission that is enormously delicate and complicated.

From an international perspective, China's experiences are consistent with those of other states that enjoy extensive discretion in formalising their own approaches to defining and applying the public policy exception in their national legal systems and national judicial practices. Chinese cases demonstrate that the distinctive features of the legislative and judicial system in China, its cultural and social traditions at its particular stage of development, and its economic and legal environment, all influence judicial practice in defining and applying the public policy exception. It is also noteworthy that conceptions of public policy that are adopted by Chinese courts are limited by the extent of advancement of China's legal profession, the development of legal education there, and the confidence Chinese judges have in discussing and



S. Zhang, *The Public Policy Exception in the Judicial Review of International Commercial Arbitral Awards*, https://doi.org/10.1007/978-3-662-67679-0

applying such a complex legal concept in rendering their decisions. As a result, these factors that are distinctive to the Chinese legal system may make it difficult for an outsider to fully understand the conception of public policy that is incorporated into Chinese law and its application in China's arbitration law in particular.

Yet the Chinese legal system, like other legal systems, has gradually acknowledged and followed international trends in defining and applying public policy in law. Pressure to comply with international obligations under the *NYC* and other bilateral or multilateral agreements, and the economic motivation to facilitate global trade and commerce, have all encouraged China to follow international trends in arbitration law. China has also made significant progress in response to these challenges since the 1990s. These include, enacting core legislation such as the *CAL* and the *CCPL* that guide arbitration practice in China; establishing the Prior Reporting system; reforming the Chinese arbitration commissions; and promoting legal education and legal research in arbitration law there, among other developments. These trends to modernise the Chinese arbitration system and to unify the practice of Chinese courts in reviewing arbitral awards—complying increasingly with international standards—demonstrate the influence that internationalisation has had on arbitration law in China. They also show how the application of public policy by Chinese courts has indirectly influenced the approach they adopt in reviewing arbitration awards.

In striving to attain international acceptance with respect to its review of arbitral awards, the Chinese legal system has also limited its intervention in the practice of arbitration in general and restricted the use of public policy arguments that limit the ambit of arbitral awards. While Chinese courts have increasingly followed these international developments, they have not done so consistently.

It is particularly noteworthy that, for countries such as China that follow rather than lead international arbitration practice, external pressures give rise to additional concerns on whether these leading practice models or notions can work well in China's legal environment, and whether they can be properly transplanted there. These concerns may contribute to hesitancy, lack of confidence and inconsistent practices of Chinese courts in defining and applying public policy.

This book stresses the need for the Chinese arbitration system and for legislators and the judiciary in particular to better understand the nature, possible elements, and limits of public policy in developing a consistent approach in judicial review of arbitration awards. The author urges Chinese legislators, the judiciary and other legal practitioners in China to provide answers or at least guidelines to address some key questions. These include, among others, the national/international nature of public policy, the key elements of public policy and their variable nature, and the appropriate boundaries of judicial review. What is also needed is for Chinese legal professionals to develop a comprehensive conception of public policy and to further improve their understanding and responses to it in the context of international arbitration.

As the Chinese economy has gradually emerged and China has become more powerful in world trade and commerce, improving China's legal environment for dispute resolution will benefit both China and its trading partners. Drawing on observations of the performance of the Chinese judicial system, the author has suggested ways of arriving at a clearer and more meaningful understanding of public policy and a more consistent approach in interpreting and applying it in the judicial review of arbitral awards. These suggestions include establishing a comprehensive set of public policy elements and applying them comprehensively and intelligibly in the judicial review of such awards. The author has also suggested that such developments should involve China's legislators, its judiciary and legal practitioners in the future reform of arbitration law and practice.

However, Chinese legal professionals can only realistically achieve these goals by balancing its domestic public policy concerns which are distinctive against an international trend that seeks to limit the application of those concerns. Their further challenge, and opportunity, is to further develop and explain the unavoidable tension between a distinctive Chinese conception of public policy and the explication of that exception in international arbitration law.

A final challenge for the Chinese legal system is to ensure that the judicial application of the public policy exception is understandable to the rest of the world. A central purpose is to demonstrate that the domestic Chinese legal environment is friendly to foreign trade and investment interests. It is important that further steps be taken in order for the Chinese legal system to respond to these challenges.

# Appendix A
# Cases Dealing with Public Policy Determined by Lower Courts

| Case number | Decided year | Name | Short title |
|---|---|---|---|
| 1 | 1992 | *Dongfeng Garments Factory of Kaifeng City and Taichu International Trade (HK) Company Ltd. v Henan Garment Import and Export Company*[1] | *Dongfeng* |
| 2 | 1994 | *New Victory Industrial Company (HK) v Jiangxi Xingwei Constructing & Industrial Materials Co Ltd.*[2] | *Xinwei* |
| 3 | 1996 | *Shanghai Dental Medical Machinery Factory v Hu Junxiong and Hong Kong Company*[3] | *Shanghai Dental* |
| 4 | 1998 | *Contestar Shipping Co Ltd., Cyprus v Zhanjiang Export Shipping Co*[4] | *Contestar* |

(continued)

[1] Yongping Xiao and Zhengxin Huo, '*Ordre Public* in China's Private International Law' (2005) 53 *American Journal of Comparative Law* 654, 660.

[2] This case is unpublished in any primary material and reported in Wang Shengchang, 'Enforcement of Foreign Arbitral Awards in the People's Republic of China', in Albert Jan van den Berg, *Improving the Efficiency of Arbitration Agreements and Awards: 40 Years of Application of the New York Convention* (Kluwer Law International, 1999) 461, 478–484.

[3]《北京市第二中级人民法院驳回上海齿科医械厂申请撤销中国国际经济贸易仲裁委员会上海分会 (1996) 沪贸仲字 038 号裁决书的裁定》[Decision Order of Beijing 2nd IPC to Refuse the Application of the Shanghai Dental Machinery Factory for Annulment of CIETAC Shanghai Award No 38] Beijing Second Intermediate People's Court, (1996) 二中经初字第 83 号 [Economic Branch, Case of First Instance No. 83].

[4] 塞浦路斯康特斯达航运有限公司申请承认和执行伦敦仲裁裁决案 [Case Concerning the Application of Cyprus Contestar Shipping Co Ltd. for Recognition and Enforcement of London Arbitral Award] Guangzhou Maritime Court, (1997) 广海发湛字 5 号 [Zhanjiang Tribunal No. 5], 15 July 1998.



S. Zhang, *The Public Policy Exception in the Judicial Review of International Commercial Arbitral Awards*, https://doi.org/10.1007/978-3-662-67679-0

(continued)

| Case number | Decided year | Name | Short title |
|---|---|---|---|
| 5 | 1999 | *Itochu Petroleum Company (Hong Kong) Ltd. v Shenzhen Petrochemical Group Corp*[5] | *Itochu* |
| 6 | 2002 | *Run'an (International) Development Co Ltd. v Dove Elevator (Far East) Co Ltd.*[6] | *Run'an* |
| 7 | 2004 | *Hehua (overseas) Land Limited v Kaige (Xiamen) Golf Club Co Ltd.*[7] | *Hehua* |
| 8 | 2005 | *Golden Sail (HK) Company v Foshan Investment Consulting Corp et al.*[8] | *Foshan* |
| 9 | 2006 | *Unknown (Dispute regarding share transfer)*[9] | *Zhejiang* |
| 10 | 2006 | *Lion Dragon v Smartdot Tech*[10] | *Lion Dragon* |

(continued)

[5] 伊藤忠石油(香港)有限公司申请承认执行英国仲裁裁决案 [Case Concerning the Application of Itochu Petroleum (Hong Kong) Co Ltd. for the Recognition and Enforcement of a UK Arbitral Award] Shenzhen Intermediate People's Court, (1999) 深中法经二初字第 190 号 [Second Economic Branch No 190], reported in 高晓力 [Gao Xiaoli],《国际私法上公共政策的运用》 [The Functioning of Public Policy in Private International Law] (China Democracy and Rule of Law Press, 2008) 259–260.

[6]《合肥润安(国际)发展有限公司与多快电梯(远东)有限公司申请撤销电梯设备合同货款争议裁决纠纷案》[Hefei Run'an (International) Development Co Ltd. v Dove Elevator (Far East) Co Ltd.—Case of Annulment of an Award dealing with Payments of Elevator Equipments Contracts Dispute] Shanghai 2nd IPC, [2002] 沪二中民五(商)初字第 55 号 [Civil Fifth Branch Commercial Dispute, Case of First Instance No. 55], 9 July 2002.

[7] Jason Blatt, 'Mutual Recognition and Enforcement of Arbitral Awards in Mainland China and Taiwan: A Breakthrough in Cross-Strait Relations' (2006) 36(3) *Hong Kong Law Journal* 585; Clarisse von Wunschheim, *Enforcement of Commercial Arbitral Awards in China: Business Laws of China* (West, 2011), App.D.36-37.

[8]《高新(香港)有限公司与佛山市投资咨询公司等申请撤销仲裁裁决纠纷案广东省佛山市中级人民法院民事裁定书》[Civil Order of the Guangdong Foshan Intermediate People's Court in regard of the Application of Goldensail (Hong Kong) Ltd. and Foshan Investment Consulting Co for Annulment of an Arbitral Award] Foshan Intermediate People's Court, (2004) 佛中法民四初字第 133 号 [Fourth Civil Branch, Case of First Instance No. 133]. It is arguable whether this case is a domestic or foreign-related case; the original award seems a domestic one, but the annulment claim was brought by a Hong Kong party. We classified it as a foreign-related case because the Foshan IPC declared it as so and might be applied to the judicial review scheme for foreign-related cases accordingly. See further Sect. 5 in Chap. 6.

[9] Wunschheim, above n 7, App.C-8, citing Honglei Yang, 'Recognition and Enforcement of Arbitration Agreements and Arbitral Awards in Chinese Courts', paper presented at the ICC-SIAC Conference: Reflections on Diverse Issues in International Arbitration, 2 September 2008.

[10] Lion Dragon v Smartdot Tech, not published, Beijing Second IPC, 13 February 2006.

(continued)

| Case number | Decided year | Name | Short title |
|---|---|---|---|
| 11 | 2008 | *Leaf Candy Co., Ltd. v Shanghai Lianfu Food Co., Ltd.*[11] | *Leaf Candy* |
| 12 | 2008 | *Pepsi Co Inc v Sichuan Pepsi (China)*[12] | *Pepsi* |
| 13 | 2009 | *Handiboke Shipping Co Ltd. v Zhoushan Zhongchang Shipping Co Ltd.*[13] | *Handiboke* |
| 14 | 2009 | *Liya Trading v Liya Capital*[14] | *Liya* |
| 15 | 2009 | *Amulong Steel Co v Yunnan Nickel and Cobalt Mining Co*[15] | *Yunnan Mining* |
| 16 | 2014 | *Maruman Co v Beijing Delin Golf Sports Development Co Ltd.*[16] | *Maruman* |
| 17 | 2014 | *Summer Maritime Ltd. v Shandong Haina Property Development Co*[17] | *Summer Maritime* |

(continued)

[11] 利夫糖果(上海)有限公司申请承认和执行新加坡国际仲裁中心仲裁裁决案 [Case Concerning the Application of Leaf Candy (Shanghai) Co Ltd. for Recognition and Enforcement of an Arbitral Award of SIAC] Shanghai Second IPC, (2008) 沪二中民五 (商) 初字 19 号 [Fifth Civil Branch (Commercial), Case of First Instance No. 19], available at <http://www.shezfy.com/view.html?id=11429>.

[12] 林一飞 [Lin Yifei],《百事公司与被申请人四川百事可乐饮料有限公司申请承认及执行外国仲裁裁决案》[Case of the Application for Recognition and Enforcement of Foreign Arbitral Award by Pepsi Co and Sichuan Pepsi Coke Co], at <http://www. cnarb.com/algy/nygyal/china/200911/12897>; Nadia Darwazeh & Friven Yeoh, 'Recognition and Enforcement of Awards under the *New York Convention*: China and Hong Kong Perspectives' (2008) 25 *Journal of International Arbitration* 837.

[13] See <http://www.wunscharb.com/court-decisions/handiboke-case-2009>; 胡建新 [Hu Jianxin],《汉迪波克公司申请承认和执行外国海事仲裁裁决案》[Handiboke Co Applying Recognition and Enforcement of a Foreign Maritime Arbitral Award] (2010) 中国水运报 China Water Transport, 16 June 2010.

[14]《加拿大利亚贸易公司与英属维尔京群岛利亚资本公司申请撤销南京仲裁委员会 (2007) 宁裁字第 266–35 号裁决纠纷案》[Liya Trading (Canada) v Liya Capital (BVI)—Case of Annulment of Nanjing Arbitration Commission's (2007) No. 2 66–35 Award] Nanjing IPC, [2009] 宁民五初字第 38 号 [Civil Fifth Branch, Case of First Instance No 38], 23 March 2009.

[15] 云南省昆明市中级人民法院阿姆龙钢铁有限公司申请执行云南镍钴矿业有限公司等仲裁裁决案 [Case Concerning Amulong Steel Co Ltd.'s Application of Enforcement of an Arbitral Award against Yunnan Nickel and Colbat Mining Co Ltd.] Yunnan Kunming Intermediate People's Court, Case Number not published, 10 November 2009.

[16]《丸万株式会社与北京德霖高尔夫体育发展有限公司申请承认和执行外国仲裁裁决一审民事裁定书》[Civil Decision of the Case of the First Instance Concerning the Application for the Recognition and Enforcement of A Foreign Arbitral Awards between Maruman Co. and Beijing Delin Golf Sports Development Co Ltd.], Beijing 2nd IPC, (2013) 二中民特字第 12593 号 [Special No. 12593], 19 May 2014.

[17]《夏长海运有限公司诉山东海纳房地产股份有限公司申请承认外国仲裁裁决纠纷一审民事裁定书》[Civil Decision on the Application for the Recognition of A Foreign Arbitral Award by Summer Maritime Ltd. against Shandong Haina Property Development Co], Qingdao Maritime Court, (2014) 青海法海商初字第 721 号 [Maritime First Instance No. 721], 22 July 2014.

(continued)

| Case number | Decided year | Name | Short title |
|---|---|---|---|
| 18 | 2014 | *Spring Maritime Ltd. v Shandong Haina Property Development Co*[18] | *Spring Maritime* |
| 19 | 2014 | *Fujian Zongheng High-Speed Information Technology Co., Ltd., Fujian Focus Media Co., Ltd., and Cheng Cheng v Starr Cayman Investment Co*[19] | *Starr Cayman* |
| 20 | 2015 | *Jacobson Golf Course Design v Sihui Zhenhuiyuan Property Development Co Ltd. et al.*[20] | *Jacobson* |
| 21 | 2016 | *Olam International Ltd. v Zibo Yinhua Cotton and Linen Co Ltd.*[21] | *Olam* |
| 22 | 2016 | *Ecom Agroindustrial Corp Ltd. Pully Switzerland v Shenzhen Guotaihua Investment Co Ltd.*[22] | *Ecom No.1* |
| 23 | 2017 | *GS Global Corporation v Shanghai Zhenrong Oil Co Ltd.*[23] | *GS Global* |

(continued)

[18] 春生海运有限公司诉山东海纳房地产股份有限公司申请承认外国仲裁裁决纠纷一审民事裁定书》[Civil Decision on the Application for the Recognition of A Foreign Arbitral Award by Spring Maritime Ltd. against Shandong Haina Property Development Co], Qingdao Maritime Court, (2013) 青海法海商初字第 1032 号 [Maritime First Instance No. 1032], (2014) 青海法海商初字第 722 号 [Maritime First Instance No. 722], 22 July 2014.

[19]《福建纵横高速信息技术有限公司、福建分众传媒有限公司等与史带开曼投资公司申请不予执行一案的执行裁定书》[Decision on the Application for Non-Enforcement of the Arbitral Award Raised by Fujian Zongheng High-Speed Information Technology Co., Ltd., Fujian Focus Media Co., Ltd., and Cheng Zheng against Starr Cayman Investment Co], Fuzhou IPC, (2014) 榕执监字第 51 号 [Enforcement Supervision No. 51], 5 November 2014.

[20]《Jacobson Golf Course Design、四会臻汇园物业发展有限公司等申请承认和执行外国仲裁裁决民事裁定书》[Decision on the Application for the Recognition and Enforcement of A Foreign Arbitral Award between Jacobson Golf Course Design and Sihui Zhenhuiyuan Property Development Co Ltd. et al.], Zhaoqing IPC, (2015) 肇中法民一仲字第 26 号 [First Branch Arbitration No. 26], 19 October 2015.

[21]《翱兰国际有限公司、淄博银花棉麻有限公司等申请承认和执行外国仲裁裁决民事裁定书》[Civil Decision on the Application for the Recognition and Enforcement of a Foreign Arbitral Award between Olam International Ltd. and Zibo Yinhua Cotton and Linen Co Ltd.], Zibo IPC, (2015) 淄民特字第 1 号 [Civil Special No. 1], 19 January 2016.

[22]《EcoM Agroindustrial 申请承认和执行外国仲裁裁决民事裁定书》[Decision on the Application for the Recognition and Enforcement of A Foreign Arbitral Awards by Ecom Agroindustrial Corp Ltd. Switzerland], Shenzhen IPC, (2014) 深中法涉外初字第 60 号 [Foreign-related First Instance No. 60], 25 May 2016.

[23]《GS Global Corporation (佳施国际株式会社)诉上海市振戎石油有限公司申请承认和执行外国仲裁裁决一案民事裁定书》[Civil Ruling on the Application for the Recognition and Enforcement of a Foreign Arbitral Award between GS Global Corporation and Shanghai Zhenrong Oil Corp], Shanghai 1st IPC, (2016)沪01协外认12号[Judicial Assistance Foreign Recognition No.12], 22 February 2017.

(continued)

| Case number | Decided year | Name | Short title |
|---|---|---|---|
| 24 | 2017 | *Sinwa Marine Pte Ltd. v Dalian Xinhe Shipping Supplies Co Ltd.*[24] | *Sinwa* |
| 25 | 2017 | *China Aviation Oil (Singapore) Corp Ltd. v Chengdu Xinhuaxin Chemical Engineering Materials Co Ltd.*[25] | *CAO Singapore* |
| 26 | 2017 | *Korea Line Corporation v HNA Group Co Ltd.*[26] | *Korea Line* |
| 27 | 2017 | *Honghe Henghao Mining Co v Ultrabulk A/S*[27] | *Henghao* |
| 28 | 2018 | *Beiliang (Hong Kong) Co Ltd. v Rizhao Xingyujia Trade Co Ltd.*[28] | *Beiliang* |
| 29 | 2018 | *Asia Maritime Pacific Chartering Ltd. v Peak International Trade (Tianjin) Co Ltd.*[29] | *Peak* |
| 30 | 2018 | *Changmyung Shipping Co Ltd. v Hebei Yuanyang Transportation Co*[30] | *Changnyung* |

(continued)

[24]《新和海事有限公司与大连新和船舶物资供应有限公司申请承认和执行外国仲裁裁决案裁定书》[Ruling on the Application for the Recognition and Enforcement of a Foreign Arbitral Award between Sinwa Marine Pte Ltd. and Dalian Xinhe Shipping Supplies Co Ltd.], Dalian IPC, (2016) 辽 02 协外认 2 号 [Judicial Assistance Foreign Recognition No. 2], 24 Feb 2017.

[25]《中国航油 (新加坡) 股份有限公司、成都欣华欣化工材料有限公司申请承认与执行外国仲裁裁决裁定书》[Decision on the Application for the Recognition and Enforcement of a Foreign Arbitral Award between China Aviation Oil (Singapore) Corp Ltd. and Chengdu Xinhuaxin Chenical Engineering Materials Co Ltd.], Chengdu IPC, (2017) 川 01 协外认1号 [Judicial Assistance Foreign Recognition No. 1], 23 June 2017.

[26]《大韩海运株式会社与海航集团有限公司船舶租用合同纠纷特别程序案件民事裁定书》[Civil Ruling on the Special Procedure Case of the Chartering Dispute between Korea Line Corp and HNA Group Co Ltd.], Haikou Maritime Court, (2016) 琼 72 协外认 1 号 [Judicial Assistance Foreign Recognition No. 1], 15 August 2017.

[27]《执行申请人奥卓布克有限公司与被申请人红河恒昊矿业股份有限公司执行异议执行裁定书》[Ruling on Enforcement Dispute between the Applicant Ultrabulk A/S and the Respondent Honghe Henghao Mining Co], Kunming IPC, (2017) 云 01 执异 54 号 [Enforcement Dispute No. 54], 18 September 2017.

[28]《北良 (香港) 有限公司、日照兴裕嘉贸易有限公司申请承认与执行法院判决、仲裁裁决案件裁定书》[Decision on the Application for the Recognition and Enforcement of Judgments or Arbitral Awards between Beiliang (Hong Kong) Co Ltd. and Rizhao Xingyujia Trade Co Ltd.], Rizhao IPC, (2016) 鲁11协外认 1 号 [Judicial Assistance Foreign Recognition No. 1], 9 January 2018.

[29]《亚洲海事太平洋租船有限公司、匹克国际贸易 (天津) 有限公司申请认可和执行香港特别行政区仲裁裁决民事裁定书》[Civil Decision on the Application for the Recognition and Enforcement of A Hong Kong SAR Arbitral Award Between Asia Maritime Pacific Chartering Ltd. and Peak International Trade (Tianjin) Co Ltd.], Tianjin Maritime Court, (2018) 津 72 民特 13, 14 号 [Civil Special No. 13 and No. 14], 30 October 2018.

[30]《沧溟海运株式会社、河北远洋运输集团股份有限公司申请承认与执行法院判决、仲裁裁决案件民事裁定书》[Civil Decision on the Application for the Recognition and Enforcement of Judgments or Arbitral Awards between Changmyung Shipping Co Ltd. and Hebei Yuanyang Transportation Co], Qingdao Maritime Court, (2018) 鲁 72 协外认 1 号-1 [Judicial Assistance Foreign Recognition No. 1–1], 5 November 2018.

(continued)

| Case number | Decided year | Name | Short title |
|---|---|---|---|
| 31 | 2018 | *Acuon Capital Ltd. v Tian et al.*[31] | *Acuon* |
| 32 | 2019 | *Rich Food v Yuan Chunqiu*[32] | *Rich Food* |
| 33 | 2019 | *Sean Inc v Tianjin Tinaduan Press Machine Co Ltd.*[33] | *Sean* |
| 34 | 2019 | *Changsheng Trading Co Inc v Henan Jianghe Mechanical Co Ltd.*[34] | *Changsheng* |
| 35 | 2019 | *Farenco Shipping Pte Ltd. and Eastern Ocean Transportation Co Ltd.*[35] | *Farence* |
| 36 | 2019 | *Automotive Gate FZCO et al. v Hebei Zhongxing Automotive Manufacture Co Ltd.*[36] | *Gate* |
| 37 | 2019 | *Noble Resources Intenrational Pte Ltd. v China Coal Jingmin (Fujian) Industry and Trade Co Ltd.*[37] | *Noble No.2* |

(continued)

[31]《株式会社 ACUON 资本申请承认和执行大韩商事仲裁院生效仲裁裁决民事裁定书》[Civil Decision on the Application for the Recognition and Enforcement of an Effective Award of Korean Commercial Arbitration Board by ACUON Capital Ltd.], Yanbian IPC, (2018) 吉 24 协外认 163 号 [Judicial Assistance Foreign Recognition No. 163], 15 November 2018.

[32]《利奇食品株式会社、元春秋申请承认与执行法院判决、仲裁裁决案件裁定书》[Decision on the Application for the Recognition and Enforcement of Judgments or Arbitral Awards between Rich Food Co Ltd. and Chunqiu Yuan], Tianjin 1st IPC, (2018) 津 01 协外认 1 号 [Judicial Assistance Foreign Recognition No. 1], 4 March 2019.

[33]《世安株式会社、天津市天锻压力机有限公司申请承认与执行法院判决、仲裁裁决案件裁定书》[Decision on the Application for the Recognition and Enforcement of A Foreign Award between Sean Inc and Tianjin Tianduan Press Machine Co Ltd.], Tianjin 1st IPC, (2018) 津 01 协外认 13 号 [Judicial Assistance Foreign Recognition No. 13], 27 March 2019.

[34]《昌盛贸易公司、河南江河机械有限责任公司申请承认和执行外国仲裁裁决裁定书》[Decision on the Application for the Recognition and Enforcement of a Foreign Arbitral Award between Changsheng Trading Co Inc and Henan Jianghe Mechanical Co Ltd.], Zhengzhou IPC, (2017) 豫 01 协外认 11 号 [Judicial Assistance Foreign Recognition No. 11], 27 March 2019.

[35]《华夏航运 (新加坡) 有限公司 (Farenco Shipping PTE Ltd.) 与东海运输有限公司 (Eastern Ocean Transportation Co., Limited) 申请认可和执行香港特别行政区仲裁裁决裁定书》[Ruling on the Application for the Recognition and Enforcement of a Hong Kong arbitral award between Farenco Shipping Pte Ltd. and Eastern Ocean Transportation Co Ltd.], Guangzhou Maritime Court, (2018) 粤 72 认港1号之一号 [Recognition Hong Kong No. 1–1], (2019) 粤 72 认港 1 号 [Recognition No. 1], 2 July 2019.

[36]《申请人盖特汽车自由贸易区公司、埃及盖特汽车制造公司等与被申请人河北中兴汽车制造有限公司申请认可和执行香港特别行政区仲裁裁决民事裁定书》[Civil Decision on the Application for the Recognition of a Hong Kong SAR Arbitral Award among Automotive Gate FZCO et al. and Hebei Zhongxing Automotive Manufacture Co Ltd.], Yichang IPC, (2015) 鄂宜昌中民认字第 00003 号之一[Civil Recognition No. 00003-A], 15 August 2019.

[37]《来宝资源国际私人有限公司、中煤京闽 (福建) 工贸有限公司申请承认与执行法院判决、仲裁裁决案件民事裁定书》[Civil Decision on the Application for the Recognition and Enforcement of Judgments or Arbitral Awards between Noble Resources International Pte Ltd. and China Coal Jingmin (Fujian) Industry and Trade Co Ltd.], Fuzhou IPC, (2019) 闽 01 认港 1 号 [Recognition Hong Kong No. 1], 29 September 2019.

(continued)

| Case number | Decided year | Name | Short title |
|---|---|---|---|
| 38 | 2019 | *South Pacific Ventures FZE v Panjin Liaohe Oilfield Kaite Oil Facilities Co Ltd.*[38] | *South Pacific Ventures* |
| 39 | 2019 | *Sinosure Fujian Co v Ping'an Bank Fujian Branch*[39] | *Sinosure* |
| 40 | 2020 | *Shanghai Jiachuan Mechanical Equipment Import and Export Co Ltd. v Meikesi Maritime Engineering Facility Co*[40] | *Jiachuan Mechanical* |
| 41 | 2020 | *Glencore Co Ltd. v Kunshan Liyi Textile Co Ltd.*[41] | *Glencore No. 2* |
| 42 | 2020 | *Octaform Systems Inc v Huajun Plastics and Building Materials Co Ltd.*[42] | *Octaform* |
| 43 | 2020 | *David Dein Consultancy Ltd. et al. v Beijing Zhonghe Guo'an Football Club Co Ltd.*[43] | *David Dein* |

(continued)

38《南太平洋风险投资有限公司、盘锦辽河油田凯特石油设备有限公司申请承认和执行外国仲裁裁决裁定书》[Decision on the Application for the Recognition and Enforcement of A Foreign Arbitral Award between South Pacific Venture FZE and Panjin Liaohe Oilfield Kaite Oil Facilities Co Ltd.], Dalian IPC, (2019) 辽 02 协外认 8 号 [Judicial Assistance Foreign Recognition No. 8], 3 December 2019.

39《中国出口信用保险公司福建分公司与平安银行股份有限公司福州分行申请撤销仲裁裁决民事裁定书》[Civil Decision on the Application for the Annulment of an Arbitral Award between Sinosure Fujian Co and Ping'an Bank Fujian Branch], Beijing 4th IPC, (2019) 京 04 民特 600 号 [Civil Special No. 600], 16 December 2019.

40《上海佳船机械设备进出口有限公司、美克斯海洋工程设备股份有限公司申请承认与执行法院判决、仲裁裁决案件其他民事裁定书》[Civil Ruling on the Application for the Recognition and Enforcement of A Foreign Arbitral Award between Shanghai jiachuan Mechanical Equipment Import and Export Co Ltd. and Meikesi Maritime Engineering Facility Co], Jiaxing IPC, (2019) 浙 04 协外认 1 号, 2 号 [Judicial Assistance Foreign Recognition No. 1 and No. 2], 1 July 2020.

41《嘉能可有限公司申请昆山立益纺织有限公司承认与执行法院判决、仲裁裁决案件民事裁定书》[Civil Decision on the Application for the Recognition and Enforcement of a Judgment or Arbitral Award by Glencore Co Ltd. against Kunshan Liyi Textile Co Ltd.], Suzhou IPC, (2019) 苏 05 协外认 2 号 [Judicial Assistance Foreign Recognition No. 2], 20 July 2020.

42《奥克塔福系统有限公司、华浚塑料建材有限公司申请承认与执行法院判决、仲裁裁决案件其他执行裁定书》[Decision on the Enforcement regarding the Application for the Recognition and Enforcement of Judgments or Arbitral Awards between Octaform Systems Inc and Huajun Plastics and Building Materials Co Ltd.], Huzhou IPC, (2019) 浙 05 协外认 1 号 [Judicial Assistance Foreign Recognition No. 1], 24 November 2020.

43《大卫戴恩咨询有限公司、布拉姆利有限公司申请执行香港仲裁裁决案》[Case of Application for the Recognition and Enforcement of a Hong Kong arbitral award by David Dein Consultancy Ltd. and Bramley Corp Ltd.], Beijing 4th IPC, 2020) 京 04 认港 5 号 [Recognition Hong Kong No. 5], date not reported, reported in the SPC,《内地与香港特别行政区发布相互执行仲裁裁决的典型案例》[Typical Cases of the Enforcement of Arbitral Awards between China Mainland and the Hong Kong SAR], 27 November 2020.

(continued)

| Case number | Decided year | Name | Short title |
|---|---|---|---|
| 44 | 2021 | *Ciming Bo'ao International Hospital Co Ltd. v HRC-Hainan Holding Company LLC et al.*[44] | *Ciming* |
| 45 | 2021 | *Stiebel-Getriebebau GmbH & Co. KG v Suzhou Kaibo Yikong Drive Technology Co Ltd.*[45] | *Stiebel* |
| 46 | 2021 | *Zhongshan Langhua Property Management Co Ltd. v Guangdong United Asia–Pacific International Investment et al.*[46] | *Langhua* |
| 47 | 2022 | *Ecom Agroindustrial Corp Ltd.. Switzerland v Qingdao Jinhuadong International Trade Co Ltd.*[47] | *Ecom No. 2* |

[44]《慈铭博鳌国际医院有限公司与海南亨延顿医院管理咨询有限公司等申请撤销仲裁裁决民事裁定书》[Civil Decision on the Application for the Annulment of An Arbitral Award between Ciming Bo'ao International Hospital Co Ltd. and HRC-Hainan Holding Company LLC et al.], Beijing 4th IPC, (2021) 京 04 民特 26 号 [Civil Special No. 26], 5 March 2021.

[45]《Stiebel-Getriebebau GmbH & Co.KG与苏州凯博易控驱动科技有限公司申请撤销仲裁裁决民事裁定书》[Civil Decision on the Application for the Annulment of An Arbitral Award between Stiebel-Getriebebau GmbH & Co. KG and Suzhou Kaibo Yikong Drive Technology Co Ltd.], Beijing 4th IPC, (2021) 京 04 民特 833 号, 28 December 2021.

[46]《中山市朗华物业管理有限公司、广东联合亚太国际投资有限公司等申请撤销仲裁裁决特别程序民事裁定书》[Civil Ruling on the Application for the Annulment of an Arbitral Award between Zhongshan Langhua Property Management Co Ltd. and Guangdong United Asia–Pacific International Investment et al.], Guangzhou IPC, (2021) 粤 01 民特 1805 号 [Civil Special No. 1805], 31 December 2021.

[47]《EcoM Agroindustrial Corp Ltd. Switzerland、青岛锦华东国际贸易有限公司申请承认与执行法院判决、仲裁裁决案件民事裁定书》[Civil Decision on the Recognition and Enforcement of Judgments and Arbitral Awards between Ecomagro Industrial Corp Ltd. Switzerland and Qingdao Jinhuadong International Trade Co Ltd.], Qingdao IPC, (2020) 鲁 02 协外认 3 号 [Shandong Judicial Assistance Foreign Recognition No. 3], 25 Feb 2022.

# Bibliography

## *English and Foreign References*

**A Articles/Books/Reports**


Ali, Shahla F., 'Barricades and Checkered Flags: An Empirical Examination of the Perceptions of Roadblocks and Facilitators of Settlement among Arbitration Practitioners in East Asia and the West' (2010) 19 *Pacific Rim Law and Policy Journal* 243

Ali, Shahla F., 'The Morality of Conciliation: An Empirical Examination of Arbitrator "Role Moralities" in East Asia and the West' (2011) 16(1) *Harvard Negotiation Law Review* 1

Al-Shareef, Naif, *Enforcement of Foreign Arbitral Awards in Saudi Arabia: Grounds for Refusal under Article V of the New York Convention* (University of Dundee, 2000)

Andrew, Romauld, 'The ILL-Favour Child of Litigation: International Commercial Arbitration and the Australian Trade Practices Act 1974' (2004) 21(3) *Journal of International Arbitration* 239

Arfazadeh, Homayoon, 'Arbitrability under the New York Convention: the *Lex Fori* Revisited' (2001) 17 *Arbitration International* 73

Arfazadeh, Homayoon, 'In the Shadow of the Unruly Horse: International Arbitration and the Public Policy Exception' (2002) 13 *American Review of International Arbitration* 43

Baamir, Abdulrahman, and Ilias Bantekas, 'Saudi Law as Lex Arbitri: Evaluation of Saudi Arbitration Law and Judicial Practice' (2009) 25(2) *Kluwer Law International* 239

Baniassadi, Mohammad Reza, 'Do Mandatory Rules of Public Law Limit Choice of Law in International Commercial Arbitration' (1992) 10 *International Tax and Business Law* 59

Barrett, Jerome T., and Joseph P. Barrett, *A History of Alternative Dispute Resolution: The Story of a Political, Cultural, and Social Movement* (Jossey-Bass, 2004)

Barnett, Peter R. *Res Judicata, Estoppel and Foreign Judgments: The Preclusive Effects of Foreign Judgments in Private International Law* (Oxford University Press, 2001)

Bartolus, *Bartolo on the Conflict of Laws* (J.A. Clarence Smith trans) (1970) 14 *The American Journal of Legal History* 157

Bermann, George A, 'Arbitration Fundamental: Arbitrability Trouble' (2012) 23 *American Review of International Arbitration* 367

Blatt, Jason, 'Mutual Recognition and Enforcement of Arbitral Awards in Mainland China and Taiwan: A Breakthrough in Cross-Strait Relations' (2006) 36(3) *Hong Kong Law Journal* 585

Böckstiegel, Karl-Heinz, 'Public Policy and Arbitrability' in Pieter Sanders (ed), *Comparative Arbitration Practice and Public Policy in Arbitration*, ICCA Congress Series (Kluwer Law International, 1987) 177

Böckstiegel, Karl-Heinz, 'Public Policy as a Limit to Arbitration and its Enforcement, presented at 11th IBA International Arbitration Day and United Nations New York Convention Day, "The






S. Zhang, *The Public Policy Exception in the Judicial Review of International Commercial Arbitral Awards*, https://doi.org/10.1007/978-3-662-67679-0

New York Convention: 50 Years" in New York on 1 February 2008, published (2008) *IBA Journal of Dispute resolution Special Issue: The New York* Convention—*50 Years* 123

Böckstiegel, Karl-Heinz, 'The Role of Party Autonomy in International Arbitration' (1997) 52(3) *Dispute Resolution Journal* 24

Boivin, Richard, and Nocola Mariani, 'International Arbitration in Canada' (2003) 20(5) *Journal of International Arbitration* 507

Born, Gary B., *International Commercial Arbitration* (Kluwer Law International, 2nd ed, 2014)

Born, Gary, 'The Different Meanings of an Arbitrator's "Evident Partiality" Under U.S. Law', blog article published in March 2013, at http://kluwerarbitrationblog.com/blog/2013/03/20/the-different-meanings-of-an-arbitrators-evident-partiality-under-u-s-law/

Brekoulakis, Stavros L., 'Chapter 2—On Arbitrability: Persisting Misconceptions and New Areas of Concern' in Loukas A. Mistelis and Stavros L. Brekoulakis (eds), *Arbitrability: International and Comparative Perspectives* (Kluwer Law International, 2009) 19

Briner, Robert, 'Switzerland' in Jan Paulsson (ed), *Internatioanl Handbook on Commerc*ial Arbitration (Kluwer International, 1992) 13

Broom, Herber, *A Selection of Legal Maxims, Illustrated and Classified* (3rd ed, Maxwell, 1858)

Brown, Erwan, 'Illegality and Public Policy: Enforcement of Arbitral Awards in England' (2000) *International Arbitration* 31

Brozolo, Luca G. Radicati di, 'Mandatory Rules and International Arbitration' (2012) 23(1) *American Review of International Arbitration* 49

Brozolo, Luca G. Radicati di, 'Arbitration and Competition Law: The Position of the Courts and of Arbitrators' (2011) 27(1) *Arbitration International* 1

Buchanan, Mark A., 'Public Policy and International Commercial Arbitration' (1988) 26(3) *American Business Law Journal* 511

Buxbaum, Richard M. 'Public Law, Ordre Public and Arbitration: A Procedural Scenario and a Suggestion' in Peter Hay et al (eds), *Resolving International Conflicts: Liber amicorum Tibor Varady* (Centre European University Press, 2009) 83

Bühring-Uhle, Christian, Lars Kirchhoff and Matthias Scherer, 'Two Surveys on Arbitration and Settlement' in Christian Bühring-Uhle, et al. (ed), *Arbitration and Mediation in International Business* (Kluwer Law International, 2006) 105

Cao, Lijun, 'A Fair Forum' (2005) 168(6) *Far Eastern Economic Review* 4

Cao, Lijun, Leilei Lu, 'To Be or Not to Be: The Practical Implications of Choosing Foreign Arbitration for Purely Domestic Contracts', at Kluwer Arbitration Blog, 6 March 2015, at http://kluwerarbitrationblog.com/blog/2015/03/06/to-be-or-not-to-be-the-practical-implications-of-choosing-foreign-arbitration-for-purely-domestic-contracts/

Carbonneau,Thomas E., 'Liberal Rules of Arbitrability and the Autonomy of Labor Arbitration in the United States' in Loukas A. Mistelis and Stavros L. Brekoulakis (eds), *Arbitrability: International and Comparative Perspectives* ( Kluwer Law International, 2009) 143

Castagno,Niccolo Pietro, 'International Commercial Arbitration and Punitive Damages' (2011) 4 *Revista de Arbitraje Comercial y de Inversiones* 729

Chamlongrasdr, Dhisadde, 'Tension in Domestic and Internatioal Law on Capacity to Enter into Artiration Agreements: A Survey on Legal Restrictions' (2005) 16 *European Business Law Review* 275

Chen, Jianfu, *Chinese Law: Context and Transfrmation* (Martinus Nijhoff, 2008)

Cheng, Dejun, Michael J. Moser and Shengchang Wang, *International Arbitration in the People's Republic of China: Commentary, Cases and Materials* (Butterworths Asia, 1995)

Cheng, Teresa, 'Features of Arbitral Practice that Contribute to System-Building' (2012) 106 *American Society of International Law Proceedings* 292

Chi, Manjiao, 'Are We "Paper Tigers"? The Limited Procedural Power of Arbitrators Under Chinese Law' (2011) 2011(2) *Journal of Dispute Resolution* 259

'China's Rising GDP and Economic Miracle', BBC News, 24 October 2012, at http://www.bbc.com/news/world-asia-china-20069627

Chukwumerije, Okezie, *Choice of Law in International Commercial Arbitration* (Quorum Books, 1994)
Clark, Daniel, 'Power and Politics in the Chinese Court System' (1996) 10(1) *Columbia Journal of Asian Law* 1
Cohen, Daniel, *Arbitrage et société* (LGDJ 1993)
Cohen, Jerome A., 'International Commercial Arbitration in China: Some Thoughts from Experience' Address at the International Economic Law and China In Its Economic Transition Joint Conference (Nov 4 and 5, 2004)
Cohen, Jerome A., 'Reforming China's Civil Procedure: Judging the Courts' (1997) 45(4) *The American Journal of Comparative Law* 793
Cohen, Jerome A., 'Time to Fix China's Arbitration' (2005) 168(2) *Far East Economic Review* 31
Cole,Richard A., 'The Public Policy Exception to the New York Convention on the Recognition and Enforcement of Arbitral Awards' (1986) *1 Ohio State Journal on Dispute Resolution* 365
Craig,W. Laurence, 'Some Trends and Developments in the Laws and Practice of International Commercial Arbitration' (1995) 20 *Texas International Law Journal* 1
Cremades, Bernardo M., and Ignacio Madalena, 'Parallel Proceedings in International Arbitration' (2008) 24 *Arbitration International* 507
Darwazeh, Nadia & Friven Yeoh, Recognition and Enforcement of Awards under the New York Convention: China and Hong Kong Perspectives (2008) 25 *Journal of International Arbitration* 837
De Ly, Filip, and Audley Sheppard, 'ILA Interim Report on Res Judicata and Arbitration' (2009) 25(1) *Arbitration International* 35
De Ly, Filip, and Audley Sheppard, 'ILA Final Report on Res Judicata and Arbitration' (2009) 25(1) *Arbitration International* 67
de Ly, Filip and Audley Sheppard, 'ILA Recommendations on Lis Pendens and Res Judicata and Arbitration' (2009) 25(1) *Arbitration International* 83
Derains,Yves, 'Public Policy and the Law Applicable to the Dispute in International Arbitration ' in Pieter Sanders (ed), *Comparative Arbitration Practice and Public Policy in Arbitration*, ICCA Congress Series (Kluwer Law International, 1987) 227
Dezalay, Yves, and Bryant G. Garth, *Dealing the Virtue: International Commercial Arbitration and the Construction of A Transnational Legal Order* (University of Chicago, 1996)
di Pietro, Domenico, 'General Remarks on Arbitrability Under the New York Convention' in Loukas A. Mistelis and Stavros L. Brekoulakis (ed), *Arbitrability: International and Comparative Perspectives* (Kluwer Law International, 2009) 85
Dolinger, Jacob, 'World Public Policy: Real International Public Policy in the Conflict of Laws' (1982) 17 *Texas International Law Journal (Austin)* 167
Drahozal, Christopher R. and Richard W. Naimark (ed.), *Toward a Science of International Arbitration: Collected Empirical Research*, (Kluwer Law International, 2005)
El-Ahdab, Jalal, 'Arbitration in Saudi Arabia under the New Arbitration Act 1983' (1986) 3 *Journal of* International Arbitration 23
El-Ahdab, Jalal, 'General Introduction on Arbitration in Arab Countries', in (1998) 27 *International Handbook on Commercial Arbitration* Annex 1
El-Ahdab, Jalal, 'Saudi Arabia Accedes to the New York Convention' (1994) 11 *Journal of International Arbitration* 87
Fan, Kun, *Arbitration in China: A Legal and Cultural Analysis* (Hart, 2013)
Fan, Kun, 'Arbitration in China, Practices, Legal Obstacles and Reforms' (2008) 19(2) *ICC International Court of Arbitration Bulletin* 25
Fan, Kun, 'Transnational Standards Struggling with Local Norms: Through the Lens of Arbitration Transplantation in China' (2013b) 18 *Harvard Negotiation Law Review* 175
Fan, Kun, 'The Risks of Apparent Bias when an Arbitrator Acts as a Mediator: Remarks on Hong Kong Court's Decision in *Gao Haiyan*' (2011) 13 *Yearbook of Private International Law* 93
Farnsworth, Allan, 'Punitive Damages in Arbitration' (1990–1991) 20 *Stetson Law Review* 395

Fry, James D., 'Desordre Public International under the New York Convention: Wither Truly International Public Policy' (2009) 8(1) *Chinese Journal of International Law* 81

Fu, Hualing, 'Putting China's Judiciary into Perspective: Is It Independent, Competent, and Fair' in Erik Jensen and Thomas Heller (eds), *Beyond Common Knowledge: Empirical Approaches to the Rule of Law* (Stanford University Press, 2003) 193

Gaillard, Emmanuel, and John Savage, *Fouchard Gaillard Goldman on International Commercial Arbitration* (Kluwer Law International, 1999)

Gaillard, Emmanuel, *Legal Theory of International Arbitration* (Martinus Nijhoff Publishers, 2010)

Garnett, Richard, 'The Legal Framework for International Arbitration in Australia: The Old and the New' in Luke Nottage and Richard Garnett (eds), *International Arbitration in Australia* (Federation, 2010)

Gemmell, Arthur J. *Western and Chinese Arbitration: the Arbitration Chain* (University Press of America, 2008)

Goldman, Berthold, '*La lex mercatoria dans les contrats et l'arbitrage internationaux : réalité et perspectives*' (1979) *Journal du Droit International* 475

Goldman,Berthold 'The Complementary Roles of Judges and Arbitrators in Ensuring that International Commercial Arbitration is Effective' in *60 Years of ICC Arbitration: A Look at the Future* (ICC Publishing, 1984) 257

Gordon, Randy D., 'Only One Kick at the Cat: A Contextual Rubric for Evaluating Res Judicata and Collateral Estoppel in International Commercial Arbitration' (2008) 18 *Florida Journal of International Law* 549

Gotanda, John Y., 'Charting Developments Concerning Punitive Damages: Is the Tide Changing?' (2007) 45 *Columbia Journal of Transnational Law* 507

Gotanda, John Y., 'Punitive Damages: A Comparative Analysis' (2003) 42 *Columbia Journal of Transnational Law* 391

Greenberg, Simon, Christopher Kee and Romesh Weeramantry, *International Commercial Arbitration: an Asia–Pacific Perspective* (Cambridge University Press, 2011)

Gu, Weixia, 'Judicial Review over Arbitration in China: Assessing the Extent of the Latest Pro-Arbitration Move by the Supreme People's Court in the People's Republic of China' (2009–2010) 27(2) *Wisconsin International Law Journal* 221

Gu, Weixia, '15 Years of the Handover: The Rise, Discontent, and Positive Interaction of Cross-border Arbitration in Hong Kong with Mainland China' (2013) 9 *East Asia Law Review* 42

Hanotiau, Bernard, "*L'arbitrabilité*", in *Recueil des Cours—Collected Courses of The Hague Academy of International Law* (Martinus Nijhoff Publishers, 2003)

Harris, Jonathan, and Frank Meisel, 'Public Policy and the Enforcement of International Arbitration Awards: Controlling the Unruly Horse' (1998) 1 *Lloyd's Maritime and Commercial Law Quarterly* 568

He, Qisheng, 'Public Policy in Enforcement of Foreign Arbitral Awards in the Supreme People's Court of China' (2013) 43 *Hong Kong Law Journal* 1037

Heller, David, 'The Public Policy Exception in Hong Kong: The Cultural Sliding Scale' (2013) 3 *The Arbitration Brief* 115

Heuman, Lars, and Göran Millqvist, 'Swedish Supreme Court Refuses to Enforce an Arbitral Award Pursuant to the Public Policy Provision of the New York Convention' (2003) 20(5) *Journal of International Arbitration* 493

Heye, William, 'Forum Selection for International Dispute Resolution in China—Chinese Courts vs CIETAC' (2003–2004) 27 *Hasting International and Comparative Law Review* 535

Holtzmann, Howard M., and Joseph E. Neuhaus, *A Guide to the UNCITRAL Model Law on International Commercial Arbitration: Legislative History and Commentary* (Kluwer Law and Taxation, 1989)

Horrigan, Brenda, Felix Hess and Siew Lin Mok, 'Chapter 5: Arbitration in China: Recent Developments' in Michael J. Moser (ed.), *Business Disputes in China* (Juris, 2009) 52

Hunter, Martin, and Gui Conde e Silva, 'Transnational Public Policy and Its Application in Investment Arbitrations' (2003) 4 *Journal of World Investment and Trade* 367

Hwang, Michael, and Shaun Lee, 'Survey of South East Asian Nations on the Application of the New York Convention' (2008) 25(6) *Journal of International Arbitration* 873

Hwang, Michael, and Rajesh C Muttath, 'Arbitration in Company Matters' (2001) 5 *International Business Law Journal* 555

International Law Institute, 'Resolution on the Autonomy of the Parties in International Contracts Between Private Persons or Entities' (1992) 64 *Annuaire de l'Institut de droit international* 383

Johnston, Graeme, 'Bridging the Gap Between Western and Chinese Arbitration Systems—A Practical Introduction for Businesses' (2007) 24(6) *Journal of International Arbitration* 565

Jones, David Phillip, and Anne S. de Villars, 'Natural Justice and the Duty to be Fair' in *Principles of Administrative Law* (Carswell, 5th ed, 2009) 208

Juenger, Friedrich K., *Choice of Law and Multistate Justice* (Martinus Nijhoff 1993)

J., S.S., Jr, 'Mandatory Arbitration as a remedy for intra-close corporate disputes' (1970) 56 *Virginia Law Review* 271

Kreindler, Richard H., 'Approaches to the Application of Transnational Public Policy by Arbitrators' (2003) 4 *Journal of World Investment and Trade* 239

Kronke, Herbert et al, *Recognition and Enforcement of Foreign Arbitral Awards* (Wolters Kluwer, 2010)

Lalive, Pierre, 'Transnational (or Truly International) Public Policy and International Arbitration' in Pieter Sanders (ed), *Comparative Arbitration Practice and Public Policy in Arbitration,*, ICCA Congress Series (Kluwer Law International, 1987)

Lasok, Paul, *The European Court of Justice: Practice and Procedure* (Butterworths 1994)

Lew, Julian D.M. *Applicable Law in International Commercial Arbitration:A Study in Commercial Arbitration Awards* (Oceana Publications, 1978)

Lew, Julian D. M., Loukas A. Mistelis and Stefan Michael Kröll, *Comparative International Commercial Arbitration* (Kluwer Law International, 2003)

Li, Yuwen 'Court Reform in China: Problems, Progress and Prospects' in Jianfu Chen, Yuwen Li and Jan Michiel Otto (eds), *Implementation of Law in the People's Republic of China* (Kluwer Law International 2002)

Liebscher, Christoph, 'European Public Policy: A Black Box?' (2000) 17(3) *Journal of International Arbitration* 73

Liu, Eric, Yaxing Zhang, Yuhao Lu and Delong Zou, 'Mainland court's standards for identifying social public interests when recognizing off-shore arbitration awards', 25 December 2014, at http://www.hankunlaw.com/downloadfile/newsAndInsights/6ac7910a05c1ec017cfde99f1de18053.pdf

Loong, Anne-Marie, 'Steps toward an International Arbitration Culture? A Dissenting View from the People's Republic of China' (2007) 1(5) *World Arbitration and Mediation Review* 665

Luttrell, Sam, *Bias Challenges in International Arbitration: The Need for a 'Real Danger' Test*, (Kluwer Law, 2009)

Luttrell, Sam, 'Public Policy Conflicts in the Arbitrability of the Trade Practice Act 1974 (Cth)' (2007) 4 *Macquarie Journal of Business Law* 139

Lynch, Katherine, *The Forces of Economic Globalization: Challenges to the Regime of International Commercial Arbitration* (Kluwer Law International, 2003)

Ma, Winnie (Jo-Mei), *Public Policy in the Judicial Enforcement of Arbitral Awards: Lessons for and from Australia* (PhD Thesis, Bond University 2005)

Malouche, Habib, 'Recent Developments in Arbitration Law in Tunisia' (1991) 8(2) *Journal of International Arbitration* 23, 29; Tarek F. Riad, 'Arbitration and the Legal Business Environment in Egypt' (2000) 17(5) *Journal of International Arbitration* 169

Martinez, Ramona, 'Recognition and Enforcement of International Arbitral Awards under the United Nations Convention of 1958: The Refusal Provisions;' (1990) 24(2) *The International Lawyer* 487

Maurer, Anton, *The Public Policy Exception under the New York Convention: History, Interpretation and Application* (Juris, 2012)

Mayer, Pierre, 'Mandatory Rules of Law in International Arbitration' (1986) 2 Arbitration International 274
Mayer, Pierre, and Audley Sheppard, 'Final Report on Public Policy as a Bar to Enforcement of International Arbitral Awards' (Paper presented at the International Law Association New Delhi Conference Committee on International Commercial Arbitration, New Delhi, 2002)
McConnaughay, Phillip J, 'The Risks and Virtues of Lawlessness: A "Second Look" at International Commercial Arbitration' (1998–1999) 93 *Northwestern University Law Review* 453
McClendon, J. Stewart, 'Enforcement of Foreign Arbitral Award s in the United States' (1982) 4 *Northwestern Journal of International Law and Business* 58
McLaughlin, Joseph T., and Laurie Genevro, 'Enforcement of Arbitral Awards under the New York Convention—Practice in U.S. Courts' (1986) 3 *International Tax and Business Law* 249
Meick, Ethan, Nargiza Salidjanova, 'China's Response to U.S.—South Korean Missile Defense System Deployment and its Implications', *US.-China Economic and Security Review Commission Staff Research Report*, 26 July 2017
Mehren, Arthur von, 'International Commercial Arbitration: The Contribution of the French Jurisprudence' (1986) 46(4) *Louisiana Law Review* 1045
Merhen, George M. von, and Alana C. Jochum, 'Is International Arbitration becoming too American?' (2011) 2 *Global Business Law Review* 47
Meidanis, Harris P. 'Public Policy and *Ordre Public* in the Private International Law of EU: Traditional Positions and Modren Trends' (2005) 30(1) *European Law Review* 95
Mistelis, Loukas A., 'Arbitrability: International and Comparative Perspectives' in Loukas A. Mistelis and Stavros L. Brekoulakis (eds), *Arbitrability: International and Comparative Perspectives* (Kluwer Law International, 2009) 1
Mistelis, Loukas A., and Stavros L. Brekoulakis (ed), *Arbitrability: International and Comparative Perspectives* (Kluwer Law International, 2009)
Morgan, Robert, and Man Sin Yeung, 'Enforcement of Foreign and Mainland Arbitral Awards in Hong Kong: Med-Arb, Public Policy and Waiver' (2012) *Asian Dispute Review* 28
Moser, Michael J. 'Chapter 1: Managing Business Disputes in Today's China: Introduction,' in Michael J. Moser (ed), *Business Disputes in China* (Juris Publishing, 2009)
Moser, Michael, and Jianlong Yu, 'CIETAC and its Work—An Interview with Vice Chairman Yu Jianlong' (2007) 24(6) *Journal of International Arbitration* 555
Moser, Michal J., 'CIETAC Arbitration:A Success Story?' (1998) 15(1) *Journal of International Arbitration* 27
Mourre, Alexis, and Luca G Radicati di Brozolo, 'Towards Finality of Arbitral Awards: Two Steps Forward, One Step Back' (2006) 23(2) *Journal of International Arbitration* 171
Mustill , Michael John, 'Transnational Arbitration and English Law' (1984) 37(1) *Current Legal Problems* 133
Nakamura, Tatsuya, 'Brief Empirical Study on Arb-Med in the JCAA Arbitration' (2009) 22 *JCAA News Letter* 10
'New World Order? How Americanised Has International Arbitration Actually Become?' (2013) 18(2) *Arbitration Newsletter*
Note, 'Arbitration as a Means of Settling Disputes within Close Corporations' (1963) 63(2) *Columbia Law Review* 267
Nussbaum, Arthur, 'Public Policy and the Political Crisis in the Conflict of Laws' (1940) 49(6) *The Yale Law Journal* 1027
Otto, Dirk, and Omaia Elwan, 'Article V(2)' in Herbert Kronke et al (eds), *Recognition and Enforcement of Foreign Arbitral Awards* (Wolter Kluwer, 2010) 345
Park, William W, *Arbitration of International Business Disputes: Studies in Law and Practice* (Oxford University, 2012)
Paulsson, Jan, 'Arbitration Unbound: An Award Detached from the Law of its Country of Origin' (1981)30 *International and Comparative Law Quaterly* 358
Paulsson, Jan, 'Delocalization of International Commercial Arbitration: When and Why It Matters' (1983) 32 *International and Comparative Law Quaterly* 53

Paulsson, Jan, 'The Extent of Independence of International Arbitration from the Law of the Situs' in Julian D. M. Lew (ed), *Contemporary Problems in International Arbitration* (Cambridge, 1986) 141

Peerenboom, Randall, 'Seek Truth From Facts: An Empirical Study of Enforcement of Arbitral Awards in the PRC' (2001) 49 *American Journal of Comparative Law* 249

Peerenboom,Randall 'Law Enforcement and the Legal Profession in China' in Jianfu Chen, Yuwen Li and Jan Michiel Otto (eds), *Implementation of Law in the People's Republic of China* (Kluwer Law International 2002)

Petsche, Markus, 'Punitive Damages in International Commercial Arbitration: Much Ado about Nothing?' (2013) 29(1) *Arbitration International* 89

Potter, Pittman B., *The Chinese Legal System: Globalization and Local Legal Culture* (Routledge, 2001)

Poudret, Jean-Francois, 'Concluding Remarks on Relationship between State Courts and Arbitral Tribunals?' in (2001) *ASA Special Series No.15: Arbitral Tribunal or State Court: Who must defer to whom?* 163

Poudret, Jean-Francois, Sébastien Besson and Stephen Birti, *Comparative Law of International Arbitration* (Sweet & Maxwell, 2nd ed, 2007)

*Pryles, Michael, The Asia–Pacific Arbitration Review 2013, at* http://www.globalarbitrationreview.com/reviews/44/sections/150/chapters/1694/preface/

Queen Mary University of London School of International Arbitration, *2021 International Arbitration Survey: Adapting arbitration to a changing world*, https://arbitration.qmul.ac.uk/media/arbitration/docs/LON0320037-QMUL-International-Arbitration-Survey-2021_19_WEB.pdf

Racine, Jean-Baptiste, *L'Arbitrage Commercial International et l'ordre Public* (LGDJ, 1999)

Redfern, Alan, Martin Hunter, Nigel Blackaby, Constantine Partasides, *Law and Practice on International Commercial Arbitration* (Oxford University, 4th ed, 2009)

Report of the United Nations Commission on International Trade Law on the Work of Its Eighteenth Session, UN GAOR, 40th sess, , UN Doc A/40/17, (21 June 1985)

Rich, Leanne, 'The Arbitrability of TPA Claims: To Stay or not to Stay?' (2010) 18 *Trade Practices Law Journal* 7

Roy,K.T., 'The New York Convention and Saudi Arabia: Can a Country Use the Public Policy Defense to Refuse Enforcement of Non-Domestic Arbitral Awards?' (1994) 18(3) *Fordham International Law Journal* 920

Sanders, Pieter (ed.), *Comparative Arbitration Practices and Public Policy in Arbitration,* ICCA Congress Series (Kluwer Law International, 1987)

Sanders, Pieter, 'Commentary' in *60 Years of ICC Arbitration—A Look at the Future* (ICC 1984)

Sanders, Pieter, 'The New York Convention' in *International Commercial Arbitration* (Martinus Nijhoff, 1960) vol II, 292

Saumier, Genevieve, 'What's in a Name—Lloyd's, International Comity and Public Policy' (2002) 37(2) *Canada Business Law Journal* 388

Savigny, Friedrich Karl, *Private International Law: A Treatise of the Conflict of Laws and the Limits of Their Operation in Respect of Time and Space* (William Guthrie trans, Nabu, 2010) [trans of: *System des Heutigen Romischen Rechts* (first published 1840)]

Sayed, Abdulhay, *Corruption in International Trade and Commercial Arbitration* (Wolters Kluwer, 2004)

Schlosser, Peter, 'Arbitral Tribunal or State Court Who Must Defer to Whom?' in (2001) *ASA Special Series No. 15: Arbitral Tribunal or State Court, Who must defer to whom?* 32

Schneider, Michael, 'Combining Arbitration with Conciliation' in Albert van den Berg (ed), *International Dispute Resolution: Towards an International Arbitration Culture*, ICCA Congress Series (1998) 57

Schwebel, Stephen M., and Susan G. Lahne, 'Public Policy and Arbitral Procedure' in Pieter Sanders (ed), *Comparative Arbitration Practices and Public Policy in Arbitration,* ICCA Congress Series (Kluwer Law International, 1987)

Seidenberg, Steven, 'International Arbitration Loses Its Grip: Are U.S. Lawyers to Blame?' (2010) 96 *ABA Journal* 50

Seriki, Hakeem, 'Enforcement of Foreign Arbitral Awards and Public Policy-A Note of Caution' (2000) 9 *The Arbitration and Dispute Resolution Law Journal* 192

Sever, Jay R, 'The Relaxation of Inarbitrability and Public Policy Checks on US and Foreign Arbtiration: Arbitration out of Control?' (1991) 65 *Tulane Law Review* 1667

Sheppard, Auldey, 'Interim Report on Public Policy as a Bar to Enforcement of International Arbitral Awards' (2000) 19(3) *Arbitration International* 217

Shore, Laurence, 'The United States' Perspective on "Arbitrability"' in Loukas A. Mistelis and Stavros L. Brekoulakis (ed), *Arbitrability: International and Comparative Perspectives* (Kluwer Law International 2009) 69

Silingardi, Gabriele *Il compromesso in arbitri nelle società di capitali* (Giuffrè 1979)

Fernando Dias Simões, 'Macau: A Seat for Sino-Lusophone Commercial Arbitration' (2012) 29(4) *Journal of International Arbitration* 375

Söderlund, Christer, 'Lis Pendens, Res Judicata and the Issue of Parallel Judicial Proceedings' (2005) 22 *Journal of International Arbitration* 301

Talmon, Stefan, *Bing Bing Jia, the South China Sea Arbitration: A Chinese Perspective* (Hart Publishing, 2014)

Tang, Houzhi, 'Is There an Expanding Culture that Favors Combining Arbitration with Conciliation or Other ADR Procedures?' in Albert Jan van den Berg (ed), *International Dispute Resolution: Towards an International Arbitration Culture*, ICCA Congress Series (Kluwer Law International, 1998) vol 8, 101

Tang, Houzhi, 'Combination of Arbitration with Conciliation—Arb-Med' in Albert Jan van den Berg (ed), *New Horizons in International Commercial Arbitration and Beyond, 2004 Bejing*, ICCA Congress Series (Kluwer Law International 2005) vol 12, 547

Tao, Jinzhou, *Arbitration Law and Practice in China* (Kluwer International, 2012)

Tao, Jingzhou, 'Enforcement of SCC Arbitration Awards in China' in Kaj Hobér, Annette Magnusson and Marie Öhrström (eds), *Between East and West: Essays in Honour of Ulf Franke* (2010)

Thirgood, Russell, 'Critique of Foreign Arbitration in China' (2000) 17(3) *Journal of International Arbitration* 89

Trakman, Leon, 'From the Medieval to the Twenty First Century Law Merchant', (2011)28(4) *American Business Law Journal* 775

Trakman, Leon, "Legal Traditions' and International Commercial Arbitration' (2006) 17 *American Review of International Arbitration* 1

UNCITRAL, *Explanatory Notes of the UNCITRAL Model Law*, http://www.uncitral.org/pdf/english/texts/arbitration/ml-arb/07-86998_Ebook.pdf

UNCITRAL, *Status: Convention on the Recognition and Enforcement of Foreign Arbitral Awards (New York,* 1958*)*, at http://www.uncitral.org/uncitral/en/uncitral_texts/arbitration/NYConvention_status.html

van den Berg, Albert Jan, *The New York Convention of 1958: Towards a Uniform Judicial Interpretation* (Kluwer Law International, 1981)

van den Berg, Albert Jan, *Improving the Efficiency of Arbitration Agreements and Awards: 40 Years of Application of the New York Convention* (Kluwer Law International, 1999)

van den Berg, Albert Jan, 'New York Convention of 1958: Refusals of Enforcement' (2007) 18(2) *ICC International Court of Arbtiration Bulletin* 1

van den Berg, Albert Jan, 'Should the Setting Aside of the Arbitral Award be Abolished?' (2014) 29(2) *ICSID Review* 263

Villiers, Luke 'Breaking in the 'unruly horse': The status of mandatory rules of law as a public policy basis for the non-enforcement of Arbitral awards' (2011) 18 Australian International Law Journal 155

Viscasillas, Pilar Perales, Arbitrability of (Intra-) Corporate Disputes, in Loukas A. Mistelis and Stavros L. Brekoulakis (eds), *Arbitrability: International and Comparative Perspectives* ( Kluwer Law International, 2009) 273

Viscasillas, Perales, *Arbitrabilidad y convenio arbitral: Ley 60/2003 de Arbitraje y Derecho Societario* (Thomson-Aranzadi 2005)

von Zumbusch, Ludwig, 'Arbitrability of Antitrust Claims under US, German and EEC Law—the "International Transaction" Criterion and Public Policy' (1997) 22 *Texas International Law Journal* 291

Voser, Nathalie, 'Mandatory Rules of Law as a Limitation on the Law Applicable in International Commercial Arbitration' (1996) 7 *American Review of International Arbitration* 319

Wade, Shai, 'Westacre v Soleimany: What policy? Which public?' (1999) *International Arbitration* 97

Wang, Shengchang, 'CIETAC's Perspective on Arbitration and Conciliation Concerning China' in Albert Jan van den Berg (ed), *New Horizons in International Commercial Arbitration and Beyond*, ICCA Congress Series (Kluwer Law International, 2005a) vol 12, 27

Wang, Shengchang, 'Enforcement of Foreign Arbitral Awards in the People's Republic of China' in Christopher R. Drahozal and Richard W. Naimark (eds), *Towards Science on International Arbitration: Collected Empirical Research* (Kulwer Law International, 2005b) 277

Wang, Shengchang, 'Recognition and Enforcement of Foreign Arbitral Awards in China' (1999) 2 *Journal of International Arbitration* 519

Ward, 'In the Matter of an arbitration between Marco Barbier and Shearon Lehman Hutton Inc' (1991) 6 *Mealey's International Arbitration Reports* 14

Watt, Horatia Muir, and Luca G. Radicati di Brozolo, 'Party Autonomy and Mandatory Rules in a Global World', (2004) 6 *International Law Forum* 90

Westlake, John, *A Treatise on Private International Law* (Sweet & Maxwell, 7th ed, 1925)

Wu, Chien-Huei, 'Mutual Recognition of Arbitral Awards among Taiwan, China, Kong Kong and Macau: Regulatory Framework and Judicial Development' (2010) 3(1) *Contemporary Asia Arbitration Journal* 65

Wunschheim, Clarisse von, *Enforcement of commercial arbitral awards in China: business laws of China* (West, 2011)

Xia, Xiaohong, 'Implementation of the New York Convention in China' (2011) 1 *International Commercial Arbitration Brief* 20

Xiao, Yongping, and Huo, Zhenxin, '*Ordre Public* in China's Private International Law' (2005) 54 *American Journal of Comparative Law* 653

Xu, Weigong, 'Definition of Arbitration in China' (2011) 30 *Journal of Law and Commerce* 107

Yang, Honglei, 'Recognition and Enforcement of Arbitration Agreements and Arbitral Awards in Chinese Courts', paper presented at the ICC-SIAC Conference: Reflections on Diverse Issues in International Arbitration, 2 September 2008.

Yeoh, Friven, and Desmond Ang, 'Reflections on Gao Haiyan—Of 'Arb-med', 'Waivers', and Cultual Contextualisation of Public Policy Arguments' (2012) 29(3) *Journal of International Arbitration* 285

Youssef, Karim, 'The Death of Inarbitrability' in Loukas A. Mistelis and Stavros L. Brekoulakis (eds), *Arbitrability: International and Comparative Perspectives* (Kluwer Law International, 2009) 47

Zhang, Mo, 'Party Autonomy and Beyond: An International Perspective of Contractual Choice of Law' (2006) 20(2) *Emory International Law Review* 511

Zhang, Shu, Peng Guo, 'The (ab)use of the public policy ground in the New York Convention in the judicial review of foreign arbitral awards: Recent developments in China', (2021) 43 *Houston Journal of International Law* 553

Zhang, Tietie, 'Enforceability of Ad Hoc Arbitration Agreements in China: China's Incomplete Ad Hoc Arbitration System' (2013) 46 *Cornell International Law Journal* 361

Zhang, Xianchu 'Enforcement of Arbitral Awards Between Mainland China and Hong Kong: Before and After Reunification' in Raymond Wacks (ed), *The New Legal Order in Hong Kong* (Hong Kong University Press, 1999) 195

**B Cases**

Arbitration Awards
ICC Case No. 5946, reported in (1991) 16 *Yearbook-Commercial Arbitration* 97
ICC Case No.1110, 15 January 1963

ICSID Case
*Ansung Housing Co., Ltd. v. People's Republic of China,* ICSID Case No. ARB/14/25
*Ping An Life Insurance Company, Limited and Ping An Insurance (Group) Company, Limited v. The Government of Belgium,* ICSID Case No. ARB/12/29
*AsiaPhos Limited and Norwest Chemicals Pte Ltd v People's Republic of China,* ICSID Case No.ADM/21/1

ICSID Annual Proceedings
*Industria Nacional de Alimentos, S.A. and Indalsa Perú, S.A. v The Republic of Peru,* ICSID Case No. ARB/03/4—Annulment Proceeding, dated 5 September 2007
Judicial Decisions
Austria
*GmbH v. O B.V. (Netherlands), O Co Ltd (Japan) and others,* Oberster Gerichtshof [Supreme Court], 4Ob80/08f, 26 August 2008
Not indicated v. Not indicated, Oberste Gerichtshof, 3, 11 June 1969
Not indicated, OGH SZ 2005, reported in (2005) 30 *Yearbook-Commercial Arbitration* 421 (Supreme Court, Austria, decided 2005) 433

Australia
*XL Petroleum NSW Pty Ltd* v *Caltex Oil (Aust.) Pty Ltd* (1985) 155 CLR 448
*Lamb* v *Cotogno* (1987) 74 ALR 188
*Walter Rau Neusser Oel und Fett AG v. Cross Pacific Trading Ltd* [2005] FAC 1102 (Federal Court Australia)

Canada
*Éditions Chouette inc. v. Desputeaux,* 2003 SCC 17
*Karaha Bodas Company LLC v Perusahaan Pertambangan Minyak Dan Gas Bumi Negara,* [2004] A.J.No.1440, (Alberta Court of Queen's Bench, Canada)
*Society of Lloyd's v Saunders* (2001) 210 PCR(4th) 519, 55 OR(3d) 688

China
*BNA v. BNB,* Shanghai 1st IPC, (2020) Hu 01 Min Te No.83, 29 June 2020
*Brentwood Industries, Inc., v. Guangdong Fa'anlong Machinery Complete Set Equipment Engineering Co Ltd.,* Enforcement of ICC Case No.18929/CYK, Guangzhou IPC, (2015) Hui Zhong Fa Min Si Chu Zi No.62, 6 Aug 2020
*Lion Dragon v Smartdot Tech,* not published, Beijing Second IPC, 13 February 2006
*Revpower Ltd. v Shanghai Far East Aviation Technology Import-Export Com,* not published
*Misuer v. Guangxia Industry et al.* Guangdong HPC [2011] [Guangdong HPC Enforcement Reply No. 43], 19 May 2011

European Court of Justice
*Eco Swiss China Time Ltd v. Benetton International NV* (C-126/97) [1999] ECR I-03055
*Elisa María Mostaza Claro v. Centro Móvil Milenium SL.* (C-168/05) [2006] ECR I-10421

*Ingmar GB Ltd v Eaton Leonard Technologies Inc,* (C-381/98) [2000] ECR I-9305

Egypt

Unpublished Case No.815/52 of May 21, 1990 (Supreme Court, Egypt)

Unpublished, Court de Cassation [Supreme Court], decided Jan 22, 2008

France

*Arrêt Dalico Cass 1ere* (1994) Rev Arb 116, 20 December 1993

*Compagnie de Saint-Gobain-Pont* à Mousson v The Fertilizer Corp of India Ltd, Cour d'appel of Paris[Paris Court of Appeal] (1st Chamber) 10 May 1971

Cour d'appel de Paris [Paris Court of Appeal] 9 II 1966 264, 9 February 1966

*Courreges Design v Andre Courreges* (1992) Rev Arb 110 (Paris Court of Appeal 5 Apr 1990)

*European Gas Turbines SA v Westman International Ltd,* (1994) Rev Arb 359

*Excelsior Film TV, srl v. UGC-PH,* Cour de Cassation [Supreme Court], 24 March 1998

*Gallay v Fabricated Metals INC [2000] Rev Arb 805,* French Cour de Cassation [French Supreme Court], 5 January 1999

*Ganz v. Nationale des Chemins de Fer Tunisiens (SNCFT),* (1991) Rev Arb 478

Siemens AG and BKMI Industrienlagen GmbH v Dutco Construction, Court of Cassation, First Civil Chamber, Decision of 7 January 1992, Case No. 89-18708/89-18726

*Linde AG v Halyvourgiki AE,* 2010 Rev arb 124 (Paris Cour d'appel, 22 October 2009)

Sonic SACI v Novokuznetsk Aluminium Plain [1998] CLC 730

*Thalès* v *Ingénierie des technologies nouvelles* (2002–2003) 2 *Cahiers de l'arbitrage* 362 (Paris, January 18, 2003)

Germany

*Billerbeck Cie v Bergaban-Handel GmbhH, Berlin-East,* Tribunal Fédéral (Bundesgericht), 3 May 1967, reported in (1976) 1 *Yearbook-Commercial Arbitration* 199

Bundesgerichtshof [Federal Court of Justice], 4 June reported in 118 *Entscheidungen des Bundesgerichtshofes in Zivilsachen* [BGHZ] 312

Czechoslovak Firm C. (claim assigned to a German Company) v. German (F.R.), Oberlandesgericht Hamburg; Bundesgerichtshof [Supreme Court], 14 October 1964

*Danish buyer v German (F.R.) seller,* Oberlandesgericht Köln [Higher Regional Court of Koeln], 10 June 1976

*Firm P v. Firm F,* Oberlandesgericht Hamburg[Higher Regional Court of Hamburg], 3 April 1975

German Charterer v. Romanian Shipowner, Bundesgerichtshof [Supreme Court], 15 May 1986

German Supreme Court, 22 June 1982, *Allg Ver. GH. v EK.*, reported in *BGHZ* 59

BGH, 27 XII 1960, BGHZ 34, 169

BGH, 24 V 1962 NJW 1962, 1436

Hong Kong SAR

*China Nanhai Oil Joint Service Corp. Shenzhen Branch v. Gee Tai Holdings Co Ltd.* [1995] 2 HKLR 215

*Gao Haiyan v Keeneye Holdings Ltd* [2012] 1 HKLRD 627 (Court of Appeal Hong Kong)

*Hebei Import and Export* v *Polytek Engineering Co.* [1999] 1 HKLRD 665 (Court of Final Appeal, Hong Kong)

*Karaha Bodas Co. LLC v Perusahaan Pertambangan Minyak Dan Gas Bumi Negara* [2007] HKCA 429 (Court of Appeal, Hong Kong)

*Paklito Investment Ltd v Klocker East Asia Ltd* [1993] 2 HKLR 39 (High Court Hong Kong)

*Shanghai City Foundation Works Corp* v *Sunlink Ltd* [2001] HCCT No. 83 of 200 (Court of First Instance Hong Kong)

India

*COSID v Steel Authority of India,* AIR 1986 Del. 8(22) (Delhi High Court, India)

*European Grain & Shipping Ltd. v. Seth Oil Mills Ltd.*, High Court of Bombay, 29 January 1983
*Renusagar Power Co Ltd v General Electric Co AIR 1994 SC 860*
*Smita Conductors Ltd v Euro Alloys Ltd*, Appeal (civil) 12930 of 1996, Supreme Court of India

Italy
*Intercommerce, Sofia v. Menaguale Eugenio*, Corte D'Appello Di Rome, 24 September 1973
*Repubblica deall' Ecuador—Casa della cultura ecuadoriana v. Danosso*, tribunal of Turin, reported in *RDIPP* 18, 25 March 1982

Japan
Buyer v Seller, High Court of Tokyo, 27 January 1994
Netherlands
*Tianjin Stationary & Sporting Goods Import and Export Corporation v Verisport BV*, Arrondissementsrechtbank [Court of First Instance], Zutphen, 3 September 1996

New Zealand
*CBI NZ Ltd* v *Badger Chiyoda* [1989] 2 NZLR 669

Spain
*English Company X v. Spanish Company Y,* Tribunal Supremo [Supreme Court], 10 February 1984
*X (Finnish shipowner) v. Y (Spanish charterer)*, Tribunal Superior [Supreme Court], 11 February 1981

Sweden
*AB Götaverken v. General National Maritime Transport Company*, Supreme Court of Sweden, 13 August 1979

Switzerland
*Dutch seller v. Swiss buyer*, Obergericht Of Basle, 3 June 1971, Obergericht of Basle [Appeal court of Basel], 3 June 1971
*Fincantieri-Cantieri Navali Italiani S.p.A. et Oto Melara S.p.A. v M. et Tribunal Arbitral,* ATF 118 II 353 (June 23, 1992)
*Inter Maritime Management SA v. Russin & Vecchi,* Tribunal Fédéral [Supreme Court], Not Indicated, 9 January 1995
*Main contractor v Subcontractor,* Tribunal Fédéral [Supreme Court of Switzerland], 14 November 1991
*Rothenberger v GEFA*, ATF 93 II 379 (Swiss Supreme Court)
*W v F and V, Decision* dated 30 Dec. 1994, reported in (1995) *ASA Bulletin* 217
Bezirksgericht [Court of First Instance], Affoltern am Albis, 26 May 1994, affirmed by the Court of Appeal in Zurich on 26 July 1995

UK
*Dalmia Bairy Industries Ltd v National Bank of Pakistan* [1978] 2 Lloyd's Rep 223
*Deutsche Schachtbau-und Tiefbohrgesellscaft mbH v Ras Al Khaimah National Oil Company* [1987] 2 *Lloyd's Rep* 246
*Egerton v Brownlow* (1853) 4 HLC 1
*Fiona Trust & Holding Corporation and Others v. Privalov and Others*, [2007] 2 Lloyd's Rep. 267 (UK)
*Kill* v *Hollister* [1746] 95 ER 532
*Minmetals Germany GmbH v Ferco Steel Ltd (1999)* [1999] 1 All ER 739
*Regazonni v KC Sthia Ltd* 1958 AC 301; [1957] 3 All ER 286
*Richardson v Melish* (1824) 2 Bing 228
*Soleimany v Soleimany* [1998] 3 WLR 811, [1999] QB 785 (CA)

*Westacre Investments Inc. v. Judoimport-SDPR Holdings Co. Ltd.*, Beogradska Banka and others, [1999] 2 Lloyd's Rep 65 High Court of Justice, Queen's Bench Division (Commercial Court), 19 December 1997
*Westacre Investments, Inc. v. Jugoimport*—SDPR Holding [2000] 1 QB 288, Court of Appeal, Civil Division, 12 May 1999

US
*AAOT Foreign Economic Association (VO) Technostroyexort v International Development and Trade Services Inc*, 139 F 3d 980 (2nd Cir, 1998)
*Action Indus., Inc. v. US Fid & Guar Co.*, 358 F 3d 337 (5th Cir. 2004)
*Andros Compania Maritime SA v Marc Rich &Co AG*, 579 F 2d 691 (2nd Cir, 1978)
*Apache Bohai Corp. LDC v. Texaco China BV*, 2007 WL 587233(5th. Cir. Feb. 27, 2007)
*Biotronik Mess-und Therapiegeraete GmbH v Medford Medical Instrument*, 415 F Supp 133 (CDNJ 1976)
*Bremen and Unterweser Reederei, GmBH v Zapata Off-Shore Co* 407 US 1 (US Supreme Court, 1972)
*Brook v. Peak Intern* Ltd. 294 F 3d 668 (5th Cir. 2002)
*Builders Federal (Hong Kong) Ltd et al v Turner Construction et al*, 655 F Supp 1400 (SDNY 1987)
*Commonwealth Coating Corp v Contiental Casualty Co*, 393 US 145, 89 S Ct 337 (1986)
*Corcoran v Ardra Ins Co Ltd*, 156 AD 2d 70 (NY 1st App Div, 1990)
*Europcar Italia S.p.A. v Maiellano Tours Inc.*, (1998) 156 F 3d 310 (US Court of Appeals for the 2nd Circuit, US)
*Fertilizwer Corp of India v IDI Management Inc*, 517 F Supp 948(1981), 530 F Supp 542
*Fritz Scherk v Alberto-Culver Co* 417 U.S. 506 (US Supreme Court, 1974)
*HRH Constr.Corp.v.Bethlehem Steel Corp.*, 384 N.E.2d 1289 (NY 1978)
*Kulukundis Shipping Co SA* v *Amtog Trading Corp* 126 F 2d 978 (2nd Cir, 1942)
*Karaha Bodas Company LLC v Perusahaan Pertambangan Minyak Dan Gas Bumi Negara*, 364 F 3d 274 (US Court of Appeals for the 5th Circuit, 2003)
*Larminoirs-Trefilieries-Cableries de Lens, S.A. v Southwire Co.*, 484 F Sup 1063(US District Court for the Northern District of Georgia, 1980)
*Mitsubishi Motors Corporation v Soler Chrysler-Plymouth Inc*105 S. Ct. 3346, 373 US 614 (US Supreme Court, 1985)
*Moses H. Cone Memorial Hospital v Mercury Construction Corp.* 460 US 1 (US Supreme Court, 1983)
*National Oil Corp. v Libyan Sun Oil Corp* 733 F Supp 800 (Del 1990)
*Parsons & Whittemore Overseas Co.v. Socie´te´ Generale de l'Industrie du Papier*, 508 F.2d 969 (2d Cir, 1974)
*Sidarma Societa* Italiana *di Armanmento v Holt Marine Indus Inc*, 515 F Supp 1302 (SDNY 1981)
*Transmaine Seaways Corp v Marc Rich & Co AG*, 480 F Supp 352 (SDNY 1979)
U.S. Biotronik Mess-und Therapiegerate GmbH & Co. v Medford Medical Instrument Com, 415 F Supp 133 (D.N.J., 1976)
*Willis* v *Shearson and American Express Inc* 569 F Supp 821 (2nd Cir, 1983)

**C Legislation**

Australia
*The International Arbitration Act 1974* (Cth)

Canada
*Professional Artists Act 1988* (Quebec)
EU

*Regulation (EC) No 593/2008 of the European Parliament and of the Council, of 17 June 2008, on the Law Applicable to Contractual Obligations (Rome I)* [2008] OJ L 177/6

Germany

*Zivilprozessordnung (ZPO)* [The German Code of Civil Procedure], promulgated on 5 December 2005 (Bundesgesetzblatt (BGBl., Federal Law Gazette) 3202; 2006, 431; 2007, 1781), last amended by Article 1 of the Act dated 31 August 2013 (Federal Law Gazette, 3533)

Hong Kong

Cap 609 Arbitration Ordinance (Hong Kong), 1 June 2011

Japan

*Arbitration Law* (Japan), enacted *on* 25 July 2005

OHADA

*Uniform Act on Arbitration*, enacted 10 March 1999, implemented on 11 June 1999

Singapore

Singapore International Arbitration Act 1994 (Chapter 143A) (Revised 2002)

Spain

*Spanish Arbitration Act* (Act 11/2011, of May 20, reforming Act 60/2003, of December 23)

Switzerland

*Federal Code on Private International Law (CPIL)* 18 December 1987

Sweden

*The Swedish Arbitration Act* (SFS 1999:116)

UNCITRAL

*Model Law on International Commercial Arbitration of the United Nations Commission on International Trade Law*, UN GAOR, 40th sess, Supp No. 17, UN Doc A/40/17, annex I (21 June 1985); passed by the GA Res 40/72, UN GAOR, 40th sess, 112th plen mtg, Agenda Item 135, UN Doc A/RES/40/72 (11 December 1985); amended by GA Res A/RES/61/33, UN GAOR, 61th sess, 64th plen mtg, Agenda Item 77, UN Doc A/RES/61/33 (4 Dec 2006)

UNIDROIT

*UNIDROIT Principles of International Commercial Contracts* (1994)

UK

*Arbitration Act 1996*

US

*Federal Arbitration Act*

**D Treaties**

*Agreement on Trade Relations Between the People's Republic of China and the United States of America*, United States-People's Republic of China, signed 7 July 1979, 1202 UNTS 179 (entered into force 1 February 1980)

*Convention Arabe D'Amman Sur L'Arbitrage Commercial* [the *Arab Convention on Commercial Arbitration*] enacted on 14 April 1987 (entered into force on 25 June 1992) ('the Amman Convention')

*Convention on Combating the Bribery of Foreign Officials in International Transactions,* OECD, signed 17 December 1997, 31 ILM 1 (entered into force 15 February 1999)
*Convention on Jurisdiction and the Enforcement of Judgments in Civil and Commercial Matters,* signed at Brussels, 27 September 1968, (entered into force on 1 Feburary 1973)
*Convention on the Recognition and Enforcement of Foreign Arbitral Awards,* opened for signature opened for signature 6 July 1958, 330 UNTS 38 (entered into force 7 June 1959)
*Geneva Convention on the Execution of Foreign Awards*, opened for signature 26 September 1927, 92 LNTS 301 (entered into force 25 July 1929)
*Geneva Protocol on Arbitration Clauses in Commercial Matters*, signed on 24 September 1923, 27 LNTS 158
*Inter-American Convention on International Commercial Arbitration*, signed at Panama, January 30 1975(entered into force on 16 June 1976)
*Inter-American Convention on Extraterritorial Validity of Foreign Judgements and Arbitral Awards,* adopted at Montevideo, Uruguay, on 8 May 1979 (entered into force on 14 June 1980)
*Protocol on the Accession of the People's Republic of China,* WT/L/432, 23 November 2001
*Riyadh Arab Agreement for Judicial Cooperation,* enacted on 6 April 1983 (entered into force 30 October 1985)
*Treaty Establishing the European Community*, opened for signature 7 February 1992, [1992] OJ C 224/6 (entered into force 1 November 1993), as amended by *Treaty of Nice Amending the Treaty on European Union, the Treaties Establishing the European Communities and Certain Related Acts*, opened for signature 26 February 2001, [2001] OJ C 80/1 (entered into force 1 February 2003)

### E Other

*AAA Arbitration Rules*
*BAC Arbitration Rules (2021)*
*CIETAC Arbitration Rules (2015)*
*HKIAC Administered Arbitration Rules*
*Hague Principles on Choice of Law in International Commercial Contracts,* The Hague Conference on Private International Law, approved 2015
*UNCITRAL Arbitration Rules*
*UNIDROIT Principles of International Contracts* (2016)

## *Chinese References*

### A Articles/Books/Reports

CIETAC,《贸仲委2022年工作报告》[CIETAC's 2022 Working Report], at: http://www.cietac.org/index.php?m=Article&a=show&id=18839
曹志勋 [Cao Zhixun],《论可仲裁性的司法审查标准—基于美国反垄断仲裁经验的考察》[Discussion on the Judicial Review Standard of Arbitrability: A Review on the Basis of US's Antitrust Law Arbitration] (2012) 83 华东政法大学学报 *East China University of Political Science and Law* 56
陈安 [Chen An]《论中国涉外仲裁的监督机制及其与国际惯例的接轨》[Discussions on the Supervision Schemes on Foreign-Related Arbitration in China and Its Connection with International Customs] (1995) 4 比较法研究 *Journal of Comparative Law* 379
陈福勇 [Chen Fuyong],《未竟的转型：中国仲裁机构现状与发展趋势实证研究》[Unfinished Transformation: An Empirical Study of the Current Status and Future Trends of China's Arbitration Institutions] (法律出版社出版社 [Law Press], 2010)

陈瑞华 [Chen Ruihua],《正义的误区—评法院审判委员会制度》[Misunderstanding of Justice: Comments on the System of Court Adjudication Committee] (1998) 1(2) 北大法律评论 *Peking University Law Review* 381

陈贤军, 张贝 [Chen Xianjun, Zhang Bei],《司法与仲裁:演变中的监督—以宁波市中级人民法院的司法实践为视角》[Judicature and Arbitration: Supervision under Evolution—From the Perspective of the Judicial Practices in Ningbo Intermediate People's Court] (2012) 30 仲裁研究 *Arbitration Study* 83

陈治东 [Chen Zhidong],《国际商事仲裁法》[International Commercial Arbitration Law] (法律出版社 [Law Press], 1998)

邓正来 [Deng Zhenglai],《中国法学向何处去—对苏力"本土资源论"的批判》[Where will the Chinese Legal Study go? Critique on Su Li's Theory of Local Resources] (2005) 23(3) 中国政法大学学报 *Journal of China University of Political Science and law* 52

杜越 [Du Yue],《大数据分析我国法院对外国仲裁裁决的承认和执行情况》[Big Data Analysis on the Recognition and Enforcement of Foreign Awards in Chinese Courts], 2020, available at: https://www.lawyers.org.cn/info/279ee53cd996446c86f5b76417a93891

法制日报 [Legal Daily],《去年全国仲裁机构受案41.5万余件》[China's Arbitration Institutions dealt with more than 415,000 cases in 2021], at: http://www.moj.gov.cn/pub/sfbgw/fzgz/fzgzggflfwx/fzgzggflfw/202203/t20220323_451264.html

傅攀峰 [Fu Panfeng], 《普通法系国际商事仲裁裁决既判力问题的处理经验及其启示—以Associated Electric v European Re为例》[Experiences of the Common Law Jurisdictions in Dealing with the Res Judicata Effect of International Commercial Arbitral Awards and Lessons from them: Taking the Associated Electric v European Re as an Example] (2012) 30 仲裁研究 *Arbitration Study* 64

Gaillard, Emmanuel, translated by 黄洁 [Huang Jie],《国际仲裁的法理思考和实践指导》[Legal Theory of International Arbitration], (北京大学出版社 [Peking University Press], 2010b)

《二十年仲裁受理案件增长近百倍, 全国仲裁机构累计受案逾80万件》["The Number of Arbitration Cases Accepted Increases nearly One Hundred Times, and Over Eight Hundred Thousand Cases Were Accepted in China's Arbitration Institutions], 法制日报 *Legal Daily*, 7 November 2014

高菲 [Gao Fei],《中国海事仲裁的理论与实践》[Theory and Practices of the Maritime Arbitration in China] (人民大学出版社 [Renmin University Press], 1998)

高薇 [Gao Wei],《论诉讼与仲裁关系中的既判力问题》[Comment on the Issue of Res Judicata in the Relation between Arbitration and Litigation], (2010) 6 法学家 *The Jurist* 153

高晓力 [Gao Xiaoli],《国际私法上公共政策的运用》[The Functioning of Public Policy in Private International Law] (中国民主法制出版社 [China Democracy and Rule of Law Press], 2008)

高晓力 [Gao Xiaoli],《最高人民法院关于适用涉外民事关系法律适用法若干问题的解释 (一) 解读》[Analysis of the Judicial Interpretation in regard of Several Issues in the Application of the Law of Application of Law in Foreign-related Civil Relationship No. 1] (2013) 3 法律适用 *Journal of Law Application* 38

葛行军 [Ge Xingjun],《关于仲裁裁决在执行中存在的有关问题—最高人民法院执行办主任葛行军在 "2003 年仲裁员实务研讨会"上的发言》[Relevant Issues in the Enforcement of Arbitral Awards: Speech of Ge Xingjun, the Chief of the Enforcement Branch of the Supreme People's Court, at the Symposium of Practices of Arbitrators 2003] (2003) 89 仲裁与法律 *Arbitration and Law* 18

顾培东 [Gu Peidong],《人民法院内部审判运行机制的构建》[The Establishment of an Internal System of the Courts for the Functioning of Judicial Power] (2011) 4 法学研究 *Chinese Journal of Law* 3

郭浩 [Guo Hao], 《我国国际商事仲裁裁决的司法审查中公共政策运用的实证研究》 [An Empirical Study of the Application of Public Policy in the Judicial Review of the International Commercial Arbitral Awards in China] (2016) 95 北京仲裁 Arbitration in Beijing 77

韩健 [Han Jian],《现代国际商事仲裁法的理论与实践》[The Theory and Practice of Modern International Commercial Arbitration], (法律出版社 [Law Press], 2000)

何其生 [He Qisheng],《国际商事仲裁司法审查中的公共政策》[Public Policy in the Judicial Review of International Commercial Arbitration Matters], (2014) 7 中国社会科学 *Social Science in China*

何勤华 [He Qinhua],《法学观念本土化考: 从新中国立宪 60 余年之视角》[Study on the Localisation of the Legal Conceptions: Perspective from the 60-year history of the Establishment of Constitutions of the PRC] (2013) 25(2) 中外法学 *Peking University Law Journal* 270

贺卫方 [He Weifang], 《中国的法院改革与司法独立—一个参与者的观察与反思》 [The Reforms in Chinese Courts and the Judicial Independence: Observations and Reflections of a Participant] (2003) 2 浙江社会科学 *Zhejiang Social Science* 83

胡建新 [Hu Jianxin],《汉迪波克公司申请承认和执行外国海事仲裁裁决案》[Handiboke Co Applying Recognition and Enforcement of a Foreign Maritime Arbitral Award] (2010) 中国水运报 China Water Transport, 16 June 2010

扈媛媛 [Hu Yuanyuan],《我国争议可仲裁性标准的确立》[Establishment of the Standard of Arbitrablity in China] (2009) 111 司法改革论评 *Judicial Reform Review* 32

黄卉 [Huang Hui],《论<纽约公约>里的不可仲裁性》[Discussion on the Inarbitrability in the New York Convention] (2011) 知识经济 *Knowledge Economy* 41

黄进, 马德才 [Huang Jin, Ma Decai],《国际商事争议可仲裁范围的扩展趋势之探析—兼评我国有关规定》[Review and Analysis of the Expanding Scope of Arbitrability of International Commercial Disputes: With Comments on Relevant Rules in Chinese Law] (2007) 143 法学评论 *Law Review* 54

黄进 [Huang Jin],《国际私法与国际商事仲裁》[Private International Law and International Commercial Arbitration] (武汉大学出版社 [Wuhan University Press], 1994)

黄文艺 [Huang Wenyi], 《新《民事诉讼法》对不予执行仲裁裁决事由修改的理解与适用》 [Understanding and Applying the Recent Amendments of the Civil Procedure Law in Regard of the Grounds of Non-Enforcement of Arbitral Awards] (2012) 81 北京仲裁 *Arbitration in Beijing* 106

黄亚英, 李薇薇 [Huang Yaying, Li Weiwei],《中国仲裁裁决在外国的承认和执行》[Enforcement of the Chinese Arbitral Awards in Foreign Jurisdictions] (2002) 6 中国对外贸易 *China's Foreign Trade* 17

姜建新, 陈立伟 [Jiang Jianxin, Chen Liwei],《关于对仲裁裁决司法审查的调查与思考—对不予执行及申请撤销仲裁审查的实证分析》[Investigations and Thoughts on the Judicial Review of Arbitral Awards: An Positive Study on the Judicial Review Practices in Annulment and Non-Enforcement of Arbitral Awards] (2013) 10 法律适用 *Application of Law* 96

江伟, 肖建国 [Jiang Wei, Xiao Jianguo],《论既判力的客观范围》[Discussing the Objective Scope of the Res Judicata Effect], (1996) 18(5) 法学研究 *CASS Journal of Law* 37

李虎 [Li Hu], 《国际商事*仲裁裁决*的强制*执行*—特别述及仲裁裁决在中国的强制执行》 [Enforcement of International Commercial Arbitration Awards: with Emphasis on Award Enforcement in the P.R. China] (法律出版社 [Law Press], 2000)

李建明 [Li Jianming],《论党领导下的司法独立》[Discussions on the Judicial Independence under the Leadership of the China Communism Party] (2003) 2 政治与法律 *Political Science and Law* 33

李娜 [Li Na], 仲裁司法审查实践中的"公共政策"研究 [Research on the Public Policy in the Judicial Review of Arbitration Matters], (2022) 119 北京仲裁 *Arbitration in Beijing* 50

梁慧星[Liang Huixing],《民法总论》[General Issues of Civil Law], (法律出版社 [Law Press], 1996)

林一飞 [Lin, Yifei],《百事公司与被申请人四川百事可乐饮料有限公司申请承认及执行外国仲裁裁决案》[Case of the Application for Recognition and Enforcement of Foreign Arbitral Award by Pepsi Co and Sichuan Pepsi Coke Co], at http://www.cnarb.com/algy/nygyal/china/200911/12897

林一飞 [Lin Yifei],《公共政策作为抗辩仲裁裁决的一项理由》[Public Policy as a Defense against Arbitral Award], at http://www.cnarb.com/Article/swzn/200807/4492.html, 15 July 2008

刘春梅 [Liu Chunmei], 《申请撤销涉外及外国仲裁裁决案件司法审查中发现的具体问题》 [Detailed Issues in Judicial Review of Cases Dealing with Application of Annulment and Enforcement of Foreign-Related and Foregin Arbitral Awards], in 韩健 [Han Jian] (ed.),《涉外仲裁司法审查》[Judicial Review of Foreign-Related Arbitral Awards] (法律出版社 [Law Press], 2006)

刘贵祥 [Liu Guixiang],《在全国海事审判工作会议上的总结讲话》[Concluding Speech at the National Maritime Judicial Practices Working Meeting] (2012) 25 涉外商事海事审判指导 *Guidance on Judicial Practices in dealing with Foreign-Related Commercial and Maritime Issues* 16

刘思达 [Liu Sida],《失落的城邦: 当代中国法律职业变迁》[The Lost Polis: Transformation of the Legal Profession in Contemporary China] (北京大学出版社 [Peking University Press], 2008)

刘想树 [Liu Xiangshu],《中国涉外仲裁制度与学理研究》[Theoretical Study on China's Foreign-Related Arbitration System] (法律出版社 [Law Press], 2001)

刘奕湛 [Liu Yizhan],《最高法: 中国法官人数已近20万人》[The Supreme People's Court: There are almost 200, 000 Judges in China], *Xinhua Net*, 25 July 2013. http://news.xinhuanet.com/legal/2013-07/25/c_116690034.htm

龙宗智, 李长青 [Long Zongzhi, Li Changqing],《论司法独立与司法受制》[Disucssion on the Judicial Independence and its Restraints] (1998) 12 法学 *Law Science* 34

陆效龙, 吴兆祥 [Lu Xiaolong, Wu Zhaoxiang],《 <关于适用仲裁法若干问题的解释>的理解与适用 》[Understanding and Applying 'Interpretation on Several Issues in regard of the Application of the China Arbitration Law'] (2006) 10 人民司法 *People's Judicature* 28

马占军 [Ma Zhanjun],《论我国仲裁裁决的撤销与不予执行制度的修改与完善—兼评<最高人民法院关于适用'中华人民共和国仲裁法'若干问题的解释>的相关规定》[Discussions on the Amendments and Perfection of China's Legal Schemes on the Annulment and Non-enforcement of Arbitral Awards—and Comments on the *SUPREME PEOPLE'S COURT's Interpretation on Several Problems in Regard of the Application of the Arbitration Law*] (2007) 2 法学杂志 *Law Science Magazine* 108

《民诉法修改不能忽略仲裁部分》[Amendment of the Civil Procedure Law shall not Ignore the Arbitration Parts], 法制日报 *Legal Daily*, 19 November 2011

孟建柱 [Meng Jianzhu],《深化司法体制改革》[Deepen the Reforms in the Judicial System], 人民日报 *People's Daily* (Beijing), 25 November 2013

牟笛 [Mou Di],《再议无涉外因素争议能否在外国机构仲裁》[A Re-Discussion on Whether A Purely Domestic Dispute without Any Foreign-Related Element Can Be Arbitrated By Foreign Arbitration Institutions], 7 January 2015, at http://www.aiweibang.com/yuedu/8943990.html

Noerr, K.W.《法律移植与 1930 年前中国对德国法的接受》[Legal Transplantation and the Acceptance of German Law in China before 1930s] (李立强、李启欣 [Li Liqiang, Li qixin] trans) (1988)2 比较法研究 *Journal of Comparative Law* 55

齐湘泉 [Qi Xiangquan],《外国仲裁裁决承认及执行论》[Study on Recognition and Enforcement of Foreign Arbitral Awards], (法律出版社 [Law Press], 2010)

钱宇宏, 马伯娟 [Qian Yuhong, Ma Bojuan],《从可仲裁性的发展看司法权的让渡》[Viewing the Alienation of Judicial Power from the Development of Arbitrability] (2004) 93 仲裁与法律 *Arbitration and Law* 18

乔欣 [Qiao Xin],《仲裁权论》[The Research on Arbitration Power], (法律出版社 [Law Press], 2000) 27

乔欣, 李莉 [Qiao Xin, Li Li],《争议可仲裁性研究》[Research on the Arbitrability of Disputes] (2004) 53 北京仲裁 *Arbitration in Beijing* 35

沈宗灵 [Shen Zongling],《当代中国借鉴外国法律的实例 (下) 》[Practical Examples the recent Chinese Legislation Learnt from Foreign Law (II)] (1997) 6(4) 中国法学 *Chinese Legal Science* 3

宋连斌 [Song Lianbin],《仲裁法》[Arbitration Law] (武汉大学出版社 [Wuhan University Press], 2010)

宋连斌 [Song Lianbin],《司法与仲裁关系的重构: "民诉法"有关仲裁新规定之解析》[Re-establishment of the Relationship between the Judicial System and Arbitration: Analysis of the New Provisions of the Civil Procedural Law Concerning Arbitration] (2013) 33 仲裁研究 *Arbitration Study* 7

宋连斌 [Song Lianbin],《中国仲裁员制度改革初探》[A preliminary exploration of Reforms of China's Arbitrator System] (2001) 4 中国国际私法和比较法年刊 *Yearbook of Chinese International Private Law and Comparative Law* 575

苏力 [Su Li],《二十世纪中国的现代化与法治》[The Modernalisation and Rule of Law in 20th Century's China] (1998a) 1 法学研究 *Chinese Journal of Law* 3

苏力 [Su Li],《法治及其本土资源》[*The Rule of Law and its Local Resources*] (中国政法大学出版社 [Chinese University of Political Science and Law Press], 2004)

苏力 [Su Li],《基层法院审判委员会的考察及思考》[Observations and Thoughts in regard of the Adjudication Committee in Basic Courts] (1998b) 1(2) 北大法律评论 *Peking University Law Review* 320

苏力 [Su Li],《送法下乡:中国基层司法制度研究》[Sending Law to the Countryside: Research on China's Basic-Level Judicial System] (中国政法大学出版社 [Chinese University of Political Science and Law Press], 2000)

万鄂湘, 夏晓红 [Wan E'xiang, Xia Xiaohong],《中国法院不予承认及执行某些外国仲裁裁决的原因—《纽约公约》相关案例分析》[Reason for the Refusals of the Recognition and Enforcement of Foreign Arbitral Awards in Chinese Courts: New York Convention Case Studies] (2010) 13 武大法学评论 *Wuhan University Law Review* 1

王红松 [Wang Hongsong],《2012年春节茶话会发言 》[Speech on the Spring Festival Party of 2012], at http://www.bjac.org.cn/page/gybh/2011zj.html

王胜明, 徐秀春 [Wang Shengming, Xu Xiuchun],《关于仲裁法的若干问题》[Several Issues in regard of the Arbitration Law], in the Research Branch of the Legislative Bureau of the State Council,《重新组建仲裁机构手册》[Handbook of the Re-Establishment of the Arbitration Institutions] (China Legal Publishing, 1995)

王胜明 [Wang Shengming],《在第六届中国仲裁论坛上的讲话》[Presentation at the 6th China Arbitration Forum] Oct 31 2012,Beijing

王亚新, 陈福勇 [Wang Yaxin, Chen Fuyong]《<民事诉讼法>修改与不予执行仲裁裁决—以北京仲裁委员会为对象的实证分析》[Amendment of the China's Civil Procedural Law and Non-Enforcement of Arbitral Awards: An Empirical Study on the Beijing Arbitration Commission] (2012) 5 法学杂志 *Law Science Magazine* 111

魏振瀛 [Wei Zhenying],《我国民法对外国法的借鉴》[Lessons drawn from Foreign Law in Our Civil Law Legislation] (2009) 5 法学家 *Jurist* 20

吴兆祥 [Wu Zhaoxiang],《在第六届中国仲裁论坛上的讲话》[Speech at the 6th China Arbitration Forum], 31 October 2012, at http://www.bjac.org.cn/news/view.asp?id=2142

武雁冰 [Wu Yanbing],《国际商事争议之可仲裁性研究》[Research on the Arbitrability of International Commercial Disputes], (Master Degree Thesis, China University of Political Science and Law, 2011)

肖永平 [Xiao Yongping],《也谈我国法院对仲裁的监督范围》[Comments on the Scope of Judicial Supervision of Arbitration by Chinese Courts] (1998) 87(1) 法学评论 *Law Review* 42

肖永平 [Xiao Yongping],《肖永平论冲突法》[Xiao Yongping on Conflict of Law], (武汉大学出版社 [Wuhan University Press], 2002)

杨宏磊 [Yang Honglei],《人民法院涉外仲裁司法审查情况的调研报告》[Investigation and Analysis Report on the Judicial Review of Foreign-Related Arbitration by the People's Courts] (2009) 9 武大国际法评论 *Wuhan University Law Review* 308

叶丹 [Ye Dan],《从现代司法理念角度探讨司法力渗透仲裁的合理度—以我国法院对涉外仲裁裁决的司法审查制度为现实载体》[Discussing Reasonable Involvement of Judicial Power in Arbitration from the Perspective of Modern Notions of Judiciality: Start from the Judicial Review System of the Foreign-Related Arbitral Awards in Our Courts], in 韩健 [Han Jian] (ed),《涉外仲裁司法审查》[Judicial Review of Foreign Arbitration] (法律出版社 [Law Press], 2006) 98

叶阳 [Ye Yang],《效力性规定在司法实践中的辨识》[Identification of "Validating Mandatory Rules" in Judicial Practices], 人民法院报 *People's Court Daily,* 23 November 2011

尹伊君 [Yin Yijun],《从"礼教风俗"到"本土资源"》[From 'Customs and Traditions' to 'Local Resources'] (1999) 3–4 比较法研究 *Journal of Comparative Law* 537

于健龙 [Yu Jianlong],《中国国际经济贸易仲裁委员会 2011年工作报告暨 2012 年工作计划》[the 2011 Working Report and 2012 Yearly Working Plan of CIETAC], at http://cn.cietac.org/AboutUs/AboutUS3.asp

于喜富 [Yu Xifu],《国际商事仲裁的司法监督与协助—兼论中国的立法与司法实践》[Judicial Supervision and Assistance of International Commercial Arbitration: Comments on China's Legislative and Judicial Practices] (Intellectual Property Rights Press, 2006)

袁发强 [Yuan Faqiang],《中国商事*仲裁机构*现状与发展趋势研究》[Research on the present of China's Commercial Arbitration Institutions and Their Development Trends in the Future] (复旦大学出版社 [Fudan University Press], 2011)

袁诗鸣 [Yuan Shiming],《在国际商事仲裁新发展高峰论坛上的讲话》[Speech at the Summit of the Recent Developments of International Commercial Arbitration] 25 March 2011, at http://ielaw.uibe.edu.cn/html/mingshijiangtang/20110503/16149.html

张贝 [Zhang Bei],《论仲裁裁决的不予执行—兼评<广东省高级人民法院关于办理申请不予执行仲裁裁决案件的若干规定 (试行) >》[Discussion on the Non-Enforcement of Arbitral Awards and Comments on the 'Several Rules of the Guangdong People's High Court in Dealing with the Application of Non-Enforcement of Arbitral Awards' (The Trial Version)'] (2013) 10 商事仲裁 *Commercial Arbitration*

张超 [Zhang Chao],《浅析我国对可仲裁争议事项的立法》[Primary Analysis of the Chinese Legislation of Arbitrable Issues] (2012) 323 法制与经济 *Rule by Law and Economics* 63

张宪初 [Zhang Xianchu], 《外国商事仲裁裁决司法审查"公共政策"理论与实践的新发展》[Recent Theoretical and Practical Developments in Applying Public Policy in Judicial Review of Arbitral Awards in Foreign Jurisdictions], in 韩健 [Han Jian] (ed),《涉外仲裁司法审查》[Judicial Review of the Foreign-Related Arbitration] (法律出版社 [Law Press], 2006) 359

赵健 [Zhao Jian],《国际商事仲裁的司法监督》[Judicial Supervision of International Commercial Arbitration] (法律出版社 [Law Press], 2000)

赵秀文 [Zhao Xiuwen], 《从宁波工艺品公司案看我国法院对涉外仲裁协议的监督》 [The Supervision of Our Courts on Foreign-Related Arbitration Agreement: Insights from the Ningbo Arts & Crafts Co Case] (2010) 5 时代法学 *Presentday Law Science* 3

赵秀文 [Zhao Xiuwen],《从永宁公司案看公共政策作为我国法院拒绝执行外国仲裁裁决的理由》[Public Policy as a Ground adopted by Our Courts for Refusal of Foreign Arbitral Award: Review from the Perspective of the *Yongning* Case] (2009) 4法学家 *Jurist* 98

赵秀文 [Zhao Xiuwen],《国际商事仲裁法》[International Commercial Arbitration Law], (人民大学出版社 [Renmin University Press], 2nd ed, 2008)

赵秀文 [Zhao Xiuwen],《中国仲裁法与建设社会主义和谐社会》[On the PRC Arbitration Law and Construction of Socialist Harmonious Society] (2006) 101 仲裁与法律 *Arbitration and Law* 5

赵秀文 [Zhao Xiuwen],《民诉法关于国际仲裁规定的不足与完善》[The Drawbacks in the CCPL's Provisions Concerning International Arbitration and Their Perfection] (2013) 9 法治研究 *Research on Rule of Law* 35

郑远民等 [Zheng Yuanmin et al.],《国际司法—国际民事诉讼与国际商事仲裁》[International Adjudication: International Civil Litigation and International Commercial Arbitration] (中信出版社 [CITIC Publishing], 2000)

中华人民共和国国务院新闻办公室 [The State Council Information Office of the People's Republic of China],《中国的司法改革》白皮书 [White Paper on China's Judicial Reforms] October 2012

中国仲裁法学研究会 [China Arbitration Academy],《2011年全国各仲裁委员会受理案件情况》[The Number of Cases Accepted by Arbitration Commissions in China in 2011], at http://www.china-arbitration.com/news.php?id=2351

周强 [Zhou Qiang],《最高人民法院工作报告》[Working Report of the Supreme People's Court], the First Meeting of the Fourteenth National People's Congress, 7 March 2023

朱华芳等 [Zhu Huafang et al.],《2021年度中国仲裁司法审查实践观察报告—大数据分析》[2021 Report on the Judicial Review Practice of Arbitration-related Cases: Analysis of Big Data], available at: http://www.tiantonglaw.com/Content/2022/09-17/2316274305.html

《专家建议出台全国统一的仲裁员行为规范》[Experts Suggests the Establishment of a Unified Ethical Code for Arbitrators], 法制网 *Legal Daily,* 9 June 2014, at http://www.legaldaily.com.cn/executive/content/2014-06/09/content_5581640.htm?node=32120
最高人民法院民四庭 [the Supreme People's Court Fourth Civil Branch],《涉外商事海事审判指导》[Guide on Foreign-Related Commercial and Maritime Trial] (人民法院出版社 [People's Court Publishing])
最高人民法院 [The Supreme People's Court],《最高人民法院中国仲裁司法审查年度报告(2019年度)》[The Supreme People's Court's 2019 Annual Report on the Judicial Review on Abitration-related Matters in China], available at: https://www.court.gov.cn/zixun-xiangqing-281031.html

**B Cases**[48]

China

《爱耳时代医疗科技 (北京) 股份有限公司与领先仿生医疗器械 (上海) 有限公司合同纠纷案》[Audonline Medical Technology (Beijing) Co. v Advanced Bionics Medical Instruments (Shanghai) Co. Ltd.—Case Concerning Contractual Disputes], 上海市高级人民法院 [Shanghai HPC, People's Republic of China], (2018) 沪民申 921 号 [Retrial No. 921], 26 June 2018
《翱兰国际有限公司、淄博银花棉麻有限公司等申请承认和执行外国仲裁裁决民事裁定书》[Civil Decision on the Application for the Recognition and Enforcement of a Foreign Arbitral Award between Olam International Ltd and Zibo Yinhua Cotton and Linen Co Ltd], Zibo IPC, (2015) 淄民特字第 1 号 [Civil Special No. 1], 19 January 2016
《奥克塔福系统有限公司、华浚塑料建材有限公司申请承认与执行法院判决、仲裁裁决案件其他执行裁定书》[Decision on the Enforcement regarding the Application for the Recognition and Enforcement of Judgments or Arbitral Awards between Octaform Systems Inc and Huajun Plastics and Building Materials Co Ltd], Huzhou IPC, (2019) 浙 05 协外认 1 号 [Judicial Assistance Foreign Recognition No. 1], 24 November 2020
《北良 (香港) 有限公司、日照兴裕嘉贸易有限公司申请承认与执行法院判决、仲裁裁决案件裁定书》[Decision on the Application for the Recognition and Enforcement of Judgments or Arbitral Awards between Beiliang (Hong Kong) Co Ltd and Rizhao Xingyujia Trade Co Ltd], Rizhao IPC, (2016) 鲁 1 1协外认 1 号 [Judicial Assistance Foreign Recognition No. 1], 9 January 2018
《北京龙盛兴业科技发展有限公司与域适都智能装备 (天津) 有限公司、霍尼韦尔自动化控制 (中国) 有限公司纵向垄断协议纠纷案民事裁定书》[Civil Ruling on the Dispute Concerning the Vertical Agreements among Beijing Longsheng Xingye Technical Co. Ltd, Resideo Smart Home Technology (Tianjin) Co Ltd and Honeywell Automation and Control Solutions (China) Co Ltd], The SPC, (2022) 最高法知民终 1276 号 [Intellectual Property Civil Final No. 1276], 19 August 2022
《北京星工场音乐娱乐有限公司诉北京中鸿房地产开发有限公司申请撤销仲裁裁决案》[Beijing Star Factory Music and Entertainment Co Ltd v Beijing Zhonghong Real Estate Development Co Ltd-Case of Annulment of Arbitral Aaward] Beijing Second IPC, 2004
《北京市第二中级人民法院驳回上海齿科医械厂申请撤销中国国际经济贸易仲裁委员会上海分会 (1996) 沪贸仲字 038 号裁决书的裁定》[Decision Order of Beijing 2nd IPC to Refuse the Application of the Shanghai Dental Machinery Factory for Annulment of CIETAC Shanghai Award Hu Mao Zhong Zi No. 038] Beijing Second Intermediate People's Court, (1996) Er Zhong Jing Chu Zi No. 83
《北京朝来新生体育休闲有限公司申请承认和执行外国仲裁裁决案》[Beijing Chaolaixinsheng Sports and Leisure Co Ltd v Beijing Suowangzhixin Investment Consulting Co Ltd – Case of Application of Recognition and Enforcement of Foreign Arbitral Awards], 北京市第

48 Some of the SPC decisions are in the form of Replies to lower courts issued by China's Supreme People's Court ('the SPC'). See the functioning of Prior Reporting System in Chap. 3.

二中级人民法院 [Beijing 2nd IPC, People's Republic of China], (2013) 二中民特字第10670号 [Special Procedure No. 10670], 20 January 2014

《沧溟海运株式会社、河北远洋运输集团股份有限公司申请承认与执行法院判决、仲裁裁决案件民事裁定书》[Civil Decision on the Application for the Recognition and Enforcement of Judgments or Arbitral Awards between Changmyung Shipping Co Ltd and Hebei Yuanyang Transportation Co], Qingdao Maritime Court, (2018) 鲁72协外认 1 号-1 [Judicial Assistance Foreign Recognition No. 1–1], 5 November 2018

昌盛贸易公司、河南江河机械有限责任公司申请承认和执行外国仲裁裁决裁定书》 [Decision on the Application for the Recognition and Enforcement of a Foreign Arbitral Award between Changsheng Trading Co Inc and Henan Jianghe Mechanical Co Ltd], Zhengzhou IPC, (2017) 豫 01 协外认 11 号 [Judicial Assistance Foreign Recognition No. 11], 27 March 2019

《春生海运有限公司诉山东海纳房地产股份有限公司申请承认外国仲裁裁决纠纷一审民事裁定书》[Civil Decision on the Application for the Recognition of A Foreign Arbitral Award by Spring Maritime Ltd against Shandong Haina Property Development Co], Qingdao Maritime Court, (2013) 青海法海商初字第 1032 号 [Maritime First Instance No. 1032], (2014) 青海法海商初字第 722 号 [Maritime First Instance No. 722], 22 July 2014

《慈铭博鳌国际医院有限公司与海南亨延顿医院管理咨询有限公司等申请撤销仲裁裁决民事裁定书》[Civil Decision on the Application for the Annulment of An Arbitral Award between Ciming Bo'ao International Hospital Co Ltd and HRC-Hainan Holding Company LLC et al.], Beijing 4th IPC, (2021) 京 04 民特 26 号 [Civil Special No. 26], 5 March 2021

《大韩海运株式会社与海航集团有限公司船舶租用合同纠纷特别程序案件民事裁定书》[Civil Ruling on the Special Procedure Case of the Chartering Dispute between Korea Line Corp and HNA Group Co Ltd], Haikou Maritime Court, (2016) 琼 72 协外认 1 号 [Judicial Assistance Foreign Recognition No. 1], 15 August 2017

《大卫戴恩咨询有限公司、布拉姆利有限公司申请执行香港仲裁裁决案》[Case of Application for the Recognition and Enforcement of a Hong Kong arbitral award by David Dein Consultancy Ltd and Bramley Corp Ltd], Beijing 4th IPC, 2020) 京 04 认港 5 号 [Recognition Hong Kong No. 5], date not reported, reported in the SPC,《内地与香港特别行政区发布相互执行仲裁裁决的典型案例》[Typical Cases of the Enforcement of Arbitral Awards between China Mainland and the Hong Kong SAR], 27 November 2020

《Ecom Agroindustrial 申请承认和执行外国仲裁裁决民事裁定书》[Decision on the Application for the Recognition and Enforcement of A Foreign Arbitral Awards by Ecom Agroindustrial Corp Ltd Switzerland], Shenzhen IPC, (2014) 深中法涉外初字第 60 号 [Foreign-related First Instance No. 60], 25 May 2016

Ecom Agroindustrial Corp Ltd Switzerland、青岛锦华东国际贸易有限公司申请承认与执行法院判决、仲裁裁决案件民事裁定书》[Civil Decision on the Recognition and Enforcement of Judgments and Arbitral Awards between Ecomagro Industrial Corp Ltd Switzerland and Qingdao Jinhuadong International Trade Co Ltd], Qingdao IPC, (2020) 鲁 02 协外认 3 号 [Shandong Judicial Assistance Foreign Recognition No. 3], 25 Feb 2022

《福建纵横高速信息技术有限公司、福建分众传媒有限公司等与史带开曼投资公司申请不予执行一案的执行裁定书》[Decision on the Application for Non-Enforcement of the Arbitral Award Raised by Fujian Zongheng High-Speed Information Technology Co., Ltd., Fujian Focus Media Co., Ltd., and Cheng Zheng against Starr Cayman Investment Co], Fuzhou IPC, (2014) 榕执监字第 51 号 [Enforcement Supervision No. 51], 5 November 2014

《高新 (香港) 有限公司与佛山市投资咨询公司等申请撤销仲裁裁决纠纷案广东省佛山市中级人民法院民事裁定书》[Civil Order of the Guangdong Foshan Intermediate People's Court in regard of the Application of Goldensail (Hong Kong) Ltd and Foshan Investment Consulting Co for Annulment of an Arbitral Award] Foshan Intermediate People's Court, (2004) Fo Zhong Fa Min Si Chu Zi No. 133

《GS Global Corporation (佳施国际株式会社)诉上海市振戎石油有限公司申请承认和执行外国仲裁裁决一案民事裁定书》[Civil Ruling on the Application for the Recognition and

Enforcement of a Foreign Arbitral Award between GS Global Corporation and Shanghai Zhenrong Oil Corp], Shanghai 1st IPC, (2016) 沪 01 协外认 12 号 [Judicial Assistance Foreign Recognition No. 12], 22 February 2017

《合肥润安 (国际) 发展有限公司与多快电梯 (远东) 有限公司申请撤销电梯设备合同货款争议裁决纠纷案》[Hefei Run'an (International) Development Co Ltd v Dove Elevator (Far East) Co Ltd- Case of Annulment of an Award dealing with Payments of Elevator Equipments Contracts Dispute] Shanghai 2nd IPC, [2002] 沪二中民五 (商) 初字第 55 号 [Civil Fitfth Branch Commercial Dispute, Case of First Instance No. 55], 9 July 2002

《华夏航运 (新加坡) 有限公司 (Farenco Shipping PTE LTD) 与东海运输有限公司 (Eastern Ocean Transportation Co., Limited) 申请认可和执行香港特别行政区仲裁裁决裁定书》[Ruling on the Application for the Recognition and Enforcement of a Hong Kong arbitral award between Farenco Shipping Pte Ltd and Eastern Ocean Transportation Co Ltd], Guangzhou Maritime Court, (2018) 粤 72 认港 1 号之一号 [Recognition Hong Kong No. 1–1], (2019) 粤 72 认港 1 号 [Recognition No. 1], 2 July 2019

《Jacobson Golf Course Design、四会臻汇园物业发展有限公司等申请承认和执行外国仲裁裁决民事裁定书》[Decision on the Application for the Recognition and Enforcement of A Foreign Arbitral Award between Jacobson Golf Course Design and Sihui Zhenhuiyuan Property Development Co Ltd et al.], Zhaoqing IPC, (2015) 肇中法民一仲字第 26 号 [First Branch Arbitration No. 26], 19 October 2015

《加拿大利亚贸易公司与英属维尔京群岛利亚资本公司申请撤销南京仲裁委员会 (2007) 宁裁字第 266–35 号裁决纠纷案》[Liya Trading (Canada) v Liya Capital (BVI)-Case of Annulment of Nanjing Arbitration Commission's (2007) Ning Cai Zi No. 266–35 Award] Nanjing IPC, [2009] 宁民五初字第 38 号 [Civil Fifth Branch, Case of First Instance No. 38], 23 March 2009

《嘉能可有限公司申请昆山立益纺织有限公司承认与执行法院判决、仲裁裁决案件民事裁定书》[Civil Decision on the Application for the Recognition and Enforcement of a Judgment or Arbitral Award by Glencore Co Ltd against Kunshan Liyi Textile Co Ltd], Suzhou IPC, (2019) 苏 05 协外认 2 号 [Judicial Assistance Foreign Recognition No. 2], 20 July 2020

《来宝资源国际私人有限公司、中煤京闽 (福建) 工贸有限公司申请承认与执行法院判决、仲裁裁决案件民事裁定书》[Civil Decision on the Application for the Recognition and Enforcement of Judgments or Arbitral Awards between Noble Resources International Pte Ltd and China Coal Jingmin (Fujian) Industry and Trade Co Ltd], Fuzhou IPC, (2019) 闽 01 认港 1 号 [Recognition Hong Kong No. 1], 29 September 2019

《利夫糖果(上海)有限公司申请承认和执行新加坡国际仲裁中心仲裁裁决案》 [Case Concerning the Application of Leaf Candy (Shanghai) Co Ltd for Recognition and Enforcement of an Arbitral Award of SIAC] Shanghai Second IPC, (2008) Hu Er Zhong Min Wu (Shang) Chu Zi No. 19, available at http://www.shezfy.com/view.html?id=11429

《利奇食品株式会社、元春秋申请承认与执行法院判决、仲裁裁决案件裁定书》 [Decision on the Application for the Recognition and Enforcement of Judgments or Arbitral Awards between Rich Food Co Ltd and Chunqiu Yuan], Tianjin 1st IPC, (2018) 津 01 协外认 1 号 [Judicial Assistance Foreign Recognition No. 1], 4 March 2019

《六盘水恒鼎实业有限公司与张洪兴采矿权转让合同争议管辖权异议案》 [Liupanshui Hengding Industry Co v Zhang Hongxing—Case of Jurisdictional Disputes Regarding a Dispute Occurred in a Transfer of a Mining Contract], reprinted in 苏泽林 [Su Zelin], 景汉朝 [Jing Hanchao] and 最高人民法院 (the Supreme People's Court) ed., 最高人民法院立案一庭、立案二庭 [the First and Second Case Filing Branches of the Supreme People's Court],《立案工作指导》[Guidance on Case Filing] (2011)(1), Vol. 28, 94–98

《南太平洋风险投资有限公司、盘锦辽河油田凯特石油设备有限公司申请承认和执行外国仲裁裁决裁定书》[Decision on the Application for the Recognition and Enforcement of A Foreign Arbitral Award between South Pacific Venture FZE and Panjin Liaohe Oilfield Kaite

Oil Facilities Co Ltd], Dalian IPC, (2019) 辽 02 协外认 8 号 [Judicial Assistance Foreign Recognition No. 8], 3 December 2019

《塞浦路斯康特斯达航运有限公司申请承认和执行伦敦仲裁裁决案》 [Case Concerning the Application of Cyprus Contestar Shipping Co Ltd for Recognition and Enforcement of London Arbitral Award] Guangzhou Maritime Court, (1997) Guang Hai Fa Zhan Zi No. 5, 15 July 1998

《山西昌林实业有限公司、壳牌 (中国) 有限公司滥用市场支配地位纠纷再审审查与审判监督民事裁定书》 [Shanxi Changlin Industrial Co. Ltd v Shell (China) Co. Ltd—Dispute Concerning Abuse of Dominance—Retrial—Civil Ruling], Supreme People's Court, (2019) 最高法民申 6242 号 [Civil Retrial No. 6242], 10 June 2020

《上海佳船机械设备进出口有限公司、美克斯海洋工程设备股份有限公司申请承认与执行法院判决、仲裁裁决案件其他民事裁定书》 [Civil Ruling on the Application for the Recognition and Enforcement of A Foreign Arbitral Award between Shanghai Jiachuan Mechanical Equipment Import and Export Co Ltd and Meikesi Maritime Engineering Facility Co], Jiaxing IPC, (2019) 浙 04 协外认 1 号, 2 号 [Judicial Assistance Foreign Recognition No. 1 and No. 2], 1 July 2020

《上诉人壳牌 (中国) 有限公司与被上诉人呼和浩特市汇力物资有限责任公司横向垄断协议纠纷民事裁定书》 [Civil Ruling Concerning the Horizontal Monopoly Agreements Between Shell (China) Co and Hohhot Huili Supplies Co Ltd—Appeal], The SPC, (2019) 最高法知民辖终 46, 47 号 [Intellectual Property Civil Jurisdiction Final No. 46, No. 47], 21 August 2019

《申请人盖特汽车自由贸易区公司、埃及盖特汽车制造公司等与被申请人河北中兴汽车制造有限公司申请认可和执行香港特别行政区仲裁裁决民事裁定书》 [Civil Decision on the Application for the Recognition of a Hong Kong SAR Arbitral Award among Automotive Gate FZCO et al. and Hebei Zhongxing Automotive Manufacture Co Ltd], Yichang IPC, (2015) 鄂宜昌中民认字第 00003 号之一[Civil Recognition No. 00003-A], 15 August 2019

《世安株式会社、天津市天锻压力机有限公司申请承认与执行法院判决、仲裁裁决案件裁定书》[Decision on the Application for the Recognition and Enforcement of A Foreign Award between Sean Inc and Tianjin Tianduan Press Machine Co Ltd, Tianjin 1st IPC, (2018) 津 01 协外认 13 号 [Judicial Assistance Foreign Recognition No. 13], 27 March 2019

Stiebel-Getriebebau GmbH & Co.KG 与苏州凯博易控驱动科技有限公司申请撤销仲裁裁决民事裁定书》 [Civil Decision on the Application for the Annulment of An Arbitral Award between Stiebel-Getriebebau GmbH & Co. KG and Suzhou Kaibo Yikong Drive Technology Co Ltd], Beijing 4th IPC, (2021) 京 04 民特 833 号, 28 December 2021

《苏州工业园区海富投资有限公司诉甘肃世恒有色资源再利用有限公司、香港迪亚有限公司、陆波公司增资纠纷案》 [Haifu Investment Co., Ltd. of Suzhou Industrial Park v Gansu Shiheng Nonferrous Metals Recycling Co., Ltd., Hong Kong Diya Co., Ltd. and Lu Bo], 最高人民法院 (the Supreme People's Court), (2012) 民提字第 11 号 [Civil Re-trial No. 11], 7 November 2011

《丸万株式会社与北京德霖高尔夫体育发展有限公司申请承认和执行外国仲裁裁决一审民事裁定书》 [Civil Decision of the Case of the First Instance Concerning the Application for the Recognition and Enforcement of A Foreign Arbitral Awards between Maruman Co. and Beijing Delin Golf Sports Development Co Ltd], Beijing 2nd IPC, (2013) 二中民特字第 12593 号 [Special No. 12593], 19 May 2014

《西门子国际贸易 (上海) 有限公司与上海黄金置地有限公司申请承认和执行外国仲裁裁决案》 [Siemens International Trade (Shanghai) Ltd Co. v. Shanghai Golden Landmark Co Ltd—Case of the Application for the Recognition and Enforcement of Foreign Arbitral Awards], 上海市第一中级人民法院 [Shanghai 1st IPC, People's Republic of China], (2013) 沪一中民认(外仲) 字第 2 号 [Recognition of Foreign Arbitral Awards No. 2], 27 Nov 2015

《夏长海运有限公司诉山东海纳房地产股份有限公司申请承认外国仲裁裁决纠纷一审民事裁定书》 [Civil Decision on the Application for the Recognition of A Foreign Arbitral Award by

Summer Maritime Ltd against Shandong Haina Property Development Co], Qingdao Maritime Court, (2014) 青海法海商初字第 721 号 [Maritime First Instance No. 721], 22 July 2014
《新和海事有限公司与大连新和船舶物资供应有限公司申请承认和执行外国仲裁裁决案裁定书》[Ruling on the Application for the Recognition and Enforcement of a Foreign Arbitral Award between Sinwa Marine Pte Ltd and Dalian Xinhe Shipping Supplies Co Ltd], Dalian IPC, (2016) 辽 02 协外认 2 号 [Judicial Assistance Foreign Recognition No. 2], 24 Feb 2017
《亚洲海事太平洋租船有限公司、匹克国际贸易 (天津) 有限公司申请认可和执行香港特别行政区仲裁裁决民事裁定书》[Civil Decision on the Application for the Recognition and Enforcement of A Hong Kong SAR Arbitral Award Between Asia Maritime Pacific Chartering Ltd and Peak International Trade (Tianjin) Co Ltd], Tianjin Maritime Court, (2018) 津 72 民特 13, 14 号 [Civil Special No. 13 and No. 14], 30 October 2018
《伊藤忠石油 (香港) 有限公司申请承认执行英国仲裁裁决案》[Case Concerning the Application of Itochu Petroleum (Hong Kong) Co Ltd for the Recognition and Enforcement of a UK Arbitral Award] Shenzhen Intermediate People's Court, (1999) Shen Zhong Fa Jing Er Chu Zi No. 190
《云南省昆明市中级人民法院阿姆龙钢铁有限公司申请执行云南镍钴矿业有限公司等仲裁裁决案》[Case Concerning Amulong Steel Co Ltd's Application of Enforcement of an Arbitral Award against Yunnan Nickel and Colbat Mining Co Ltd] Yunnan Kunming Intermediate People's Court, 10 November 2009
《执行申请人奥卓布克有限公司与被申请人红河恒昊矿业股份有限公司执行异议执行裁定书》[Ruling on Enforcement Dispute between the Applicant Ultrabulk A/S and the Respondent Honghe Henghao Mining Co], Kunming IPC, (2017) 云 01 执异 54 号 [Enforcement Dispute No. 54], 18 September 2017
《中国出口信用保险公司福建分公司与平安银行股份有限公司福州分行申请撤销仲裁裁决民事裁定书》[Civil Decision on the Application for the Annulment of an Arbitral Award between Sinosure Fujian Co and Ping'an Bank Fujian Branch], Beijing 4th IPC, (2019) 京 04 民特 600 号 [Civil Special No. 600], 16 December 2019
《中国航油 (新加坡) 股份有限公司、成都欣华欣化工材料有限公司申请承认与执行外国仲裁裁决裁定书》[Decision on the Application for the Recognition and Enforcement of a Foreign Arbitral Award between China Aviation Oil (Singapore) Corp Ltd and Chengdu Xinhuaxin Chenical Engineering Materials Co Ltd], Chengdu IPC, (2017) 川 01 协外认 1 号 [Judicial Assistance Foreign Recognition No. 1], 23 June 2017
《中国技术进出口总公司诉瑞士工业资源公司侵权损害赔偿案》[China National Technical Import & Export Corp. v. Swiss Industrial Resources Corp—Case of Appeal for Damages in Tort)] [1989] 1 中华人民共和国最高人民法院公报 [Gazette of Supreme People's Court of People's Republic of China] 26
《中山市朗华物业管理有限公司、广东联合亚太国际投资有限公司等申请撤销仲裁裁决特别程序民事裁定书》[Civil Ruling on the Application for the Annulment of an Arbitral Award between Zhongshan Langhua Property Management Co Ltd and Guangdong United Asia-Pacific International Investment et al.], Guangzhou IPC, (2021) 粤 01 民特 1805 号 [Civil Special No. 1805], 31 December 2021
《株式会社ACUON资本申请承认和执行大韩商事仲裁院生效仲裁裁决民事裁定书》[Civil Decision on the Application for the Recognition and Enforcement of an Effective Award of Korean Commercial Arbitration Board by ACUON Capital Ltd], Yanbian IPC, (2018) 吉 24 协外认 163 号 [Judicial Assistance Foreign Recognition No. 163], 15 November 2018
《最高人民法院关于申请人DMT有限公司 (法国) 与被申请人潮州市华业包装材料有限公司、被申请人潮安县华业包装材料有限公司申请承认和执行外国仲裁裁决一案请示的复函》[Reply of the Supreme People's Court to the Request Concerning the Application of a Foreign Arbitral Award between the Applicant, DMT S.A. (France) and the Respondents, Huaye Packing Materials Company of Chaozhou City and Huaye Packing Materials Company of Chao'an County] Supreme People's Court, [2010] Min Si Ta Zi No 51, 12 October 2010

《最高人民法院关于申请人安徽省龙利得包装印刷有限公司与被申请人 BP Agnati S.R.L 申请确认仲裁协议效力案的请示的复函》[Reply of the Supreme People's Court Concerning the Application to Confirm the Validity of the Arbitration Agreement between Applicant, Anhui Longlide Packing and Printing Co Ltd and Respondent, BP Agnati S.R.L] Supreme People's Court, Min Si Ta Zi [2013] No. 13, 25 March 2013

《最高人民法院关于宁波市北仑利成润滑油有限公司与法莫万驰公司买卖合同纠纷一案仲裁条款效力问题的批复》[Reply of the Supreme People's Court Concerning the Validity of the Arbitration Agreement in the Contractrual Dispute between Ningbo Beilun Licheng Lubricant Oil Co and Formal Venture Corp]Supreme People's Court, Min Si Ta Zi [2013] No. 74, 5 December 2013

《最高人民法院关于德国旭普林国际有限责任公司与无锡沃可通用工程橡胶有限公司申请确认仲裁协议效力一案的请示的复函》[Letter of Reply of the Supreme People's Court to the Request for Instructions on the Case Concerning the Application of Züblin International GmbH and Wuxi Woke General Engineering Rubber Co., Ltd. for Determining the Validity of the Arbitration Agreement] Supreme People's Court, [2004] 民四他字第 23 号 [Fourth Civil Branch No. 23], 8 July 2004

《最高人民法院关于清华同方股份有限公司、清华同方光盘股份有限公司申请撤销 [2002] 贸仲裁字第 0095 号仲裁裁决一案的请示的复函》[Reply of the Supreme People's Court upon the Request in regard of the Application to annul the Award of [2002] Mao Zhong Cai Zi No. 0095 by Qinghua Tongfang Co Ltd and Qinghua Tongfang CD Co Ltd] Supreme People's Court, (2003) Min Si Ta Zi No. 2, 28 February 2003

《最高人民法院关于德宝 (远东) 有限公司申请执行湖北省鹰台经济发展公司合作合同纠纷一案中不予执行涉外仲裁裁决的请示的复函》[Reply of the Supreme People's Court to the Request Concerning the Non-Enforcement of a Foreign-Related Arbitral Award in the Disputes Regarding Hubei Yingtai Economic Development Co's Contract of Coordination], Supreme People' Court, [2011] 民四他字第 62 号 [Fourth Civil Branch No. 62], 14 December 2011

《最高人民法院关于上诉人利比里亚·利比里亚力量船务公司与被上诉人中国·重庆新涪食品有限公司海上货物运输合同纠纷管辖权异议一案的请示的复函》[Reply of the Supreme People's Court in regard of the Jurisdictional Challenge of the Dispute on a Shipping Contract between the Appellant, (Liberia) Liberia Power Shipping Co and Appellate, (China) Chongqing Xinfu Food Co Ltd] the Supreme People's Court, [2006] Min Si Ta Zi No. 26, 21 December 2006

《最高人民法院关于原告中国·北京埃力生进出口有限公司诉被告日本·太阳航行贸易有限公司、新加坡·松加船务有限公司海上运输合同管辖权异议上诉一案的请示的复函》[Reply of the Supreme People's Court in regard of the Jurisdictional Challenge of the Dispute on a Shipping Contract between the Plaintiff, (China) Beijing Ailisheng Import & Export Co Ltd, and Defendants, (Japan) Solar Shipping and Trading S.A. and (Singapore) Songa Shipping Pte Ltd] Supreme People's Court, [2007] Min Si Ta Zi No. 14, 29 September 2007

《最高人民法院关于上诉人武钢集团国际经济贸易总公司与被上诉人福州天恒船务有限公司、被上诉人财富国际船务有限公司海上货物运输合同纠纷管辖权异议一案的请示的复函》[Reply of the Supreme People's Court in regard of the Jurisdictional Challenge of the Dispute on a Shipping Contract between the Appellant, Wugang International Economic and Trading Co and Appellate, Fuzhou Tianheng Shipping Co Ltd and Fortune International Shipping Ltd] Supreme People's Court, [2009] Min Si Ta Zi No. 36, 4 November 2009

《最高人民法院关于北京市第一中级人民法院不予执行美国制作公司和汤姆·胡莱特公司诉中国妇女旅行社演出合同纠纷仲裁裁决请示的批复》[Reply of the Supreme People's Court to the Request of the Beijing First Intermediate People's Court in regard of the Non-Enforcement of the Arbitral Award regarding the Dispute between USA Production Co, Tom Hulett & Asso and Chinese Women Travel Agency] Supreme People's Court, Ta [1997] No. 35, 26 December 1997

《最高人民法院关于英国嘉能可有限公司申请承认和执行英国伦敦金属交易所仲裁裁决一案请示的复函》[Reply of the SPC on the Recognition and Enforcement of an Arbitral Award

Made by the UK London Metal Exchange Applied by Glencore UK] Supreme People's Court, [2001] 民四他字第 2 号 [Fourth Civil Branch No. 2, 19 April 2001

《最高人民法院关于深圳市广夏文化实业总公司、宁夏伊斯兰国际信托投资公司、深圳兴庆电子公司与密苏尔有限公司仲裁裁决不予执行案的复函》 [Reply of the Supreme People's Court on the Non-enforcement of an Arbitral Award concerning Shenzhen Guangxia Culture Industry Company, Ningxia Islamic International Trust and Investment Company, Shenzhen Xingqing Electronics Company and Misuer Co Ltd] Supreme People's Court, [2000] Zhi Jian Zi No. 96–2, 20 April 2002

《最高人民法院执行工作办公室关于澳门大明集团有限公司与广州市东建实业总公司合作开发房地产纠纷仲裁裁决执行案的复函》 [Reply of the Supreme People's Court Enforcement Branch Concerning Macau Daming Group Co. Ltd v Guangzhou Dongjian Real Estate Co Dipustes on Developments of Real Estates] Supreme People's Court, [2003] Zhi Ta Zi No. 9, 5 August 2003

《最高人民法院关于浙江省天河房地产联合发展公司申请撤销中国经济贸易仲裁委员会上海分会仲裁裁决案的复函》[Reply of the Supreme People's Court Concerning the Application of Zhejiang Tianhe Real Estate Developments Co for Annulment of the CIETAC Shanghai Award] Supreme People's Court, [2003] Min Si Ta Zi No. 19, 10 November 2003

《最高人民法院关于ED&F曼氏 (香港) 有限公司申请承认和执行伦敦糖业协会仲裁裁决案的复函》 [Reply of the Supreme People's Courting Concerning the Application of ED & F Man (Hong Kong) for Recognition and Enforcement of an Arbitral Award of London Sugar Association] Supreme People's Court, [2003] Min Si Ta Zi No. 3, 1 July 2003

《最高人民法院关于香港享进粮油食品有限公司申请执行香港国际仲裁中心仲裁裁决案的复函》 [Reply of the Supreme People's Court Concerning the Application of Hong Kong Xiangjin Food & Oil Co Ltd for Enforcement of an Arbitral Award of HKIAC] Supreme People's Court, [2003] Min Si Ta Zi No. 9, 4 November 2003

《最高人民法院关于不予执行国际商会仲裁院 10334/AMW/BWD/TE最终裁决一案的请示的复函》[Reply of the Supreme People's Court Concerning the Non-Enforcement of ICC Final Award No. 10334/AMW/BWD/TE] Supreme People's Court, [2004] Min Si Ta Zi No. 6, 5 July 2004

《最高人民法院关于天津先达大酒店申请撤销 [2003] 津仲裁字第 364 号仲裁裁决一案的请示的复函》[Reply of the Supreme People's Court to the Request Concerning the Application of Tianjin Xianda Hotel for Annulment of [2003] Jin Zhong Cai Award No. 364] Supreme People's Court, [2005] Min Si Ta Zi No. 26, 民四他字第 26 号), 11 August 2005

《最高人民法院关于对海口中院不予承认和执行瑞典斯德哥尔摩商会仲裁院仲裁裁决请示的复函》 [Reply of the Supreme People's Court to the Haikou Itermediate People's Court's Request Concerning the Non-Enforcement of SCC's Arbitral Award] Supreme People's Court, [2001] Min Si Ta Zi No. 12, 13 July 2005

《最高人民法院关于是否裁定不予执行中国国际经济贸易仲裁委员会仲裁裁决的复函》 [Reply of the Supreme People's Court Concerning Non-Enforcement of CIETAC's Award] Supreme People's Court, [2005] Min Si Ta Zi No. 45, 23 January 2006

《最高人民法院关于是否裁定撤销中国国际经济贸易仲裁委员会华南分会仲裁裁决的请示的复函》 [Reply of the Supreme People's Court Concerning the Annulment of CIETAC South Branch's Arbitral Awards] Supreme People's Court, [2005] Min Si Ta Zi No. 47, 1 March 2006

《最高人民法院关于是否裁定撤销中国国际经济贸易仲裁委员会 [2004] 中国贸仲京裁字第 0222 号仲裁裁决请示的复函》 [Reply of the Supreme People's Court Concerning the Annulment of CIETAC Award [2004] Zhong Guo Mao Zhong Jing Cai Zi No. 0222]Supreme People's Court, [2006] Min Si Ta Zi No. 2, 7 March 2006

《最高人民法院关于邦基农贸新加坡私人有限公司申请承认和执行英国仲裁裁决一案的请示和复函》 [Reply of the Supreme People's Court Concerning the Application of Bunge Agribusiness Pte Ltd (Singapore) for Recognition and Enforcement of a British Arbitral Award] The Supreme People's Court, [2006] Min Si Ta Zi No. 41, 25 June 2006

《最高人民法院关于马绍尔群岛第一投资公司申请承认和执行英国伦敦临时仲裁庭仲裁裁决案的复函》[Reply of the Supreme People's Court Concerning First Investment Co of Marshall Islands' Application for Recognition and Enforcement of an Ad-hoc Arbitral Award of London, UK] Supreme People's Court, [2007] Min Si Ta Zi No. 35, 27 February 2008

《最高人民法院关于不予承认日本商事仲裁协会东京 04–05 号仲裁裁决的报告的复函》[Reply of the Supreme People's Court to the Request Concerning the Non-Recognition of JACC's Tokyo Award No. 04–05] Supreme People's Court, [2007] Min Si Ta Zi No. 26, 3 March 2008

《最高人民法院关于裁定不予承认和执行社团法人日本商事仲裁协会东京 05–03 号仲裁裁决的报告的答复》[Reply of the SPC to the Order to Refuse the Recognition and Enforcment of JACC Tokyo Award No. 05–03], Supreme People's Court, [2008] 民四他字第 18 号 [Fourth Civil Branch No. 18], 10 September 2008

《最高人民法院关于不予承认和执行国际商会仲裁院仲裁裁决的请示的复函》[Reply of the Supreme People's Court Concerning Non-Enforcement of an ICC Arbitral Award] Supreme People's Court, [2008] Min Si Ta Zi No. 11, 2 June 2008

《最高人民法院关于舟山中海粮油工业有限公司申请不予执行香港国际仲裁中心仲裁裁决一案的请示报告的复函》[Reply of the Supreme People's Court to the Request Concerning the Application of Zhoushan Zhonghai Food & Oil Industrial Co Ltd for Non-Enforcment of a HKIAC's Arbitral Award] Supreme People's Court, [2009] Min Si Ta Zi No. 2, 18 March 2009

《最高人民法院关于GRD Minproc有限公司申请承认并执行瑞典斯德哥尔摩商会仲裁院仲裁裁决一案的请示的复函》[Reply of the Supreme People's Court Concerning the Application of GRD Minproc Co Ltd for Recognition and Enforcement of SCC's Arbitral Award] The Supreme People's Court, [2008] Min Si Ta Zi No. 48, 13 March 2009

《最高人民法院关于不予承认及执行蒙古国家仲裁庭仲裁裁决的请示的复函》[Reply of the Supreme People's Court Concerning Non-Enforcement of Mongolian National Arbitration Court's Arbitral Award] The Supreme People's Court, [2009] Min Si Ta Zi No. 33, 2 September 2009

《最高人民法院关于宁波永信汽车部件制造有限公司申请撤销宁波仲裁委员会甬仲裁字 [2007] 第 44 号裁决一案的请示报告的复函》[Reply of the Supreme People's Court Concerning the Application of Ningbo Yongxin Motor Components Production Co for Annulment of Ningbo Arbitration Commission's Award Yong Zhong Cai Zi [2007] No. 44] Supreme People's Court, [2009] Min Si Ta Zi No. 45, 29 October 2009

《最高人民法院关于是否不予承认和执行国际商会洛桑 12330/TE/MW/AVH仲裁裁决的请示的复函》[Reply of the Supreme People's Court to the Request Concerning Non-Recognition and Non-Enforcement of ICC Award No. 12330/TE/MW/AVH (Lousanne)] Supreme People's Court, [2012] Min Si Ta Zi No. 38, 5 November 2009

《最高人民法院关于路易达孚商品亚洲有限公司申请承认和执行国际油、种子和脂肪协会作出的第 3980 号仲裁裁决请示一案的复函》[Reply of the Supreme People's Court Concerning the Application of Louis Dreyfus Commodity Asia Co Ltd for Recognition and Enforcement of International Federation of Oils, Seeds & Fats Association' s Arbitral Award No. 3980] Supreme People's Court, [2010] Min Si Ta Zi No. 48, 10 October 2010

《最高人民法院关于申请人天瑞酒店投资有限公司与被申请人杭州易居酒店管理有限公司申请承认仲裁裁决一案的请示报告的复函》[Reply of the Supreme People's Court to Request Concerning Application of Tianrui Hotel Investment Co Ltd for Enforcement of Arbitral Award against Hangzhou Yiju Hotel Management Co Ltd] Supreme People's Court, [2010] Min Si Ta Zi No. 18, 18 May 2010

《最高人民法院关于不予承认日本商事仲裁协会东京 07–11 号仲裁裁决一案的请示的复函》[Reply of the Supreme People's Court to the Request Concerning the Non-Recognition of JACC's Tokyo No. 07–11 Arbitral Award] Supreme People's Court, [2010] Min Si Ta Zi No. 32, 29 June 2010

《最高人民法院关于撤销中国国际经济贸易仲裁委员会 (2009) CIETACBJ裁决 (0355) 号裁决案的请示的复函》[Reply of the Supreme People's Court to the Request Concerning the Annulment of CIETAC's (2009) CIETACBJ Award No. 0355] Supreme People's Court, [2011] Min Si Ta Zi No. 13, 22 April 2011

《最高人民法院关于德宝 (远东) 有限公司申请执行湖北省鹰台经济发展公司合作合同纠纷一案中不予执行涉外仲裁裁决的请示的复函》[Reply of the Supreme People's Court to the Request Concerning the Non-Enforcement of a Foreign-Related Arbitral Award in the Disputes Regarding Hubei YIngtai Economic Development Co's Contract of Coordination]Supreme People's Court, [2011] Min Si Ta Zi No. 62, 14 December 2011

《最高人民法院关于韦斯顿瓦克公司申请承认与执行英国仲裁裁决案的请示的复函》[Reply of the Supreme People's Court to the Request Concerning the Application of Western Bulk Co Ltd for Recognition and Enforcement of a British Arbitral Award] Supreme People's Court, [2012] Min Si Ta Zi No. 12, 21 May 2012

《最高人民法院关于宁夏高院请示不予执行 (2011) 中国贸仲深裁字第 36 号仲裁裁决的复函》[Reply of the SPC to Ningxia HPC Concerning the Non-enforcement of CIETAC Shen Cai Award No (2011) 36], Supreme People's Court, [2012] 民四他字第 27 号 [Fourth Civil Branch No. 27], 30 July 2012

《最高人民法院关于新加坡中天投资 (集团) 有限公司申请撤销中国国际经济贸易仲裁委员会仲裁裁决一案的复函》[Reply of the Supreme People's Court to the Request Concerning the Application of Singapore Zhongtian Investment (Group) Co Ltd for Annulment of CIETAC's Awards] Supreme People's Court, [2012] Min Si Ta Zi No. 47, 25 October 2012

《最高人民法院关于北京康卫医药咨询服务中心有限公司申请撤销中国国际经济贸易仲裁委员会仲裁裁决案件的请示的复函》[Reply of the Supreme People's Court to the Request Concerning the Application of Beijing Kangwei Medical Consulting Service Centre Co Ltd for Annulment of CIETAC's Arbitral Award] Supreme People's Court, [2012] Min Si Ta Zi No. 57, 19 December 2012

《最高人民法院关于申请人北方万邦物流有限公司申请撤销 (2012) 海仲京裁字第 001 号仲裁裁决一案的请示的复函》[The Reply of the SPC Concerning the Request to Set Aside CMAC Jing Cai Award No. (2012) 001 submitted by Beifang Wanbang Logistics Co Ltd], Supreme People's Court, [2013] 民四他字第 5 号 [Fourth Civil Branch No. 5], 22 January 2013

《最高人民法院关于对诗董橡胶股份有限公司与三角轮胎股份有限公司涉外仲裁一案不予执行的请示的复函》[Reply of the Supreme People's Court to the Request for Instructions on Non-Enforcement of the Foreign-Related Arbitral Award between Sri Trang Agro-Industry Plc. and Triangle Tyre Co., Ltd], Supreme People's Court, [2013] 民四他字第 12 号 [Fourth Civil Branch No. 12] 22 March 2013

《申请人厦门湖里山炮台管理处申请撤销 (2011) 中国贸仲京裁字第 343 号仲裁裁决案》[Case Concerning the Application for the Annulment of (2011) CIETAC Beijing Arbitration Award No. 343 by Xiamen Hulishan Fortress Management Bureau], Supreme People's Court, [2013] 民四他字第 27 号, date not reported

《最高人民法院关于申请人 Castel Electronics Pty Ltd 申请承认和执行外国仲裁裁决一案请示的复函》[Reply of the Supreme People's Court Concerning the Applicant, Castel Electronics Pty Ltd's Application to Recognise and Enforce a Foreign Arbitral Award] Supreme People's Court, [2013] Min Si Ta Zi No. 46, 10 October 2013

《最高人民法院关于北京朝来新生体育休闲有限公司申请承认大韩商事仲裁院作出的第 12113–0011 号、第 12112–0012 号仲裁裁决案件请示的复函》[Reply of the SPC Concerning the Enforcement of KCAB Awards 12113–0011, 12112–0012 Requested by Beijing Chaolaixinsheng Sports and Leisure Co Ltd], Supreme People's Court, [2013] 民四他字第 64 号 [Fourth Civil Branch No. 64], 18 December 2013

《最高人民法院关于西门子国际贸易(上海)有限公司申请承认与执行外国仲裁裁决一案的请示的复函》[Reply of the SPC Concerning the Recognition and Enforcement of a Foreign

Award Requested by Siemens International Trade (Shanghai) Co Ltd], Supreme People's Court, [2015] 民四他字第 5 号 [Fourth Civil Branch No. 5], 10 October 2015

《最高人民法院关于对北京市高级人民法院就轮台县绿源农林开发有限责任公司申请撤销中国国际经济贸易仲裁委员会 [2014] 中国贸仲京裁字第 0526 号仲裁裁决案件的请示的复函》[Reply of the SPC Concerning the Report from the Beijing HPC Regarding the Request to Set Aside CIETAC Jing Cai Award No. [2014] 0526 by Luntai County Lvyuan Agriculture and Forestry Development Co Ltd], Supreme People's Court, [2015] 民四他字第 40 号 [Fourth Civil Branch No. 40], 28 Oct 2015

《最高人民法院关于湖北省高级人民法院就申请人 FSG 汽车工业控股公司与被申请人武汉泛洲机械制造有限公司申请承认和执行奥地利联邦经济会仲裁中心 SCH-5239 号仲裁裁决一案请示的答复》[Reply of the SPC Concerning the Report from Hubei HPC Regarding the Request to Recognition and Enforcement of International Arbitral Centre of the Austrian Federal Economic Chamber Vienna Award No. SCH-5239 between FSG Automotive Holding AG and Wuhan Fanzhou Mechanic Manufacturing Co Ltd], Supreme People's Court, [2015] 民四他字第 46 号 [Fourth Civil Branch No. 46], 24 December 2015

《最高人民法院关于西特福船运公司申请承认英国伦敦仲裁庭作出的 "HULL XXK06–039" 号仲裁裁决案件请示的复函》[Reply of the SPC Concerning the Report Regarding the Recognition of an Award made in London UK No. HULL XXK06–039 Requested by Spliethoff's Bevrachtingskantoor B.V.], Supreme People's Court, [2015] 民四他字第 48 号 [Fourth Civil Branch No. 48], 25 December 2015

《最高人民法院关于东成国际贸易有限公司申请执行涉外仲裁裁决一案的请示的答复》[Reply of the SPC to the Report Concerning the Enforcement of A Foreign-related Arbitral Award Requested by Dongcheng International Trade Co Ltd], Supreme People's Court, [2015] 民四他字第 53 号 [Fourth Civil Branch No. 53], 9 December 2015

《最高人民法院关于不予执行国际商会仲裁院第 18295/CYK 号仲裁裁决一案请示的复函》[Reply of the SPC to the Report Concerning the Non-enforcement of the ICC Award No. 18295/CYK], Supreme People's Court, [2016] 最高法民他字第 8 号 [SPC Civil Other Cases No. 8], 22 March 2016

《最高人民法院关于株式会社 J&D IB 申请承认国外仲裁裁决一案请示的答复》[Reply of the SPC to the Report Concerning the Recognition and Enforcement of a Foreign Award Requested by J&D IB Ltd], Supreme People's Court, [2016] 最高法民他 38 号 [SPC Civil Branch Other Cases, No. 38], 17 May 2016

《最高人民法院关于对河南省高级人民法院就申请人成可化学工程和咨询公司与被申请人多氟多化工股份有限公司申请承认和执行外国仲裁裁决纠纷一案请示的复函》 [The Reply of the SPC to the Report from Henan HPC Concerning the Recognition and Enforcement of a Foreign Award Regarding the Dispute between the Applicant Chenco Chemical Engineering and Consulting GmbH and Respondent Duofuduo Chenical Engineering Co], the Supreme People's Court, [2016] 最高法民他 66 号 [SPC Civil Branch Other Cases No. 66], 20 December 2016

《最高人民法院关于江苏省高级人民法院就申请人 Bright Morning Limited 与被申请人宜兴乐祺纺织集团有限公司申请承认和执行新加坡国际仲裁中心 2011 年第 130 号 (ARB130/11/MJL) 仲裁裁决一案请示的复函》[The Reply of the SPC to the Report from Jiangsu HPC Concerning the Recognition and Enforcement of SIAC 2011 Award No. ARB130/11/MJL Regarding the Dispute between the Applicant Bright Morning Limited and Respondent Yixing Leqi Textile Group Co Ltd], Supreme People's Court, [2017] 最高法民他 44 号 [SPC Civil Branch Other Cases No. 44], 23 June 2017

《最高人民法院关于广东省高级人民法院就广东三茂铁路实业发展有限公司与珠海经济特区香洲金都房产开发有限公司、佳建亚洲有限公司申请不予执行仲裁裁决一案请示的复函》 [Reply of the SPC to the Report from Guangdong HPC Concerning the Non-enforcement of an Arbitral Award Regarding the Disputes between the Applicant Guangdong Sanmao Railway Industrial Development Co Ltd and Respondents Zhuhai Special Economic Zone Ciangzhou Jindu Real Estate Development Co Ltd and Best Fair Asia Limited], Supreme

People's Court, [2017] 最高法民他 115 号 [SPC Civil Branch Other Cases No. 115], 26 December 2017

《最高人民法院关于北京市高级人民法院就英属盖曼群岛商智龙二基金公司申请认可和执行香港特别行政区仲裁裁决一案请示的复函》[Reply of the SPC to the Report from Beijing HPC Concerning the Recognition and Enforcement of a Hong Kong Arbitral Award Requested by IP Cathay II, L. P., Cayman Island], Supreme People's Court, [2017] 最高法民他 131 号 [SPC Civil Branch Other Cases No. 131], 25 December 2017

《最高人民法院关于天津市高级人民法院就申请人帕尔默海运公司与被申请人中牧实业股份有限公司申请承认和执行外国仲裁裁决一案请示的复函》[Reply of the SPC to the Report from Tianjin HPC Concerning the Recognition and Enforcement of a Foreign Arbitral Award Regarding the Dispute between the Applicant Palmer Maritime Inc and the Respondent Zhongmu Industrial Co] Supreme People's Court, [2017] 最高法民他 140 号 [SPC Civil Branch Other Cases No. 140], 9 March 2018

《最高人民法院关于广东省高级人民法院就派视尔有限责任公司申请承认和执行韩国商事仲裁院仲裁裁决一案的请示的复函》[Reply of the SPC to the Report from Guangdong HPC Concerning the Recognition and Enforcement of an KCAB Award Requested by Pixelplus Co. Ltd], Supreme People's Court, [2018] 最高法民他 15 号 [SPC Civil Branch Other Cases No. 15], 29 March 2018

《最高人民法院关于海南省高级人民法院就承认与执行美国国际争议解决中心 50–125–T-00029–13 号仲裁裁决一案再次请示的复函》[Reply of the SPC Concerning the Second Report from Hainan HPC regarding the Recognition and Enforcement of ICDR Award No. 50–125–T-00029–13], Supreme People's Court, (2018) 最高法民他 108 号 [SPC Civil Branch Other Cases No. 108], 21 December 2018

《张兰、盛兰控股集团 (BVI) 有限公司 [Grand Lan Holdings Group] 申请撤销仲裁裁决特别程序民事裁定书》[Civil Order of Special Procedure on the Setting Aside of An Arbitral Award Requested by Zhang Lan and Grand Lan Holdings Group], Supreme People's Court, [2019] 最高法民特4号, 5 号 [SPC Civil Special Procedure No. 4, 5], 29 December 2020

《申请人盖特汽车自由贸易区公司、埃及盖特汽车制造公司等与被申请人河北中兴汽车制造有限公司申请认可和执行香港特别行政区仲裁裁决民事裁定书》[Civil Decision on the Application for the Recognition of a Hong Kong SAR Arbitral Award among Automotive Gate FZCO et al. and Hebei Zhongxing Automotive Manufacture Co Ltd], Yichang IPC, (2015) 鄂宜昌中民认字第 00003 号之一[Civil Recognition No. 00003-A], 15 August 2019

《上海绿叶风学生营养配膳有限公司与上海华富士素食有限公司》[Shanghai Green Leaves Wind Food Co Ltd v Shanghai Huafushi Fast Food Co] Shanghai Second IPC, [2002] 沪二中民五 (商) 初字 [Shanghai Second IPC Civil Fifth Branch (Commercial), Case of First Instance] No. 79, 21 October 2002

《江苏省物资集团轻工纺织总公司诉 (香港) 裕亿集团有限公司、 (加拿大) 太子发展有限公司侵权损害赔偿纠纷上诉案》[Textile & Other Light Industries Co. Ltd. of the Commodities Group (Jiangsu Province) vs. Topcapital **Holdings** Ltd. (Hong Kong) and Prince Development Ltd. (Canada)-Case of Appeal for Dispute of Liabilities of Tort], [1998] 3 中华人民共和国最高人民法院公报 [Gazette of Supreme People's Court of People's Republic of China] 109

《中国石化集团国际石油勘探开发有限公司与UNI-TOP Asia Investment Limited申请撤销仲裁裁决案裁定书》[Decision on the Application for the Annulment of the Arbitral Award between SINOPEC Group International Petroleum Exploration and Production Corp. and UNI-TOP Asia Investment Limited], Beijing 4th IPC, (2017) 京04民特39号[Civil Special Procedure No.39], 27 April 2020

Hong Kong SAR

宫本海 對 香港國際仲裁中心 [Gong Benhai v Hong Kong International Arbitration Centre], High Court of Hong Kong Special Administrative Region, Court of the First Instance, HCMP 325/2014, 28 April 2014

## C Legislation

Mainland China

《中华人民共和国宪法》[The Constitutional Law of the People's Republic of China] (People's Republic of China)

《中华人民共和国立法法》[The Legislation Law of the People's Republic of China] (People's Republic of China) National People's Congress, Order No. 31, 15 March 2000

《中华人民共和国人民法院组织法》[The People's Courts Organisation Law of the People's Republic of China] (People's Republic of China), National People's Congress, Order No. 3, 1 July 1979 (Most Recent Amendment by National People's Congress Standing Committee, 26 October 2018)

《中华人民共和国民事诉讼法》[The Civil Procedure Law of the People's Republic of China] (People's Republic of China) National People's Congress, Order No 44, 9 April 1991 (Recently amended by National People's Congress Standing Committee, Order 106, 24 Dec 2021)

《中华人民共和国刑事诉讼法》[The Criminal Procedure Law of the People's Republic of China] (People's Republic of China) National People's Congress, Order No. 6, 1 July 1979 (Recently amended by National People's Congress, Order No. 55, 14 March 2012)

《中华人民共和国法官法》[The Law of Judges of the People's Republic of China] (People's Republic of China) National People's Congress Standing Committee, Order No. 38, 28 Feburary 1995 (Recently Amended by National People's Congress Standing Committee, Order No. 53, 30 June 2001)

《中华人民共和国香港特别行政区基本法》[The Basic Law of the Hong Kong Special Administrative Region of the People's Republic of China] (People's Republic of China) National People's Congress, Order No. 26, 4 April 1990

《中华人民共和国澳门特别行政区基本法》[The Basic Law of the Macao Special Administrative Region of the People's Republic of China] (People's Republic of China) National People's Congress, Order No. 3, 31 March 1993

《中华人民共和国民法通则》[General Principle of Civil Law of the People's Republic of China] (People's Republic of China) National People's Congress, Order No. 37, 12 April 1986

《中华人民共和国合同法》[Contract Law of the People's Republic of China] (People's Republic of China) National People's Congress, Order No. 15, 15 March 1999

《中华人民共和国仲裁法》[Arbitration Law of the People's Republic of China] (People's Republic of China) National People's Congress Standing Committee, Order No. 31, 31 August 1994

《中华人民共和国公司法》[Company Law of the People's Republic of China] (People's Republic of China) National People's Congress Standing Committee, Order No. 16, 29 December 1993, recently amended by the National People's Congress Standing Committee, Oder No. 8, 28 December 2013

《中华人民共和国中外合资经营企业法》[Law of the People's Republic of China on China-foreign Equity Joint Ventures] (People's Republic of China) National People's Congress, Order No. 7, 1 July 1979

《中华人民共和国涉外民事关系法律适用法》[Law of the People's Republic of China on the Application of Law for Foreign-Related Civil Relations] (People's Republic of China) National People's Congress Standing Committee, Order No. 36, 28 October 2010

《中华人民共和国各级人民代表大会常务委员会监督法》[Law of the People's Republic of China on the Supervision of All Levels of People's Congress Standing Committee] (People's Republic of China) National People's Congress Standing Committee, Order No.10, 27 August 2006

《中华人民共和国进出口商品检验法》[the Law of People's Republic of China on Import and Export Commodity Inspection] (People's Republic of China) National People's Congress Standing Committee, Order No. 14, 21 February 1989 (amended in 2002)
《中华人民共和国政府采购法》[Law of People's Republic of China in regard of Government Procurement] (People's Republic of China) National People's Congress Standing Committee, Order No. 69, 29 June 2002
《中华人民共和国海商法》[The Maritime Law of the People's Republic of China] (People's Republic of China) National People's Congress Standing Committee, Order No. 64, 7 November 1992
《中华人民共和国民用航空法》[The Civil Aviation Law of the People's Republic of China] (People's Republic of China) National People's Congress Standing Committee, Order No. 56, 30 October 1995
《中华人民共和国进出口商品检验法》[Law of the People's Republic of China on Import and Export Commodity Inspection] National People's Congress Standing Committee, Order No. 14, 21 February 1989; Modified by National People's Congress Standing Committee, Order No. 67, 28 April 2002
《中华人民共和国著作权法》[The Copyright Law of the People's Republic of China] (People's Republic of China) National People's Congress Standing Committee, Order No. 31, 7 September 1990, recently amended by National People's Congress Standing Committee, Order No. 26, 26 February 2010
《中华人民共和国商标法》[Trademark Law of the People's Republic of China] (People's Republic of China) National People's Congress Standing Committee, Order No. 59, 23 August 1982, recently amended by the National People's Congress Standing Committee, Order No. 6, 30 August 2013
《中华人民共和国专利法》[Patent Law of the People's Republic of China] (People's Republic of China) National People's Congress Standing Committee, Order No. 11, 12 March 1984, recently amended by the National People's Congress Standing Committee, Order No. 8, 27 December 2008
《中华人民共和国消费者权益保护法》[the Protection of Consumer Rights Act of the People's Republic of China] (People's Republic of China) National People's Congress Standing Committee, Order No. 18, 31 October 1993, recently amended by Order No. 7, 25 October 2013
《中华人民共和国反垄断法》[Antitrust Law of People's Republic of China] (People's Republic of China) National People's Congress Standing Committee, Order No. 68, 30 August 2007
《中华人民共和国企业破产法》[The Law of People's Republic of China Concerning Bankruptcy of Enterprises] (People's Republic of China) National People's Congress Standing Committee, Order No. 54, 27 August 2006
《中华人民共和国外商投资法》[Foreign Investment Law of the People's Republic of China] (People's Republic of China) National People's Congress, Order No 26, passed on 15 March 2019, effective on 1 January 2020
《中华人民共和国民法典》[Civil Code of the People's Republic of China] (People's Republic of China) National People's Congress, Order No. 45, 1 Jan 2021
《全国人大常委会关于进一步加强法律解释工作的决议》[Statement on the National People's Congress Standing Committee in regard of Further Enhancing the Practice of the Interpretation of Law] National People's Congress Standing Committee, 10 June 1981

Republic of China and Taiwan Region

《中華民國憲法》[The Constitution of the Republic of China] (Republic of China), National Constitutional Convention, 25 December 1947

《中華民國憲法增修條文》[The Additional Articles of the Constitution of the Republic of China], Legislative Yuan, 10 June 2005

**D Treaties/Multi-jurisdictional Arrangements**

《海峡两岸共同打击犯罪及司法互助协议》[Cross-strait Joint Fight against Crime and Mutual Legal Assistance Agreement] Cross-Strait Relation Association and Cross-Strait Communication Foundation, 26 April 2009

《最高人民法院关于内地与香港特别行政区相互执行仲裁裁决的安排》 [Supreme People's Court's Arrangements of the Supreme People's Court on the Mutual Enforcement of Arbitral Awards between the Mainland and the Hong Kong Special Administrative Region] Supreme People's Court, Fa Shi [2000] No. 3, 18 June 1999

《最高人民法院关于内地与澳门特别行政区相互认可和执行仲裁裁决的安排》 [Arrangement between the Mainland and the Macau SAR on Reciprocal Recognition and Enforcement of Arbitration Awards], Supreme People's Court, Fa Shi [2007] No. 17, 17 September 2007

《最高人民法院关于人民法院认可台湾地区有关法院民事判决的规定》 [Provisions of the Supreme People's Court Concerning the Recognition of the Civil Judgments of the Courts in Taiwan Region by the People's Courts] Supreme People's Court, Fa Shi [1998] No. 11, 22 May 1998

《最高人民法院关于人民法院认可台湾地区有关法院民事判决的补充规定》[Supplementary Provisions of the Supreme People's Court Concerning the Recognition of the Civil Judgments of the Courts in Taiwan Region by the People's Courts] Supreme People's Court, Fa Shi [2009] No. 4, 14 May 2009

《最高人民法院关于认可和执行台湾地区仲裁裁决的规定》[Regulations on the Recognition and Enforcement of Arbitral Awards Made in Taiwan by the Supreme People's Court]Supreme People's Court, 法释 [2015] 14 号 [Judicial Interpretation No. 14], 2 June 2015

**E Other**

Drafts of Legislation

《中华人民共和国外商投资法 (草案征求意见稿》[The Foreign Investment of the People's Republic of China (Draft for Comments)] (People's Republic of China) Ministry of Commerce, 19 January 2015, at http://www.mofcom.gov.cn/article/ae/ag/201501/20150100871007.shtml

《<中华人民共和国仲裁法 (修订) >征求意见稿》[Draft of the Modified Arbitration Law of the People's Republic of China] (People's Republic of China), Ministry of Justice, 30 July 2021, available at: http://www.moj.gov.cn/pub/sfbgw/zlk/202107/t20210730_432958.html

Government Decisions and Regulations

《中华人民共和国外资企业法实施细则》[Detailed Rules for the Implementation of the Foreign-Invested Enterprise Law of the People's Republic of China] State Council, 28 October 1990, amended in 12 April 2001, 19 February 2014

《中华人民共和国进出口商品检验法实施条例》[Regulations for the Implementation of the Law of People's Republic of China on Import and Export Commodity Inspection] State Council, 31 August 2005

《中华人民共和国经济合同仲裁条例》[Regulations of the PRC on the Arbitration of Disputes Involving Economic Contracts] (People's Republic of China) State Council, 22 August 1983

《股票发行与交易管理暂行条例》[Trial Rules for Management of Share Issuance and Trade] (People's Republic of China) State Council, 22 April 1993

《中央人民政府政务院关于在中国国际贸易促进委员会内设立对外贸易仲裁委员会的决定》[Decision of the Administrative Council of the Central People's Government Concerning the Establishment of a Foreign Trade Arbitration Commission Within the China Council for the

Promotion of International Trade] (People's Republic of China), Administrative Council of the Central People's Government, 6 May 1954

《中华人民共和国国务院关于在中国国际贸易促进委员会内设立海事仲裁委员会的决定》[Decision of the State Council of the People's Republic of China Concerning the Establishment of a Maritime Arbitration Commission Within the China Council for the Promotion of International Trade] (People's Republic of China), State Council of the People's Republic of China, 21 November 1958

《国务院办公厅关于印发<新组建仲裁机构方案><仲裁委员会登记暂行办法><仲裁委员会仲裁收费办法>的通知》[Notice of the General Office of State Council in regard of the Issuance of 'Plan of the Newly Established Arbitration Institutions', 'Interim Plan for the Registration of the Arbitration Commissions' and 'Regulations of the Charging Measures of the Arbitration Commissions'] State Council, Guo Ban Fa [1995] No. 44, 28 July 1995

《国务院办公厅关于贯彻实施<中华人民共和国仲裁法>需要明确的几个问题的通知》[Notice on Clarifying A Few Problems in the Enactment of the Arbitration Act of PRC by the General Office of the State Council] State Council, 8 June 1996

《对外经济贸易部关于认真做好执行<华盛顿公约>工作的通知》[Notice of the Ministry of Foreign Trade and Economic Co-operation in regard of the Implementation of the Washington Convention] The Ministry of Foreign Trade and Economic Co-operation, 1 August 1992

《司法部关于威海仲裁委员会是否可以聘任外籍人士担任仲裁员的批复》[Reply of the Ministry of Justice in regard of whether Weihai Arbitration Commission can employ foreign arbitrators] Ministry of Justice, 20 Aug 1996

《山东省参照<中华人民共和国公务员法>管理的单位审批办法》[Regulation of the Shandong Province in regard of the Approval of the Bodies that Managed in Accordance with the Public Servants Law of the People's Republic of China] Shandong Province Human Resources Bureau, Lu Fa(鲁发) [2006] No. 19

Judicial Interpretations, Judiciaries' Notices, Regulations and Decisions

《最高人民法院关于修改<关于审理民间借贷案件适用法律若干问题的规定>的决定》[Decision of the Supreme People's Court to Amend the Regulations on Several Issues Concerning the Application of Law in the Adjudication of Loan Disputes between Private Parties] Supreme People's Court, Judicial Interpretation [2020] No.6, effective 20 August 2020

《全国法院涉外商事海事审判工作座谈会会议纪要》[Minutes of the National Symposium of the Chinese Court System on the Adjudication of Foreign-related Commercial and Maritime Law Matters], the SPC, released 31 December 2021

《最高人民法院关于执行我国加入的<承认及执行外国仲裁裁决公约>的通知》[Notice of the Supreme People's Court in regard of the Implementation of the 'Convention on the Recognition and Enforcement of Foreign Arbitral Award'] Supreme People's Court, 法(经)发 (1987) 5 号 [Supreme Court (Economic) Notice No. 5], 10 April 1987

《最高人民法院关于司法解释工作的若干规定》[Several Regulations Issued by the Supreme People' Court in regard of the Practices of Judicial Interpretation] Supreme People's Court, Fa Fa [1997] No. 15, 23 June 1997

《最高人民法院关于司法解释工作的规定》[Regulations Issued by the Supreme People's Court in regard of the Practices of Judicial Interpretation], Supreme People's Court, Fa Fa [2007] No. 12, 23 March 2007

《最高人民法院关于适用〈中华人民共和国仲裁法〉若干问题的解释》[Supreme People's Court's Interpretation on Several Issues in regard of the Application of the China Arbitration Law] (People's Republic of China), Supreme People's Court, Fa Shi [2006] No. 7, 26 December 2005

《最高人民法院关于实施<中华人民共和国仲裁法>几个问题的通知》 [Supreme People's Court's Notice Concerning Several Issues in the Implementation of the China Arbitration Law] (People's Republic of China) the Supreme People's Court, Fa Fa [1997] No. 4, 26 March 1997

《最高人民法院关于司法解释工作的若干规定》[Several Regulations Issued by the Supreme People' Court in regard of the Practices of Judicial Interpretation] Supreme People's Court, Fa Fa [1997] No. 15, 23 June 1997

《最高人民法院关于当事人对驳回其申请撤销仲裁裁决的裁定不服而申请再审，人民法院不予受理问题的批复》[Reply by the Supreme People's Court in regard of the Application for Retrial of the Cases in which an Arbitral Award was Annulled and Such Application was Not Accepted by the People's Court] Supreme People's Court, Fa Shi [2004] No. 9, 29 July 2004

《最高人民法院关于仲裁协议无效是否可以裁定不予执行的处理意见》 [Opinions of the Supreme People's Court in regard of whether the Enforcement of an Arbitral Award should be Refused on the Basis of a Invalid Arbitration Agreement] Supreme People's Court, 20 June 2002

《最高人民法院关于正确审理仲裁司法审查案件有关问题的通知》[Notice of the Supreme People's Court in Regard of Correct Judicial Review of Arbitral Awards] Supreme People's Court, Fa (2013) No. 194, 4 September 2013

《最高人民法院关于人民法院处理与涉外仲裁及外国仲裁事项有关问题的通知》[Notice of the Supreme People's Court in regard of Relevant Issues in the People's Courts' Practices in dealing with Foreign-related Arbitration and Foreign Arbitration] Supreme People's Court, Fa Fa [1995] No. 18, 28 August 1995

《最高人民法院关于人民法院撤销涉外仲裁裁决有关事项的通知》[Notice of the Supreme People's Court in regard of Relevant Issues in the People's Courts' Practices of Annulment of Foreign-Related Arbitral Awards] Supreme People's Court, Fa (1998) No. 40, 22 April 1998

《最高人民法院关于审理和执行涉外民商事案件应当注意的几个问题的通知》[Notice of the Supreme People's Court in regard of Several Issues in regard of the Judicial Review and Enforcement of Foreign-related Civil and Commercial Cases] Supreme People's Court, Fa (2000) No. 51, 17 April 2000

《最高人民法院民事案件案由规定》[Rules of the Supreme People's Court in regard of the Cause of Action in Civil Litigation] Supreme People's Court, Fa Fa [2008] No. 11, 29 October 2007, recently amended by Fa (2007) No. 41, 18 February 2011

《最高人民法院关于贯彻执行<中华人民共和国民法通则>若干问题的意见（试行）》[Opinions of the Supreme People's Court in regard of the Implementation of the 'Genera Rules of the Civil Law of the People's Republic of China' (the Trial Version)] Supreme People's Court, Fa (Ban) Fa [1988] No. 6, 2 April 1988

《最高人民法院关于适用<中华人民共和国民事诉讼法>若干问题的意见》[Opinions of the Supreme People's Court in regard of Several Issues on the Application of the Civil Procedure Law of the People's Republic of China] Supreme People's Court, Fa Fa [1992] No. 22, 14 July 1992

《最高人民法院关于适用《中华人民共和国民事诉讼法》的解释》[Judicial Interpretation of the Supreme People's Court on the Application of the Civil Procedure Law of the People's Republic of China] (People's Republic of China), Supreme People's Court, 法释 (2015) 5 号 [Judicial Interpretation No 2015–5], 30 January 2015, modified on 23 December 2020 and then 22 March 2022, effective 10 April 2022

《最高人民法院关于适用涉外民事关系法律适用法若干问题的解释（一）》[Judicial Interpretation of the Supreme People's Court in regard of Several Issues in the Application of the Law of Application of Law in Foreign-related Civil Relationship No. 1] (Supreme People's Court), Fa Shi [2012] No. 24, 28 December 2012

《最高人民法院关于确认仲裁条款效力几个问题批复》[Reply of the Supreme People's Court Concerning the Confirmation of the Effects of Arbitration Clause] Supreme People's Court, 5 November 1998

《最高人民法院关于适用<中华人民共和国合同法>若干问题的解释 (二) 》[Interpretations of the Supreme People's Court on Several Issues in the Application of the Contract Law of the People's Republic of China (Second)] Supreme People's Court, 法释 (2009) 5 号 [Judicial Interpretation No. 5], 24 April 2009

《最高人民法院关于当前形势下审理民商事合同纠纷案件若干问题的规定》[Regulations of the Supreme People's Court in regard of the Judicial Review of Civil and Commercial Contractual Disputes under Recent Circumstances] Supreme People's Court, Fa Fa [2009] No. 40

《最高人民法院关于人民法院审理借贷案件的若干意见》[Opinions of the Supreme People's Court Concerning the Judicial Review on Loan Disputes] Supreme People's Court, Fa Min Fa [1991] No. 21, 2 July 1991

《最高人民法院关于统一法律适用加强类案检索的指导意见(试行)>》[Guiding Opinions of the Supreme People's Court on Unifying the Application of Laws to Strengthen the Retrieval of Similar Cases (for Trial Implementation)], Supreme People's Court, 31 July 31, 2020

《最高人民法院关于设立国际商事法庭若干问题的规定》[Provisions of the Supreme People's Court on Several Issues concerning the Establishment of International Commercial Courts] Supreme People's Court, Fa Shi [2018] No. 11, 27 June 2018

《最高人民法院印发《关于案例指导工作的规定》的通知》[Notice of the Supreme People's Court on Issuing the Provisions on Case Guidance] Supreme People's Court, Fa Fa [2010] No. 51, 26 November 2010

《最高人民法院印发<关于建立法律适用分歧解决机制的实施办法>的通知》[Notice by the Supreme People's Court of Issuing the Implementation Measures for Establishing the Mechanism for Resolving Differences in the Application of Laws], Supreme People's Court, ), Fa Fa [2019] No. 23, 28 October 2019

《最高人民法院关于仲裁司法审查案件报核问题的有关规定》[Supreme People's Court's Regelation on the Reports and Approvals in the Judicial Review of Arbitration-related Cases] (People's Republic of China) the Supreme People's Court, 法释 [2017] 21 号 [SPC Interpretation No. 21], 4 December 2017, modified by《最高人民法院关于修改〈最高人民法院关于仲裁司法审查案件报核问题的有关规定〉的决定》[Supreme People's Court's Decision to Modify the Supreme People's Court's Regelation on the Reports and Approvals in the Judicial Review of Arbitration-related Cases] (People's Republic of China) the Supreme People's Court, 法释 [2021] 21 号 [SPC Interpretation No. 21], 15 November 2021

《最高人民法院关于审理仲裁司法审查若干问题的规定》[Supreme People's Court's Regulation on Several Several Matters in the Judicial Review of Arbitration-related Cases] (People's Republic of China) the Supreme People's Court, 法释 [2017] 22 号 [SPC Interpretation No. 22], 4 December 2017

《最高人民法院关于人民法院为中国 (上海) 自由贸易试验区临港新片区建设提供司法服务和保障的意见》[The Supreme People's Court's Opinion on the Judicial Services Supporting the Development of the Chinese (Shanghai) Free Trade Trial Zone Lingang New District]] (People's Republic of China) the Supreme People's Court, 法发 [2019] 31 号 [SPC Notice No. 31], 13 December 2019

《最高人民法院关于为自由贸易试验区建设提供司法保障的意见》[Supreme People's Courts Opinion on the Judicial Services Promoting and Supporting the Development of the Free Trade Trial Zone], Fa Fa [2016] No. 34, 30 December 2016

《最高人民法院关于人民法院在互联网公布裁判文书的规定》[Provisions of the Supreme People's Court on the Issuance of Judgments on the Internet by the People's Courts], 21 November 2013, Interpretation No. 26 [2013], updated 10 January 2016

最高人民法院关于审理垄断民事纠纷案件适用法律若干问题的规定 (公开征求意见稿) 》[The Supreme People's Court's Rules Concerning Various Matters on the Application of Law in the Adjudication of Civil Disputes in Relation to Antitrust Law (Draft for Public Consultation)], The SPC, 18 November 2022

《广东省高级人民法院关于印发<广东省高级人民法院关于办理申请不予执行仲裁裁决案件的若干规定 (试行) >的通知》[The Notice of the Guangdong People's High Court in regard of the Issuance of 'Several Rules of the Guangdong People's High Court in Dealing with the Application of Non-Enforcement of Arbitral Awards' (The Trial Version)] Guangdong People's High Court, Yue Gao Fa Fa [2009] No. 17, 2 March 2009

Arbitration Rules and Regulations of Arbitration Institutions

《北京仲裁委员会仲裁规则》[Beijing Arbitration Commission Arbitration Rules 2008], Beijing Arbitration Commission, 20 September 2007

《北京仲裁委员会仲裁员守则》[Beijing Arbitration Commission Code of Conducts of Arbitrators 2006], Beijing Arbitration Commission, 14 August 2006

《北京仲裁委员会关于提高仲裁效率的若干规定》[Several Regulations of the BAC for the Enhancement of Arbitration Efficiency] (2003)

《西安仲裁委员会仲裁规则》[Xi'an Arbitration Commission Arbitration Rules] Xi'an Arbitration Commission, 1 February 2008

《中国国际经济贸易仲裁委员会仲裁规则 (2012)》[China International Economic and Trade Arbitration Commission Arbitration Rules (2012)] CIETAC, 3 February 2012

《横琴自由贸易试验区临时仲裁规则》[Hengqin Free Trade Zone Ad-hoc Arbitration Rules], effective April 2017

《中国海商法协会临时仲裁规则》[China Maritime Law Association Ad Hoc Arbitration Rules], effective 18 March 2022